The Korean War

ASIA/PACIFIC/PERSPECTIVES
Series Editor: Mark Selden

The Korean War

An International History

Wada Haruki

Translated by Frank Baldwin

ROWMAN & LITTLEFIELD
Lanham • Boulder • New York • Toronto • Plymouth, UK

Published by Rowman & Littlefield
4501 Forbes Boulevard, Suite 200, Lanham, Maryland 20706
www.rowman.com

10 Thornbury Road, Plymouth PL6 7PP, United Kingdom

British Library Cataloguing in Publication Information Available

Library of Congress Cataloging-in-Publication Data
Wada, Haruki.
[Chosen Senso zenshi. English]
The Korean War : an international history / Wada Haruki.
pages cm. -- (Asia/Pacific/perspectives)
Includes bibliographical references and index.
ISBN 978-1-4422-2329-5 (cloth : alk. paper) -- ISBN 978-1-4422-2330-1 (electronic)
1. Korean War, 1950-1953. I. Title.
DS918.W33613 2013
951.904'2--dc23
2013027920

Printed in the United States of America

Contents

Acknowledgments

This volume took shape over more than two decades through extraordinary collaboration. After my first article on North Korean history appeared in 1981–1982, I spent two months at the University of Washington in 1984 at the invitation of Bruce Cumings, whose monumental two-volume work *The Origins of the Korean War* inspired my interest in the conflict. Although our understandings of the war differ in several respects, I deeply appreciate his support and friendship.

While working on captured North Korean materials at the Washington National Records Center, Suitland, Maryland in 1983, I became acquainted with independent Korean scholar Pang Sun-joo, who shared his peerless familiarity with the collection. I was assisted at the Russian archives in Moscow by the late Grant Adibekov, archivist of Russian State Archives of Social-Political History, and Gennadii Boldiugov, President of AIRO XX, an independent association of Russian historians on twentieth-century Russia.

Kathryn Weathersby and the Cold War International History Project provided a set of declassified Soviet documents on the war. Without these records this book could not have been written. I treasure the exciting discussions with her and other CWIHP colleagues—Chen Jian, Vladislav Zubok, Odd Arne Westad, Aleksandre Mansourov, and David Wolf. I would also like to thank Yurii V. Vanin, Charles Armstrong, Okonogi Masao, and Mizuno Naoki. Korean scholars were particularly generous with insights and assistance, including Moon Jong-in, Park Myung-lim, Yi Chong-sok, Chong Hyon-su, Lee Jong-won, Nam Ki-jong, and the late Suh Dong-man.

This book is an expanded version and translation of *Chosen Senso Zenshi* (The Korean War: A History) published in 2002 by Iwanami Shoten, whose kind permission made it possible. Gavan McCormack and Mark Selden encouraged me to publish an English version. I am greatly indebted to Frank

Baldwin for the translation, accomplished over several years as we struggled to mesh schedules. Chen Jian, as one of the first readers of my manuscript, encouraged the publication and gave important revision advice. Mark Selden's dedicated editing greatly improved the narrative. Tom Wells read the manuscript and made many useful suggestions. I alone am responsible for any errors that remain.

Abbreviations

APRF	Russian Presidential Archives
AVPRF	Russian Archives of Foreign Policy
CC	Central Committee
CCP	Chinese Communist Party
CPSU	Communist Party of the Soviet Union
CPV	Chinese People's Volunteers
CWIHP	Cold War International History Project
DPRK	Democratic People's Republic of Korea
FEAF	Far East Air Forces
FRUS	*Foreign Relations of the United States*
GELC	General Election Leading Committee
GHQ	General Headquarters
JCP	Japanese Communist Party
JCS	Joint Chiefs of Staff
KLO	Korean Liaison Office
KMAG	Korean Military Advisory Group
KPA	Korean People's Army (DPRK)
KWP	Korean Workers' Party
MSB	Maritime Safety Board (Japan)
NDC	National Defense Corps (ROK)

NEBDA	Northeast Border Defense Army (China)
NKWP	North Korean Workers' Party
NSC	National Security Council
PLA	People's Liberation Army (China)
PRC	People's Republic of China
RGASPI	Russian State Archives on Social-Political History
ROC	Republic of China
ROK	Republic of Korea
ROKA	Republic of Korea Army
SCAP	Supreme Commander for the Allied Powers
SKWP	South Korean Workers' Party
TLO	Tactical Intelligence Liaison Office
TsKhSD	Center for storage of contemporary documents (Russia)
UNC	United Nations Command
UNCURK	United Nations Commission for the Unification and Rehabilitation of Korea
USSR	Union of Soviet Socialist Republics

Romanization and Expression of Names

THE ROMANIZATION OF KOREAN NAMES

This book uses elements of the McCune-Reischauer system of romanizing Korean. But I dropped the diacritical marks (breve and apostrophe) used to distinguish unaspirated consonants from aspirated consonants and simple vowels from compound vowels. When a specific romanization usage has been sanctioned by history and personal choice, I have not changed that usage.

THE EXPRESSION OF ASIAN NAMES

All Asian names are given in normal order, family name first and given name second, such as Kim Il Sung, Mao Zedong, and Yoshida Shigeru. In these cases, Kim, Mao, and Yoshida are family names. But some people express their names in English form, such as Shu Guang Zhang. Here Zhang is the family name.

Preface: The Korean War: Its Origins and Legacy

Though it began more than six decades ago and was suspended by a truce agreement in 1953, the Korean War is still not safely in the past. Its legacy continues to affect the people of Northeast Asia, the Asia-Pacific region, and indeed the whole world. With tensions on the Korean Peninsula continuing to flare, this unfinished war deserves careful scrutiny.

From the first Sino-Japanese War (1894–1895) to its defeat in World War II in 1945, an expansive Japan was at war, often aggressively. In the final chapter of this epoch, an attempt to create the Greater East Asia Co-prosperity Sphere as part of a Japanese pan-Asian empire, ended in Japan's defeat on August 15, 1945. Surrender followed the fall of Okinawa and US bombing that devastated cities across the Japanese mainland and culminated in the atomic bombing of Hiroshima and Nagasaki.

Since 1945, Japan has not gone to war. Not a single Japanese has been killed in war, nor have Japanese killed any enemy soldiers or civilians. The demise of the Japanese empire did not, however, bring peace to Northeast Asia. In contrast to Europe at the end of World War II, new conflicts immediately erupted across Northeast and Southeast Asia. In China, Nationalist and Chinese Communist Party forces waged war across the mainland from Manchuria to Hainan Island. In Vietnam, the Communist-led Democratic Republic of Vietnam fought the French colonialists who returned after World War II.

As for Korea, it was liberated from Japan's colonial rule in 1945, only to be divided at the 38th parallel by the United States and the Soviet Union, which controlled their respective zones. A struggle ensued to establish a unified, independent nation, with Communist nationalists in the north pitted against non- and anti-Communist nationalists in the south. Each sought domination. In 1948, two countries were established, the Democratic People's Republic of Korea (DPRK) and the Republic of Korea (ROK), supported by Moscow and Washington, respectively. Both Korean states sought legitimacy and to unify the peninsula by force, taking advantage of the growing confrontation between the United States and the USSR. ROK President Syngman Rhee and DPRK Prime Minister Kim Il Sung and his deputy Pak Hon-yong, who was born in South Korea, each shared this aspiration.

In September 1949, the Soviet Union successfully tested an atomic bomb, and the following month the Chinese Communists declared victory over the Nationalists. Amid such fundamentally changed international circumstances, on June 25, 1950, the Korean War burst forth with an attack by the North that was endorsed and aided by the Soviet Union.

With DPRK forces advancing rapidly across the South, the United States immediately gained UN Security Council resolutions on June 25 and 27 demanding that it end the invasion. Under cover of these resolutions, the United States entered the conflict to save the ROK, using bases in Japan and Okinawa for logistical support—as staging grounds for combat operations against DPRK forces and bombardment of North Korea. The Truman administration simultaneously intervened in the continuing Chinese civil war by sending the 7th Fleet to patrol the Taiwan Straits and defend the Nationalist government that had fled to Taiwan. Initially, the Korean People's Army (KPA) of the North pushed American and ROK forces as far south as the Pusan Perimeter. But US forces regrouped and repulsed the attack, and this time ROK forces along with the Americans drove north across the 38th parallel. In October 1950 they were on the verge of destroying the DPRK when China entered the war and forced US and ROK units to retreat. From this stage the Korean War, although it had been fought from the outset within the framework of great-power conflict, changed from a Korean civil war to a Sino-American war in the Korean Peninsula. The Soviet Air Force also covertly joined the conflict in disguised aircraft with Chinese markers, and US and Soviet pilots dueled in the skies over North Korea.

The entire region was drawn into what may be called the Northeast Asian War. The Chinese Revolution and the Korean War established a new regional order: two hostile states on the Korean Peninsula, a face-off between the two Korean foes with Washington, with ties with Japan and Taiwan, on one side and Beijing and Moscow on the other. The Northeast Asian War escalated US-Soviet confrontation into a global struggle, creating the Cold War system. Military confrontations were centered in East Asia, while Europe remained in an uneasy state of armed peace.

Although truce talks in the Korean War began in June 1951, the fighting continued back and forth near the prewar border until a truce was finally signed in July 1953. The ceasefire did not, however, lead to a peace treaty.

Rather, the fighting has simply remained suspended for sixty years, with the two sides in a state of permanent war readiness and hostility.

Like the Korean War, the Indochina War was halted by a truce, in 1954. France pulled out of Indochina, and the United States, which had been supporting France, intervened directly. The Vietnam War heated to a full boil in the 1960s. South Korea sent fifty thousand troops to assist US forces in Vietnam. Beijing and Moscow supported North Vietnam, and Pyongyang sent its pilots to fight in the skies over Vietnam. The Vietnam War was, from a global geopolitical perspective, a continuation of the Korean War. During the final stage of that cruel war, Beijing and Washington achieved détente, and in 1975 the Vietnamese Communists at last triumphed over the Americans. The thirty-year hot-war phase of New Asian Wars, which began with the Chinese civil war and continued in Korea and Indochina, had finally ended. The opening of US-China relations and Japan-China relations in the years 1970–1972 signaled the possibilities for change in Asia. In the late 1970s, China's new leader, Deng Xiaoping, launched economic reform and opening. South Korean President Park Chung-hee, who was weakened by his association with the abortive war in Vietnam, was killed by his secret police chief as democratic movements surged in 1979. And South Korea's democratic revolution followed in 1987.

In the late 1980s, the Cold War ended, too. Moscow and Beijing established diplomatic ties with Seoul, and China's "socialist market economy" surged. The Soviet Union collapsed in 1991, and Russia began its own transition from socialism, deepening North Korea's isolation and anxiety as Russia cut back on aid. But the United States remained a military superpower in the Asia-Pacific, and the essential structure of US-North Korea conflict remained intact. In 1993–1994, tensions between Washington and Pyongyang grew nearly to the point of open hostilities, making clear that the Korean War could flare up again. In the nearly twenty years since, hopes of ending the conflict in Korea have been repeatedly dashed. In 2000 the historic conference between the leaders of South and North Korea brought a breakthrough in North-South mutual recognition and reconciliation. But in 2006 and 2009, North Korea announced that it tested its nuclear weapons, insisting that they were needed to counter the US nuclear threat. In this dangerous stalemate in the Korean Peninsula, violence has even erupted on occasion. In November 2010, North Korea bombarded the South's Yeonpyeong Island off the west coast, killing three South Korean civilians. In 2011 Kim Jong-il passed away and the age of two "Great Leaders" ended. But although now headed by the young successor, Kim Jong-un, the son of Kim Jong-il and the grandson of Kim Il-sung, North Korea has adopted seemingly a more hostile and confrontational stance, and tensions between North and South—and the United States, remain high.

In short, the Korean conflict has never really ended. Despite the 1953 armistice, Washington and Pyongyang, as well as Seoul and Pyongyang, remain in conflict. Therefore we must now address the origins of the Korean War, the nature of the confrontation, and the ways in which it has affected and continues to affect the geopolitical landscape of Northeast Asia and the Pacific region if we are to finally end the war and give birth to a more harmonious era.

CLASHING INTERPRETATIONS OF THE KOREAN WAR

With both sides in Korea insisting that the other started the war, from the outset research on the war was extremely politicized. For decades the central issue debated was who launched the initial attack? In North Korea, the Soviet Union, and China, the official line was that South Korea, acting on instructions from Washington, was the aggressor. But in the United States and South Korea, the generally accepted view was that the North attacked the South, either on orders from the Kremlin or as part of a Sino-Soviet plot.

Skeptics in the United States, on the other hand, suggested that even if North Korea struck first, Washington had laid a trap and induced the attack. I. F. Stone's *Hidden History of the Korean War* (1952) is the classic work in this genre.[1] In 1960, Allen S. Whiting's *China Crosses the Yalu: The Decision to Enter the Korean War* showed that Beijing did not press to start the conflict.[2] The following year, the first volume of the official US Army history of the war, covering the six months from the start of hostilities to China's intervention, presented new information about US military operations.[3] Roy E. Appleman vividly depicted how four US infantry divisions, seriously understrength and only partially trained and equipped to fight, retreated before North Korea's determined attacks. An official history of the air war in Korea—a major study based on classified information—was published the same year.[4] In this work, author Robert F. Futrell provided a detailed picture of the hidden war.

In Japan, the writings of Shinobu Seizaburo provoked controversy. In a penetrating 1965 essay and a book four years later, Shinobu characterized the conflict as a civil war, culminating in a revolutionary attempt by Kim Il Sung to unify Korea by force.[5] The Korean War, in his view, was neither part of an expansionist strategy by Moscow nor the result of a trap set by Washington. Defenders of the orthodox leftist view in Japan—that the United States and South Korea invaded the North in June 1950—disputed Shinobu's interpretation, but his argument remains compelling. A study by Kamiya Fuji (1966) and an essay by Okonogi Masao (1975) reinforced Shinobu's interpretation in Japanese academia.[6]

Until the mid-to-late 1970s, as shown below, the diplomatic record on the Korean War was essentially closed, and scholars had to rely on personal memoirs and secondary sources. But with the end of the twenty-year classification period for many US records, from the mid-1970s US archives began to open to researchers: State Department and US Army records, captured North Korean documents, and the personal papers of American politicians became available. *The Foreign Relations of the United States* (hereafter *FRUS*) volume for 1950 appeared in 1976.[7] Two Americans, William W. Stueck Jr. and James I. Matray, published books based on State Department records in 1981 and 1985,[8] respectively, as did Okonogi Masao in 1986.[9] These works are all first-rate scholarship. The State Department records showed that a rattled Truman administration quickly changed policy toward Korea.

From the 1980s, the most important "revisionist" scholars to emerge out of the political conflicts and reflections of the Vietnam War era used declassified official documents to criticize conventional interpretations of the Cold War, which portrayed the Soviet Union as an aggressor and the main cause of the Cold War, and the DPRK as a proxy. These scholars investigated hitherto uncontested justifications of US actions abroad in order to show Washington's policy errors and its responsibility for the outbreak of war. Bruce Cumings, who provided the most comprehensive analysis of personal papers and diplomatic, military, and intelligence records, is representative of this group. His monumental research on the Korean War appeared in two volumes in 1981 and 1990.[10] The first volume, a brilliant eye-opening account based on US Army records, described the activities of People's Committees in South Korea in the years 1945–1947 and their suppression by the US Military Government. In volume two, covering 1947 to 1950, Cumings took the position that the Korean War had begun in 1945. "From the start of this project it has been our position that the question pregnant with ideological dynamite, 'who started the Korean War,' is the wrong question," he wrote. "Who started the Korean War? This question should not be asked."[11] Cumings accepted I. F. Stone's hypothesis of an American "rollback" strategy in the years 1945–1950. Specifically, turning to June 1950, Cumings paid special attention to what happened at Ongjin at 4:00 a.m. on June 25. He suggested that the South Korean 17th Regiment might have started to occupy Haeju prior to the North Korean attack. He also addressed issues ignored by other writers, including the North Korean occupation of South Korea, Taiwan's role in the start of the war, and the US-ROK occupation of the North.

Pang Sun-joo, a Korean scholar living in the United States, examined captured North Korean documents that Cumings had not fully utilized, and in his 1986 study he published the text of two KPA orders to frontline units to attack, showing that the KPA had opened the fighting.[12] Poring over US intelligence reports from Korea, Pang also concluded that the United States had been aware of North Korean battle preparations and allowed Pyongyang to attack.

Cumings and Jon Halliday, a British researcher, worked on a television program about the Korean War by Thames Productions in the early 1980s and jointly authored *Korea: The Unknown War* (1988). This book-length photo essay reiterated Cumings' contention that "Who started the Korean War?" was the wrong question.[13]

Gavan McCormack, in Australia, published *Cold War, Hot War* in 1983.[14] While presenting both of the two dominant interpretations of which side started the war, he doubted that the North was guilty as charged. He was inclined to think that the militarily inferior South Korean side deliberately provoked a counterattack from the North by partially occupying Haeju. He also urged examination of allegations that the United States had used biological weapons in Korea.

Korea: The War before Vietnam by Callum A. MacDonald, a critical English specialist on the United States, accepted the theory that North Korea started the war. But he emphasized the cruelty of the US "limited war" against the North.[15]

Additional FRUS volumes—*Korea and China in 1951* and *Korea 1952–1954*—appeared in 1983 and 1984, respectively.[16] Also, Rosemary Foot's study of the Korean armistice negotiations, *A Substitute for Victory: The Politics of Peacemaking at the Korean Armistice Talks*, appeared in 1990.[17] Another major work was published that same year: the second volume of the US Army official history of the Korean War.[18]

Many researchers on the Korean War in the 1980s, typified by Cumings, were critical of Cold War America. These works were based primarily on US materials—only Cumings could read Korean—and lacked a thorough analysis of internal developments in North Korea.

Also in Japan, a three-volume account of the Korean War by Sasaki Harutaka, based on Republic of Korea Army (ROKA) materials and interviews, was published in 1976.[19] Fifteen years later, in 1991, a Japanese translation of Kim Hak-joon's general treatment of the Korean War appeared. A South Korean, Kim's major finding was that the North Korean leadership had split in 1951 over whether to continue the fighting; the Pak Hon-yong faction favored continuing to fight, while the realist faction of Kim Il Sung and Choe Yong-gon opposed this course.[20]

THE NEW CHINESE SOURCES AND CAPTURED DOCUMENTS

In China in the 1980s, in the wake of reforms initiated by Deng Xiaoping, fascinating new primary materials became available. Using these materials, scholars studied the role of Chinese Koreans in Manchuria during the second

Sino-Japanese War of 1937–1945, the armed struggle against Japan in Manchuria, and the Korean War.

I wrote my first article on the Korean War in 1990, using the North Korean materials discovered by Pang Sun-joo and new research and primary materials in China.[21] My view was that after 1948, with the two Korean states competing for legitimacy, there was no alternative to unification by force. The showdown was framed by rhetoric in the South about "advancing North" and unifying the country and by the North's call to "complete the national territory." Based on captured North Korean documents, I argued that the KPA, acting on orders from the government, started the Korean War.

Afterward, in the 1990s, many new materials related to the war appeared, including the memoirs of Chinese generals, the declassified papers of Mao Zedong, and historical accounts. Books by Xu Yan, Qi Dexue, and Heng Xueming advanced our understanding of China's role.[22] Scholars could now interview veterans of the war in Beijing and Yanchi. In the Soviet Union, a memoir on the Soviet Air Force's participation in the war appeared, as did fragmentary materials about Stalin by Soviet historians.

The first person to use the Chinese materials extensively was Shu Ken'ei (Zhu Jianrong), a Chinese scholar in Japan. His 1991 study described how Mao Zedong overrode the opposition of colleagues and dispatched Chinese troops into the conflict.[23] In 1993, I wrote three articles based on the new scholarship in China and the first Soviet documents opened for scholarly use.[24] At about the same time, two Chinese scholars in the United States, Chen Jian and Zhang Shu Guang, published rigorous studies on China and the war.[25]

My first book on the war, published in 1995, combined the earlier essays and new writing.[26] Among the topics covered were President Syngman Rhee's state of mind and strategy in June 1950, the Japanese Communist Party (JCP) and the "Japan factor," Japan's cooperation with US military operations, and the occupations of southern and northern Korea (extending Cumings' account). I also discussed the establishment of a joint North Korean–Chinese command, conditions in wartime North Korea based on Soviet archival materials, the suppression of the Pak Hon-yong faction, and the clash between US officials and Syngman Rhee over a truce agreement. I tried to elucidate some of the most contentious or elusive issues.

Hagiwara Ryo, Park Myung-lim, and Suh Dong-man studied captured North Korean documents extensively. Hagiwara's study (1993) showed the disposition of frontline KPA divisions, including their code names, and the collapse of KPA units after US and ROKA forces landed at Inchon in September 1950. Former JCP writer Hagiwara called the conflict a "conspiratorial war launched by Kim Il Sung." Yet he also concluded that the United States was aware of KPA preparations and used the DPRK's attack to intervene in Korea. To Hagiwara, the "great conspiracy" was undertaken by Washington. But there is no proof for this assertion.[27]

Park Myung-lim's book (1996), a revised version of his doctoral thesis at Korea University, following Cumings' work, presented a different historical paradigm. It also set a new standard for research on the war.[28] Park's examination of captured North Korean documents and South Korean materials depicted internal conditions on both sides. The division of Korea into two separate states in 1948 set the stage for the conflict, but Park attributes the outbreak of fighting to a decision by northern leadership, which was inclined toward "radical militarism," with the exception of Defense Minister Choe Yong-gon, who opposed the war policy. Park also meticulously examined advocacy in South Korea of unification by force as well as the political situation on the eve of war.

Suh Dong-man's doctoral dissertation at the University of Tokyo (1995) thoroughly analyzed changes in the party, state, and military system in North Korea. He also provided the first description of the Korean Workers' Party apparatus within the KPA.[29]

THE DECLASSIFIED RUSSIAN MATERIALS

Russian archival material about the war was made public sporadically after the start of Perestroika in the late 1980s. But with the end of the Soviet Union in 1991, a fundamental change occurred. In June 1994, President Boris Yeltsin presented ROK President Kim Yong-sam with a collection of key records, which was publicized by the ROK Foreign Ministry on July 20 that year. The collection consisted of 216 documents, a total of 548 pages; however, the full text of only four documents was made public. Among the released materials was a chronological description of the events from January 1949 to October 1950 (running sixty-three pages in Russian) prepared by a Soviet Foreign Ministry official. I obtained this description when my earlier book was in proofs and was able to include only a commentary on the Russian documents in a postscript.

The ROK government kept the remainder of the Russian documents closed to scholarly research. In 1995, American scholar Kathryn Weathersby and others who used these materials in Moscow obtained a complete set of copies for the Cold War International History Project (CWIHP), however, in cooperation with the Korean Research Center at Columbia University. The CWIHP translated a number of important documents and provided the set of original documents to scholars around the world. Exegeses soon began.

In January 1996, at a CWIHP symposium on the "Cold War in Asia" at Hong Kong University, several scholars discussed the Russian materials, including Weathersby and Alexandre Mansourov, a PhD candidate at Columbia University. In addition, they distributed proof issue 6–7 of the *CWIHP Bulletin*, which contains their translations of 115 and 21 documents, respectively.[30] Using the documents from 1949, Mansourov showed that the Kremlin feared a ROKA attack on the North. I made a presentation at the symposium on my book and a 1995 article on Japanese Communist Party leader Nosaka Sanzo. Judging from subsequent developments, I argued, when Stalin and Zhou Enlai met in September 1952, Chinese leaders were concerned about Kim Il Sung's wish to end the war immediately by accepting the US proposal on the POW problem. Stalin unhesitatingly supported the Chinese position that the war should continue until the US abandoned its position on POWs, though he was sympathetic to Kim Il Sung's wish to end the war. At the same time, Stalin, seeking scapegoats for the failures of the Korean War and the Japanese revolution among those who called for continuing the war, agreed to the removal of both Ito Ritsu from the Japanese Communist Party and Pak Hon-yong from the North Korean government as traitors or foreign agents. This reflected the Soviet leader's view that the war could be ended.[31] Some participants at the symposium considered my assessments of Stalin's views speculation unsubstantiated by documentation. This discussion triggered my subsequent work.

The CWIHP kindly provided me with copies of all the Russian materials it possessed, and I began to work on them. There were 406 items, a total of 1,118 pages. In addition, the *Seoul Shinmun* published certain Soviet materials related to the Korean War in a series from May 15 to August 1, 1995. With few exceptions, these were documents that had been made available by the CWIHP.

Not all of the relevant Russian materials were made public, however. For example, neither the CWIHP nor *Seoul Shinmun* publications included any documents from June 1950. But in the summer of 1995, the Moscow bureau of the *Sankei Shimbun* and the British Broadcasting Corporation (BBC) obtained a report from Soviet Ambassador Shtykov to Vice-Chief of Staff Zaharov dated June 26, 1950.[32] Sent immediately after the start of hostilities, this document is extremely valuable, clearly conveying the initial operations of the KPA attack. The Moscow bureau of the *Sankei Shimbun* also obtained materials related to biological warfare in Korea that were published in January 1998. Weathersby authenticated them and published a translation in the *CWIHP Bulletin*.[33]

In March 1998, a book entitled *The Korean War as Seen in Soviet Documents* by Evgenii Bajanov, vice-president of the Russian Foreign Affairs Academy, and his wife, Natalia, was published in Seoul. A documentary collection with brief explanations, the book includes some documents not contained in the CWIHP collection.[34]

Then, in 2000, Alexander Torkunov, president of the Moscow State University of International Relations, published, in Moscow, *The Enigmatic*

War: The Korean Conflict, 1950–1953. This book also contains original Russian materials, including more than a dozen items not in the CWIHP collection.[35] Therefore, it is useful as a collection of Russian documents, but the academic level is rather low. Torkunov makes the dubious assertion that Stalin insisted on continuing the war during the truce conferences. A Japanese translation of Torkunov's book was published in November 2001.[36]

Analysis of the new Russian materials contributed greatly to the understanding of the war. They consist mainly of telegrams from Stalin, Mao Zedong, Kim Il Sung, and Soviet ambassadors Shtykov and Razuvaev in Pyongyang. The thinking, mindsets, and styles of Stalin, Mao, Kim Il Sung, and Pak Hon-yong were revealed for the first time.

The new Russian materials cover almost every aspect of the start of the war. They show that Kim Il Sung and Pak Hon-yong wanted to unify the peninsula by force. Initially opposed, Stalin in early 1950 approved the attack. With aid from Stalin and Mao, North Korea then struck against the South. These materials are also a window on relations between Stalin and Mao. Stalin took the initiative for the truce conference in May 1951, but once it started consistently supported Mao's position on negotiations. As noted, the Soviet leader was also sympathetic to Kim Il Sung, who wanted to stop the fighting in 1952.

Kathryn Weathersby, who used these materials in a series of articles, tended to conclude that Stalin never agreed to end the war,[37] contradicting my view. At one time, Bruce Cumings disputed the very use of these Russian materials and clashed with Weathersby.[38] In my view, he should have examined the Russian materials and revised his interpretation of the origins of the war at the time. But in his 2012 book, *The Korean War: A History,* he acknowledged that "It is now clear from Soviet documents that Pyongyang had made a decision to escalate a civil conflict to the level of conventional warfare."[39] Alexandre Mansourov, who used new Soviet documents and others for his dissertation, drew upon Cumings' research for his interpretation of the 1949 crisis and made a compelling argument that Stalin and Ambassador Shtykov were concerned about a possible attack by Seoul in 1949. However, Mansourov seems to have overlooked the fact that Kim Il Sung and other North Korean leaders were not greatly alarmed by this prospect.[40] A 1996 book by Vojtech Mastny, *The Cold War and Soviet Insecurity: The Stalin Years,* also used the Russian materials and addressed my presentation at the Hong Kong symposium.[41] Mastny holds that Stalin was opposed to stopping the war in 1952.

Chinese researcher Shen Zhihua presented new Russian materials in his book *The Sino-Soviet Alliance and the Korean War.*[42]

When a Korean translation of my 1995 book, *The Korean War,* by Suh Dong-man appeared in 1999, I added a chapter on the new Russian materials.[43] However, in light of these materials, the book needed extensive revision, which I began in 1998. Meanwhile, new materials continued to appear in China, and many books were published in 2000 to commemorate the fiftieth anniversary of China's entry into the war. Among them, a study by the Academy of Military Sciences, *A History of the War to Resist America and Aid Korea*, is an outstanding three-volume study.[44] Also, Pang Xianzhi and Li Jie used new materials about Mao Zedong in *Mao Zedong and the Cause of Resistance to America and Aid to Korea*,[45] as did Chen Jian in *Mao's China and the Cold War*.[46]

Although I discussed aspects of Japan's involvement in the war, mainly the Japanese Communist Party and Korean residents in Japan, in *The Korean War*, in 1998 I took up the Japan factor more extensively in an essay on Stalin's policy.[47] More recently, with growing interest in Japan's cooperation with the United States in the conflict, Yamazaki Shizuo published a book on Japan's wartime role.[48] Although written as a political protest, Yamazaki's *Japan's Cooperation in the Korean War* used military histories and municipal, prefectural, and central government records. Nam Ki-jong's PhD dissertation, "The Korean War and Japan," is a scholarly analysis of the issues based on archival materials of General Headquarters (GHQ), the Allied Forces in Japan.[49] Aided by these works, I have comprehensively covered the Japan factor in this study.

A symposium held in Seoul in 2000 to commemorate the fiftieth anniversary of the start of the Korean War included a very informative presentation by Paul G. Pierpaoli on how the United States was profoundly changed by the war.[50] Pierpaoli's 1999 book, *Truman and Korea: The Political Culture of the Early Cold War*, is also a major work.[51] Papers by South Korean scholars on social transformation and legacies, atrocities against civilians, and South Korean prisoners of war detained in North Korea illuminate other dimensions of the conflict.[52] In addition, Kim Tong-chun has written an acclaimed book on the war's social impact: *The War and Society: What Was the Korean War to Us?*[53] At the symposium and at another meeting in Taiwan in March 2002, I gave papers that portrayed Japan and Taiwan as beneficiaries of the war.

In March 2002, studying all the new Russian documents and all new scholarly works, I published a new Japanese book, *Chosen Senso Zenshi* [The Korean War: A History], from Iwanami Shoten. One year later Chinese researcher Shen Zhihua presented his interpretations based on new Russian documents in his book *Mao Zedong, Stalin and the Korean War*. Among others, he too mentioned the disagreement in 1952 between Kim Il Sung, who wished to end the war immediately, and Mao Zedong, who opposed accepting the US demand about repatriation of war prisoners, but Shen rejected my argument, supporting Weatherby's stance about Stalin's willingness to continue the war.[54]

Since then, in the second half of the first decade of the new millennium, important studies were published in South Korea. Chong Pyong-jun's *The Korean War: Clashes at the 38 ᵗʰ Parallel and Formation of the War* (2006) is a meticulous analysis of the border clashes of 1947–1949 preceding the war.[55] With assistance from Pang Sun-joo, Chong examined captured North Korean documents in the US National Archives more thoroughly than earlier researchers. He also used reports by V. N. Razuvaev, head of the Soviet military advisory group in North Korea, that were published by the War History Compilation Committee, Ministry of National Defense, Republic of Korea.[56] Yom In-ho's *Another Korean War: The Fatherland for Manchurian Koreans and the War* (2010) is an exhaustive study, based on Chinese sources, of the transfer of Korean units in the People's Liberation Army to North Korea.[57] Park Myong-lim's *Korea 1950: War and Peace* (2002), an extension of his earlier research, covers the period from June 25, 1950, to the retreat of the Korean People's Army in September 1950 and China's subsequent entry into the war.[58] Park takes up the issue of wartime atrocities, previously addressed by Kim Tong-chun, and provides greater detail on atrocities committed by North Korea. All of these studies were consulted in preparing the present work.

This work is a translation of my Japanese book, *Chosen senso zenshii* [The Korean War: a history] (Iwanami Shoten, 2002), but in a revised and enlarged version. In particular, this work incorporates the newly available Soviet materials about the critical meeting between Stalin, Kim Il Sung, and Pak Hon-yong in September 1952. These records provide the documentary foundation for my understanding of the relationship between Stalin and Kim Il Sung at critical junctures of the war.[59] This document was also published in Chinese at the same time in Shen Zihua's collection of Soviet archival materials concerning the Korean War, which contains new documents from Foreign Ministry and Defense Ministry archives.[60]

TOWARD A NEW INTERPRETATION OF THE KOREAN WAR

This book treats the Korean War as a regional conflict, a "Northeast Asian War." In *The Korean War: An International History*, William Stueck writes, "In its timing, its course and its outcome, the Korean War served as a substitute for World War III."[61] I sympathize with his perspective. In fact, in earlier writing, I called Korea a "semi-world war." But, upon reflection, the concept "Northeast Asian War" seems more meaningful.[62] North and South Korea, the USSR, China, the United States, Taiwan, and Japan were the nations that were most deeply involved in and most deeply affected by the war. The conflict reshaped the nations, people, and political alignments of the whole Northeast Asian region.[63] However, taking into account such participants in the United Nations forces as Canada, Australia, New Zealand, the Philippines, and Thailand, it may be better to call it an "Asia-Pacific War." Yet, from still other angles—the war's shaping of the early years of the Cold War, with the United Nations as an umbrella for the US-led forces, and the participation of European and Asian nations—the conflict displays many features of a world war. I nevertheless place special importance to the character of the Korean War as a Northeast Asian War, because Northeast Asia, with the United States' participation, was the region in which the most fundamental changes occurred as the legacies of that war.

This book describes the Korean War from its outbreak to the truce in July 1953. As we will see, the character of the hostilities in Northeast Asia as a result of the war changed dramatically through a series of critical events. These events included US-Chinese reconciliation, democratic revolution in South Korea, the end of the Cold War, the normalization of ROK-Soviet and ROK-Chinese relations, the demise of the Soviet Union, the North-South rapprochement in Korea, and the rise of China. But, despite these developments, North Korea and the United States remain hostile antagonists. Their antagonism, combined with the lingering abnormality of North Korean relations with Japan, its former colonial ruler, challenges in no small measure the North Korean state and people, with implications for the entire Korean Peninsula, Northeast Asia, and the Asia-Pacific. The legacy of the Korean War remains a fundamental reality for the peoples of Northeast Asia and the Asia-Pacific.

Chapter One

Two States and Unification by Force

Japan's surrender in World War II on August 15, 1945, freed Korea from Japanese colonial rule. However, the surrender was followed by the division of the Korean Peninsula into two zones and their occupation by the United States and the Soviet Union. The timing of Japan's capitulation was consequential for Korea: had the Suzuki cabinet accepted the Potsdam Declaration in early August, the United States would not have dropped atomic bombs on Hiroshima and Nagasaki. Nor would the Soviet Union have entered the conflict against Japan. And Korea probably would not have been divided into two occupied zones at the 38th parallel.

Moscow accepted Washington's proposal on August 15 for a division of occupied zones of Korea as part of an agreement that led to the creation of a divided country and two spheres of influence in Northeast Asia. Korean hopes for a single independent country had been dashed. Three years later, in August and September 1948, Seoul and Pyongyang declared the creation of the Republic of Korea (ROK) and the Democratic People's Republic of Korea (DPRK). Each state claimed the entire peninsula and denounced the other as a puppet of a foreign power holding a part of its territory. It was a recipe for rancor and continued conflict.

Adopted at a constitutional assembly in Seoul on July 12, 1948, Article 3 of the ROK Constitution specified that the territory of the Republic of Korea "shall consist of the Korean Peninsula and its adjacent islands." At the opening ceremony of the ROK's National Assembly in December, President Syngman Rhee declared that, in cooperation with the United Nations, South Korea would hold free elections in the North to select about one hundred members to complete the assembly.[1] In Pyongyang on September 8, 1948, the Supreme People's Assembly adopted a constitution for the DPRK. Arti-

1

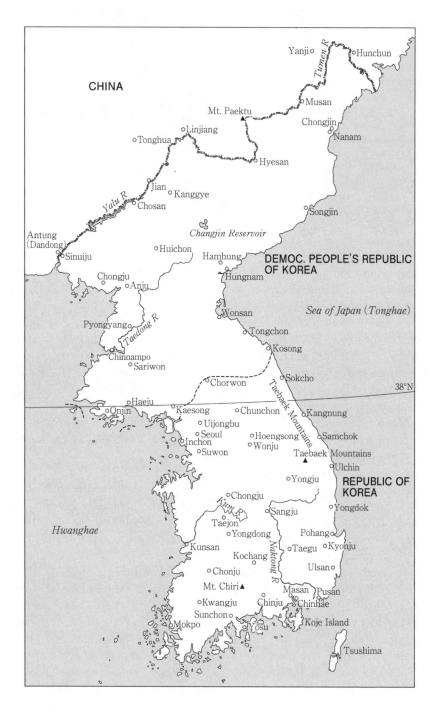

Map of Korea

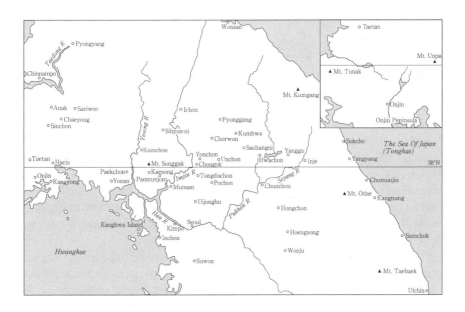

North and South of the 38th Parallel

cle 103 stated bluntly: "The capital of the Democratic People's Republic of Korea is Seoul."

A month later, DPRK Prime Minister Kim Il Sung announced the following political program: "The central government, established with the consent of South and North Koreans, will unify all the Korean people and use all its power for the rapid construction of a unified, democratic, autonomous and independent nation. We shall make every effort to realize the proposal of the Soviet government for the simultaneous withdrawal of both [American and Soviet] forces, the most urgent condition to guarantee the completion of national territory and the unification of the fatherland."[2]

The two Korean governments shared a common goal, but it was an antagonistic one: to remove the other by any means available. From the outset, the North called for "completion of the national territory" (*kukdo wanjong*), a euphemism for destroying the Rhee regime. A little later, the South adopted the slogan "Advance North, Unify the Nation" (*pukchin tongil*), code words for unification by force. But Korean aspirations for a single nation collided with the US-Soviet agreement on postwar Northeast Asia. This agreement—shaped by the Yalta Agreement, General Order No. 1 of the Supreme Commander of the Allied Powers (SCAP), and the Moscow Foreign Ministers' Conference of December 1945—called for the United States to occupy Japan. The Soviet Union agreed to participate in the administration of Japan through the Allied Council for Japan, an advisory body to SCAP. The Soviets acquired southern Sakhalin and the Kurile Islands, while the United States detached Okinawa from Japan and ruled it as a military colony. Moscow recognized the legitimacy of Chiang Kai-shek's Kuomintang government in China in return for rights in Manchuria and recognition by the United States and Chiang of the independence of Outer Mongolia. Taiwan reverted from Japan to China. And, of course, Korea was divided into two zones, respectively by the two powers.

Despite the start of the Cold War in Europe, Stalin respected this framework in Asia. His policy toward the Japanese Communist Party (JCP) showed the extent of his commitment. The Communist Party of the Soviet Union (CPSU) had no overt ties to the JCP from 1946 to 1949. All contacts were handled secretly by agents of the Red Army Main Intelligence Department (GRU) and JCP leader Nosaka Sanzo. Stalin wanted to avoid any indication that the Kremlin was manipulating the JCP to challenge American hegemony.[3]

Why was Stalin so cautious? By defeating Germany, the Soviet Union had brought Eastern Europe under its sway; the Soviet camp stretched from North Korea to East Germany. Yet this expansion strained Russian finances, and the Kremlin wanted to avoid a confrontation with Washington. The postwar Soviet Union, overwhelmed by heavy war damages, could not directly challenge the United States. Above all, Stalin feared the American atomic bomb.[4]

The presence of foreign forces in the two Koreas may have also acted as a barrier to conflict. In October 1948, the Soviet command in North Korea started to withdraw its troops, completing the drawdown in late December. About this time, the United States finally began to remove its forces from the South. At this stage, the South was militarily superior to the North.

But Communist successes in the Chinese civil war encouraged North Korean leaders to pursue unification by force. The People's Liberation Army (PLA) gained complete control of Manchuria in October–November 1948, inspiring North Korea, which had allowed the Chinese Communists to operate from its territory. The United States had not intervened militarily in China, but it now reacted swiftly to the specter of an imminent Communist victory. On October 9, 1948, President Harry S. Truman approved National Security Council (NSC) report 13/2 and changed occupation priorities in Japan from democratization to economic recovery, an attempt to make the former enemy a non-Communist regional outpost. Washington announced nine principles to stabilize Japan's economy, and in February 1949, Joseph Dodge, a Detroit banker, arrived in Tokyo to implement a tough recovery policy, ensuring a direct clash with the JCP and organized labor. In the January 1949 election in Japan, the JCP increased its Diet seats from four to thirty-five, boosting the party leadership's morale and determination. To deny public sector employees the right to strike and reduce the workforce at the Japan National Railways, the occupation authorities had to attack the JCP and the unions under the party's control.[5] Korean members of the party must have reported the conflict to the DPRK leadership in Pyongyang, providing further incentive for action against the South.

Mao Zedong had wanted to meet Stalin since 1947 to discuss support and solicit advice in the war against the Nationalists, who the USSR still recognized as the legitimate government of China. Stalin approved a secret meeting, but postponed the trip throughout 1948.[6] At year's end, the Kremlin apparently acceded to Mao's wishes. Then, on December 31, the Kuomintang asked Stalin to help arrange an end to the civil war. Between January 10 and 15, 1949, Stalin and Mao exchanged six cables, agreeing that, in order to have a pretext for the USSR to avoid responding directly to the KMT request, the Chinese Communists would offer to negotiate with the Nationalists if Chiang Kai-shek and other top figures were excluded.[7] On January 26, Stalin sent Anastas Mikoyan (under the alias Andreev) to Chinese Communist Party (CCP) headquarters at Xibaipo in Hebei Province to meet Mao and other Chinese leaders for the first time. Mikoyan advised the Chinese Communists to occupy Shanghai, Nanjing, and other cities quickly, create a functioning political structure, and allow other political parties and groups to operate after the revolution.[8] At this point the Soviet Union secretly changed its China policy from recognizing the KMT government as a legitimate authority to supporting the Communist revolutionary war.

In 1948, the Soviet Union had suffered several setbacks: it had failed to crush Tito's revolt in Yugoslavia, prevent West Berlin's independence through the Berlin Blockade, and gain influence over the new state of Israel.[9] Acutely aware of US military power, the Kremlin feared that the advances of the Chinese revolution would break its postwar agreement on Asia with Washington. Soviet accusations that Jewish doctors in the USSR were American spies signaled its misgivings about the United States. In January 1949, Solomon A. Lozovskii, a Jew and the deputy people's commissar of foreign affairs, was ousted from the CPSU and arrested, along with people associated with the Jewish Anti-Fascist Committee, including Polina Zhemchuzhina, the wife of People's Commissar of Foreign Affairs Vyacheslav Molotov. An article accusing Jewish theater critics of being "rootless cosmopolitans" appeared in *Pravda* on January 28, 1949. It ushered in a widespread anti-Semitic campaign.[10]

But regardless of the international situation, the fate of the Korean Peninsula would not be resolved independent of the intentions of the leadership of the two states. In the DPRK, Kim Il Sung was both the prime minister and secretary general of the North Korean Workers' Party (NKWP). Born in 1912, Kim had fought against the Japanese in Manchuria under the direction of the CCP and served as commander of the 2nd Front, 1st Route Army, before fleeing to Soviet territory in 1940. Deputy Premier and Foreign Minister Pak Hon-yong (born 1900), the number two leader in the DPRK, was a longtime Communist activist who had reorganized the Communist Party in Seoul in August 1945 before moving to the North in 1948. After the merger of the South Korean Workers' Party and the North Korean Workers' Party in June 1949, Pak became vice-chairman of the Korean Workers' Party (KWP). Until 1948, Kim Il Sung had been the top leader in the North, but from early 1949, Kim and Pak shared authority. They consulted on major matters and both participated in negotiations with China and the USSR.

Returnees from China, Manchuria, and the Soviet Union formed the second tier of leadership in North Korea. Ho Ka-i (born 1908), a Soviet citizen, was second vice-chairman and secretary of the KWP. From the Yan'an group, Kim Tu-bong (born 1889) chaired the Standing Committee of the Supreme People's Assembly, and Pak Il-u (born 1912) was minister of internal affairs and a member of the KWP's Political Committee. The Manchurian faction was concentrated in the military, except for Kim Il Sung and Kim Chaek (born 1903), the vice-premier and minister of industry. The Soviet and Yan'an groups ran the government and KWP. Several military men came from the Yan'an group, like Pang Ho-san (born 1916), a division commander, while Defense Minister Choe Yong-gon (born 1900) and Chief of Staff Kang Kon (born 1918) were both from the Manchurian faction. Mu Chong (born 1905) and Kim Ung (born 1912) from the Yan'an group were vice-ministers in the Ministry of National Defense, and Yu Song-chol (born 1918) and other Soviet Koreans headed the ministry's bureaus. After the DPRK was established in 1948, some members of the Southern Workers' Party also joined the leadership. Yi Sung-yob (born 1905), for example, was justice minister. This influx seemingly reduced the influence of the Yan'an group.[11]

The dominant political figure in the Republic of Korea was President Syngman Rhee. Born in 1875, Rhee had a long record of nationalistic activity that included serving as the first president of the Provisional Korean Government in Shanghai. He had lived in exile in Hawaii and the United States for more than twenty years. Prime Minister and Defense Minister Yi Pom-sok (born 1898), a nationalist who had been active in China in the Kwangbok Army, was a close associate of Rhee who often clashed with American officials. Shin Sung-mo (born 1891), another important senior official, had participated in the movement for Korean independence in Vladivostok with Shin Chae-ho. Later he graduated from a maritime school in Shanghai and captained British merchant vessels. A supporter of the Korean independence movement, Shin had ties to Rhee that probably dated from the 1920s. After August 1945, Shin headed the Korean Youth Corps, was minister of internal affairs, and in March 1949 was named defense minister. Shin's competence in English and ability to get along with Americans explains the bizarre appointment of a neophyte in military matters to head the Defense Ministry.[12]

The men who actually ran the army under Shin Sung-mo were profession-al soldiers who had been trained at Japanese military schools and served as officers in the Imperial Japanese Army. The first ROKA chief of staff, Chae Pyong-dok, graduated from the Imperial Army Officer's School (49th class) and had been a major in command of the Inchon Arsenal in August 1945. Chae had no combat experience, and was removed as ROKA chief of staff but reappointed in December 1948. Chong Il-gwon, the deputy chief of staff, attended the Mukden Officer's School of the Manchukuo Army and graduat-ed from the Imperial Officer's School six classes after Chae Pyong-dok; he served in the Manchukuo Army in August 1945.

The most famous ROKA division commander was Kim Sok-won, also a graduate of the Imperial Army Officer's School, who had served in Manchu-ria and bragged of hunting down Kim Il Sung's guerrilla unit. US officers were especially wary of Kim. Other former officers in the Japanese military included two who had served against the Communists in the Kanto (Chien-tao) Special Unit in Manchuria. Kim Paek-il graduated from the Shenyang Officer's School and Paek Sun-yop graduated from the Manchukuo Army Officer's School. His younger brother Paek In-yop, a regimental commander in the ROKA, had also served in the Kanto Special Unit. [13]

Yun Chi-yong, the first ROK minister of internal affairs, had been Syng-man Rhee's personal secretary in Hawaii. Kim Hyo-sok, Shin Sung-mo's successor as minister of internal affairs, was one of the founders of the Korean Democratic Party, a member of the National Assembly, and in 1949 vice-minister to Shin, who seems to have recommended him for the position of minister. Shin Sung-mo and Kim Hyo-sok appear to have been closely related. When the Korean War started, Kim, who had pushed for the purge of South Korean Workers' Party (SKWP) members from the ROKA on the eve of the war, stayed in Seoul and supported the North. [14]

The tightly knit northern regime under Kim Il Sung and Pak Hon-yong seemed much stronger than the Rhee administration in the South.

CROSS-BORDER ATTACKS BY SOUTH KOREA

In January 1949, Kim Il Sung and Pak Hon-yong were preparing for their first trip to the Soviet Union since the establishment of the DPRK. They hoped to conclude a friendship treaty between Pyongyang and Moscow that would serve as a military alliance. The pact would be a security guarantee now that Soviet troops had been withdrawn from the North the month before. Kim and Pak must have also seen a treaty as assurance of Soviet support in the event that North Korea moved against the South. But their hopes were frustrated.

Soviet ambassador to the DPRK Terentii Shtykov met with Kim Il Sung and Pak Hon-yong on January 17. Shtykov informed them that the Soviet government had agreed to their proposal for a visit to the USSR by a Korean government delegation. Kim and Pak were delighted and asked when they could go. Shtykov replied that they should prepare all the issues they intended to raise in Moscow, and when that work was completed, the date would be set. He suggested a provisional date of February. However, the ambassador also explained to Kim and Pak that with Korea divided, early conclusion of a treaty of friendship and mutual assistance with the Soviet Union was not appropriate. Such a treaty might be used by reactionary forces in South Korea in propaganda campaigns against the Democratic People's Republic of Korea.

Shtykov's stance was troubling to Kim and Pak. Kim timidly argued for the necessity of such a treaty, one involving Soviet military support, but Shtykov managed to persuade them that it was premature.[15]

Ambassador Shtykov was no ordinary diplomat. Born in 1907, he had been second secretary of the Communist Party in Leningrad under Andrei A. Zhdanov from 1938. Shtykov had been in the Red Army at the time of the Soviet-Finland War and later fought against the Germans. During the Soviet campaign against Japan in August 1945, he had been a member of the military council of Gen. K. A. Meretskov's First Far Eastern Front and was the chief formulator and executor of Soviet policy toward North Korea. Shtykov had headed the Soviet delegation to the Joint US-Soviet Commission to assist the formation of a provisional Korean government in 1946 and then became the first Soviet ambassador to the DPRK.[16] He was an important patron of Kim Il Sung and North Korea, and DPRK leaders had to defer to his wishes.

While Shtykov's reticence about a treaty was disappointing to Kim and Pak, some belligerent moves by ROK forces around the time of their meeting only deepened Shtykov's concern. The South launched repeated attacks across the 38th parallel. On January 27, 1949, Shtykov reported several recent incidents to Moscow. On January 15, a South Korean police unit crossed the parallel in the Sachangni district, Kangwon Province, and attacked the home of the chairman of the district People's Committee. A DPRK police unit counterattacked. Then, on January 18, a thirty-man South Korean police unit armed with light machine guns again crossed the border in the Sachangni district and attacked a district KWP office. A northern police unit drove them off. On January 20, the ROKA struck again: a forty-man unit attacked a northern guard outpost in the Chongok district. The northern unit suffered four dead and two severely wounded; two men were missing. On the same date, a sixty-man ROKA unit attacked villages in the Yanggu district, killing one villager and wounding others. And on January 23, a ROKA unit of eighty to ninety men in vehicles attempted to cross the border in the Chongok district, but was driven off. Southern military units were stationed right below the 38th parallel and an attack on the North was rumored, Shtykov reported. But he concluded: "At the present time an attack by the Southern army is not likely. Internal and external circumstances would not permit it."[17]

Although northern guard units had repulsed the southern police and army incursions, the situation was dangerous, as Shtykov cautioned Vyacheslav Molotov on February 3: "The 38th parallel is defended by two North Korean police brigades armed with only Japanese army rifles. Moreover, they have only three to ten rounds per rifle. They do not have automatic rifles. If attacked by Southern police, the Northern police cannot counterattack and must withdraw. When they ran out of ammunition, some were captured by the South Korean police."[18]

Shtykov also noted that although the Soviet government had approved weapons for northern police brigades, the USSR's Maritime Military District had not shipped the arms, despite repeated appeals to do so. If a vessel was made available, Shtykov said, the weapons would arrive by the end of February. He asked Molotov to intervene.

The same day, Shtykov reported that at 9:00 a.m. six trucks loaded with ROKA soldiers and police had crossed the border on a coastal road near the Japan Sea and been driven back by North Korean guards. At 10:00 a.m. in the same area, thirty-five vehicles with ROKA troops and police had moved four kilometers inside North Korea. Northern guards had retreated; the intruders remained until 6:00 p.m. In a different area on the Japan Sea at 9:00 a.m., ROKA troops had fired rifles at a northern police outpost. And at 10:00 a.m. the village of Taepo, fifteen kilometers north of the parallel on the coast, had been fired on by a South Korean trawler and small vessel.[19]

Apparently alarmed by these attacks and where they might lead, Moscow reacted swiftly. The next day, a message reached Pyongyang from the port of Vladivostok in the Maritime Military District that a Soviet vessel would leave for North Korea on February 17 with 1,500 rifles, 400 portable machine guns, 2,500,000 rounds of rifle ammunition, 3,200,000 rounds of the other ammunition, and other equipment.[20]

Also on February 4, Shtykov reported that a ROK police unit had entered the Yangyang district near the 38th parallel on February 2, occupied high ground, and attacked a northern guard unit, which suffered eight dead and four wounded. Northern guards drove off the attackers, but the South Koreans returned and set up an observation post on Hill 198.5. A ROKA battalion was stationed south of the border there, Shtykov relayed, and a KPA battalion would be sent to the area.[21]

Although Shtykov was sending such detailed reports to Moscow, Kim Il Sung did not mention the clashes near the 38th parallel in his speech on February 1 to the Supreme People's Assembly. He denounced the South

Korean leadership's call for the long-term presence of US troops in the South. "There are daily calls to 'subjugate the North,'" Kim said, but "if they try they will be crushed completely."[22] On February 26, the DPRK Ministry of Internal Affairs finally issued a report on the cross-border attacks.[23] The provocations were intended to justify the stationing of US troops in South Korea, the ministry asserted.[24] Yet Kim Il Sung and Pak Hon-yong apparently did not regard the situation as very serious. In their meeting with Shtykov on February 3, the seven topics they listed for discussion in Moscow all concerned economic and cultural support.[25]

Whether the southern attacks were initiated by local commanders or ordered by Seoul is unclear. The ROK government itself seemed uncertain whether the objective was to create tension at the border to prevent the withdrawal of US troops from the South and obtain more weapons from Washington or to prepare for an "advance" into the North.

At a meeting with visiting US Secretary of the Army Kenneth C. Royall and US Ambassador John Muccio in Seoul on February 28, President Syngman Rhee's first request was for rifles to arm ROK police at the 38th parallel. Rhee said between 150,000 and 300,000 South Koreans had served in the Imperial Army and, if necessary, within six weeks the ROKA could be increased by 100,000 men. Morale was a problem in the North, Rhee claimed: "If North Korea were invaded by South Korea, a large proportion of the North Korean Army would desert to the South Korean Army." The South Korean president indicated that "he would like to increase the Army, provide equipment and arms for it, then in a short time move north into North Korea." An uneasy Ambassador Muccio responded that as long as there was a chance of peaceful negotiations with North Korea, "no such action should be taken." Secretary Royall reinforced his sentiment: as long as US combat troops were in South Korea, Royall stated, "no invasion of North Korea could in any event take place." President Rhee's remarks amounted to "a request for the removal of all American combat troops," Royall said. Rhee replied that he had no objection to an immediate withdrawal if the United States would increase the number of its military advisers and "agree to provide a reasonable amount of additional weapons." Rhee criticized the vacillation of the US State Department as being largely responsible for the loss of China and warned that such vacillation "might be seriously harmful to Korea."[26] The meeting ended on an acrimonious note.

The capital most worried about Korea was Moscow. Stalin seems to have been extremely concerned over the reports from North Korea on the border clashes. On February 9, Air Force Major General Serbin, commander of the Air Force of the Pacific Fleet, abruptly arrived in Pyongyang on orders from the Soviet General Staff to negotiate the return of a Soviet fighter regiment to Wonsan. Serbin wanted an air base, now used by the KPA 2nd Division, turned over to the Soviet air force. Shtykov strongly opposed this: "The return of a Soviet air regiment to Korea is both politically disadvantageous to us and completely unnecessary." In his view, the South Korean government was not likely to be planning a grave step like an invasion of North Korea in the near future. "Regarding provocations north of the 38th parallel, the Northern army and police can repulse them."[27]

For Soviet forces to return to Korea in the middle of a US withdrawal was strange. Stalin clearly sought to halt the American pull-out, presumably to prevent a South Korean attack on the North.[28] Shtykov's protest reflected the strong opposition of the North Korean leadership, whose first priority was the departure of US forces; it is inconceivable that they would have welcomed any action that prolonged the American presence.

In a cable to Moscow on February 14, Ambassador Shtykov endorsed a North Korean request that the UN Security Council ensure the withdrawal of US forces from the South. Shtykov explained that the North Koreans thought a US military presence "was an obstacle to the unification of national territory and the creation of an independent democratic Korean state."[29] In response, on March 23 Moscow informed Shtykov of a discussion on February 16 between General Kuz'ma Derevianko, the Soviet representative on the Allied Council for Japan, and Gen. Douglas MacArthur. The withdrawal of US troops would soon be completed, MacArthur had said; most units had already left, and the former commander of US forces in Korea had moved to Tokyo. The sole duty of the US brigadier general remaining in South Korea was to lead a group of officers training the ROKA.[30] There was thus no need for the UN Security Council to press for a US withdrawal.

On February 24, M. A. Purkaev, the chief of staff of the Soviet Union's Far Eastern Army, asked Shtykov to send him all the information he had about the South Korean police and security system at the 38th parallel.[31] The Soviet military authorities in the Far East, who took their orders from Moscow, were also concerned about the situation after US troops left.

Meanwhile, Moscow was suffering internal tensions. On February 15, A. A. Kuznetsov, formerly Communist Party first secretary in Leningrad and now central party secretary and a member of the organization bureau, and two others were found guilty of antiparty activity. On March 5, N. A. Voznesensky, who had formerly served in Leningrad, was dismissed from his positions as a member of the Politburo, chief of Gosplan, and vice-premier. Enemy suspects had been discovered in the very heart of the CPSU. This was the beginning of the so-called "Leningrad Incident."[32]

A NORTH KOREAN DELEGATION VISITS THE SOVIET UNION

North Korean leaders visited Moscow amid these political intrigues. Led by Kim Il Sung, the seven-man delegation left Pyongyang on February 22. They flew to Voroshilov, where they boarded the Siberian railway for the ten-day trip, arriving in Moscow on March 3. After visits to Lenin's mausoleum and the Kremlin, and meetings with Molotov and N. M. Shvernik, chairman of the Presidium of the Supreme Soviet, the delegation, accompanied by Chu Nyong-ha, the DPRK's ambassador to the Soviet Union, met Stalin on March 5. It was the very day Stalin had removed Voznesensky. Also present were Andrei Vyshinsky, who had just replaced Molotov as foreign minister, and Shtykov.

According to the official record, the meeting began with small talk. Then Stalin and Kim Il Sung discussed economic and cultural assistance to North Korea. After a review of other topics such as trade and credits, Kim Il Sung raised military issues. Kim pointed out that American troops were still in South Korea and that the provocations by the reactionaries were becoming bolder. North Korea had ground forces, but virtually no naval strength, Kim said, and it needed Soviet aid to bolster its navy. Stalin asked how many US troops were in South Korea, and whether the South had its own troops. He also asked whether the North was afraid of the South. Kim replied that they were not afraid, but that it would be good to have naval units. Pak Hon-yong said that the North's army was stronger than the South's.

Stalin promised assistance for the North Korean navy and mentioned the possibility of assistance for the North Korean Air Force as well. When Stalin asked whether the South Korean army had been infiltrated by North Korean supporters, Pak said yes, but that so far the northern agents had not exposed themselves. Stalin said that was appropriate, that there was no need to expose themselves now, and that the South had apparently placed its own agents in northern units. The North should exercise caution.

Stalin also asked about the situation at the 38th parallel. Kim told him that there had been clashes with the South in Kangwon Province near the parallel. But the South Korean police were poorly armed and had retreated when regular North Korean army units were dispatched.

Stalin's last question was about officer training in North Korea. Kim informed him that the North had an officer training school, but no military academy, and that not one senior officer had graduated from a military academy. He requested that Korean officers be allowed to study in a Soviet military academy, and Stalin said he would approve the request.[33]

That was the extent of the one-hour meeting. Based on the official record, the US scholar Alexandre Mansourov concluded that Kim Il Sung did not bring up Korean unification by force.[34] According to the declassified visitor's list kept at Stalin's secretariat, Kim Il Sung and Pak Hon-yong (accompanied by interpreter Mun Il) also met with Stalin on March 14 at 7 p.m. for an hour and forty-five minutes. Molotov and Shtykov were also present.[35] But the fact of this meeting remains secret.

Some researchers in Russia hold that Stalin, Kim Il Sung, and others also met on March 7 and discussed military unification.[36] An account in the *Seoul Shinmun* newspaper in South Korea, reportedly from the record of the March 7 meeting, contains an exchange between Stalin and Kim Il Sung. According to this account, Kim told Stalin that the Korean situation had heated up and that the North could liberate the whole peninsula by force. The reactionaries in South Korea would not agree to peaceful unification and were trying to keep the country divided until they were strong enough to attack the North, Kim argued. Now was the best time for the North to attack. Northern forces were strong, Kim said, and the North had powerful partisan units in South Korea.

Stalin replied that there should be no attack on the South for three reasons, according to the newspaper's account. First, the northern People's Army had not attained conclusive superiority over the South Korean army, and was inferior in terms of numbers. Second, US forces were still in South Korea and would probably intervene if a war started. Third, the agreement between the Soviet Union and the United States to divide Korea at the 38th parallel was still in effect, and if the Soviet Union violated it first, there would be no grounds for blocking US intervention.

Kim responded that then North Korea would have no chance in the near future to unify Korea, although the South Korean people wanted unification as soon as possible in order to liberate themselves from the reactionary government in Seoul and American imperialist rule. To this, Stalin replied that if the enemy had plans to invade the North, they would probably attack first and soon. That would be the best opportunity for North Korea to strike back because a defensive response would gain widespread support.[37]

This account of the supposed March 7 meeting accords with what Kim Il Sung later told Ambassador Shtykov that Stalin had said in Moscow. The document used by the *Seoul Shinmun* newspaper that was purported to be a record of the March 7 meeting is actually of the March 14 meeting.

Kim Il Sung's argument that now was the best time for the North to attack the South casts doubt on his qualifications as a military leader, one who could objectively judge the relative strength of his own and hostile forces. Trying to gain Stalin's support for an attack, he probably overstated the case, and Stalin's reasoned response left no room for argument.

On March 17, the North Korean delegation to the Soviet Union concluded a ten-year agreement on the general principles of DPRK-Soviet cooperation on economic and cultural matters. Other agreements signed the same day specified the details of commercial transactions and payments, long-term loans, and technical aid. Under the loan agreement, which was the most important one, the Soviet Union provided North Korea with 212 million rubles.[38]

In February and March of 1949, then, the leaders of both Koreas had expressed a desire to unify the peninsula by force. But their superpower patrons in Washington and Moscow had reined them in.

On March 22, the Truman administration decided its policy toward the ROK in NSC report 8/2. Three courses of action were considered: "abandon Korea to Communist domination," "guarantee unconditionally the political independence and territorial integrity of south Korea," or "as a middle course, to establish within practicable and feasible limits conditions of support" for South Korea. NSC 8/2 recommended the middle course, withdrawal of US forces, transfer of weapons and equipment to South Korea, and the continued presence of a military advisory group.[39] Having lost China, the United States would guarantee Japan's security, but was uncertain of a commitment to the Republic of Korea.

INFORMATION OF AN IMMINENT SOUTH KOREAN INVASION

After Kim Il Sung and Pak Hon-yong departed home, an alarming report reached Moscow, and on April 17 Stalin directed Ambassador Shtykov to investigate. According to the report, US forces were expected to withdraw from South Korea to Japan in May, which would give the South Korean military freedom of action. During the same period, the UN Commission on Korea would leave Korea. From April to May, the report said, South Korea would concentrate its forces near the 38th parallel and then launch a sudden attack on the North in June. The South expected to destroy northern forces by August, according to the report.

On April 16, the South Koreans had assembled about 8,000 troops in the Kaesong district and about 10,000 in the Uijongbu district directly below the 38th parallel in the west. Six days earlier, on April 10, two tanks had been unloaded from a railroad flatcar in Tongduchon.[40]

Four days previously, the US secretary of state had written the US embassy in Seoul: "1. The Department has received a report from a source in the Far East, who has an excellent reputation for accurate reporting, to the effect that he expects serious trouble in Korea within a 60-day period. 2. He said the initiative will be taken by the south Koreans. 3. This information ties in with reports from the same source received during the middle of February 1949."

The gist of the source's February reports was that North Korean military preparations had "intensified," and that the esprit de corps of South Korean troops was high after suppressing uprisings in Yosu and Sunchon. ROK Prime Minister Yi Pom-sok had tightened the South's military organization "to the point where the South Koreans think they could not only defend but even attack. . . . A feeling out process has for some time been under way in the frequent forays by both sides into the 'target range' neighborhood of the 38th parallel—no longer guarded by American troops."[41]

The information contained in the source's reports may have been gleaned in Washington by a Soviet spy. Or in South Korea such information could have been picked up by spies for the United States or for the Soviet Union.

Concerned about a possible southern invasion of the North, Stalin also asked the Soviet General Staff for a report on the situation at the 38th parallel. Chief of Staff A. M. Vasilevsky and Vice-Chief S. M. Shtemenko replied on April 20 that from January 15 to April 15, 1949, there had been thirty-seven border violations by the South; twenty-four had occurred between March 15 and April 15. The South had placed part of the ROKA at the parallel, notably the First Brigade in the Kaesong area. A larger-scale provocation was possible, they warned, and they advised that the North Korean military command be instructed to prepare for such an attack.[42] Since January 1949, the ROKA First Brigade had been led by the very hawkish Brig. Gen. Kim Sok-won.[43]

Ambassador Shtykov told the Soviet Foreign Ministry on April 20 that he was trying to confirm the information in the General Staff's report. "The Korean People's Army has major deficiencies in combat readiness," he added. Shtykov listed five unfulfilled promises to North Korea by Moscow. First, although in North Korea an air force training regiment was organized in charge of training pilots, in seven months only eight of eighty North Korean cadets had qualified as pilots because of shortages of training aircraft and gasoline. Promised trainers had not arrived, and when they would was unknown; three hundred tons of aircraft fuel purchased from the Soviet Trade Corporation were unusable. Second, Lieutenant General Smirnov, chief military adviser to the KPA commander, was qualified to command only division-level units, was arrogant, and should be transferred. Also, Soviet advisers on joint naval and ground operations had not yet arrived, and two of the three army divisions did not have a military adviser assigned to the commander. Third, instead of the two hundred military-use motorcycles promised, the moskvich model unsuitable for army operations had been delivered; the motorcycle battalion thus had no motorcycles. Fourth, though most of the material for a plant to make Shipagin-model automatic rifles had arrived as promised in July 1948, there were no technical experts and the plant was not functioning. Fifth, there had been no response to the North's request for a naval antiaircraft regiment. With the situation in Korea considered dangerous, the ambassador wanted Moscow to meet its obligations.[44]

Stalin removed Lieutenant General Smirnov as chief military adviser to the KPA commander and named Shtykov to the post instead. Chief of Staff Vasilevsky conveyed this change in a telegram dated April 21.[45]

In Seoul, meanwhile, President Syngman Rhee and US Ambassador John Muccio were quarreling daily. On April 14, Rhee showed Muccio the draft of a letter to the US government that included this paragraph: "We will feel strong enough to not have to count on support by an American security force when we have sufficient weapons for a standing army of 65,000 men and for an armed and equipped reserve force of 200,000 men. As you know, Mr. Ambassador, we are far from having reached that point now." Muccio assured Rhee verbally of continued US support and later the same day wrote, "It is the United States intention to continue to provide economic, technical, military, and other assistance regarded as essential to economic and political stability of the newborn Republic."[46] Mollified by Muccio's assurances, Rhee announced at a press conference on April 18 that "American troops would be withdrawn during the course of the next several months," but that an American military mission would remain in Korea.[47] From Rhee's standpoint, the situation was not conducive to an advance to the North.

CHINESE COMMUNISTS CROSS THE YANGTZE

The major event that spring in Northeast Asia occurred elsewhere. The one million troops of the Chinese People's Liberation Army crossed the Yangtze River, and on April 23 they captured Nanjing, Chiang Kai-shek's capital, in the decisive battle of the Chinese civil war. Enormously buoyed by this triumph, the North Korean leadership prepared for action.

On April 27 or 28, Kim Il Sung and Pak Hon-yong discussed the reorganization of North Korean forces with Soviet Ambassador Shtykov and asked for powerful weapons. Shtykov reported the meeting to Stalin employing deferential wording—"In accordance with your instructions . . . I met with [Kim and Pak]," and so on—giving the impression that Shtykov presented Stalin's instructions and the Koreans accepted his terms. However, the request Kim and Pak made was for offensive units and must have originated with the North Korean leaders.

Shtykov described to Stalin the units requested: 1. a mechanized brigade to be formed by May 1949, composed of, among other things, two tank regiments each with thirty-three tanks, a self-propelled artillery division, other artillery divisions, including an antitank division, a self-propelled artillery regiment, and a motorcycle battalion; 2. a special army tank regiment with thirty-three tanks to be stationed at Wonsan; 3. a continued tank training regiment; 4. self-propelled artillery battalions within each infantry division; 5. an army artillery regiment; 6. an engineer battalion; 7. a mixed aerial division of two regiments (with forty-three fighter-bomber aircraft per regiment) to be organized by September and a continued pilot training regiment. The North Koreans were now recruiting sixteen thousand volunteers for these units, Shtykov reported. To pay for the weapons, they had promised to deliver thirty thousand tons of rice to the Soviet Union immediately and to transfer the balance in September and October.

Shtykov included with his report a letter from Kim Il Sung to Stalin: "Given the changed situation in Korea it is of vital necessity that the North Korea People's Army be strengthened and equipped. Comrade Stalin, please grant this additional request, which is related to organizational measures. With the exception of aerial units, I anticipate that the formation of mechanized and other units will be completed by May 1949. The air force units should be complete in September."

Shtykov provided Stalin an attached list of weapons that contained 136 categories. It included aircraft—30 Ilyushin-10 and Yak-9, and 24 UT-2 or Yak-18—87 T-34 tanks; 102 SU-76 self-propelled artillery guns; small arms and ammunition, including 25,000 7.62 mm rifles and 7,000 7.62 mm pistols; construction equipment for army engineers; and communications equipment.[48]

Alexandre Mansourov believes that this list was inspired by the Soviets and that the objective was "strengthening the counteroffensive capabilities of the KPA."[49] But if the request indeed originated in Moscow, it is strange that there would be no response until June 4, 1949, some five weeks later.

TRANSFER OF KOREAN UNITS FROM CHINA'S PLA

The North Korean leadership also requested troops from China. Kim Il, a trusted colleague of Kim Il Sung from the Manchurian faction, left Pyongyang for China on April 28. The DPRK deputy defense minister and director of the Political Department of the KPA, Kim Il was accompanied by the North Korean commercial representative to China. At Mukden, Kim Il conferred with Gao Gang, who was in charge of the Chinese Communist Party, military, and government in Manchuria. In Beijing, Kim Il met with Zhu De and Zhou Enlai four times and Mao Zedong once. He returned to North Korea by May 13.

According to a report by I. V. Kovalev, CPSU representative to the CCP, on May 17 Mao Zedong asked him to convey to Stalin the details of Kim Il's visit. Kovalev recounted that Kim Il had told the Chinese leaders that he was authorized to discuss the following issues with the CCP's Central Committee: the situation in the East, the establishment of an Information Bureau there, and assistance to North Korea of officers and weapons. But Mao told Kim Il that it was "premature" to establish an Information Bureau for the East. "Of the twelve countries in the East," Mao pointed out, according to Kovalev's report, "the CCP has ties only to five: Mongolia, Thailand, Indochina, the Philippines and Korea. China does not have normal relations with [the communist party in] Japan and Indonesia and is not well informed about these countries." Thus, he said, "it would be better to establish ties, study the situation, and then start to set up a Cominform for the East. At this point, we should establish a Mutual Wireless Communication Bureau to exchange views on specific issues as they arise."

As for North Korea's request for officers and weapons, Mao said that China could probably provide such assistance. One and a half million Koreans lived in Manchuria, and there were two Korean divisions (each with about ten thousand troops) in the PLA, one of which had combat experience in Manchuria against Nationalist forces. These divisions could be transferred at any time that North Korea requested them. "In addition, we trained 200 officers, who are now receiving advanced instruction and can be sent to Korea in a month," Mao said. "If a war starts between North and South Korea, we will help to the extent possible. We are prepared to provide food and weapons for the two divisions noted."

According to Kovalev's report, Mao also said that "our Korean comrades believe there is a possibility U.S. troops will be withdrawn from South Korea in the near future and are worried that they will be replaced by Japanese forces with whose help the South will plan to attack North Korea." Mao advised Kim Il to counterattack against these forces. "They must be very careful about whether Japanese units are with the South Korean forces. If they are, the North Koreans should be cautious." "If American forces leave and are not replaced by Japanese units," he advised Korean comrades "not to plan an attack on South Korea but to wait for more favorable conditions." "In the course of an attack, General MacArthur might quickly commit Japanese units to Korea. We could not provide rapid, effective support because our basic military strength is now on the other side of the Yangtze River."

In addition, Mao said that if the international situation improved in early 1950, North Korea could probably plan an attack on South Korea. "If Japanese troops enter Korea, we would quickly send elite troops and destroy the Japanese units," he assured Kim Il, according to Kovalev's report. Mao added that any action of this nature would be taken only after coordination with Moscow.[50]

In his account to Kovalev of his exchange with Kim Il about a Cominform for the East, Mao portrayed himself as responding to a topic initiated by Kim Il. But according to a report by Ambassador Shtykov to Foreign Minister Vyshinsky, "Mao Zedong showed his concern by asking [Kim Il] if the matter was raised when the North Korean government delegation visited Moscow. Mao asked the views of the North Korean Workers Party's Central Committee on this issue." According to Shtykov, Mao said that he had received letters from four Communist parties—those in Burma, Malaya, Indochina, and one other country—with "proposals to start an Information Bureau of Communist parties in the East." But "Kim Il replied that he knew nothing about the issue and would report the conversation to Kim Il Sung."[51]

Both Kovalev's and Shtykov's accounts indicate that Mao Zedong said he thought it was too early to start an Eastern Cominform. Shtykov explained Mao's reasoning this way: "China and Indochina are still at war and the situation in Korea is tense. Creation of an Eastern Information Bureau would be seen as the formation of a military alliance."

Four Communist parties had indeed proposed the establishment of an Asian version of the Cominform, and Mao asked Kim Il about the KWP's view on it to get a sense of sentiment in the CPSU. Mao wanted China to lead an Asian/Far Eastern Cominform, but his approach was to consult Moscow on everything and to prepare carefully. His willingness to consult was equivalent to asserting the equality of the Chinese and Soviet Communist parties in the world revolutionary movement.

Shtykov, whose account of Mao's reply to Kim Il's request is more accurate than Kovalev's, said that the purpose of Kim Il's visit was to request the transfer of the "Korean divisions in the People's Liberation Army" to North Korea. One of the divisions was stationed at Mukden, another at Changchun (both in Manchuria), and a third was in combat operations. Mao said that he "was prepared to transfer the two divisions in Manchuria at any time," Shtykov wrote.

Subsequently, China portrayed this transfer inaccurately as Koreans "returning to their homeland." But these divisions of Koreans living in Manchuria were CCP forces that had fought in China's revolution. The staff officers were all members of the CCP. If the revolution triumphed and a Communist state was established, they would be citizens in the new China with a preferential status to benefit from state-led land reform.

Still, Koreans in Manchuria had been overjoyed at the creation of the DPRK. Yanbian (Yonbyon in Korean) was the region in East Manchuria where a majority of inhabitants were Korean. A Korean newspaper of this region, the *Yonbyon Ilbo*, published a roundtable discussion in September 1948 to mark the formation of the DPRK. The participants expressed their happiness and support for the struggle against Syngman Rhee. Yet chief editorial writer Lim In-ho, a former activist in the Manchurian General Bureau of the Korean Communist Party who had joined the CCP in 1945, wrote: "Koreans in Manchuria must understand their duty is to join in the Chinese revolution here. This commitment will help the fatherland." Yang Hwan-jun, another longtime activist in the Korean Communist Party in Manchuria, wrote: "There is no need to debate the question of whether to go to Korea. . . . Redoubled courage and determination in our efforts to support the Chinese revolution are the way to protect the new Democratic People's Republic of Korea."[52] On the other hand, another Korean expressed great emotion "at first seeing the national flag" of the DPRK and lamented the hardships facing the families of Koreans serving with Chinese forces. An official of Yanji (Yongil in Korean) city, the central city of the Yanbian region, responded that they were taking steps to alleviate such suffering and criticized the *Yonbyon Ilbo* for inaccurate reporting.[53] Many Koreans apparently believed that their soldiers were not treated properly. Yet Korean nationalism rang out at a rally to celebrate the birth of the DPRK, "The Korean people already have our own free fatherland and government" and there were appeals to rally around "our hero and leader General Kim Il Sung."[54]

Korean loyalties were complicated. The head of the Yanbian regional committee of the CCP, Han Liu Jun-xiu, obtained approval from the central authorities in Beijing for dual citizenship for Koreans.[55] But this status was not always recognized, and Koreans in Manchuria who fought in the Chinese civil war were linked to the CCP, the Chinese army, and the Chinese revolution.

Viewed from Pyongyang, Koreans living in Manchuria were still Korean. Kim Il Sung, Kim Chaek, and Choe Yong-gon had all lived there and fought against Japan. North Korean leaders wanted "their troops" back.

The Chinese Communists understood this and decided to send the two PLA divisions to Korea. Individual Korean soldiers did not volunteer to go. Without a decision by the CCP and orders from PLA headquarters, there would be no transfer.[56]

During his meeting with Kim Il in the spring of 1949, Mao Zedong had urged the North Koreans to limit themselves to counterattack the South. If attacked by the South, Mao advised, the North should resist and strike back. But Kim Il Sung presented the attitude of Chinese leaders as very favorable to his cause. He told Shtykov: "Mao Zedong said who knows when a military clash will occur in Korea. Koreans must carefully consider every factor and secretly prepare. In Korea, there could be a surprise attack or a drawn out conflict. The latter would not be advantageous to us, he said; Japanese forces could be sent in to help the South Korean 'government' side. Mao Zedong told Kim Il, 'you should not worry because the Soviet Union is next door and China is in Manchuria. If necessary China will secretly send troops. Chinese have black hair, Mao said, and can't be distinguished from Koreans.'"[57]

Kim Il Sung obviously wanted to conceal China's caution from Stalin. Mao Zedong had promised the Korean divisions, but had opposed an attack on the South in the spring of 1949 and recommended that military action not be considered until 1950.

The North Koreans believed that it was unlikely that US forces would return to South Korea if they were once removed, and were only worried about Japanese forces entering the picture. As Mao indicated, the Chinese, too, thought Japanese troops might be committed. An article by Shin Yom entitled "The American Expansionists' Policy toward Japan" in the March 1948 issue of the North Korean Workers' Party's journal *Kulloja* shows the depth of North Korean misperceptions about Japanese forces. Full of propaganda, the piece claimed that former high-ranking Japanese officers from the

Imperial Headquarters were serving in the Japanese government's Demobilization Bureau, that "Japanese regular army units and regiments were kept intact" on farms in "remote areas" in Japan, and that a group of officers was organizing a "secret government" that was opposed to democratization in Japan and had fifty-five thousand followers in Tokyo alone. Shin concluded that the United States was about to revive "Japanese militarism" and use Japanese forces as a "U.S. gendarmerie" to police the Far East and Pacific region.[58]

In reality, there was no Japanese army in May 1949. The Supreme Commander for the Allied Powers had totally disarmed and demobilized Japanese forces several years before. To organize former soldiers quickly for a war would have been impossible. But the North Koreans, with no experience with the American military but with memories of the ferocity of Japanese soldiers, believed that the United States had secretly preserved part of the Imperial Army as the nucleus for a new force. Frightened by phantom Japanese infantrymen, they were less concerned about US forces. At this stage, Kim Il Sung and his comrades started to prepare for unification by force of arms.

THE BORDER CLASHES ESCALATE

Meanwhile Soviet Ambassador Shtykov was reading reports of US troop withdrawals from the South and a possible attack by the South on the North after the withdrawals. On May 2, he forwarded information obtained in April by the Political Security Bureau, Ministry of Internal Affairs, DPRK, which ran espionage operations in the South. This information was originally not reported to the DPRK minister, vice-minister, or Kim Il Sung. Political Security Bureau chief Pang Hak-se, a Soviet Korean, had passed it to a representative of the Main Intelligence Department of the Soviet Red Army in North Korea. Pang's action showed where his loyalty lay. That he sent the information to Moscow through the Soviet Army Intelligence Department rather than via the Soviet ambassador is also significant. Shtykov showed his displeasure; Kim Il Sung could not have been happy either.

Shtykov reported that US-ROK negotiations on US troop withdrawals were moving ahead and that US Ambassador Muccio had said on April 19 that the pull-out would be completed in a few months. Shtykov was concerned by remarks made at a press conference by Shin Sung-mo, the newly appointed ROK defense minister. The Republic of Korea "has sufficient troops to maintain public order after U.S. forces withdraw," Shin stated. "If North Korea invades the South, our military can not only defend themselves but deliver a heavy blow." Quoting reports confirmed by Soviet Army Intelligence, Shtykov said that the South Korean army had been increased from

53,600 men on January 1, 1949, to 70,000 men by the end of March. More-over, mechanized units had been expanded by two to four times, and subversive elements were being purged from the military. A ROKA battalion commander told a DPRK agent that 30,000 troops were positioned to move on Pyongyang, that plans for an attack had been distributed to the battalion level, and that the offensive was scheduled for June. Agents were setting up cells in every northern province in preparation for an uprising when southern forces crossed the border. Shtykov, Kim Il Sung, and Pak Hon-yong had agreed to take certain "necessary preliminary measures" before the South struck.[59]

But a meeting in Seoul the same day that Shtykov wrote the Foreign Ministry shows that Shtykov's fears were exaggerated. Present were Rhee, Yi Pom-sok, Shin Sung-mo, Muccio, Korean Military Advisory Group head Brig. Gen. William L. Roberts, and US Embassy Counselor Everett Drumright. According to the meeting notes, referring to the political situation in China, Shin asked Muccio if relations between Korea and the United States should not be reconsidered. Muccio deplored recent events in China, but thought they would have no appreciable impact on the Korean problem. "A world conflict apart, he did not think there would be an invasion of South Korea from the north." Distrustful of American assurances, Shin said that Korea had twice sought guidance and assistance from the United States, which had not responded. Rhee, too, was unconvinced. "He [Rhee] went on [to] say that there was a question in the minds of the Korean people whether the United States can be relied upon. The Korean people never thought, he said, that the United States would drop China." Rhee requested that Korea be kept within the US defense line.[60]

Major border clashes occurred immediately after this meeting. Both the North and South blamed the attacks on the other. Though the US Army G-2 in South Korea confidently concluded that ROK units had struck first,[61] the North, too, was acting aggressively. On May 3, three companies of North Korean border guards drove South Korean troops from the 292 Meter Hill adjoining Mt. Songak, which was south of the 38th parallel. The South Koreans counterattacked the next day, and then selected troops were brought in to recapture the Hill. The ROKA commander was Kim Sok-won, who led the 1st Division. On May 5, two battalions of the ROKA 8th Regiment in the Chunchon area led by the battalion commanders crossed the border to join the North. They were welcomed as heroes. On May 7, the South destroyed a northern border guard unit near Uijongbu. The North struck back in the Paekchon area and the Ongjin Peninsula. In the former, northern forces crossed the Yesong River on May 18 and occupied Yonan. South Koreans counterattacked and pursued the northern forces across the border until driven back themselves. Although partly below the 38th parallel, the Ongjin Peninsula was an extension of North Korean territory and far from Seoul—an enclave and a perfect target. On May 21, two northern battalions attacked Mt. Tunak. The South threw eight battalions into the battle, but could not dislodge the intruders; the fighting continued until June.[62]

Alexandre Mansourov contends that Kim Il Sung, Pak Hon-yong, and Shtykov feared "the Rhee government might launch an all-out attack against the North sometime at the end of June or early July 1949."[63] I disagree. Recalling Stalin's injunction not to attack unless attacked first, Kim Il Sung and Pak Hon-yong seem to have regarded the southern attacks as an opportunity, which would explain why they did not inform Shtykov of the border incidents in early May. Finally, on May 27, Kim Il Sung told Shtykov of an intrusion in the Shiokenri (Chikyonni) area by an ROKA battalion. Kim also said that two ROKA battalions in the Kaesong district had crossed the border and were trying to seize ridges, and that three ROKA battalions were in Chunchon in the Chorwon area.[64] Shtykov immediately reported this information to Moscow.

In Seoul, a worried John Muccio was restraining Rhee, who had chided Washington in a May 7 press statement that said, in part: "We do not propose to fight the North Korean Communists or their foreign overlords. We will continue our efforts to unify the North and South by peaceful means. At the same time, we are responsible for the protections of the lives and property of our people; and when the Korean Communists come over the 38th parallel and destroy us, we cannot sit still and allow them to harm us without resistance; we must make their invasion of the South costly to them. For this purpose we need a sufficient supply of adequate weapons for our defense."[65]

Muccio protested Rhee's statement two days later. With the clash at Kaesong in mind, the ambassador urged "Rhee to restrain ROK forces from taking any aggressive action." President Rhee responded that the "ROK harbors no aggressive aims, had not taken initiative at Kaesong, but would never yield inch [of] ROK territory to invaders. Rhee asserted over and over again his government would fight to last man against Communist aggression no matter what help might be received from US."[66] Rhee said that the Kaesong incident had put him in a difficult position, and Muccio agreed that it was a very serious matter, adding that General Roberts was setting up an investigation. Rhee stressed the strategic importance of Kaesong and that the Korean government would not yield it "inch by inch." But Muccio urged Rhee to stop the border clashes: "the United States supported the Korean Government firmly on its defensive measures. But should the Korean Government resort to aggressive measures, Mr. Muccio said he wished to point out the U.S. could not be of any assistance in this regard."[67] The ambassador was desperately trying to prevent the South from attacking the North.

FORMATION OF THE FATHERLAND FRONT

In Pyongyang, preparations were then under way for forming a broad front organization for Korean unification. On May 12, eight political parties and social organizations in South Korea proposed to North and South political parties and social organizations formation of a unified Democratic Front for the Attainment of the Unification of the Fatherland (Fatherland Front) "to unite the struggle for U.S. troop withdrawal and unification of the fatherland." After US troops left the South, the front's target would be "the enemies of the people—the traitorous, pro-Japanese Syngman Rhee clique." On May 16, the North's front organization, the Democratic National United Front, accepted the South's proposal for the Fatherland Front. But this was all for show. Kim Il Sung and Pak Hon-yong were behind the joint initiative.

On May 25, a preparatory committee of representatives from the South and North met for the first time and announced its plan to form the Fatherland Front. The front aimed to achieve "complete independence" for Korea, which entailed the removal of US troops. The Fatherland Front would "oppose traitors to the Fatherland who block unification," accomplish democratic reforms in the north, and "support the republic's government (that is the DPRK)." It also sought to expand democratic reforms throughout Korea, revive People's Committees in South Korea, and free "imprisoned patriots" in the South.[68] In fact, the front was a militant organization that brought all north and south Korean Communist social organizations under one umbrella to attain "completion of the national territory."

On May 31, Ambassador Shtykov, Kim Il Sung, and Pak Hon-yong reviewed an appeal to be issued that day by the Fatherland Front, which proposed a general election throughout Korea as a means for peaceful unification. Representatives of pro-unification political parties and organizations would create a General Election Leading Committee (GELC) to implement the election. There would be a ban on pro-Japan elements; direct attachment of police in the North and South to the GELC, with pro-Japan elements purged from their ranks; and disbandment of ROKA units that had suppressed the Cheju rebellion. Some southern representatives strongly supported peaceful unification, Shtykov pointed out. He thought a concrete proposal would "be tactically advantageous."

Shtykov reported this fact without stating who presented the proposal for the general election. But Kim Il Sung and Pak Hon-yong were confident that if an election were held in September, the left would win in both zones of Korea, Shtykov reported to the Soviet Foreign Ministry. He asked Moscow for instructions.

The call for peninsula-wide elections was pure propaganda. Shtykov himself came to feel misled by the front's repeated use of the term "peaceful unification."[69] Mansourov sees the Fatherland Front as a move to thwart a southern attack on the North and seems to attribute the election scheme to Shtykov.[70] But the proposal, which was unpalatable to the Rhee regime, need not be seen as advocated by Shtykov alone.

On June 4, Moscow informed Shtykov that the weapons and aid Kim Il Sung had asked for in early May to organize new units would be delivered by the end of 1949. Kim would get the aircraft, tanks, and self-propelled artillery he sought. But he would only get ten thousand rifles; he had wanted twenty-five thousand. North Korea was to deliver thirty thousand tons of rice by October 1; the two sides would agree by then on a delivery date for the remainder of the rice.[71]

ROK SUPERIORITY

The withdrawal of US forces from the South had by now entered the final stage, and South Korean government dissatisfaction with the United States was growing. Because ROK forces had not been reinforced, US Ambassador Muccio persuaded Washington to provide $200,000 to strengthen the ROK's coast guard, and Washington considered the transfer of aircraft to the ROK. Weapons transfers seemed to be stalled.

On May 17, Muccio informed Syngman Rhee that the last US forces would depart in a few weeks. Two days later, ROK Foreign Minister Yim Pyong-jik and Defense Minister Shin Sung-mo issued a joint press statement. The United States should take moral responsibility with the Soviet Union for dividing Korea at the 38th parallel, they said. The Republic of Korea had requested from the United States the minimum requirements needed by its forces. Citing reliable sources, they said the USSR had agreed to arm DPRK's six Korean People's Army (KPA) infantry divisions and three motorized divisions, and to provide twenty patrol boats, one hundred fighter planes, twenty bombers, and one hundred reconnaissance planes. The United States should at least provide comparable equipment.[72]

When Muccio protested the statement to Rhee the next day, the ROK president summoned Ministers Yim and Shin and told them no press releases were to be issued without his prior approval. Muccio later recounted the scene: "Foreign Minister thereupon flew into rage, declared United States had sold China down river and were pressing same course respecting Korea. Both Rhee and Defense Minister were obviously embarrassed at the spectacle."[73]

Defense Minister Shin Sung-mo pleaded his case again to Muccio the next week. After lengthy preliminary remarks, he asked that the withdrawal of the US Regimental Combat Team be postponed for six months. According to Muccio, Shin expressed a belief that the withdrawal of the RCT "at this time would be followed at once by North Korean invasion." Muccio assured

Shin: "I expressed belief North Koreans could not risk all-out invasion [of] South Korea, it would no doubt pursue current infiltration activities."[74]

On May 31, Muccio attributed the "clamor and fear aroused by troop withdrawal to the ROK government's propaganda line to retain US troops, defection of ROKA troops to the north, and the China debacle." In addition to economic assistance, he recommended provision of vessels and planes to the ROK coast guard, and port calls by US naval forces.[75] But South Korean leaders wanted much more.

Yet South Korea fared well in the early fighting on the Ongjin Peninsula in June. After an Ongjin District Combat Command led by Major Kim Paek-il was established on June 5,[76] ROKA units drove the North Koreans back, pushed into the North, and on June 17 occupied Mt. Unpa eight hundred meters north of the 38th parallel. In an assessment the next day, Shtykov saw the danger of an invasion by the South when the US troops left, which would probably be by July. The ambassador wrote: "Withdrawal should give free-dom of action to the Southern reactionaries who want to resolve unification by force. This is advocated by Syngman Rhee, Yi Pom-sok, Shin Sung-mo, and the leaders of the National Democratic Party. They agree on everything except when to attack. . . . The ROKA is concentrated near the 38th parallel. According to agent reports, only one battalion remains on Cheju Island . . . and the ROKA will attack three days before the official announcement that U.S. troops have left." Noting the fighting on Ongjin, Shtykov reported that on June 11 Syngman Rhee had announced "a plan to inflict heavy damage on the Communists that would be implemented in two or three weeks. . . . Under the circumstances, the South Korean authorities may launch a larger scale military provocation than we have seen to date. According to public sources, the Southern army has six divisions."[77]

In an analysis of North-South military strength on June 11, Muccio out-lined the border clashes, acknowledged the danger inherent in "two native forces facing each other," and observed that with both Russian and US troops gone there would no longer be a "restraining force." Yet, unlike Shtykov, Muccio was sanguine: "Nevertheless, it is the considered view of this Mis-sion that neither South Korea nor North Korea, with what appear to be fairly evenly balanced military forces, is likely in the foreseeable future to assume the risks associated with a deliberate all-out invasion." The North Koreans had precipitated the fighting on the Ongjin Peninsula, Muccio thought, "ei-ther to test South Korean defenses and capabilities or to intensify the 'war of nerves' . . . along the parallel."[78]

By contrast, when Shtykov considered the comparative military strengths of the South and North, he was horror-struck at ROK preparations to move north, and he quickly sent an analysis to Moscow on June 22. The ROKA had six infantry divisions, while the NKPA had only three and one brigade, he reported. Two of the NKPA infantry divisions were stationed at Nanam and Wonsan, with one division and a regiment near Pyongyang. As of mid-June these units would be fully equipped, Shtykov noted. An NKPA tank regiment had thirty tanks. A mechanized brigade lacked equipment, and air units had not received enough new aircraft. A force redeployment was under way in anticipation of a southern invasion, Ambassador Shtykov reported: in the Pyongyang area the 2nd Infantry Regiment, a tank battalion, and a self-propelled artillery division would be deployed close to the 38th parallel; one regiment would be sent from Nanam to Pyongyang; from Wonsan the 9th Regiment would move to Pyongyang; and a tank regiment would go to Chorwon. If fighting began, Shtykov said, the Korean divisions in Manchuria at Mukden and Changchun would be thrown into the action. [79]

In Pyongyang, Kim Il Sung and Pak Hon-yong were then under popular pressure for unification. A secret report dated June 21 from the head of the Propaganda and Agitation section of NKWP Hwanghae Province Committee to the Party Center noted that the public considered unification by force inevitable. The report quoted a worker in Suan County: "If a peaceful solution is arranged and the Americans interfere . . . we'll have to drive them out." A clerical employee in the same county said, "Basically I want a peaceful solution, but if the Southern clique's last-ditch struggle goes on, we'll have to lower the hammer on them." A merchant in Suan County stated: "Unless we get rid of the border, a general election can't be held. U.S. troops and Syngman Rhee's forces are there and won't just go away, so there probably will be a lot of casualties." And a farmer in Yonbaek County declared: "Peaceful unification clearly won't work. Unification is always possible through military force." [80]

If such sentiment was widespread in North Korea, senior KWP leaders must have concluded that there was popular support for unification by force. Their mind-set was totally different from that of the fearful Shtykov and other concerned Russians.

THE FOUNDING CONGRESS OF THE FATHERLAND FRONT

On June 24, the day before the Founding Congress to establish the Fatherland Front, Moscow approved the idea of a nationwide election in September. [81] At the Founding Congress, held in Pyongyang, 704 representatives from 71 political parties and organizations in South and North Korea were present, according to the announcement for the gathering. In opening remarks, Kim Tu-bong said, "We will crush the traitorous, degenerate policy of the puppet Syngman Rhee 'government' and fight to perfect national territory and to establish a unified, independent fatherland." Ho Hon proclaimed, "If peaceful methods do not achieve unification of the fatherland, we will achieve it by struggle!" [82]

On June 26 the Congress was not in session. Kim Il Sung held a meeting of the NKWP Central Committee and presented the proposal for a nation-wide election. According to Shtykov, "This proposal was a complete surprise; some committee members were confused and doubtful." Still, the Central Committee unanimously approved its inclusion in a draft declaration to be presented to the Fatherland Front. That evening, when Kim Il Sung explained the NKWP's policy to representatives from other political parties in North Korea, some reacted similarly. A number of the representatives said it was impossible to hold free elections in the South, while others objected that the proposal was tantamount to recognizing Syngman Rhee's administration as the legal government of the Republic of Korea. In the end, however, the party representatives accepted Kim Il Sung's explanation and adopted the proposal.[83]

On the same day in South Korea, a major political figure was assassinated. Kim Ku, a respected nationalist leader and rival of Syngman Rhee, who advocated cooperation between the two Koreas, was shot on a street in Seoul. Nevertheless, the Fatherland Front's Founding Congress reconvened on June 27. Chang Sun-myong, representing the NKWP, proposed a policy of peaceful unification through the nationwide election. Despite some confusion among the delegates, the proposal attracted wide support, and the next day the Fatherland Front called for a general election to unify Korea.[84] As Mansourov says, while Shtykov may have interpreted "peaceful unification" as a ploy to prevent a southern invasion of the North, Kim Il Sung and Pak Hon-yong most likely saw an election as a pretense to justify unification by force. Of course, the proposal for a general election was not extended to the ROK government, which would have rejected it.

The Founding Congress selected ninety-nine representatives for the central committee of the Fatherland Front, fifty from the North and forty-nine from the South. Among forty-nine from the South Han Tok-su, the representative of the League of Koreans in Japan (Choren) was named. The preliminary list of members from the South included Song Sung-chol, representing that organization.[85] But he had been sent to Seoul in the spring of 1946. Therefore it was natural that Han Tok-su who had just arrived from Japan, was put in the list of the central committee.[86]

On June 30, immediately after creation of the Fatherland Front, the southern and northern Workers' Parties covertly merged into the Korean Workers' Party, with Kim Il Sung as chairman and Pak Hon-yong and Ho Ka-i as vice-chairmen. Ho Ka-i and Pak Chong-ae from the North Korean Workers' Party and Yi Sung-yop from the South Korean Workers' Party were chosen as party secretaries.[87] These moves solidified the control of Kim Il Sung and Pak Hon-yong over the government and party in the DPRK.

THE COMPLETION OF US TROOP WITHDRAWALS

The last US troops left South Korea on June 29, 1949 (except for a small advisory and training contingent). The US Army Department submitted a memorandum to the State Department on the possibility of a northern invasion of the South after this removal. As of May 30, South Korean forces consisted of 71,086 army personnel, 5,450 coast guard personnel, and 50,434 national police—for a total of 126,970. North Korean forces consisted of 46,000 army personnel and 56,350 police and paramilitary forces—for a total of 102,350. In a section entitled "Possible Courses of Action," the US Army memorandum stated: "Apparently South Korean security forces are sufficiently organized, trained, and equipped to meet external aggression precipitated by North Korean armed forces as now constituted. . . . The People's Army of North Korea hardly retains the capability of sustained and comprehensive military operations without Chinese Communist and Soviet-Manchurian aid and support." But, the memorandum warned, "If the U.S. does not adopt a course of action to counter full scale invasion by Communist forces, the Republic of Korea might be overthrown." Of the five options listed, Option C was presented as the least difficult: "To initiate police action with U.N. sanction by the introduction of a military task force into Korea composed of U.S. units and units of other member nations of the United Nations."

In a separate memorandum, the Joint Chiefs of Staff rejected reconstitution of a "U.S. joint task force in South Korea" at the request of the ROK government or application of the Truman Doctrine to Korea. The Chiefs argued that "Korea is of little strategic value to the United States and that any commitment to United States use of military force in Korea would be ill-advised and impracticable in view of the potentialities of the over-all world situation and of our heavy international obligations as compared with our current military strength."[88]

Soviet Ambassador Shtykov was still uneasy in mid-July. He reported the interrogation of three captured soldiers from the ROKA 18th Regiment who said that rather than wait for the North to invade the South, their unit would strike first and that North Korea would be conquered by August 15. The regiment's objective, in conjunction with the ROKA 13th Regiment, was to occupy Haeju. Shtykov appended a report from a source in the Southern Workers' Party that quoted Syngman Rhee as saying that the Fatherland Front's proposal for a national election would be an ultimatum to South Korea. North Korea would invade in September, Rhee said, so the South should strike first in July.[89]

But Shtykov's anxiety proved unwarranted. After US forces departed, the ROKA took no decisive action. On July 17, Shin Sung-mo, the ROK defense minister, told the Korean Youth Corps: "Our forces are waiting for the president's order. If we receive the order, we can take Pyongyang and Wonsan in one day."[90] But it was an empty threat.

FIGHTING ON ONGJIN

Amid the mounting tensions on the Korean Peninsula, the Soviet Union had begun to strengthen cooperation with China, putting the Kremlin on a collision course with Washington in Asia. On July 1, 1949, Mao declared his "lean-to-one-side" approach toward the Soviet Union. At that time, CCP Politburo member Liu Shaoqi was already in Moscow, and, accompanied by Gao Gang and Wang Jiaxiang, had met with Stalin on June 27. At another meeting with Liu on August 5,[91] Stalin apologized for mistaken Soviet policies toward China.[92] But despite the USSR's budding relationship with the Chinese Communists, Stalin still wanted to avoid a confrontation with the United States in Korea.

Thus, South Korean rhetoric and border attacks were a matter of concern to the Soviet Union. On August 3, Moscow passed on to Shtykov information obtained in New York. An Associated Press story quoted an important ROK official as advocating an invasion of the North, and a United Press article predicted a major military clash soon. Shtykov was to verify the situation along the 38th parallel and comment on the reports from New York.[93]

On August 4, KPA units from the North crossed the 38th parallel on the Ongjin Peninsula and destroyed two ROKA companies with an artillery attack. The assault may have been related to an impending conference between President Rhee and Chiang Kai-shek at the Chinhae naval base in South Korea.[94] Bruce Cumings found an important report from John Muccio in the State Department archives in which Muccio recounted a meeting with Shin Sung-mo on August 13. Shin told Muccio that the northern attack on August 4 was "most alarming." The ROKA General Staff "were insistent that the only way to relieve the pressure on Ongjin would be to drive North." The military urged an immediate attack in the Chorwon area. Recalling General Roberts' advice not to attack the North, Shin opposed the plan and decided to send reinforcements to Ongjin. But Prime Minister Yi Pom-sok and President Rhee, who had returned from the Chinhae conference, opposed that course of action. On August 16, Rhee astonished Muccio by saying that he wanted to replace Army Chief of Staff Chae Pyong-dok with Kim Sok-won, commander of the 1st Division, who was known as an advocate of attacking the North. Muccio objected, and the change was not carried out.[95]

The Rhee-Chiang conference was held on August 7–8. On arrival in South Korea, the generalissimo stressed the shared destiny of Chinese and Koreans and lauded the ROK's independence. "The Chinese and Korean peoples are brothers who for 3000 years have shared a relationship as close as lips and teeth," Chiang stated. "Unfortunately we are both threatened by Communist aggression." He cited an old Chinese saying about the "friendship of men together in a storm tossed boat." A postconference joint statement of Rhee and Chiang extolled the formation of the Asian Anti-Communist Federation agreed by President Elpidio Quirino of the Philippines and Chiang on July 12.[96] Behind the scenes, there had been delicate negotiations that not even US Ambassador Muccio had known of. On August 27, Muccio belatedly reported to Washington that at the Chinhae conference Chiang Kai-shek had offered Taiwan's air support for an invasion of North Korea and that South Koreans were greatly encouraged by his offer. "More and more people feel that the only way unification can be brought about is by moving North by force . . . ," Muccio wrote. "I doubt whether Rhee would actually order a move North in his saner moments. Captain Shin, I know, is dead against it. Lee Bum-sok (Yi Pom-sok) would love it. However, should we have another Kaesong or Ongjin flare-up, a counterattack might lead to all sorts of unpredictable developments."[97]

NORTHERN INTENTIONS

The fighting on the Ongjin Peninsula demonstrated the will of the North Korean leadership, who had good reason to be confident: they now possessed twenty-eight thousand seasoned Korean troops from the PLA. The PLA's 166th Division had arrived in Korea from Shenyang, Manchuria, in late July and became the KPA 6th Division. It was commanded by Pang Ho-san. The PLA's 164th Division arrived from Changchun, Manchuria, in August and was redesignated the KPA 5th Division. It was commanded by Yi Tok-san (whose real name was Kim Chang-dok). The KPA now had five infantry divisions.[98]

Gen. Pang Ho-san typified the North Korean military. Born to a farm family in Baoqing Province, Manchuria, in 1916, he had joined a partisan group sponsored by the CCP after Japan seized Manchuria in 1931, and entered the CCP five years later. Pang was selected for training at the Communist University of the Toilers of the East (KUTV) in Moscow. Returning to China in 1939, he had been assigned to a Korean research team of the Overseas Committee, CCP, at Yan'an. When the Northeast Korean Volunteers were established in 1945, Pang was the political commissar of the 1st Unit, which became later the independent 4th Division of the Northeast Field Army, and finally the PLA 166th Division in 1948. Pang was its political commissar throughout these years.[99]

With two crack Korean divisions from the PLA in hand, the upbeat Kim Il Sung and Pak Hon-yong now clearly intended to liberate the South by force.

Shtykov recounted a meeting with them on August 12 before he returned to Moscow on leave: "They said it is now clear that Seoul had rejected the proposal for peaceful unification and the North has no choice but to prepare for an attack on the South. The Korean people would not understand why they did not attack. We would lose the people's trust and the historical chance to unify the fatherland. Comrade Stalin, who has always been supportive of Koreans, should understand our feelings."

Shtykov replied to them: "Comrade Stalin stated his position at the meeting in Moscow on March 11 [*sic*—March 14], 1949. The Northern military forces do not have clear superiority over the potential enemy. In addition, there is the Soviet-U.S. agreement about the 38th parallel. An attack will only have legitimacy if the South strikes first." But Kim Il Sung countered that the 38th parallel was only a meaningful line of division as long as US troops remained. With US troops now gone, the parallel was no longer an obstacle to invasion. Kim and Pak argued that the South had postponed an invasion of the North and was building powerful defenses, similar to a Maginot Line, along the 38th parallel that would make it impossible for the KPA to counterattack, as Stalin had recommended. The combat along the parallel showed that the KPA was superior militarily to the ROKA, they said. Shtykov wrote: "I expressed my doubts about the feasibility of the North's plan. I pointed out that the evaluation of the situation by Kim Il Sung and Pak Honyong was too optimistic and ideological. Kim Il Sung had not expected such a response and looked hurt." [100]

Kim Il Sung then broached the creation of a liberated zone in the Samchok area of southern Kangwon Province. Samchok is a coastal city in the South close to Mt. Taebaek and some distance from the 38th parallel. Kim was probably thinking of it as a base for partisan activity. Shtykov replied that the idea required careful study. [101] The next day, Kim Il Sung again argued strongly for an advance southward. This time the plan was to occupy the Ongjin Peninsula and narrow the distance to the South's defense line by 120 kilometers. Shtykov repeated that the idea had to be examined fully. [102]

In Moscow on August 27, Shtykov briefed Stalin on the North Korean leaders' desire to attack the South and listed the reasons why he disagreed with them. First, there were two states on the Korean Peninsula, and South Korea was recognized by the United States and other countries. If the North took military action, the United States would intervene, not only providing weapons and ammunition to South Korea but also possibly sending Japanese troops to aid Seoul. Second, the United States would probably use an invasion of the South to start a massive propaganda campaign to vilify the Soviet Union. Third, an invasion of the South might have the political support of a large majority of Koreans across the peninsula, but the KPA did not have overwhelming military superiority over the southern forces. Fourth, South Korea had already created a powerful army and police force. Surprisingly, however, Shtykov supported Kim Il Sung's idea of making Samchok a liberated zone and occupying the Ongjin Peninsula below the 38th parallel. [103]

At the same time, in his letter dated August 20, South Korean President Rhee appealed to President Truman for additional military support, including arms and ammunition. He rejected American advisers' assurances that the Communists would never attack in force, and wrote: "I have stated before, and I state categorically again, that the Republic of Korea will not attack the territory north of the 38th parallel. But if the Communist forces do make an all out attempt to drive south and capture our capital, we shall use every strength we possess not only to defeat them and hurl them back, but also to attack their retreating forces and in so doing to liberate our enslaved countrymen in the north." [104]

At this stage in the Korean conflict, both the North and South—aware that the Soviet Union and the United States opposed unilateral action—had stated the same policy: if attacked, they would counterattack and unify the peninsula by force.

Of course, in Moscow there was concern not only about Korea's impact on US relations, but the impact of developments in China as well. On August 4, the 4th Field Army of the PLA led by Lin Biao liberated Changsha, the capital of Hunan Province. [105] What would the United States do? Then, on August 13, A. A. Kuznetsov, secretary of the CPSU, whose daughter was married to Anastas Mikoyan's son, was arrested. The wave of arrests among former and present Leningrad party leaders was spreading. [106] Further, on August 29, the Soviet Union conducted its first test of an atomic bomb. It was unclear how Washington would react to this landmark. But, of course, the United States already had an atomic arsenal, and it would take considerable time for the Soviets to actually produce atomic weapons. [107]

Japan's political situation also attracted the attention of Soviet leaders. Tokuda Kyuichi, secretary of the Japanese Communist Party, predicted that the Yoshida cabinet would be toppled by September. The JCP spread rumors of a developing revolution and formation of a people's government in September. But a series of mysterious events involving the Japan National Railways—the death of JNR president Shimoyama on the tracks, the sudden start of a train without an engineer at Mitaka station in July, and the attempt to wreck a train near Matsukawa station in August—were blamed on the JCP, whose campaign to stop the dismissal of public service employees, especially members of the national railway union, failed. Also, on September 8, the Japanese government and the Supreme Commander for the Allied Powers disbanded the League of Koreans in Japan, and the Korean Democratic Youth Union—the most militant organizations controlled by the JCP. Top league leader Han Tok-su and adviser Kim Chon-hae and twenty-eight other league leaders were purged from public employment. [108] The Soviet Union was on the verge of adopting a new policy toward Japan.

Adding to the Kremlin's political concerns, North Korea was continuing to press Moscow to support an attack on the South. On September 3, Kim Il Sung sent his secretary Mun Il to speak with Soviet Minister G. I. Tunkin, the senior embassy officer in Pyongyang in Shtykov's absence, to follow up on the August exchange with the ambassador. Mun told Tunkin that Kim Il Sung had received reliable intelligence that the ROK planned to occupy the Ongjin Peninsula north of the 38th parallel and bombard a cement factory in Haeju. Kim Il Sung wanted permission to strike first, seize the peninsula, and occupy South Korean territory as far as Kaesong. Tunkin reported to Moscow: "Kim Il Sung thinks that, the international situation permitting, it is possible to move further South. He is firmly convinced that South Korea can be brought under control in from two weeks to at most two months."

Tunkin advised caution on such a grave matter, saying North Korea should not make a hasty decision. But Mun Il said the ROKA unit commander on Ongjin had written orders to fire on the Haeju cement factory at 8 a.m. on September 20.[109] There was no time to waste.

Stalin directed Tunkin to assess North Korean thinking on five points: (1) evaluation of ROKA numbers, arms, and combat capability; (2) the partisan movement in the South and the degree of expected public support; (3) the popular reaction in the South and the extent of real support for KPA military units if the North attacked first; (4) the presence of US forces in the South and Kim Il Sung's opinion on what measures the United States might take if North Korea attacked; and (5) evaluation of the North's strength, military readiness, equipment, and combat capability.[110]

Tunkin questioned Kim Il Sung and Pak Hon-yong on September 12 and 13 and reported to Moscow on September 14. The North Korean leaders put ROKA strength at seven divisions, plus a Capital Guards force, for a total of twenty-three regiments and two special battalions. Including the air force, the ROKA had between eighty thousand and eighty-five thousand men, Kim and Pak said. It was equipped with ninety-three 105 mm cannons, forty-seven 37 mm cannons, thirty armored cars, twenty light tanks, ten L-4 aircraft, nine L-5 aircraft, and three cargo airplanes, with a total of forty-two aircraft in all. In addition, Kim and Pak reported the South had about fifty thousand police and between forty thousand and fifty thousand Fatherland Defense Corps members. "Kim Il Sung is convinced from the skirmishes at the 38th parallel that the South Korean army's combat capability is poor," Tunkin wrote. "Kim Il Sung and Pak Hon-yong said there are Northern agents in every Southern unit, but refrained from saying that in a civil war these agents could work to destroy Southern units."

On the partisan movement in the South, Kim and Pak told Tunkin that the fifteen thousand to twenty thousand partisans had been recently strengthened somewhat. Kim Il Sung did not expect major contributions from them, but Pak Hon-yong, a southerner, believed that partisan support would be huge.

Both Kim and Pak expected the partisans would cut communications and hoped that they would seize the major ports. They would probably not seize the ports in the initial period of military action, Kim and Pak said, but perhaps they could later.

As for the response of the southern populace if the North started a civil war, Tunkin wrote: "Kim Il Sung vacillated. At the first meeting on September 12, he said that for the North to take military action first would definitely create a negative impression among the people and be politically disadvantageous." Kim Il Sung cited Mao Zedong's statement to Kim Il in the spring of 1949 that Korean comrades should not attack South Korea but wait for more favorable conditions, and that Chinese friends could not provide rapid, effective support at present. But the next day, according to Tunkin, "Kim Il Sung, clearly influenced by Ho Ka-i [present as an interpreter], said first the people would probably welcome military action by the North, and the North would probably suffer no political loss by striking first. However, later . . . Kim Il Sung said that if a civil war is drawn out, it would be politically disadvantageous, and since a quick victory could not be expected under the present conditions, he also did not advocate the North start a civil war. He proposes to seize South Korean territory on the Ongjin Peninsula and from east of the peninsula to Kaesong."

The notion that Kim Il Sung's attitude changed because of Ho Ka-i, a Soviet Korean, as Tunkin alleged, is doubtful. Ho Ka-i was in no position to advise Kim Il Sung on the political reaction in the South. By saying the people would probably welcome an invasion, Kim Il Sung may have simply been trying to make a stronger case to the Soviets. But Kim Il Sung had not forgotten Mao Zedong's advice, nor did he count on much help from southern partisans, making him more cautious than his colleague Pak Hon-yong.

Northern intelligence sources had put the number of US military advisers in the South at 900, along with 1,500 US soldiers (the official US figure for military advisers was 500). Tunkin reported to Moscow: "If a civil war occurs in Korea, in the opinion of Kim Il Sung and Pak Hon-yong, the United States can dispatch Japanese and [nationalist] Chinese troops and itself provide sea and air support. U.S. military advisers would probably directly organize military operations." Kim and Pak did not believe that US ground forces would be committed, given their assumption that Japanese and Nationalist Chinese troops would be sent.

According to Tunkin, Kim Il Sung and Pak Hon-yong numbered North Korean forces, including air and coast guard units, at 97,500, with sixty-four tanks, fifty-nine armored cars, and seventy-five aircraft. "Kim Il Sung regards the North's military as superior to the South's in equipment, . . . morale, training and political consciousness." But Kim acknowledged that they were deficient in air and naval forces and lacked heavy artillery and ammunition.

Occupying Ongjin, as Kim Il Sung proposed, amounted to a probe, Tunkin wrote Moscow: "The South Korean forces under attack may lose the will to fight. In that case [the North] will continue to push southward. If the South Korean forces . . . do not collapse, [the North] will hold the occupied area. The defense line will have been reduced by a third. The operation on the Ongjin Peninsula should not be rushed. They [North Koreans] should wait until additional equipment arrives from the Soviet Union. . . . Kim Il Sung recognizes that operations in Ongjin have the potential to turn into a civil war, but he does not expect that to happen because the South lacks the courage to attack elsewhere along the 38th parallel."

Tunkin's personal assessment was that an attack on Ongjin would lead to prolonged civil war. Having failed in China, the United States would probably intervene strongly to save Syngman Rhee, and might also take advantage of the war to inflame international hostility against the Soviet Union. It was inadvisable for the North to start a civil war, Tunkin said. Even if a limited intrusion were successful, the North would be criticized and suffer a huge political setback.[111]

MOSCOW REMAINS OPPOSED TO AN INVASION

On September 16, two days after Tunkin reported to Moscow on Kim Il Sung's and Pak Hon-yong's views on the Korean situation, the show trial opened in Budapest of former Hungarian Interior Minister Lazlo Rajk. Rajk testified that he had been a spy for the former Hungarian police, that he had been threatened by US and Yugoslav intelligence, and worked for them to overthrow the Hungarian People's Democratic system.[112] In Europe the Cold War was being waged with increasing ferocity. In Moscow, the day before the Rajk trial began, Soviet Ambassador to North Korea Terentii Shtykov submitted a long personal memorandum to Stalin to supplement one he had written in late August.[113] He covered many topics, including the political and economic situation in South Korea, oppressive measures taken by the Rhee regime, and an assessment of the South's and North's military strength.

Shtykov put the ROKA at eighty-five thousand men (with seven infantry divisions and five special regiments or battalions) and the Fatherland Defense Corps at fifty thousand, the same numbers as Kim Il Sung. Shtykov listed North Korean troop strength at 80,000 (17,500 less than Kim Il Sung's figures). It included five infantry divisions and two brigades. Shtykov also listed thirty-three T-34 tanks for the North—much lower than Kim Il Sung's sixty-four tanks—and seventy-four aircraft. As for the North's combat readiness, the NKPA had not been tested in battle, Shtykov observed, but units fighting in the Kaesong area had done well. He noted the capabilities of the two additional divisions from China.

Shtykov's evaluation of North Korean readiness was objective: the troops were not adequately trained and would suffer heavy casualties in combat. On the other hand, their élan and political consciousness were good and few would surrender or defect. Plus northern agents had induced defections from the ROKA.

Shtykov reported that Kim Il Sung and Pak Hon-yong thought that unification could not be accomplished by peaceful measures, and that the Fatherland Front initiative did not ensure unification. Their premise was that a large majority of Koreans wanted to end the division of their country. American forces were an obstacle, Kim and Pak said, but with them out of the way the people would now ask what was preventing unification. Kim Il Sung and Pak Hon-yong did not want to be responsible for prolonging the division and had reached the point of seeking unification by force. If the North did not strike now, they argued, the peninsula would remain divided for many years, and the southern reactionaries would crush left-wing elements, build a powerful military force, and perhaps invade the North. As for his own views, Ambassador Shtykov wrote:

> I . . . regard the internal political situation in both the south and north as favorable to our friends . . . but the reactionary imperialist countries may use a first strike by the People's Army against the Soviet Union. I do not regard American intervention and support for the South as impossible. Nor do I regard the personnel of the People's Army and the equipment our friends now have as sufficient to guarantee that they can completely destroy Southern forces and acquire all of South Korea.
>
> Therefore, it is both possible and feasible to develop support extensively, and direct a partisan movement in the South. If conditions are favorable, the limited tactic of occupying the Ongjin Peninsula and the Kaesong area could be carried out. Southern provocations at the 38th parallel can be exploited to punish the South, occupy these two areas, and shorten the battle lines.

Shtykov, unlike Tunkin, thus favored the Ongjin strategy.

Stalin directed Vyacheslav Molotov, the first deputy prime minister and party Politburo member to have former Minister for the Armed Forces Nikolai Bulganin, Vice-Foreign Minister Andrei Gromyko, and Ambassador Shtykov draft a response to North Korea as a Politburo decision. Four drafts from this process survive, and all follow the same basic line of analysis. The first lists four types of reasons for opposing a northern invasion of the South, in this order: political reasons, military reasons, the danger of US intervention, and the potential for peaceful unification. In the second draft, military reasons preceded political ones, but it concluded with the following recommendation: "Of course [the North] must always be prepared if the Southern authorities attack first to destroy their military forces and unify the country under the leadership of a people's democratic government." Revisions were then made in this text and the retyped version became the third draft. Stalin himself made a change in the conclusion: "Of course, in the event South Korean forces attack first, [North Korea] must be prepared to defeat them and act as the situation allows." This wording is also included in the fourth and final draft, which bears written comments by several people. One comment was to remove the recommendation to be prepared to counterattack.[114] On September 23, Molotov sent this draft, with Stalin's changes, along with a request for comments to members of the Politburo.[115]

At a Politburo meeting on September 24, three sections were cut from this fourth draft. The following wording on potential northern military action was removed: "The attacking forces must have at least twice the troop strength of the enemy." Also eliminated was this wording on a northern invasion of the South: "This will give the United States an excuse to commit its own forces to Korea in the name of supporting the South." Finally, the section quoted above that North Korea must be prepared to destroy the South's military forces in the event the South attacked was taken out. The effect of these deletions was to make the document vaguer. Stalin must have deleted his own addition to the conclusion about the North needing to be prepared to defeat the South if the South attacked; no one else could have removed it.

The Politburo Central Committee directed Ambassador Shtykov to convey the following statement to Kim Il Sung and Pak Hon-yong:

> From a military perspective, we cannot regard the KPA as prepared for such an attack southward. To attack without the appropriate preparation would almost certainly result in prolonged military operations. This would lead to major political and economic difficulties for North Korea and not result in the enemy's defeat, and of course cannot be permitted. At present North Korea does not have the requisite superiority in troop strength over South Korea and no preparations have been made for a military attack on the South. . . .
>
> Politically as well [North Korea] is unprepared for a military attack on the South. Of course, the people hope for national unification, and we agree with your view that the South is waiting for liberation from an increasingly reactionary system. However, to date there has been little effort to organize a popular uprising to arouse the masses to the struggle, extend the partisan movement throughout Korea, and create liberated zones. . . . Thus it must be recognized that politically, too, there are no preparations for the proposed attack on the South.

The Politburo also rejected the limited strategy of seizing the Ongjin Peninsula and Kaesong area, since this would be regarded as the start of a war between the North and South. The Politburo once more stressed Soviet apprehension that a military action initiated by the North would provide the Americans with an excuse to intervene in Korea. It recommended that resources be concentrated on: (1) developing a South Korean partisan movement, creating liberated zones, and preparing for a mass armed uprising; and (2) an extensive buildup of the KPA.[116]

In the autumn of 1949, then, Stalin and the CPSU—worried that the United States would intervene in a Korean conflict—rejected the North Korean leaders' proposal for liberation by force. Ambassador Shtykov concurred completely.

Just before the Politburo decision, President Truman on September 23 announced to the world that the Soviet Union had tested an atomic bomb. Two days later, the Soviet news agency TASS issued a statement that the Soviet Union now possessed atomic bombs.[117] This was exciting news in Beijing and Pyongyang, as was Mao Zedong's declaration on October 1 from Tiananmen Gate on the founding of the People's Republic of China.

Two days later, Ambassador Shtykov, now back in Pyongyang, informed Kim Il Sung and Pak Hon-yong of the Politburo decision. He later reported their reaction to Moscow: "Kim Il Sung and Pak Hon-yong were reserved. They listened to me, and Kim Il Sung said only 'Okay' (*Khorosho*). Pak Hon-yong responded more fully, saying the conclusion was correct and they had to develop a broader partisan movement in the South. Guerilla activity was expanding and they have sent about 800 organizers to the south."[118]

Yet Kim Il Sung and Pak Hon-yong thought the time was ripe to act. They must have wondered why Moscow withheld its permission and been deeply disappointed. On the other hand, Pak Hon-yong was probably encouraged by the recommendation to strengthen the southern partisans.

SOUTHERN PARTISANS

The Cheju Island uprising—the first full-scale action by partisans in the South—had started over a year earlier, on April 3, 1948, on orders from the Southern Workers' Party (SWP). The next partisan campaign had begun on October 20, 1948, when the ROKA 14th Regiment at Yosu refused orders to suppress the revolt on Cheju. Remnants of the regiment had fled to the Chiri mountains and formed the Mt. Chiri Guerrilla Unit; by about April 1949, only two hundred members of the unit remained. Yi Hyong-sang, a leader of the SWP, went to the Chiri mountains and formed a new unit around the survivors. Two months later, the People's Guerrilla Unit, 2nd Corps, was organized with five hundred members.

After the Southern and Northern Workers' Parties merged on June 30, 1949, former leaders of the SWP, such as Pak Hon-yong and Yi Sung-yop, controlled the partisans. Yi organized 360 graduates of the Kangdong Political Academy into the 1st Corps (with Yi Ho-chae as commander) and sent it to the Mt. Odae area in May 1949. The 3rd Corps, comprising about three hundred fighters and commanded by Kim Tal-sam, leader of the Cheju revolt, was sent to Mt. Taebaek in August 1949.

But the ROKA, using relentless counter-guerrilla tactics, destroyed the 1st Corps in December 1949. And the 3rd Corps, which had grown to more than six hundred men, was reduced to sixty by March 1950. Only the 2nd Corps continued to operate from its base in the Chiri mountains.[119] In short, the partisan movement did not become the potent force that Moscow and Pak Hon-yong had expected.

SOVIET POLICY TOWARD JAPAN CHANGES

The Soviet Union's recognition of the People's Republic of China and alliance with the PRC required a review of its policy toward Northeast Asia, starting with subtle changes toward Japan. At Stalin's request, in late October 1949, K. Ses'kin, the chief of the Japan Section of the Main Intelligence Department of the Red Army Headquarters, who was in charge of liaison with the Japanese Communist Party, evaluated JCP leader Nosaka Sanzo, his agent in Japan. Ses'kin favorably assessed Nosaka's strategy of peaceful revolution under the Allied Occupation.[120] But Stalin apparently had asked for the review in order to change policy toward the JCP. When K. Derevianko, the Soviet representative on the Allied Council for Japan, met with Tokuda Kyuichi, general secretary of the JCP, and his deputy Nosaka on November 11, they were confident that the Supreme Commander for the Allied Powers would not outlaw the party.[121]

At about this time, Nosaka wrote to Derevianko that the funds the JCP had received from the Soviet party a year earlier had been used up, and asked for additional financial support. Derevianko transmitted this request to Moscow. On November 25, G. M. Grigor'ian, the chairman of the External Policy Committee, CC of the CPSU, proposed to Stalin that they tell Nosaka that "financial support for operating expenses is not appropriate."[122] Top CPSU leaders had already reached a consensus opposing the JCP's political strategy and its request for further financial assistance. In December, they publicly criticized the JCP's strategy of peaceful revolution and ordered it to confront US occupation forces through illegal struggle.

A militant strategy in Japan was consistent with support of the Chinese revolution and required no sacrifice or even expense for the Soviet Union. But approval of armed unification in Korea was a different matter. Stalin was determined not to allow events there to take an unacceptable direction.

THE CAMPAIGN TO RECOVER MT. UNPA

On October 15, DPRK Foreign Minister Pak Hon-yong submitted to the United Nations a report by the Fatherland Front on southern violations of the 38th parallel. In fact, the day before, on October 14, two battalions of the North's 3rd Police Brigade started a drive to retake Mt. Unpa; northern troops forced ROKA units to withdraw from this high ground north of the parallel, which they had held since June.[123] On October 26, an alarmed Stalin told Ambassador Shtykov: "You are forbidden to advise the North Korean government to take aggressive military action against South Korean forces without permission from the Center and are under instructions to report to the Center in a timely manner all planned actions and incidents at the 38th parallel. You have not complied with these instructions."[124] Shtykov had not reported the North's preparations for the attack or the fighting. Stalin, who was angry because he had heard of the incident from a different source, demanded that Shtykov explain and follow orders. Shtykov prevailed on the Defense Ministry to provide information about the incident and apparently reported to Moscow on October 20.

On October 31, Shtykov reported again, saying that he had heard on October 11 from Bodiagin, adviser to the police brigade, that DPRK Interior Minister Pak Il-u had ordered Mt. Unpa be retaken. Shtykov had confirmed that the area was on the northern side of the parallel and emphatically directed North Korean forces not to cross the border. He had never urged aggressive military action, the ambassador said. But he acknowledged three errors: failure to appreciate the significance of this action, failure to direct Bodiagin to stop the operation until he was certain of its scope, and submission of a late report that omitted the clash.[125] The mea culpa did not satisfy Stalin. On November 20, Gromyko conveyed to Shtykov Stalin's anger that he had failed to follow "the Center's instructions not to provoke incidents along the 38th parallel."[126] The "Center" meant Stalin. He still did not support Kim and Pak's plan to unify Korea by force.

BLUSTER AND APPEAL FROM SEOUL

In Seoul on September 16, US Ambassador Muccio endorsed a proposal by General Roberts to the Pentagon for additional military assistance to the ROK in fiscal year 1950, noting that a limit of $10 million would be inadequate if large-scale hostilities broke out between North and South Korea. The ambassador took strong exception to the mere $26,956 that Roberts had requested to purchase seven L-4 aircraft. According to intelligence reports, Muccio said, the Soviet Union was supplying North Korea with "a relatively sizeable number of comparatively high-performance military aircraft." If the reports were confirmed, the United States should consider strengthening the ROK air force.[127] Muccio, who had earlier cautioned against boosting South Korea's military capability, partly out of concern about a secret agreement between Syngman Rhee and Chiang Kai-shek, now seems to have had a change of heart. Muccio reported to Washington that at the Chinhae conference, Dr. K. C. Wu, a former ROC vice-foreign minister, had requested Nationalist air bases on Cheju Island. Nationalist Chinese officials were surprised at the ROK's lack of naval forces and inability to defend such bases. On the other hand, when the ROK foreign minister Yim Pyong-jik asked how much air support the Nationalists could provide if the South moved against the North, the meager assistance proffered left ROK officials disillusioned. No agreement on military cooperation was reached at the Chinhae meeting. Despite a flurry of rumors that suggested otherwise, Muccio said Rhee was very cautious and had no intention of becoming involved in the Chinese civil war.[128]

Although he was certain that the United States would not support an attack on the North, Rhee publicly still spoke of "advancing north to unify the country." At a press conference with foreign correspondents on September 30, he said, "The great majority of South Koreans fervently want the overthrow of the North Korean communist regime, and if such action started the United Nations would surely approve." He added that "time helps the communists."[129] Rhee wrote to Robert Oliver, his adviser and publicist, that same day:

I feel strongly that now is the most psychological moment when we should take an aggressive measure and join with our loyal communist army in the north to clean up the rest of them in Pyongyang. We will drive some of Kim Il Sung's men to the mountain region and where we will gradually starve them out. Then our line of defense must be strengthened along the Tumen and Yalu Rivers. We will be in a 100% better position. The natural boundary line along the river and the Paikdoo (Paektu) Mts. can be made almost impenetrable with sufficient number of planes and two or three fast running naval vessels standing at the mouths of the two rivers with fighting planes defending all the coast lines including Cheju Island.[130]

Toward the end of this letter, Rhee wrote that in the Cold War the Soviet Union always was waging an advantageous war, while the United States' war was doomed to be defeated. He appealed that now was the time for Koreans to rise up and struggle against their enemies.

In response, Oliver wrote:

I sympathize with the feeling that offense is the best and sometimes the only defense. However, it is very evident to us here that any such attack now, or even to talk of such an attack, is to lose American official and public support and will weaken our position among other nations. . . . The strong feeling in

American official and public circles is that we should continue to lean way over backward to avoid any semblance of aggression and make sure the blame for what happens is upon Russia. I can fully concur in your disgust that we must still continue to retreat and appease, after four years . . . but I do think the time is not too far away when a turn will come and Russia will be thrown back.[131]

If Russia and North Korea attacked, Oliver tacitly suggested, the United States would support an ROK counterattack and occupation of the North. In response to Oliver's letter dated October 24, Rhee wrote: "Unless they [South Koreans] have at least the moral support of the United States, not to speak of the material support, nothing can be done." But, "If Korea had the assurance that if attacked the United States would stand by [it] and would not sacrifice Korea, it would be a different matter."[132]

A week later, on board the visiting cruiser USS *St. Paul*, Rhee called the Soviet Union an imperialist power that occupied the northern half of Korea and had designs on the rest of Korea. South Korea would fight to the end against Soviet aggression, Rhee said, by itself if necessary, but preferably with support from the United States and the United Nations. Korea is "a body cut in half," Rhee said, and "we can't live much longer this way." When Muccio met Rhee to confirm this statement, the president "explained that in talk he wished to convey [the] idea he had no plan to move north today or tomorrow but that [the] Republic of Korea would have to be prepared to fight and unify the country by force if necessary."[133]

Syngman Rhee knew that he needed not only American moral empathy but also US troops, who would only be forthcoming if the North attacked and the Americans came to the South's aid. At a year-end press conference, Rhee declared, "We must accomplish unification in the new year. When that inevitable time comes, we cannot avoid bloodshed and civil war. . . . We must on our own unify our land."[134] Rhee remained committed to unification by force.

A week earlier, the US National Security Council had completed NSC report 48/1, and Truman approved it on December 29. As the NSC report stated, US policy makers saw the Soviet Union as the greatest threat in Asia, and their objective was "to contain and where feasible to reduce" Soviet expansionism. To that end, the "Asian off-shore island chain" would be held, as well as Japan, the Philippines, and Okinawa. Japan was crucial, the United States believed, and must not fall into the Soviet bloc.[135] The statuses of Taiwan and South Korea were left up in the air.

On the other side, although the Soviet Union had endorsed the Chinese revolution and begun to challenge the US occupation of Japan, as 1949 came to an end Stalin still refused to give Pyongyang the green light for unification by force.

Chapter Two

North Korea Goes to War

THE SINO-SOVIET SUMMIT

Mao Zedong's meeting with Joseph Stalin in late 1949 changed the political landscape of Northeast Asia. Leaving Beijing by train on December 6, Mao, accompanied by his secretary Chen Boda, interpreter Shi Zhe, and other aides, arrived in Moscow on December 16. The two Communist leaders lost no time getting acquainted, meeting that evening at six o'clock at Stalin's dacha. Vyacheslav Molotov, Georgii Malenkov, Nikolai Bulganin, and Andrei Vyshinsky were also present. After an exchange of greetings, Mao presented China's agenda to the Soviets. "The most important issue now is to secure peace," Mao said. "China needs a long peaceful breathing spell, three to five years." He then asked, "How and for how long can international peace be achieved?" Stalin replied:

> We have been at peace for four years already, but we are also concerned about peace. There are no direct threats to China. Japan has not recovered so it is not yet prepared for war. America talks a lot about war but fears it the most. Europe is frightened by war. There is no one to fight China. Maybe Kim Il Sung will take on China? Peace depends on our efforts. If we work well together, we can have peace not for five or ten years, but for twenty or twenty-five years, or even longer.

Although the triumph of the Chinese revolution seemed to please Stalin, when Mao got down to brass tacks about Soviet-Chinese relations, the Soviet leader had some reservations about Mao's agenda. Stalin said:

> We must decide whether to announce the continuation of the 1945 treaty of alliance and friendship between the USSR and China, announce that it will be revised, or make the needed revisions now. . . . As you know, the major

45

provisions of this treaty [on the Kurile Islands, South Sakhalin, Port Arthur, and other issues] were the result of the Yalta Agreement. This treaty was concluded, so to speak, with the approval of the United States and England. Taking this situation into consideration, we, in our inner circle, have decided not to modify any of the points now. The reason is that if even one clause is revised, it would give the United States and England legal grounds to propose revision of the clauses covering the Kurile Islands, Southern Sakhalin and other provisions. Therefore, we have decided to continue nominally the present treaty but in actuality revise it, that is to say, leave as is the Soviet Union's right to station troops at Port Arthur but, at the request of the Chinese government, withdraw the units currently stationed there. This can be done as a request from China. Regarding the Chinese Eastern Railroad [from Siberia's Chita to Vladivostok via Harbin], in this case too, we can maintain the formal agreement while actually modifying certain clauses at China's request. However, if the Chinese comrades are not satisfied with this arrangement, I would like you to make a proposal. [1]

Stalin's attitude was contradictory. On the one hand, he acknowledged the achievements of the Chinese revolution; on the other, he insisted on affirming the Yalta Agreement, which secured for the Soviet Union not only territorial gains from Japan but also Soviet interests in Manchuria. Stunned by Stalin's position, Mao hid his disappointment behind a noncommittal reply. "It's clear the treaty should not be revised now," Mao stated. But Mao was determined to get a revised treaty. He convinced Stalin to defer the issues and accept a visit by Zhou Enlai.

The conversation then moved to other topics, including Soviet loans to China, requests for Soviet support for construction of naval and air force facilities in China, the possibility of developing mineral resources and rubber plantations there, and the translation and editing of Mao's writings.

Hitherto there has been no adequate account of the subsequent Mao-Stalin meetings. The diary of Chinese security official Wang Dongxing first clarified the situation. On December 18, Politburo member Anastas Mikoyan and Foreign Minister Vyshinsky dined with Mao. After they left, Mao issued orders to launch the Chinese campaign against Hainan Island. The next day, he prepared instructions on China's domestic issues, and on December 20 Molotov and Mikoyan visited Mao to discuss arrangements for Stalin's seventieth birthday.

At the official birthday ceremony on December 21 at the Bolshoi Theater, Mao was the first foreign guest to speak in praise of Stalin. A huge birthday banquet was also held in the Kremlin's hall the following day. The second Stalin-Mao conference was December 24 and lasted five hours. Stalin telephoned Mao the next day and they talked through an interpreter. The third face-to-face meeting was on the evening of December 26. It also lasted five hours. Wang's diary entry is unclear, but there seems to have been a meeting on December 27 as well. Afterwards, Mao Zedong informed Wang that he told Stalin, "If there are areas where [our] authority has not been established, we'll ask the Soviets, our senior colleagues, for help [in resolving the issue]. But we will never abandon our sovereignty." Stalin was deferential to Mao, saying "my understanding was deepened." On December 28, Stalin disclosed to Mao a memorandum by I. V. Kovalev, his emissary in China, critical of the Chinese leadership.[2]

Stalin and Mao had avoided acrimonious confrontation over a Sino-Soviet treaty, but what, exactly, did they discuss during these lengthy meetings? According to the Soviet interpreter Fedorenko, all the meetings were held at night at Stalin's dacha at Kuntsevo. "Many themes were discussed. There was not a strict agenda. . . . The topics were always chosen by the hosts."[3]

Years later Mao told the Soviet philosopher Pavel Iudin that he was displeased with Stalin during the first stage of his visit because the Soviet leader did not want to invite Zhou Enlai to Moscow and "avoided any meeting with me."[4] German researcher Dieter Heinzig found the following comment in a handwritten insertion by Iudin in his record of his meeting with Mao: "Concerning the Korean question, when I [Mao] was in Moscow there was no talk of conquering South Korea, but rather of strengthening North Korea significantly."[5]

The very fact that the nighttime meetings between Mao and Stalin took place was long kept secret. Fedorenko, in the memorandum quoted above, also wrote: "In the course of the free conversations they exchanged views on many issues—military, political, economic, and ideological. . . . For example, the problem of language and programs of thinking were also discussed."[6] M. V. Gorbanevskii, who researched Stalin's essay on linguistics, has surmised that Stalin was inspired by his discussion with Mao Zedong on the problematic nature of N. I. Marr' s theory.[7] The talks with Mao were important to Stalin.

That the two leaders talked about the situation in Asia, and the United Nations, is beyond dispute. On December 25, in the course of their meetings, the Soviet Union put senior officers of Japan's former Kwantung Army Unit 731 on trial for bacteriological warfare activities in China during World War II. At the International Military Tribunal for the Far East (the Tokyo Trials) earlier, in return for receiving the unit's experimental data, the United States blocked the court from prosecuting central figures of the unit. At that time, the Soviet prosecutor had accepted this agreement. The Soviets' decision to publicize the hidden atrocities of the Japanese Imperial Army was a clear indication that the Soviet Union was moving away from cooperation with the United States in the occupation policy toward Japan. At that time, Stalin was preparing an article denouncing Japanese Communist Party leader Nosaka Sanzo's strategy of peaceful revolution under the US occupation for the Cominform organ, *For Eternal Peace and Democracy*, which he may have discussed with Mao.

On January 1, 1950, Molotov and Mikoyan spoke with Mao at his quarters in Moscow about his trip to Leningrad. One purpose was to counter a British news service report that day that Stalin was holding Mao under house arrest. On January 2, an interview with Mao appeared in *Pravda*. It clearly indicated his desire to resolve the issue of a Sino-Soviet alliance treaty. Molotov and Mikoyan solicited Mao's views that day.[8] According to Shi Zhe's memoirs, Mao offered three proposals for consideration: conclude a new treaty between China and the Soviet Union, announce that there had been an exchange of views on the old treaty, or issue a statement regarding relations between the two countries. If the second option were chosen, Zhou Enlai need not come to Moscow. But Molotov agreed that a new treaty should be concluded, and Zhou Enlai was summoned.[9]

Korea was surely discussed during Mao and Stalin's nightly conferences. The Soviets were aware of the contents of a telegram from Chinese military leader Lin Biao to Mao in Moscow in early January 1950. Stalin informed Soviet Ambassador to North Korea Terentii Shtykov on January 8 that some of the 16,000 Korean troops in Lin Biao's 4th Route Army "expressed a desire to return to their homeland after the offensive in South China. The war is almost over and Lin Biao wishes to send a division or four or five regiments of Koreans to Korea." Stalin directed Shtykov to consult with Kim Il Sung on the matter. In 1949, it will be recalled, Kim Il, Kim Il Sung's aide, and Mao had come to an agreement on the transfer of Korean troops and Mao might have referred to Lin Biao's telegram to bring up Korea to Stalin.[10]

The Chinese government had already informed Kim Il Sung that the troops were available when he met Shtykov on January 19. Kim asked the ambassador for advice, a clever ploy. Kim wanted the troops quickly and said a three-man delegation would soon be sent to China. He planned to form one division and two regiments with the Korean soldiers and use the remainder to form a motorcycle regiment and a mechanized brigade.

Kim Il Sung wanted the troops to remain in China until April.[11] Mao made the final decision in Moscow on January 22 to send the troops to North Korea along with their weapons.[12] In March, 17,000 Korean troops were assembled in Zhengzhou and formed into the 15th Independent Division and an independent regiment; they departed for North Korea in April, per Kim's request.[13]

On January 4, *Pravda* carried a militant speech by Liu Shaoqi, Mao's second in command of the CCP, to an Asia-Pacific conference of the World Federation of Trade Unions in Beijing, which is evidence that the CPSU supported the line of the Chinese revolution. That line advocated a combination of armed and mass struggle to liberate the peoples of Asia.[14] Mao and Stalin must have conferred on this, too. On January 6 the Cominform organ carried an article by "Observer" entitled "The Situation in Japan" that castigated the Japanese Communist Party (JCP). The article was reprinted in *Pravda* the next day.

This attack on the JCP revealed the secret connection between the CPSU and JCP and Moscow's control of the JCP. The article called on the JCP to abandon the Nosaka line of peaceful revolution and adopt a policy of confrontation with US occupation forces in Japan. The anonymous author scathingly condemned Nosaka's "peaceful revolution as a form of Japanized Marxism-Leninism. . . . 'Japanized' Marxism-Leninism is nothing more than a Japanese version of an anti-Marxist and anti-socialist theory that claims that reaction can become democracy and imperialism can peacefully evolve into socialism. The Nosaka 'theory' whitewashes the imperialists who occupy Japan, extolls American imperialism and deceives the Japanese masses."[15]

Condemnation of Nosaka signified Stalin's endorsement of Mao's armed-struggle path to power and the applicability of the radical line of the Chinese revolution to Japan. The article was also a subtle bid by the Cominform (Communist Information Bureau), basically a Soviet-dominated organization concerned with European affairs, to intervene directly in the Asian Communist movement. Mao's favorable reaction to the Cominform attack is evident in a message he sent to Hu Qiaomu, head of the PRC's press department, from Moscow on January 14, 1950: "Our party must publish its view and support the Cominform attack on Okano Susumu. I want to say that it is regrettable that the JCP Politburo has not accepted this criticism and that the JCP must take appropriate steps and quickly correct Okano Susumu's mistakes."[16] (Okano Susumu was Nosaka Sanzo's pseudonym during the Comintern era.) The Soviets' attack on the JCP checked China's move to create an Eastern Cominform, yet among those most excited by the article surely were Kim Il Sung and Pak Hon-yong.

ACHESON DRAWS A LINE

Secretary of State Dean Acheson, speaking at the National Press Club in Washington, DC, on January 12, 1950, placed the Aleutian Islands, Japan, Okinawa, and the Philippines within a US defense perimeter that left Taiwan and Korea outside it. According to Bruce Cumings, Acheson intended to induce a Communist attack on South Korea, but North Korea did not interpret the speech as a green light.[17] Park Myung-lim basically agrees with Cumings that North Korea did not see the speech as a green light, and also suggests that South Korea continued to regard itself as inside the defense line even after the speech and did not protest it.[18] According to Cumings, North Korea initially reported that Acheson had included South Korea in the perimeter. In an earlier work, I suggested that North Korea might have feigned misunderstanding of the Acheson speech and downplayed its importance, but that the speech may have inspired Kim Il Sung's boldness on January 17, when he conveyed to Shtykov his wish to begin action against the South.[19] In any case, the fact that Kim Il Sung and DPRK Foreign Minister Pak Hon-yong did not anticipate American intervention if the North attacked the South, and believed that the Truman administration would send Japanese forces instead, helps explain why Kim evinced little interest in the speech.

Kim Il Sung and other leaders in Pyongyang may have been influenced by a recent analysis of the political situation in Japan by Song Sung-chol. In March 1949, Song, a candidate for the JCP Central Committee in 1945–1946, had been named head of the Japan section of the DPRK Foreign Ministry. His analysis had appeared in *Kulloja* on October 15, 1949. Song called Japanese Prime Minister Yoshida Shigeru's disbandment of the League of Koreans in Japan (Choren) in 1949 "fascist." Song also described how conservative parties in Japan had merged in a bid to control two-thirds of the seats in the Diet and revise the new constitution.[20] But unless Article 9 of the constitution requiring "renunciation of war" and "non-possession of war potential" was revised, Song asserted, Japan could not rearm and swiftly deploy troops to fight in Korea.

Stalin, however, was preoccupied with American intentions, and Acheson's speech appeared to be a hint that Washington would not interfere militarily. On January 8, the Soviet Union supported the PRC's demand for a seat at the United Nations, and five days later it announced that it would not attend the Security Council until Beijing's right to represent China was recognized. The Soviet actions were probably planned well in advance. Stalin also planned a strong protest against Acheson's statement that the Soviet Union intended to annex Inner Mongolia and Xinjiang. On January 17, he sent Molotov and Vyshinsky to see Mao, who had just returned to Moscow from Leningrad. They gave Mao a copy of Acheson's speech and proposed that the USSR, PRC, and Mongolia all issue statements in response, which Vyshinsky and the foreign minister of Mongolia did on January 21. Mao drafted a statement on January 19 that was released under the name of Hu Qiaomu. Moscow was displeased that the statement did not appear under the name of the PRC's foreign minister, overtly criticizing Mao. Mao got angry at Molotov and Stalin, but did not say a word. Vyshinsky charged Acheson with camouflaging his intentions by saying that the United States was a "friend" of Asian peoples; thus "U.S. aggressive plans for Japan, the Ryukyus, and the Philippines" were revealed.[21] Vyshinsky did not dare mention the fact that South Korea was not included among the countries within the US defense perimeter. If there had been an emotional clash with Mao Zedong on this issue, the Soviets might not have even been able to give him their interpretation of the speech.

Zhou Enlai arrived in Moscow on January 20, 1950, and negotiations started on a revised Sino-Soviet treaty. Agreement was reached on the basic issues at the first official meeting on January 22. The participants focused on Stalin's statement at the meeting that the Alliance and Friendship treaty between the Soviet Union and Kuomintang government was an "unequal treaty." A surprised Mao Zedong asked, "Wouldn't a change [in the existing treaty] run counter to decisions at the Yalta conference?" Stalin replied, "True, it does. Once we take the position to amend the treaty, we must go all the way. Indeed, this is somewhat inconvenient for us, and we will have to go to fight against the Americans. We are already reconciled to that."[22]

Stalin made clear to Mao that he intended to confront the United States in Asia. In reply to Mao's comment that preventing Japanese aggression should be incorporated in the new treaty, Stalin stated, "That is right—and to hell with it. Japan still has cadres remaining. If the Americans continue their policy toward Japan, these people will probably gain power."[23] Stalin foresaw that in the future Washington would probably advocate Japan's rearmament, but in 1950 there were no Japanese armed forces. Only the United States could intervene in Korea, Stalin believed. Stalin interpreted Acheson's speech as an indication that the Truman administration was washing its hands of South Korea, however, and must have judged that he could make a strong pressure on the United States. In the treaty negotiations, Stalin basically accepted all the Chinese requests regarding Chinese control of Port Arthur, Dalian, and the Chinese Changchun Railroad (Chinese Eastern Railway).[24]

KIM IL SUNG APPEALS TO MOSCOW FOR ENDORSEMENT

Kim Il Sung had been disappointed when the Soviet Politburo the previous September had rejected unification of Korea by force. On December 29, he had sent Soviet Ambassador Shtykov an additional request for weapons and ammunition worth 112 million rubles, promising to pay in nonferrous metals and precious metals. In April 1949, when making the request, Kim had not offered to pay for the weapons, but Moscow's lack of enthusiasm for war with South Korea probably forced him to try a different approach. Shtykov recommended approval of Kim's request.[25]

The Cominform's attack on the Japanese Communist Party in early January had given Kim Il Sung and Pak Hon-yong fresh hope for gaining Soviet support for a move against the South. If the Soviet Union supported the path of the Chinese revolution and ordered the JCP to challenge US occupation forces, there must be a new attitude in Moscow toward unification by force in Korea. What's more, the military balance of forces between the South and North was changing; the DPRK was gaining the upper hand. Kim Il Sung and other senior North Koreans seem to have thought the time was ripe to ask Stalin again for permission to attack the South.

According to a report by Shtykov on January 19, on January 17 DPRK Foreign Minister Pak Hon-yong hosted a small farewell party for Yi Chu-yon, the newly appointed DPRK ambassador to the Chinese People's Republic. Present on the Korean side were Kim Tu-bong, Kim Il Sung, Pak Hon-yong, Deputy Foreign Minister Pak Tong-cho, and Yi Chu-yon. Wen Shi-zhen, the PRC commercial trade representative, Ambassador Shtykov, and Soviet Embassy counselors A. M. Ignat'ev and V. I. Pelishenko were also present. Shtykov recounted:

> During the party Kim Il Sung spoke fervently several times in Chinese with the trade representative. From snatches of the conversation I could understand, they were talking about the triumph in China and the situation in Korea. In a reception room after the party, Kim Il Sung gave Yi Chu-yon advice on his assignment in China. Speaking in Korean, Kim Il Sung frequently inserted phrases in Russian about how Mao Zedong is his friend and has always helped Korea, so Yi Chu-yon should act boldly.
>
> After Yi Chu-yon left, Kim excitedly told counselors Ignat'ev and Peli-shenko that now that China was completely liberated, the liberation of Korean people in the south of the country is next in line. He said: "The people of southern Korea believe in me and expect support through our military forces. The partisans can't decide the question on their own. The Southerners know we have a good army. I can't sleep at night recently thinking about how to resolve the question of the unification of the whole country. If liberation of the Southern people and unification of the country is postponed, I will lose the confidence of the Korean people." Kim Il Sung went on to say that when he visited Moscow, Comrade Stalin said he should not attack the South, but if Syngman Rhee's forces attacked the North, we could counter-attack the South. However, Syngman Rhee has not attacked and liberation of the Southerners and unification of the country has been put off. Kim Il Sung thinks he should visit Comrade Stalin again and obtain direction and permission for an offensive by the People's Army for the purpose of the liberation of the people of South Korea. In addition, Kim Il Sung said he cannot start the attack on his own because he is a disciplined communist and Comrade Stalin's instructions are the law to him. Kim said that if he cannot meet Comrade Stalin now, he intends to see Mao Zedong when the Chinese leader returns from Moscow. Kim Il Sung said forcefully that Mao Zedong had promised to provide aid when the war in China is over.
>
> Kim Il Sung said he had other issues to discuss with Mao, including the possibility of creating an eastern bureau of the Cominform.
>
> Kim Il Sung also said he intended to discuss everything with Comrade Shtykov and have me arrange a meeting with Comrade Stalin.
>
> Counselors Ignat'ev and Pelishenko tried to steer the conversation away from these topics. Then Kim Il Sung took me aside and began the following conversation: "Can I meet Comrade Stalin and talk about the situation in the South and [word missing] the question of an offensive against Syngman

Rhee's forces? The people's army now is significantly stronger than the army of Syngman Rhee." Kim Il Sung said if he could not talk with Comrade Stalin, he wanted to meet Mao Zedong who would have received instructions on many issues in Moscow.

Then Kim Il Sung brought up the Ongjin Peninsula, asking why I had not allowed him to attack it, adding that the People's Army could take Ongjin in three days and in an all-out offensive could also enter Seoul in several days.

I answered that he had not raised the question of a meeting with Comrade Stalin and if he proposed such a meeting, Comrade Stalin would probably agree. Regarding an attack on the Ongjin Peninsula, I said it was impossible to do so. I tried to end the discussion of these subjects, saying it was late and we should all head home. With this the conversation ended.

Kim Il Sung was a bit drunk after the party and spoke in an excited fashion, but it was not accidental that he began the conversation. He obviously had thought the issues through and his objective was to explain his attitude and sound out our response.

During the conversation Kim Il Sung repeatedly stressed that he wanted Comrade Stalin's advice on the situation in South Korea. He is always thinking about how to launch an attack, he said.[26]

Kim Il Sung told Yi Chu-yon in Russian that "Mao Zedong is my friend" to be sure that Shtykov and the other Soviet officials would understand him. His comment to Shtykov that if Stalin would not meet him, he wanted to confer with Mao left no doubt about his strategy: he might get Mao's support for an invasion if Stalin would not give it. His statement that he wanted to discuss with Mao establishing an Eastern Cominform reflected the same strategy.

STALIN APPROVES AN ATTACK BY THE NORTH

On January 28, Shtykov sent Moscow an agent's report about a South Korean cabinet meeting on January 6. During a discussion of the British government's recognition of the People's Republic of China, ROK Prime Minister Yi Pom-sok said they should assume the United States would soon follow suit and recognize the PRC as well. Yi also stated that President Truman had abandoned Taiwan and that South Korea would share the same fate as the Kuomintang government. "Thus we should not expect too much from America," Yi Pom-sok reportedly said. "We have to create a broad united front and with its help peacefully unify the North and South."

Syngman Rhee declared, according to the report: "The international situation is dictated by U.S.-Soviet relations . . . and the present political situation is extremely disadvantageous to South Korea. America showed from the start it would not fight for the Republic of Korea. Fortunately, the ROK is close to Japan and so long as the United States has not resolved the Japan problem, it will not abandon the Republic of Korea. Even if the South suddenly unified

Korea, unless the issue of Japan is settled in a way consistent with our interests, Korea's situation could deteriorate again. South Korea had to get the Japanese government and the United States involved in a broad anti-Communist movement."[27]

This report on the isolated mood of the ROK cabinet might have encouraged Stalin's new attitude. On January 30, Stalin responded to Shtykov's report on his discussion with Kim Il Sung at the farewell party for Yi Chu-yon in his own name: "Your message was received. I understand Comrade Kim Il Sung's dissatisfaction. However, the huge undertaking he wants to carry out toward South Korea requires enormous preparations. It must be organized in a way that avoids excessive risk. If he wishes to discuss this matter with me, I will prepare for such a meeting. Inform Kim Il Sung that I am prepared to assist him in this matter."[28]

This was the first paragraph of Stalin's telegram. The next paragraph was a business-like request that Shtykov pass on a request that North Korea provide 25,000 tons of lead annually and assurance that technical assistance and experts would be provided upon request. Stalin wanted strategic materials in return for military assistance.

On January 30, Shtykov related Stalin's message to a delighted Kim Il Sung, who asked the ambassador if it really meant he could meet Comrade Stalin.[29] Kim Il Sung must have been almost incredulous at the good news and promised to act on the request for lead in ten to fifteen days.

On February 2, Stalin sent supplementary instructions to Shtykov: "Explain the following to Comrade Kim Il Sung. At present our consultation must be kept secret. The meeting must not be revealed to other North Korean leaders or our Chinese comrades. It is essential that the meeting be completely concealed from our enemies. In meetings with Mao Zedong in Moscow we exchanged views on the necessity and feasibility of providing assistance in order to raise the military strength and improve the national defense of the Democratic People's Republic of Korea."[30]

This telegram, which was first made public by A. V. Torkunov, of course shows Stalin's fear that information about the meeting would leak out. Though Kim Il Sung told Pak Hon-yong everything, Stalin himself did not inform Mao at this time that he supported Pyongyang's aspirations.

WAR PREPARATIONS

With Stalin's assent in hand, Kim Il Sung asked Shtykov on February 4 if the CPSU Central Committee had approved an earlier DPRK request for a loan of 2.1 billion won. Was it all right to create three new infantry divisions, increasing the KPA to ten divisions? Kim Il Sung asked the ambassador. Shtykov cautioned Kim Il Sung to consider whether North Korea had the material resources for such a huge increase in forces, and said an answer would take time. Under a 1949 credit agreement with the Soviet Union, North Korea was to receive seventy million seven hundred thousand rubles annually for three years. Kim Il Sung wanted Stalin's permission to use, in 1950, the Soviet credit allocated for 1950 and 1951 to purchase arms and equipment for the three divisions. He also sought Stalin's views on three matters to be taken up by the DPRK's Supreme People's Assembly on February 25. Shtykov promised to seek a decision from Moscow.[31]

In reply to a report from Shtykov on February 9, Stalin promised that the CPSU Central Committee would favorably consider North Korea's loan request, approval of formation of the three new KPA divisions, and payment of the 1951 credit allocation in 1950; he also raised no objection to the agenda for the Supreme People's Assembly. Stalin was amazingly magnanimous, and Kim Il Sung was deliriously happy.[32]

"Kim Il Sung was ecstatic at my report and repeatedly asked me to convey his gratitude to Comrade Stalin for his assistance," Shtykov reported to Soviet Minister of Foreign Affairs Andrei Vyshinsky.[33]

On February 20, Lt. Gen. N. A. Vasil'ev arrived in Pyongyang to assume the post of chief military adviser to the KPA,[34] tangible support for Kim Il Sung's plans. Vasil'ev had commanded the 298th Division in the final Soviet counterattack on the Germans in the defense of Moscow during World War II. As a major general, he had led the division in the defense of Stalingrad from August 1942 until the victorious Soviet breakout in February 1943, and in 1944 commanded the First Infantry Corps, First Baltic Coast Front in the battle for Vilnius.[35]

On March 3, Shtykov transmitted Kim Il Sung's letter to Moscow. In accordance with the credit request for 1950, it sought 120 to 130 million rubles worth of arms. In return, North Korea agreed to transfer to the Soviets gold, silver, and monazite worth 133 million rubles.[36]

On March 12, Stalin instructed Shtykov to inform Kim Il Sung that he approved disbursement of the 1951 credit installment in 1950. Kim Il Sung followed up two days later with a detailed order for weapons and ammunition for delivery in 1950.[37]

The Korean Liaison Office (KLO), an American intelligence unit that had remained in Seoul after the withdrawal of US troops, acquired valuable information about a conference of DPRK Interior Ministry unit commanders held on March 10–15. KLO agents reported to General Willoughby, head of G-2, Far East Command, the gist of Kim Il Sung's March 15 speech to the conference:

> The South Korean army, which is supported by the Americans, has poor morale and is defending South Korea rather than intending to attack North Korea. Even if the SK Army attacks NK, we shall easily repulse that puppet group.

In 1949, we defended the North only; however, in 1950, we will begin the heroic struggle to merge the divided Korea and will achieve glorious complete independence.

The only way to obtain a glorious victory is to cause disturbances at the 38th Parallel and have the South Korean army devote all of its attention to that area while our guerrilla units attack the puppets from the rear. This is the only way to unify our divided country. [38]

Southern guerrillas would strike the decisive blow after a border clash, Kim said, concealing Stalin's apparent approval of a conventional assault by regular KPA units. Kim's real strategy involved moving from defense to offense.

That February and March, KLO agents ominously reported construction of roads and bridges leading from North Korea to the 38th parallel, including bridges over the Hantan River in Kangwon Province and the Imjin River in Kyonggi Province. [39]

The G-2 section of Gen. Douglas MacArthur's headquarters in Tokyo also had intelligence indicative of an impending North Korean invasion. A report dated March 10 predicted, "The KPA will invade South Korea in 1950." An evaluation followed: "The Soviet Union's intentions in Korea are believed to be closely related to Communist program in Southeast Asia. If Soviet [Union] is satisfied they are winning in struggle for those places, they probably will be content to wait a while longer and let South Korea ripen for future harvest. If checked or defeated in their operation in these countries in Asia, [Soviets] may divert large share of their effort to South Korea, which could result in PA invasion of South Korea." [40]

Yet a report from G-2, Tokyo, MacArthur's headquarters, dated March 25 said, "It is believed that there will be no civil war in Korea this spring or summer." North Korea's probable strategy was to use guerrilla attacks and psychological warfare to create instability and topple the South Korean government, the report stated. [41] At this stage of the unfolding events, this assessment was probably as far as the intelligence analysts could go.

ANOTHER TRIP TO MOSCOW BY NORTH KOREAN LEADERS

Kim Il Sung and Pak Hon-yong told Shtykov on March 20 that they wanted to meet Stalin in early April. The visit should be unofficial, they said, as in 1949, and they had three issues they wished to discuss. [42] Stalin received Shtykov's message about their request for a meeting and their agenda issues on March 23. A handwritten memorandum inserted at the end of the record of the Stalin–Kim Il Sung conference is regarded by Evgenii Bajanov as a compilation of the contents of Shtykov's telegram (Anatolii Torkunov quoted from the telegram itself).[43] I quote below the photographic copy printed in the *Seoul Shinmun* newspaper:

Issues for Comrade Stalin to resolve.

1. The paths and methods to achieve unification. We [North Koreans] intend to carry out unification by force.[44]
2. Economic matters.

   a. Prospects for economic development of Korea. What kind of plan and for what duration—two, three, or five years—should be implemented? How should southern Korea be regarded?
   b. Electrification of Korean railroads.
   c. Increased import of industrial facilities, automobiles and tractors from the Soviet Union.
   d. Prospects for development of Korean agriculture.
   e. Soviet technical experts.
   f. Training Korean workers in the Soviet Union.

3. Sino-Korean relations.

   a. Conference with Mao Zedong.
   b. Treaty with China.
   c. Status of Korean residents of China and Chinese residents of Korea.
   d. An information bureau for Communist and Worker parties in Asia.
   e. Reconsideration of the contracts for marine transportation companies.

Before Kim Il Sung's visit, Stalin summoned D. N. Mel'nik, party first secretary in Sakhalin Province, who arrived in Moscow on March 26 and was immediately taken to a night meeting attended by Stalin, Malenkov, Molotov, Kaganovich, Mikoyan, Bulganin, and Nikita Khrushchev. Stalin asked about the situation in the island of Sakhalin, particularly the military forces, and about the defensive capabilities of the Kurile Islands and Sakhalin. "Plans to strengthen the defense of the Kuriles are inadequate," Stalin said. Using material and maps prepared by the military, Stalin proposed construction of a railway tunnel from the continent to Sakhalin. The Politburo members were instructed to draft a plan to support Sakhalin and build a railway tunnel across the straits. At a Politburo meeting on April 2, Stalin spoke about the project: "We have no right to rely on the La Perouse Strait as a connection with the east coast of Sakhalin and the Kuriles. There we must always fear mines and bombardment from both banks. To defend our country at the Far Eastern boundary and protect the Kuriles and Sakhalin, we must establish a secure link with Sakhalin." The Politburo approved construction of a tunnel under the Tatar Strait; Stalin wanted it completed between 1953 and 1955. The objective was to strengthen the military defenses of the Kuriles for the expected confrontation with the United States over Korea. Construction with convict labor began shortly thereafter.[45]

Kim Il Sung and Pak Hon-yong left Pyongyang for the Soviet Union on March 30 in a special airplane provided by the Soviet Union. They boarded the Siberian Railway at Voroshilov and reached Moscow ten days later. On April 10, they met Stalin, accompanied by Shtykov and interpreter Mun Il. Also present were Malenkov, Molotov, and Vyshinky.[46]

As Stalin told Beijing later, he approved the liberation of South Korea at this fateful meeting. Actually, Stalin gave his conditional approval. The Korean leaders were told that the decision hinged upon consultation with Mao Zedong.

My account of this meeting here is based on a report compiled by the International Division, Central Committee, CPSU that appeared in the *Seoul Shinmun*, which Bajanov also quoted.[47] According to the report, Stalin told Kim Il Sung that changes in the international environment and the Soviet Union's domestic situation allowed him to be more positive about the unification of Korea. He cited several factors in his thinking. They included the triumph of the Chinese Communist Party, which could now direct its attention and energy to support of Korea; China could now release troops to Korea, and the victory of the Chinese revolution proved that, psychologically, the time was ripe for the liberation of Asia. The Chinese revolution frightened the reactionary forces and America, Stalin said. Unable to intervene in the Chinese revolution, the United States could not now challenge the new Chinese state; within America anti-intervention sentiment now prevailed. Stalin also said that the Soviet Union's possession of the atomic bomb was intensifying anti-interventionist feeling in the United States. However, the North Koreans should weigh the circumstances carefully and study the possibility of US intervention, Stalin advised Kim Il Sung. They must also gain the approval of Chinese leaders. Combat operations could not commence without Chinese backing, Stalin told Kim Il Sung.

The United States was unlikely to intervene, Kim Il Sung responded, because the Soviet Union and China were behind North Korea and Washington could not become involved in a major conflict. Furthermore, Mao Zedong had always supported Korean hopes for unification and frequently said that upon completion of the Chinese revolution, troops would be provided. But Kim Il Sung believed Koreans could unify the country on their own.

Stalin outlined a three-stage plan of attack. First, troops would be assembled near the 38th parallel. Next, the North would issue proposals for peaceful unification, which the South would have to dismiss. Third, the offensive should start with seizure of the Ongjin Peninsula. This strategy could help conceal the North's intentions, in Stalin's view. A counterattack by the South would be an opportunity to expand the battlefield. The war had to be executed with surprise and speed, Stalin said: catch the South and the Americans off guard and allow them no time to organize resistance and mobilize international support.

Stalin emphasized that the Soviet Union could not directly intervene in the conflict. He also stressed the importance of Mao Zedong's support. If the United States got involved, North Korea would need Chinese help, he said. But Kim Il Sung, counting heavily on the partisans in the South, rejected the possibility of US intervention, and claimed that the North would win in three days. Pak Hon-yong elaborated on the role of the partisans, saying 200,000 Korean Workers' Party members in the South would unleash large-scale uprisings.

Although this account cannot be verified from the original documents, it is consistent with earlier and subsequent revelations. The key point: Stalin gave the North Korean leaders the final permission to attack conditional upon Chinese support.

Politburo members held a farewell party for Kim Il Sung and Pak Hon-yong at Stalin's dacha before they departed the Soviet Union. According to Khrushchev's memoirs, Kim Il Sung declared that "after the unification of South and North Korea, Korea as a whole would benefit." Khrushchev and other members of the Politburo wished Kim Il Sung every success.[48] The train had left the station.

ON TO BEIJING

The Korean leaders next had to consult with Mao Zedong. As they left Moscow, DPRK Ambassador Yi Chu-yon in Beijing, without mentioning their trip to the Soviet Union, informed Mao Zedong that Kim Il Sung wanted to meet with him. If Kim Il Sung had concrete plans to unify Korea, the visit should be kept secret, Mao told Yi.[49] An initial visit of Korean leaders to the new People's Republic of China ordinarily would have been public; but a parley on war demanded total secrecy. Mao also said that if World War III broke out, North Korea would be drawn in and thus must build up its military strength. After a four-day stay in Moscow, Kim Il Sung and Pak Hon-yong returned to North Korea on April 25.[50] They would visit Mao in about three weeks.

Kim and Pak told Terentii Shtykov on May 12 that Ambassador Yi Chu-yon had acted on his own in meeting Mao and had been recalled to Pyongyang and cautioned as a result. They also reported that Mao had told the ambassador that Korea could not be unified by peaceful means. North Korea need not fear US intervention, Mao had said, in their rendition; the Americans would not risk World War III for such small territory as the southern half of the Korean Peninsula.[51]

This account of Kim and Pak's discussion with Shtykov, including their recounting of Mao's statement to Yi about the United States not risking a world war for South Korea, is based on a Soviet Foreign Ministry report dated August 10, 1966. In an earlier work, I expressed doubt that Mao had said this in Beijing, because it does not reflect his sense of probable US actions. I still have doubts about it. It is plausible that Kim spun the chairman's comments to impress Ambassador Shtykov and influence his thinking on a northern attack.

Kim Il Sung's decision to go to China with Pak Hon-yong was not discussed by the KWP Central Committee; Kim had told only Deputy Prime Minister Kim Chaek. A meeting with Mao was tantamount to a decision for war, and it had been made by only Kim Il Sung, Pak Hon-yong, and Kim Chaek. Choe Yon-gon, defense minister, did not participate, probably because he was not a party member. Kim Il Sung told Shtykov that he would not ask Mao for aid because the Soviet Union had granted all his requests and was providing vital assistance.[52]

Kim Il Sung and Pak Hon-yong arrived in Beijing on May 13 and conferred with Mao that evening. Mao questioned the Koreans about their understanding with Stalin, and he immediately tried to ask the Soviet leader about his intentions—Soviet Ambassador to China N. V. Roshchin queried Moscow the same day.[53] Andrei Vyshinsky sent Stalin's response: "Comrade Mao Zedong. At the meeting with Korean comrades, Comrade Filippov [Stalin] and friends, due to the changed international environment, expressed agreement with the Koreans' proposal to start unification. However, a reservation was attached: Ultimately this problem must be decided jointly by Chinese and Korean comrades and if Chinese comrades do not agree the decision must be postponed until a new assessment is made. Our Korean comrades can explain the details of the meeting."[54]

The records of the conversations between Mao and Kim Il Sung have not been disclosed. Pak Hon-yong and Zhou Enlai respectively recounted the content of Mao and Kim's conversations to Roshchin and each talk was recorded and reported to Moscow on May 15.[55]

According to Pak Hon-yong, Kim Il Sung first described to Mao the three-stage plan Stalin had proposed in Moscow and said that they agreed with it. Mao Zedong indicated his overall approval of the plan and made several suggestions: they should train every Korean People's Army soldier and officer thoroughly in their assignments, and the KPA should move with great speed, avoiding delay by skirting the major cities, and annihilate enemy military forces. Mao Zedong speculated that Japanese forces might be deployed in Korea. Kim Il Sung thought it unlikely, but conceded that the United States could dispatch 20,000 to 30,000 Japanese troops. Their involvement would not be decisive, he said, because Koreans would fight even more fiercely. Mao thought intervention by Japanese units would probably prolong the war, but agreed that their involvement was not likely, adding, significantly, that if US troops were committed, China would probably send its forces to northern Korea. The constraints on the Soviet Union posed by the agreement with the United States on separate occupation zones in Korea did not apply to China, which could thus help North Korea, Mao said.

According to Zhou Enlai, Mao warned Kim Il Sung that if Japanese troops *were* sent to Korea, the war would be prolonged and there was a greater likelihood of US intervention. Kim Il Sung reportedly said in reply that the United States showed no sign of intervening militarily in the Far East, having withdrawn from China without fighting, and would probably stay out of Korea as well.

Mao had previously thought the North Koreans would start operations against the South after Taiwan was liberated, whereupon China could provide ample support. But since they had decided to act now, he agreed to cooperate in the joint undertaking. He asked Kim Il Sung if additional Chinese troops would be needed along the Sino-Korean border. Kim Il Sung declined the offer, thanking him for it.

At this stage, Kim Il Sung and Mao Zedong both thought Japanese forces would probably not be introduced into Korea, an obvious conclusion if they understood the situation in occupied Japan, which of course no longer had any armed forces. Kim Il Sung reasoned that if Japanese forces were ruled out, no foreign troops would intervene. But Mao had begun to think that US units might well return to the South. In any case, he promised all-out support for Kim Il Sung's attempt to unify Korea, including Chinese forces if Washington entered the fighting.

BUILDUP

Kim Il Sung and Pak Hon-yong returned to Pyongyang on May 16, and the buildup for war began. The fully equipped Chinese PLA 15th Independent Division, a Korean division that had left Zhengzhou in April, arrived in Wonsan on May 18 and was redesignated the KPA 12th Division. The division commander was Tao Kefu (also known as Chon U) and the chief of staff was Chi Pyong-hak. Kim Kang, the assistant chief of the KPA Cultural Bureau, was named political commissar of the division. Choe A-rip became commander of the artillery regiment. The Independent Regiment that left Zhengzhou at the same time was included in the 4th Division commanded by Yi Kwon-mu (Yan'an group).[56] The KPA now had seven divisions.

The scholar Alexandre Mansourov, who had access to documents in the Soviet Defense Ministry archives , writes that on May 17 Soviet Defense Minister A. M. Vasilevskii and Chief of Staff S. M. Shtemenko ordered Adviser N. A. Vasil'ev to draw up an operational plan for a northern attack.

Applying lessons learned in the war against Germany, the defense minister directed Vasil'ev to guard against a surprise attack by the enemy, not underestimate enemy troop strength, deceive the enemy at the moment of attack, execute the assault with lightning speed, and capture Seoul. All North Korean forces should be mobilized before the attack. [57]

On May 29, Soviet Ambassador Shtykov reported the preparations to Stalin. According to Mansourov, Shtykov's report was the outcome of a conference that day attended by Shtykov, Kim Il Sung, Soviet advisers Vasil'ev and Postnikov, Kim Chaek, Chief of Staff Kang Kon, Defense Minister Choe Yong-gon, and others. [58] I quote below Shtykov's telegram as reprinted in Torkunov's book *An Enigmatic War: The Korean Conflict, 1950–1953:*

> Kim Il Sung informed me of the attack preparations. The agreed upon weapons and equipment have arrived. Kim Il Sung inspected the supplementary divisions and said they too would be ready for combat by the end of June. As ordered by Kim Il Sung, the KPA General Staff, with the advice of Gen. Vasil'ev, has completed a comprehensive operational plan. Kim Il Sung has approved the plan. Force organization must be resolved by June 1. The KPA will probably be fully mobilized in June. Kim Il Sung thinks the attack should begin in late June. A later date is undesirable for two reasons; the enemy may learn of the military preparations and the rainy season starts in July. Kim Il Sung proposes to begin the movement of troops to forward assembly areas from June 8 to June 10. [59]

After meeting with Kim Il Sung, Shtykov spoke with Vasil'ev and Postnikov, who had favored July for the attack. Persuaded by Kim Il Sung's reasoning, they were now inclined toward June, as was Shtykov. The operational plan began with a limited strike on the Ongjin Peninsula, followed by an attack on the eastern coast and a frontal assault on Seoul. [60]

Park Myung-lim argues that Defense Minister Choe Yong-gon opposed the attack at this late May meeting and notes that important orders issued by the DPRK Ministry of National Defense from May to September were not in the name of Minister Choe Yong-gon, but in the names of Vice-Minister Kim Il, Artillery Commander Mu Chong, and others. [61] Mansourov says that Choe Yong-gon stressed the potential of peace talks and opposed hasty military action. [62] But if Choe Yong-gon had not supported war at this meeting, he probably would have been excluded from subsequent planning . Despite any earlier differences of opinion, a consensus was reached on May 29.

Kim Il Sung and Pak Hon-yong then began a campaign to camouflage military preparations. On June 2, Kim Il Sung, using the Fatherland Front, the front group initiated by the North, called for immediate peaceful unification. On June 7, the Fatherland Front issued an appeal for a general election throughout the peninsula in August, not in September as proposed earlier, to be preceded by a preparatory conference of northern and southern political parties and organizations in mid-June in Haeju or Kaesong. On June 10, Pyongyang Radio called for a prisoner exchange: Kim Sam-yong and Yi Chu-ha, Southern Workers' Party leaders imprisoned in the South, for Cho Man-sik, a Christian nationalist leader held in Pyongyang. On June 11, three emissaries from the Fatherland Front were arrested when they crossed the 38th parallel to meet with antigovernment groups in the South. The same day, the ROK government predictably rejected the Fatherland Front's proposal for nationwide elections.

At a conference convened on June 12 by KPA Chief of Staff Kang Kon, Kim Il Sung presented the operational plan for the North's attack on the South to all division commanders, their chiefs of staff, and artillery commanders. Among the division commanders present were Choe Kwang of the 1st Division (Manchurian faction); Yi Chong-song of the 2nd Division (a Soviet Korean); Yi Yong-ho of the 3rd Division (Manchurian faction); Yi Kwon-mu of the 4th Division (Yan'an group); Kim Chang-dok of the 5th Division (Yan'an group); Pang Ho-san of the 6th Division (Yan'an group); and Chon U of the 12th Division (Yan'an group).[63] Defense Minister Choe Yong-gon, Vice-Defense Minister Kim Il, artillery commander Mu Chong, Kim Ung, and other heads of departments of the Defense Ministry should have been present. Mansourov says that Soviet Ambassador Shtykov and the Chinese chargé d'affaires also attended. This was probably the first explanation of war policy at the division command level. Some division commanders from the Yan'an group complained at the meeting that they had been kept in the dark on the North's plans.[64] Orders for the divisions to commence field exercises and move to advanced positions near the parallel were probably issued at this meeting. Meanwhile, Shtykov informed Stalin that from June 13 KPA units would be moved to within ten to fifteen kilometers of the parallel.[65]

According to Bruce Cumings, a highly classified twelve-page captured document dated June 13 and entitled "Politico-Cultural Work in Wartime (reference materials)" from the Cultural Section of the KPA's 655th Detachment "documents KPA planning for an assault on the South, which is no surprise, but it does not prove that they attacked first, or indeed had plans to in June."[66] By contrast, Hagiwara Ryo considers this the most important of the captured documents he discovered and terms it "the 6th Division's operational plan to move south." And Park Myung-lim regards it as the smoking gun—"the core proof that the North attacked first."[67] However, it would have been physically impossible to take the operational plan for the North's attack to the KPA divisions' Cultural (but in fact Political) Sections and for the 655th Detachment to prepare a twelve-page document, mimeograph copies, assemble them into pamphlets, and distribute them by the next day after the conference of division commanders and their heads of staff.

The document divided the KPA detachment's political activities into five stages: those en route to the assembly area, prior to the receipt of attack orders, before the attack began, from the attack until regrouping, and post-combat. In other words, the document listed political work from the time of the secret assembly to after the fighting. Tellingly, the Chinese word "jiedan" was used for "stage," not the Korean "tangkye." The first-stage instructions included the need to take specific precautions against noise and lights to maintain secrecy on night marches. "In an emergency such as an enemy air raid during the march, maintain absolute obedience to orders," the instructions stated.[68] This did not reflect the situation in North Korea, but rather was a general guideline based on the combat experience of a Korean division in China. The fourth-stage instructions are also curious: "The regimental and battalion personnel in charge of culture should form a staff to consolidate occupied areas, manage the dead and wounded and collect captured material. In cooperation with local political parties, political authorities, and security personnel, they should mobilize the people and arrest disruptive elements." But there were no collaborating "local political parties and political authorities" in South Korea. For the fifth stage, entitled "Stabilizing Occupied Areas," the only instructions were to "conduct ideological indoctrination and set up a tight defensive organization that can repulse an enemy counterattack." The document concludes: "These materials for wartime political cultural activities should be used to supervise staff training, studied thoroughly and improved on the basis of experience gained through actual training."[69] Previous researchers overlooked this part about training. At two places in stage three, the expression "combat order (training)" is used. This document was obviously for training, not an operational plan to liberate the South.

On June 16, Shtykov sent a three-stage operational plan of attack to Moscow. According to the quotation by Torkunov, the plan was as follows: "The attack begins early in the morning of June 25. KPA units attack first on the Ongjin Peninsula and then launch major blows along the west coast. Seoul is occupied and the Han River seized. At the same time the Eastern KPA liberates Chunchon and Kangnung. Enemy main forces are surrounded and destroyed in the Seoul area. In the final stage of the operation remnants of the enemy army are destroyed and, by the occupation of cities and ports, the remainder of Korea is liberated."[70]

Among the captured documents which were translated by the US Army is one with handwritten notes entitled "Reconnaissance Plan for the KPA's Attack Operation." It was prepared in Russian by the chief of the KPA Reconnaissance Department. Cumings has disputed the document because it is in Russian; however, the use of Russian is quite plausible in a memorandum prepared before an order is issued. Classified "Sov. Sekretno," an abbreviation of "Sovershenno sekretno" (Top Secret), the document is a reconnaissance plan in response to the three-stage operational plan. In the first stage,

"The enemy's defense line is breached and the enemy's main-strength units are crushed." In the second stage, "the attack on southern Korea continues and the enemy's reserve forces are crushed." In the third stage, "Remnants of the shattered enemy forces are swept to the southern coast."[71] The stages differ from those in the three-stage operational plan Shtykov sent to Moscow. This version is for an all-out attack. Thus, in addition to the operational plan that started with an attack on the Ongjin Peninsula, there was a variation that specified a comprehensive attack along the 38th parallel.

Both plans called for destruction of the main ROKA forces in the Seoul area. Chief Soviet Military Adviser Vasil'ev assumed the ROKA would defend the approach to the capital at all costs. By destroying organized resistance there, Seoul could be occupied, Vasil'ev reasoned, leaving only ROKA reserve units, a scenario probably derived from his experience fighting the Germans. As mentioned, Vasil'ev had participated in the desperate defenses of both Moscow and Stalingrad, where a German breakthrough probably would have dealt a fatal blow to the Soviet Union. The chief military adviser had forgotten, however, that when Napoleon invaded Russia in 1812, Marshal Kutuzov withdrew his forces from Moscow and later attacked the retreating, demoralized French.

Another captured document, also in Russian, and dated June 18, shows that the reconnaissance plan was sent to the 3rd Police Brigade, the 1st, 4th, 5th, 6th, and 12th divisions, and the 12th Motorcycle Regiment.[72]

KPA DEPLOYS TO THE PARALLEL

The deployment of KPA units close to the 38th parallel around June 10 is well known.[73] Pang Sun-joo unearthed a report dated June 22, 1950, by O I-sam, assistant commander in charge of the Cultural Section of Unit 353, sent to the assistant commander in charge of the Cultural Section of Unit 395. The Cultural Section was the political section of each of these units. The report sheds additional light on KPA troop movements. It stated:

Ideological trends of military personnel.

1. On the march.
    Since the proposals for peaceful unification by the Fatherland Unification Front failed and the delegates sent to the South to transmit the Front's statement were arrested, our servicemen may have anticipated action at some point. Although prepared to move at any time, with maneuvers underway they did not think action was imminent. Finally, after the noon meal on June 17, vehicles were loaded and march preparations were ordered. The troops were not rattled. Calmly but rapidly, they checked their personal equipment, burned all trash, removed all graffiti to maintain secrecy, and were ready to function as units in the field.

March preparations were finished in four to five hours, by dinner time, and units moved out at 1930 hours. All personnel in our unit rode in new-model gun carriages bearing the name of the famous Morozov factory. The cannon were loaded with rounds. Prepared for battle, on command the unit headed for the objective . . . arriving at 0200 hours, June 18 . . .

2. Morale at the assembly area.

Upon arrival at the objective, artillery positions were constructed, vehicles camouflaged, emplacements and economic organizations quickly prepared under the supervision of commanding officers . . .

On June 19, again on orders from a higher command, the unit advanced to a new position 500 meters forward. The unit calmly shifted to night action and worked well to set up the gun emplacements, camouflage vehicles and escort lights. The men were in good spirits . . . especially on the 20th when rain fell all day. Élan was high as the men checked their weapons and vehicles and were ready to defend their gun emplacements. On that day the drivers and gun crews transported the river crossing equipment and then, in their soaked uniforms, listened to the proposal sent by the Supreme People's Assembly to the Southern National Assembly. Their morale strong, they ignored the harsh conditions and completed combat preparations . . . [74]

In a diversionary move on June 19, the DPRK Supreme People's Assembly made an unconditional proposal to the ROK National Assembly that the South could never accept. The KPA soldiers all might understand that war was drawing closer.

On June 20, Shtykov urged Moscow to approve Kim Il Sung's request for Soviet naval personnel to operate vessels; North Korea lacked sailors. [75] At 10:00 p.m. Moscow time that day, in a highly unusual move, Shtykov called Moscow and reported that two hours earlier the ROKA had been ordered to attack North Korea at 11:00 p.m. Moscow time. But Shtykov said the attack order was not encoded and "dubious." [76]

On June 21, Shtykov sent a decisive telegram: "Kim Il Sung said the North, based on intercepted Southern broadcasts and reports from intelligence agents, has apparently obtained the details of an imminent attack by the South on the KPA. According to his information, the South is increasing the combat capability of its military forces. The South's defensive positions have been strengthened and additional troops have been sent to the Ongjin Peninsula. Consequently, Kim Il Sung proposed a change in the original operational plan: a simultaneous attack all along the 38th parallel." [77]

Stalin quickly approved a simultaneous assault across the front, but rejected Kim Il Sung's plea for Soviet naval personnel to transport KPA troops in landing operations because it would give the United States a justification for intervention. [78]

Kim Il Sung believed the North's plans had leaked to the South and that the KPA should strike before Seoul could implement counter moves. But I doubt that the South really had such intelligence. As we have seen, North Korean leaders had already planned for the option of a widespread offensive, and they may have persistently advocated a simultaneous offensive. An attack on the Ongjin Peninsula, a limited offensive in an area where there had been repeated clashes, could easily have been presented to Stalin as a counterblow to a southern assault. But an all-out offensive as a response to a southern border raid strained credulity. Nevertheless, North Korea chose that option.

WASHINGTON ON THE BRINK

The key to US actions lies in NSC 68, adopted by the National Security Council on April 14, 1950. The centerpiece of subsequent US national security policy, NSC 68 recognized that the Soviet Union had the atomic bomb and would soon have the hydrogen bomb as well, and concluded that by 1954 Moscow would be capable of unleashing a devastating preemptive attack on the United States. The Soviet threat was "more immediate than had previously been estimated," the report said. In order to counter the threat, NSC 68 called for a massive US military buildup. But the large expenditures this entailed ran counter to President Harry Truman's conservative fiscal policy, and "in the meantime, NSC-68 was shelved," Paul Pierpaoli wrote.[79]

The question of whether Washington was unaware of North Korean preparations for an attack on the South, or whether it knew of them and allowed Pyongyang to strike, has long fascinated researchers. The truth is that the United States knew of North Korean military activities but did not take them seriously.

The Far Eastern Command's intelligence unit in Korea, the Korean Liaison Office, was aware of the North Korean military buildup and changes along the 38th parallel. From the end of March 1950, intelligence agents reported that residents were being removed from the area just north of the 38th parallel. On March 31, an agent reported that on February 10, 30 percent of the residents of Tongchon, twenty kilometers north of the parallel, had been ordered to relocate to Wonsan and Chorwon by March 31.[80] Another agent reported that all residents in the Haeju area had been directed to leave by March 15.[81] One agent reported: "The North Korean Puppet Government has issued an order for the evacuation of residents who live within 4 km of the 38th parallel. The evacuation was to take place between 15 March and 30 March 1950. . . . It is reported that the strength of the armed forces along the 38th Parallel has been augmented [to] three times that of last year and that it is the intention of the NK regime that no ordinary citizens will be permitted in the area within 4 km of the border."[82] In April the KLO received word that a unit from China, originally the 166th Division, was now the KPA 4th

Division.[83] There was also a report that the North Korean government had ordered local authorities to repair all main roads and construct bridges near the 38th parallel.[84]

The intelligence reports increased exponentially in May. The most comprehensive was KLO Report 518, based on an agent report dated May 10. It said that in addition to the two divisions from China that had entered North Korea in August 1949, three more divisions had arrived in December 1949 and were incorporated into the KPA, which now had seven divisions and reportedly "would be raised to 13 in the future." The G-2, Far East Command, appended the following comment:

> The existence of 6 regular army divisions has been recognized to date, and the garrisons are located roughly in a cross country belt between the 38th and 39th parallels. I have long suspected that our secret agents, both Army and KLO were not able to make deep penetrations and some of these men, who were sent into the North-eastern corner of Korea, adjacent to the Russian Border, have disappeared. I consider it likely therefore that this northern area with the important ports of Chongjin and Najin are not only recruiting and organization areas, but are probably the points of entry for Russian equipment, particularly tanks and heavy weapons . . .
>
> We could therefore speculate reasonably that a greater total than 13 divisions may be in the process of formation.
>
> This is consistent with the theory that the offensive requires a 2 to 1 superiority, for any degree of calculated success. The present strength of the South Korean forces . . . is completely known to Communist North Korea. Consequently they are not likely to make an attack with lesser strength; on the other hand, they are more than likely to double their own forces . . .
>
> Previous evidence of the entry from Manchuria of trained Communists of ethnic Korean origin would furnish the necessary manpower and there have been many reports of such entry across the Yalu River. In addition, we have current reports (KLO #507) of continuous compulsory recruitment of N-Koreans in the period June 1949 to March 1950 inclusive. . . . There have been intermittent rumors of N-Korean invasion threats, accentuated by the reported movement of the 3rd and 2nd divisions into the western 38th parallel area. On 5 January we reported "N-Korean Government has set March and April 1950 as a time to invade S-Korea." We reported again on 10 March that "report received that PA will invade S-Korea." Under date of 8 Dec 49, we reported to the D/A as follows: "No invasion appears imminent, and no long range prediction on the timing of an overt invasion would be valid in view of rapidly changing factors. . . . With the conclusion of the Chinese Communist campaign in China, more troops and supplies may be channeled into N-Korea; it appears that the danger to the Southern Republic will mount at that time.
>
> Climactic conditions most favorable to military operations have passed (Dec 1949). The most favorable period for any such action will occur in April and May, 1950.[85]

North Korea indeed had seven divisions, as US intelligence indicated, and if an additional three divisions were in fact ready, the agents were correct on the scale of the North's buildup. Yet the G-2 assessment was that the North would not attack without double the strength of ROKA forces. Though favorable weather conditions in April and May were noted, as well as the earlier speculation about an attack, G-2 concluded that the situation was not dangerous. A later evaluation of General MacArthur's intelligence coverage said: "In dealing with the North Korean invasion potential G-2 was never deceived into believing that the offensive posture of the North Korean Government was self-generated and inspired. It was constantly realized and consistently reported that behind any action of the North Korean puppet government lay the strong and purposeful direction of the Soviet master minds in the Kremlin. G-2 . . . was careful to point out that the time of the North Korean invasion of South Korea would depend upon the dictates of the Russian high command in Moscow, on the Soviet estimate of the world situation and on the communist struggle in other countries of Asia."[86]

Some scholars think the G-2 assessment was intentionally added to the agent's report, a view Cumings is inclined to agree with. He cautions that a conclusive judgment must await declassification of all the relevant materials, but writes: "It makes legitimate, however, the speculation that a small group of officials in Tokyo and Washington saw the attack coming, prepared to meet it, and then let it happen—while keeping Congress in the dark, then and thereafter."[87]

Pang Son-joo conjectures that "the United States knew the general outline of the attack on the South, and the Far East Command knew at least by June 23 that [the North] would attack within a day or two."[88] Judging from MacArthur's behavior immediately after the war started, however, he was a prisoner of the notion that the Soviet Union controlled North Korea's actions and might have thought that Moscow would not support an attack in the early summer of 1950. On this point I agree with Okonogi: "Immediately before the war started U.S. intelligence analysts knew a considerable amount about North Korea's offensive capability but not enough. Intelligence agencies and the relevant administration officials doubted the Communists' intentions [were to attack]."[89]

A June 14 CIA report concluded that the North had the capability to attack the South, but was silent on the North's intentions.[90] John Foster Dulles, an adviser to the State Department, reportedly read the CIA report before he left for Seoul in mid-June. That North Korea paid close attention to Dulles's visit is well known. On June 19, Dulles spoke to the South Korean National Assembly: "Already [in the 20th century] the U.S. has twice intervened with armed might in defense of freedom when it was hard pressed by unprovoked military aggression. We were not bound by any treaty to do this. . . . You are not alone. You will never be alone as long as you continue to play worthily your part in the great design of human freedom." South Koreans interpreted the speech as a guarantee of their security. Cumings holds that Dulles did not think war was imminent, though.[91]

KMAG commander Brig. Gen. William L. Roberts, who had gone to Tokyo to escort Dulles to Seoul, returned again to Japan to see him off back to Washington and then left Tokyo for retirement in the United States before his successor arrived. Col. W. H. Stirling Wright, the acting KMAG commander, received orders to go to Tokyo on June 19 and left Seoul on June 24. According to one account, Wright was on leave when the war started.[92]

On June 19 the CIA released a second report entitled "Current Capabilities of the Northern Korean Regime." The report said: "Thus, northern Korea's armed forces, even as presently constituted and supported, have a capability for obtaining limited objectives in short-term military operations against southern Korea, including the capture of Seoul. . . . At the present time, the northern Korean armed forces are probably psychologically prepared to fight wholeheartedly against southern Korean troops." The report concluded, however, that "it is not certain that the northern regime, lacking the active participation of Soviet and Chinese Communist military units, would be able to gain effective control over all of southern Korea." Again, the analysts did not comment on whether an attack was imminent.[93]

SEOUL ON THE BRINK

As North Korea rapidly prepared for war, South Korea grew more unstable. Inflation spiraled out of control, and President Syngman Rhee tried to postpone National Assembly elections. But Rhee still hoped to unify the peninsula by force and saw a first strike by Pyongyang as a golden opportunity. In February 1950, Chong Il-gwon, vice-chief of staff of the ROKA, accompanied the president on a visit to General MacArthur in Tokyo. Rhee told the general that the Soviet Union was "instigating the North to challenge the Republic of Korea in a proxy war." The only deterrent was a firm US Korea policy, Rhee said. MacArthur replied that if the Soviet Union or China started a war, they should be stopped even if it meant using nuclear weapons.[94]

In March 1950, an operational plan against a northern attack was prepared under the supervision of ROKA Chief of Staff Shin Tae-yong and Vice-Chief of Staff Chong Il-gwon. ROKA Operational Plan 38 was highly classified and only made public in 1995 in a study published by the ROK Ministry of Defense. The study's authors write, "The plan was to create a defense zone centered on the Uijongbu area, repulse the KPA attack, and secure the 38th parallel."[95] According to Chong Il-gwon: "The concept established main and secondary defense lines centered on the probable approach routes."[96]

Park Myung-lim was the first scholar to categorize the plan as calling for a withdrawal after a North Korean attack followed by a counterattack. The plan envisioned three stages of resistance—at the border, the main defense line, and the final defense line—followed by the withdrawal and, at the appropriate time, the counterattack. ROKA headquarters and every division had a similar operational plan.[97] This contingency planning was fully consistent with Rhee's strategy.

Relations between Seoul and Washington, already frayed, were further strained on April 3 when Secretary of State Dean Acheson threatened Rhee with a reassessment of US economic assistance if stringent measures were not taken to control inflation in South Korea, and warned against postponing the National Assembly elections.[98] As a bow to Washington, Rhee replaced Yi Pom-sok, who had antagonized the US Embassy in Seoul, as prime minister with Yi Yun-yong. But on April 6, by a four-vote margin, the National Assembly rejected Yi Yun-yong's appointment.[99]

Rhee then removed Yi Pom-sok and named Defense Minister Shin Sung-mo interim prime minister. Acheson's objection to postponing the National Assembly elections made it impossible to delay them. When Home Minister Kim Hyo-sok used the national police to strengthen the position of the Democratic National Party, Rhee's party, the president replaced him with Paek Song-uk, a former Buddhist priest. Although Kim Hyo-sok had aggressively purged members of the Southern Workers' Party from the ROKA, he proved to be a secret agent for the North and would flee there during the war. On April 10, Chae Pyong-dok was reappointed ROKA chief of staff, replacing Shin Tae-yong.[100] Also that month, Vice-Chief of Staff Chong Il-gwon left Seoul on the pretext of attending the US Army's Command and General Staff School in Ft. Leavenworth, Kansas. In fact, Shin Sung-mo had sent Chong to the United States "to explain to leaders in the Defense Department the dangerous situation at the 38th parallel and persuade them of the importance of military aid," according to Chong Il-gwon.[101] To send the vice-chief of staff on an overseas mission for more than two months at such a critical moment was strange.

In early May, Senator Tom Connally, chairman of the Senate Foreign Relations Committee, made provocative comments in an interview with *U.S. News and World Report*. Asked whether Korea was an essential part of US defense strategy, he answered:

> No. Of course, any position like that is of some strategic importance. But I don't think it is very greatly important. It has been testified before us that Japan, Okinawa and the Philippines make the chain of defense which is absolutely necessary. And, of course, any additional territory along in that area would be that much more, but it's not absolutely essential.[102]

South Korean leaders angrily denounced the United States as untrustworthy; Acheson and US Ambassador to South Korea John Muccio strenuously disavowed Connally's views.

At a news conference on May 10, Shin Sung-mo announced that two infantry divisions from China had arrived in North Korea. The North's military strength had increased to a total of 183,100 troops and now included 173 tanks and 195 military aircraft.[103] Two days later, Rhee held a press conference and said: "A few days ago one American friend said that if the United States gave weapons to South Korea, she feared that South Korea would invade North Korea. This is a useless worry of some Americans who do not know South Korea. Our present war is not a cold war, but a real shooting war. Our troops will take all possible counter-measures. . . . North Korea is concentrating near the 38th parallel. I do not think these North Korean troops are concentrating near the 38th parallel to invade Japan or China. . . . I daresay that if the United States wants to aid our country it should not be only lip-service."[104]

US Embassy Counselor Everett Drumright reported to the State Department that Shin Sung-mo's statement on the North's military strength was an exaggeration in a bid for more military aid. North Korea actually had 103,000 troops and 65 tanks, he said.[105] In reality, the South Korean figures were correct.

In the second National Assembly elections on May 30, the ruling parties could not win despite extensive interference in the elections by the Home Ministry. Of 210 assembly members, only 21 incumbents retained their seats. In the new assembly, the ruling parties held 57 seats and the opposition captured 26 seats, but 127 seats were occupied by independent members. They included prominent figures, such as moderates An Chae-hong, Won Se-hun, and Yo Un-hong, and progressives Cho Bong-am and Chang Kon-sang. The anti-Rhee cast of the assembly was evident in the election of a speaker. In the first vote, Shin Ik-hui (Minguk Party) received ninety-six votes and Cho So-ang (Socialist Party) got forty-eight. Independent O Ui-yong, who had government support, won forty-six votes, and the ruling party candidate Yi Kap-sung got only eleven. In the final vote, Shin Ik-hui was elected speaker and Cho Pong-am was elected one of the vice-speakers.[106] From Pyongyang, South Korea must have appeared to be disintegrating and Rhee's authority even weaker.

Operational Plan SL-17, a refinement of ROKA Operational Plan 38 against an attack by the North, was completed in the Defense Ministry on June 19.[107] According to Clay Blair, the plan stipulated that if the North attacked, US and ROK forces would retreat to Pusan, establish a defense line, and then counterattack with a landing at Inchon to cut off northern forces. Given the weaponry of the time, a last-ditch stand near Seoul was unrealistic and a retreat-counterattack strategy made sense. The South Koreans were a step ahead of KPA Chief Military Adviser Gen. N. A. Vasil'ev.

As for the big question—did South Korea induce an attack by the North?—Park Myung-lim argues that North Korean agents in the ROKA paved the way for Pyongyang to attack. Citing the northern agent Kim Hyo-sok as an example, Park concludes that "some South Koreans were rather a fifth column than inducing the DPRK to strike." North Korean agents had undoubtedly infiltrated the higher echelons of the ROK government and military,[108] and some ROK leaders were indeed behaving strangely. For example, on April 22, newly reappointed Chief of Staff Chae Pyon-dok shuffled many senior officers: Paek Sung-yop from command of the 5th Division to the 1st Division, Yu Sung-yol from the 1st Division to the 3rd Division, Yi Ung-chun to head the 5th Division, and Kim Paek-il from the 3rd Division to vice-chief of staff at ROKA headquarters.[109] In themselves such transfers were not remarkable. However, the possibility of a northern attack was openly discussed—this became known as the "May-June crisis"—and Chae himself on May 13 had anticipated an attack on May 30. Then, on June 10, Chae again shifted senior officers: Yi Hyung-gun, commander of the 8th Division stationed at the 38th parallel, was replaced with Yi Song-ga; Yi Chun-sik left the 7th Division in favor of Yu Chae-hun; and Shin Sang-chol was replaced as commander of the 6th Division by Kim Chong-o. Though one interpretation is that more competent officers were placed in command, the new generals never had a chance to inspect their areas of responsibility before North Korea attacked on June 25.[110]

Any special measures taken by the ROK government and military after June 20 are unknown. The special alert that was put into effect on June 11 was lifted on Friday, June 23. The ROKA Intelligence Bureau reported suspicious activities by the KPA, but the chief of staff reportedly was not overly concerned.[111]

Chapter Three

Attack

In June of 1950, ordered to commence field exercises, the DPRK's Korean People's Army had moved close to the 38th parallel. The 6th and 1st Divisions faced the southern city of Kaesong beyond the parallel. The 105th Tank Brigade and the 4th and 3rd Divisions assembled in front of Tongduchon, and the 2nd Division faced Chunchon, both cities in the South beyond the parallel. The 12th Division gathered near Inje, and the 5th Division was on the East Sea coast. It was a formidable presence.

Of the twenty-one KPA regiments near the parallel, ten were composed of veteran Korean troops from China. They included regiments of Pang Ho-san's 6th Division, Chon U's 12th Division, and Kim Chang-dok's 5th Division, as well as the 18th Regiment. In addition, three brigades of police from the DPRK's Internal Affairs Ministry were to be reorganized into the 7th, 8th, and 9th KPA Divisions, but had not yet been deployed.

According to captured North Korean documents, Unit 657, that is the 13th Regiment, 6th Division, received verbal orders at 6:35 p.m. on June 23 to seize enemy dugouts and sixteen fortified positions, then occupy Kaesong and secure the road to Seoul. Attack preparations were to be completed by midnight.[1] In Unit 251, that is the 3rd Engineer Battalion, 2nd Division, the 1st Company dismantled mines from 7:00 p.m. on June 24 to 4:00 a.m. on June 25 to enable an infantry regiment to pass through on the road to Chunchon. The battalion's 2nd Company, on orders from an infantry regiment commander, removed mines from 10:00 p.m. on June 24 to 4:00 a.m. on June 25 to clear the way. The battalion commander recorded these activities in a report dated June 29.[2]

The captured North Korean documents show that KPA infantry regiments that had been ordered to commence field exercises first advanced to the front, then received battle orders the evening of June 23, and then on the evening of

June 24 were ordered to attack at 4:00 a.m. the following morning. Engineer battalions began to remove mines the evening of June 24.[3]

About 4:40 a.m. on Sunday, June 25, North Korean forces simultaneously attacked South Korean positions along the 38th parallel. The most incontrovertible documentary evidence that North Korea started the war is a telegram dated June 26 from Soviet Ambassador Terentii Shtykov in Pyongyang to First Deputy Chief of the Soviet General Staff Matvei Vasil'evich Zakharov in Moscow.[4] The telegram, which also describes some of the fighting (from the DPRK's perspective), is worth quoting at length:

> I am reporting on the preparation and progress of the operational plan of the Korean People's Army. In accordance with the plan prepared by the General Staff Headquarters, the Korean People's Army began to assemble near the 38th parallel on June 12 and completed the movement on June 23. Unit movements were coordinated and carried out without incident. Enemy spies probably discovered unit movements, but we were able to keep secret the operational plan and time of attack. Soviet advisers participated in division-level operational planning and area reconnaissance.
>
> All operational preparations were completed on June 24. Orders with the date and time of attack were issued to division commanders on that date.
>
> A political order from the Minister of National Defense was read to every unit explaining that because South Korean military forces had violated the 38th parallel and launched a military attack, the government of the Democratic People's Republic of Korea has ordered the Korean People's Army to counterattack. The order to counterattack was enthusiastically welcomed by the officers and men of the Korean People's Army.
>
> Units reached their departure points by midnight June 24. Military action commenced at 4:40 a.m. local time [June 25]. When preparations for an artillery attack were ready, bombardment was carried out from twenty to forty minutes; barrages were fired at ten-minute intervals. Then the infantry rose up and charged with great élan. Some units advanced three to five kilometers in the first three hours.
>
> The attack by the Korean People's Army was a complete surprise to the enemy. The enemy showed strong resistance in only three areas: Ongjin, Kaijin [Kaesong], and the approach to Seoul. After noon on the first day, the enemy began organized resistance. The following towns were occupied the first day: Oshin [Ongjin] (Ongjin area), Kaesong, and Sinupni.
>
> In the Chunchon area, units of the Korean People's Army advanced twelve kilometers. On the East Sea coast the advance was eight kilometers.
>
> On the first day [North] Korean naval forces carried out two amphibious operations on the Japan Sea coast. Two marine battalions and 1000 partisans were landed in the Kangnung area and 600 partisans went ashore successfully in Ulchin area at 5:25 a.m. The partisans occupied the Ulchin city office and many nearby areas.
>
> The landing was accomplished during a battle between People's Army warships and South Korean warships. A South Korean trawler was sunk and

another vessel was heavily damaged; the North Korean Navy had no casualties.

On June 26 units of the Korean People's Army fought their way deeper into South Korean territory. (Looking from left to right), [T]he Ongjin Peninsula and the Kaishin [Kangyong] Peninsula were completely liberated, and a unit of the 6th Division forced its way across the bay and occupied a populated area near Kimpo Airport.

The 1st and 4th divisions occupied Munsan and Tongduchon in the Seoul area, and the 2nd Division seized the prefectural center Chunchon. The advances continued on the Japan Sea coast, too. Toupuiri [Chumunjin] harbor was seized.

All day today communications were cut with the 12th Division headed for Kosen [Hongchon] and with the 3rd Division and the Mechanized Brigade, which had passed through Sinupni-attacking in the Uijongbu area.

Shtykov's report along with captured North Korean documents make it abundantly clear that the attack order itself—the command to "counterattack" the invading ROKA—and indeed every aspect of the North Korean offensive was meticulously planned by the DPRK military in conjunction with Soviet advisers.

Shtykov also candidly wrote General Zakharov:

The following deficiencies in the operations of the People's Army must be noted:

1. As the units advanced, higher echelon staff lost communication with lower levels. The People's Army General Staff Headquarters already on the first day was not directing the fighting because there were no reliable communications with any division. . . .
2. The Korean People's Army command staff has no combat experience and after Soviet military advisers were withdrawn, combat leadership was poorly organized, the use of artillery and tanks in combat was inadequate, and communications broke down.
3. However, our military advisers report great enthusiasm and a sense of common purpose to carry out the mission in Korean People's Army units.
4. In connection with the start of military operations the political support among the North Korean people, the widespread enthusiasm for and confidence in the North Korean government and in victory by the Korean People's Army, are noteworthy. . . .
5. Korean People's Army headquarters took steps to establish communications with and control of subordinate units. The army command center was moved to the Tepugesu [Chorwon] area. The Defense Minister, chief of staff, and the chief Soviet military adviser will probably go there with a group of officers.

Shtykov's report to Zakharov also summarized ROKA performance in the first two days of military operations. He concluded:

1. The enemy is resisting and fighting while retreating deep into South Korean territory. Large numbers of South Korean soldiers have not been taken prisoner.
2. The puppet authorities of South Korea have started to commit units from rear areas and are trying to stop the advance of the People's Army.
3. On the first day the People's Army attack caused confusion in the South. South Korean authorities and the U.S. Ambassador broadcast appeals for the populace to be calm. ROKA headquarters broadcast false reports of ROKA successes.

On June 26, DPRK Prime Minister Kim Il Sung issued a statement in which he asserted that northern police units had stopped the "full scale attack" by the "puppet forces of the traitor Syngman Rhee," and that the People's Army had been ordered to launch "a decisive counterattack . . . [to] liberate the South and unify the fatherland under the flag of the Democratic People's Republic of Korea." Kim also declared, "We are waging a just war for the unification and independence of the fatherland, freedom, and democracy."[5] Kim announced formation of a Military Committee "to mobilize rapidly the entire people." He was the committee's chairman; the other members were the three DPRK vice-premiers—Pak Hon-yong, Hong Myong-hui, and Kim Chaek—and Defense Minister Choe Yong-gon, Interior Minister Pak Il-u, and State Planning Committee Chairman Chong Chun-taek. The omission of Ho Ka-i, the third-ranking member in the KWP, suggests that the committee was a war cabinet.[6]

THE ROKA RESPONDS, BUT SEOUL IS ABANDONED

The KPA's attack caught the ROKA off guard. Only three ROKA divisions and three regiments in other divisions—a total of twelve regiments—were stationed on the southern side of the 38th parallel. The 17th Regiment, Capital Division, was on the Ongjin Peninsula; its regimental commander was Paek In-yop. The 1st Division was at Kaesong; its commander was Paek Sun-yop. The 7th Division, under CO Yu Chae-hung, was at Tongduchon. The 6th Division, under CO Kim Chong-o, was at Chunchon. And the 10th and 21st regiments of the 8th Division were stationed on the East Sea coast. Three other divisions were based far southward at Taejon, Taegu, and Kwangju.

When the twenty-one KPA regiments launched their blitzkrieg, they outnumbered the defenders by two to one. Moreover, while the ROK had no tanks, the KPA's Tank Brigade possessed 258 tanks.[7] No wonder the ROKA could not withstand the attack.

When ROKA Chief of Staff Chae Pyong-dok rushed into ROKA headquarters at 7:00 a.m. on June 25, the KPA already held Kaesong. ROK

Defense Minister Shin Sung-mo, a civilian, did not take command of military operations. That task fell to Chae, a specialist in procurement without combat experience. Chae was confused about what to do. Chae personally went to the 7th Division headquarters in Uijongbu and confirmed that the North had launched an all-out offensive, returning to ROKA headquarters at 10:00 a.m.[8]

After a report from Minister Shin, President Rhee immediately sought a meeting with US Ambassador John J. Muccio, who arrived at Rhee's office shortly before noon. Rhee requested ammunition and equipment from the United States. He also said that a cabinet meeting would be convened at 2:00 p.m. and that he intended to declare martial law in Seoul. Rhee's last words to Muccio were remarkably calm and analytical. According to Muccio,

> He stated that he had been trying to avoid making Korea a second Sarajevo; but perhaps the present crisis presented the best opportunity for settling the Korean problem for once and all. He commented that American public opinion seemed to be growing stronger day by day vis-à-vis Communist aggression. He hopes the US would take action to "maintain the present situation in Formosa," because he would "like to see the Chinese Communists kept occupied for a while."[9]

Rhee believed the start of hostilities was making Korea a second Sarajevo in the sense that a clash in Korea would lead to a world war. He also felt that expansion of a local conflict into a world war would open the way for the ROK to unify the country.

In his command position, ROKA Chief of Staff Chae considered organizing a swift counterattack by recalling hastily the three divisions from the southern part of South Korea. At the 2:00 p.m. cabinet meeting, Chae's report of the North Korean offensive was confirmed, and President Rhee's order to declare a state of emergency was adopted. Although ROKA units continued to fight north of Seoul, by evening the KPA was in front of Uijongbu, a city located thirty kilometers south of the parallel. Rhee unilaterally decided to move the government to Taejon, startling the cabinet and Ambassador Muccio, who urged the president to remain in Seoul. Rhee repeatedly insisted that he was not concerned for his personal safety, but said that government leaders should not risk capture.

At 1:00 p.m. on June 26, the day after the cabinet meeting, Uijongbu fell, endangering Seoul. Rhee left the capital before dawn on June 27. Acting Prime Minister Shin Sung-mo called an emergency cabinet meeting and ordered the government to move to Suwon, a city closer to Seoul than Taejon. Rhee headed for the naval base at Chinhae, at the far end of the Korean Peninsula, but at Taegu he decided that he had fled too far, and he returned to Taejon.[10]

Rhee probably thought that as long as he was not captured, he could return to Seoul when US forces intervened and then attack the North together with his forces. If Rhee had been considering unification by force, the northern attack played into his hands. But American aid had to arrive quickly. At 5:00 p.m. on June 27, US Embassy Counselor Everett Drumright caught up with Rhee in Taejon, where the president castigated him and the United States for not fulfilling their earlier promises of military aid. [11]

OCCUPIED SEOUL

On June 28, a unit of the KPA's 105th Tank Brigade and the 18th Regiment, 4th Division, from China, captured Seoul. The 18th Regiment set up headquarters in the Toksugung Palace, where Emperor Kojong, forced to abdicate, lived until his death. [12] Then the 3rd Division, under Yi Yong-ho, entered Seoul. Some capital residents who had fled the fighting returned to their homes that evening. Kim Song-chil, a history professor at Seoul National University, recorded the scene in his diary:

> About noon, a group of children in the lead, residents left Tonamdong and headed home. There were already people in the street waving red flags and shouting "Mansei" (hurrah). A DPRK flag hung from a school flagpole. When the crowd crossed the Miari pass and headed for Tongsomun, there were tanks, cars, horse-drawn carts and clusters of KPA troops. The soldiers were speaking in their hard Sobuk accent, but to us they were compatriots who spoke the same language, had the same customs, and had Korean blood in their veins. . . . They seemed like long-lost brothers who had finally come home from some far-away place. Seeing them talk quietly and laugh, no one was frightened. [13]

Yi Sung-yop, the minister of justice in the DPRK, and formerly a leader of the South Korean Workers' Party (SKWP), was appointed chairman of the Seoul Provisional People's Committee (SPPC). Given his southern roots, that was to be expected. The vice-chairman of the SPPC, however, was Soviet Korean Pak Chang-sik, the vice-chairman of the Pyongyang City People's Committee, and Pak Hyo-sam , who having fought in China during the anti-Japanese resistance, was a member of the Yan'an group and was named Seoul garrison commander. Seoul was taking on the color of Pyongyang. [14]

On June 30, SPCC Directive 3 ordered all political parties and social organizations in the South to register and submit rosters of their members and officers. Directive 6, issued the same day, ordered individuals connected with the ROK government to turn themselves in. The directive stated:

> Now the people have been liberated from reactionary rule. Individuals who want to cleanse themselves of past crimes of acts inimical to the sovereignty of the DPRK and support the policies of the DPRK and contribute to the unifica-

tion of the fatherland should acknowledge their past offenses and submit a petition to a city office or police station.

Seoul residents were obligated to report "reactionary elements" that were in hiding. A curfew was established from 9:00 p.m. to 4:00 a.m., and "anyone who spreads reactionary propaganda by repeating rumors or distributing leaflets is to be regarded as hostile to the policies of the Republic and the KPA," the directive declared.[15]

All newspapers and magazines in the South were now banned. In their place, the occupiers launched the *Haebang Ilbo* [Liberation Daily], the organ of the former SKWP; the *Choson Inminpo* [Korean People's News]; and the Pyongyang *Nodong Sinmun* [Worker's News].[16] On the front page of the first issue of the *Haebang Ilbo* on July 2 was a photo of Kim Il Sung, his June 26 statement, and a congratulatory message he issued on June 28 on the liberation of Seoul. In his June 26 speech, Kim urged the partisans to "expand liberated zones . . . deal with traitors and revive People's Committees, the sovereign organs of the people." A speech by Yi Sung-yop, chairman of the Seoul Provisional People's Committee, was on the second page:

> Koreans, from today you begin a new life of freedom and prosperity as citizens of a unified, liberated, and glorious republic under the flag of the Democratic People's Republic of Korea and the guidance of the national patriot and hero Premier of the DPRK, General Kim Il Sung. . . . Citizens of Seoul, rally around the People's Committee and we will bravely sweep away the traitors who block the unification and independence of the fatherland. The people are victorious. In days the flag of our Republic will wave over Cheju Island and all of Korea.[17]

On July 3, the *Haebang Ilbo* carried the complete text of the DPRK Constitution on the front page. The next day, the left half of page one was devoted to a large photograph of Pak Hon-yong and the text of a radio address he gave. Pak was identified with the honorary suffix *sonsaeng* (elder); his position and record in the North were not mentioned. In his address, Pak said that he was entrusted to speak by the Workers' Party Central Committee, and he recalled the earlier struggles in the South for liberation and unification. Pak appealed to party members and all southerners to rise up: "The hour of great change has arrived, the final victory wrested in battle awaits the fighting and patriotic people." The KPA would soon end the fraternal civil war provoked by Syngman Rhee, Pak said. "At this grave moment why do the people of the south not rise up? Why do they hesitate? Everyone should join in this just war of all the people to save the country." Speed was crucial: "It is in the people's interest to end the war as soon as possible. . . . Your bitter enemy is the traitor Syngman Rhee, the tool of American imperialism. If you do not join the side of the people now, when

will you? . . . The time for unification and independence is here. People of
the South, rise up, join in solidarity with the DPRK, and take your honored
place in the great work of the unification of the fatherland under the flag of
the Republic."[18]

Not mentioning Kim Il Sung, Pak appealed to Southern Workers' Party
members in his own name as purportedly a Communist leader of the South.
But what he appealed for was expansion of the DPRK and its absorption of
the South.

THE UNITED STATES REACTS

A report of the North Korean attack reached Gen. Douglas MacArthur, the
Supreme Commander of the Allied Powers (SCAP) and the commander in
chief, Far East, the US Army, in Tokyo the morning of June 25. MacArthur
informed US State Department adviser John Foster Dulles and John Allison,
chief of the State Department's Northeast Asia Division, who were still in
Tokyo after visiting South Korea, about the attack. In MacArthur's view, the
attack was not an all-out effort, the Soviets were not necessarily behind it,
and the Republic of Korea would be victorious.[19] MacArthur's initial actions
were to send transport aircraft and US Navy vessels to South Korea in response to Ambassador Muccio's request at about 10:00 p.m. that evening to
evacuate American women and children.[20]

MacArthur neither anticipated the North Korean attack nor immediately
prepared for an all-out counterattack. In an analysis four days later, Dulles
pointed out that MacArthur had failed to evaluate properly intelligence data
showing the North Korean military buildup near the 38th parallel. There was
a mood of complacency among the US military advisers in the General
Headquarters (GHQ). SCAP, Dulles said, had induced overconfidence in the
morale and discipline of the South Korean troops:

> GHQ Tokyo was not informed promptly, and when informed did not evaluate
> the attack as serious until the third day when Seoul was within the enemy
> grasp. It seems to have been assumed that the attack was a purely North
> Korean adventure, carried out without the Soviet planning, preparation and
> backing which would assure its success as against any resistance that the South
> Koreans could interpose.[21]

On June 25, however, Dulles concurred with MacArthur's optimistic
view and also thought that South Korea might repulse the attack. But he
wrote to Washington that if Seoul could not stave off the assault, US forces
should be used. Even if US intervention invited action by the Soviet Union,
Dulles said, rather dramatically, to do nothing and watch South Korea de-

stroyed "would start disastrous chain of events leading most probably to world war."[22]

Ambassador Muccio's first report to Washington from Seoul was sent at 10:00 a.m. on June 25 and reached Washington at 9:26 p.m. on June 24. He outlined military developments and concluded: "It would appear from nature of attack and manner in which it was launched that it constitutes all out offensive against ROK."[23] The reaction of the Truman administration was to take the problem to the UN Security Council. Secretary of State Dean Acheson made a preliminary contact with UN Secretary General Trygve Lie from the State Department at 11:30 p.m. on June 24, and at 2:00 a.m. on June 25 he officially requested a meeting of the Security Council. President Truman was in Missouri for the weekend. "In succeeding days, Acheson dominated the decision making," according to Bruce Cumings.[24]

The Security Council convened at 2 p.m. on June 25, minus the Soviet delegate (the Soviet Union was then boycotting the Council), and adopted a resolution drafted by the United States. The resolution called upon the authorities of North Korea to cease hostilities and withdraw to the 38th parallel. It also called upon all UN members to render every assistance to the United Nations in the execution of the resolution. At the objection of other countries, the original US wording of "unprovoked act of aggression" was dropped.[25]

President Truman returned to Washington the evening of June 25 and presided over a meeting of senior officials at Blair House. Acheson recommended provision of weapons and supplies to South Korea, US air cover to support the evacuation of American women and children, and attacks on North Korean tanks and aircraft that tried to interrupt the US evacuation. He also recommended additional assistance to South Korea under the Security Council resolution, deployment of the 7th Fleet to the Taiwan Straits, and increased aid to Indochina. Acheson initially saw the attack in Korea as the start of a Communist offensive against the Asian continent, not merely South Korea. Secretary of Defense Louis A. Johnson supported his proposals, and Truman approved them.[26]

Acheson further conceived the US government's response on the following afternoon of June 26. Cumings quotes George Kennan's memoirs: "the course actually taken by this Government was not something pressed upon [Acheson] by the military leaders, but rather something arrived at by himself, in solitary deliberation." Cumings pointed out that "these decisions followed on Acheson's logic of containment in Korea, elaborated first in 1947 and structuring his Press Club speech" the previous January.[27] Acheson's ideas were again adopted at a second Blair House conference that evening: deployment of US air and naval forces in support of ROK forces, orders to the 7th Fleet to prevent an attack on Taiwan from mainland China, an increase in US military forces in and aid to the Philippines, and dispatch of a military mission to Indochina. Acheson drafted a statement of these policies that Truman announced at noon on June 27.[28]

"The attack upon Korea makes it plain beyond all doubt that Communism has passed beyond the use of subversion to conquer independent nations and will now use armed invasion and war," Truman said. "It has defied the orders of the Security Council of the United Nations to preserve international peace and security." In response to the Security Council call for member assistance to the United Nations, and in line with Acheson's recommendations, the US government ordered air and naval units to give cover and support to South Korea. "In these circumstances the occupation of Formosa by Communist forces would be a direct threat to the security of the Pacific area and to the United States . . ." Truman also stated. "Accordingly I have ordered the Seventh Fleet to prevent any attack on Formosa." Truman called on the Nationalist government "to cease all naval and air operations against the mainland."[29]

Many participants in the Blair House meetings saw these moves as "limited intervention" in Korea, and optimistically thought that they would stabilize the military situation there.[30] However, Acheson saw a global Communist offensive afoot. Cumings quotes Acheson's statement in 1951 congressional hearings: "Korea is not a local situation. It is not the great value of Korea itself which led to the attack. . . . But it was the spearpoint of a drive made by the whole Communist control group on the entire power position of the West—primarily in the East, but also affecting the whole world. . . . That is the global strategy of the global purpose of both sides. It isn't a Korean war on either side."[31]

Cumings disagrees: "Acheson was wrong. It was a *Korean* war on the northern side, and for much of the southern population." Yet to Kim Il Sung, Pak Hon-yong, and other leaders in Pyongyang, the conflict was unquestionably both a civil war in Korea and an extension of the Chinese revolution. And, in view of Stalin's secret multifaceted support for the North Korean attack, Acheson's interpretation had some basis in fact.

The resolute change of US foreign policy expressed in the decision to defend Taiwan from the Chinese Communists had enormous implications for international relations. The Chiang Kai-shek regime in Taipei was ecstatic, the Communists in Beijing enraged. On June 28, PRC Premier Zhou Enlai condemned Truman's decision as "aggression against China's territory and an utter violation of the UN Charter."[32]

The evening of June 27, the UN Security Council, with the Soviet delegate still absent, adopted a resolution proposed by the United States that called on member states to "furnish such assistance to the Republic of Korea as may be necessary to repel the armed attack."[33] The resolution gave UN approval to US military actions under way and to those on the drawing board.

THE SOVIET UNION REACTS

From January 13, 1950, the Soviet Union, based on a declaration by the Chinese People's Republic on January 8, had demanded the expulsion of the Kuomintang representative from the UN Security Council and boycotted the Council. Mao Zedong was in Moscow that January and the Soviets' demand was probably an expression of solidarity with the PRC. Since there was no possibility that the Sino-Soviet position would prevail in the Security Council, eventually Moscow would have to lift the boycott. However, it was still in effect on June 25 when North Korea launched its attack.

After January 30, when Stalin had endorsed North Korea's policy of armed unification, he may have seen the boycott in a different light than he had earlier. If war started in Korea, the problem would be taken to the Security Council, he doubtless realized. And if the Soviet Union returned to the Council and supported Pyongyang against a critical motion by the United States, international public opinion would turn sharply against Moscow for using its veto to block a resolution. Moscow might be condemned as a partner in aggression with North Korea. It would thus be better to be absent. Although the boycott was started to support the PRC, Stalin may well have continued it in anticipation of a North Korean attack. [34]

Andrei Gromyko, the Soviet Union's first vice-minister of foreign affairs in 1950, recounted in his memoirs an exchange with Stalin about the Security Council's emergency session on June 25. Gromyko presented the foreign ministry's position to Stalin: "We have prepared official instructions that firmly reject criticism of North Korea and the Soviet Union [expressed] in the American letter requesting a Security Council meeting." Those instructions attacked "U.S. participation in the invasion of North Korea" and invoked "our veto if sanctions are proposed against North Korea," Gromyko said. Stalin replied: "I think the Soviet representative should not appear at the Security Council meeting." Gromyko argued that in the absence of Soviet representative to the UN Jacob Malik, there might be proposals to send UN forces to the Republic of Korea. Unpersuaded, Stalin dictated orders to Malik to continue the boycott. [35]

Malik thus stayed away from the Security Council meeting on June 25, and the first resolution—calling on North Korea to cease hostilities and withdraw to the 38th parallel and for member states to assist the UN in execution of the resolution—was adopted, with Yugoslavia abstaining. The same day, Acheson directed the US ambassador in Moscow to protest Malik's absence to the Soviet foreign minister and "ask assurance USSR disavows responsibility" for the North Korean attack and would "use its influence with North Korean authorities to withdraw their invading forces immediately." [36]

On June 27, following Truman's commitment of US naval and air force units to support ROK forces, Malik conferred with UN Secretary General Lie and others over lunch. Malik attacked the June 25 resolution as one-sided and illegal because both the Soviet delegate and the legitimate representative of China were absent. Malik insisted that the North Korean action was a response to a southern attack across the border and objected to US intervention, including bombing of the North. Malik was silent when Lie and Ernest A. Gross, the US deputy representative to the UN, countered his assertions. To Lie's question about mediation of the dispute by a UN agency, Gross said a precondition was that North Korea cease fighting and withdraw its forces. Finding himself in an untenable position, Malik said nothing. Gross asked Malik whether he had any suggestions to terminate a situation which the United States considered so grave that American lives were being jeopardized on behalf of a UN decision. Upon Malik's evasive reply, Lie pressed him to answer the question. Malik again argued that the Security Council's decision was illegal. The conversation terminated with Gross pointing out that the question of Korea clearly involved protection of the UN Charter and hence world peace, and that the time had passed when debate on the question of Chinese representation could take the place of compliance on the part of North Korea with the decision of the Security Council. Malik told Gross he still intended to leave New York for the USSR in the first week of July, as planned, and he evaded replying to the question of how long his absence was going to be.[37]

It is clear that Malik was making every effort to evade responding to the situation. The Soviet Union responded to the US request for assurance that it was not responsible for the North Korean attack and that it would use its influence to get North Korea to withdraw from the South on June 29. Gromyko presented a memorandum on that day to US Ambassador to the Soviet Union Alan Kirk. The memorandum made three points:

1. In accordance with facts verified by the Soviet Government, the events taking place in Korea were provoked by an attack by forces of the South Korean authorities on border regions of North Korea. Therefore the responsibility for these events rests upon the South Korean authorities and upon those who stand behind their back.

2. As is known, the Soviet Government withdrew its troops from Korea earlier than the Government of the US and thereby confirmed its traditional principle of non-interference in the internal affairs of other states. And now as well the Soviet Government adheres to the principle of the impermissibility of interference by foreign powers in the internal affairs of Korea.

3. It is not true that the Soviet Government refused to participate in meetings of the Security Council. In spite of its full willingness, the Soviet Government has not been able to take part in the meetings of the Security Council in as much as, because of the position of the Government of the US, China, a permanent member of the Security Council, has not been admitted to the

Council which has made it impossible for the Security Council to take decisions having legal force.[38]

THE UNITED STATES ENTERS THE WAR

On June 28, upon learning that the KPA had entered Seoul at dawn, ROKA Chief of Staff Chae Pyong-dok left the capital and ordered the bridge across the Han River destroyed immediately. People and vehicles were on the bridge when it exploded; a single steel span remained standing. US Ambassador to South Korea John Muccio caught up with President Syngman Rhee in Taejon and spoke to him, his cabinet, and members of the National Assembly. The ambassador found that "Koreans from Rhee down were seriously dispirited by course [of] hostilities, especially loss [of] Seoul. They [were] also disheartened by lack [of] actual US military aid."[39]

Ambassador Kirk's report of his meeting with Gromyko reached Washington at 1:00 p.m. on June 29. Acheson was convinced that Gromyko's wording of the Soviet Union's traditional principle of noninterference in the internal affairs of other states meant that Moscow would not intervene in Korea.[40] An emergency US National Security Council meeting on the evening of June 29 directed General MacArthur to expand US air operations north of the 38th parallel—a significant expansion—and to commit US ground forces to the Pusan-Chinhae area.[41]

MacArthur flew from the Haneda Airport in Tokyo to Suwon, South Korea, on June 29 for a personal look at the battlefield. He reported that South Korean forces were incapable of mounting a counterattack and in danger of being destroyed and that the Republic of Korea might collapse. To hold present lines and push the enemy back, the use of US ground forces was unavoidable, the general said. MacArthur recommended that a regimental combat team be committed immediately and that two divisions be readied for action.

MacArthur's report, sent about noon on June 30, reached Washington at 1:31 a.m. on June 30.[42] Truman received it before dawn and approved dispatch of the regimental combat team. At a White House conference that morning, MacArthur was also authorized to deploy ground forces under his command, and a naval blockade of North Korea was ordered. These decisions committed all three branches of the US military to the battle. But an offer by Chiang Kai-shek, who was elated that the United States had intervened by sending the vessels of the 7th Fleet, to send 33,000 troops to South Korea within five days was declined.[43] Truman was inclined to accept Nationalist troops, but Acheson cautioned that it would invite intervention by the Chinese Communists.

After Seoul fell on June 28, the difficult ROKA retreat continued. On June 30, Syngman Rhee replaced Chae Pyong-dok as ROKA chief of staff with Deputy Chief of Staff Chong Il-gwon, who had rushed back from the United States. Chong's first order was to gain time and to "preserve forces" in the withdrawal. He later explained in his memoirs that the order corresponded to ROKA General Staff Order 38.[44] Rhee basically agreed with his new chief of staff, but declared that he would die in Taejon rather than flee further. US Embassy First Secretary Harold Noble, acting on orders from Ambassador Muccio, and Shin Sung-mo and Chong Il-gwon all dissuaded Rhee, who finally relented on July 1 and agreed to leave Taejon. But Rhee said that he would not leave Taejon while the US ambassador and embassy staff were there. Then Rhee and his wife Francesca left for Mokpo by car, with Pusan the ultimate destination. After learning of the commitment of US forces to Korea, Noble hurried after the presidential entourage.[45]

Of the US Army's ten divisions in 1950, four were in the 8th Army assigned to occupation duty in Japan. Each division was understrength, with two battalions per regiment instead of three. The 24th Division, commanded by Maj. Gen. William Dean, was based in Kyushu with its headquarters in Kokura. On MacArthur's orders, the division's 21st Regiment of 440 men in Kumamoto was flown from Itazuke Air Base to South Korea the morning of July 1; the remainder of the unit sailed from Sasebo on July 3. The 34th Regiment of the 24th Division, based in Sasebo, had embarked the evening of July 1. General Dean himself arrived in Korea on July 3. The 24th Division, comprising 15,965 men with World War II equipment, was the first US ground unit to fight in the Korean War.[46]

The United States had decided to intervene in Korea within five days of the North's attack and had forces on the ground in about ten days. The American commitment, approved by the UN Security Council, started to become multinational when Australia sent two warships on June 29 and an air force unit on June 30.[47]

On July 3, Dean Acheson had the US representative at the United Nations, Warren Austin, propose that military forces contributed by UN member states in accordance with the Security Council resolution on member assistance to South Korea be placed under American command. Austin also proposed that the United States report regularly to the Security Council on the military activities of the unified command and that a five-nation subcommittee be formed within the Council.[48] These proposals were intended to convert unilateral US military intervention to a multilateral UN action. On July 4, the 25th Infantry Division, whose units had been stationed at Gifu, Sakai, Otsu, and Nara in Japan, left by sea for South Korea from Kyushu. The same day, Acheson moved to strengthen the Security Council resolution by proposing that the unified force operate under the UN flag. The British and French representatives agreed to sponsor the resolution.[49]

The Soviet Union then made a countermove outside the United Nations. On July 6, Andrei Gromyko summoned the British ambassador to the Soviet

Union, expressed the Kremlin's wish for a peaceful settlement, and solicited "specific proposals."[50] Prime Minister of the United Kingdom Clement Atlee regarded this as a serious initiative and suggested to Truman a discussion to coordinate views toward Moscow. On July 7, British Foreign Minister Ernest Bevin said that the entrance of the People's Republic of China into the United Nations could be a negotiating card with Moscow. Britain, which had already recognized the PRC, disagreed with the US position on Taiwan.[51] But Acheson rejected the British proposal, saying that discussions with the Soviet Union should be based on the Security Council resolutions to date.[52] The new resolution to create a unified military command was submitted to the Security Council on July 7 as an Anglo-French proposal, and passed by a seven to nothing vote with three abstentions (Egypt, India, and Yugoslavia). The Soviet Union was still absent from the Council.[53]

This resolution meant that American forces now wore a UN mantle. On July 14, Syngman Rhee, on the recommendation of Chong Il-gwon, sent a letter from Taegu to MacArthur that transferred command of ROK forces to UN Commander MacArthur, transforming South Korean troops into UN soldiers.[54] Many nations subsequently contributed ground forces: Thailand, Turkey, Australia, New Zealand, the Philippines, Canada, France, England, Greece, the Netherlands, Belgium, Ethiopia, Colombia, and Luxembourg. Sixteen nations in all sent troops to Korea.

On July 12 and 14, the US 1st Cavalry Division stationed at Asaka near Tokyo left for Korea from Yokohama. Initially slated for a later landing operation at Inchon, the division was hastily diverted to support the two US divisions already in Korea. Of the US occupation forces in Japan, only the 7th Division, with headquarters at Makomanai, Hokkaido, now remained there.[55]

JAPAN AND WAR

In Japan noon radio broadcasts broke the news of fighting in Korea on June 25, and newspapers printed extra editions. But there were no evening editions in 1950, and thus extensive press coverage began on June 26. The headlines in the *Asahi Shimbun* that day read: "North Korea Declares War on South Korea," "Keijo [Seoul] Threatened," "Full-scale Offensive at 38th Parallel," and "Invaders Smash Across Imjin River."[56] Japan did not have diplomatic relations with the Republic of Korea; there were no Japanese diplomats, wire services, or newspaper reporters in Seoul. All accounts consequently came from non-Japanese sources; nevertheless, every Japanese newspaper carried war news on the front page for fifteen days.

Still surrounded by signs of wartime devastation, most Japanese were apprehensive about the fighting in nearby Korea. The exception was a segment of the left linked to the Japanese Communist Party. At Waseda University, a student ran up to the leftist student union office, a copy of an extra edition in hand, yelling "They did it!" Students on campus that day were enormously excited by the North Korean attack.[57] At the University of Tokyo, students rallied in front of the office of the student union of the Faculty of Economics. JCP cell leader Totsuka Hideo shouted that the struggle of the Korean People's Army was a civil and revolutionary war, not a defensive battle, and urged everyone to support the liberation and unification of the Korean people.[58] The two university unions were strongholds of the internationalist faction of the JCP, which was condemned as a deviationist faction by the Party's mainstream.

Some three weeks earlier, on June 6, the Supreme Commander for the Allied Powers had banned twenty-four JCP leading members from public employment. The following day SCAP had purged seventeen people on the editorial board of *Akahata*, the JCP's newspaper. Mainstream JCP faction leaders Tokuda Kyuichi and Nosaka Sanzo went underground. The remainder of the party's provisional central bureau became cautious. On June 26, *Akahata* carried DPRK announcements: "Korean People's Army, massive counterattack ordered," "ROKA invasion repulsed everywhere," "Artillery bombardment by ROKA," "People's Republic forces advance in seven places," "Syngman Rhee flees to Japan?" "Smashing unification obstructionist Syngman Rhee," and "A beacon for people's liberation."[59] But *Akahata* did not declare a party position on the war.

SCAP immediately struck hard against this kind of news coverage. MacArthur suspended publication of *Akahata* for thirty days on the grounds that *Akahata* "had perverted the truth in discussing the Korean situation," and that its coverage "showed the newspaper was an instrument of subversion." Yoshikawa Mitsusada, chief of the Investigation Bureau of the Legal Affairs Agency in Japan, led a company of riot police in a raid on JCP headquarters and confiscated rotary presses.[60] The first political crackdown after the start of the Korean War, the raid looked like another step in SCAP's suppression of the Communist Party that began earlier in the month. Later, on July 18, MacArthur directed the Yoshida administration to suspend publication of *Akahata* indefinitely. And the so-called "Red purge" started. JCP members were purged from newspapers and the broadcasting corporation (NHK). On July 15, JCP members in the Osaka Branch of NHK (Japan Broadcasting Corporation) were banned in the name of General MacArthur's directive.

On July 24, Lt. Col. Jack P. Napier, executive officer of the Government Section of GHQ, assembled executives of newspapers and radio stations and hinted at the dismissal of Communist employees. Four days later, 336 Communists and suspected sympathizers were fired from eight major newspapers in Japan, including 104 employees of the liberal *Asahi Shimbun*. By the end of August, 704 people nationwide had been fired from fifty companies; the purge was later extended to other companies and government employees. By the end of 1950, about 13,000 people would be dismissed.[61]

But the Japanese government was silent on Korea that June after the North's attack on the South. The chief cabinet secretary, the official spokesman for the Yoshida administration, made no comment. Only the head of the Metropolitan Police issued a statement, assuring the country that "all necessary steps would be taken to maintain public security" and cautioning against spreading rumors.[62] The political parties, too, were silent. The *Asahi Shimbun* editorialized on June 26 and 28 that "unification is probably the great aspiration" of the Korean people, but "there is no justification for armed conflict" and urged a peaceful settlement and restitution of the status quo ante. On July 1, the paper said that despite sympathy for the suffering people of Korea, "Japan is a third party not involved in the war. . . . We should redeem alien to us what is not directly related to us. We must not forget that we no longer live in a militaristic Japan." The next paragraph expressed an all-too-typical Japanese way of thinking: "The Korean situation may become even graver and, depending on circumstances, a fighter aircraft might stray into our territory. The fires of war burn nearby. But now it is not our business and we cannot become involved."[63] Initially, the government and public opinion wanted Japan to be neutral and stay out of the war.

But cooperation with GHQ's war efforts had already begun. At 6:00 p.m. on June 26, the Maritime Safety Force (MSF) placed all regional districts on alert. Four districts—Otaru, Moji, Maizuru, and Niigata—were ordered to report any unusual incidents to the local occupation headquarters, request instructions, take appropriate action, and inform MSF headquarters.[64] GHQ ordered the Moji district to maintain a strict watch in the coasts of northern Kyushu.[65] This was an extraordinary measure; usually Japanese government cooperation with GHQ for war was carried out by secret compliance with SCAP orders. The GHQ Civil Transport Section, the US 8th Army, and the 3rd Railway Headquarters all asked the Japanese government to facilitate military freight shipments by train. On June 29, a senior official of the Japanese Ministry of Transport issued instructions, entitled "Emergency Freight Shipments Related to the Outbreak of Hostilities in Korea," to the head of each National Railway branch that shipments of US military personnel and equipment had priority under SCAP's orders.[66] After Japan's surrender in 1945, all Japanese vessels over one hundred tons had been put under the control of SCAP/GHQ's Mercantile Section. Using occupation authority, the US military mobilized Japanese vessels and established the Commercial Maritime Management Committee (CMMC) within the Mercantile Section.[67]

Japan became a launching pad for US air attacks in Korea. In June 1950, Lt. Gen. George E. Stratemeyer commanded the Far East Air Forces, which consisted of the 5th Air Force (Nagoya), the 20th Air Force (Kadena Air

Base, Okinawa), and the 13th Air Force (Clark Air Base, Philippines). These US air forces included a total of 1,172 aircraft, including 365 F-80Cs. Of the eighteen fighter squadrons, the four stationed at Itazuke Air Base, Kyushu, were closest to Korea. The other fourteen squadrons were at Yokota Air Base, Misawa Air Base, Kadena, and Clark. A unit of B-26 light bombers was at Johnson Air Base, Saitama Prefecture. All B-29s were at Anderson Air Base in Guam. When the war started, fighters and a squadron of fighter-bombers were moved to Itazuke and Ashiya in northern Kyushu and the 19th Bomber Squadron of twenty B-29s was shifted to Kadena. By June 29, US pilots had flown 172 sorties in support of South Korean forces. On that day, the B-26s that had shifted from Johnson to Itazuke bombed Pyongyang Airfield.[68] Japanese media coverage of US air operations was severely restricted. For example, the _Asahi Shimbun_ carried an Associated Press story from "an air base in southern Japan" (not naming it) with a photograph of a "U.S. bomber squadron passing over Fukuoka city en route to counter-attack North Korean forces."[69]

In July, two B-29 Bombardment Groups arrived from the US west coast. The 22nd went to Kadena, Okinawa, and the 92nd went to Yokota, each with about twenty aircraft. On July 14, ten B-29s took off from Yokota at nine-minute intervals and bombed KPA units in the outskirts of Chonju in the South. On July 16, forty-seven aircraft from Kadena attacked the Seoul railway marshaling yards.[70] In August more B-29s from stateside bases joined the air war in Korea. The 98th Bombardment Group operated from Yokota, and the 307th Bombardment Group from Kadena. By mid-August, ninety-eight B-29s were flying missions from the two bases.[71]

Ammunition and fuel from the United States for the B-29s were unloaded at Oppama, Kanagawa Prefecture, and moved by train to Yokota Air Base on the Nambu Line, which operated at full capacity. Another key function of the Yokota base was aerial surveillance. The 31st Photo Reconnaissance Squadron of RB-29s was transferred there from Kadena and flew daily missions over Korea.

Meanwhile, on July 3 the Japanese government finally began to hold meetings at the ministerial and vice-ministerial levels to consider air defense measures, a declaration of a state of emergency, and assistance with US military operations. The next day the Yoshida cabinet decided for the time being to cooperate with US military actions "within the scope of administrative measures"—in other words, without seeking Diet approval or new legislation.[72]

The Japanese Communist Party issued its first statement on Korea on July 5: "There is a danger the war may spread to Japanese territory. . . . Japan must not become involved directly or indirectly in the Korean Civil War. . . . We oppose any involvement in the Korean Civil War."[73] The same day, the Japan Socialist Party's executive committee decided that party's position, which was officially approved on July 8 by the central committee. The Socialists would "protect international peace based on justice . . . oppose aggression through the use of military power and support in spirit the maintenance of law and order by the United Nations." Regarding the Korean conflict specifically, "the direct cause is the resort to force by the Democratic People's Republic of Korea in an attempt to unify Korea," the JSP declared. While Japan was occupied by the Allied Nations and the government and people must comply with occupation orders, the JSP stated, "the government's position of positive cooperation with the United Nations goes beyond the obligation of compliance and amounts to intervention in an international dispute, which, given the spirit of our new Constitution and our international environment, is imprudent." The party advocated a comprehensive peace settlement with all the belligerents.[74]

On July 8, MacArthur ordered the Japanese government to establish a 75,000-man National Police Reserve and increase the Maritime Safety Force by 8,000 men. MacArthur somewhat cryptically explained that Japan's "police system has reached that degree of efficiency in organization and training which will permit its augmentation to a strength which will bring it within the limits experience has shown to be essential to the safeguard of the public welfare in a democratic society."[75] SCAP's true objectives here were threefold: (1) to protect US bases in Japan depleted by the deployment of American troops to Korea; (2) to defend against attacks by Communists and pro–North Korea elements; and (3) to strengthen security in northern Kyushu. These goals clearly showed the role which Japan should perform for the US war in Korea.

For SCAP to order the Japanese government publicly to take such actions was unusual. Yet the Yoshida administration, which was obliged to perform every order of SCAP as a result of the acceptance of the Potsdam Declaration, complied fully and moved to establish the National Police Reserve without Diet approval as an administrative procedure.

Prime Minister Yoshida officially stated his position on the Korean War in a policy speech to the Japanese House of Representatives on July 14. The UN decision to impose military sanctions against North Korean "aggression" was appropriate, Yoshida said; "the Red invaders" were exerting "an evil power . . . and Japan itself is already endangered." Action by the international alliance had alleviated anxiety about how a "disarmed Japan could be secure." "Although Japan is not in a position to participate positively, to join in actions by the United Nations, it is wholly appropriate for Japan to cooperate to the extent possible," Yoshida concluded. Yoshida dismissed notions of a "peace treaty with all the belligerents or permanent neutrality" as "divorced from reality." He also attacked the "dangerous ideology behind the strategy of the Japanese Communist Party" and promised to crack down on the Communist movement. [76] Yoshida did not spell out the difference between participating "positively" in the war and cooperating to "the extent possible."

An *Asahi Shimbun* editorial questioned Japan's qualifications to cooperate with the United Nations, however, and cautioned that while the "JCP's anti-American activities should be denounced . . . liberal ideology must not be suppressed in the name of anticommunism." [77] In a parliamentary interpellation on July 15, Socialist Suzuki Mosaburo charged that the prime minister was ignoring the spirit of the preface and Article 9 of the Constitution, which called for peace and neutrality, and demanded that the new constitutional commitments be preserved. "Japan's territory and people must be protected from the wretched havoc of world disputes, internal violence, and war by the collective security of the United Nations," said Suzuki, citing a national consensus against involvement in another war. Japanese supported in spirit "the UN policy of trying to halt the spread of aggression by force," he said, but Japan "is an occupied country and unable to express its national will and must obey the orders of the Occupation forces based on the terms of surrender. No other attitude or course of action is possible." [78]

Yoshida had clarified his stance to some degree earlier that day in a reply to a question from Kawasaki Hideji of the Japan Democratic Party: "Your question is what is cooperation with the United Nations, what is the substance of cooperation. . . . My thinking is as follows: our people are willing not only to express approval of the United Nations action but also to cooperate to the extent possible to attain the United Nations' objective. There is no reason for Japan to take any positive actions." [79]

Thus, Yoshida wanted Japan to support the United States and South Korea spiritually, oppose the Communist camp, and cooperate with the United Nations "to the extent possible," whereas the Socialist Party called for spiritual support of the United Nations but adherence to the Constitution and strict neutrality. The two sides, then, agreed on one point: Japan should cooperate with the United Nations spiritually, but not actually participate in UN actions.

On July 21, in the Foreign Affairs Committee in the House of Representatives, Premier Yoshida commented on the issue of recruitment of Japanese volunteers to serve in South Korea:

> We consider this impermissible. . . . Such action would raise suspicion that Japan was rearming or would again threaten world peace . . . which would impede an early peace settlement. Accordingly, I think for the government to approve something like volunteers would be politically unwise, thus . . . it is impermissible, and I do not want to allow it. . . . Rearmament . . . has clearly been renounced in the Constitution. I think the article in the Constitution that renounces military forces and war is a very good provision and as a people we should preserve it forever, so even if a request were made by other countries . . . the Japanese people should not agree to it. [80]

During parliamentary interpellations the same day, Liberal Party (Jiyuto) Diet member Nakamura Torakichi said North Kyushu was an Allied base and that an attack by North Korea on it thus "was not out of the question." Could it be stopped? Nakamura asked. Premier Yoshida replied vaguely: "I too can imagine how worried the people of Kyushu must be, but I think they will be reassured as the Americans gradually move north [in Korea]." Talk of the future was hypothetical and not useful at this time, said Yoshida, who thought an attack on northern Kyushu by Communist forces unlikely. [81]

The Japanese government and the Socialists both held that Japan had to obey occupation orders. On July 26, Communist Party Diet member Watanabe Yoshimichi raised the issue of MacArthur's status as Supreme Commander for the Allied Powers and commander in chief of the United Nations' Command in the Lower House Foreign Affairs Committee. Ohashi Takeo, director general of the Legal Affairs Agency, responded: "All directives issued in Japan by General MacArthur rest not on his authority as UN Commander but on his authority as Supreme Commander for the Allied Powers and derive from General Order No. 1, Clause 12, issued in 1945. The Japanese government and individuals are obliged to respond to them swiftly and sincerely."[82] On July 29, Communist Diet member Kazahaya Yasoji said Ohashi spoke of "compliance with directives," but asked, "Was there not a limit to compliance?" Ohashi replied, "We should only check directives formally. Therefore, in practice no such distinction is possible." Ohashi continued: "Regarding the Korean problem, spiritual cooperation with the United Nations is entirely different from carrying out instructions based on Occupation directives."[83] The former was Japanese government "policy," whereas the latter was a government "obligation."

Cooperation as a policy was spiritual, while in practice unlimited cooperation as a duty was just obedience to Occupation orders. The conservatives and Socialists shared a similar logic on spiritual cooperation with the UN but obedience to occupation orders, though they sought different outcomes: Yoshida wanted covert cooperation with the United States. The Socialist Party affected not to notice that Japan was deeply involved in the war.

Japan had by now become not only a base for US bombing of North Korea but a military camp organized to support the war more broadly. From the coast guard and national railways to merchant marine vessels and Red Cross nurses, Japan was mobilized and duty bound to comply with SCAP orders. But the government did not acknowledge the nation's role in the war, and the people were unaware of it.

TAIWAN

War in Korea was a godsend to the Nationalist Chinese government on Taiwan. On the eve of the conflict, relations between Chiang Kai-shek and Washington had been tense. Truman and Acheson did not want Taiwan to fall to Communism, but according to Bruce Cumings, were loath to defend the corrupt, undemocratic Chiang regime. Although a Communist attack on Taiwan was possible from early 1950, Truman and Acheson banned weapons sales to Taiwan and indicated that the United States would not defend the island. The Nationalist regime was anxious, as was the Taiwan lobby in the United States.[84] A group of prominent men, including William Donovan, founder of the wartime Office of Strategic Services; Millard Goodfellow, formerly head of special operations at OSS; Gen. Claire Chennault, head of the Flying Tigers; and Adm. Charles Cooke, commander of the Western Pacific Fleet, were critical of Acheson's policy. They sought to link Taiwan and South Korea and wanted the United States to defend them both in order to block Soviet expansion in the Far East.[85]

In May 1950, the US chargé d'affaires to Taiwan, Robert Strong, reported to Washington that Taiwan would be attacked in June or July. The State Department wanted a way out of the situation and was inclined to support a plan submitted that month to oust Chiang. The question was whether replacing the generalissimo with more palatable leadership would justify US military support for Taiwan. Dean Rusk, assistant secretary of state, favored the idea, which was endorsed by Acheson and Dulles. The sticking point was who would replace Chiang. The American choices, Sun Li-jen and Hu Shih, both declined. Rusk made a final attempt to persuade Hu Shih on June 23, but in vain.[86]

Shao Yulin, the Nationalist Chinese ambassador to South Korea, recalled his thoughts on the night of June 25 following the North's attack on the South:

> The Korean War was a total boon to Taiwan. We had faced an immediate military threat from the Communist Chinese and our friend America might have abandoned us and recognized the bandit pretenders. The outbreak of war was the turning point; the situation changed completely. Chinese and Koreans share joy and anguish. If the war became advantageous for South Korea, it would certainly be to our advantage, too. If the Korean conflict turned into a world war between America and the Soviet Union, not only will South and North Korea immediately be united, but we might be able to cross the Yalu River and the Northeast region, and return to China proper. Even if the war goes badly for South Korea, America and the Free World should be more concerned [about the spread of communism] and increase their support for South Korea, and then international communism probably would not attack Taiwan.

Shao feared that because of ROK President Syngman Rhee's weak political base and military forces, not only Seoul but all of South Korea might fall into the hands of the North Korean Communists and "again fall victim to tragic national ruin." But "America should be the first to help," he believed, and Nationalist China would be next to provide assistance to the South. [87]

On June 26, Chiang cabled a message of encouragement to Rhee. The next day Taiwanese Prime Minister Chen Cheng expressed hope that every effort be made to support the Republic of Korea. [88] The Kuomintang was overjoyed when Truman sent the 7th Fleet to the Taiwan Straits. Direct US military intervention was more than the Nationalists had expected. On June 28, Ye Gongchao, Taiwan's minister of foreign affairs, accepted Truman's declaration of June 27 in principle, promising that Nationalist naval and air units would not attack the mainland. The next day the Nationalist government, in response to the UN Security Council's appeal for member support for the defense of South Korea, offered to send 33,000 ground forces to South Korea. Wellington Koo, the Nationalist ambassador in Washington, immediately began talks with the State Department. [89] But the Truman administration, fearful that Communist China would intervene, rejected Taiwan's offer of troops.

Yet, without sending one soldier or bearing any sacrifice over Korea, Taiwan's security was now guaranteed. With South Korea threatened by Communism, Washington wasn't going to let Taiwan fall. War in Korea was a windfall for the Chinese Nationalists.

THE SOVIET UNION AND CHINA RESPOND
TO US INTERVENTION

At the eighth session of the Chinese central government council on June 28, Mao Zedong denounced Truman's statement of June 27 and "American imperialism" and vowed to liberate Taiwan. [90] PRC planning for an assault across the Taiwan Straits was then under way. Documents from the 3rd Field Army dated May 17, 1950, show that training was scheduled to start that July for an assault in April or May 1951. But on the same day, Zhou Enlai informed Xiao Jinguang, the Chinese Navy commander, of a new policy: "to continue demobilization of our land forces while strengthening our naval and air forces, and the liberation of Taiwan will be postponed." [91] Although Chinese leaders may have already recognized the difficulty of liberating Taiwan, US intervention in the Taiwan Straits forced a change in policy.

Meanwhile, Stalin was irritated about US moves toward military intervention in Korea. On July 1, Stalin complained that his ambassador to North Korea Terentii Shtykov had reported "nothing about the plans of the KPA general staff headquarters." Would the KPA continue to move forward or halt? Stalin demanded to know. "In our view, the attack should absolutely continue. The sooner southern Korea is liberated, the less chance of [U.S.] intervention," Stalin said. He instructed Shtykov to inform DPRK Prime Minister Kim Il Sung that the weapons and ammunition Kim had earlier requested would be shipped by July 10.[92]

Shtykov reported to Stalin that day that there was both good news and bad news. In the liberated areas of South Korea, Shtykov related, people had welcomed the KPA, People's Committees had been reestablished, and the partisans were active. But there were also ominous signs. US broadcasts of anti-DPRK propaganda and US air raids were having an effect: "political sentiment has become somewhat negative . . . with signs of uncertainty about final victory." Some people in the liberated areas showed a wait-and-see attitude, Shtykov reported. In Pyongyang, DPRK leaders Kim Il Sung, Pak Hon-yong, Pak Il-u, Kim Chaek, Choe Yong-gon, and Kang Kon were confident of victory, but "some leaders, Kim Tu-bong and Hong Myong-hui, were cautious, saying North Korea by itself could not wage war against the United States and had reportedly asked Kim Il Sung about the Soviet Union's position under these conditions." Shtykov said that he had promised Kim weapons and ammunition, and ended on an upbeat note: "Overall the situation continues to be favorable."[93] And, indeed, the KPA 4th Division seized Suwon three days later.

The People's Republic of China had apparently not been informed in advance of the date of the North's attack on South Korea. In a discussion on July 2 with Soviet Ambassador to China Nikolai Roshchin, Premier Zhou Enlai speculated that the United States could send half of the 120,000-man US occupation force in Japan to Korea; land them at Pusan, Masan, and Mokpo; and transport them north by railway. The North Korean military must advance rapidly and seize these harbors, Zhou said. To hold Seoul, the North Koreans had to build powerful defenses in the Inchon area where US forces might land. Will Japan enter the war? Roshchin asked Zhou. China had no intelligence reports that Japan was in any condition to enter the fighting, Zhou replied. If the Americans cross the 38th parallel, he said, China would send volunteers, perhaps disguised as Koreans, to stop them. Three Chinese armies, a total of 120,000 troops, were already assembled in the Mukden area, Zhou stated. (This assertion was untrue. It was probably meant to keep China in the unfolding strategic game.) Zhou wanted Roshchin to inquire if the Soviet Union could provide air cover for the Chinese troops. The North Koreans had underestimated the possibility of US intervention, Zhou said; Mao had warned them about US intervention in May of 1949 and again this May.[94]

THE KPA'S ONSLAUGHT AND THE US RESPONSE

Caught off guard by the US intervention, Kim Il Sung was confused. Shty-kov met him and DPRK Vice-Premier Pak Hon-yong on July 3. Kim was very worried about the slow pace of the KPA advance, complaining that although Defense Minister Choe Yong-gon had personally directed the Han River crossing, the operation was disorganized. Fearful that US forces would land behind the KPA or at a harbor in North Korea, endangering frontline units and liberated areas, Kim asked for swift delivery of weapons and am-munition from the Soviet Union in order to organize two new infantry divi-sions, i.e., twelve battalions. Kim sought Shtykov's advice on how to strengthen the North's military leadership because the KPA would be fight-ing against US forces. Shtykov and Soviet Chief Military Adviser N. A. Vasil'ev suggested changes in the command structure. The DPRK, they ad-vised, should (1) form two Army Groups each comprised of four to six divisions; (2) reorganize the General Staff Headquarters into a Frontline Headquarters; (3) retain the Ministry of National Defense and put it in charge of supply, training, and coastal defense; (4) designate Kim Il Sung supreme commander; and (5) shift senior officers to other positions. On this last point, they said Deputy Minister for Artillery Mu Chong should become command-er of the Left Wing Group; Vice-Chief of Staff Kim Ung should become commander of the Right Wing Group; Vice-Premier and Minister of Industry Kim Chaek should become frontline commander; and Chief of Staff Kang Kon should move to frontline command chief of staff. But Choe Yong-gon should be retained as defense minister.

North Korean leaders had prepared their wartime military organization before the start of the North's military actions against the South, but they were obliged to reorganize it in haste according to Soviet guidance after US intervention became apparent. Accepting the Soviet plan, Kim and Pak told Shtykov that a meeting of the Military Committee would be held tomorrow or the day after. Shtykov expected the Frontline Headquarters to move to Seoul and requested permission for Vasil'ev to go there.[95]

The North's reorganization was announced on July 4.[96] Both Army Group commanders were from the Yan'an group. Mu Chong (born 1905) had studied at the Chungang high school in Seoul, gone to China in 1925, and entered the artillery course at the Chinese Northern Military Academy. Mu joined the Chinese Communist Party two years later, served as a senior artillery officer in Peng Dehuai's 5th Army, and participated in the Long March. He was a founding member in 1942 of the Korean Independence League, and in 1945 of the Korean Volunteers Army (KVA). Mu led the KVA from Yan'an to Mukden. Ordered to return to North Korea, he immedi-ately joined the Korean Communist Party (North Korean Bureau) and was appointed chief of the cadre section. Mu was unsuited to Party work, howev-

er, and switched back to the military; he was named KPA artillery commander.[97] But Mu had never commanded a large unit in the Chinese civil war,
fueling doubts about his ability.

By contrast, Kim Ung (born 1912) was a real soldier who had studied
from 1933 to 1937 at the Huangpo Military Academy in China and later at
the Anti-Japanese Military-Political College in Yan'an. He too had joined the
CCP. Kim had commanded the 1st Unit of the Korean Volunteer Corps.
Later he served in the New 4th Army, fought against the Japanese, and
became the highest ranking Korean in the unit. After the Northeast Korean
Volunteer Army was formed in 1945, Kim commanded the 1st Detachment.
Pang Ho-san was the detachment's political commissar. Kim fought in Manchuria in the Chinese civil war and returned to Korea about the same time as
Kang Kon. He was involved in formation of the KPA and served as chief of
the Combat Training Bureau, Ministry of National Defense, and later as vice-
minister.[98] Kim seems to have been a better soldier than Mu.

Stalin denied Ambassador Shtykov's request that Vasil'ev move to Seoul.
Soviet forces were not to become directly involved in the fighting, Stalin
ordered.[99] The uneasy Soviet leader wrote to Ambassador Roshchin applaud-
ing China's plan. Stalin knew that Zhou Enlai had claimed to have assembled
nine divisions near the Sino-Korean border in order to send volunteers to
North Korea in the event that enemy forces crossed the 38th parallel. Stalin
promised "to try to provide air support for the [Chinese] units."[100]

On July 7, the Chinese Communist Party's Military Committee decided to
create a Northeast Border Defense Army (NEBDA) from the 38th, 39th, and
40th armies of the 13th Army Group under the Fourth Field Army. Deng
Hua, commander of the 15th Army Group, who had led the operation to
liberate Hainan Island, was named to lead the new force. Mao approved these
decisions.[101]

On July 8, Kim Il Sung again asked Stalin to authorize twenty-five to
thirty-five Soviet military advisers to serve with the KPA Frontline Headquarters and the headquarters of the two Army Groups.[102] Stalin's reply is
unknown. But on July 13, Stalin informed Chinese leaders of a British proposal for a peaceful resolution of the Korean problem if North Korean forces
withdrew to the 38th parallel. Stalin intended to make a counterproposal that
Chinese and North Korean representatives be added to the UN Security
Council to debate the issue. He wondered what Mao thought of the idea. On
the military situation, Stalin told the Chinese leaders: "We do not know if
you have decided to deploy nine divisions at the Korean border. If you have
made such a decision, we are prepared to send an air division of 124 jet
fighters to provide air cover for those units."[103] The same day, Stalin directed
Shtykov to ask Kim Il Sung's view on his proposed response to the British
proposal. Kim expressed full agreement with Stalin's strategy on July 14.[104]

As the KPA pushed ahead despite US intervention in the fighting, southern refugees fled southward, children on their backs and meager possessions in hand. Retreating South Korean police murdered leftist political prisoners.

On July 20, the KPA shattered the US 24th Division and captured Taejon, capital of South Chungchong province in the South. Gen. William Dean was missing for several days and taken prisoner by the KPA.[105] In a three-day period, South Korean military and police murdered about 1,800 political prisoners in Taejon Prison, an atrocity that only came fully to light in January 2000 in declassified US Army documents.[106]

Advance elements of the US 1st Cavalry Division landed at Pohang on July 18. The 5th Cavalry Regiment reached Yongdong south of Taejon the day the city fell and was assigned to defend the highway from Taejon to block the North Korean advance. After fierce fighting on July 25, Yongdong was abandoned. A total of 39,000 US troops were now in Korea, yet the North Koreans pushed ahead.[107]

According to the official US Army history, Roy E. Appleman's *South to the Naktong, North to the Yalu* (1992), "The large numbers of Korean refugees crowding the Yongdong area undoubtedly helped the enemy infiltrate the 1st Cavalry Division positions." Appleman writes of an apparently pregnant woman who was discovered to be carrying a small radio and using it to aid the northern army. The "Eighth Army tried to control the refugee movement through the Korean police, permitting it only during daylight hours and along predetermined routes," Appleman recounts.[108] From July 26 to 29, US troops who regarded refugees as enemy soldiers in mufti killed about one hundred people who had taken shelter in a railroad tunnel at Nogulli, twenty kilometers east of Yongdong. The North Korean newspaper *Choson Inminpo* first reported the killings on August 10, 1950; the incident became a cause celebre in South Korea in 1999 when the Associated Press exposed the massacre.[109]

The Rhee government meanwhile fled farther south, pursued by the KPA. On July 26, the 3rd Battalion of the US Army's 29th Regiment, assigned to defend Chinju, was destroyed in a KPA ambush. Former ROKA Chief of Staff Chae Pyong-dok, who was with the regiment, was killed in the attack.[110]

Senior KPA officers were also killed in the push south. On July 30, Choe Chun-guk, who had replaced Chon U in early July as commander of the KPA's 12th Division, was killed by a landmine. KPA Frontline Command Chief of Staff Kang Kon was also killed by a landmine on the bank of the Naktong River shortly after the capture of Taejon. Kang had earlier joined the Northeast Anti-Japanese Allied Army and distinguished himself in combat in the Chinese civil war. His death was kept secret until early September when Yu Song-chol was named acting chief of staff. He reportedly held the position about a month.[111] Yu, a Soviet Korean, had been assigned to the

Intelligence Bureau of the Soviet Union's Far East Army during World War II, and when the Northeast Anti-Japanese Allied Army had fled to the Soviet Union and was reorganized into the 88th Special Brigade, he had been attached to it as Kim Il Sung's interpreter.[112] In North Korea he served as chief of the Operations Bureau of the DPRK's Ministry of National Defense. Lacking combat experience, Yu's real function as acting KPA chief of staff was probably to interpret between Kim Il Sung and Soviet Chief Military Adviser N. A. Vasil'ev.

At the start of the North's offensive against the South, the North Korean Air Force had 132 combat aircraft, and its pilots bombed southern targets, including Seoul. Though US attacks destroyed many North Korean planes on the ground, DPRK pilots dueled with Americans in the skies over Korea in mid-July. However, in attacks and clashes from July 18 to 20, US pilots decimated the DPRK air force. Thus established from the get-go, US air supremacy became a decisive factor in the war.[113]

On July 24, General MacArthur announced the establishment of a United Nations Command for UN actions in Korea, with its headquarters in Tokyo.[114] Three days later, Australia dispatched an artillery battalion to Korea from its forces in Japan.[115] The same day, Soviet representative to the UN Jacob Malik informed UN Secretary General Trygve Lie that he would return to the Security Council within five days, which he did on August 1. Formation of the UN Command was a serious setback for the Communist bloc.

Also in late July, the KPA 6th Division led by Pang Ho-san, which had earlier occupied Kwangju in South Cholla Province, broke through to Chinju from the southern side of the Chiri mountains and pushed to the north of Masan. In early August, the KPA's 4th Division, led by Yi Kwon-mu, was west of Yongsan in the Naktong River area. Pang and Yi were both in the forefront of the KPA drive southward. They were from Manchuria and had been sent by the Chinese Communists to study at the Communist University for Toilers of the East in Moscow. Back in China, they had then worked in the Korean group of the research section of the Overseas Committee of the CCP's Central Committee in Yan'an.[116]

As the KPA's 6th and 4th Divisions were moving south, the KPA's 3rd, 10th, 2nd, and 15th Divisions were deployed west of Taegu, while the 13th, 1st, 8th, 12th, and 5th Divisions were strung out on a line from Sangju to Yongdok.[117] The novelist Kim Sa-ryang was with troops of the 6th Division on Mt. Sobuk within shouting distance of Masan. "I can see the ocean," he wrote. "I can see Koje Island. This is the South Sea."[118] Unification must have seemed so close.

On August 3, the US Air Force started an interdiction campaign to cut KPA supply lines, targeting major railway switching yards and forty-four rail and highway bridges. Raids on August 3 and 4, which included planes dispatched from Yokota Air Base near Tokyo, rained bombs on the Seoul marshaling yards. Then, on August 7, B-29s from Yokota and Kadena, Okinawa, attacked the marshaling yards up in Pyongyang. On August 10, the refinery and marshaling yards in Wonsan were struck. Over a month and a half, 1,761 tons of bombs were dropped on a petrochemical complex in Hungnam. These raids destroyed an enormous number of supplies in North Korea's transportation centers. Thirty-seven bridges were knocked out between August 12 and September 4. By the end of August, the FEAF Bomber Command reported that 140 bridges between Seoul and the front lines were impassable. Roy Appleman evaluated the August bombing raids as the most effective of the air offensives that influenced the outcome of the war.[119]

KPA units tried to avoid the bombing by moving supplies at night. In August the US Air Force thus began night attacks, which proved ineffective, as the KPA continued to advance.[120]

On the ground, the KPA drive toward Pusan was a spectacular success. Yet Chinese leaders in Beijing were concerned about the next phase of the war. At a meeting on August 6 of the CCP Politburo, Mao apparently said that the United States might use atomic bombs in Korea, but that China must be unafraid and prepare for war.[121] The next day new orders were issued to Nie Rongzhen, acting PLA chief of staff. Nie later wrote in his memoirs: "U.S. imperialism never makes failure with easy mind. The Americans had naval and air superiority. They could counterattack. The KPA forces were in isolated advanced positions and had few reserves. The military situation in Korea was susceptible to complications and reverses. On August 5, based on decisions of the Central Military Commission, I ordered the Strategic Reserve to 'complete all preparations this month and wait for operational orders.'"[122]

On August 13, China's NEBDA staff held the first joint Chinese military conference on intervention in Korea. The generals in attendance held that China possessed numerical and qualitative superiority over the United Nations in ground forces and supply capability, and had a more just cause. As for America's atomic weapons, they concluded: (1) victory in war was decided by men, not one or two atomic bombs; (2) the use of nuclear weapons on the battlefield would cause casualties not only to the Chinese but to the Americans as well; and (3) the United States could not ignore worldwide opposition to nuclear weapons.[123] Despite these confident assertions, US atomic weapons remained very worrisome to the Chinese.

On August 18, Nie gave Deng Hua, commander of the NEBDA, until September 30 to complete preparations for Chinese ground participation in the war. Presumably Mao was optimistic about the conflict at the time.[124] On August 19, Mao discussed with Soviet philosopher P. F. Iudin the two options he thought were available to the United States: fight at present troop levels and be forced to withdraw from Korea or persist regardless of casualties and commit another thirty to forty divisions. In the latter scenario, North

Korea could not withstand the enemy by itself and would need Chinese assistance. But if China provided help, Mao told Iudin, US forces would be defeated, postponing World War III.[125] Mao apparently thought an intensive international propaganda campaign could foreclose the second US option.

THE NORTH KOREAN OCCUPATION

North Korea recruited "volunteers" for military service in the occupied areas of the South. In Seoul on July 3, 16,000 students were assembled at the Kumhwa elementary school and marched through the streets with banners that said, "Let's Volunteer for the Front." After the demonstration, "patriotic" students participating in rallies at Tongdaemun (East Big Gate) and Kwanghamun resolved to join the volunteers. On July 6, the Korean Workers' Party announced conscription of so-called volunteers: each prefecture in South Korea was assigned a quota for males eighteen years of age and older. A headline in the North's *Minju Choson* newspaper on July 10 proclaimed, "Young Men in Liberated Areas to the Front! Volunteers Rush to Serve." The article described a big rally of 3,000 students from more than twenty high schools and colleges in Seoul which was held on July 6 to "exterminate U.S. imperialism."[126] A CIA report also noted the volunteers' enthusiasm.[127] Stirred by skillful appeals, many idealistic students enlisted on the spot and left for the battlefield without a word to their parents. Of course, psychological pressure was organized by Communists behind the scenes.[128]

People's Committees were elected and land reform implemented swiftly in the liberated areas. On July 4, the Standing Committee of the DPRK's Supreme People's Assembly, acting in accordance with Article 7 of the DPRK constitution, extended land reform—whereby land was confiscated without compensation and redistributed without payment—to the South. As was done in North Korea in 1946, all tenant land would be confiscated and distributed to farm laborers, landless farmers, and tenants. The People's Committees would hold meetings in every village to decide how to implement the reform and elect village committees. Higher-level People's Committees had to ratify their actions.[129] Swift implementation was ordered. Land transfers were to be completed in Kyonggi, South Kangwon, and Hwanghae Provinces by August 20 and then started in Cholla and Kyongsang Provinces. In South Kangwon Province, a mass meeting of farmers was held in late July, and land reform was completed in Kyonggi Province by early August.[130]

A directive from the Standing Committee of the DPRK's Supreme People's Assembly on July 14 called for election of People's Committees in every county, township, and village of South Korea.[131] Province-level committees were comprised mainly of people chosen in an underground election in 1948. Elections for People's Committees in thirteen counties of Kyonggi Province and ten counties of South Kangwon Province were completed by late August and held in all districts of South Cholla Province by early September.[132]

On August 18, North Korea also extended its labor law to the South. When the North was liberated by "the great military power of the Soviet Union," the announcement for the extension said that workers had received an eight-hour workday and compulsory social insurance, which would now be implemented in the South. In addition, key North Korean officials were appointed to administer equitable collection of taxes-in-kind on agricultural crops in the South.[133]

Expansion of the DPRK's economic and social framework to the South left the approximately sixty ROK National Assembly members who had remained in Seoul no scope for independent political activity. What's more, the northern authorities called on them to make radio addresses. Kim Song-chil, an associate professor at Seoul National University, recounted:

> They could not speak freely. Kim Hyo-sok, former Minister of Home Affairs, was too obsequious and articulately disingenuous. By comparison, however, the remarks by neutrals like An Chae-hong, Cho So-ang, and others proved to be agreeable to me. They disparaged the ROK less and curried favor with the DPRK less than Kim Hyo-sok. Perhaps the problem was their individual personalities, but I had thought their positions as neutrals was honorable. . . . Dr. Kim Kyu-sik spoke in a stern tone. . . . He seemed to be profoundly disappointed. I was deeply moved.[134]

Venerable veteran of the Korean nationalist movement Kim Kyu-sik appeared on the radio on July 16. In humble opening comments, he described himself as a person with no talent who had striven for Korean independence and freedom. He and others had refused to participate in the unilateral 1948 election in the South and opposed the establishment of the Republic of Korea under Syngman Rhee, he said, because the election and the ROK's establishment were "not only illegal and totally disregarded the aspirations and interests of the Korean people but also hardened the division of the nation at the 38th parallel." The Rhee regime, under the US-ROK agreement, had sold out Korean interests, he said, imprisoned and killed patriots, and engaged in political terrorism. They were "enemies of the nation and people." Kim criticized the United States for arrogant "military intervention in another country's civil conflict and bombing innocent people" in the name of the United Nations. "We must appeal to international justice to stop this illegal foreign military intervention immediately and remove all foreign troops, and we must hold elections across Korea on the principles of unification of the fatherland and democracy and establish a completely independent, unified government," Kim said.[135]

At a public rally in late July, forty-eight ROK National Assembly members declared their support for the DPRK. According to Bruce Cumings, assemblymen Kim Yong-mu, Won Se-hun, Paek Sang-gyu, Chang Kon-sang, Cho So-ang, Kim Kyu-sik, and An Chae-hong participated in the rally.[136]

On August 14, the Fatherland Unification Democratic Front, the front group created by the North, appealed for signatures to a "Declaration of the Korean People" to drive US forces out of Korea and "put traitors who aided the United States on trial by People's Courts."[137] The campaign was conducted in the South, too, and well-known intellectuals signed the declaration. On August 23, the *Haebang Ilbo*, a newspaper published by the North during its occupation of Seoul, carried a photograph of Kim Kyu-sik, Cho So-ang, An Chae-hong, and others signing the appeal. Kim Kyu-sik again reportedly condemned the US invaders who had unilaterally intervened militarily in an internal dispute among Koreans, demanded that Syngman Rhee—instigator of a civil war and traitor—be put on trial in the name of the people, and proposed a mass meeting of representatives of all groups in the South to censure Rhee and other traitors. An Chae-hong reportedly blamed foreign interference for the loss of life and destruction of national facilities in Korea, and said, "Syngman Rhee and his supporters-traitors must face the people's judgment."[138] It is doubtful that Kim and An wrote such speeches by themselves; their statements show the North's control of political life in the South. There was simply no place in the liberated South for anti-Rhee, non-Communist politicians.

THE KPA HITS THE WALL

The ROK government celebrated August 15 (Liberation Day) in the temporary capital of Taegu, then fled to Pusan two days later.[139] US and ROKA forces meanwhile withdrew to east of the Naktong River and set up a final defense line. The US 25th, 24th, and 1st Cavalry Divisions, as well as the 2nd Division, which had recently arrived from the United States, along with the ROKA's 1st, 6th, 8th, Capital, and 3rd Divisions, established the line.[140] US air attacks were then intensifying, with B-29 carpet bombing of North Korean positions. In a thirty-minute period on August 16, B-29s from the Yokota and Kadena Air Bases dropped 3,084 five-hundred-pound bombs and 150 one-thousand-pound bombs on KPA forces in the Waegwan area.[141] The *Asahi Shimbun* in Japan ran the headline "Furious B-29 attack on Waegwan area," and reported that ninety-nine B-29 bombers dropped 850 tons of five-hundred-pound bombs; planes came from "a base in Okinawa" and from another base in Japan.[142] Censors blocked mention of use of Yokota Air Base near Tokyo.

US and ROKA forces were increased and reequipped during the battle for Taegu. In August, combined Allied forces totaled 141,808 men. On September 1, Allied strength was 86,655 US forces, 91,696 ROKA forces, and 1,578 British forces, for a total of 179,929.[143] US tanks exceeded KPA tanks by five to one.[144]

Outnumbered and without air cover, the KPA could not break through the US-ROKA defenses at the Naktong River, which held for a month. At the end of August, the Communist camp was becoming pessimistic. Mao told Pavel Iudin that the United States had increased its forces in Korea and that the second scenario he'd mentioned—which involved intervention by Chinese forces—could not be excluded.[145] PLA commander Deng Hua also submitted a pessimistic analysis of the Korean situation on August 31. The Korean Peninsula was long, narrow, and mountainous, Deng observed, limiting the attainment of numerical superiority. "We would operate on interior lines with a strategy of attacking with our main force, but three sides of [the battlefield] are surrounded by ocean and the enemy has air and sea superiority and could attack at our weak points. If the enemy lands on our flank and rear, he will have the advantage of exterior lines. . . . The enemy will leave a small force in place . . . to battle the KPA and land its main force on the flank (the Pyongyang or Seoul area) in a major amphibious operation and attack the KPA from the front and rear. In this case, the KPA would be in an extremely difficult position."[146]

Kim Il Sung was the most apprehensive. On August 25 he told Soviet Ambassador Shtykov that two US divisions had arrived in South Korea, that all KPA divisions had been committed to the North's offensive, and that an enemy counterattack could not be stopped. Shtykov said that several KPA divisions should be withdrawn from the front and brought up to full strength with replacements and equipment. Kim Chaek, KPA frontline commander, had ignored instructions to withdraw, Kim Il Sung said tearfully, bemoaning how difficult his job had become:

> There is no one to consult with. The vice-premiers are no help. Cabinet ministers are doing a poor job. . . . I trusted Pak Hon-yong, but Pak was not up to the tasks and could not handle problems himself. When I assigned something to him, Pak immediately delegated it to subordinates. When I tried to discuss a difficult issue, Pak always agreed and never expressed his own opinion.

Shtykov reported to Moscow:

> Some of the North Korean leadership who expected an easy victory are confused, starting to lose confidence in their own [North Korea's] capability, and fear the war will be prolonged. In an attempt to evade responsibility they do not exert leadership and just follow Kim Il Sung's orders. Kim Il Sung and Pak Hon-yong disagree sharply on the situation in the South. Kim criticized Pak,

saying there is no Workers' Party organization in the south, many former members have betrayed the cause, and despite appeals to rise up and help the KPA, the partisans do nothing. . . . Kim is generally correct, but does not acknowledge the severe terror and violence in the South and that the best Workers' Party activists were killed or arrested. Pak feels responsible for the situation in the South and has begun to waver a bit. . . . Kim has thrown himself completely into the task. He is concentrating on military matters and has postponed urgent public welfare measures. One senses in his work style a lack of experience and maturity. We are trying to support him as far as possible on everything. I request permission to urge Pak discreetly to become more engaged and exert leadership. [147]

On August 28, the same day Shtykov sent this message, Stalin directed the ambassador to relay his congratulations, in the name of the Central Committee of the CPSU, to Kim Il Sung on his conduct of the war. The message was to be delivered verbally unless the North Korean side asked for it in written form, in which case Stalin's name was to be removed. Stalin understood Kim's emotional state and tried to encourage him. The message began: "The Central Committee, All Union Communist Party, send Congratulations to Comrade Kim Il Sung and his friends on the brilliant success of the Korean people in their great war of liberation. The Committee is confident those interfering [in Korea] will soon be forced into an ignominious retreat from Korea."

Stalin said that Kim should not be unduly worried about military setbacks. There had been defeats in the Russian civil war and the war against Germany, Stalin pointed out. He praised North Korea for being the standard bearer of the Asian anti-imperialist liberation movement, whose military forces would learn from the North Koreans how to strike decisive blows against the imperialists. [148]

After getting Shtykov's okay, a deeply grateful Kim Il Sung asked permission to read the cable to Pak Hon-yong and to inform the Political Committee of the Central Committee of the KWP about it. Some members of the Political Committee had a bad attitude, Kim had told Shtykov; reporting the congratulatory message would be helpful. [149] On August 31, the Political Committee endorsed Kim's wish to express their appreciation to Stalin: "We are totally committed to a final victory over the American interventionists who are again trying to enslave Korea. We are very grateful for your constant fatherly concern and assistance in this noble struggle for independence and freedom." [150]

Mao's military advice to DPRK representatives from August to early September is recounted in a report to Moscow by Soviet Ambassador to China Nikolai Roshchin on September 3. [151] Mao told the North Koreans about his analysis of the two options he thought were available to the United States and said that the enemy was most likely to adopt the second option:

increase its forces by thirty or forty divisions. The North should create a strong reserve force and prepare defenses at two potential amphibious landing sites: Inchon-Seoul and Chinnampo-Pyongyang, Mao advised. The KPA had mistakenly committed all its forces to the offensive and hurriedly liberated territory rather than destroying enemy forces, Mao said. The KPA had already been stalled in one area for more than a month. Mao asked the North Koreans to consider a swift withdrawal in order to reorganize their forces and prepare new battle lines.

THE JAPANESE FOREIGN MINISTRY AND THE PEACE PROBLEMS DISCUSSION GROUP

On August 19, with Communist forces threatening Pusan, the Japanese Foreign Ministry issued a statement entitled "Japan's Position on the Korean War." The timing reflected the sense of crisis in Tokyo over the military situation in Korea. To stand idly by as North Korean Communist forces invaded the South "would be suicidal for democracy," the ministry warned. The United States "had stood up to military power with military power in defense of world peace and democracy" and an "international alliance had taken effective measures." The power struggle between the two worlds, the Communist and Free worlds, was accompanied by an ideological struggle, the Japanese Foreign Ministry noted, and "as part of the democratic world, Japanese were already in the battle." Ambiguity would aid the Communist camp and be "equivalent to fleeing the battlefield before the enemy." The war showed that Japan's security could not be jointly guaranteed by the Communist and Free worlds, the ministry observed. The stark choice was to surrender to the Communists or to cooperate with the United Nations: "The battle for democracy in Korea is a battle to protect Japan's democracy. If Japan does not cooperate with the international alliance to the fullest extent permitted, how would its security be safeguarded?"[152]

Although the rhetoric of cooperation with the UN in Japan had escalated from "spiritual cooperation" or "cooperation to the extent possible" to "cooperation to the fullest extent permitted," there was still no concrete indication of what Japan was doing, or would do in the future. The lack of clarity was consistent with basic government policy.

On August 29, Premier Yoshida Shigeru secretly wrote to SCAP Douglas MacArthur. "Let me assure you that the Japanese government and people are ever ready and anxious to furnish whatever facilities and services that you may require. I only regret that we cannot do more by way of cooperating with the U.N. in its Crusade against Communist aggression."[153] In short, Japan would comply with any order by SCAP for facilities and labor, but regretfully could not go beyond that.

Katsumata Seiichi, chairman of the Japan Socialist Party's Policy Council, told a newspaper reporter that the Foreign Ministry's statement on Japan's position on the war was one-sided in three respects. First, it "totally ignored the fact that the world was now desperately trying to maintain peace through the United Nations." Second, "reaction and fascism cause war," Katsumata said, and the "Yoshida Cabinet has not reflected in the slightest on their own roles in encouraging this tendency." Third, the "freedom" in the ministry's statement "benefited the capitalist class and was not the 'freedom' sought by the working class." But the stance of the Socialist Party's left wing, as reflected in Katsumata's remarks, was purely ideological and unrealistic.

Party Secretary Asanuma Inejiro, leader of the JSP's right wing, held a press conference on August 20 during a speaking tour in Kyushu. "The position of the Socialist Party on Korea is that we condemn the invasion by armed force and we support in spirit the maintenance of law and order by the United Nations," he said. "The government position paper divides the world into two [camps] and says Japan should be part of one. The government is fanning jingoistic sentiment among the people, a sign of its enthusiasm to get involved in an international dispute."[154]

Thus, while the Foreign Ministry's statement dismissed neutrality and advocated cooperation with UN forces, but was silent on what Japan was actually doing, Asanuma supported UN forces but opposed Japan's involvement in the conflict. Both were essentially consistent with Yoshida's position.

Meanwhile, a group of Japanese intellectuals was preparing a famous statement calling for peaceful coexistence between the United States and the Soviet Union, and a peaceful and neutral Japan. In the spring of 1948, over two years earlier, eight social scientists from the East and West had met under the aegis of UNESCO and issued a call for peace. Japanese social scientists, persuaded by Yoshino Genzaburo, editor in chief of the magazine *Sekai*, responded with a joint statement published in 1949 in the magazine. This was the origin of the Peace Problems Discussion Group in Japan, which published its first commentary on the post–World War II peace settlement in the March 1950 issue of *Sekai*. The group sought a settlement with all belligerents (including the Soviet Union and China); called for Japan's security to be based on neutrality, nonaggression, and UN membership; and opposed granting any country military bases in Japan. Article 9 of the Japanese Constitution, stipulating renunciation of war and nonpossession of war potentials were strongly endorsed. The key person behind the group's statement was Shimizu Ikutaro, a radical professor; the signers included such respected conservatives as Abe Yoshishige, Amano Teiyu, Watsuji Tetsuro, and Ryu Shintaro. Some Communists were also involved.[155]

The Peace Problems Discussion Group met again in August and drafted another statement in September, "A Third Peace Proposal," that appeared in the December issue of *Sekai*. Shimizu and the liberal professors Maruyama Masao, Tsuru Shigeto, and Ukai Nobushige played important roles in drafting this statement.[156] Although prepared during the KPA onslaught on South Korea, the statement made no reference to the Korean War except for praising Indian diplomacy that sought a negotiated resolution and expressing doubts about how to deal with the conflict, or to an appropriate outcome. Peace was discussed in abstract terms, i.e., "War . . . is the worst evil on earth." Avoiding a showdown between the United States and the Soviet Union was crucial, the statement argued. Coexistence between the Communist and non-Communist worlds had to be the highest priority for those concerned with peace and a mission for the United Nations. Peaceful coexistence might lead to the convergence or fusion of the two systems, the authors maintained. Their major concern was a US-Soviet nuclear war.[157] They optimistically believed that the Korean War would not escalate to a US-Soviet conflict, a perspective they shared with Premier Yoshida.

The drafters of the statement essentially detached themselves from the immediate reality of the hot war in Korea just across the Tsushima Straits to address a more fundamental global reality—the Cold War. They focused on future possibilities to criticize current realities, a form of utopianism. Rooted in the new Japanese Constitution's renunciation of war and hopes for "permanent peace," the statement advocated neutrality between the two worlds and entrusted Japan's security completely to the United Nations. But their United Nations was an idealized organization, not the actual world body waging war to achieve peace and unification for Korea.[158] They repeatedly insisted on the Japanese constitutional ban on military forces and endorsed police power for the United Nations. Uncompromising utopian pacifism was a central thread of their statement.

This peace manifesto was intrinsically limited and could not affect realpolitik. But it was a good fit for the left wing of the Japanese Socialist Party and its political base, Sohyo (The General Federation of Trade Unions). Never a "conceptual basis of the Japanese state,"[159] utopian pacifism was the ideological raison d'etre of opposition political parties in Japan at the time.

Part of the electorate passionately supported the Socialists on pacifism, though, and many intellectuals agreed with the Peace Problems Discussion Group. While the Yoshida administration trumpeted spiritual cooperation with the UN and secretly provided human and material assistance to SCAP, it never sought public endorsement of this policy. For the suffering of World War II had generated intense antipathy to war and the military in Japan, and though Japan could not stay completely out of the Korean War, the same popular sentiment that condemned involvement in any conflict and embraced pacifism shaped Yoshida's strategy. The public could enjoy the economic boom brought by this invisible war as it was "happening across the river."

THE INCHON LANDING

With its supply lines virtually destroyed, and its forces under attack from the air by the United States Air Force day and night, the KPA had to win quickly or it never would. On Kim Il Sung's orders, the KPA launched a final offensive to break through the US-ROKA Naktong River defense line. The 1st Army Group struck on August 31, and the 2nd Army Group two days later. Under furious attack, the US 2nd and 25th Divisions called in air power. On September 1, 5th Air Force fighter-bombers flew 167 close-support sorties. On September 2, twenty-five B-29s bombed Kumchon, Kochang, and Chinju; a total of three hundred sorties were flown in support of the two US divisions, which held their positions.[160]

From September 4 to 6, the 5th Air Force flew 394 sorties in support of ROKA units fighting the KPA east of Taegu, and South Korean troops counterattacked the KPA on September 6. Five days later, US planes flew 683 sorties against KPA troops in the Waegwan area. The next day the North Koreans retreated in despair; the KPA's final two-week offensive had ended in failure. So did their hope of unification. According to Robert Futrell, "The momentum of the Communist attacks was spent by 12 September, and the enemy was falling back in the face of counterattacking Eighth Army forces. Looking backward at the successful accomplishment of the Eighth Army's magnificent defensive effort, General Walker had nothing but praise for the air support which the Fifth Air Force had provided to the Eighth Army."[161]

Meanwhile, in Tokyo, General MacArthur, following conventional counterattack strategy, had been planning an amphibious landing behind enemy lines at the southern port city of Inchon since early July.[162] The Chinese had cautioned North Korean leaders against the possibility of such encirclement; Kim Il Sung too worried about a US landing behind his main forces.

The US Defense Department approved MacArthur's plan on August 21. The remaining US forces in Japan had already begun preparations. The main US troops that would be involved in the assault were the 1st Marine Division, which had arrived in Japan on August 10, and the 7th Infantry Division.[163] The Japanese ports of Kobe, Sasebo, and Yokohama would be the chief staging areas for the attack. The 1st Marine Division would ship out from Kobe, and the 7th Infantry Division would ship from Yokohama. The 5th Marine Regiment would leave from Pusan; artillery and support units would sail from Sasebo. The landing was set for September 15, with departure from Japan on September 10. But Typhoon Jane delayed the sailings by a day.

Of the forty-seven LSTs (landing ship tanks) that carried marine units in the Inchon landing, thirty-seven had Japanese crews.[164] These World War II–vintage vessels had been transferred to Japan's merchant marines.[165] On orders from the Commercial Maritime Committee, Japanese crews transported 79 percent of the US Marine landing force at Inchon.[166] Familiar with the long shallow harbor, they steered the LSTs to shore in Japan's biggest direct participation in the Korean War.

The United States assembled a total of 260 vessels and 75,000 men off Inchon. The first assault wave landed on Wolmi Island before dawn on September 15. A second wave waited until high tide in the evening and then landed at another beach. The attacking US forces shattered the KPA's defenses and advanced toward Seoul. On September 22, Premier Yoshida congratulated MacArthur on the "bold stroke in your strategy," which "has changed overnight the whole picture of the Korean situation" and brightened "the prospect of an early restoration of peace to the peninsula."[167]

On September 16, Joseph Stalin told N. A. Vasil'ev and Terentii Shtykov that the objective of the amphibious landing was to cut off the KPA from North Korea. Stalin said that at least four KPA divisions should be withdrawn from their positions immediately to establish a battle line east and north of Seoul, enabling the remainder of the KPA to withdraw and hold at the 38th parallel.[168]

On September 18, Chinese Premier Zhou Enlai queried Ambassador Roshchin and Soviet military advisers P. M. Kotov and I. P. Konnov about the US landing at Inchon. Their only sources of information were newspaper reports and Radio Pyongyang, the ambassador and the advisers said. Complaining that the North had ignored Mao's advice to create a strong reserve force and prepare a defense at Inchon, Zhou said that if the North had 100,000 reserve troops in the Seoul and Pyongyang areas, they could crush the US landing force. But if there were no reserves, the main KPA units should be withdrawn northward to a defense line, where they should stop the Americans and then separate the US divisions and destroy them one by one. A new attack corps should be organized, Zhou further advised, concealed, and then prepared for the decisive battle. The United States, Great Britain, and France were worried that the Soviet Union and China might enter the war in Korea, Zhou said. The West could not fight a long war; the Communists must take advantage of that fear and show that they will intervene. Chinese forces had been assembled in Manchuria to intimidate the Americans and British, Zhou indicated.[169]

The same day in Pyongyang, Kim Il Sung told Chinese Ambassador to the DPRK Ni Zhiliang that North Korea was preparing for a long war. After reading a report of the conversation, Zhou got Mao's approval to advise Kim Il Sung on the war through the ambassador, and on September 20 he laid out his views on the need for a protracted war.[170] Also on September 20, Stalin instructed Soviet Ambassador to China Roshchin to inform Zhou that North Korea's "abnormal" failure to inform China of the war situation stemmed not from unwillingness by Kim Il Sung but from the breakdown in communications with the front lines.[171] Stalin attributed North Korea's defeat at Inchon to the presence of US and British troops with ROKA units, and stated that he had urged North Korea to withdraw its main forces and establish strong positions east and north of Seoul. On September 21 Roshchin gave a telegram expressing this view to Zhou, who said that China and the Soviet Union were in complete agreement on strategy. He had sent a similar message to Pyongyang two days earlier.[172]

On September 20, the US troops from the Inchon landing crossed the Han River and launched an attack to retake Seoul. At this critical moment, Stalin made a bold decision: he ordered the Soviet General Staff to send a fighter aviation regiment to Pyongyang as soon as possible. The next day, Soviet Defense Minister A. M. Vasilevsky recommended the 34th Fighter Aviation Regiment of the 147th Fighter Aviation Division (forty Yak-9s) for the mission. Two days later, Vasilevsky changed the recommendation to the 304th Fighter Aviation Regiment of the 32nd Fighter Aviation Division (forty LA-9s).[173]

Soviet philosopher Pavel Iudin met Mao Zedong on September 22 and reported the conversation to Moscow. According to Iudin, Mao noted that Great Britain stood with the Truman administration in Korea, but had recognized the People's Republic of China and would not support a US invasion of China. America could not fight a protracted, large-scale war in Korea, Mao told Iudin, which would be a test of strength; Washington would judge the Sino-Soviet response and perhaps then compromise. At that point, China would probably be allowed to enter the United Nations, Mao believed. But as long as Beijing was kept out of the world body, it would challenge US imperialism in Asia. Although UN membership might be given to China as a "dog collar," Mao said, it would be valuable.[174] The chairman was still optimistic.

Yet the war was going badly for the Communist side. Stalin sent a military mission to Pyongyang led by Gen. Matvei Vasil'evich Zakharov, deputy chief of the General Staff. Zakharov had been chief of staff in the 2nd Ukraine Front Army at the end of World War II and chief of staff for R. I. Malinovskii's Zabaikal Front Army in the fighting against Japanese forces in August 1945. In his first report from North Korea on September 26, Zakharov said that KPA units in the Seoul and Pusan areas were at great risk. The US landing force at Inchon and units attacking northwest of Taegu were moving toward Chungju to surround and destroy the KPA main force. The United States had total air superiority, Zakharov noted; KPA personnel were terrified of the bombings. The 1st Army Group was in danger of encirclement. "KPA units have suffered heavy casualties mainly from enemy air raids, lost nearly all their tanks and most of their artillery, and are fighting a difficult delaying action," Zakharov wrote. "KPA units lack ammunition and fuel; deliveries have virtually halted. Accounting for present quantities of weapons and ammunition is badly organized. Command control from top to bottom is poor."[175]

At a meeting on September 26 of the Soviet military mission with Kim Il Sung and Pak Hon-yong, it was decided to name Kim supreme commander in chief and defense minister, and to establish a Staff Office to command troops under him. The participants also decided to strengthen rear area organization. In addition, six new divisions would be organized in North Korea. But plans to form nine divisions from southerners were dropped. Nevertheless, Kim directed that mobilized southerners be taken to the North to create the new divisions. There were no trained drivers for the 3,400 trucks the Soviet Union had provided and General Zakharov suggested to Stalin that Kim Il Sung be encouraged to request 1,500 truck drivers from China.

Before seeing the Zakharov report from Pyongyang, Stalin sent a long message, based on a Politburo decision, to Zakharov and Shtykov. The KPA's difficulty was the result of "major mistakes" in command and tactics by its Frontline Headquarters, Army Group headquarters, and division headquarters, Stalin said. In a stinging rebuke to his own advisers, Stalin wrote, "Primary responsibility for these errors lies with our military advisers," who wasted a week by ignoring orders from the supreme commander to withdraw four divisions from the central front for the defense of Seoul. What's more, reconnaissance was inadequate and tanks had been used improperly and destroyed because artillery bombardment had not cleared the enemy from the battlefield. Stalin spelled out the errors of Soviet military advisers: "They had not realized the strategic significance of the enemy landing operation at Inchon and denied its importance. Shtykov had even suggested that the author of an article in *Pravda* about the Inchon landing be put on trial. Because of blindness and lack of strategic experience, the advisers questioned the transfer of forces from the south to the Seoul area, the redeployment was delayed . . . and seven days were lost." The military advisers were not properly assisting KPA commanders: "KPA troops are undirected and fighting blindly, and cannot coordinate joint operations between different branches." Stalin ordered that his message, which included eight specific directives, be transmitted to the Soviet military advisers, especially to Chief Military Adviser N. A. Vasil'iev.[176] Stalin was enormously sympathetic to the North Korean leadership.

SEOUL IS ABANDONED, AND REINFORCEMENTS ARE SOUGHT

North Korean authorities began to withdraw from Seoul after the US landing at Inchon. South Koreans imprisoned as "reactionary elements" were taken to the North; some political prisoners were executed. Many South Korean notables were persuaded or forced to go to the DPRK. There were a large number of "rabuk insa" (abductees) to the North. Pro-North sympathizers feared retribution in the South. Some collaborators, like former ROK Internal Affairs minister Kim Hyo-sok, had no choice but to flee to the North, whereas such persons as Dr. Kim Kyu-sik who probably acted from conviction also left Seoul. In all, sixteen of the forty-eight National Assembly members who stayed in Seoul in June went to the North: Kim Yong-mu, Won Se-hun, Paek Sang-gyu, Cho So-ang, An Chae-hong, Kim Kyong-bae, Kim Ung-chin, Kim Chil-song, Yu Ki-su, Yi Sang-gyong, Yi Chong-song, Chong In-sik, Cho Kyu-sol, Cho Chong-sung, Cho Hon-yong, and Choe Pyong-ju.[177]

Southerners who genuinely identified with the DPRK and volunteered for military service left the South with the KPA, believing that someday they would return to Seoul. Kim Song-chil's diary entry for September 23 recounts:

> At night the traffic crossing Miari pass was reportedly bumper to bumper with automobiles and trucks heading north. This happened every night so the number of people and amount of goods taken to the North is unknown. A pathetic stream of prisoners were marched north nightly. Most seemed to be relatively well off and educated. They were tied together in a row. . . . The guards yelled insults at the weak and laggards who fell behind, ordering them to keep moving. Those who did not obey were reportedly executed on the spot.[178]

US and ROKA units recaptured Seoul on September 27. Two days later, with MacArthur and Syngman Rhee present, the South Korean government was formally reinstalled in the capital. After the ceremony, Rhee requested that MacArthur permit the ROKA to pursue the enemy north across the 38th parallel. MacArthur wanted to issue a surrender ultimatum to North Korea and asked Rhee to wait two days for a response. But the next day Rhee ordered ROKA Chief of Staff Chong Il-gwon to advance north immediately.[179]

On September 29, Shtykov met in Pyongyang with Kim Il Sung and Pak Hon-yong at their request. The situation was grave, Kim said, because the enemy held the Charyong mountain range and was at the rear of the 2nd Army Group. An orderly withdrawal had seemed feasible, but discipline had broken down and orders were not executed. The enemy had cut off the 1st Army Group and fragmented the 2nd Army Group, Kim said, and the situation in Seoul was unclear. Choe Yong-gon was in the field, but unreachable by radio. Unaware of each division's location and situation, Shtykov could only say with certainty that the defense of the 38th parallel had to be strengthened. Kim asked Shtykov if the enemy would cross the parallel. Still hoping for national unification, Kim had wanted to create fifteen divisions and continue the fight. If the enemy crossed the parallel, Kim said, he would be pessimistic, as neither new divisions nor a counterattack could be organized. Kim's hope that the enemy would stop at the parallel, despite his own violation of the border, shows his confusion.

Shtykov refused Kim's request to look at the draft of a letter by Kim and Pak to Stalin. Pak persisted, saying the letter had been reviewed by the KWP Political Committee. Shtykov again declined, saying that reviewing the contents of such a letter was up to the Politburo, CPSU. "Kim Il Sung and Pak Hon-yong are agitated. One senses they are overwhelmed by confusing events and uncertain of the future," Shtykov reported.[180]

The next day Shtykov received the letter to Stalin, written in Korean and signed by Kim and Pak, and appended it to his report.[181] Kim and Pak wrote:

Moscow, Kremlin
DEEPLY RESPECTED Iosif Vissarionovich STALIN
On behalf of the Workers' Party of Korea, we express to You, the liberator of the Korean people and the leader of the working peoples of the entire world, our profound gratitude for compassion and assistance which You constantly provide to our people struggling for the freedom and independence of its Fatherland.

In this letter, we would like to brief You on the current situation at the fronts of the liberation war of our people against the American aggressors.

Prior to the assault landing at Inchon (Chemulpo) one could not judge the situation at the fronts as unfavorable to us. The adversary, suffering one defeat after another, was cornered into a tiny piece of land at the southern-most tip of South Korea and we had a great chance of winning a victory in the last decisive battles.

Such a situation considerably damaged the military authority of the United States. Therefore, in those conditions, in order to restore its prestige and implement by any means its long-held plans of conquering Korea and transforming it into its military-strategic bridgehead, on September 16 the U.S. performed an assault landing operation and landed a considerable number of troops and armaments in the vicinity of Inchon after having mobilized almost all its land, naval, and air troops deployed in the Pacific ocean. . . .

The units of our People's Army heroically fight against advance assault landing units of the enemy. However, we consider it necessary to report to You about the emergence of very unfavorable conditions for us.

The enemy's air force numbering about a thousand airplanes of various types, facing no rebuff from our side, totally dominate the air space and perform air raids at the fronts and in the rear day and night. . . . Having cut off all the communications lines of our troops and joined the assault force that landed in Inchon with the units of their southern front that broke through our frontline, the adversary has a real opportunity to take over the city of Seoul completely.

As a result, the units of the People's Army that are still fighting in the southern part of Korea have been cut off from the northern part of Korea, they are torn into pieces. . . . After taking over Seoul completely, the enemy is likely to launch a further offensive into North Korea. Therefore, we believe that if in future the above-mentioned conditions unfavorable to us continue, then the Americans' aggression ultimately will be successful. . . .

Dear Iosif Vissarionvich, we are determined to overcome all the difficulties facing us so that Korea will not be a colony and a military springboard of the U.S. imperialists. We will fight for the independence, democracy and happiness of our people to the last drop of blood. . . . This not withstanding, if the enemy does not give us time to implement the measures which we plan, and, making use of our extremely grave situation, steps up its offensive operations into North Korea, then we will not be able to stop the enemy troops solely with our own forces.

Therefore, we cannot help asking You to provide us with special assistance. In other words, at the moment when the enemy troops cross over the 38th parallel we will badly need direct military assistance from the Soviet Union.

If for any reason this is impossible, please assist us by forming international volunteer units in China and other countries of people's democracy for rendering military assistance to our struggle.

We request Your directive regarding the aforementioned proposal.

Respectfully,

September 29, 1950

The CC of the Workers' Party of Korea.

KIM IL SUNG,
PAK HON-YONG

Kim Il Sung, Pak Hon-yong, and other KWP leaders did not actually expect the Soviet Union to commit forces to the war. Rather, they wanted Stalin to use his influence to secure military help from China. On October 1, Pak Il-u arrived in Beijing with a request signed by Kim Il Sung and Pak Hon-yong for troops from the People's Liberation Army. The entreaty was identical to that in Kim and Pak's message to Stalin, except for this provision: "We earnestly request that when enemy forces advance north of the 38th parallel, PLA units be deployed and support the military operations of our forces."[182]

On September 30, the Politburo of the CPSU endorsed the decisions made four days earlier that Kim Il Sung be both supreme commander and defense minister, and that South Korean men be moved to the North to form six new KPA divisions.[183] The following day, senior officials were shuffled: Choe Yong-gon went from defense minister to western region commander, and Frontline Commander Kim Chaek was concurrently named eastern regional commander.[184] Kim Ung, who had led the now dissolved 2nd Army Group, became KPA chief of staff.[185]

In a long cable on October 1, Stalin rebuked Shtykov for not previewing the letter from Kim and Pak: "Under the extremely difficult circumstances Korean comrades naturally seek our advice and support." To have refused it would have exacerbated their loss of self-confidence, Stalin said. He directed Shtykov to convey four points to Kim and Pak immediately:

1. The enemy's intentions were to cross the 38th parallel and try to conquer North Korea, so the North must mobilize all its resources and stop the attack. The North's strength and ability must not be underestimated by the North Korean leaders. The North Koreans could resist at and above the 38th parallel. They should organize new divisions, and the Soviet Union would provide the equipment.
2. Partisan warfare should be organized behind enemy forces in the South, using local partisans and KPA units still there.
3. Tough leadership and an unyielding defense were crucial. The first priority was to stop the collapse of confidence among leaders. Assignments must be strict and precise. Everyone had to understand that defense of the country was a personal responsibility: Defend the major ports and probable landing areas on the coast.
4. Regarding military support, Stalin considered volunteer military units most useful, and he promised to discuss it with "our Chinese comrades" and reply in a few days.[186]

Stalin, who was probably uncertain about the war prospects himself, tried to encourage the rattled North Korean leaders and restore their confidence. The same day, he requested troops from Mao and Zhou: "In my judgment . . . the situation of our Korean comrades is becoming desperate." Stalin told the two Chinese leaders that Army Group commanders had not complied with Kim Il Sung's instructions to withdraw northward after the Inchon landing. Stalin wrote:

Our Korean friends have no troops capable of resistance in the vicinity of Seoul. Hence, one needs to consider the way toward the 38th parallel as wide open.

If in the current situation you consider it possible to send troops [to] help the Koreans then you should move at least five or six divisions toward the 38th parallel at once so our Korean comrades [will have] an opportunity to organize reserves north of the 38th parallel under the cover of your troops. China's divisions should probably be volunteers and of course have their own command structure.[187]

The appeals for China's help from Moscow and Pyongyang reached Beijing on the same day. Unlike in July, Stalin did not mention Soviet air cover for Chinese forces.

THE KPA'S RETREAT

Cut off from communications and supplies, the KPA collapsed and retreated from South Korea. Novelist Kim Sa-ryang, who was attached to the KPA's 6th Division, went missing and was reportedly killed. Dancer Choe Sung-hui and her daughter An Song-hui, who were entertaining troops at the front, narrowly escaped death.[188]

A large number of South Koreans worked for the People's Committees and Workers' Party organizations set up in occupied areas in the South, and most of them evacuated to the North, but still many were left with the remnants of KPA in the South. Some of those who stayed behind joined the partisans and fought against ROKA and US forces. Yi Tae, author of *Nambugun* [Southern Forces] was a reporter for the Seoul *Hapdong Shinmun* newspaper when the war started. A left-wing sympathizer, Yi joined the North Korean Central News Service and reported from Chongju, North Chungchong Province, in the South. While making his way north, Yi was helped by partisans on Mt. Hoemun and joined them.[189]

Discipline broke down during the KPA retreat. Some leaders in Pyongyang, probably including Ho Ka-i, then in charge of Korean Workers' Party affairs, sought to reestablish control by tightening KWP leadership within the military. He reorganized the Ministry of National Defense's Culture Department into a Political Department and renamed the Culture Section in every army unit the Political Section. In the chaos of the retreat, however, a larger organizational reshuffle was unrealistic. What could be done was dismiss Kim Il, chief of the Culture Training Department, and appoint a new head of the KPA Political Department. Pak Hon-yong, vice-chairman of the KWP and the second most important person in the government behind Kim Il Sung, was named to the post. Documents show that the reorganization was decided on October 21 by the Political Committee, CC KWP.[190] For the moment, Supreme Commander Kim and Pak, the two men who had advocated war, were still leading the defeated army. Given Pak's avoidance of responsibility that Kim complained about earlier, Pak must have been pressured into taking the position of head of the KPA Political Department.[191]

Kim and Pak signed an order on October 14 that was simply draconian. Blame for the North's failure in the war was placed on KPA officers and political cadres "who were disoriented by the new situation, showed cowardice in combat with the enemy, abandoned their command function . . . disguised themselves as [ordinary] soldiers, went into hiding or discarded their weapons and ripped off their rank epaulettes to save their disgraceful lives. . . . By abandoning their troops and not taking appropriate measures to deal with the confusion in their units they failed to maintain discipline, improve vigilance, deal with cowards and despondent elements, and organize units under their command for combat and effective defense." The cowardice of frontline leaders had allowed the enemy to take territory where 17 million people lived. The six-part order authorized the execution by firing squad of commanding officers who deserted their positions, or of anyone else who discarded their weapon and quit fighting. The order read:

1. No retreat. We now have nowhere to withdraw to. The Korean People's Army is the military power of the fatherland and the people, who ask you to defend your positions to the death.
2. Defeatists and those who mislead the people are a dangerous enemy in combat. Anyone, regardless of rank, who causes confusion in a unit, discards his weapon, or leaves combat without authorization is an enemy of the people and will be summarily executed.
3. Officers of all ranks will join combat units and exercise command on the battlefield, actively lead in their area of responsibility, become role models, initiate a powerful counterattack, close on the enemy, and strike severe blows. . . .
4. Frontline, army group and division commanders will organize supervisory units and attach them to rear area defense units and regiments by October 15. Supervisory commanders, with military inspectors and court officers, are authorized to execute, remand to punishment units, or return to their units any officer or soldier who deserts the battlefield.
5. All senior officers, including unit commanders and assistant commanders, will sign this order and transmit it to subordinate units. All recipients will read this order to their units and ensure that all personnel with military duties understand its significance. [192]

Historically, armies have regularly resorted to summary execution of deserters to maintain discipline. But the immediate prototype for the Kim-Pak order was Supreme Command Order 81, dated August 13 and issued during the battle at the Naktong River: "Do not withdraw one step from the occupied area and your position." According to the order, personnel who left combat positions without authorization from higher headquarters or abandoned their weapons were to be court-martialed and executed. [193]

Stalin's leadership in the war against Germany provided an earlier model for Kim and Pak's order. Order 270 was issued by the Supreme Commander Headquarters of the Red Army on August 16, 1941, after Soviet forces had suffered defeats. The order not only called for summary execution of commanders and political officers who in combat removed rank markings, withdrew to the rear, or surrendered to the enemy; it also called for the arrest of their families. The family members of soldiers who surrendered were stripped of state entitlements and assistance as well. [194] Then there was Order 227, which was issued on July 28, 1942, at the start of the battle for Stalingrad, by the Soviet People's Commissariat for Defense, acting on Stalin's instructions: "It is time to stop withdrawals. Do not retreat one step. This must be our major appeal. . . . Unit commanders and political officers are forbidden to leave their posts. . . . Officers and soldiers who were caught by panic, and cowards must be summarily executed. Commanders, commissars, and political officers . . . who leave their combat assignments without orders from higher authority are traitors who betray the fatherland." Such commanders were to be relieved, sent to punishment battalions, and assigned to the front lines.[195] Military historians in Russia regard this harsh order as having been necessary to maintain the Soviets' battle line during the war. Soviet military advisers in Korea, familiar with the extreme steps taken by the Red Army in the war against Nazi Germany, probably drafted the October 14 order for Kim and Pak.

But the effectiveness of this order is unclear. KPA units in the South with weak leadership were destroyed. At the same time, well-trained units like Pang Ho-san's 6th Division maintained a chain of command and retreated to the North along the Taebaek mountain range.

On October 21, one week after Kim and Pak issued their order, the KWP Political Committee established a party organization within the military. This marked the start of KWP control over the army, which in some ways had previously seemed to be less the Party's army than the army of the Manchurian faction.[196] The rebuilding of the KPA would now begin.

Chapter Four

US-ROK Forces Reach the Yalu and China Enters the War

US-ROK FORCES MOVE NORTHWARD

American policy makers pondered whether US and ROK troops moving northward in the South should halt at the 38th parallel or advance into North Korea after the KPA was routed. John Allison, chief of the State Department's Northeast Asia Division, a proponent of rolling back Communism, spelled out his view in a memorandum on August 12, 1950: "The situation in Korea now provides the United States and the free world with the first opportunity to regain territory from the Soviet bloc. Since a basic policy of the United States is to check and reduce the preponderant power of the USSR in Asia and elsewhere, then UN operations in Korea can set the stage for the non-communist penetration into an area under Soviet control."[1]

George Kennan, the architect of the US policy of containment, a cautious strategy to prevent the expansion of Soviet influence around the world, opposed rollback in Korea too. He had recently resigned as head of the State Department's Policy Planning Division, but was still at the State Department until the end of August. Convinced that Moscow would react to a US provocation, Kennan wanted to maintain the Cold War status quo. If US troops crossed the 38th parallel, Soviet or Chinese forces would intervene in Korea, he believed. Kennan was disturbed by the position expressed in a draft government memorandum on July 31 that North Korean forces should not only withdraw to the 38th parallel, but also "surrender their arms to the United Nations commander and relinquish authority to him in order that he might create order throughout all of Korea." Kennan worried that "this could be interpreted by the Russians only to mean that we were pressing for the establishment of full military and police authority of General MacArthur right up to the northern borders of Korea, at the gates of Vladivostok. The Russians would never under any circumstances agree to this."[2]

By mid-August 1950 the Allison faction in the US government had the support of Secretary of State Dean Acheson and President Harry Truman.[3] According to Bruce Cumings, "The problem that remained was not whether to roll back the North, but who should control it."[4] But in reality a fight was still being waged inside the government over whether to let Gen. Douglas MacArthur, the China Lobby, and ROK President Syngman Rhee have their way and overthrow the DPRK, or whether to stop them.

Defense Secretary Louis Johnson's aides told Nationalist Chinese embassy officials in Washington on July 20 that the Truman administration had decided to advance into North Korea. Cumings speculates that the Chinese Communists of the People's Republic, who had agents inside the Nationalist government on Taiwan, may have learned of Washington's intentions from this discussion.[5]

On July 13, MacArthur told Gen. Joseph Collins, the US Army chief of staff, and others that he intended to occupy all of North Korea.[6] MacArthur told in a teleconference on July 17 that "the problem is to compose and unite Korea."[7] MacArthur saw the war in Korea as an opportunity to recover the Chinese mainland, and in late July he visited Chiang Kai-shek on Taiwan.

Alarmed, Truman and Acheson sent Averill Harriman, the former US ambassador to Moscow, to Japan in early August to tell MacArthur that the conflict must be limited to Korea.[8] But the general told Harriman that North Korean forces "must be destroyed as early as possible," that elections could be held in North Korea within two months of Seoul's recapture to fill the seats in the National Assembly reserved for northern delegates, and that Korea must be reunified.[9] MacArthur also argued that the United States "should be more aggressive in promoting dissension within China." Even if Chiang's planned counterattack against the PRC failed, he said, "it might be a good idea to let him land and get rid of him that way."[10] MacArthur assumed that neither the Soviet Union nor China would intervene directly in Korea if US troops moved north, and he openly criticized the Truman administration's cautious defense of Taiwan in a message to the Veterans of Foreign Wars on August 27. Truman decided on September 1 to replace Defense Secretary Johnson, but did not rebuke MacArthur.[11]

The US National Security Council staff completed a draft policy statement on Korea, NSC 81, on September 1. "Final decisions cannot be made at this time concerning the future course of action in Korea," the report said, because US policy would have to be reexamined if the Chinese Communists or the Soviet Union entered the war. "The United Nations forces have a legal basis for conducting operations north of the 38th parallel to compel the withdrawal of the North Korean forces behind this line or to defeat these forces," the report maintained. General MacArthur "should be authorized to conduct military operations, including amphibious or airborne landings or ground operations in pursuance of a roll-back north of the 38th parallel for the purpose of destroying the North Korean forces." However, since the United Nations Security Council resolution on Korea calling on member states to help the ROK repel the North's attack did not clearly authorize an advance into northern Korea for the purpose of "unifying Korea under the Republic of Korea . . . the execution of such plans [to occupy North Korea] should take place only with the explicit approval of the President, and would be dependent upon prior consultation with and the approval of the U.N. members." But if China and the Soviet Union did not intervene or threaten to intervene, the report argued, driving North Korean forces back to the North or expanding the ground campaign above the 38th parallel to defeat the North would be permitted, with the caveat that "U.N. operations should not be extended to areas close to the Manchurian and U.S.S.R. borders of Korea." If the Soviet Union or Chinese Communists reoccupied northern Korea, the report advised, the UN Command was not to extend ground operations above the 38th parallel. The US government was very cautious on this point. If organized resistance by North Korean forces ceased, NSC 81 called for the United States to "attempt to reduce its share of the U.N. responsibilities for Korea," and on the basis of a new UN resolution the ROKA should disarm the KPA. Free elections should be held under UN auspices and Korea unified, with UN forces to remain in Korea until a stable unified state was established. [12]

At an NSC meeting on September 7, the US Joint Chiefs of Staff (JCS) called the policy proposal in NSC 81 "unrealistic," a view that reflected MacArthur's strong opposition to the report. MacArthur insisted that the US objective should be the "destruction of North Korean forces," and thus that operations should be conducted north of the 38th parallel, mainly by the ROKA. He and Syngman Rhee had agreed that, once reestablished in Seoul, the ROK would declare itself the "only government of all Korea." If UN forces shattered the KPA, the ROKA would mop up. Rhee intended to hold elections in the North for the one hundred vacant seats in the ROK National Assembly. [13]

Secretary of State Acheson was coming to respond to the views of the military and inclined to allow the US Air Force to bomb the North, including Najin (Rashin) and other places near the Soviet border, and sought revisions in the NSC report. [14] A provision was then added that UN Commander General MacArthur had to obtain President Truman's approval before advancing northward. UN forces were not permitted to cross the Korean borders with Manchuria (China) or the Soviet Union. However, UN land forces, minus ROKA units, were permitted to approach the borders. The revised report, now NSC 81/1, was presented to Truman on September 9. [15]

The JCS began planning military operations on the basis of NSC 81/1. After the success at Inchon, they obtained Truman's approval on September

27 for the following order to MacArthur: "Your military objective is the destruction of the North Korean armed forces."[16]

In a meeting on September 18 at the US Mission to the UN attended by State Department adviser John Foster Dulles and Allison, South Korean Ambassador to the United States Chang Myon strongly requested that UN forces advance into North Korea. He also urged that elections be held there under UN supervision and that ROK jurisdiction be extended to the North.[17]

The next day, the US Mission prepared a position paper that called for a UN resolution to assist the Korean people to be free, independent, and unified. Although the paper said that the United States "must avoid commitment with regard to bringing about unification of Korea through military means," asking the UN General Assembly to resolve to unify Korea was tantamount to legitimizing an advance by UN forces into the North. The paper emphasized that ROK jurisdiction was limited to south of the 38th parallel, which was very different from the South Korean position.[18] While agreeing to the new objective of unification of Korea for UN forces, Dulles recognized that its attainment depended on the attitudes of the Soviet Union and China, and he proposed that the United States not take the initiative on it.[19]

After consultation with Washington, on October 1 MacArthur broadcast a surrender demand to Kim Il Sung, the commander in chief of North Korean forces: "The early and total defeat and complete destruction of your armed forces and war making potential is now inevitable."[20] MacArthur called upon Kim "at once to liberate all United Nations prisoners of war and civilian internees under your control and to make adequate provision for their protection, care, maintenance and immediate transportation to such places as I indicate." On the same day, the ROKA I Corps, commanded by Kim Paek-il, crossed the parallel and moved toward Wonsan.[21]

On October 2 MacArthur issued a general directive to all elements of the UN Command:

> Under the provision of the United Nations Security Council Resolution of 27 June, the field of our military operations is limited only by military exigencies and the international boundaries of Korea. The so-called 38th Parallel, accordingly, is not a factor in the military employment of our forces. To accomplish the enemy's complete defeat, your troops may cross the border at any time, either in exploratory probing or exploiting local tactical conditions. If the enemy fails to accept the terms of surrender set forth in my message to him of 1 October, our forces, in due process of campaign will seek out and destroy the enemy's armed forces in whatever part of Korea they may be located.[22]

The order sanctioned the ROKA's advance into North Korea. MacArthur directed the US Army's X Corps to move from Seoul to Pusan and then proceed by sea to attack Wonsan.[23] The ROKA I Corps, operating independently, continued to advance on Wonsan.

The UN General Assembly on October 7 adopted a new resolution on Korea sponsored by eight countries, including Great Britain and Australia, by a vote of forty-seven to five, with seven abstentions. The Soviet Union and its allies opposed the resolution; Yugoslavia, India, and five Arab nations abstained. Without mentioning MacArthur's order for UN forces to advance into North Korea, Resolution 376(V) confirmed it and stated an objective for the attack on North Korea. The resolution referred to the General Assembly resolution of December 12, 1948 (No. 195, III) that recognized the Republic of Korea as "a lawful government . . . based on elections which were a valid expression of the free will of the electorate of that part of Korea and which were observed by the Temporary Commission." Based on the Security Council recommendations of June 27, 1950, the new resolution said, UN forces were reacting to "an armed attack [on the Republic of Korea] and to restore international peace and security in that area." The resolution recommended that "all appropriate steps be taken to ensure conditions of stability throughout Korea" and confirmed that the "essential objective" of the General Assembly's resolutions on Korea was "the establishment of a unified, independent and democratic Government of Korea." The United Nations Commission for the Unification and Rehabilitation of Korea (UNCURK) was established to replace the UN Commission in Korea. Australia, Chile, the Netherlands, Pakistan, the Philippines, Thailand, and Turkey were appointed to it. [24] The United Nations was on a course to replace a Communist administration and unify Korea by force.

On October 9, MacArthur broadcast a revised final surrender demand to North Korea. To implement the new UN resolution, he called "upon all north Koreans to cooperate fully with the United Nations in establishing a unified, independent and democratic government of Korea." If there was no response immediately, MacArthur warned, "I shall at once proceed to take such military actions as may be necessary to enforce the decrees of the United Nations." [25] That morning, the US 1st Cavalry Division crossed the 38th parallel in force and headed for Kumchon. It was the start of a drive on Pyongyang. [26]

On October 10, the ROKA 3rd and Capital Divisions of I Corps occupied Wonsan, a major port city. [27] The next day the ROKA 1st Division crossed the parallel as well. Division commander Paek Sun-yop had worked in Pyongyang for a while after the end of World War II [28] and wanted his division to be the first to enter the North Korean capital.

In a radio broadcast that day, Kim Il Sung said because of the enemy offensive "the Korean People's Army is obliged to withdraw [but it] must continue fighting. . . . Our front-line forces are in a very difficult situation. Our fatherland faces a deep crisis." He appealed to the soldiers of the KPA to "fight to the last drop of blood" and to partisans in the South to organize attacks in occupied areas. He also called for the arrest and "removal" of spies and "subversive elements" in rear areas. Kim defiantly rejected MacArthur's surrender demand and declared: "We must deal unmercifully with rumor mongers, defeatists, doubters, deserters, and cowards." Far from giving up, Kim threatened to launch a counterattack: "Our task today is to defend every inch of the fatherland with our blood. To deal a new decisive blow to the enemy, we must gather all our strength and quickly drive the American military interventionists and the puppet Syngman Rhee clique out of our country forever."[29]

On October 15, Truman and MacArthur met on Wake Island. The president repeatedly asked the general if China would enter the war. MacArthur painted a rosy picture: Pyongyang would soon fall, there was no possibility of intervention by the Soviet Union or China, US forces would complete basic operations and be withdrawn by Christmas, and the UN could probably hold a general election in 1951. In a joint announcement, the two leaders said they "had reached full agreement."

It proved to be a fragile understanding.[30]

CHINA WEIGHS INTERVENTION

On October 2, the day after ROKA forces crossed the 38th parallel, an expanded meeting of the Chinese Communist Party Politburo took up the issue of intervention in Korea. A memorandum by Mao Zedong dated October 2, about the decision to intervene, which was first published in *Mao Zedong junshi wenxuan* [Selected Military Papers of Mao Zedong] in 1981, reads:

1. We decided to send part of the army to Korean territory to fight the forces of America and the puppet Syngman Rhee in support of our Korean comrades. We regard this mission as essential because if all of Korea is occupied by the Americans, the revolutionary power of Korea will be completely defeated. In that case the American aggressors will become increasingly frenzied to the detriment of the entire East.
2. We think as follows. We decided to send Chinese troops to Korea to fight American forces. (1) Therefore, the following problems must be resolved: We must prepare to destroy and drive out the American forces and those of other nations on Korean territory. (2) Once Chinese forces are fighting American forces in Korean territory, we must be prepared to face Americans' declaration that America is at war with China. We must be prepared for America to employ its air force to bomb many of China's major cities and industrial centers and use its naval forces to attack our coastal areas.
3. Of these two questions, the first is whether Chinese troops can destroy American troops in Korea and we can effectively resolve the Korean problem. . . .[31]

Sections 4, 5, and 6 of the memorandum covered the dispatch of twelve Chinese divisions and combat operations against US forces.

According to the researchers who first published this memorandum, it was a telegram to Stalin. Zhu Jianrong, author of *Mao Zedong's Korean War*, quotes a military researcher in Beijing who said that parts of the telegram are omitted, including a request for Soviet weapons and air support. Zhu doubts the telegram was actually sent on October 2, as do I.[32] Zhu and I believe that the omitted parts described countermeasures against US attacks on Chinese cities, industrial centers, and coastal areas. Pang Xianzhi and Li Jie, the authors of *Mao Zedong and the Cause of Resistance to America and Aid to Korea* (2000), showing a photocopy of the first and last pages of the original material, conclude that the memorandum was written by Mao prior to the October 2 CCP Politburo conference.[33] When the proposal ran into strong opposition, they argue, Mao did not send it to Stalin. The opening sentence in the memorandum reads: "Comrade Filippov, I received your telegram dated October 1 and herewith respond with our opinion." Mao Zedong clearly wrote it before the October 2 conference in response to Stalin's October 1 request that China send troops to Korea. The final page says: "Please tell us whether or not you can deploy large numbers of air force units to help us protect the cities listed above. (We have no air defenses.) Be well. Mao Zedong. October 2, 1950."

Mao wanted the Soviet Union to send air force units to China to defend against US attacks on its cities, industrial centers, and coastal areas. Chen Jian read the original text of this telegram in Mao's own handwriting at the CCP's Central Archives. Although he was not permitted to copy the last two sentences, Chen has written that Mao requested, as a condition of China's entry into the war, that the Soviet air force defend China's entire coastline against expected US attacks.[34]

Mao Zedong thus wanted the Soviet Union to promise air cover. Moreover, under the Sino-Soviet Treaty on Alliance and Friendship, Moscow would be obligated to send such air force units to China. But the result would be a world war between the United States and the Soviet Union, which Stalin was determined to avoid.

Faced with strong opposition to Chinese intervention at the October 2 CCP Politburo conference, Mao scrapped the draft message to Stalin and took the opposite position in a telegram sent through Soviet Ambassador to China Nikolai Roshchin on October 3:

> I received your telegram dated October 1. We initially planned to send several divisions to North Korea to assist our Korean comrades if the enemy attacked north of the 38th parallel.

However, upon closer consideration, we now think such action would have extremely serious consequences. First, it would be extremely difficult to resolve the Korean problem with several divisions. . . .

Secondly, [intervention] would bring on an open conflict between China and the United States that would also drag the Soviet Union into the war. . . .

Many Central Committee comrades think we should be cautious.

Of course, to our Korean comrades who are in such a difficult situation, not to get our troops in support would be very bad. We ourselves think it would be regrettable. . . .

Korea will be temporarily defeated, but the form of struggle will change to partisan war.

We will hold a general meeting of the Central Committee attended by the responsible comrades from each bureau. A final decision has not yet been made on this problem. This is a preliminary telegram and we wish to consult with you. If you concur, we will send comrades Zhou Enlai and Lin Biao to your vacation place. They are prepared to consult with you on this problem and to report on the situation in China and Korea.

I await your response.

October 2, 1950

Mao Zedong[35]

Ambassador Roshchin commented to Stalin that "China has changed its initial position." He added that the Chinese could send more than five or six divisions to Korea, although the PLA lacked equipment, antitank weapons, and so forth. Roshchin could not account for the about-face.

Mao's message was unpersuasive to the Soviets. Although resigned to not getting everything he wanted from the Soviet Union, he was trying to probe what China could obtain. The crux of the matter was that a final decision on Chinese intervention had not yet been made and Zhou Enlai would seek better terms from the Soviets.

In a telegram to Stalin on October 4, Mao asked that Soviet philosopher Pavel Iudin be permitted to stay in China four months longer to travel around the country. Iudin had come to China to assist with the editing of Mao's writings.[36] Stalin's response to Mao's telegram of October 3,[37] apparently sent on October 3 or 4, affected a pivotal decision on Korea that the CCP would make on October 5.[38] Stalin told Mao that he had requested that five or six Chinese divisions be sent to Korea because the Chinese had previously asserted several times that they would send them. He added four points:

1. The events in Korea show that the United States is not now prepared for a big war.
2. Japan, whose militaristic potential has not yet recovered, cannot provide military assistance to the Americans.
3. The United States inevitably will be compelled to yield on the Korean question to China, which has the backing of its ally, the Soviet Union, and

will probably accept a settlement favorable to [North] Korea that does not allow the enemies to use Korea as a springboard.

4. For the same reason, the United States will not only have to abandon Taiwan but also drop the idea of a separate peace settlement with the Japanese reactionaries as well as give up their plans to revive Japanese imperialism and make Japan a springboard into the Far East.

China could not obtain these four points by adopting a "wait and see" attitude, Stalin said—"serious struggle" and an "impressive display of power" were the way to win concessions from the Americans. Otherwise China would not recover Taiwan. In order to persuade China to send several divisions to North Korea, Stalin promised to come to China's aid in a "big war," which he had hoped to avoid:

> Of course, I am concerned that even if the United States is not prepared for a big war, it could be brought into a big war for reasons of prestige and that would bring China into the war and then the USSR, which is bound by a Mutual Assistance Pact with China, would probably also be brought into the war. Should we fear this? In my view, we should not. Our countries are stronger than the USA and England, and the other capitalist countries of Europe, with the exception of Germany which cannot at present assist the United States, are not serious military powers. If a war is unavoidable, it is better to have it now than later. In several years Japanese militarism will be restored as an ally of the United States, and the USA and Japan will probably have a ready-made springboard on the continent in the form of Syngman Rhee's Korea.

But Stalin did not actually believe that if the United States expanded the war and attacked China, and the Soviet Union entered the war on China's behalf, that they would win. Nor did he, in fact, intend to enter the conflict at all and fight America. And he did not want the war expanded to the Chinese mainland. His suggestion that the Soviet Union would fight alongside China was an empty promise designed to get Beijing to send several divisions to North Korea.

On October 4, the expanded CCP Politburo conference reconvened. Opposition to intervention in the Korean conflict was strong in the CCP and the government, and Mao, who wanted to send some divisions despite his telegram to Moscow the day before through Ambassador Roshchin suggesting otherwise, was unable to persuade waverers. The next day, October 5, People's Liberation Army leader Peng Dehuai, who had said nothing in the debate, took Mao's side and advocated intervention. The Politburo ultimately approved Mao's proposal to send Chinese troops to North Korea, which included designation of Peng Dehuai as commander of the Chinese People's Volunteers (CPV). In conversations after the meeting, Mao suggested that Zhou Enlai be sent to the Soviet Union to consult on Moscow's participation in the war.[39] Mao probably thought from the wording of Stalin's telegram that at least the Soviet air force would join military operations.

On October 7, Mao informed Stalin of China's decision to send troops to Korea. Mao would dispatch nine divisions, not the six discussed earlier, but there would be a delay, Stalin informed Kim Il Sung on October 8. The tenacious Mao first wanted to send Zhou Enlai to the Soviet Union for negotiations. Stalin exhorted Kim Il Sung: "You must hold your positions and not give up one inch of territory."[40]

ZHOU ENLAI VISITS THE SOVIET UNION

October 8 was a busy day for Mao Zedong. The Chinese People's Volunteers headed by Peng Dehuai were established, Mao instructed Chinese Ambassador to the DPRK Ni Zhiliang to tell Kim Il Sung that Chinese troops would be sent,[41] and he dispatched Zhou Enlai to meet Stalin. Zhou took along General Lin Biao, who like Peng Dehuai was a major PLA leader, but was not an enthusiast of intervention.[42]

Zhou and Lin arrived in Moscow on October 10 and flew to a health resort on the Black Sea, accompanied by Vice-Premier Nikolai Bulganin.[43] Nearly all members of the Soviet Politburo were present at the meeting held there, which began with Stalin's review of the military situation in Korea. Because of the DPRK's early victories, the Korean comrades had underestimated the enemy, Stalin said. Since the US landing at Inchon, North Korea had suffered extremely heavy losses and the battlefield situation was critical, he asserted. Stalin then asked for the views of his Chinese comrades. Zhou Enlai responded that a careful assessment of China's domestic conditions and other factors had led the CCP Politburo to conclude that Chinese troops could not be sent to Korea after all. Zhou listed the reasons: China had suffered enormous damage from its prolonged civil war; serious problems of state management and living conditions remained; war in Korea would consume resources and be a heavy burden on the new regime; the military lacked weapons, equipment, and supplies; and if China entered the war, it might become bogged down in Korea. Plus, if the issues in Korea were not resolved, the fighting might extend to fraternal countries as well.[44]

The CCP Politburo had actually already approved dispatch of the Chinese People's Volunteers to Korea. Zhou's strategy was to induce Stalin to say the Soviet Union would join the war, and he wanted China to commit troops.

Stalin launched into a strong discourse on why intervention was in China's national interests. If the enemy occupied all of Korea, and US and ROK troops were stationed on the Yalu and Tumen rivers, Northeast China would never be secure and economic development was out of the question, Stalin argued. If the Korean comrades could not hold out and were to be sacrificed, their withdrawal from Korea should be planned and organized, however, Stalin said. China and the Soviet Union should agree that "the main military forces, weapons, equipment, and some cadres and staff should be withdrawn to Northeast China and the infirm and wounded moved to Soviet territory. It is much easier to enter Korea from Northeast China than the Soviet Union. In short, we must agree to share this heavy burden." Kim Il Sung had to be notified immediately of China's and the Soviet Union's plans, Stalin said. What did the Chinese leaders think?

Lin Biao answered with a question: Given the mountainous terrain in northern Korea, could the Koreans establish strongholds there and sustain partisan warfare? No, Stalin said, the partisans would be annihilated. Stalin continued:

> We long ago announced the prompt, complete withdrawal of our forces from Korea. It is difficult for us to send troops there again. It would be tantamount to a state of war with the United States. China can deploy a certain level of troops, I think. We can provide weapons and equipment and at a strategic time a certain level of aircraft to provide cover. Of course, [the cover] will be limited to rear areas and this side of the battlefield. We cannot go into enemy rear areas. We must avoid aircraft being shot down and pilots being taken prisoner by the enemy. [Soviet pilots] becoming prisoners of war would have a bad effect internationally.

Stalin then played his aid card more directly. On the assumption that China would send troops, he asked Zhou to provide a list of needed equipment and weapons and to work out the details with Bulganin. However, if China could not commit troops to Korea, "we should immediately inform our Korean comrades of the results of this discussion and our proposal and urge them to prepare for evacuation as quickly as possible."[45]

A later cable from Mao to Zhou on October 12 puts Stalin's exchange with Zhou and Lin over Soviet air support in a different light. According to this cable, not only did Zhou Enlai ask for Soviet air support for Chinese ground operations in Korea, he also reiterated Mao's request for Soviet protection from US attacks against the Chinese mainland. Stalin apparently replied that even preparations for air cover in Korea would take two to two and a half months.[46] One can reasonably assume that his wording about sending aircraft to China was vague. Zhou would not have accepted such thin assurance, and he did not carelessly accede to intervention. The agreement he came to with Stalin covered only the provision of Chinese and Soviet military equipment and joint Soviet-Chinese advice that North Koreans take refuge in Soviet territory and Manchuria if the enemy occupied all of Korea. Stalin and Zhou sent a joint telegram to Beijing on October 11 about the provision of the military equipment, and Zhou probably also informed Beijing separately. Stalin may have informed Kim Il Sung on his own about the advice of Chinese and Soviet leaders to prepare for evacuation. Zhou left for Moscow the day after meeting with Stalin.

Stalin ordered Kim Il Sung on October 13: "We see no prospect of continued resistance. Our Chinese comrades decline to intervene militarily. You and your colleagues must prepare for a complete evacuation to China and the Soviet Union or to China or the Soviet Union. It is imperative that all forces and equipment be transported out. Create and execute a detailed operation plan. Potential power to fight the enemy in the future must be preserved."[47]

Soviet Ambassador to North Korea Terentii Shtykov reported the reaction in Pyongyang to Moscow: "Kim Il Sung and Pak Hon-yong were both present. I read your telegram. Neither expected such a message. Kim Il Sung said it was extremely painful but they would implement your advice. Kim asked me to read just the actual recommendations again and had Pak write them down. They asked for assistance in drafting a plan."[48]

In Beijing, where an emergency meeting of the Politburo was held the evening of October 12, the situation was about to change dramatically. Peng Dehuai objected strongly to the attitude of Soviet leaders, but Mao explained the Soviet position on assistance and urged intervention. The Politburo agreed with Mao, and the final decision was made to go to war in Korea. Mao instructed Zhou in Moscow to reopen talks with Stalin:

1. With Comrades Gao Gang, Peng Dehuai and other comrades on the Politburo I reviewed the situation and concluded it is advantageous to send our forces to Korea after all. In the first stage we can strike at the puppet troops (ROK Army). Our army is confident they can cope with the puppet troops. We can establish bases in the mountainous region north of Wonsan and Pyongyang, rally the Korean people, and reorganize the Korean People's Army. . . . If we can just annihilate several divisions of puppet troops in the first phase, we can change the Korean situation to our advantage.

2. Our choice of this positive policy is advantageous for China, Korea, Asia, and the world. If we do not send troops, the enemy would gain control up to the Yalu River, reactionary forces at home and abroad would become stronger, and our position everywhere would suffer. The Northeast [Manchuria] especially would be at a disadvantage, our Northeast defense forces would be tied down, and the electric power facilities in southern Manchuria, too, would be controlled by the enemy.

3. As noted in the telegram yesterday jointly signed by Filippov and you regarding whether the Soviet side can fully satisfy our request for airplanes, cannons, tanks, and so forth . . . if the Soviet side can do that, our army can enter Korea confidently and conduct a long war, and maintain the solidarity of the great majority of the people at home.

4. But if in addition to deploying Soviet volunteer pilots in two or two and a half months in support of our operations in Korea, Soviet aircraft could be assigned to protect Beijing, Tientsin, Shenyang, Shanghai, Nanjing, Tsingtao, and other places, we would not fear any air attacks. But if U.S. air

forces attack during that interval of two months to two and a half months, we must endure a certain amount of damage.
5. In short, I think we should enter the war and must enter the war. If we go to war the gain will be very large; if we do not enter the war, the loss will be very large.[49]

Mao had gradually persuaded his Politburo colleagues that intervention in Korea was in China's national interests, and he apparently sent a telegram to Stalin on China's decision that has not been made public. On October 13, Stalin informed Kim Il Sung via Shtykov: "I just received a telegram from Mao Zedong. The message informs that the CCP Central Committee has reexamined the situation and decided, although its forces are inadequately equipped, to provide military support to the Korean comrades. I am waiting for detailed reports from Mao Zedong. In connection with this new decision by our Chinese comrades, I ask You to cancel temporarily implementation of the telegram sent to You yesterday about the evacuation of North Korea and the withdrawal of the KPA to the north. Fyn Si."[50]

According to Shi Zhe's memoirs, Zhou Enlai, surprised to learn from Mao that the decision for war had been made without an assurance of Soviet air cover, began negotiations with First Vice-Premier Vyacheslav Molotov.[51] In addition to providing Soviet air support for field operations in Korea within two to two and a half months, Zhou asked that the Soviets send air units to China. Stalin responded that the units could be stationed on Chinese territory and provide cover, but that it would take them sixty to seventy-five days to begin operations over Korea.[52]

On October 14, Ambassador Roshchin reported a meeting with Mao Zedong and quoted him as saying:

> Our comrades hesitated because of various problems in the international situation and the question of provision by the Soviet Union of weapons and air cover. These problems have all been clarified.
> . . . Of greatest importance are air force units to protect us. We hope they will arrive quickly, within two months at the latest.[53]

Also on October 14, Stalin again informed Kim Il Sung of developments: "After vacillation and a series of tentative decisions the Chinese comrades made a final decision to assist Korea with troops. I am glad that a final decision advantageous to Korea has been made at last. You must regard the advice from the leading Chinese and Soviet comrades as hereby cancelled."[54]

Kim Il Sung and Pak Hon-yong must have been overjoyed at the Chinese decision and thus Stalin's cancellation of his order to evacuate.

JAPANESE PARTICIPATION IN THE WAR

The Japanese breathed a collective sigh of relief at the successful Inchon landing. An opinion poll conducted by the *Asahi Shimbun* newspaper on September 21–24 asked respondents if Japan should cooperate with the United Nations in Korea: 58.6 percent were in favor and 9.2 percent were opposed. Those who approved of cooperation with the UN were asked what form it should take, and the results ran as follows: complete cooperation—10.9 percent; provide military forces—11.3 percent; oppose Communist ideology—6.1 percent; provide military bases—4.1 percent; provide human resources—2.9 percent; economic cooperation—17.5 percent; spiritual cooperation—11.4 percent; other forms—7.6 percent; and "don't know"—28.3 percent. Aggregated figures showed 28.3 percent endorsed active cooperation, whereas 35.9 percent favored passive cooperation. When the undecided were included, an overwhelming 64.2 percent of respondents did not support direct involvement in Korea, evidence that Premier Yoshida's policy had broad support.

Nearly half of the public—45.6 percent—also favored Yoshida's approach to a peace treaty, which would exclude the Soviet Union and China. Those who favored a comprehensive settlement with all the belligerents totaled 21.4 percent, and 33.3 percent were undecided. As for Japanese rearmament, 53.8 percent of respondents approved of it, 27.6 percent were opposed, and 18.6 percent were undecided. But when it came to the post–World War II settlement's provision of bases in Japan to the United States, only 29.9 percent of respondents were in favor, 37.5 percent were opposed, and 32.9 percent were undecided. The bulk of the public favored an independent security policy rather than the military ties to Washington that Yoshida wanted. As for Japan's military obligations, 37.9 percent favored exclusively defensive operations (to repulse an attack on Japan); only 18.5 percent endorsed the dispatch of Japanese troops overseas.[55]

Meanwhile, the US government had been conducting secret talks with several countries on the post–World War II peace settlement with Japan, and it officially announced the start of multilateral negotiations. In Tokyo in early October 1950, the Ministry of Foreign Affairs began to prepare position papers for the final stage of negotiations. Nishimura Kumao, the director of the Treaty Department, Foreign Ministry, and his colleagues thought the postwar settlement on the stationing of US forces in Japan should be within a UN framework. According to recent research by Toyoshita Narahiko, at a meeting on October 5 with such veteran scholars and high officials as Koizumi Shinzo, Itakura Takuzo, Arita Hachiro, and Tsushima Juichi, Premier Yoshida said, "The security arrangements must take the Soviet Union into consideration and reassure the public." He instructed them "to prepare ideal security arrangements for Japan that could be presented upon a request from

Washington," and to "consider the disarmament of Korea and the disarmament of a part of the Soviet Union."

On October 21, Prime Minister Yoshida ordered Nishimura to draft a treaty with three points: "(A.) disarmament of Japan and Korea; (B.) the removal of air bases from a specified region; and (C.) reduction of naval forces in the Western Pacific." The Treaty Department prepared a draft by October 31 entitled "Northern Pacific Six Nation Treaty" partially based on the advice of military experts, including two former Japanese Imperial Army generals, Shimomura Sadamu and Kawabe Torashiro. The Nishimura draft assumed six signatories: Japan, Republic of Korea, Republic of China (Taiwan), Great Britain, the United States, and the Soviet Union. Among the provisions were disarmament of Japan and the Republic of Korea; a demilitarized region extending one thousand kilometers from the international border shared by the People's Republic of China, the Soviet Union, and the Republic of Korea to the Southern Kuriles; and supervision of the treaty provisions by the United Nations.

Toyoshita Narahiko, who first made public this secret Japanese drafting of a peace treaty, dismissed it as a "dream-like fantasy." The "China" the planners had in mind as one of the six signers was of course Chiang Kai-shek's Republic of China (Taiwan), as Toyoshita pointed out, not the regime of Mao Zedong and Zhou Enlai that actually shared a border with the Soviet Union. The operative premise of the draft treaty was that the US and ROK forces would soon defeat North Korea and eradicate the DPRK, enabling the victors to force the USSR and PRC to demilitarize part of their territory. China's entry into the war demonstrated the utter unreality of the draft most clearly.

Nevertheless, the draft, after being revised and now entitled "A Proposal to Enhance Peace and Security in the North Pacific Region," was presented to Yoshida on December 26. At one point during the drafting process, a provision was added to demilitarize all areas stripped from Japan in the postwar settlement except for Okinawa because of US military concerns. In the final version, only Japan and Korea were to be disarmed,[56] yet the aborted wording shows how strongly Yoshida and his advisers felt about demilitarization.

As the Yoshida administration worked on post–World War II peace terms, Japan's clandestine involvement in the Korean War increased. US and ROK forces pushing northward after the Inchon victory discovered that North Korean coastal areas had been mined when three warships were damaged. The mines had to be removed before US troops could land at Wonsan in the North. In early October, the US 7th Fleet formed Joint Task Force 7 with US, Japanese, and ROK minesweepers to clear the Wonsan area.[57] The eight Japanese minesweepers were from the Maritime Safety Board (MSB), a fledgling coast guard, and had removed mines from Japan's coastal waters since World War II. On October 2, Adm. Arleigh A. Burke, deputy chief of staff to the commander of Naval Forces Far East, had summoned MSB Director Okubo Takeo and ordered him to assign minesweepers to the task force. Okubo reported the matter to Yoshida, who said: "The policy of the Japanese government is to cooperate with United Nations' forces." Yoshida "authorized [me] to carry out Burke's proposal," Okubo recounted. "At the time Dulles was frequently visiting Japan. . . . Yoshida and Dulles conferred [on a peace treaty]. . . . Japan was in delicate position internationally so the special minesweeping operation was kept secret."[58]

What Okubo called Burke's "proposal" was actually an order. Okubo then sent all twenty MSB minesweepers to Moji on the island of Kyushu, where they were formed into two units and sent to Pusan in South Korea. The official directive for Japan to participate in the minesweeping operation was issued on October 4 by Vice-Admiral Turner Joy, commander of the Naval Forces Far East, to Minister of Transportation Yamazaki Takeshi. Joy's directive ordered the Japanese government to assemble twenty minesweepers and five patrol vessels at Moji.[59] A directive from Gen. Douglas MacArthur dated October 6 states: "The Supreme Commander Allied Forces authorizes the use in Korean waters of twenty Japanese minesweepers . . . and directs the government of Japan to issue the required orders to vessels assembled at Moji."[60] Okubo issued the order to the minesweeper captains.[61]

Ten minesweepers and a tender left Moji the same day Okubo issued his order. Eight minesweepers joined the 7th Fleet's operations unit and began clearing the Wonsan area on October 10. A total of 207 MSB personnel—all government employees serving as an extension of their normal duties—participated in the operation.

ROKA troops occupied Wonsan on October 10, as resistance continued in nearby areas. The minesweeping was difficult and very dangerous. After mines near the shore were removed, thirty-nine planes from two US aircraft carriers bombed a minefield further offshore on October 12. When minesweepers moved in to complete the job, two US vessels hit mines and were sunk; thirteen men died and thirty-three were wounded. A third vessel was hit by North Korean shore batteries. Although ROKA units suppressed the batteries on October 17, the minesweeping remained quite hazardous.[62] A Japanese minesweeper, MS-14, that started operations that day was destroyed by a mine. Chief Steward Nakatani Sakataro, twenty-five, was killed, and eighteen crewmen were wounded. An ROK vessel was sunk by a mine the same day. Given the dangers, the crews of three MSB minesweepers refused orders and the vessels returned to Japan.

On October 20, the second contingent of Japanese minesweepers joined the operation,[63] which continued when the US landing at Wonsan started six days later. On November 26, a tugboat pulling a crane vessel hit a mine and thirty US crewmen were killed.[64] The second MSB contingent ended operations that day and withdrew; there were no more Japanese casualties. The operation in North Korean waters and the death of Nakatani were hidden from the Japanese public. At a secret funeral ceremony on October 27, MSB Director Okubo said Nakatani was "killed in an important special minesweeping operation ordered by Headquarters, U.S. Naval Forces Far East."[65] Okubo was later elected to the Diet and served as minister of labor. In 1978 he wrote his memoirs, *Roaring Waves*, and revealed the minesweeping operations. A year later, Nakatani was honored along with three other MSB personnel killed in domestic minesweeping operations; they were awarded the Order of the Paulownia Flowers, Eighth Degree.[66] MSB special minesweeping units also conducted other operations in the fall of 1950, including at Inchon, Kunsan, Haeju, and Chinnampo. A total of fifty-four minesweepers and 1,200 personnel were involved; fifty-four former Imperial Navy officers served on the Joint Task Force.[67]

Participation in the minesweeping operations, which assisted the US-ROK attack on North Korean territory, presented a most clear example of Japanese real collaboration in the war in Korea.

PYONGYANG FALLS

The ROKA 3rd and Capital Divisions occupied Hamhung and Hungnam, two major industrial centers in North Korea, on October 17.[68] US bombing had devastated North Korean cities. An Associated Press reporter on an observer flight over Pyongyang described the destruction:

> The besieged capital of North Korea looks from the air like an empty citadel where death is king. It seems no longer to be a city at all. It is more like a blackened community of the dead, a charred ghost town from which all the living have fled before a sudden plague. . . . Two rail lines converge in the heart of the city and the marshaling yards are a great black stain. The hulks of twisted and overturned locomotives and freight and passenger cars rest on their sides. Other patches of blaze-blackened buildings and industrial plants cancer the city, and the city itself is now a cancer without hope.[69]

The ROKA 1st Division started the assault on Pyongyang on October 19, and with the US 1st Cavalry Division captured the capital the next day.[70] But military victory brought a civil dilemma, one that would plague the United States in many other countries it occupied over the years: Who would govern occupied North Korea?

Seoul and Washington had already clashed over administration of the North. The Republic of Korea considered itself the only legal government on the peninsula. On October 10, ROK Home Minister Cho Pyong-ok announced that South Korean National Police were patrolling nine "liberated" towns in North Korea and that 30,000 policemen "were being recruited to keep order in all Red territory as it is freed from Communist rule."[71] But the UN General Assembly resolution on October 7 had limited ROK jurisdiction to southern Korea and stipulated that a unified, independent, and democratic Korean government would be established by elections supervised by the United Nations. On October 12, the UN Interim Committee on Korea advised the UN Unified Command "to assume provisionally all responsibilities for the government and civil administration" of North Korea and recommended that "officers from the several forces of the members of the UN serving under the Unified Command in Korea" be assigned to civil administration.[72] On October 16, ROK President Syngman Rhee wrote to MacArthur that the UN Interim Committee's "proposal to protect and revive Communism in the north is unthinkable" and that his government would take over civilian administration there by dispatching governors appointed two years earlier to the five northern provinces.[73] The US government desperately tried to dissuade Rhee from disputing the UN Command's authority in North Korea, warning that the ROK's reputation would suffer in the United Nations and urging him not to rock the boat. On October 20, US Ambassador to the ROK John Muccio reported that Rhee had agreed not to make public comments about civil authority in the North and not to send officials and police there without a request from MacArthur.[74]

However, the UN Command's policy—i.e., the US military's policy—on civil administration in the North was overly optimistic and unrealistic. Maj. Gen. Frank W. Milburn, whose I Corps was advancing northward, issued Proclamation No. 1 at Munsan in South Korea on October 13. "All laws and ordinances remain in effect unless rescinded, suspended, or banned by UN Forces," the proclamation stated, and "North Korean officials must carry out their administrative functions until replaced by the Allied Command."[75] The North Koreans were not going to obey that order.

General Milburn issued a second proclamation eight days later, after Pyongyang was occupied. He appointed an administrative committee for Pyongyang and ordered all residents of the city to comply with its orders. Among the committee's members were Yim Chong-duk as mayor, U Che-sun and O Chin-hwan as vice-mayors, and Kim Yong-il as chief of police.[76] They were selected by Col. Archibald W. Melchior, a US Army civil affairs officer.[77] According to a reporter for the *New York Times*, Mayor Yim Chong-duk was a sixty-five-year-old school teacher who had never held public office. The *London Times* reported that Vice-Mayor U Che-sun was a businessman who had previously owned a tungsten mine and was a friend of the famous North Korean nationalist Cho Man-sik. Another vice-mayor, O Chin-hwan, had managed two firms in Manchuria until the end of World War II and owned two large houses in Pyongyang.[78] On October 26, Colonel

Melchior named Kim Song-ju governor of South Pyongan Province in the North, although Kim Pyong-yon, a friend of U Che-sun, had been designated provisional governor of this province by the ROK government two years earlier.[79] While Kim Pyong-yon was a member of Cho Man-sik's first South Pyongan Province committee for the Preparation of Korean Independence in 1945, Kim Song-ju was a key member of the militantly anti-Communist Northwest Youth League, an association of North Koreans who had fled to the South after 1945.[80]

Syngman Rhee returned to Pyongyang for the first time in thirty-nine years at 8:30 a.m. on October 27 and spoke to fifty thousand people in the plaza in front of the former city hall. Banners proclaimed "The Republic of Korea Government is our Government" and "Our Leader President Yi Sung-man (Syngman Rhee) Mansei!"[81] Rhee warned the crowd that some Koreans were vicious animals with human faces that would enslave them. Communist Party members would not be treated as Koreans, he said. Rhee stated that he had left Seoul after the North's attack, been a refugee, and led a scaled-down government in the South. Fifty-three countries had provided the Republic of Korea with weapons and supplies, he told the crowd, and the Republic had counterattacked. The United Nations had decided that until a general election was held, administration of the North would be conducted mainly by a military government, Rhee said. He was complying with that decision, he indicated, while negotiating with the United Nations. Rhee also declared that the citizens of Pyongyang should no longer think in terms of North or South, or factions and parties, but about living together. They must not allow themselves to be manipulated by the Communist Party or let the Communists destroy their freedom. Rhee ended with another admonition: "All the misguided people who were deceived by the Communist Party must repent and preserve this land bequeathed by our forefathers. Those who truly repented will be embraced and pardoned, but those who have committed murder and arson must be apprehended, brought to trial, and punished. We will never forgive traitors who betrayed the nation and took up the cause of foreign countries."[82] Rhee flew back to Seoul at 12:20 p.m.

As the US 1st Cavalry Division and the ROKA 7th Division remained in Pyongyang, the US 24th Division, the ROKA 1st Division, and the 27th British Commonwealth Brigade occupied Anju on October 23–24. They captured Chongju on October 30 and then advanced to Chongchadong. Sinuiju lay just ahead. The ROKA 6th Division meanwhile advanced due north from Wonsan and reached Chosan near the Yalu River on the border with China.[83]

The US Air Force had by now run out of strategic targets in North Korea. On October 25, the 92nd Bombardment Group at Yokota returned to Fairchild Air Force Base in Washington state, and the 22nd Bombardment Group was transferred from Kadena to March Field, California.[84] The three remaining squadrons were supplemented with B-29s: the total number of B-29s available for service in Korea was kept at ninety-five.

The UN Command's civil administration was then functioning poorly in North Korea. Plans to utilize the existing administrative structure had failed completely. A *New York Times* reporter described the confusion in Pyongyang on October 30:

> Although less than half of the population of 600,000 stayed behind when the United States and South Korean troops entered the city, thousands of refugees are returning daily, aggravating the difficulties.
>
> Under the Communist Government, all civil positions were held by party members and even jobs requiring some "know-how" were limited to those believed to be reliable politically. The result was that when Communist troops left the city all civilians capable of running the municipal services took off with them.[85]

On October 25, South Korean newspaper editors visited Pyongyang and Hamhung at the invitation of the UN Command. In a series of articles about the trip, Kim Sam-gyu, editor in chief of *Tong'a Ilbo*, wrote that in both cities municipal committees and self-defense units composed of young men had been set up. US civil affairs officers and ROKA officers told the editors that the system of consultation and oversight worked well. The system was very similar to that in South Korea, and coordination and control were easy, they said, although ROK officials could not participate directly.[86] However, Kim Sam-gyu pointed out problems with the so-called cleansing operation: "The people of North Korea, perhaps because of five years of oppression and terror, have thought the Republic of Korea was heaven on earth. After our troops entered the North, the price of daily necessities rose sharply and living conditions deteriorated. Occupation officials are privileged, arrogant and contemptuous of North Koreans as a defeated people. . . . Ordinary North Koreans, with serious expressions on their faces, emphasized that the great majority of KPA soldiers are young boys who were forced into military service. They request magnanimous treatment for KPA prisoners of war. When asked how you distinguish 'pargeni' (Reds) who must be cleansed, the response was that a party member in a position of responsibility should be cleansed, while rank-and-file members can be tolerated for awhile. Actually, the really bad elements have already fled, they said."[87]

US Ambassador Muccio told the UN Interim Committee on Korea that the police officers sent from the South to the North "were not under the South Korean Government" and were "working under Gen. Douglas MacArthur's Unified Command." "The South Korean Government was making every effort to treat its prisoners fairly," Muccio said.[88] But South Korean historian An Yong-hyon describes a different reality. The ROKA military police commander in Pyongyang, Kim Chong-won, "announced that not only members of the communist party but everyone in affiliated organizations such as professional associations and confederations of women, youth, and farmers would be executed," An Yong-hyon wrote. "Terror gripped Pyongyang."[89]

The ROK National Assembly passed a law on September 28, 1950, that was intended to punish collaborators in areas of South Korea that had been overrun by the KPA. Screening committees were established in each locality to indict accused collaborators.[90] The law was applied in occupied areas of the North as well. During a visit to Wonsan on October 16, ROK Interior Minister Cho Pyong-ok ordered the execution by this law of people who had worked for North Korean administrative organs.[91]

CHINA CROSSES THE YALU

On October 25, the Communist Party of the Soviet Union Politburo decided to support, at the United Nations and the Far Eastern Commission in Washington, a charge by DPRK Foreign Minister Pak Hon-yong that US forces in Korea were using Japanese troops. Pak alleged that Japanese soldiers were fighting alongside US troops in the Seoul area, that a company of Japanese troops was in the Chorwon area, and that many Japanese troops were with the ROKA 7th and 8th Divisions.[92]

According to Nam Ki-jong's dissertation, Koreans living in Japan had volunteered for the ROKA. Five hundred and forty-six members of the pro-Seoul Association for Korean Residents in Japan (Mindan) had been trained at Camp Drake, Asaka, in September 1950. They had been formed into the First Volunteer Contingent of Koreans in Japan and had served in the Inchon landing.[93] The US 8th Army had planned to incorporate 30,000 to 40,000 ROK recruits in the five American divisions. The first Korean augmentation recruits were assigned to the US 7th Division in Japan. In addition, 8,625 South Korean recruits had been brought from Pusan to Yokohama from August 15 to 24, given rudimentary training at the Higashi Fuji maneuver area, and shipped out with the division for Inchon on September 11.[94]

North Korea probably mistook the Koreans from Japan, usually of smaller stature than Americans, for Japanese. A total of about 8,300 South Koreans were attached to three other US divisions besides the 7th, creating the impression that Japanese soldiers were in Korea. But there is no evidence that Japanese soldiers participated in ground operations in Korea. North Korea and the Soviet Union may have made this charge to set the stage for the entry of Chinese forces into the war.

With North Korea's survival hanging in the balance, on October 19 six Chinese divisions from the 40th and 39th Armies crossed the Yalu River on the border between China and North Korea at Antung, and six divisions from the 42nd and 38th Armies crossed at Jian. A week later, six more Chinese divisions from the 66th and 50th Armies crossed the Yalu at Antung. China had committed eighteen divisions and 260,000 troops.[95]

At a meeting between CPV commander Peng Dehuai and Kim Il Sung on October 21, Peng asked Kim to admit Korean comrades in CPV command. Kim agreed, and Pak Il-u became a senior officer in the Chinese People's Volunteers.[96] A member of the Yan'an group and the Korean most trusted by the Chinese Communist Party, Pak was the DPRK interior minister and had served in the security and police fields, but never in the military. The selection of a person with Pak's background to serve in a senior position in the CPV undoubtedly made a strong impression on Kim Il Sung. On October 25, Mao Zedong officially appointed Pak Il-u, together with Deng Hua, commander of the 13th Army Group, vice-commander and vice-political commissar of the CPV. The two were jointly named to these posts. Peng Dehuai was appointed secretary of the CPV, while Deng Hua and Pak Il-u were appointed vice-secretaries.[97] Pak Il-u became the third-ranking officer in the CPV.

Advancing at night to avoid detection, the CPV on October 25 made contact with the ROKA 1st Division in the Unsan area in North Pyongan Province. Peng ordered field positions set up quickly and prepared for an attack on November 1. The large surprise assault that day by Communist Chinese forces pushed US and ROK units back in the west to the towns of Tokchon, Kaechon, and Anju. This first Chinese offensive in the Korean War ended on November 4.[98]

Mao then increased CPV forces in Korea from November 7 to 19, with the 9th Army Group, consisting of three armies (each four divisions)—the 20th, 26th, and 27th—a total of twelve divisions—crossing into Korea from Jian and Linjiang. China by this time had committed thirty divisions and more than 380,000 troops.[99]

A new air war started on October 31 when Soviet-made MiG-15s (far superior to the US older F-80C) marked as Chinese air force planes attacked US aircraft in the Sinuiju area of the North. According to US military records, on November 8, seventy-nine B-29 bombers attempting to destroy the steel bridge from Andung to Sinuiju were intercepted by MiG-15s. US F-80s came to the rescue of the bombers, filling the sky with deadly dogfights.[100] Soviet records show that the Soviet General Staff on November 15 sent the 64th Fighter Group commanded by General Belov to Andung, China, under orders to engage in combat operations until November 24.[101] The US-Soviet air war in Korea was now under way. Meanwhile, the Sino-American ground war was entering the second phase.

US forces had drawn up an operational plan based on MacArthur's proposal for a full-scale attack to start on November 24 to liberate North Korea up to the Yalu River. Leaders in Washington were concerned about whether to continue the offensive if contact was unexpectedly made with Chinese forces. On November 9, the US National Security Council approved MacArthur's plan. The 8th Army estimated Chinese forces at a maximum of 70,000 troops, far less than the 380,000 it had actually committed.[102]

On November 24, a UN force comprised of seven US divisions, six ROKA divisions, and three brigades of British and Turkish troops attacked Chinese forces. Arrayed against them was a vastly larger force of thirty CPV divisions. Peng Dehuai's strategy was to lure UN forces deep into his lines on the east and west of North Korea and then strike a decisive blow. Peng ordered the CPV's IX Army Group to ambush the enemy in the Lake Changjin (Changjin Reservoir) area. On November 25–26, the CPV launched a second offensive, inflicting heavy casualties on US and ROK units, which began to fall back. The 1st Marine Division, the main force of US X Corps, lost half its men in the snowy retreat. The CPV also suffered heavy casualties.[103] At this moment Mao Zedong's son, Mao Anying, was killed in an air raid on CPV headquarters on November 25.[104]

Though Chinese troops were the main force in the CPV's second offensive, they were supplemented by KPA remnants that had made their way north from the South. On November 15, Pang Ho-sang, who led the KPA's 6th Division back to North Korea, was named a Hero of the Republic and awarded the Order of the National Flag, first class; the unit was renamed the Guards Division.[105] On November 22, the KPA's 5th and 10th Divisions were also honored for fighting their way home, and their commanders, Kim Chang-dok and Yi Pang-nam (both from the Yan'an group), respectively, received the Order of the National Flag, first class.[106]

In preparation for a third offensive against US and ROKA forces, the KPA's 6th Division became the main force of a new 5th Corps commanded by Pang Ho-sang. A second corps was organized under the command of Choe Hyon, who formerly led the KPA's 2nd Division, and both corps were placed in the east. Yi Kwon-mu, commander of the KPA's 4th Division, was named to lead the 1st Corps, which was sent to the west.[107] A Chinese estimate put KPA troop strength at 75,000.[108]

New KPA divisions were then being organized and trained in Manchuria. On October 31, Soviet Ambassador to the DPRK Shtykov reported to Moscow the location and scale of the training: there were three KPA divisions in Wangou; three in Huolong; and three in Yanji as well, along with 5,000 service troops. In Tonghua, there was an infantry school (5,000 troops) and a school for political officers (1,500 candidates). In Wangqing there was a tank school (1,500 troops), and Yanji had a flight school (2,600 trainees). Choe Yong-gon, once again DPRK defense minister, had overall responsibility for rebuilding the KPA. Shtykov requested Soviet advisers to assist with the KPA's training.[109] Stalin asked him what the North Korean government thought and warned Shtykov not to force his ideas on Kim Il Sung, who the next day asked Stalin for the advisers. [110]

China desperately needed arms and ammunition from the Soviet Union. On November 8, Mao told Stalin that the CPV force in Korea had reached twelve armies of thirty-six divisions. (Actually, at that point there were thirty divisions.) The troops were armed with weapons captured from the Japanese and Nationalist Chinese units, Mao said; it was difficult to manufacture ammunition. Mao wanted to equip the CPV divisions with standardized Soviet weapons. For 1951, he requested 140,000 rifles (58 million rounds) and 26,000 automatic rifles (80 million rounds), among other arms. Reminding Stalin that Zhou Enlai had been promised five thousand trucks, Mao asked for ten thousand tons of gasoline. Nine days later, Mao requested quick delivery of at least five hundred trucks. [111] Stalin promised the five hundred trucks by November 26. [112]

Frustrated by US air superiority since June following the start of hostilities, on November 18 Kim Il Sung asked Stalin to allow two hundred to three hundred Korean students in the Soviet Union to be trained as pilots. [113] Stalin agreed, suggested the flight training be conducted in Manchuria, and expedited departure procedures for the Koreans. [114]

Zhou asked Stalin's advice on China's participation in the UN Security Council. Stalin replied on November 10, based on a Politburo decision, and suggested China choose from two possible courses of action. China could reject its invitation to address the Security Council because it would not be allowed to speak on the Korean War or the issue of Taiwan. The alternative was to accept the invitation, make a statement, and withdraw if the PRC was not allowed to state its positions. [115] Stalin preferred the former course; China chose the latter and named Wu Xiuquan its representative to the United Nations. Wu made his first speech to the Security Council on November 28. [116]

US-ROK RETREAT

The US 8th Army abandoned Pyongyang on December 5, moving first to the south bank of the Taedong River. "Much of the city was afire by 0730 on 5 December when the rear guards destroyed the last bridges over the Taedong and set off final demolitions in the section of Pyongyang below the river," Billy Mossman recounted. The US withdrawal from Chinnampo was completed by December 11 in a makeshift armada comprised of "LSTs, transports of the Japanese merchant marine, a squadron of U.S. Navy troop and cargo transports and at least a hundred Korean sailboats," Mossman wrote. The unlikely flotilla transported casualties, prisoners of war, material removed from Pyongyang, and about thirty thousand Korean refugees. Supplies that could not be removed and the port facilities were destroyed.[117]

Losing hope of unification, US and ROK units headed south toward the 38th parallel. In the east on December 8, General MacArthur ordered the X Corps to evacuate the North through Hungnam. A total of 105,000 troops, 18,000 vehicles, 350,000 tons of bulk cargo, and 86,000 refugees were removed to safety in the South. Dynamite, ammunition, and gasoline were used to destroy Hungnam and port facilties.[118] To US forces, Pyongyang and Hungnam were mere enemy cities, and they followed a scorched-earth policy in them.

A large number of refugees fled to South Korea by sea or overland on foot. Those evacuated by US and ROK forces probably had worked for or cooperated with the US occupiers in the North. Civilians who walked south had a range of motives, from antipathy to Communism and a desire to join family members in the South to rumor-fed fear that the Americans would drop atomic bombs on the North. In the chaos, few families escaped together. Husbands left wives and children behind; separated from their parents, children went south alone. Just how many North Koreans crossed to South Korea in the early winter of 1950 is unknown. South Korean writers have chronicled this human flow and the fate of the refugees. One of the best-known accounts is *Hanssi nyondaegi* [The Han family chronicle] by Hwang Sok-yong. Another novelist, Yi Ho-chol, named these people *wollam silhyang-min*—people who went over to the South and lost their home forever.[119]

PYONGYANG IS "LIBERATED"

Following the US-ROKA retreat, Chinese and North Korean forces recaptured Pyongyang on December 6. "Democratic Capital Pyongyang Liberated" proclaimed the KPA's newspaper.[120] Although the DPRK constitution designated Seoul the nation's future capital, the loss and recovery of Pyongyang apparently intensified identification with it.

A week earlier, Stalin had congratulated Mao: "Your successes gladden not only me and my comrades in the leadership, but also all Soviet people." Just as the Soviet army had gained experience in modern warfare in the war against Germany during World War II, Stalin said, the Chinese army, through the war against the United States, would be transformed into an "up-to-date, well-armed powerful army."[121]

North Korean leaders, of course, were the most delighted by these successes. At a meeting in Beijing on December 3 with Mao Zedong, Liu Shaoqi, and Zhou Enlai, Kim Il Sung must have expressed his heartfelt thanks for the CPV and their battlefield performance. The Chinese seized the opportunity to bring up the question of a unified military command.[122] For the KPA, including new divisions then being formed in Manchuria, to engage in combat operations, Mao said, a unified headquarters was necessary. Friendly-fire incidents had occurred when the KPA mistakenly attacked the CPV.[123] Probably not enthusiastic, Kim had no choice but to agree. Later in the month in North Korea, Peng and Kim worked out the arrangements for a CPV-KPA Joint Headquarters based on a six-point agreement drafted by Zhou Enlai:

1. To deal more effective blows against our common enemy, China and Korea agree to establish a Joint Headquarters to unify all operations and related matters within Korean territory.
2. China and Korea mutually agree to designate Peng Dehuai as commander of the Joint Headquarters and Political Commissar, Kim Ung as vice-commander of the Joint Headquarters, and Pak Il-u as vice-Political Commissar, Joint Headquarters.
3. The Korean People's Army and all guerrilla units and the Chinese People's Volunteers are under the unified control of the Joint Headquarters. The Joint Headquarters will issue all orders through the General Headquarters, Korean People's Army and the Headquarters, Chinese People's Volunteers.
4. The Joint Headquarters has authority in all operations to control transportation (public roads, railroads, ports, airfields, wire and wireless telephone and telegraph communications), planning for provisions, mobilization of personnel and materials, etc.
5. Regarding activities for mobilization in rear areas of Korea to support the front lines, supplementary training, and the reestablishment of local administration, and related matters, the Joint Headquarters will report and make proposals to the Korean government, based on the situation and war needs.
6. As for newspaper reporting of operations, an organization designated by the Joint Headquarters will be responsible for the preparation of news, which will be released to Korean newspaper agencies in the name of General Headquarters, Korean People's Army.

Note: To maintain secrecy, orders in the names of Peng Dehuai, Kim Ung, and Pak Il-u will be issued only to the General Headquarters of the Korean People's Army and the Headquarters of Chinese People's Volunteers. Their names will not appear on orders to subordinate units, which will be from the Joint Headquarters.[124]

According to Du Ping, "after establishment of the Joint Headquarters, all operational matters and frontline activities were under its authority, while mobilization, training, and military/civilian security measures in rear areas were under the direct jurisdiction of the North Korean government. The existence of the Joint Headquarters was kept secret."[125]

For Kim Ung, the KPA chief of staff and an able soldier, to be named vice-commander of the Joint Headquarters was appropriate; the fact that he was in the Yan'an group and had worked with the Chinese Communists for years was also a factor in his appointment. When Kim Ung and Pak Il-u were in the joint chain of command, Kim Il Sung was excluded completely from operational leadership, although he was still nominally KPA supreme commander.

After Kim Ung moved to the Joint Headquarters, former vice-minister of education Nam Il was appointed KPA chief of staff. Nam Il, a Soviet Korean, had been an educator in the Soviet Union and had no military experience. "Nam Il had no knowledge of the military, but he was highly intelligent, cultured, and wise," Yu Song-chol wrote. "Those qualities enabled him to serve as chief of staff with distinction at that difficult time."[126] The talented Nam Il probably got along amicably with Kim Il Sung. Nam Il could have had a good relationship with the Soviet military advisers, and he probably was effective as liaison between the Joint Headquarters and KPA units. The fact that Nam Il was appointed KPA chief of staff meant that the KPA no longer played a role in formulating strategy.

SHOCK IN WASHINGTON

Chinese intervention in the Korean War was a devastating setback for American leaders. Just when the UN Command had reached the Yalu River, the North Korean state was all but destroyed, and the peninsula almost unified under the UN flag, Chinese troops had suddenly appeared on the battlefield and routed UN forces. MacArthur, Truman, and the United Nations were staggered. On November 28, MacArthur bluntly told the Joint Chiefs of Staff, "We face an entirely new war." The ultimate objective of Chinese forces "was undoubtedly a decisive effort aimed at the complete destruction of all United Nations forces in Korea . . ." MacArthur stated. "It is quite evident that our present strength of forces is not sufficient to meet this undeclared war by the Chinese. . . . This command has done everything humanly possible within its capabilities but is now faced with conditions beyond its control and its strength."[127] At an emergency NSC meeting that day in Washington, military leaders, fearful of attacks from Chinese airfields in Manchuria, said the United States should neither become engaged in a general war against China nor attack inside Chinese territory. Secretary of State Dean Acheson agreed with the cautious approach against war with China as summarized by Defense Secretary George C. Marshall. The meeting ended without a recommendation to Truman.[128]

MacArthur strongly disagreed with the cautious consensus in Washington and thought that the UN Command could salvage victory by expanding the war. On November 29, the general informed the JCS that a significant number of Nationalist Chinese troops on Formosa could be available within two weeks and asked for authority to negotiate directly with the Nationalist government.[129] The JCS immediately rejected the request on the grounds that British Commonwealth forces could not be employed with Nationalist troops given Britain's recognition of the PRC and that the policy MacArthur espoused would isolate the United States at the United Nations.[130]

At a press conference on November 30, Truman said that the mission of UN forces in Korea was to "repulse aggression that threatens not only the whole fabric of the United Nations, but all human hopes of peace and justice. . . . We shall intensify our efforts to help other free nations strengthen their defenses in order to meet the threat of aggression elsewhere. We shall rapidly increase our own military strength." Truman said he intended to ask Congress for additional funds "to increase the size and effectiveness of our armed forces."[131] In response to a question about consideration of the use of the atomic bomb, Truman replied, "There has always been active consideration of its use. I don't want to see it used. It is a terrible weapon." When asked if atomic weapons would only be used with UN approval, Truman said, "Responsibility for the use of weapons ordinarily rests with the field commander."[132]

China's entry into the war triggered a full-scale review of the use of atomic weapons. At a Pentagon conference on December 1, Army Chief of Staff Lawton Collins said that attacks on bases in China might bring Chinese and Soviet airpower into the war: "The only chance then left to save us is the use or the threat of the use of the A-bomb. We should therefore hold back from bombing in China even if it means that our ground forces must take some punishment from the air." Collins favored the defense of Japan but thought Korea of little strategic value, "not worth a nickel while the Russians hold Vladivostok and positions on the other flank."[133]

Concerned that Truman's comments at the press conference might be misinterpreted, the White House issued a clarification the same day that said "only the President can authorize the use of the atomic bomb, and no such authorization has been given."[134] The British government was not reassured. Prime Minister Clement Attlee flew to Washington to meet Truman, who on December 7 promised to consult with Great Britain and Canada before using atomic bombs. Attlee wanted a written assurance, but had to settle for an oral promise.[135]

MacArthur asked the JCS to reassign to his command the two bomber groups that had returned to the United States from Japan. Concerned about a potential Soviet attack in Europe, the Joint Chiefs would not put the bombers on bases vulnerable to an "all-out Communist air attack" and denied the request.[136] To contend with the Soviets' MiG-15s, General Stratemayer assigned the latest US fighters, the F-86A Sabre and F-84E Thunderjet fighter-bomber, to action in Korea, intensifying US-Soviet aerial warfare over the peninsula.[137] But MacArthur thought US airpower insufficient. On December 9, he sought commander's discretion to use atomic bombs. On December 24, he submitted "a list of retardation targets" and requested twenty-six atomic bombs.[138]

Chong Il-gwon asserts in the revised version of his memoirs that President Rhee had anticipated China's military intervention. Unperturbed about the Chinese offensive from Unsan to Lake Changjin, Rhee told Chong the Chinese action might give the cowardly Truman some guts. There was nothing to worry about, Rhee said, because MacArthur understood and would handle the situation. MacArthur himself had foreseen the possibility of China's action, but told Truman that Beijing would not enter the war, in order to avoid criticism of his advance north of the 38th parallel. Rhee showed Chong an exchange of correspondence with the general, Chong recalls.[139] It is reasonable to assume that Rhee, who saw the North Korean attack as another Sarajevo that might bring Korean unification, thought a clash with the PLA was inevitable. Rhee wanted the United States to keep open the atomic option and expand the war, and he welcomed Truman's statement on November 30.

Rhee also told Chong he understood that the atomic bomb was a terrible, sinful weapon, but that the bomb would be useful to save mankind from wicked, irrational aggression.[140]

When MacArthur's views were rejected in Washington and US-ROK forces were pushed back by the CPV, Rhee's irritation with the cautious approach in Washington grew.

Editorial writers in Tokyo had no sense of crisis over Korea. The *Asahi Shimbun* opined on October 21 that after the capture of Pyongyang UN forces only had to "mop up a defeated enemy," and that the Communists should have learned a painful lesson from "the defeat in Korea." The newspaper optimistically looked ahead: "The United Nations faces a difficult test in the reconstruction of a free, self-sufficient, unified Korea. UN success in creating a new Korea should also contribute to the democratic development of Japan." On November 7, two days after the newspaper reported that China had entered the war, an editorial said that Beijing had "ignored international law. To equate the destruction of North Korea with a threat to China . . . was paranoid." China should immediately stop "playing with fire," the editorial stated.[141] It was all empty talk.

HOT OR CAUTIOUS PURSUIT?

On December 4, before returning to Beijing, Chinese Ambassador to the Soviet Union Wang Jiaxiang posed two questions to First Deputy Minister of Foreign Affairs Andrei Gromyko: Will the United States seek negotiations with China and the Soviet Union over Korea? And should China attack south of the 38th parallel? Any answer to the first question would be conjecture, Gromyko responded; there had been no approach so far. On the second, the diplomat offered as his personal opinion that "one should strike while the iron is hot." Wang said that even within the ranks of the non-Communist parties supporting the PRC government, spirits were on the rise. Reading a letter from the front in Korea, Wang told Gromyko that the Americans were poor soldiers (*voiaki*) whose fighting skills were far inferior to those of the Japanese.[142]

The Chinese and Soviets were then debating whether Chinese forces should press the attack. A disagreement between CPV commander Peng Dehuai and Soviet Ambassador Terentii Shtykov has been discussed at length in the Chinese literature on the war. After driving US-ROK forces back to the 38th parallel, Peng halted the attack to rest and resupply his troops. Shtykov reportedly wanted the Chinese to continue the offensive across the 38th parallel and take Seoul.[143] The last two messages on the issue available to researchers are a telegram from Shytkov in Pyongyang to Moscow on November 22 and a letter from Kim Il Sung to the ambassador dated November 27. Subsequent communication between Pyongyang and Moscow, or within Pyongyang, remains classified up until a report from the new Soviet Ambassador to the DPRK Vladimir Razuvaev, which Andrei Vyshinskii sent to Stalin's secretary on January 5, 1951.[144] In general, communication between Beijing and Moscow from December 7, 1950, until January 5, 1951, remains closed. Many sensitive materials are hidden from scholarly perusal.

The Russian journal *Istochnik* published documents related to the Korean War in 1996. An editor's note says Shtykov was transferred from Korea on November 29 (which may be a bit early),[145] when he was named first secretary of the Far Eastern Maritime Region Communist Party committee.[146] This was not a punitive reassignment. His replacement, Gen. Vladimir N. Razuvaev, was fifty (seven years older than Shtykov), and a career soldier who at the end of World War II had commanded the First Shock Army.[147] It seemed only that a military officer had succeeded a Party functionary. Nevertheless, the disagreement between Peng Dehuai and Shtykov was probably a factor.

The Chinese, of course, still had to consider North Korean wishes. Kim Il Sung reportedly urged Peng on December 7 to press the attack on the retreating enemy.[148] The next day, however, Peng proposed to Mao that the Chinese People's Volunteers not cross the 38th parallel, and then awaited orders.[149] Three days later, Mao sent Peng a secret intelligence report about a visit by US Army Chief of Staff Collins to Japan and the front lines in Korea, and about his conferences with MacArthur and US 8th Army Commander Walton Walker. Impressed by the speed and scale of the Chinese–North Korean attack, Collins reportedly said that American forces had suffered very heavy losses in personnel and equipment, that morale was extremely bad, and that they could not defend Korea for long. Collins had already informed the Joint Chiefs of Staff of his views, the report said, and MacArthur had been ordered to assemble warships in South Korean ports for an evacuation. Articles in the foreign press reported that preparations for a retreat from Seoul were under way. The accuracy of this information should be established shortly, Mao told Peng. [150]

The intelligence Mao sent Peng was exaggerated and inaccurate. Collins did visit Japan and the Republic of Korea from December 4 to 6, met General Walker and his staff, and conferred with MacArthur and other senior commanders in Tokyo on December 7. The resulting plan, however, was to halt the Chinese attack north of Seoul. Withdrawal from the capital would occur only if the 8th Army's redeployment south was in jeopardy, the planners decided. [151]

But, convinced that one more push might force the United States out of Korea, Mao recklessly thought China should press on. Because the United States and Great Britain had asked for a ceasefire north of the 38th parallel, on December 13 Mao ordered Peng to cross the parallel and advance to Kaesong in the South. [152] Peng reported two days later, "In obedience to Chairman Mao's order, I resolved . . . to advance south of the 38th parallel." [153]

Yet Peng was cautious, as evident in a long telegram (2,200 characters) he sent to Mao on December 19:

> Since the second victory the spirits of the Korean party, government, military, and people and the prestige of the CPV are very high. However, expectations of quick victory and blind optimism are widespread. The Soviet ambassador says U.S. forces are trying to escape and we must pursue them. . . . In my view, the Korean War will be fairly long and difficult. If the enemy shifts from the offensive to defense, shortens the battlefield, concentrates troops, and narrows the front, the situation will be advantageous to combined-arms operations. The morale of American and puppet troops has fallen, but the enemy still has about 260,000 troops. On the political side, it would be very disadvantageous to the imperialist camp to abandon Korea immediately. Britain and France are not asking America to do that. Even if the enemy suffers one or two more defeats and another two or three divisions are exterminated, they may withdraw and defend several bridgeheads (Pusan, Inchon, Kunsan). A complete and immediate withdrawal can hardly be expected. At present, our forces must advance cautiously. [154]

Mao "completely agreed" with Peng two days later: "America and Britain plan to use the old image that people have of the 38th parallel and conduct political propaganda to lure us into a ceasefire," Mao said. "Thus it is necessary for our forces to cross the 38th parallel, attack again, and then rest and regroup." [155]

Mao agreed with Peng that Seoul need not be reoccupied.

On December 29, Mao informed Peng that Stalin had written him that "the leadership of the CPV is correct and he had criticized the many mistaken opinions." In short, Stalin agreed with Peng.[156] But the North Koreans and Terentii Shtykov clearly favored hot pursuit of the enemy and wanted to retake and hold Seoul. Mao apparently had told Stalin that Shytkov did not understand military matters. Stalin acknowledged the criticism and decided to replace Shtykov.[157] Of course, Stalin also wanted Seoul recaptured. But Shtykov had to go.

A confused United Nations was then vacillating over a response to China's intervention. Representatives from India, England, and Sweden, and Secretary General Trygve Lie sounded out Chinese representative to the UN Wu Xiuquan on the conditions for a halt to the fighting in Korea. Zhou Enlai told Soviet Ambassador to the PRC Nikolai Roshchin China's position on December 7. Representatives from India, England, and Sweden and Trygve Lie sought to save the situation at the 38th parallel, Zhou said. To avoid putting Chinese forces in an unfavorable position and to hold the initiative, Zhou intended to give Wu the following terms for a ceasefire:

1. The withdrawal of all foreign troops from Korea.
2. The withdrawal of U.S. military forces from the Taiwan Straits.
3. The Korean question must be resolved by the Korean people themselves.
4. Admission of the Chinese People's Republic to the United Nations and expulsion of Chiang Kai-shek's representative from the United Nations.
5. Convene a conference of the foreign ministers of the four major powers to prepare a peace treaty with Japan.

   If these five conditions for the cessation of military operations are accepted, the five great powers can send their representatives to a conference to sign a ceasefire agreement.[158]

Zhou asked for a Soviet response that day. Stalin immediately instructed Roshchin to inform Zhou that the Soviet Union agreed completely with the proposal. To conceal China's intentions, Stalin suggested they welcome an immediate cessation of military activities in Korea and ask about the conditions for a ceasefire that were under consideration by the United Nations or the United States.[159] However, that same day, instructions were sent to Soviet Foreign Minister Vyshinsky at the United Nations that points one and three were the conditions for a ceasefire, not all five.[160] At a press conference on December 16, Wu Xiuquan gave points one, two, and five.[161]

THE KWP CENTRAL COMMITTEE THIRD PLENUM

Removed from day-to-day military leadership, DPRK leaders Kim Il Sung and Pak Hon-yong reviewed the war to date and concentrated on party affairs. The third plenary session of the KWP Central Committee was held on December 21. It was the first full committee meeting in a year. In a report on the war,[162] Kim Il Sung recounted the early victories and praised the 3rd, 4th, and 6th Divisions and the 105th Tank regiment, led by Yi Yong-ho, Yi Kwon-mu, Pang Ho-san, and Yu Kyong-su, respectively. As supreme commander, Kim Il Sung bore responsibility for the subsequent setbacks, but he blamed everything on the frontline commanders and his vice-minister of defense. The 2nd Corps commander, Mu Chong, had rashly executed his subordinate during the chaotic retreat from the South. Kim Il, the vice-minister of defense and in charge of the KPA's Political Department, was a defeatist who said the army could not fight the enemy without air support, Kim Il Sung stated. Choe Kwang, commander of the 1st Division, and Kim Han-jung, commander of a reserve division, had abandoned their units and fled to save their lives, Kim Il Sung charged. Yim Chun-chu, chairman of the KWP Committee in North Kangwon Province, had panicked and failed to prepare for a withdrawal. The five men, of whom Choe Kwang, Kim Il, and Yim Chun-chu were members of the Manchurian faction, were dismissed from their positions. Kim Il Sung blamed all failures on cowardly commanders and avoided mentioning the systemic errors of the KWP and government leaders. The dismissal of Kim Il was also related to the KWP takeover of the military, which Kim Il Sung did not mention.

Kim Il Sung had harsh comments on the partisans in the South, too: "When the Korean People's Army attacked, we expected the underground party organization in South Korea to rise up everywhere, rapidly expand partisan warfare, strengthen the movement, create confusion in the enemy's rear areas, and thereby contribute to an easy victory by the Korean People's Army." However, many party members had been killed by the oppressive Syngman Rhee government, Kim said:

> Under the difficult conditions, our party organization in South Korea could not rapidly mobilize the people and organize extensive partisan warfare, with the result that the Korean People's Army faced additional difficulties in accomplishing its mission. . . . The Party Political Committee recognized the importance of a powerful partisan organization that could disrupt enemy rear areas and on its own organized special partisan units under the leadership of the most powerful member of the Central Committee and sent them [to the South]. However, the leaders of partisan units, including Comrade Ho Song-taek, did not follow Party instructions and fight in enemy rear areas.[163]

Kim ignored his own fundamental misjudgment of the political situation in the South and focused on the failure of partisan units sent from North Korea. With the blame shifted to others, Kim Il Sung and Pak Hon-yong were safe from criticism.[164] The dismissed Mu Chong was put in command of the 7th KPA Corps and assigned to train the new units in Manchuria, and Kim Il became chief of the Political Bureau, Interior Ministry.[165]

SEOUL IS RECAPTURED

Peng Dehuai issued orders for the third Chinese–North Korean offensive on December 22: the 42nd and 66th Armies of the CPV were assembled northwest of Chunchon as a left column, and the 38th, 39th, 40th, and 50th Armies formed a right column headed for Seoul. The KPA's 5th and 2nd Corps were assigned the area near the East Sea coast.

The Chinese attacked with overwhelming numerical superiority on New Year's Eve.[166] General Matthew Ridgway had by now succeeded Walton Walker as 8th Army commander; Walker was killed nine days earlier when his jeep collided with a truck. US 5th Air Force fighters and fighter-bombers, favored by five days of clear weather, furiously attacked the Chinese troops. American pilots flew 564 sorties on January 1, 1951; 531 on January 2; 556 on January 3; 498 on January 4; and 447 on January 5. Pyongyang was hit by 63 B-29s on January 3 and by 60 Superfortresses two days later.

Still, the Chinese–North Korean offensive rolled on.[167] Peng's strategy, as proposed to Mao on December 28, was to seize the 38th parallel. If US-ROK forces abandoned Seoul, the KPA 1st Corps would occupy the capital and the main forces would regroup north of the 38th parallel.[168] General Ridgway ordered a withdrawal from Seoul on January 1. The last bridge across the Han River was destroyed three days later, and Seoul was reoccupied the same day,[169] this time by Chinese and North Korean troops.

A report of Seoul's liberation to Mao from Peng Dehuai, Kim Ung, and Pak Il-u, all of the Joint Headquarters, was forwarded to Moscow on January 8. Stalin congratulated the Chinese on "the great victory of the people—the patriotic forces—over the reactionary forces."[170]

Advanced Chinese units had reached the 37th parallel in the South when Peng ended the third offensive on January 7. He suspected that US strategy was to entice him southward and then cut off CPV-KPA forces with another Inchon-like landing behind their lines.

Some Chinese scholars claim that Ambassador Shtykov advocated that the offensive continue. However, he had, of course, been replaced by then as ambassador, and it would be strange for a new ambassador (Vladimir Razuvaev) to insist that the army of an ally take risks. The North Koreans were probably the advocates.

Although the Chinese writer Ye Yumeng and scholar Heng Xueming differ on many points, they agree that the North Koreans referred to the opinion of a Soviet ambassador in support of continuing the offensive beyond Seoul, and that Pak Hon-yong was a more forceful proponent than Kim Il Sung. Heng concludes that the North Koreans backed down from this position, but that Peng Dehuai had to promise to hold a joint conference of senior North Korean and Chinese military leaders. [171]

Though the accuracy of these accounts is difficult to assess (Soviet documents provide no verification), Kim Il Sung undoubtedly wanted the third offensive to continue until total victory. But he was a failed commander and had to moderate his views. By contrast, Pak Hon-yong was unyielding and more of a thorn in the Chinese side. After consultation with Mao Zedong, Peng convened a joint Sino-Korean military meeting to resolve their differences of opinion.

AMERICAN VACILLATION, JAPANESE SENTIMENT

December 1950 to January 1951 was a period of intense crisis in Washington. After all, the enemy had broken through the 38th parallel and recaptured Seoul. On December 15, President Truman finally addressed America on national television and radio and explained the grave situation in Korea. The next day he declared a national emergency, vowed to fight against "world domination by Communist imperialism," and announced the establishment of the Office of Defense Mobilization. By these steps, Truman accepted the mobilization recommendations in NSC 68. [172] But he did not have a policy to resolve the precarious military situation in Korea. Defense Secretary George Marshall and the three Joint Chiefs of Staff were inclined toward US withdrawal and deployment of forces to Japan, where they expected the Soviet Union to attack. [173] The JCS sent new instructions to MacArthur on December 29: While striking as hard as possible against the enemy, they said, if MacArthur was forced back to near the Kum River and a line to the east, and the Chinese massed "large forces against your position with an evident capability of forcing us out of Korea, it then would be necessary . . . to direct you to commence a withdrawal to Japan." [174] MacArthur, of course, saw the policy as totally defensive and negative.

The general had an ally in Ashida Hitoshi, president of the Democratic Party in Japan. At the request of MacArthur's GHQ in Tokyo, Ashida submitted a memorandum in early December to the Government Section of the GHQ:

The Korean Incident clearly shows the aggressive intentions of the Communist countries and Japan is also directly threatened. There is a very strong possibility that World War III will occur in a few years. When other countries diligent-

ly prepare for this probability, it is unacceptable for Japan alone to act like a
bystander. We must have a national consensus. . . . I want Premier Yoshida to
lead public opinion in this direction. The government's urgent task is to explain to the people that Japan faces a crisis and that Japanese must defend the
country with their own hands, and the government should be in the vanguard
of this movement. . . . Both the Liberal Party and Socialist Party advocate
"cooperation with the United Nations." But if we ask what concretely Japan
has contributed, the answer is . . . nothing. Can this earn the trust of the United
States and Great Britain?

Ashida wanted the Yoshida administration to lead a broad-based national
movement for defense of Japan against Communism that would include the
Liberal, Socialist, Democratic, and other parties. He sent his memorandum to
Premier Yoshida on December 7,[175] and met with him at Yoshida's residence
a week later. Ashida reiterated that the war in Korea was a crisis for Japan
and urged Yoshida to form a national unity cabinet. Yoshida hinted that the
Communist Party should be outlawed, but was averse to talks with the Socialists. Ashida recommended bold action and appealed to Yoshida's patriot-
ism in colorful language: "For the sake of the country you might even run
down Ginza in a loin cloth!"[176] But dramatic gestures to show desperate
determination were not Yoshida's style.

Despite Chinese intervention in Korea, Yoshida did not consider the military situation there all that crucial. When the Diet session ended for the year-
end recess on December 16, he convened a secret plenary session of Liberal
Party Diet members and denounced Ashida's proposal for a unity cabinet as
"inappropriate speech and behavior in Japan's current circumstances" because the Korean War did not pose such a danger for Japan. "Some people
say the Korean problem is entering a crucial phase and World War III is
inevitable. I do not think wars occur so easily. The situation is not that grave.
I do not think the Chinese Communists will triumph in the end or that the
Korean disturbance will go on indefinitely. At the appropriate point there
will be a settlement."[177]

Ashida made public his memorandum to GHQ and made a statement in
the *Asahi Shimbun* on December 28: "The Chinese Communists not only aim
to control Korea but next will call for the liberation of Japan from U.S.
occupation. . . . It is rare for one country to sacrifice its young men and fight
to the death to protect another people who will not defend themselves."
Ashida's formula for his broad-based national defense movement: exclude
the Communist Party, bring the Socialist Party into the picture, and strength-
en independent self-defense forces.[178]

Japanese Socialist Party Secretary Asanuma Inejiro weighed in from the
left against Ashida: "That Japan cannot be indifferent to recent trends in
Korea is true. But as a country that has pledged peace and demilitarization in
our new constitution we must always have convictions and confidence in

peace. . . . Japan is under the supervision of the Allied Powers and I firmly believe that our security should be guaranteed by the United Nations and we should closely observe trends in Asia. When the Allies have as yet said nothing about rearmament, politicians concerned about the nation should not raise the issue."

At a press conference on December 28, Prime Minister Yoshida derided fear-mongering politicians who shout "'Oh, my god! Oh, my god!' Shouting in such way, they brought forth the Great East Asia War." Instead of spouting overheated rhetoric, Yoshida said, "We should uphold the spirit of the Constitution for the time being and not talk rashly about rearmament." He called for a crackdown on the Communist Party and pro-Pyongyang Korean rioters in Japan. "It is particularly outrageous for people from another country like some Koreans to disturb public order. Even from the perspective of national self-defense we must take strong measures."[179] Yoshida and the Socialists thought alike: protect the constitution and oppose rearmament. Ashida and his call for a military buildup were politically isolated.

Renunciation of war and nonpossession of war potentials in Article 9 of the new constitution was only feasible if Japan's security was to be guaranteed by the United States, the Soviet Union, China, and Great Britain. But war in Korea among these former Allies had destroyed the pacifist premise of Article 9 and undermined the postwar structure for guaranteeing Japan's security. Wishful thinking about a guarantee from the United Nations did not alter a fundamental reality: the world body and China were at war. If Japan expected to be safe behind a UN shield, it had to cooperate when the organization was in peril. Yoshida had in mind a security guarantee from the United States, a step down the path toward a US-Japan security treaty. The Socialist Party was headed toward utopian pacifism with no discussion of realistic security provisions. On December 28, the JSP central committee adopted a bill sponsored by the party's left wing to be submitted to the upcoming party congress. The bill had three principles: a peace treaty with all belligerent nations, neutrality, and no foreign military bases in Japan. The party's right wing had a nuanced position: after a peace settlement, Japan would seek inclusion in a UN collective security guarantee, join the United Nations, and request that it recognize the special features of the new Japanese constitution. Japan retained the right of self-defense at this time, but given Article 9, rearmament was not an issue.[180]

On December 30, MacArthur presented the JCS with a stark choice: Withdraw from Korea and reinforce the defense of Japan, or launch a limited war against the Chinese mainland. The latter choice included "retaliatory measures within our capability": blockade China's coast, destroy China's war industries by naval bombardment and air attacks, obtain Nationalist troops on Formosa to serve in Korea, and permit Nationalist forces to attack the Chinese mainland.[181] The JCS rejected the general's retaliatory measures on January 9.[182] The next day, MacArthur angrily responded: "The issue really boils down to the question of whether or not the United States intends to evacuate Korea. . . . My query therefore amounts to this: Is it the present objective of United States policy to maintain a military position in Korea—indefinitely, for a limited time, or to minimize losses by evacuation as soon as it can be accomplished?"[183]

The United Nations wanted an end to the fighting. Having readily endorsed US sanctions against North Korea, the UN was now enmeshed in a war that might become worldwide and even nuclear. The three-member Cease-Fire Group at the UN—Iran, Canada, and India—that was established in December submitted five principles to the First Committee of the General Assembly as the basis for negotiations after a ceasefire: (1) There should be an assurance that an immediate ceasefire would not be used as a screen to conceal a new offensive; (2) If a truce were arranged, it should be used to consider steps to restore peace; (3) There should be phased withdrawal of non-Korean armed forces, and the Korean people should be able to express their will freely regarding a future government; (4) Provisional steps, in accord with UN principles, should be considered for the administration of Korea, and the United States, Soviet Union, and China should guarantee that administration; (5) A body should be established including representatives of the governments of the United Kingdom, United States, Soviet Union, and the People's Republic of China to settle problems in the Far East, including Taiwan and the representation of China in the United Nations. US. Secretary of State Acheson quickly expressed support for the principles, and US Ambassador to the UN Warren Austin agreed in the First Committee that they be sent to China.[184]

A JCS memorandum entitled "Courses of Action Relative to Communist China and Korea," dated January 11, 1951, shows clearly how seriously the US government was cornered by the military situation in Korea . The Joint Chiefs listed US objectives in the region: "a. Maintain the security of the off-shore defense line: Japan—Ryukyus—Philippines; b. Deny Formosa to the Communists; c. Delay a general war with Russia until we have achieved the requisite degree of military and industrial mobilization; d. Prevent, by all appropriate means, the further spread by force of Communism on the mainland of Asia: particularly into Indochina, Siam and Malaya; e. Support the South Koreans as much and as long as practicable; keeping alive an exile government of Korea, if forced to evacuate Korean territory; f. Support establishment in China of a government friendly to the United States."[185]

The memorandum also shows the confused, sometimes wishful thinking in some segments of Washington. If conditions deteriorated to the point that the ROK was lost and a government in exile was established, creation of a pro-American regime in Beijing was not in the cards. Nor was establishing a pro-American regime in China likely even if the ROK was healthy.

A DETERMINED MAO

Stalin sent Mao a memorandum on a possible truce on January 11 that has not been made public; it probably concerned moves by the United Nations. Soviet Ambassador to China Nikolai Roshchin reported Zhou Enlai's reaction to the memorandum on January 13 to Moscow.[186] Zhou thanked Stalin for his advice, said that their Korean comrades would be informed, and indicated that Mao had requested that Kim Il Sung and Peng Dehuai come to Beijing for consultations on the memorandum.[187]

Mao, of course, intended to win the war and was not interested in a truce. On January 14, he sent instructions to Peng with a copy to Stalin:

> Comrade Peng Dehuai,
> I ask that the contents of this message be transmitted to Comrade Kim Il Sung.
> The approximately 100,000 Korean recruits now being trained in Northeast China must be incorporated into KPA corps over the next two to three months, during the period for rest and reorganization . . .
> The CPV and Korean forces must complete very important work during the next two to three months. Units must be brought up to strength with the new trainees, who should learn the experiences of the veterans, the army must be reequipped, the railroads made serviceable, provisions and ammunition stockpiled, and transportation and services improved in rear areas. By completion of this work, we can achieve final victory.
> The enemy command probably has two options for military action.
>
> 1. After light resistance to pressure from Chinese and Korean troops, the enemy will withdraw from Korea. In this case, it would be due to our thorough preparations. Having obtained intelligence information about our thorough preparatory measures, the enemy will be convinced that our forces are even stronger and fearing difficulty will withdraw from Korea.
> 2. The enemy will continue stiff resistance in the Pusan-Taegu area until convinced that resistance is useless and then he will withdraw from Korea. In this case, we must be fully prepared so we can continue to fight. Otherwise, we will repeat the same mistake the Korean forces made from June to September 1950.
>
> But it is also possible that objective circumstances may force us to conduct a single offensive in February and then rest and regroup to complete preparations necessary for a final operation. This must also be included in our calculation. However, if this does not happen, after completing the necessary preparations in two to three months, it will be both necessary and feasible to carry out the final decisive offensive. . . .[188]

Mao intended with a fourth or fifth offensive to compel US forces to pull out of Korea, win the "final victory," and accomplish the "goal of finally resolving the Korea problem." He and Zhou prepared a ceasefire counterproposal they knew would be unacceptable to Washington:

1. China agrees to discussions by the relevant parties to end the Korean War on the basis of the withdrawal of all foreign troops from Korea and the resolution of internal political problems by the Korean people.
2. The conference agenda will include the removal of U.S. military forces from Taiwan and the Taiwan Straits and other Far eastern problems.
3. The seven countries to participate in the conference are the People's Republic of China, Soviet Union, Great Britain, United States, France, India, and Egypt. The legal status of China in the United Nations is to be confirmed by the fact of opening the conference.
4. The site of the seven-nation conference is China. [189]

Mao told Zhou to request Kim Il Song's agreement with their ceasefire counterproposal.[190] Kim was informed on January 14 and apparently told that the Soviet Union had already approved the terms.[191] Documents related to this exchange have not yet been made public; but we may safely assume that Kim assented.

The UN First Committee of the General Assembly approved a draft resolution, based on the Cease-Fire Group's report, on January 13 by a vote of fifty (including the United States) to seven, with one abstention.[192] Four days later, Zhou rejected the UN proposal and announced China's terms. Dean Acheson issued a protest statement, and there matters stood.[193]

Gen. Lawton Collins, the US Army chief of staff, conferred with MacArthur in Tokyo again on January 15 and presented the policy on Korea that had been worked out with President Truman. "Evacuation would be delayed as long as possible without endangering the Eighth Army or the security of Japan," Collins informed MacArthur. The 8th Army's "objective was to permit the longest time possible for political action by the United Nations and the fullest opportunity to punish the Chinese." If evacuation became necessary, "President Truman wanted not only the ROKA but also members of the ROK government and the ROK police force, altogether more than a million people, taken out of Korea," Collins added. Collins flew to Taegu and met with Gen. Matthew Ridgway, the new 8th Army commander, who was full of fighting spirit. Collins seemed encouraged by Ridgway's determination to improve the combat performance of US troops, particularly general officers.[194]

A confidence gap was then emerging on the Chinese side. CPV commander Peng Dehuai did not share Mao's bullish outlook. On January 16, Peng visited Kim Il Sung to inform Kim of Mao's instructions to him on the war two days earlier and added his own views. Peng returned to his headquarters on January 18, and the next day he wrote to Mao, who forwarded the letter to Stalin on January 27. Peng wrote:

Comrade Kim Il Sung and his comrades think it is impossible for the KPA alone to pursue and attack the retreating U.S. army and puppet troops. This would also be adventuresome. They said the Politburo regard as correct my proposal about the need for two months to rest and regroup in order to advance cautiously, without haste. Comrade Pak Hon-yong had a different opinion. On January 17, I again explained the options to him: make a dangerous advance without preparations or prepare first and advance cautiously. There were positive and negative aspects to both choices. Pak was then satisfied with my explanation.

The Soviet advisers also agreed that because the next offensive is decisive, approval from the Politburo of the Korean Worker's Party would probably contribute to effective implementation.[195]

Peng's letter confirms the rift that was opening between Pak and Kim on liberation of the South.

CHINESE-KOREAN SENIOR MILITARY LEADERS' CONFERENCE

CPV and KPA senior leaders met on January 25 to reach a consensus on the next offensive. In attendance were Peng Dehuai, Gao Gang, Deng Hua, Song Shilun, Kim Il Sung, Kim Tu-bong, Pak Hon-yong, Kim Ung, Du Ping, and Pak Il-u. Du Ping headed the secretariat of the conference. After welcoming remarks from Kim Tu-bong, Peng Dehuai reported on the third offensive and current tasks. Pak Hon-yong reviewed the KPA's political work. Deng Hua spoke on the initial experiences of the operations of US and ROK forces, and Du Ping, who was also chief of the political section of the CPV, reported on the CPV's political work in the third offensive.[196]

The third offensive was a "great victory," Peng said. More than seventy thousand enemy troops were annihilated and two-thirds of Korea was "recovered and liberated." He stressed that the offensive was a "foundation for greater victories" and had "strengthened China's national defense and exposed the weakness of American imperialism." Peng, a realist, attributed the victory to correct "principles of military leadership," specifically "concentration of numerically stronger forces that separate, surround, and exterminate individual enemy units." Pursuit of a retreating enemy was a different matter: "Pursuit on foot of any enemy with modern equipment cannot achieve great results. . . . In consideration of the fact that we had to solve transportation and supply problems, rest troops, improve coastal defenses, and strengthen security in rear areas, our decision not to continue a furious pursuit was completely correct." Peng added: "To ignore an enemy's superior equipment and neglect tactics is incorrect." Peng listed examples of correct tactics: night attacks, bold encirclement to cut off enemy units, attacks behind enemy lines, and attacks by small elite units on artillery emplacements and headquarters.[197] Du Ping emphasized the need to "discard the notion of quick victory . . . and plan for a prolonged campaign."[198] Pak Hon-yong's response is unknown. He may have expressed mild dissatisfaction that the enemy had not been vigorously pursued at the end of the third offensive.

The next day, Jie Fang spoke on training plans and operations, Han Xian-chu discussed tactical issues, and Hong Xuezhi talked about supply operations and problems. Hong said: "Soldiers universally worry about three things: first, no cooked rice; second, lack of ammunition; and third, not being sent to the rear if wounded."[199] Jie, Han, and Hong defended Peng's strategy. Just as the Chinese–North Korean military leaders' conference had begun, Gen. Matthew Ridgway launched a counterattack, including a reconnaissance probe of Chinese-Korean positions, called "Operation Thunderbolt." US forces attacked toward Seoul from Osan to Suwon. Retaking the capital was not the objective, but caught by surprise, Chinese and North Korean units withdrew.[200]

On the third day of the Chinese–North Korean conference, the participants divided into groups and continued the discussion. Concerned about the UN Command's latest attack in Korea, Peng cabled Mao and asked him to consider a truce:

> To increase the internal contradictions of imperialism can we broadcast an announcement that Chinese and North Korean forces support a truce and the KPA and CPVA have withdrawn from fifteen to thirty kilometers north of the Osan-Taipyongni-Tanguni line? If you agree, please broadcast the announcement from Beijing. . . . If the enemy continues to attack northward and we strike with full force, we cannot eliminate more than one division. It will be extremely difficult to hold the bridgehead. If we attack, our plans to equip and train units will be ruined. . . .[201]

On January 28, Kim Il Sung reported on "Future Activities of the Korean Workers' Party" and, as if disregarding the advance of UN forces, declared that "we will surely win the war."[202] Northeast China party representative Gao Gang, calling himself "a cadre supporting the Chinese People's Volunteers in the rear area," said: "We have everything necessary to achieve the final extermination of the enemy."[203] He argued that the enemy had proposed peace negotiations because they feared the power of China and Korea and wanted a lull in order to strengthen their own forces.[204]

Mao rejected Peng's entreaty to consider a truce and on January 28 ordered him to prepare for a counterattack:

> Our forces must immediately prepare for the fourth offensive. The objective is to exterminate 20,000 to 30,000 U.S. and Rhee troops and occupy the area north of Taejon-Andong. . . .
>
> After Chinese and North Korean forces have occupied the area north of the Taejon-Andong line, they should again prepare for two to three months and

then execute the last and decisive fifth offensive. This is advantageous in all aspects.[205]

Stalin agreed with Mao's instructions to Peng: "From an international perspective, it is absolutely advisable that Chemulpo and Seoul should not be recaptured by the enemy and for Chinese-Korean forces to strike a major blow against the enemy."[206] Zhang Shu Guang is surely correct that Mao's order to Peng was "ambitious but unrealistic."[207]

On January 29, the fifth and final day of the Chinese–North Korean conference, KPA 5th Corps commander Pang Ho-san reported on the tactical experiences of the KPA 6th Division, and two CPV assistant division commanders described their tactics and those of the enemy.[208] The conference ended with these reports, and the participants quickly departed. In Korea, meanwhile, the US drive continued, forcing Chinese and Korean units to retreat to north of Suwon.

On January 31, Kim Chaek, the KPA frontline commander immediately after the outbreak of the war and a major figure in the Manchurian faction, died in his quarters of a heart attack. His death was a great loss to Kim Il Sung.[209]

That same day, Peng reported an acute threat posed by the UN Command: "The enemy is advancing with a large number of aircraft, tanks, and artillery. We are resisting with only rifles, machineguns, mortars, and a small number of mountain guns, and we are short of ammunition. . . . Because of [the enemy's] intense firepower, our losses in dead and wounded are heavy. . . . Our forces have not received supplies of shoes, ammunition, and food. . . . It is impossible to march barefoot in the snow." Ordered by Mao to prepare for the fourth offensive, Peng reported that by great effort the supplies would arrive by February 6. He gave marching orders for the CPV's 13th Army Group effective the night of February 7; the fourth offensive would commence five days later.[210]

The Joint Headquarters desperately reorganized their forces. The problem was how to integrate the KPA into the CPV. On January 30, Stalin instructed new Soviet Ambassador Razuvaev to confer with Kim Il Sung about restructuring the KPA. The North Korean army had too many divisions (nineteen on the battlefield and nine being trained in Manchuria) and an insufficient number of trained, able officers, in Stalin's view. The ambassador was to persuade Kim to reduce the number of divisions to a maximum of twenty-three.[211] Stalin's message was also forwarded to Mao.[212] On January 31, Razuvaev reported that Kim Il Sung had quickly accepted Stalin's suggestion.[213]

The Han Group, a combined CPV-KPA unit, was formed on the western front under the command of Han Xianchu and included the KPA First Corps led by Yi Kwon-mu. The KPA 6th Corps was held in reserve. On the eastern front, the Deng Group of the CPV was created under the command of Deng Hua, and the Kim Group, led by Kim Ung and made up of the KPA's 2nd, 3rd, and 5th Corps, was assigned to it. The newly organized KPA 3rd Corps was led by Kim Kwang-hyop.[214]

Peng reported to Mao on February 5 about field operations and a meeting he had held with Kim Il Sung. Peng had told the North Korean leader his plan that they should first stop the enemy's present attack and that thus they should improve the situation. The Joint Headquarters would now take time to prepare for the decisive offensive. Kim agreed with the plan. Peng reported a change in Kim's attitude: "The exultation borne of the easy victories in the first three offensives is gone."[215] Kim Il Sung had come to his senses.

The battlefield setbacks incurred by the Chinese and North Koreans were undeniable. US-ROK forces had started the second phase of Operation Thunderbolt on February 1, pushed the frontline toward the suburbs of Seoul, and reached the southern bank of the Han River on February 11. They were within sight of the capital. Kim Il Sung no longer had any illusion about a quick triumph. Peng had clearly revised Kim's objectives.

The fourth offensive kicked off on February 11. On the eastern front, Chinese and North Korean units decimated the ROKA 8th Division, took Hoengsong, and advanced toward Wonju, where the UN Command held and the surge ended on February 16. The Joint Headquarters had to adopt a mobile defense line in front of Wonju.[216] US-ROK units counterattacked on February 20 in "Operation Killer," and the Chinese and North Koreans fell back.

Peng returned to Beijing on February 20 to dissuade Mao from continuing the offensive. Forced to rethink his strategy, Mao on March 2 informed Stalin: "The most recent offensive on the Korean battlefield shows that unless the bulk of enemy forces are destroyed, the enemy will not withdraw from Korea. A certain amount of time is needed to destroy the bulk of enemy forces. Thus it is possible that military operations in Korea may be of a prolonged character. We should assume military operations in Korea will take at least two years."[217]

Chinese leaders had already implemented measures for a long war. They intended to adopt a troop rotation system whose objective was "to smash enemy intentions, maintain long-term operations, and exterminate the enemy a step at a time." Kim Il Sung agreed to the rotation system. The Joint Headquarters formed Group One from the nine army groups of the thirty Chinese divisions in Korea, and Group Two from six army groups that were to be moved from China to Korea and three army groups already there. The two Groups would be rotated in early April 1951. The eight KPA corps were reduced to six and included in the rotation system. Group Two was to take over frontline positions and then go on the offensive because enemy recapture of Seoul would badly affect Chinese-Korean morale. Mao wanted the

Soviet air force to defend Pyongyang and a line north of Wonsan, and he requested that Soviet aircraft be based in Korea.[218]

Stalin promptly responded to Mao on March 3 that two Soviet air divisions under General Belov's command would move to Korean territory. However, there is no indication that Soviet air units left Andung in Manchuria. The initial operational area from Antung to Sonchon may have been enlarged to cover Pyongyang.[219]

Operation Killer on the eastern front ended in early March and Chinese-Korean troops were forced to abandon Hoengsong. On March 7, the UN Command started Operation Ripper on the western front and Communist forces had to abandon Seoul. By the end of March, they had been driven back all along the front to north of the 38th parallel. A fresh start was out of the question; the fourth Chinese–North Korean offensive ended on April 21.[220] There was no Chinese victory. The Sino-American War would end in a draw.

Chapter Five

Fighting while Negotiating

WASHINGTON AND MOSCOW

When the UN Command recaptured Seoul in March 1951 and pushed close to the 38th parallel, the US State Department again prepared a presidential statement calling for ceasefire talks. Secretary of State Dean Acheson gave President Harry Truman a draft on March 23: "United Nations forces in Korea are engaged in repelling the aggression committed against the Republic of Korea and the United Nations. . . . There remains the problem of restoring international peace and security in the area in accordance with the terms of the Security Council resolution of June 27, 1950."[1]

During a tour of the front lines in Korea the next day, UN Commander Douglas MacArthur threatened expansion of the war to China:

> The enemy therefore must by now be painfully aware that a decision of the United Nations to depart from its tolerant effort to contain the war to the area of Korea through expansion of our military operations to his coastal areas and interior bases would doom Red China to the risk of imminent military collapse.
>
> These basic facts being established, there should be no insuperable difficulty arriving at decisions on the Korean problem if the issues are resolved on their own merits without being burdened by extraneous matters not directly related to Korea, such as Formosa and China's seat in the United Nations.[2]

Truman, though enraged by MacArthur's threat to expand the war, bided his time. On April 5, Congressman Joseph H. Martin, Jr., in a speech in the House of Representatives, read a letter from MacArthur that supported Martin's advocacy of using Chinese Nationalist forces to open a second front in Asia "to relieve the pressure on our forces in Korea." The general wrote: "It seems strangely difficult for some to realize that here in Asia is where the Communist conspirators have elected to make their play for global conquest. . . . If we lose the war to communism in Asia the fall of Europe is inevitable."[3]

Open insubordination in the form of his letter to Martin sealed MacArthur's fate. Truman relieved him of his command on April 11. In a radio address to the nation, Truman explained that the "United States was trying to prevent the spread of hostilities in Asia into a third world war." A negotiated peace could be achieved, the president said, based on a ceasefire, steps to prevent another outbreak of fighting, and an end to aggression.[4] US 8th Army Commander Matthew Ridgway replaced MacArthur as UN commander, and the United States intensified efforts to start ceasefire talks, encouraged by Soviet peace feelers.

Joseph Stalin's fears of a wider war were temporarily eased by Truman's dismissal of MacArthur and his favorable comments about negotiations. Yet according to the historian Bruce Cumings, "The United States came closest to using atomic weapons in early April 1951." And, indeed, that month, the US government again considered using the atomic bomb. On March 31, Commander of the Far East Air Forces Lt. Gen. George Stratemeyer had reported to MacArthur that the atomic bomb storage facility at Kadena Air Base in Okinawa was ready for use. On April 5, the Joint Chiefs of Staff ordered immediate retaliation with atomic bombs if China committed new large forces to the fighting or if bombers from China attacked US forces. On April 6, Truman approved the JCS's request to carry out such retaliation and authorized the transfer from the Atomic Energy Commission to the military of a certain number of complete atomic bombs. In the confusion following MacArthur's dismissal, however, the transfer was not carried out.[5] Yet, depending on the circumstances, there was still a real possibility that the United States would use atomic bombs, and not only North Korea but China and the Soviet Union would be on the target list. Stalin presumably thought the Communist bloc had gotten a reprieve but that the bomb was still an option for Washington.

THE FIFTH CHINESE–NORTH KOREAN OFFENSIVE

The fifth offensive by Chinese and North Korean forces began on April 22, eleven days after MacArthur was fired. What Mao Zedong had called "the last offensive" was supposed to drive the Americans out of Korea. Chinese-Korean forces broke through the 38th parallel again from the North and crossed the Imjin River. Starting at dawn on April 23, the US Air Force flew 1,100 sorties and reportedly killed or wounded 2,000 enemy troops. Fighters, fighter-bombers, and bombers continued the aerial assault day and night, dropping proximity-fused bombs, flares, and napalm in close support of ground operations.[6]

The Korean People's Army's 1st Corps and the Chinese People's Volunteers' 63rd, 64th, and 65th Armies of the 19th Army Group, despite very heavy losses, advanced to Mt. Pukhan north of Seoul. To the east, eight armies of the 3rd and 9th Army Groups of the CPV broke through the 38th parallel and put pressure on Seoul. In one week of combat, Chinese and North Korean forces claimed to have exterminated 23,000 of the enemy. The US 8th Army reported American casualties of 314 dead and 1,600 wounded, with 13,349 known Chinese and North Korean dead and 23,829 estimated enemy dead. The UN Command's headquarters in Tokyo estimated 75,000 to 80,000 enemy killed or wounded.[7] The number of ROKA casualties is unclear.

The UN Command stopped the Chinese–North Korean fifth offensive north of Seoul on April 29. After a short break in the fighting, on the eastern sector the CPV's 3rd and 9th Army Groups and the KPA's 2nd, 3rd, and 5th Corps resumed the incursion, mainly in the area south of the Soyang River. In five days of round-the-clock assaults, they pushed UN forces fairly far to the south before losing momentum. On May 19–20, American B-29s dropped radar-aimed bombs on massed Chinese and Korean units and broke up the attack. Chinese commander Peng Dehuai halted the offensive on May 21.[8] Chinese and North Korean losses were severe, while the UN Command had conserved its strength.

On May 23, the US 8th Army, now led by Gen. James Van Fleet, launched a coordinated counterattack. Twenty-two B-29s from Kadena paved the way in the largest one-night close-support attack of the Korean War. Saturation bombing pulverized the battlefield.[9]

Chinese and North Korean forces were forced back toward the 38th parallel, and the CPV's 180th Division—encircled by US armored units—was almost annihilated. Only one thousand of the nine thousand men escaped.

At the end of May, the UN Command crossed the prewar boundary of the 38th parallel from the south for the third time. In mid-June, the KPA's 1st Corps penetrated south of the parallel from the north in the western sector, and other units got close to the line in the east, but they were unable to recover the territory that they had taken in mid-January.[10] The fifth Chinese–North Korean offensive ended in total failure.

Stalin must have realized not only that the objective of driving the United States out of Korea was unattainable, but that he had to check the impulse in Washington to broaden the war. While the fifth offensive was still under way, he directed Jacob Malik, the Permanent Soviet Representative to the United Nations, to contact the US Mission at the UN. On May 2, Malik invited two members of the Mission to ride with him into Manhattan. In the course of a wide-ranging informal discussion of the world situation, Malik told them that many outstanding issues—including the war in Korea—could be settled by discussion between the US and Soviet governments.[11] Without a word to China, Stalin took the initiative to determine US intentions about a ceasefire.

A PEACE SETTLEMENT WITH JAPAN

Preparations for a post–World War II peace settlement with Japan had meanwhile reached the critical stage. With Japan still an occupied country, the United States had enjoyed unfettered use of bases and facilities throughout the archipelago to prosecute the war in Korea. In Okinawa, which was under direct US military control, airbases were substantially expanded. A peace settlement with Japan had to allow continued US use of the bases in Japan after the occupation ended, and keep Okinawa under exclusive US administration to be turned into a major military outpost for the United States. But Washington policymakers wanted to exempt Japan from paying war reparations in order to stimulate economic recovery in Japan and to facilitate Japanese rearmament.[12] Communist China could be excluded from the postwar negotiations over Japan, but not the Soviet Union, which enormously complicated the international politics of a settlement.

In January 1951, the Dulles Mission headed by State Department adviser John Foster Dulles visited Tokyo for peace talks. Upon arriving, the mission received a memorandum from Japanese Prime Minister Yoshida Shigeru on "our views." The memorandum said: "Japan will ensure internal security by itself. But as regards external security, the cooperation of the United Nations and, especially, of the United States is desired through appropriate means such as the stationing of troops." This arrangement "should be made apart from the peace treaty, as providing for cooperation for mutual security between Japan and America as equal partners," the memorandum stated. Yoshida also sought reconsideration of an earlier US proposal for a UN trusteeship of Okinawa with the United States as administrating authority and asked that the Ryukyu Islands be returned to Japanese sovereignty "as soon as the need of a trusteeship disappears." As for Japanese rearmament, the Yoshida administration said that it was "impossible at present" for three reasons: the "sentiment of the masses" could not be ignored, the financial burden would impoverish the population and provoke the social unrest sought by the Communists, and neighboring countries feared the "recurrence of Japanese aggression, when internally Japanese had reasons for exercising caution against the possibility of the reappearance of old militarism."[13]

Dulles was pleased with Yoshida's consent to a security guarantee that accepted the stationing of US forces, but unhappy with the notion that Japan and the United States would be "equal partners." Dulles refused to reconsider his position that Okinawa should be under US administration—and pushed Japan to rearm.

What Yoshida meant by "the sentiment of the masses" against Japanese rearmament is clear from his conversation with the US State Department's John Allison shortly before the peace conference . Prominent Americans had recently called for rearming Japan, Yoshida told Allison, and former Japanese military men had been quite active on this front, too. But the Japanese people did not follow them, Yoshida pointed out, nor support political leaders who advocated rearmament, like ex-premier Ashida Hitoshi. The people were wiser, Yoshida said.[14]

Yoshida understood the public's emotional antipathy to the military and war. But, faced with Dulles's insistence on rearmament, Yoshida hurriedly prepared a blueprint for a fifty thousand-man emergency security force, "Initial Steps for Rearmament Program," that was shown to US negotiators on February 3.[15] At the same time, he fundamentally respected public sensibilities and was determined to delay rearmament. The Yoshida Doctrine was to offer bases to the United States, rely on a treaty with Washington for national security, agree to lightly armed Japanese forces that did not require revision of the country's constitution, and focus national energies on economic reconstruction.

After Dulles returned to Washington, he drafted the first peace proposal in March. The provisional draft placed Okinawa under potential UN trusteeship—but with the United States as the administering authority—and gave the Soviet Union the southern half of Sakhalin Island and the Kurile Islands. It also acknowledged that Japan lacked the financial resources to pay reparations. The draft was transmitted to other Allied Powers on March 23.[16] US strategy was to entice the Soviet Union with the territorial provisions and rupture the Sino-Soviet relationship.

The Soviet Union was obligated by the Sino-Soviet friendship treaty to collaborate with Beijing in a peace settlement with Japan. Having gotten the PRC to intervene in Korea, Stalin was now doubly obligated to support Beijing, which was excluded from the peace talks. It would have been inconceivable for the Soviet Union to betray China just to get southern Sakhalin and the Kuriles. Therefore Stalin determined to boycott the US and British efforts for peace talks with Japan and strengthen the Japanese Communist Party's struggle against the United States in order to undermine the US rear in Japan.

The mainstream JCP leadership had gone underground on June 24, 1950, the eve of the Korean War, as a result of the party's suppression by the Supreme Commander for the Allied Powers. Splintered and confused, the party did not take a clear position on the war. Only rank-and-file party members, including Koreans, and the internationalist faction of students, publicly supported North Korea. JCP leaders Tokuda Kyuichi and Nosaka

Sanzo had fled by sea to Beijing and switched to the Chinese line of armed struggle against the US occupation of Japan. [17]

At the JCP's Fourth National Conference, held underground on February 23–25, 1951, the JCP adopted a policy that stated: "Korea is the focus of worldwide class struggle and will decide the outcome of the confrontation between the two camps over 'Peace' or 'War.'" To "regard the Korean War as a distant conflict or cooperate [with U.S./UN forces] would deepen the 'national crisis' and collaborate in the 'nation's destruction,'" the JCP declared. Japan had two choices: "One path leads to acquiescence in 'war and slavery' under the control of international monopoly capital. The other is the path of 'peace and independence' through ties to the peace-loving democratic forces of the world. There is no third way."[18] The reality was that the JCP faced a choice between the Yoshida government's support of the United States and cooperation with the war, or alignment with the Soviet Union, China, and North Korea in struggle against the United States.

The party's resolution adopted at the conference advocated armed struggle against the US occupation of Japan through the formation of an underground apparatus—Core Self-Defense Units, Combat Groups for Peace, Patriotic Struggle groups, and guerrilla units—and by combining labor and farmer movements. The guerrilla units were "a weapon to create a national united front to oppose the United States, rescue the nation, and become a People's Liberation Army." The resolution recommended special activities toward US forces, the new Japanese National Police Reserve, and the national police force. [19]

In April, Stalin summoned to Moscow mainstream JCP leaders Tokuda, Nosaka, and Nishizawa Takaji, and, separately, Hakamada Satomi from the opposition internationalist faction. Chinese Communist Party Liaison Department chief Wang Jiaxiang and assistant chief Li Chuli accompanied the Japanese Communists. Stalin directed the mainstream JCP leaders to implement the Fourth National Conference resolution on armed struggle and prepare a new party program, and told Hakamada to cooperate with them. [20] Stalin hoped the JCP would intensify the anti-American struggle in Japan. The Soviet and Chinese Communist parties echoed his appeal.

On May 3, a joint United States–United Kingdom draft peace treaty with the same three basic principles over Okinawa, Japan's cession of territories to the Soviet Union, and Japan's exemption from war reparations that John Foster Dulles had included in his March draft was ready. [21] Forced to respond, Stalin told Mao on May 6 how he would reply and requested his support. The gist of the Soviet reaction to the peace treaty draft was: (1) opposition to a unilateral peace treaty written primarily by Washington and a request for joint preparation by China, the Soviet Union, the United States, and the United Kingdom; (2) a request for recognition of China's right to Taiwan; (3) opposition to US control of the Ryukyus; (4) advocacy of a specified limit to Japan's military power; and (5) opposition to Japan's join-ing a military alliance and support for removal of the occupation forces from Japan one year after a peace settlement.[22] Mao immediately concurred,[23] and on May 7 the Soviet response was handed to the US ambassador in Mos-cow.[24] Although in the US-UK draft Japan ceded southern Sakhalin and the Kuriles to the Soviet Union, in the interest of solidarity with Beijing, Stalin turned down the opportunity for this territorial gain.

Since the Soviet Union would not join the peace process, on June 14 the United States changed the draft wording from "Japan cedes" to the Soviet Union southern Sakhalin and the Kuriles to Japan "renounces all rights" to the territory.[25] Now Soviet ownership of these territories was not to be recog-nized.

POLITICAL CRISIS IN SOUTH KOREA

Republic of Korea President Syngman Rhee faced his worst wartime crisis in late March 1951 when the ROK National Assembly revealed two damaging incidents: the National Defense Corps scandal and the Kochang massacre.

A National Defense Corps law promulgated on December 21, 1950, had authorized the mobilization of 500,000 able-bodied men between the ages of seventeen and thirty-nine (except active-duty military, police, and students) into a second national force to complement the ROKA. Korean Youth Group officials became the NDC leaders, and KYG head Kim Yun-gun was ap-pointed commander with the rank of brigadier general.[26] On January 9, Syngman Rhee said he expected the National Defense Corps to respond in kind to the "human wave" tactics of the Chinese Communists. In an appeal for volunteers, General Kim said that rather than "wait to be killed," South Koreans would strike first. The general also claimed that another million able-bodied men were available to supplement the new force.[27]

A favorite of President Rhee, Kim Yun-gun had earlier been a Korean-style wrestler. He possessed only a primary school education and was un-qualified to lead a large military organization like the NDC. NDC trainees were ordered to march to fifty-one training unit locations in North and South Kyongsang provinces and were caught up in the exodus from the capital of Seoul after CPV and KPA units recaptured it on January 4, 1951. The hastily mobilized recruits had no uniforms or food rations. Units became disorga-nized and separated from each other, and the force soon disintegrated into a horde of refugees. Government and military officials had embezzled much of the funds allocated to the NDC. The would-be rescuers of Seoul were a pathetic spectacle.[28]

Yi Yong-hui, a future South Korean radical intellectual leader, was then an interpreter with the 9th Regiment, 11th Division, of the ROKA, which was clearing Communist guerillas from the Chiri mountains. He described the scene: "All the school buildings and athletic fields in and near Chinju were full of emaciated men. For the first time I smelled the stench of the dead and dying. Their clothes were tattered and their shoes had fallen apart during the long forced march over frozen dirt roads." More than one thousand men died and many were sick. [29]

Despite the obvious disaster, on January 20 Gen. Kim Yun-gun told a press conference: "A million National Defense soldiers are in training. Unfortunately a few impure [subversive] elements are spreading negative stories." In response to a question in the National Assembly on January 26, ROK Defense Minister Shin Sung-mo dismissed criticism of the NDC as a "fifth column plot." When the National Assembly censured Shin, Syngman Rhee was forced to order Provost Marshal General Choe Kyong-nok to investigate. But he showed his intention to protect Gen. Kim Yun-gun, and aware of Rhee's real wishes, Shin intervened in the probe. [30] Chang Myon, the former ambassador to Washington and a favorite of the Americans, became ROK prime minister in late January 1951, but apparently did not intervene. [31]

More trouble loomed for Syngman Rhee when from February 10 through the night of February 11 soldiers from the ROKA's 3rd Battalion, 9th Regiment, 11th Division, massacred a large number of innocent civilians in Sinwon township, Kochang County, South Kyongsang Province, during a counterguerilla sweep. National Assembly members learned of the atrocity in late February and Defense Minister Shin was forced to investigate. Predictably, he tried to cover up this incident, too. On March 29, the National Assembly unanimously authorized an onsite investigation in Kochang and established a committee to probe the NDC. [32] The ROK military staged an attack by men disguised as Communist guerillas to disrupt the investigation. In early April a joint National Assembly–government investigation was established. The Defense Ministry assigned Kim Chong-won ("Tiger Kim"), vice-commander of the military police, Civil Affairs Department, South Kyongsang Province Martial Law Command, to the inquiry. Kim had commanded the military police during the US-ROKA occupation of Pyongyang and, following instructions from Defense Minister Shin, whitewashed the killings. The official report concluded that eighty-seven "secret communist collaborators were legally executed," [33] not innocent civilians.

The attempted cover-up sparked public outrage at the Rhee administration; National Assembly members and the press demanded the truth. When an infuriated "Tiger Kim" beat up two Yonhap Press reporters on April 24, journalists broke through security guards and handed Rhee a written protest. That same day, Rhee had to ask for the resignations of Shin Sung-mo, Interior Minister Cho Pyong-ok, and Justice Minister Kim Chun-yon. Cho Pyong-ok and Kim Chun-yon, both affiliated with the Hanmin Party and critical of

Rhee, immediately stepped down. The three ROK service chiefs of staff and every ROKA division commander signed an appeal to Rhee to keep Shin in office. But the National Assembly strongly protested military interference in politics and demanded Shin's ouster. Bowing to the pressure, Shin resigned and became Seoul's diplomatic representative to Japan.

On April 26, an interim report from the National Assembly's Special Investigation Committee blamed the National Defense Corps scandal. Twenty percent of the Corps was dead or dying, and the rest were unfit for duty, according to the report, which recommended that the culpable officers "commit hara-kiri or be executed." Six days later, the National Assembly passed a resolution to abolish the Corps.[34]

Yi Ki-bong, who had been Rhee's private secretary during his exile years until the end of World War II, was appointed defense minister on May 7. Although without any military experience, Yi had to deal with the investigation into the NDC scandal.[35] On May 9, Vice-President Yi Si-yong resigned to take responsibility for the corruption in the NDC. Eight days later, Gen. Kim Yun-gun was finally taken into custody because of the NDC's corruption, and the same day the National Assembly elected a new vice-president. On the third ballot, by a margin of three votes, Kim Song-su, leader of the Min'guk Party, defeated Rhee's candidate, Kim Kap-song, yet another blow to the president.[36]

Because of the ongoing political crisis in South Korea, the United States rejected nearly all of the many requests from the ROK government on war matters. On April 16, the Rhee administration queried Washington's policy. Would the United States seek to induce a ceasefire before UN forces reached the Yalu River? If ROK forces advanced to the Manchurian border, would the United States induce UN forces to withdraw from Korea? If UN forces were inadequate, was there any possibility that the United States might permit the United Nations to invite Japanese armed forces to land in Korea? The State Department replied that the first two questions were hypothetical and that there were "no Japanese forces in existence."[37] The ROKA asked for more weapons. On May 2, General Van Fleet wrote ROKA Chief of Staff Chong Il-gwon, "The primary problem in the ROK is to secure competent leadership in their army." Without it, further provision of arms and equipment would be "a criminal waste of badly needed equipment."[38]

The NDC's corruption and the Kochang massacre had undermined American confidence in the ROK military. On May 5, US Ambassador to South Korea John Muccio told Rhee he was "against foreign interference in Korean affairs," but offered some advice: "It is fundamental that in the long run no country is militarily defensible unless it is in good health socially, economically and politically." The ambassador criticized the formation of the National Defense Corps without consulting UN or US officials, the refusal to explain what steps had been taken for land reform, and the tendency to believe so-called intelligence reports from paramilitary and private groups, such as the Youth Group and "Tiger Kim" rather than official information from the ROK government and the United Nations.[39] Secretary of State Acheson was angered by Rhee's comment to the press on May 18 that if ROKA arms and equipment were upgraded, South Korea could request the withdrawal of US forces. Acheson ordered Muccio to warn Rhee of "the damaging effect his ill-advised statements" could have on the war effort.[40] Dissatisfied with the ROK government and military, the Truman administration saw no need to consult South Koreans on peace talks.

Muccio reminded Acheson on June 1 that newspaper reports and rumors that the United Nations was considering a ceasefire had "frightened, baffled, and infuriated" South Koreans, and warned: "Attitude of Koreans in post-hostilities period should not be overlooked. If they feel they have been sold out, no amount of pressure or cajolery likely to keep them quiet."[41]

President Truman promised Rhee on June 5 that the United States would continue to train and equip the ROK military, but did not mention a possible ceasefire.[42] ROK Ambassador to the United States Yang Yu-chan asked Assistant Secretary of State Dean Rusk four days later if ceasefire negotiations had been proposed on the basis of a "new five-point peace proposal." Rusk "categorically denied" knowledge of any such plan. The State Department completely shut out the ROK government.[43] Besieged by questions from Rhee, ROK cabinet members, and other Koreans about US policy, Muccio appealed to Acheson that same day for guidance on "how to calm fears [of] Koreans."[44] Washington was unmoved.

The political turmoil in South Korea dragged on. Eleven NDC officers, including Kim Yun-gun, were ordered on June 15 to face a court-martial for the NDC's corruption. Chong Il-gwon was relieved as ROKA chief of staff and left for advanced training in the United States eight days later. His right-hand man, Kang Mun-bong, chief of the operations section of the ROKA General Staff, was also relieved and sent to the United States. Yi Chong-chan was appointed the new chief of staff.[45] Accountability finally touched top ROKA leaders.

The public court-martial of NDC leaders began in the auditorium of the Tongin Elementary School in Taegu on July 5. Two weeks later, Kim Yun-gun and four subordinates were found guilty and sentenced to death. In July court-martial proceedings began in the Kochang massacre.[46]

THE SOVIET UNION BROKERS A CEASEFIRE

On May 17, a Democratic US senator introduced a resolution in the US Congress to end the fighting in Korea that *Pravda* reported two days later as a sign of American war weariness.[47] The State Department designated

George Kennan, a known critic of US policy, who had left the department in 1950, to convey a message to the Kremlin. Kennan explained US willingness for a ceasefire at a secret meeting with Soviet representative to the UN Jacob Malik on May 31.[48] Moscow did not inform Beijing of the approach.

Meanwhile, the UN Command was driving Chinese and North Korean forces back above the 38th parallel. Stalin told Mao on May 22 that the Soviet Union would replace the MiG-9s it had previously provided to China with MiG-15s at no cost to China because the former were inferior to the latest US jet fighters. Stalin asked only that China cover the transportation costs for the 372 planes. Mao cabled his appreciation on May 25,[49] and the following day Stalin repeated his apology about the MiG-9s. The Soviets had mistakenly believed that MiG-9s could compete with the newest British and American jets, an error that set back China's air defense, and they were obligated to make amends.[50] Stalin was uncharacteristically contrite, perhaps in part because he had started Korean truce talks with Washington behind the back of China.

On May 27, when it was clear that the fifth Chinese–North Korean offensive had failed, Mao forwarded a letter he had sent to Peng Dehuai the previous day to Stalin. "American forces still have fighting spirit and confidence," Mao said, and it was difficult to encircle and destroy even one regiment, to say nothing of mounting a large-scale operation against several divisions. If one PLA army corps could destroy one or two US battalions in an operation, Mao wrote, Chinese commanders should consider it a success. If each of the eight Chinese armies at the front in Korea could destroy one or two US battalions, he argued, they could decimate eight to sixteen enemy battalions in all. The Communists had defeated Chiang Kai-shek's New 1st and New 6th Armies, its 5th and 18th Armies, and the 7th Army of the Guangxi group by first inflicting a small number of casualties and then increasing the toll until large numbers of the enemy were annihilated. Mao wrote: "Our five offensives in Korea have completed this first stage of small destructive operations. However, these have not been sufficient. To advance to the stage of large-scale destructive operations will require many more offensives. . . . If the enemy has the courage to continue the advance, the further north they go, the better. However, the enemy does not have to move north of a Pyongyang-Wonsan line. Please consider the situation and inform me of your views."[51]

Mao thought victory was not impossible but may have been reluctant to admit to the possibility of defeat. The core issue: should China try to draw US forces into North Korea again and inflict small but significant losses on them there?[52]

Stalin immediately disagreed with that idea. On May 29 he told Mao: "Your plan seems very dangerous. This kind of plan might succeed once or twice. But British and U.S. forces will easily see through it." If there were strong defensive positions in the rear areas, such a plan might work, Stalin said, but "as far as I know, there are none in Korea." He continued: "The British and American forces that advance into the north will build new defensive fortifications and you and the North Koreans will probably be unable to break through their lines without heavy losses. . . . The analogy of the experience with Chiang Kai-shek's forces is not persuasive. . . . You should be aware that if Pyongyang falls into enemy hands again, not only will the North Korean populace and military suffer a loss of morale but British and American forces will be exultant."[53]

Stalin had consistently agreed with Mao on strategy in Korea. But this time he flatly opposed the view of his comrade in arms, probably because Mao's strategy ignored the plight of North Koreans and was so dangerous. Stalin was also skeptical about the likelihood of big victories in the future.

On May 29 Stalin told Soviet Ambassador to the DPRK Vladimir Razuvaev (Terentii Shtykov's replacement) to inform Kim Il Sung that Soviet carbines and machine guns would be provided to the North, but not mortars.[54] Although more cautious about war strategy than Mao, Kim was delighted because he thought getting the weapons meant the Chinese–North Korean offensive would definitely continue.[55] On May 30 Kim wrote to Peng Dehuai that he had heard Peng's assessment of the situation and operational plans from Pak Il-u and Deng Hua and agreed with them. The war had become more difficult and costly in human terms, Kim said; nevertheless, military action should continue. A peaceful resolution of the Korean problem was impossible, Kim said, and the war could not be stopped at the 38th parallel; thus the attack on the enemy must continue. Kim suggested a temporary suspension of operations to prepare for a large-scale offensive in late June.[56]

On May 31–June 1, Peng sent a comprehensive analysis of the war situation to Mao. In the first of two letters, Peng reported that because bridges over the many rivers south of the 38th parallel were destroyed, supplies were low, and the troops were exhausted; he had curtailed the second stage of the fifth offensive and withdrawn his forces to the positions they had held at the start of the third offensive. In short, Peng had not crossed the 38th parallel, and he explained why: "Courage alone is not enough to fight an enemy equipped with [modern] technology; the leadership must be brave and rational."[57]

In his second letter to Mao, Peng described the military situation in more detail. He could hold the Mundungni-Kumhwa-Chorwon line until June 10, the Kosong-Pyonggang-Kumchon line until the end of June or early July, and the Tongchon-Ichon-Haeju line until the end of July (all of these lines were in the North). The Pyongyang-Wonsan line could probably be maintained if three CPV armies were replaced, more antitank weapons and antiaircraft guns were supplied, partisans struck behind enemy lines, and the UN Command forces did not greatly increase, Peng said. The battlefield was narrow and Chinese lines of communications were extended, Peng advised Mao. The enemy had large forces backed by aircraft, tanks, and powerful artillery, and the morale of British and US troops was "relatively high." Chinese-Korean forces could not operate in daylight or attack individual enemy units, he noted. In a mobile defense, an experienced force could inflict casualties on the enemy at a two-to-one ratio, but with inexperienced forces the casualty rate was probably about even, Peng wrote.[58] Partisan units had not yet been committed. Overall, Peng painted a grim picture of the war.

On June 4, Mao forwarded Peng's pessimistic letters without any comment to Stalin, who responded the next day. "I, too, think you should not try to conclude the war in Korea hastily," Stalin wrote Mao. "My reasons are, first, a prolonged war affords the Chinese military an opportunity to learn modern warfare on the battlefield. Second, you can destabilize the Truman administration and destroy the military reputation of British-U.S. forces." This was probably Stalin's real objective. The Soviet military could also obtain intelligence about the latest US weapons and some actual equipment. With a rear defense line, Peng could fight without fear of encirclement, Stalin said, endorsing Peng's own judgment. Since Mao had complained of shortages of artillery, antitank weapons, and other equipment, Stalin asked why he had not sought them. Stalin strongly seconded Peng's wish for partisan warfare and in relation with "relatively high" morale of British and US troops attributed the loss of morale among Chinese and North Korean troops to the see-saw pattern of advances and retreats. Somehow, three or four enemy divisions had to be destroyed.[59]

Stalin favored continuing the war while negotiating with the enemy, but still had told Mao nothing about the start of ceasefire talks with Washington. At a second meeting with George Kennan on June 5, Jacob Malik confirmed that the Kremlin wanted peace.[60]

KIM IL SUNG AND GAO GANG VISIT MOSCOW

On June 3, Kim Il Sung met with Mao Zedong and Zhou Enlai in Beijing. Some scholars argue that Chinese leaders persuaded Kim to accept the start of truce talks, with the 38th parallel as the military demarcation line, at this meeting.[61] But Mao had not previously mentioned truce negotiations on any occasion, and the day before he wrote Peng Dehuai that Kim "might express his views on operational matters." On June 11, Mao informed Peng that he had reached an understanding with Kim that a counterattack would be deferred until August and that they would prepare a sound operational plan with offensive and defensive components that could succeed.[62] But Mao said nothing about truce talks.

On June 5, Mao requested that Stalin meet with Chinese Communist Party leader Gao Gang and Kim Il Sung: "In the course of prosecuting the war in Korea we have faced many important problems, including financial issues, military problems on the battlefield, and the danger the enemy might land marines in rear areas. In a few days we will send Comrade Gao Gang to Moscow by airplane to inform you of these problems. We would like your advice on how to resolve them." Mao added that Comrade Kim Il Sung was now in Beijing and wanted to accompany Gao Gang and consult with Stalin.[63] Mao did not mention truce negotiations. He intended to have Gao Gang request Soviet equipment for sixty Chinese divisions in fiscal 1951.

Stalin replied affirmatively to the request for the meeting on June 7. Two days later, Mao told Stalin that Gao and Kim had decided to depart on June 10, and added several supplementary points: "Comrade Gao Gang will report directly to you about the problem of war and peace and Soviet advisers for the volunteer force, so I will not touch on them here."[64]

Gao Gang and Kim Il Sung left for Moscow on a Soviet aircraft on June 10 and met Stalin three days later. There is no record of this meeting; I rely here on the account in the memoirs of interpreter Shi Zhe. After a briefing on the military situation in Korea, Stalin asked the visitors which option they preferred: seek an immediate ceasefire or continue to fight until the situation on the front lines improved and then start truce negotiations. The responses from Gao and Kim were unclear. They used various expressions, such as "stop the fighting," "ceasefire," "peace" (reconciliation), "armistice," and "peace treaty." Stalin explained what these words actually meant and asked about their intentions, best-case goals, and demands. When Kim and Gao said they wanted a ceasefire, Stalin explained that it was a suspension of military activity for a fairly long period. The two sides in Korea would still negotiate, the war was not over, and the fighting could resume at any time, he said. A ceasefire was not peace.[65] Kim and Gao probably accepted this kind of ceasefire; Stalin persuaded them to begin negotiations. Although Shi Zhe does not mention the Malik-Kennan contacts, Stalin must have explained what Kennan said about US peace terms.

Stalin cabled a succinct postmeeting summary to Mao: "Three problems were raised. We agreed that a ceasefire is now advantageous. Second, about military advisers, if you think Soviet military advisers are really necessary, the Soviet Union is prepared to supply them. Third, regarding weapons for sixty divisions, we have no objection." In the final paragraph, Stalin returned to a ceasefire: "After the meeting we received information that Britain and the United States, in the name of the sixteen countries fighting in Korea, will soon make a ceasefire proposal to you and the Koreans. Prior to the proposal, they want to strike a blow against your forces (including Koreans). This may be a rumor. However, it is a rumor consistent with the known facts and highly plausible. I advise you to strengthen your defenses and prevent an enemy advance."[66]

Mao, too, did not mince words. In a quick reply to Stalin, he said that Gao Gang knew his views on a ceasefire.[67] In a cable to Gao and Kim, Mao said the timing was wrong to raise the ceasefire issue because the KPA and CPV could not take the offensive for two months. The UN Command would see a ceasefire initiative as a sign of weakness. Mao gave them detailed instructions.

1. We should wait for an enemy statement.
2. An inquiry by the Soviet government to the American government regarding a ceasefire based on Kennan's comments is welcome. The two methods noted can be simultaneously implemented. Namely, on the one hand the Soviet government makes an inquiry. On the other, if the enemy presses for an armistice, Korea and China will express willingness to open negotiations. Discuss this with Stalin and decide which way is advisable.
3. Ceasefire conditions. Restoration of the boundary at the 38th parallel. North Korea and South Korea each provide a small amount of territory to create a neutral zone. . . . We consider it unnecessary to raise the problem of China's entry into the United Nations as a condition. . . . We must consider if the Taiwan problem should be raised as a condition. We think this problem should be raised as a way to bargain with them. If America strongly insists that the Taiwan problem be resolved separately, we will make an appropriate concession.

On June 14, Gao and Kim forwarded Mao's cable to Stalin. They asked for and got a meeting that day,[68] and apparently left for China the next day.

In a June 21 cable to the Kremlin, Mao said that Gao Gang had reported Stalin's views to him, which he thought were correct and what China must do. The eight months of warfare in Korea had shown the great disparity in weapons and equipment between Chinese forces and the enemy, Mao said, and he thanked Stalin for the Soviet Union's positive response to China's request for the equipment for the sixty divisions.[69] PLA Chief of Staff Xu Xiangqian, who was then visiting the Soviet Union, would handle further negotiations, Mao indicated. Although Mao did not specifically refer to a ceasefire, he tacitly accepted Stalin's proposal to pursue one.

DPRK Foreign Minister Pak Hon-yong was not present at the meeting with Stalin when Kim Il Sung agreed to the start of armistice talks and may have been somewhat dissatisfied. But since it was just the start of negotiations, and the fighting would continue during the talks, Pak was probably not adamantly opposed.

PREPARATION FOR THE ARMISTICE TALKS

With China and North Korea on board, Soviet representative to the UN Jacob Malik hinted in a radio address over the UN network on June 23 at the possibility of a ceasefire.[70] The next day, Stalin told Mao that the Soviet Union had carried out its promise to initiate talks and that a halt in the fighting was possible. He dashed Mao's immediate hopes for weapons and equipment: the Soviet Union, he now said, could not equip sixty divisions in a year. That was "out of the question" because Soviet experts had concluded that equipment for only ten divisions could be provided in the current fiscal year; to fulfill the complete request would take three years. Stalin hoped to shorten the period by six months, but that seemed unlikely.[71] Stalin had led Mao to believe the CPV would be rearmed and re-outfitted. As soon as China agreed to armistice talks, Stalin had changed his tune. Ruthless bargaining was his norm.

Moscow, Beijing, and Pyongyang were finally largely on the same page on war strategy, but Washington kept Seoul in the dark about the impending armistice talks until Malik's radio address. At the request of the ROK Embassy, on June 25 Dean Rusk, Assistant Secretary of State for Far Eastern Affairs, and U. Alexis Johnson, director of the State Department's Office of Northeast Asian Affairs, met with ROK Embassy Counselor Kim Sae-sun and First Secretary Han Pyo-uk to discuss Malik's proposal.[72] Three days later, John D. Hickerson, Assistant Secretary of State for UN Affairs, explained recent developments to ROK Ambassador to the United States Dr. Yang Yu-chan, who was shown the original copies of cables between the State Department and Moscow and given paraphrased copies of portions.[73]

In a top-secret cable on June 29, Secretary of State Dean Acheson informed Ambassador John Muccio that ceasefire talks might get under way: "Dept aware this is an explosive issue with ROK. You will have to muster every available resource[s] and argument to avoid development ugly situation which might jeopardize security UN forces and their lines of communication in ROK. Dept can understand basis for Rhee's and other leaders' opposition to any settlement Korean war leaving country divided and with risk of new invasion omni-present." Acheson praised Muccio's efforts to prevent the situation from "getting out of hand" and directed him to "constantly hammer" the following points: (1) There was no international recognition of the authority of the Republic of Korea north of the 38th parallel; (2) a unified Korea was a UN and US objective, but neither had ever taken the "position that unification [should] be achieved by force regardless of circumstances"; (3) the military situation had changed since UN forces entered North Korea in October because of China's intervention; (4) ROK leaders "must be brought [to] realize outbreak of world war [would] be for them a disaster"; (5) the ROK's future rests on the ability of the Free World to negotiate a lasting settlement with the Soviet bloc; and (6) reconstruction in the immediate postsettlement period depends on the United States, and "intransigent and inflammatory statements and provocative or violent actions" would trigger "revulsion" by the American public against the ROK.[74]

On June 30, UN Commander Matthew Ridgway broadcast an offer to discuss an armistice to the commander in chief of Communist forces in Korea. The same day in Washington, Ambassador Yang presented the ROK's conditions for talks to the State Department. They included the withdrawal of all foreign troops from both North and South Korea, suspension of Soviet support to North Korea, ROK participation in the armistice negotiations, and the unification of Korea.[75] The South Koreans did not actually want ceasefire talks, but they were too weak to reject them outright.

Immediately after the Ridgway broadcast, Muccio telephoned Syngman Rhee for an urgent meeting. ROK Prime Minister Chang Myon, Foreign Minister Byun Yong-tae, and Defense Minister Yi Ki-bong were already present when the ambassador arrived. Rhee read Ridgway's communiqué aloud and wanted to call a cabinet meeting immediately to decide South Korea's terms for talks. Muccio cautioned against snap decisions and public announcements; Rhee ordered the foreign minister to cancel a scheduled press conference. Chang Myon said that they "should not talk to Commies until all had been driven from Korea," according to Muccio, who warned of an adverse reaction to intransigence on an armistice.[76]

On July 1, the *Tong'a Ilbo* newspaper in South Korea reported that President Truman would personally lead the armistice negotiations and editorialized against a ceasefire without unification. A mass rally in Pusan that afternoon rejected an armistice and demanded Korean unification.[77] As news of the Ridgway broadcast spread, the ROK National Assembly started to debate a truce. Muccio thought the voices of caution outweighed rash elements and was "reasonably certain that negotiation [of] ceasefire presents no insuperable difficulties in relations" with the ROK, "provided: (1) ROK military officer participates; (2) no use 38th Parallel as delineation, but rather actual front."[78] On July 2, Muccio reported that Rhee had "concluded that ROK [would] of course have to go along with US and UN decisions. He added that in order [to] prevent loose talk he today told Cabinet to preserve public silence on ceasefire issue."[79]

Although South Korean views had been ignored, the Rhee regime could not oppose the start of peace talks. When they began on July 10, a *Tong'a Ilbo* editorial reflected the public mood: "Our people are near despair because a ceasefire will indefinitely delay the cherished unification of the fatherland until an unknown future. . . . Yet not only our democratic allies but also the Communist camp want to avoid expansion [of the fighting] to a major war and to try a ceasefire. To insist on just what we want would be unreasonable."[80]

On June 29, Kim Il Sung forwarded to Mao a UP story about Ridgway's moves toward a ceasefire offer and asked how China and North Korea should respond to a proposal. Mao quickly sent the message to Stalin,[81] and early on June 30 in another cable Mao told Stalin that he understood that to equip sixty divisions would take three years and asked how they should respond if Ridgway offered talks.[82] Upon learning of Ridgway's broadcast, Mao sent Stalin a draft response that he would tell Kim Il Sung to accept. Mao preferred Kaesong as the venue for the talks, not Wonsan as Ridgway wanted, and to gain time for preparations, he set July 15 as the starting date. Mao attached an intriguing suggestion to Stalin: "In view of the short time before the starting date and the importance of the conference, I request that you contact Comrade Kim Il Sung directly and personally lead the talks, and keep me informed of developments."[83] In other words, Mao was going to force North Korea to conduct the ceasefire negotiations, but wanted Stalin to actually direct them.

Stalin replied that their answer to Ridgway had to be in the names of the commanders of both the Chinese and Korean forces. The US command would put no credence in a response from just the North Koreans, Stalin said, and he attached a draft in the names of Kim Il Sung and Peng Dehuai. Stalin declined Mao's request that he lead the talks: "In your telegram you suggest that I direct the ceasefire negotiations from Moscow. That is of course unthinkable and unnecessary. The person to lead is you, Comrade Mao Zedong. Our greatest contribution is advice on particular issues. We cannot yet maintain direct liaison with Kim Il Sung. You should maintain contact."[84]

Kim Il Sung tried to get Stalin's ear. On July 1, Soviet Ambassador to the DPRK Razuvaev forwarded to Moscow a draft response to Ridgway from Kim and asked for its approval "as soon as possible." KPA Chief of Staff Nam Il would represent North Korea in the truce negotiations, Razuvaev said, and he listed six negotiating points.[85] Nam Il's designation as the DPRK's representative probably owed more to his personal abilities than his status as KPA chief of staff. Stalin told Razuvaev the next day that Kim Il Sung's response to Ridgway differed from that of Mao Zedong, and that Kim should confer with the Chinese. The two governments should issue a joint response, Stalin said.[86] The answer to Ridgway prepared by China in the names of Kim Il Sung and Peng Dehuai was announced on July 2 and called for armistice talks to begin on July 10 at Kaesong.

Stalin moved ahead cautiously, with full regard for Mao's feelings, while giving neither encouragement nor instruction to Kim Il Sung independently of the Chinese leader. The courtesy that Stalin and Mao afforded Kim contrasts with the high-handed way the United States brushed aside Syngman Rhee's objections to a ceasefire.

Kim Il Sung, on knowing Stalin's message on responding to Ridgway, changed Nam Il's six negotiating points to seven and sent the text to Mao.

Mao appended his views and forwarded it to Stalin on July 3.[87] Kim and Mao were not in complete agreement. Kim's text called for: (1) a set time for the ceasefire to start, (2) a buffer zone ten kilometers from the 38th parallel on each side, (3) no movement across the 38th parallel, (4) withdrawal of foreign warships from North Korean territorial waters, (5) withdrawal of all foreign troops from both South and North Korea within two months of an armistice, (6) exchange of prisoners within two months of a ceasefire, and (7) repatriation of civilians forcibly removed from the North by US and ROK forces. Mao's draft specified: (1) the date for the start of ceasefire talks, (2) a buffer zone ten miles from the 38th parallel on each side, (3) suspension of transfer of weapons and armed troops from outside into Korea, (4) establishment of a neutral nations supervisory committee, and (5) repatriation of prisoners of war within four months of a truce. Mao also mentioned two additional points: (1) the withdrawal of all foreign forces from both North and South Korea and (2) the repatriation of northern and southern refugees within several months. Mao noted that both these issues which Kim Il Sung insisted on posing were problematical and that it would be difficult to attain their demands. Insistence would jeopardize the negotiations, Mao said, and he asked Stalin to intervene.[88]

Stalin suggested the same day that Mao hold back the third and fourth points (suspension of transfer of weapons and troops from outside and establishment of a neutral nations supervisory committee). If the US side raised these issues, Mao could agree or make a counterproposal. Stalin supported Kim Il Sung on the two supplementary points—that all foreign troops should be withdrawn from Korea within two months of an armistice, and that forcibly removed northern civilians should be repatriated—and asked Mao to support these positions.[89]

On July 2 Mao sent detailed instructions to Peng Dehuai, Gao Gang, and Kim Il Sung and informed them that Li Kenong, first deputy foreign minister of the PRC and Qiao Guanhua, director of the press bureau of the PRC's Ministry of Foreign Affairs, would be sent to oversee the negotiations.[90] Mao sent military orders related to the armistice negotiations to Stalin the next day,[91] and mailed telegrams to Kim Il Sung, Peng Dehuai, Li Kenong, and Qiao Guanhua on July 4.[92] On the eve of the armistice talks, Mao read the drafts of the opening speeches by Nam Il and Deng Hua, and ordered deletion of a paragraph from Nam Il's speech that credited the Soviet Union's Jacob Malik for the peace talks on the grounds that it would attract needless criticism.[93] Mao completely managed the truce preparations.

THE ARMISTICE TALKS START

On July 7, Moscow was informed of the deletion of Japan "cedes" southern Sakhalin Island and the Kurile archipelago to the Soviet Union from the post–World War II peace treaty with Japan in favor of Japan "renounces all rights" to the territory.[94] Moscow now knew that it had lost a chance for international recognition of a coveted territorial acquisition. But solidarity with China was more important to the Kremlin, so it did not fight the change. It would continue to boycott the postwar peace talks since Beijing was excluded.

Three days later, on July 10, the Korean Armistice Conference opened at Kaesong. As the existence of the CPV-KPA Joint Headquarters was kept secret, the Communist side was formed by representatives of both armies and led by Gen. Nam Il, the KPA chief of staff. The Communist contingent also included Deng Hua, vice-commander of the CPV; Yi Sang-jo, chief of staff of the auxiliary headquarters of the KPA; Xie Fang, chief of staff of the CPV; and Chang Pyong-san, chief of staff of the First Corps of the KPA. The chief liaison officer for the Communist side was Kim Chang-man, who was chief of the mobilization bureau of the Supreme Headquarters of the KPA. He was assisted by the chief KPA liaison officer, Kim Pa, and the CPV liaison officer, Chai Junwu (also known as Chai Chengwen), the counselor at the PRC Embassy in Pyongyang.[95] Nam Il and Kim Pa were Soviet Koreans, and Kim Chang-man, Yi Sang-jo, and Chang Pyong-san were from the Yan'an group. Although three of the Communist delegates to the armistice conference were Koreans, including the chief negotiator, the Chinese were in charge, without doubt.

The UN Command side was led by Vice-Adm. Charles Turner Joy, who was aided by three US generals and Gen. Paek Sun-yop, commander of the First Corps of the ROKA. Syngman Rhee had summoned Paek from the front lines to Pusan and ordered him to join the negotiations. Rhee told Paek that he himself opposed a truce because it would result in continued division of the peninsula.[96] Paek's basic attitude was uncertain.

Li Kenong prepared a daily record of the talks for Mao, who forwarded copies to Stalin, Kim Il Sung, and Peng Dehuai. Li sent reports to Mao on July 10, 11, 13, 16, and 17.[97] They included a summary of a disagreement about the agenda. Chief Communist negotiator Nam Il thought the issue of refugee repatriation was disadvantageous to North Korea, and thus it was removed. Mao asked Stalin if they were taking the right approach.[98] Stalin assured him on July 14 that they were.[99]

On July 18, Mao forwarded to Stalin his instructions to Li Kenong to keep the withdrawal of all foreign troops from Korea on the agenda.[100] Then, after reading the conference reports for July 19 and 21,[101] Mao told Li Kenong that a stalemate on foreign troop withdrawals for a day or two was all right, but that the negotiators should then drop direct reference to the issue.[102] Mao informed Stalin that to avoid a breakdown in the talks he would no longer insist on foreign troop withdrawals from Korea.[103] Stalin concurred on July 21, saying the issue of troop withdrawals had served its purpose of demonstrating the Communist side's position.[104] The Communists and UN Command settled the conference agenda on July 26.

Mao also received reports on the armistice conference for July 26–27 and 29–31.[105] Mao personally directed the Communist positions in the talks through instructions to Li Kenong, who in turn informed the rest of the Communist team. Mao reported his moves to Stalin, who agreed with them and took no initiatives. Kim Il Sung and Peng Dehuai also received Mao's instructions; they neither demurred nor made recommendations. Mao was in charge of strategy not only on the battlefield but at the peace table as well.

Mao continued to forward Li Kenong's reports on the talks to Stalin in August.[106] At the Kaesong conference, the major issue was the location of the military demarcation line (i.e., the truce line). The Communists wanted the 38th parallel; the UN Command insisted on the actual battle line, which was mostly north of the parallel. With air and naval superiority, the UN Command controlled the skies and coastal waters and argued that the demarcation line should be north of positions held on the ground.[107] On August 2, Mao ruled out any concession on this point, even at the risk of a deadlock. We must persist, he told Li Kenong, forwarding a copy of his instructions to Stalin.[108] Mao repeated his order to hold firm on August 4.[109]

A week later, when the UN Command had not yielded, Mao sent fresh instructions. The United States wanted the actual battlefield positions to be the military demarcation line, Mao advised Li, and had created the impression that China and Korea would reject anything except the 38th parallel. Li was to insist on the legitimacy of their proposal; however, if the UN Command dropped the demand for a line north of current positions and accepted the actual status quo, the Communists could compromise by calling the 38th parallel the "basic military boundary" and propose creation of a "buffer zone" north and south of it.[110]

The same day, Mao asked Stalin to construct three airfields in the Anju district in North Korea by October 20 so Chinese and North Korean aircraft could be transferred from Chinese territory in November.[111] Mao intended to increase Communist air power and stubbornly fight on against the United States.

But, on August 12, Li Kenong reported: "It is clear from the process of the talks and the general [military] situation that we cannot get the enemy to accept our proposal for the 38th parallel. . . . If the ultimate objective of our struggle is to establish the 38th parallel as the military boundary and we will only accept minor changes in this objective, we must be prepared for a rupture in the negotiations. If that is not our objective, we must make an explicit compromise proposal. . . . In our view (Li Kenong, Deng Huai, Xie Fang, Qiao Guanhua) the enemy's ultimate objective is to stop military operations at the present battle lines. . . . Judging on the basis of the limited materials we have, the general world situation, the needs of our country, and [North] Korea's inability to continue the war, we think that finding a solution based on a halt of military operations somewhere along the present front lines is the best course of action."[112]

The Chinese delegation did not consult their North Korean colleagues on this matter, probably because the Koreans opposed a compromise. Mao immediately instructed the negotiators to confirm that the UN Command had dropped its earlier demand for a line far north of the fighting area on the ground. If that was the case, the negotiators were to link the 38th parallel with present battle lines, the military demarcation line with the buffer zone, in order to suggest a variant of compromise, which he proposed previously.[113] Mao rejected the compromise suggested by his team at Kaesong, which was based on the recognition of the present front line as the military demarcation line.

Li Kenong sent three reports to Mao on the talks on August 13 and another four reports from August 14 to August 17. Following Mao's instructions, the Chinese–North Korean side was unyielding. On August 17, Stalin replied affirmatively to Mao's request six days earlier to construct three airfields in the Anju district of North Korea: Soviet aid would include the assignment of two antiaircraft regiments in direct support of the three airfields.[114]

Neither the United States nor China would concede on the military demarcation line, and the talks were consequently at an impasse. On August 22, the Communist negotiators broke off the meetings. Mao did not consult with Stalin beforehand or report the breakdown to him until August 27. The enemy had committed "a series of provocative acts" while the negotiations were stalled, Mao told Stalin that day. Enemy soldiers disguised as civilians had entered the neutral zone on August 19 and attacked Chinese guards, killing one, Mao reported. An enemy aircraft on August 22 bombed the living quarters of the Chinese delegation to the talks. These incidents could be an attempt by the ROK to thwart an armistice, Mao thought, but the air attack was impossible without US approval: "We have decided to make a strong response to the enemy's provocative actions. We announced a suspension of the talks until the enemy accepts responsibility for these incidents." Mao outlined two scenarios and sought Stalin's opinion: in one scenario, the negotiations would break down; in the other, after a delay, the enemy would offer a compromise on the military demarcation line that might require the participation of neutral nations in the talks.[115]

Stalin referred Mao's cable to the Soviet Politburo, which concurred with Mao's assessment and believed negotiations were more important to the

United States than the Communist side. The Americans might interpret an invitation to representatives from neutral nations to join the armistice talks as a sign that China and North Korea wished to make a quick compromise, Stalin told Mao. He thus advised against the move. If Mao was of the same mind, Kim Il Sung must be informed, Stalin said. The central issue—a military demarcation line—was not mentioned by Stalin.[116] He apparently shared Mao's conviction that the Communists should press hard on basic principles and show no weakness to the United States.[117]

KOREAN ASPIRATIONS

What had begun as a civil war between Koreans to unify the peninsula had become a Sino-American war. The leaders of both South and North Korea passionately believed that a military stalemate meant that all of the sacrifices Koreans had made would be for nothing. On July 16, Gen. Matthew Ridgway tried for two hours to persuade Rhee to accept negotiations that would break the deadlock. US Ambassador John Muccio filed a detailed report on the president's response:

> Rhee warned that cease fire would be used by Russians for propaganda and Commies everywhere wld believe they were victors and that US had sued for peace. Soviet objective was to eject US from South Korea and he saw no polit possibility ever inducing Soviets get out of Korea. Thus if Korea ever to be united short of world war III it must be done now by mil means. . . . Rhee insisted Koreans desired to reunite at any cost and obliterate memory of thirty-eighth parallel. He said that in signing cease fire UN would be helping Commies and WW III could never be avoided that way.[118]

Rhee pleaded again for unification in a letter to Ridgway four days later:

> Substance of position of my Govt is that we cannot maintain our nation in half of our country. A divided Korea is a ruined Korea, unstable economically, politically, and militarily. . . . Fact is clear to us that Korean nation must be committed to simple but vital principle of reunification. . . . Separate maintenance of north and south divisions cld only be by sufferance of and through direct support by foreign powers. Korea must in effect either cease to be independent entity or it must become all one body—all Democratic or all Communistic.

According to Muccio, Rhee said these views were "shared by almost all Koreans North or South who believe reunification inevitable either through democratic means or through Commie aggression."[119]

Taking his cue from Rhee, Gen. Paek Sun-yop stayed away from the truce talks when a military demarcation line was on the agenda. Rhee wrote to

President Harry Truman on July 28 that "Koreans regard the continuance of a dividing line as a death warrant for our nation."[120] The South Korean leader preferred that the talks failed.

Pak Hon-yong and Kim Il Sung of the DPRK also still wanted to fight for unification. Pak, the North's foreign minister, had been head of the Political Department of the KPA until February 1951, when Kim Chae-uk (a Soviet Korean) had replaced him.[121] Pak was implacably committed to reviving guerrilla operations in the South. A Korean Workers' Party decision on August 31, right after the truce talks were broken off, was surely Pak's handiwork. Entitled "Party Activities and Organization in the Unliberated Zone," the new plan had three objectives: reconstruct the underground party organization in the South and strengthen the Fatherland Front, expose the US military and the Rhee regime, and strengthen the partisan struggle behind UN lines. The document began with an overview of positive and negative aspects of the KWP's work in the South prior to the war. The southern organization of the Korean Workers' Party had struggled heroically, but failed "to carry out assignments in the war for the fatherland at the level required by the party," the KWP document stated. The partisan struggle did not achieve "decisive results," popular uprisings were not organized, and operations were not mounted to destroy the National Defense Corps. "The Party policy and political course were correct, however, our party organization in the South was ineffective in actual operations and did not create its own clandestine activities, preserve strength, organize, respond to the new situation, and fight flexibly," the document observed. The lower-level organization of the party was blamed, not the leaders like Pak Hon-yong and Yi Sung-yob.

In the new KWP plan, the southern area was divided into five districts, each with an organizational committee that had authority over partisan activity. Large partisan units were reorganized into highly mobile company-size detachments. Party members were to be armed with the "world view of Marxism-Leninism whose theories . . . should become a reliable compass." Kim Il Sung was not mentioned, a sign that Pak Hon-yong and his colleagues wrote the document. A Liaison Department was established in the KWP Central Committee to oversee the party organization and partisan units in the South. The Flying Column command at the Supreme Headquarters of the KPA was absorbed into the Liaison Department. The plan established an institute to train up to one thousand underground agents and partisan leaders for missions in the ROK.[122]

Pae Chol, the head of the Flying Column command, was appointed chief of the KWP's Liaison Department. His deputy was Pak Sung-won, who had headed the People's Committee in Kyonggi Province in the South immediately after the war started and was political commissar of the Independent First Unit of the Southern Flying Column. The training institute, the Kumgang Political Institute, a large facility for preparing agents and partisan leaders for missions in the South, opened in October 1951 in Yulli-myon, Sohung County, Hwanghae Province. Kim Ung-bin, formerly chief of the Independent First Unit, was named director. Pae Chol had earlier been the Seoul representative of the Korean Federation in Japan, had worked with the Southern Korean Workers' Party (SKWP), and had headed the KWP committee in North Kyongsang Province before the war. Kim Ung-bin had led the Seoul committee of the SKWP. All three were close associates of Pak Hon-yong.[123]

Despite the new initiatives, Pak and his southern colleagues failed to restart guerrilla operations in South Korea except for activities at Mt. Chiri by the 4th Unit of the Southern Army, commanded by Yi Hyon-sang. The Flying Column accomplished nothing. Only the Kumgang Political Institute functioned as planned. About 900 men originally from South Korea were assembled from all over the North and trained for missions against the ROK.[124]

On September 13, Pak Hon-yong told a delegation from the Democratic Republic of Vietnam that "the Korean people are annihilating the American invaders and we will continue this heroic struggle until they are driven from our land."[125] Pak wanted to continue the war and guerrilla operations during the armistice talks, and would have sympathized with Rhee's plea for unification to Ridgway.

US Ambassador Muccio was annoyed that North Korea did not criticize Rhee's obstructionist tactics. On August 11 the ambassador told the State Department that "North Korean aspirations for a unified country just strong as South Koreans. . . . ROK activities opposing cease-fire demanding unity thus have effect stealing thunder from North Koreans." Muccio suggested that the State Department exploit ROK attitudes to counter Communist propaganda that the United States was the obstacle to progress at the Kaesong truce talks.[126]

In a speech on August 14, Kim Il Sung explained why North Korea had entered the armistice talks:

Whatever the intention of the American imperialists in asking for a ceasefire, when a person who has always broken the peace says he wants to solve the problem peacefully, there is no reason why we, who have proposed a peaceful solution to the Korean problem, still desire it, and will continue to advocate it, should not respond. Furthermore, we did not attack America. The American imperialists crossed the Pacific Ocean to subjugate Korea. They failed and now say they want to stop the war. There is no reason why Koreans, as a peace-loving people, cannot agree to an offer to halt the war. The Korean people desire armistice talks. The Korean people have always wanted peace and we seek peace now.[127]

But it would be rash to conclude from these remarks that Kim differed with Pak Hon-yong on continuing the war.[128] At heart, Kim must have still hoped for unification and shared Rhee's anguish at the thought of permanent division.[129]

In a report to a KWP cadres meeting in Pyongyang on October 21, Pak Hon-yong declared that the United States wanted to continue the Korean War in order to provoke a Third World War. To attain "final victory" and "exterminate the enemy," Pak called for "strengthening the home front and total mobilization of the country's material and financial resources."[130] Kim Il Sung told the cadres, "To avoid enslavement by the American imperialists and the running-dog Syngman Rhee . . . we must fight on in this difficult situation for the long term."[131] Pak and Kim were of one mind: the war must go on.

Pak Il-u, the third-ranking person at the CPV-KPA Joint Headquarters, which had been established at Mao's urging the previous December, had a somewhat divergent attitude. In a pamphlet to commemorate the sixth anniversary (August 15, 1951) of Korea's liberation from Japan, Pak wrote: "Reviewing the results of five offensives, Korean and Chinese forces achieved a decisive victory in the Korean War and U.S. imperialism suffered a defeat from which it will not recover.[132] That is to say, unable to recover from failure in Korea the United States will never triumph over China. And the Soviet Union has become so powerful the United States will never be able to overcome and invade it."[133]

From Pak Il-u's essentially Chinese perspective, the PRC had stopped the rollback strategy of the United States, held its own against the UN Command, and won the war against the United States. Pak had a sense of accomplishment not shared by other Korean leaders.

Kim Il Sung, the North's supreme commander in name only, had been excluded from the military side of the war and now had little to say in the armistice talks. As Mao Zedong pulled the strings at Kaesong through Li Kenong, Kim Il Sung and Pak Hon-yong were both relegated to the sidelines, where they read reports of the negotiations and grew increasingly displeased with Pak Il-u.

THE SAN FRANCISCO PEACE TREATY AND THE JAPANESE COMMUNIST PARTY

As a post–World War II peace settlement with Japan was taking shape, Stalin was helping the Japanese Communist Party challenge the US occupation. He urged three mainstream JCP leaders whom he had summoned to Moscow to prepare a party program based on decisions by the JCP's Fourth National Party Conference. Dissatisfied with their first attempt, Stalin rewrote it, and the leaders accepted his version. Stalin next invited the antimainstream JCP leader Hakamada Satomi to a meeting with Tokuda Kyuichi, Nosaka Sanzo, and Nishizawa Takaji, and got Hakamada's assent to his version. N. B. Adyrkhaev, the interpreter at the meetings, says the whole process of preparing a party program took six weeks. Hakamada recalled being in Moscow four months at the time of the meeting. The group departed from Moscow in the summer of 1951.[134]

Radio Moscow broadcast a commentary from the August 14 Cominform publication that said the JCP should unite on the policy adopted at the Fourth National Party Conference,[135] meaning the official agreement that party leaders had endorsed in Moscow. Domestic JCP factions in Japan then engaged in self-criticism and united with the mainstream faction. The Central Committee of the JCP mainstream faction met on August 19–20, studied the new Moscow-made program draft, and passed a resolution on party unity.[136]

Meanwhile, Stalin prepared to use the San Francisco Peace Conference, which had been scheduled to begin on September 4 to conclude the postwar peace treaty with Japan, as a stage for propaganda. On August 8, the Soviet Foreign Ministry gave him a draft peace treaty with a preface that explicitly blamed Tokyo for World War II. Japan had signed the Tripartite Treaty of Alliance with Germany and Italy, the draft stated, "planned aggressive war and brought about war with the Allied Nations, and was responsible for war in Asia and the Pacific." This analysis was absent from the draft treaty circulated by the United States and Great Britain. With an eye on the international situation, Stalin decided against a separate Soviet treaty draft and ordered the Foreign Ministry to prepare suggested revisions to the Anglo-American draft.[137]

At the peace conference, Soviet Deputy Foreign Minister Andrei Gromyko's numerous objections to the Anglo-American draft were rejected, and he soon walked out, together with representatives from the Soviet republics of Ukraine and Belarus, as well as those from Poland and Czechoslovakia. Japan and forty-eight other nations signed the Treaty of Peace with Japan on September 8, and two hours later Prime Minister Yoshida and John Foster Dulles signed a separate United States–Japan Security Pact.

The peace treaty was very lenient toward Japan. War responsibility for World War II was not explicitly placed on Japan; the preface was silent on the historical background of the war. Guilt and blame were covered only in Article 11, where Japan accepted the judgments of the International Military Tribunal for the Far East and other Allied War Crimes courts. By contrast, the territorial provisions were harsh. Japan renounced inter alia all claims to the Kurile Islands and southern Sakhalin. Japan agreed to place the Ryukyu Island (Okinawa) under a UN trusteeship and temporary US administrative control, and transferred formerly mandated territories to the United States. But the various claims for Japanese reparations were greatly reduced. Article

14(a) recognized Japan's obligation to pay reparations, but also recognized that Japan's resources were insufficient to "make complete reparations." Clause 1 stipulated that Japan should assist in compensating for the cost of repairing the damage done, by making available the "services of the Japanese people." Clause 2 provided that the Allied Nations could dispose of the property of Japan and Japanese nationals under the control of the Allies. Finally, in Clause 1(b), the Allied Nations waived all other reparation claims. Yoshida acknowledged the mild conditions. The treaty contained no "punitive or retaliatory clauses" and was "not a treaty of vengeance but an instrument of reconciliation," he said. "The Japanese Delegation gladly accepts this fair and generous treaty."

Many of the signatories had not engaged in hostilities with Japan. Those with a direct stake worked out the final conditions: the United States, Great Britain, Australia, New Zealand, the Netherlands, and France. Five countries in Southeast Asia that had been colonies of western imperialist powers but were occupied by Japan during World War II—Indonesia, the Philippines, Vietnam, Cambodia, and Laos—insisted on reparations and demanded special agreements with Japan on reparations.[138]

Peace and security were a package. Premier Yoshida's objectives were to avoid rearmament in the near future and to prolong the presence of US troops in Japan as a security guarantee. The crucial goal for US leaders was the continued use of bases in Japan, under the same conditions as during the occupation, after Japan regained sovereignty. The peace treaty gave the United States administrative authority over Okinawa and enabled the US military to utilize the whole Ryukyu archipelago, and the US-Japan Security Pact extended that right of keeping US military bases to all of Japan. The United States could operate these bases to "contribute to the maintenance of international peace and security in the Far East and to the security of Japan against armed attack from without," the security pact stated, as well as to help "put down large-scale internal riots and disturbances in Japan." No expiration date was specified. A separate administrative agreement was to be concluded. Thus the use of Japanese territory for military operations in Korea was secured. The United States, not obliged by any duty, was willing to maintain its armed forces in and about Japan, in the interest of peace and security.

On the same day that the peace treaty and security pact were signed, US Secretary of State Dean Acheson and Yoshida exchanged notes that allowed UN members to station troops assigned to UN activities in the Far East in Japan, and obligated Japan to provide facilities and services. Acheson's note said: "armed aggression has occurred in Korea, against which the United Nations and its members are taking action . . . and the General Assembly . . . has called upon all states . . . to lend every assistance to the United Nations action. . . . Japan has been and now is rendering important assistance . . . in the form of facilities and services made available to the members of the

United Nations. . . . I would appreciate confirmation, on behalf of your Government, that if and when the forces of a member or members of the United Nations are engaged in any United Nations action in the Far East after the Treaty of Peace comes into force, Japan will permit and facilitate the support in and about Japan, by the member of the forces engaged in such United Nations action." Replicating Acheson's wording, Yoshida confirmed that assistance would continue after the peace treaty came into effect.[139] The security pact and the exchanged note established Japan as Washington's subordinate ally.

The Soviet Union, which was not a party to the peace treaty, meanwhile followed a two-track policy on Korea of waging war while negotiating. On the one hand, Moscow promoted truce negotiations in Korea. On the other, it intensified the JCP's struggle against SCAP in Japan mainly to undermine logistical support for UN military action in Korea and to assist China's and North Korea's war efforts. The truce talks were an insurance policy against an expanded conflict while Stalin fomented revolution behind US lines in Japan.

The New Program adopted at the Fifth National Party Conference of the JCP on October 16–17 said that the Yoshida regime was "the moral and political pillar of the U.S. Occupation authorities" and was "enslaving the Japanese people for the American imperialists." Yoshida and the Liberal Party had to be overthrown by a "national-liberation democratic revolution," the JCP declared. The New Program also proclaimed that "to think liberation and democratic reform can be achieved by peaceful means is a mistake" and called for violent revolution.[140] But this kind of program could hardly attract popular support in Japan.

SPECIAL PROCUREMENTS

The unprecedented economic boom in Japan sparked by the Korean War had an enormous impact on living standards and political consciousness in the country. Many US bases emptied out in the summer of 1950 when units were rushed to Korea, but they filled up again as replacements arrived from the United States, trained for battle, and were deployed to the front. Casualties from Korea convalesced in field hospitals around Japan.[141] Hundreds of thousands of GIs came to Japan on five-day rest and recuperation leave from Korea. In June 1950 there were 125,000 US troops in Japan. And at the high point during the war, in July 1951, 350,000 US servicemen were in Korea, and they all passed through Japan. The number of "panpan" girls, the prostitutes who worked near US bases, increased enormously.[142]

The Korean War was a "divine wind" (kamikaze) that brought prosperity to Japan. "Our business and financial world was rescued," wrote Ichimanda

Naoto, governor of the Bank of Japan.[143] In 1950 the economy was plagued by a credit squeeze, bankruptcies, and unemployment as a result of severe retrenchment under the Dodge Plan to counter inflation. Suddenly, special procurements by US forces and a boost in exports tipped the country's economy from bust to boom. Textiles and metals led the recovery with rapid price increases from July to December 1950: rayon tripled in price, cotton thread doubled, raw silk thread rose 180 percent, and the price of sheet and bar steel more than doubled.[144]

A popular phrase captured the gold rush atmosphere. *Gatchaman* combined the sound of a loom with the vernacular name for a 10,000 (man) yen note (about US$278), and meant every turn of a loom earned that much profit. Pundits spoke of "textile prosperity" because the top four Japanese corporations in earnings were all textile makers: Toyobo Co. Ltd., Toyo Rayon, Kanebo Ltd., and Teijin Ltd. Synthetic fiber makers Toyo Rayon and Teijin had gross profits of over 45 percent in 1950.[145]

Scrap iron and metal dealers scoured the country to keep blast furnaces operating. The Toyota Motor Corporation exemplifies the dramatic turnaround that resulted from war orders. In 1949 Toyota's annual sales of trucks and automobiles had reached ten thousand vehicles, but in 1950 the company was hard hit by a sharp drop in sales, compounded by the credit squeeze and the lifting of price controls on steel. In late 1949 SCAP had removed price controls on automobile manufacturing, which had encouraged competition and market forces. From November 1949 to March 1950, Toyota lost 76 million yen, and management wanted to lay off workers and cut costs. The company union staged a series of work stoppages to protest dismissals, but on June 10 called off the strikes and accepted the firing of 1,600 workers.[146]

The outbreak of the Korean War two weeks later was manna from heaven. On July 31, the US 8th Army ordered 1,000 trucks from Toyota, and it placed another order on March 1, 1951, for 3,679 trucks. "These orders saved us from the crisis," the company history recounts. "The Korean War boom stimulated general demand, and production could not keep up with orders." Formation of the National Police Reserve also boosted orders for automobiles; Toyota sold 950 vehicles to the NPR from December 1950 to June 1951.[147] Producing vehicles with fewer employees and lower labor costs improved profits. Toyota, which for a long time had not paid a dividend to stockholders, had a pretax profit of 249.3 million yen for the quarter ending March 1951 and paid a 20 percent dividend.[148] Simply put, the Korean War was the midwife to Toyota's emergence as an auto giant.

Special US and Japanese procurements resulting from the Korean War in the first two years after June 25, 1950, totaled $660 million. They reached $480 million in 1953.[149] Some economists believe the Dodge Plan aided recovery in 1949, but the majority hold that the retrenchment under the plan worked well only after the start of the Korean War. Japan's economy benefited substantially from Korea's tragedy; it recovered to prewar levels and was poised for the rapid growth that began in 1955.

The Korean War boom also turned public attention to economic well-being. This mind-set was consistent with Premier Yoshida's goals of pursuing limited cooperation on security with the United States and nonmilitary economic development. That combination also became the cornerstone of postwar leftist pacifism.

THE PRELIMINARY JAPAN-ROK CONFERENCE

Japan recognized Korea's independence in the San Francisco peace treaty and now had to establish diplomatic relations with its neighbor, the Republic of Korea. That entailed navigating the thorny issue of Japan's thirty-five-year colonial reign over the peninsula; plus, of course, the two Korean states were at war. The United States wanted Japan to open negotiations with South Korea, establish diplomatic relations, and then politically support and provide material aid to the ROK.

The Rhee government had sought to join the peace settlement with Japan as an Allied Nation, but John Foster Dulles had refused it on the grounds that the ROK had not been in a state of hostilities with Japan during the Pacific War and that Washington represented its interests. At South Korea's request, Dulles did make several changes in the draft treaty, most importantly to Article 4(b). The final text states: "Japan recognized the validity of dispositions of property of Japan and Japanese nationals made by or pursuant to the directives of the United States Military Government." This article forced Japan to accept a fait accompli: The US military government in South Korea had seized Japanese property there and transferred it to the ROK. The Japanese side deeply resented this provision. [150]

As early as February 1950, Gen. Douglas MacArthur, in the hope that Japan and South Korea could develop a cooperative relationship, had arranged a meeting between Premier Yoshida and President Rhee in Tokyo. Eighteen months later, on August 16, 1951, SCAP informed the ROK government that the United States was prepared to offer its offices for talks with Japan, and in mid-September the ROK accepted. The Yoshida administration replied affirmatively on September 29. [151]

Japan wanted to discuss with the ROK the issue of Koreans in Japan. Between late August and early September 1949, Yoshida had sent a famous letter to MacArthur advocating the return of Koreans to their homeland. The premier cited several reasons. First, with a food shortage in Japan, the diversion of imported foodstuffs to feed Koreans was a burden. Second, "A great majority of the Koreans are not contributing at all to the economic reconstruction of Japan." Third, "There is a large percentage of criminal elements among the Koreans. They are habitual violators of our economic laws and regulations. A great many are Communists and fellow-travellers prone to commit political offenses of the most vicious kind."[152] On September 8, 1949, the Yoshida administration disbanded the League of Koreans in Japan and the Democratic Youth Union of Koreans in Japan. But MacArthur disapproved Yoshida's attempt to expel Koreans forcibly.[153]

With the Korean War under way and many Koreans in Japan supporting the North and engaged in subversive activities, Yoshida was more determined than ever to deal with this inconvenient minority. In a meeting with Dulles in April 1951, Yoshida had objected to ROK participation in the San Francisco Peace Conference and then returned to the issue of Koreans in Japan. Yoshida said that the Japanese government would like to send almost all Koreans in Japan "to their home." The government had long been concerned over their illegal activities, he said. He had raised the matter with General MacArthur, who had opposed their forced repatriation, partly on the grounds that they were mostly North Koreans and "would have their heads cut[s] off" by the ROK if sent there. Yoshida said that the government had determined that the assassination of the president of the Japanese National Railways in the summer of 1949 had been committed by a Korean, but that it been unable to catch the guilty party, who was believed to have fled to Korea.[154]

Yet it was unrealistic to suggest that pro-Pyongyang Koreans be sent to South Korea in wartime. That Yoshida repeatedly brought up the issue shows his dismissive attitude toward other Asians in general. And while the Japanese government would discuss the legal status of the Korean community in Japan with the ROK, it apparently had no interest in taking up other matters before resolving the post–World War II peace settlement, whereas the ROK saw an advantage to early resolution of bilateral issues.[155]

Nonetheless, Japan-ROK preliminary talks began in a room at the Diplomatic Section of SCAP in Tokyo on October 20, 1951. William Sebald, chief of the section, was present, along with Yang Yu-chan, the ROK ambassador to Washington, who represented his government, and Iguchi Sadao, the Japanese vice-minister of foreign affairs, who represented Japan. In his opening remarks, Ambassador Yang read a speech by President Rhee. We want peace in the Far East, Rhee's speech declared. Korea and Japan must forge friendly relations now, Rhee said. Korea has never invaded Japan, he stated, but Japan has often caused suffering to Koreans and invaded Korea. You have committed such violent and illegal acts as murder, torture, conscription, and forced sale of rice against peace-loving Koreans, Rhee told the Japanese. But we will forgo enmity toward Japan, and by resolving all the problems between us we hope for a new start. Finally, Ambassador Yang read President Rhee's last words. "We do not seek compensation for the acts you committed in the past. Let us bury the hatchet."[156] ROK delegation member Yu Chin-o later recalled that Councillor Chiba Hiroshi of the Japanese Ministry of Foreign Affairs asked, pretending to be perplexed, "What does 'Let us bury the hatchet' mean?"

The ROK wanted full-scale negotiations on the establishment of diplomatic relations between Japan and the ROK, Korean claims rights, and other matters. But Japan would only discuss the legal status of Koreans in Japan and shipping problems. The preliminary talks on the agenda for the Japan-ROK conference ended on December 4, 1951. Formal negotiations between the two countries were scheduled to begin in February 1952.[157]

South Korean leaders, who did not believe ties with Tokyo would enhance the ROK's international position, were angered by the attitude of Japanese diplomats.[158] In a memorandum on the preliminary talks sent to ROK diplomatic posts abroad, Syngman Rhee said: "What we most need from Japan is not an offer to send soldiers onto our shores, but a concrete and constructive evidence of repentance for past misdeeds and of a new determination to deal fairly with us now and in the future. Convincing evidence that this change of heart has occurred and has become deeply rooted in Japan would not only strengthen us but would also greatly improve the situation of Japan itself. . . . We are still waiting and hoping that this evidence will be shown."[159] The two neighbors were very far apart.

RESUMPTION OF THE KOREAN ARMISTICE TALKS

The UN Command had meanwhile seized the initiative in Korea during the truce talks in Kaesong. In the eastern front, the US 2nd Division attacked the KPA 2nd Corps from July 26 to 30. Furious fighting centered on a ridgeline overlooking a crater twenty-five miles north of Inje nicknamed the Punchbowl by US troops, who held the highest peak, Mt. Taeu (Hill 1179). A peak to the west held by Chinese troops was dubbed Bloody Ridge. Intensive fighting also raged in central Korea in an area bounded by Kumhwa, Chorwon, and Pyonggang known as the Iron Triangle, where the opposing forces attempted to capture or defend ridgelines. Here, on August 18, during the UN Command's summer offensive, three US divisions attacked three KPA corps. The fighting continued until late in the month.

After the truce talks were suspended in late August, the attacks resumed from September 1 to 18. Chinese–North Korean forces, entrenched in strong positions connected by a network of narrow tunnels six to nine feet underground, stubbornly resisted, and the battle lines barely changed.[160]

In response to a message from the Chinese–North Korean delegation at Kaesong on August 27 that the armistice talks were suspended, Mao said that in preparation for a renewed full-scale offensive, he was considering how to deal with enemy ground tactics, get stronger air defenses, and other measures. Mao indicated that he wanted Soviet military advisers for the Chinese People's Volunteers.[161] On September 8, Mao asked Stalin for eighty-three advisers: ten for CPV staff, ten for the five army groups of the CPV, and sixty-three for twenty-one CPV armies.[162] Such a large request implied that the front had stabilized into trench warfare, and that the Soviet Union need not fear that its advisers would be taken prisoner by the United States. By making the request, Mao also probably wanted to confirm Moscow's commitment to the war.

Less than enthusiastic, Stalin said that a team of officers under Gen. Matvey Vasil'evich Zakharov, the senior Soviet military adviser in Korea, would be sent to the CPV staff and that assignment of advisers to the army group or army level would depend on Zakharov's recommendation.[163] Two days later, Stalin told Mao that five officers would be sent to the CPV staff, but that advisers were not customarily assigned at the army group or army level.[164] Mao then reiterated the request for five advisers for the five army groups.[165] However, Stalin refused and Mao had to back off.[166] Mao then requested that the 3,510 automobiles and 1,900 bicycles China had previously agreed to purchase separately from the Soviet Union be included in its credits for military equipment. That would violate the purchase agreement, said Stalin, and he again refused.[167]

Far above the furious ground fighting in Korea, the air war had escalated. The US Air Force unleashed Operation Strangle in June 1951 to interdict supply routes to the front, first attacking roads and then railroads. The Soviet air force committed more pilots and support personnel, facilitated by a new airbase in Miaogou twenty kilometers west of Antung.[168] The Soviet MiG-15 outperformed the Americans' F-80, and a fairly good air defense was established.[169] In a telegram to Stalin on October 24, Mao said the Soviet air force led by General G. Lobov and the Chinese air force had achieved excellent results, and that Soviet and Chinese antiaircraft batteries had also done well.[170] A Soviet air force report for the period from November 1, 1950, to September 15, 1951, says the Soviets downed an average of 28.6 US aircraft per month and had a favorable kill-to-loss ratio of 6.4 to 1. For the period from September 1951 to January 1952, the monthly average of downed US aircraft rose to 74, including bombers and fighter-bombers, and the kill-to-loss ratio increased to 9.2 to 1.[171] From autumn 1951 to early 1952, Soviet pilots outfought the Americans.

The Chinese–North Korean Joint Headquarters was concerned about a flanking attack from the sea. Soviet intelligence reported in early September that US forces in Japan were training for another amphibious landing. On September 17, the Central Military Committee in Beijing ordered PLA commander Peng Dehuai to improve defenses on the east and west coasts of Korea. Peng asked Choe Yong-gon, the DPRK defense minister, to provide personnel to establish a West Coast Command and an East Coast Defense

Headquarters, and for Choe Yong-gon himself to lead the former. After Peng and Kim Il Sung consulted, Peng named Han Xian-chu to lead the West Coast Command. The deputy was Pak Chong-dok, commander of the 4th Corps of the KPA. Song Shilun, commander of the 9th Army Group of the CPV was put in command of the East Coast Defense Headquarters, and his deputy was Yi Ri-bop, commander of the 7th Corps of the KPA.[172] But, while the Chinese–North Korean military made efforts to improve their defenses, the US military was not planning an amphibious assault at the time.

The UN Command opened an autumn offensive on September 29 and gained ground in the Kumsong area from October 8 on. Across the entire front, however, Chinese–North Korean forces held firm.[173]

Mao wanted to restart the armistice talks, and the Communist delegation asked for a resumption at Kaesong on September 20. They rejected a US request to shift the venue to Panmunjom, a small village north of the 38th parallel.[174] On October 18, Mao instructed Li Kenong on tactics for an upcoming Liaison Officers Conference to prepare for the talks: do not appear overeager and push for rapid resumption, nor procrastinate, Mao said. The chairman also decided to approve a move to Panmunjom and informed Stalin.[175]

On October 22, CPV and KPA liaison officers agreed on the conditions to resume talks, and Li Kenong outlined to Mao the delegation's strategy. When the issue of the military demarcation line was raised at the subdelegation level, they would no longer insist on the 38th parallel; instead, they would wait a while and then propose, based on a proposal Kim Il Sung had made on August 16, the present battle lines as the military demarcation line. Mao apparently endorsed this approach,[176] and on October 25 he informed Stalin of the plan and sought advice on how to proceed. Mao also asked Stalin for information about the reaction of Kim Il Sung to these developments.[177]

Kim Il Sung cabled Mao that same day, when the armistice talks resumed at Panmunjom, that he agreed with this strategy.[178] The Communist side now sought an agreement with the UN negotiators to designate the present battle lines the military demarcation line. On November 14, Mao again asked Stalin's views on this and other issues that he thought could be resolved. Mao was optimistic about coming to an agreement on an exchange of prisoners. "We are opposed to the principle of one for one and intend to propose an exchange based on the principle that both sides return all prisoners. On this problem, too, an agreement should not be difficult."

Mao also anticipated that an early truce agreement was possible. "We are trying to achieve a suspension of military activity within this year," he wrote Stalin. "At the same time, we are making the necessary preparations in the event the enemy delays or breaks off the negotiations. In anticipation that the negotiations will be prolonged half a year or a year, we have begun to conserve human and material resources in the Korean theater. We will hold the positions now occupied and use a protracted active defense to inflict heavy losses in manpower on the enemy to win the war."

Mao ended his cable to Stalin with a complaint about the economic impact of the war on China: China's national expenditures for 1951 had increased 60 percent over the previous year, and the fiscal outlook for 1952 was dire. Yet Mao was guardedly optimistic: "Peace through the armistice talks would be advantageous for us, however, we do not fear a delay in negotiations. By proceeding this way, we will certainly gain victory. At the same time, domestically we will carry out successfully various measures and in the political and economic spheres we can attain stability and greater development."[179]

In a cable to Kim Il Sung on November 13, Stalin criticized the Chinese for failing to provide the North Koreans with military equipment they had promised them, and expressed good will toward the Korean leader. A month earlier, Soviet Ambassador to the DPRK Vladimir Razuvaev, on Kim's behalf, had inquired about the promised Chinese equipment for three divisions. Stalin apologized to Kim for the tardy response, explaining that he had been away from the capital. Gao Gang had assured him at their meeting in Moscow that China would transfer to North Korea equipment for three divisions from the thirty divisions' worth of equipment that China had requested from the Soviet Union, Stalin said. (The request was subsequently raised to provide equipment for sixty divisions). China's failure to fulfill its promise to the North Koreans was regrettable, Stalin said; Kim should query the Chinese about the equipment.[180] Kim told Razuvaev he would write to Mao.[181] Stalin continued to support Mao, but was not always happy with Chinese methods and empathized on this matter with Kim Il Sung.

Stalin naturally took Mao's side in disagreements over basic issues, however. For example, Kim Il Sung wanted to submit an appeal from the DPRK to the Sixth Session of the UN General Assembly to expedite the armistice talks. On November 19, on the basis of a decision by the Politburo of the CPSU, Stalin told Kim he fundamentally agreed with Mao's approach to the truce negotiations, which he described as: "Use flexible tactics, carry through with strong action, and show no sign of impatience or concern about achieving a rapid conclusion to the armistice talks."[182] Acting on another Politburo decision the same day, Andrei Gromyko instructed Razuvaev to block the DPRK's appeal to the General Assembly because "at the present time when the Americans are making threats it would be seen as a sign of Chinese-Korean weakness and politically disadvantageous." Moscow was unaware of how the Chinese would react to the appeal or the North Koreans' motives, Gromyko said; Razuvaev should advise the North Koreans to postpone the appeal.[183] This first indication that Kim Il Sung was inclined toward an armistice ran afoul of Stalin.

But before Gromyko's instructions arrived on November 19, DPRK Foreign Minister Pak Hon-yong sent the appeal to the General Assembly. Furious that Razuvaev had not stopped the North Koreans, Gromyko the next day severely rebuked the ambassador for "unacceptable" performance of his duties.[184]

In the DPRK's appeal, Pak protested to the General Assembly that the US side, as a tactic to prolong the war, was spreading rumors that UN prisoners of war were being executed in North Korea. Actually, it was the UN side that was killing prisoners, Pak said, and UN forces were bombing and using naval gunfire against North Korea. Pyongyang was already in ruins: over the last four and a half months, 25,000 bombs had been dropped on the capital and caused 3,500 casualties, Pak stated. The DPRK sought an immediate halt to military activity as a first step toward a peaceful resolution of the Korean problem.[185] US air raids were obviously inflicting great pain on North Korea.

KIM IL SUNG CONTROLS THE KWP

Kim Il Sung gained undisputed control of the KWP in late 1951 by discrediting Ho Ka-i (a Soviet Korean), the third-ranking member of the KWP as vice-chairman and secretary of the party's Central Committee, and forcing him to undergo self-criticism. Born in 1908, Ho Ka-i had been second secretary of the party committee in the Pos'et Korean district, Primorsky krai (region), USSR, in 1937. After Soviet Koreans were forcibly resettled in Central Asia, Ho Ka-i led the organization section of the party committee in the Yangiiul' district in Uzbek SSR. Sent to North Korea in 1945, he became head of the party labor department and then the organization department.[186] It is no exaggeration to say that Ho was the architect of the Workers' Party in North Korea.

At the Fourth Plenum of the Party Central Committee on November 1–4, Kim Il Sung presented a report entitled "Some Deficiencies in Party Organizational Activities." The report launched an attack on Ho over the party's handling of members' behavior during the US-ROK occupation of parts of North Korea in autumn 1950 and the methods used to rebuild the party later. More than four-fifths of the party members disciplined for actions during the occupation were charged with losing or destroying their party membership certificates. Kim Il Sung thought the Fatherland Front, the front organization created by the North that called for Korean unification, was still needed and opposed treating the Chong'u Party (an outgrowth of the Chondogyo religion) and the Democratic Party, which were part of the Fatherland Front, as reactionary organizations because they had collaborated with US and South Korean forces during the occupation. Kim wanted to open the KWP to the peasantry and make it a mass political party; opposed sweeping disciplinary measures; called for strengthening unity from below with supporters of other parties in the Fatherland Front; and criticized party bureaucratism and formalism.[187] Kim never mentioned Ho Ka-i by name, but his speech was clearly an attack on the party secretary who had overall responsibility for organizational matters.

During the debate at the Fourth Plenum on party practices, Chang Yun-pil, the chairman of the party committee in Taedong County in South Pyongan Province, said that before the US-ROK occupation there had been 8,857 party members in the county. But there were just 5,178 now, and only 600 recruits had joined the party since. The party had discussed attracting new members since May 1951, he said, but few had been recruited: 80 in June, 90 in July, and 140 in August. The numbers were low because eligibility was restricted to relatives of revolutionaries and KPA soldiers, he stated. Seventy-seven percent of current party members had been punished after the occupation, Chang said, and in almost half of these cases the offense was related to the party card. In Taedong County, he stated, rank-and-file members rarely challenged senior cadres, a submissive obedience that weakened ties with the masses. Party leaders tended to be coercive, insisting that farmers plant more crops and provide more cloth to the government. Some farmers bought fabric at the market to meet their quota or turned over cloth they had saved for weddings, he revealed. The party organization must correct its high-handed bureaucratic style, Chang asserted.[188]

Kang Sol-mo, chief of the organization department in the KWP's South Hamgyong Province committee, admitted that he "blindly and mechanically" implemented the party's organizational policy. Almost a third of applicants for party membership were rejected, and disciplinary actions excluded many members from active participation, he said.[189] Kim Paek-en, chairman of the KWP's Sonchon County committee in North Pyongan Province, said that before October 1950 the Chong'u Party's county organization had seven thousand members; the figure was now down to three thousand. The leaders disappeared, and party members went into hiding. Further, he said, membership in the Democratic Party's county organization had dropped from four thousand to four hundred.[190] In the parts of North Korea that had been occupied by US-ROK forces, loyalty to the regime was severely shaken, and the KWP feared that it was isolated from the populace.

Ho Ka-i admitted that his accomplishments were outweighed by his failures. As Kim Il Sung had noted, Ho stated at the Fourth Plenum, the KWP had not understood that strengthening the Fatherland Front was the way to win the war. Ho acknowledged an "incorrect tendency" to close the door to would-be party members and to admit only those with a proletarian background. Under various pretexts, he said, many party cells had impeded party growth. Even the physically handicapped had been rejected. In the KWP's failure to distinguish between education and consciousness, Ho pointed out, illiterate people had been barred from membership. Disciplinary action against those who made mistakes during the occupation was appropriate, Ho insisted, but punishing half the party was wrong. While the destruction of party membership cards was an important issue, he said, "we took the wrong approach." Moreover, "Ignoring the views of the masses and solving problems subjectively isolates the party from the masses." Ho argued that the KWP's Central Committee was responsible for the failure of some party organizations to lead the masses by education and persuasion instead of by threats and abuse. Although the committee's decisions and instructions were basically correct, it had failed to provide adequate guidance and control of implementation. "We must learn from Central Committee activities led by Comrade Kim Il Sung," Ho said, noting that when Kim received an unsatisfactory answer from committee cadres, he went immediately to the countryside and talked to farmers. That was how Kim had discovered shortcomings in the collection of taxes-in-kind and in party organizational activities. Ho admitted that he had previously thought that the party's disciplinary measures were implemented correctly. He concluded by suggesting that provincial and county committee leaders emulate Kim Il Sung's leadership style.[191]

Ho Ka-i was stripped of his party posts and demoted to the unimportant slot of vice-premier of the DPRK.[192] Other party reassignments were also made: Pak Chong-ae was moved from secretary to the Political Committee; Pak Chang-ok was switched from chief of the propaganda department to secretary; Yi Hyo-sun (a member of the Kapsan faction) was promoted to the organization committee; Pak Yong-bin (a Soviet Korean) became chief of the organization department; and Kim Chon-hae, who had returned to North Korea from Japan, was named chief of the social department. Also, Pae Chol's appointment to lead the Liaison Department was approved.[193]

This radical redirection of the KWP through fundamental changes and criticism by lower-ranking members made Kim Il Sung the most powerful figure in the party. Stalin must have authorized the removal of Ho Ka-i, the top Soviet Korean, from the party leadership. Kim Il (a main figure of the Manchurian faction) was reassigned from military matters to chairman of the party committee in South Pyongan Province evidently after Ho Ka-i's fall.[194]

As Kim Il Sung was strengthening his power base, South Korean President Syngman Rhee was engaged in a fierce battle for political survival with the ROK National Assembly. Under the ROK's constitution, the president was elected by the National Assembly; Rhee's term was scheduled to end in August 1952, and the Assembly was not going to reelect him. Rhee had put himself above any party or political faction and relied on five core social organizations for political support: the Kungmin Society, Taehan Youth Corps, Federation of Korean Trade Unions, Federation of Korean Agricultural Cooperatives, and the Taehan Women's Association. In a speech on August 15, 1951, Rhee indicated that he might form a new party "to improve the position of workers and farmers." Pro-Rhee legislators rallied to his side, and to no one's surprise his five mainstay organizations formed a preparatory council to establish the Liberal Party.[195]

On November 30, Rhee supporters introduced a bill in the National Assembly to revise the ROK's constitution and elect the president by direct popular vote and to dilute the power of the National Assembly by making it a legislature with two chambers. Some opposition assembly members vowed to block the changes, and a group of assemblymen led by O Ui-yong split off from the five social organizations outside the assembly. On December 23, two Liberal Parties were formed, one outside the assembly and one inside. The Liberal Party of civil organizations named Rhee party president and Yi Pom-sok vice-president. The Liberal Party of National Assembly members named Kim Tong-song and Yi Kap-song vice-cochairmen, with the top post left vacant. A small number of ruling party representatives joined Rhee's Liberal Party. Amidst this jockeying for power, Rhee used his popular coalition to harass opponents. Nevertheless, on January 18, 1952, the National Assembly overwhelmingly rejected the constitutional revisions by a vote of 143 to 19, with one abstention.[196] Rhee ordered the external Liberal Party to mount a popular protest against "disloyal" members of the National Assembly. Violent extremist groups such as the Paekkol (Skeleton) Group and the Minjun Chagyol (People's Self-Determination) Group intimidated and attacked defiant assemblymen.[197]

STALEMATE AT PANMUNJOM

Disagreement over the repatriation of prisoners of war halted the armistice talks at Panmunjom in February 1952 and was potentially irresolvable. About 104,000 KPA troops had surrendered to UN forces by October 1950 during their retreat northward after the Inchon landing the previous month, and about 15,000 CPV soldiers had surrendered during the fifth offensive of the Chinese and North Koreans in April–June 1951. From 50 to 70 percent of the CPV had previously been in Kuomintang armies, and former KMT officers who had been demoted to enlisted men in the CPV formed anti-Communist organizations in the prisoner camps, aided by personnel sent from Nationalist Taiwan.[198]

Lacking Chinese-speaking personnel to interrogate and exploit CPV prisoners for psychological warfare purposes, US forces had asked the Nationalist embassy in Seoul to provide fluent speakers of Chinese and English; the embassy sent the first interpreter by November 6, 1950. In late January 1951, the US 8th Army, through US Ambassador John Muccio, had requested that the Nationalist embassy, now relocated in Pusan, help with psychological warfare. Nationalist Ambassador Shao Yulin sent Secretary Chen and Assistant Military Attaché Du of the embassy to meet with 8th Army personnel. Drawing on his experiences in the Sino-Japanese War, Shao suggested that the United States undertake ground and airborne propaganda broadcasts, including the use of leaflets and nursery rhymes. The 8th Army also consulted with experts in Washington and Tokyo and held a conference of psywar officers.

At the request of the 8th Army, on February 16 Ambassador Shao picked fourteen teachers and students from the Overseas Chinese School who understood English or Japanese to serve as interpreters. After a short course of military training in Taegu, the newly minted interpreters were sent to the front to assist with interrogations of enemy prisoners. The Nationalist government offered fifty trained personnel, and by June 1951 sixty-six Chinese were assigned to psychological operations, thirty-nine with US forces and twenty-seven with the ROKA. Nationalist Chinese specialists had suffered casualties of one dead, seven wounded, and one missing.[199]

The 8th Army's Civil Intelligence and Education program used Nationalist Chinese personnel to conduct anti-Communist propaganda in the prison camps. Starting in autumn 1951, they persuaded prisoners to sign requests for repatriation to Taiwan. These statements often were obtained through violent intimidation, including murder.[200] Repatriation of Chinese POWs was a very complicated issue. Article 118 of the Geneva Convention requires that "prisoners of war shall be released and repatriated without delay after cessation of active hostilities." President Truman said in May 1951 that prisoners who surrendered and cooperated with the UN side should not be returned to Communism. On January 2, 1952, the UN Command formally took the position at the Panmunjom truce talks of nonforcible repatriation: only prisoners who wanted to return to China or North Korea would be exchanged on a one-for-one basis. The Communist side immediately rejected this principle as a violation of the Geneva Convention.[201]

At first, Mao, of course, as he had earlier indicated to Stalin, did not realize that the disposition of prisoners would be a critical impediment to a ceasefire. In a review of the armistice talks on January 31, 1952, Mao told Stalin that a final agreement had not been reached because the UN side had intentionally delayed the negotiations. Three basic issues had been resolved, and three remained: the voluntary repatriation of prisoners, rehabilitation of airfields, and restrictions on construction of new airfields. The other side stands firm on these points, Mao said, yet say they can be removed from the agenda. The possibility of an overall agreement was improving, Mao told Stalin. But China and North Korea were not counting on it. There was a "conspiracy" in American ruling circles to sabotage the ceasefire negotiations, Mao said: "We are prepared to strike a decisive blow." He included in his cable to Stalin a draft proposition on the composition and functions of a neutral nations supervisory committee and asked for concrete advice. If Stalin agreed with the proposition, Mao wanted the Kremlin to ask the Communist parties in Poland and Czechoslovakia to serve on the committee.[202]

Stalin agreed to contact Poland and Czechoslovakia: "Your firm stance has already achieved positive results and should force the enemy to make further concessions."[203] Neither Mao nor Stalin yet understood the seriousness of differences with the UN Command over prisoner repatriation.

Signs of dissatisfaction at the prospect of a compromise settlement surfaced in North Korea when Pak Hon-yong paid a strange private visit to Peng Dehuai on January 16, 1952. Pak told Peng that all Koreans wanted peace and continuation of the war was undesirable; however, if the Soviet Union and China thought the fighting should go on, the KWP Central Committee would surmount all difficulties and the KPA would hold their present positions. On his way out, Pak told Peng that the visit was just a personal get-together and his comments were only his personal opinions and not those of the KWP Central Committee or the government.[204] In fact, Pak sought to learn China's position on continuing the war and to ingratiate himself with the Chinese.

Peng reported the conversation to Mao on January 22: "I replied that a peaceful adjustment on a just and reasonable basis was advantageous to China. I explained that the present war situation has conditions advantageous to our side and increases the difficulties of the Americans. Thus there can be an agreement in the armistice negotiations. However, on the military side, in order to continue military activity we are upgrading our troop strength. . . . As he left, Foreign Minister Pak Hon-yong said he agreed with my assessment of the overall situation."[205] Mao's reaction is unknown, but one can imagine Stalin's doubts about Pak upon reading of his visit.

Peng also described to Mao the widespread hardship that then existed in North Korea, which had collected an excessive 650,000 tons of agricultural production in taxes. Ten percent of the population was starving and the majority had only enough food to last until April or May. Peng hoped the Chinese government would quickly deliver the 30,000 tons of grain already approved for North Korea. Despite China's own fiscal plight, Peng urged that the level of Chinese aid to North Korea in 1952 remain the same as in 1951—1600 billion yuan (237 million rubles).[206]

Mao replied to Peng on February 4 that the 1952 aid budget for Korea was 1500 billion yuan (222 million rubles) and that assistance would be increased if the fighting ended. From February to May 1962, Mao said, five thousand tons of both rice and foxtail millet per month and two hundred tons of soybean oil would be delivered. In February alone, 3.3 million meters of cotton cloth would be provided. Mao asked himself what the first priority for North Korea's economic recovery would be if the fighting stopped, and said that the CPV could provide manpower.[207]

Mao shared this exchange with Stalin to show China's determination to help alleviate the terrible human suffering in Korea and to fight on rather than accept an unjust compromise at Panmunjom. The Soviet Politburo approved on April 1 a promise by Stalin to Kim Il Sung of fifty thousand tons of wheat flour from Siberia, for which Kim expressed gratitude.[208]

In mid-January 1952, a far-ranging review of the UN Command's position on nonforcible repatriation of prisoners began in Washington. On February 4, the secretaries of Defense and State submitted a joint position paper to the president; prisoners would be rescreened; those who refused repatriation would be screened out, i.e., removed from the list of prisoners; and all the prisoners still on the list would be repatriated. The pros and cons of this course were enumerated. The draft recommended that the president confirm the principle of no forced repatriation.[209] The Defense Department subsequently had second thoughts and withdrew from the paper,[210] but the State Department stuck to its original position. On February 8 a memorandum from Secretary of State Acheson was handed to President Truman: "It is therefore recommended that you approve the maintenance of the present United States position, namely that we will not accept Communist proposals which would require the use of force to repatriate the Communist prisoners of war held by the United Nations Command." There would be no compromise; the United States would adhere to principle. Truman approved the policy that day.[211]

Communist Party members among the UN's prisoners fiercely resisted the rescreening of them by UN forces in February. Sixty-nine prisoners were killed in a riot in a POW camp in South Korea on February 18, and many other bloody confrontations erupted in March.[212]

By February 1952, Stalin, Mao, and Kim Il Sung understood that the armistice talks were deadlocked over the prisoner issue.

Chapter Six

The Third Year

By early 1952 the Korean battlefield had stabilized into trench warfare. Despite US ability to bomb at will, the Communists held their front line because Chinese and North Korean troops had dug an extensive network of underground fortifications that withstood bombing and artillery. By May 1952, Chinese troops had burrowed 7,789 tunnels stretching a total of 199 kilometers, and the Korean People's Army had built 1,730 tunnels that extended 89 kilometers. By August the Communists had finished constructing an underground labyrinth that stretched 250 kilometers from east to west and 20–30 kilometers from south to north.[1] US and South Korean troops excavated comparable tunnel systems.

Max Hastings described the battlefield as US troops saw it:

> Along most of the line, the United Nations and the Chinese faced each other a mile or so apart, from foxholes and observation points sited on the forward slopes. But these were no longer the casual scrapes of troops in constant motion across a battlefield; they were fortresses, honeycombs of bunkers and tunnels bored into earth and rock by engineers with bulldozers and drills, roofed with steel supports and timber, surmounted by many feet of earth or sandbags. They resembled the diggings of an army of monstrous moles, the setts of a great legion of badgers.[2]

With the trench warfare came stalemate on the battlefield, which was of course conducive to truce negotiations. All parties had been forced to abandon hopes of victory, or at least the United States and China had, and they were now the major protagonists. But they fought on to try to set favorable terms for a ceasefire. The original foes, the two Koreas, considered an outcome short of unification unacceptable. The differences in war goals inevitably brought disagreements in each camp. There were leadership struggles in both Koreas and divergent interests and goals among allies in both the Communist and US camps.

Skirmishes on the battlefield were not only waged at the front lines but in rear areas. The United States intensified its bombing campaign deep into North Korea, and the Communists fomented guerrilla activities in South Korea. The emphasis began to shift from conventional warfare to propagandizing and pursuing diplomatic strategies to discredit the enemy while undermining their will to fight.

THE GERM WARFARE CAMPAIGN

Early in the third calendar year of the conflict, the Communist side alleged that the United States was waging biological warfare in Korea. On February 21, 1952, Mao Zedong told Joseph Stalin that eight times from January 28 to February 17 of that year US forces had dropped bacteriological agents from airplanes or fired them at Chinese or North Korean troops in artillery shells. China intended to publicize US actions.[3]

The memoirs of senior Chinese officials contain accounts of the alleged biological warfare. Yang Dezhi, commander of the 19th Army Group of the Chinese People's Volunteers, wrote that on January 28 the CPV headquarters reported that US aircraft had scattered a large quantity of virus-laden insects—carpenter ants, fleas, and spiders—over Kumgonni and several other places southeast of Ichon in North Korea. On February 11, four US aircraft flew over Yang's headquarters and dropped a milky slime that stuck to his uniform sleeve, Yang wrote. Analysis showed that the substance contained bacteria.[4]

According to CPV commander Peng Dehuai's chronology, on January 29 he alerted the CPV to the biological warfare, organized anti-epidemiological units, and ordered them to neutralize the enemy's attack. Peng also said he convened an emergency conference to implement epidemic control measures on February 7. But neither episode is mentioned in *History of the War to Resist America*, China's official history published in 2000.[5] And Peng did not send Beijing a report on biological warfare at this time.

In Beijing, Nie Rongzhen, the PLA chief of staff, reported American use of insects to the Chinese Communist Party's Central Committee on February 18. The next day, Mao Zedong told Chinese Premier Zhou Enlai to formulate countermeasures. Zhou immediately drafted a six-point plan: laboratory testing of the insects, dispatching anti-epidemiological units and vaccine to the front lines, a protest statement by North Korean Foreign Minister Pak Honyong, a supporting statement from the PRC foreign minister, an appeal by the China People's Committee for World Peace to the World Peace Council protesting the US biological warfare, and participation by the Soviet Union in the campaign.[6] Mao's February 21 cable to Stalin reporting the biological warfare was based on this plan.

The same day that Mao cabled Stalin, the Central Military Commission of the People's Republic of China sent a cable to Peng Dehuai, Deng Hua, Gan Siqi, and Gao Gang that stated: "Judging from the widespread symptoms, the enemy has recently spread many kinds of insects throughout Korea and is clearly conducting bacteriological warfare." In a cable written by Zhou Enlai, Mao informed Kim Il Sung and Peng Dehuai, "Since January 28 poisonous bacteria have been dropped from airplanes on the front lines in Korea. Analysis has shown that some insects carry the plague bacillus." Mao's message to Stalin must have contained similar details.[7]

But it strains credulity to think that Kim Il Sung, the leader of North Korea, and Peng Dehuai, the supreme commander of Communist forces in North Korea, would have been first informed of the germ warfare in North Korea by Beijing, as the above two cables might suggest, if indeed it occurred. North Korea would later claim that Kim Il Sung had reported US use of bacteriological weapons to the DPRK Military Committee on February 20.[8]

DPRK Foreign Minister Pak Hon-yong protested US biological warfare to the UN Secretariat on February 22.[9] The next day, the *Nodong Shinmun* newspaper in North Korea, the official paper of the Korean Workers' Party, carried Pak Hon-yong's protest to the United Nations in the lower left-hand corner of page one. It was the first newspaper report of germ warfare in Korea. No other articles about germ warfare appeared in the paper that day. The announcement of Pak's protest was overshadowed in the paper by a commemoration of the thirty-fourth anniversary of the establishment of the Soviet Red Army and a large photograph of Joseph Stalin.

The *Sankei Shimbun* newspaper in Japan later wrote of a note by Glukhov, former adviser to the DPRK Ministry of Public Security, to L. P. Beria, the deputy chairman of the USSR Council of Ministers, dated April 13, 1953. It stated that when Beijing had informed the North Korean government of American use of bacteriological weapons, the North Koreans had insisted on publishing their own statement first.[10] And Zhou Enlai's plan was for Foreign Minister Pak to release a statement ahead of China. But Pyongyang may have rushed its statement, as Stalin had not approved Pak's protest beforehand. For North Korea to act without Soviet approval was highly unusual.

The Soviet Politburo considered China's request for the Soviet Union to join the campaign against US biological warfare on February 23.[11] It apparently agreed with Zhou Enlai's plan for extensive countermeasures. Also, *Pravda* published Pak Hon-yong's protest statement.[12]

Zhou issued a statement on February 24 that the Chinese government and people supported the DPRK government's protest and urged the peace-loving people of the world to protest American bacteriological warfare and stop America's "insane criminal acts."[13] The *Nodong Shinmun* carried Zhou's statement on February 27 and for the first time published related articles on the alleged warfare.[14]

On February 28, Nie Rongzhen informed Mao and Zhou that vaccine had been shipped to the front lines and that forty-four health specialists had been sent to Korea. Huge amounts of vaccine and other medical supplies were needed, Nie said.[15]

The CPV set up a Comprehensive Epidemic Prevention Committee on March 1 with Deng Hua in charge and Pak Il-u as vice-chief. Similar committees were established at the army group, army, and division levels. On March 3, China's Northeast (Manchurian) Military Command reported to the central PLA General Staff Headquarters the discovery of bags dropped by aircraft that contained small rodents infected with bacteria. Acting on Mao's instructions, Zhou Enlai on March 6 cabled Lu Dingyi, chief of the propaganda department of the CCP's Central Committee, that the Chinese Central Military Commission's Epidemic Prevention Office should direct antibacteriological warfare propaganda.[16] The Xinhua News Agency disseminated the report from Manchuria that day. In the Soviet Union on March 2, the Politburo decided on its response to the alleged US bacteriological warfare,[17] and on March 8 *Pravda* carried the Xinhua story.[18] Zhou Enlai charged that between February 29 and March 5, 448 US aircraft had dropped a large number of germ-carrying insects on Manchuria.[19]

North Korea started its own propaganda campaign against US germ warfare on March 2 with reports by correspondents in the *Nodong Shinmun* of "the people's outrage at the use of bacteriological weapons by the murderous American imperialist devils." The "American imperialist wild beasts continue to use barbaric germs," the *Nodong Shinmun* declared.[20]

Kim Il Sung then wanted to do an interview with the TASS news agency in the Soviet Union as a way to criticize US policy in Korea. Ambassador Razuvaev informed Moscow that Kim would make three points: the United States was prolonging the truce talks, the Soviet Union wanted to involve a neutral nations supervisory commission in the talks, and if the United States broke off the negotiations North Korea was determined to continue the war. But Kim apparently did not intend to mention germ warfare. This perhaps suggests that North Korean leaders were not paying much attention to germ warfare. On March 5, Soviet Deputy Foreign Minister Andrei Gromyko reported to Stalin that the idea of an interview had been rejected because it would show Chinese and Korean "impatience and irritation" at the war dragging on, and because the third point Kim intended to make could be interpreted as a threat.[21] Stalin agreed, and on March 7 the Politburo informed Razuvaev. The interview was dropped.[22]

On March 9, Zhou Enlai conferred with Nie Rongzhen, He Cheng, and others about the apparently expanded US bacteriological offensive in Manchuria and epidemic prevention measures by China. Four days later, Zhou ordered the collection of evidence of US germ warfare. On March 14, the Chinese government established a Central Epidemic Prevention Committee. This new committee was headed by Zhou Enlai, with Guo Moruo and Nie Rongzhen as deputies and He Cheng in charge of its secretariat.

The next day, an Inquiry Commission on the Bacteriological War Crimes of US Imperialism headed by Li Dequan and Liao Chengzhi left Beijing for Korea and Manchuria. Four days later, on March 19, a Chinese government directive on anti-epidemic measures was issued in the name of the Central Epidemic Prevention Committee. Zhou then ordered the Northeast Military District and CPV to gather proof of germ warfare for the upcoming arrival in Manchuria and North Korea of two international investigation teams.[23]

A delegation for the International Association of Democratic Lawyers, one of the teams, visited Korea from March 5 to March 19. After going to China, it issued reports on March 31 and April 2. The second group, the International Scientific Commission for the Investigation of the Facts Concerning Bacterial Warfare (ISC), was organized by the pro-Soviet World Peace Council and led by Dr. Joseph Needham. The ISC issued a report of the investigations it conducted in Korea and China from June 23 to August 31.[24]

According to newly released documents, Soviet adviser to the Ministry of Public Security of the DPRK Glukhov and Soviet Ambassador to the DPRK Vladimir Razuvaev later reported that Soviet advisers, at the request of Kim Il Sung and Pak Hon-yong, helped the DPRK Ministry of Health create a fake contaminated zone to show the ISC. "Victims" were produced by infecting condemned prisoners with cholera and plague bacilli. To frighten the ISC and curtail its investigation, "explosions were set off near the place where the delegation was staying," Glukhov wrote.[25]

Chen Jian has written that "what really happened in Korea in the winter of 1951–52 must be regarded as one of the most mysterious aspects of the Korean War history. . . . I found enough evidence to show that in early 1952 both CPV commanders and Beijing's leaders *truly believed* that the Americans had used biological weapons against the Chinese and the North Koreans. . . . However, no convincing evidence has ever been produced on the American side"—including independent researchers—"to confirm the Chinese version of this story or to explain what really happened." On the other hand, Milton Leitenberg shows that as early as January to May 1951, Chinese press and radio accounts alleged that US forces were using experimental data collected during World War II by Unit 731, a Japanese Imperial Army biological warfare research unit in Manchuria, to conduct experiments on Chinese prisoners.[26]

The documents published by the *Sankei Shimbun* newspaper in Japan on this episode indicate that the germ warfare charges originated in Beijing. My own examination of Chinese documents confirms this. Kim Il Sung's apparent lack of enthusiasm for the Communist campaign against germ warfare also makes one wonder if the warfare actually occurred. Although further research is needed, my conclusion is that the charges of germ warfare were unfounded. In any event, the propaganda campaign failed to discredit the United States.

Meanwhile, on March 8, 1952, Andrei Gromyko instructed Vladimir Razuvaev to tell Mao Zedong or Zhou Enlai that it was "not the right time" for attacks that Peng Dehuai was then planning against a US division.[27] Two days later, Mao cabled Stalin that he had heard nothing about the attacks from Peng. Mao also thought the timing was wrong and intended to contact Peng.[28] On March 18 the CPV's 63rd Army attacked not US forces but ROKA units on heights south of Kumgok. CPV headquarters reported that "this kind of prepared, planned, and limited attack" was effective, and suggested that if each CPV army organized one or two such small attacks from the end of March to April, the results would be helpful for negotiations at Panmunjom.[29] But these limited offensive operations did not change US policy on prisoners of war, the biggest sticking point in the truce talks.

On March 28, Mao wrote Stalin: "An agreement on the negotiations in Korea is conceivable. If agreement is reached in April we intend to send a responsible comrade to Moscow as early as mid-May."[30] But Mao's optimism about a settlement in Korea was unwarranted.

In the same message, Mao told Stalin that in light of the San Francisco peace treaty and the Japan-US security treaty, he no longer wanted Soviet naval forces to withdraw from Port Arthur in China. Stalin agreed on April 2, adding that a logical explanation for keeping the Soviet naval forces there—a new Soviet-PRC treaty—was needed to convince the world.[31]

REPUBLIC OF CHINA–JAPAN PEACE TREATY

The Truman administration was meanwhile pressuring Japan to show its opposition to Communist China and support Generalissimo Chiang Kai-shek in the Republic of China (Taiwan) by establishing diplomatic relations with the ROC. But Japanese Premier Yoshida Shigeru was bent on avoiding ties with Taiwan that would antagonize Beijing. The US State Department's John Foster Dulles told Yoshida in Tokyo on December 10, 1951, that US Senate ratification of the Treaty of Peace with Japan that had been signed in San Francisco the previous September was in danger, and Dulles showed Yoshida a draft letter he should send to the US government to assure its passage. In accordance with the principles of the San Francisco peace treaty, the letter said, a treaty would be concluded between Japan and the Republic of China whose provisions would apply to territory under the control of the government of the Republic of China and "all the territory that henceforth comes under it." Yoshida especially objected to the latter point, because if an attack by the Chiang administration on the mainland of China succeeded, the treaty would extend to the seized area and could be seen as Japan's endorsement of an attempt to retake all of China by force. But, unable to withstand US pressure to align against Beijing, Yoshida conceded all points, and on December 24 he sent a letter to the US government based on the Dulles draft.[32]

Negotiations on a peace treaty between Taiwan and Japan began in Taipei on February 20, 1952.[33] Yoshida's reluctance to establish a treaty was shown by naming a former Japanese colonial official as plenipotentiary for the talks. Kawada Isao had been president of the Taiwan Colonization Company and finance minister during the Asia-Pacific War. ROC Foreign Minister Ye Gongchao led the Chinese delegation. The Chiang Kai-shek regime, a remnant of the Republic of China that the Communists had driven from the mainland, hoped to gain international support by engaging in the negotiations. It also hoped that the negotiations would end the era of Japanese aggression against China that had started with the Manchurian Incident in 1931.

Ye Gongchao proposed that Article 14 on Japanese war reparations in the San Francisco peace treaty with Japan be included in the bilateral peace settlement. Japan should pay reparations, Ye said, but because of its weak economic condition he acknowledged it could not pay all that was due to the Republic of China. Instead, Ye sought a provision in the treaty that Japan would supplement reparations with "the services of the Japanese people."[34] Kawada Isao, however, rejected a "one-sided obligation," and said that the inclusion of "restrictive" provisions such as those imposed by the Allies on defeated Japan in the San Francisco treaty "would disappoint" the Japanese people: "Therefore I hope that you will understand that it is necessary to give the contents of the treaty such form as will not arouse our national feelings so far as is possible."[35]

Ye rejected this position on March 1: "The relations between China and Japan have in the past few decades been marred by two wars and many unfortunate incidents. Indeed, from the Mukden [Manchurian] Incident of September 18, 1931 to V-J day the Chinese people, particularly those in our Northeastern provinces, were made the hopeless victims of continuous Japanese militarist aggression. The long years of war with Japan have so depleted China's resources and eaten into her vitals that at the close of hostilities she was left with little more will than power to resist the onrushing tide of Red aggression. The war with Japan has, indeed, cost us dearly."[36]

Ye blamed Japan for the Kuomintang's defeat in the Chinese civil war, a dubious explanation. Nonetheless, all Chinese on both sides of the Taiwan

Straits shared his condemnation of Japanese aggression against China. Ye concluded on a positive note: "True to the spirit of magnanimity and reconciliation, which China has adopted toward Japan since V-J Day, we have, of our own volition, chosen to follow the spirit of the San Francisco Treaty."[37]

Unmoved by Ye's remarks, Kawada Isao flatly rejected the provision calling for supplementing Japanese reparations with "the services of the Japanese people." Even if a claim for such services was put in the text, he argued, they were not practical. Yet Japan had just expressed a willingness to provide "services" to the Philippines and Indonesia; Kawada's cavalier rejection took advantage of the Kuomintang's weakness. Later, Wajima Eiji, chief of the Asian Department of the Japanese Ministry of Foreign Affairs, went to Taiwan and met with Zhang Qun, former ROC prime minister. But there were no concessions in Wajima's briefcase.

With Japan unyielding, on March 19 the Chinese moved the "services" article from the ROC-Japan treaty text to the protocol (i.e., annexed document) and dropped the claim. They still wanted Japan to acknowledge a basic obligation to provide reparations,[38] but the Japanese side refused again. This was too much for Ye, who on April 2 presented another written statement critical of Japan:

> It must be remembered that, of all the Allied Powers the Republic of China fought the war against Japan the longest, incurred the heaviest damage, and her people suffered the most. It is therefore only fair that Japan should recognize her obligations to pay reparations to the Republic of China for the damage and suffering caused by Japan, an obligation Japan agreed to in the San Francisco Treaty. The Republic of China, on her part, would be willing to waive the benefit of services which Japan has promised to make available to the other Allied Powers whose territories were once occupied and damaged by Japanese Forces. In order to do so, the Republic of China must first be given an opportunity to accept the rights and obligations under Article 14 of the San Francisco Treaty. Such is the spirit that has guided the drafting at subparagraph (c) paragraph one of the draft protocol. The Japan version of the said subparagraph, fails to provide for the recognition by Japan of her obligation to pay reparations and attempts to deny China's position as one of the Allies. This is unacceptable to the Chinese government.[39]

The Japanese delegation disregarded Ye's statement and insisted that the Republic of China state in the protocol that it relinquished the "services of the Japanese people" and the right to seek reparations. Unable to break off the negotiations, the Chiang regime complied. The official treaty documents contain this exchange:

Japanese delegate: It is my understanding that since the Republic of China has voluntarily waived the service compensation as stated in Article 1 (b) of the protocol of the present Treaty, and the only benefit that remains to be extended to her under Article 14 (a) of the San Francisco Treaty is Japan's external assets as stipulated in Article 14 (a) of the same treaty. Is it so?

Chinese delegate: Yes, it is.[40]

With those words, the Republic of China gave up all rights to seek reparations from Japan for acts committed in China. On April 28, after only two months of negotiations, the draft treaty was finished. At the signing ceremony, Kawada said: "The magnanimous attitude of His Excellency the Generalissimo of the Republic of China is fully expressed in the provisions that especially concern our people." Japan was thankful and would remember his generosity, Kawada stated, and would play an appropriate role in promoting "the unity of the peace-loving nations of the world."[41]

But the notion that a "magnanimous" Chiang Kai-shek had willingly foregone redress was a myth. The ROC had no other choice given Japan's rigidity. The outcome of the treaty negotiations may rank as a greater success for Japanese diplomacy than the San Francisco peace treaty. Nonetheless, the result proved to be the root of future trouble. The ROC's diplomatic ties to Tokyo helped the Kuomintang regime survive, but the relinquishing of the ROC's rights to compensation for the enormous wartime devastation inflicted by Japan meant also the relinquishing of the People's Republic of China's rights to compensation, which scarred future Sino-Japanese relations.

On April 28, the same day that the ROC-Japan treaty was concluded, the San Francisco peace treaty and the US-Japan security pact—the legal authority for the US Air Force to use Yokota Air Base for bombing raids over Korea—came into effect.

A week later, Premier Zhou Enlai of the PRC attacked a US statement hailing effectuation of the San Francisco treaty. Far from restoring Japan's sovereignty and independence, Zhou said, the treaty prepared Japan for war as a US military base and dependency, and it enslaved the Japanese people. And the so-called peace treaty between the "Taiwan Kuomintang remnant clique" and Japan was a military threat to the People's Republic of China and would never be recognized by it, Zhou declared.[42]

In the meantime, negotiations to normalize relations between Japan and the Republic of Korea had started in Tokyo on February 15, five days ahead of the start of talks in Taipei between the ROC and Japan. Japan's impressive delegation was led by Matsumoto Shunichi, who had been vice-foreign minister in August 1945 when Japan had surrendered to the Allies. The Japanese delegation also included such distinguished officials as Iguchi Sadao, then the vice-foreign minister; Nishimura Kumao, the head of the Treaty Department; and Wajima Eiji, chief of the Asian Department in the Ministry of

Foreign Affairs. South Korean Ambassador to the United States Yang Yu-chan still led the ROK side.

The month before, in mid-January 1952, South Korea had declared a maritime demarcation line in the ocean around the Korean Peninsula that it called a "Peace Line" (it was known in Japan as the "Rhee Line"). Liancourt Rocks, known by the Japanese as Takeshima and by Koreans as Dokdo, was on the Korean side behind this line; Japan and the ROK had disputed dominion of the Rocks since the end of Japanese colonial rule. The ROK had banned Japanese fishing vessels from the zone and begun to seize violators. Japan strongly protested the South Korean actions.[43]

The diplomats at the ROK-Japan negotiations to normalize their relations discussed issues that needed to be addressed to complete a basic normalization treaty. They especially discussed the legal status of the 1910 Treaty of Annexation, which the Korean side insisted had been imposed on Korea by force. But the most contentious issue was Seoul's right to claim the property of Japanese in Korea. The crux of the dispute was interpretation of the term "recognizes" in Article 4(b) of the San Francisco peace treaty: "Japan recognizes the validity of dispositions of property of Japan and Japanese nationals made by . . . the United States Military Government." The ROK's representatives at the negotiations with Japan contended that Japan's colonial rule of Korea was illegal from the outset, that property accumulated by Japanese there was ill gotten, and that Japan had no right to the assets disposed of by US military authorities. But Japanese delegation head Matsumoto Shunichi insisted that Japanese citizens retained personal property rights in Korea, and that when Japanese property was sold, its citizens were entitled to the proceeds.

The first round of talks between the ROK and Japan foundered over this fundamental issue.[44] The negotiations were broken off on April 21. The contrast between Japan's quick peace treaty with Nationalist China and its suspended talks with South Korea is striking.

KIM IL SUNG SEEKS AN IMMEDIATE TRUCE

In the spring of 1952, the Korean War truce talks at Panmunjom were also stalled, and a rift developed between Kim Il Sung and Foreign Minister Pak Hon-yong in the North Korean camp. Kim was inclined to seek an early truce, while Pak wanted to continue the war. Pak and KWP Secretary Yi Sung-yop, both of whom came from the South, continued to prepare for operations against the South. In February, three hundred trainees were sent from the Kumgang Political Institute, which prepared agents and partisans for missions in the South, to near the front lines in the Yongbaek area of Hwanghae Province. The 10th Detachment of partisans was reactivated under the command of Maeng Chong-ho. Six hundred other men reportedly were in training at the institute.[45]

But in March the situation changed abruptly. The institute was abolished on orders from the KWP central committee, and the trainees were moved to the newly constructed First Branch School at the Central Party Institute in North Pyongan Province.[46] This was a direct attack on Pak Hon-yong and his close associates, who sought to continue guerrilla warfare in the South.

A campaign to create a personality cult around Kim Il Sung surfaced in connection with Kim's fortieth birthday on April 15, exacerbating his break with Pak Hon-yong. On April 10, the *Nodong Shinmun* newspaper in the DPRK carried a hagiographic biography of "General Kim Il Sung."[47] On Kim's birthday five days later, the newspaper featured congratulatory essays by Pak Hon-yong and Korean Workers' Party Secretary Pak Chong-ae.[48]

Pak Hon-yong's piece used the expression "Comrade Kim Il Sung our respected leader," but the tone was not reverential. Comrade Kim, together with the party and government, Pak said, had displayed unprecedented heroism in the fierce test of war and prevailed. And thanks to the great Joseph Stalin's theory of revolution, they had led the people on the correct path. Amazingly, the final sentence of Pak Hon-yong's essay praised not Kim Il Sung, but Stalin: "Today as we celebrate the fortieth birthday of our own national leader, we send warm greetings and respect to Field Marshal Stalin who liberated us and supported our heroic undertaking and is the brilliant leader and teacher of the working people of the world." Pak was displeased with the emerging personality cult of Kim Il Sung, and thus chose to offer Stalin as the icon. By contrast, Party Secretary Pak Chong-ae effusively referred to "Comrade Kim Il Sung, the leader of the party and the people," reiterated his official biography, and concluded with praise of Kim.

In May, Gen. Mark Wayne Clark became the third commander in chief of the United Nations Command in Korea, replacing Gen. Matthew Ridgway. Days later, Communist prisoners at the Koje Island POW camp off the coast of South Korea revolted and took the camp commander, Brig. Gen. Francis T. Dodd, hostage. With no prospect of a compromise on the prisoner issue at the armistice talks, Clark decided on a forceful military response to the stalemated negotiations: intensified bombing of North Korea.

On May 13, Far East Air Force Commander Gen. Otto P. Weyland requested permission to renew the bombing of Pyongyang, which had been suspended for the last year. Clark ordered Weyland to wait until the UN armistice delegation could get the Communists to mark all prisoner-of-war camps, as both sides had agreed to do.[49] On June 6, Weyland proposed a general attack on North Korea's hydroelectric power complex, which included all of the plants on the Yalu River except Suiho. Clark gave him the green light, and the aerial assault started ten days later. On June 19, the US Joint Chiefs of Staff added Suiho to the target list.

On June 23, the US 5th Air Force and 7th Fleet naval aircraft attacked thirteen hydroelectric plants in North Korea, including Suiho, Nos. 3 and 4 at Pujon, and Nos. 3 and 4 at Changjin. Eleven power plants were completely destroyed. "For more than two weeks North Korea sustained an almost complete power blackout and after that the production of small thermoelectric plants plus some limited use of the lesser damaged hydroelectric plants restored North Korea's power to perhaps 10 percent of its former capacity," the official US Air Force history of the war recounts.[50] Great Britain and other countries criticized the attacks. Japanese newspapers reported that the raids were carried out by US naval aircraft and the 5th Air Force without mentioning that some aircraft were from Yokota Air Base in Japan.[51]

On June 25, Japanese Diet member Tokano Satoko of the right wing of the Japan Socialist Party raised the following questions in the Lower House Foreign Affairs Committee: As a result of the Suiho Dam attack, was the government concerned about retaliatory bombing of US bases in Japan? And why had Japanese communities near Tachikawa and other bases been asked to participate in blackouts? Vice-Foreign Minister Ishihara Kanichiro responded that he had no details of the bombing of Suiho Dam and that the Foreign Ministry had asked certain local communities to cooperate with blackouts at the request of the US military.[52] The idea was that the blackouts would make retaliatory strikes more difficult.

On July 4, US planes attacked North Korea's Military Academy located fifty kilometers northeast of Antung in China, one day after the JCS gave permission for the strikes. Four days later, US planes struck an iron bridge between Kanggye and Kunuri and the Nos. 1 and 2 power plants at Changjin River.[53] The Japanese press carried short articles reporting that US planes bombed three power plants.[54]

The bombing of Pyongyang, dubbed "Operation Pressure Pump," resumed on July 11. Planes from US 7th Fleet aircraft carriers, the US 5th Air Force, and the ROK Air Force struck at 10 a.m., 2 p.m., and 6 p.m., followed by night attacks from fifty-four B-29s based at Yokota and Kadena in Japan and Okinawa, respectively. The 1,254 sorties constituted the biggest bombing raid so far in the Korean War. A total of 23,000 gallons of napalm were dropped. Two days later, Radio Pyongyang announced that "brutal" strikes had destroyed 1,500 buildings and killed or wounded seven thousand people.[55] Japanese newspapers, citing Radio Pyongyang, reported that two thousand people were killed in the capital.[56]

The bombing attacks on North Korea continued that month, with the Sunghori cement plant hit on July 15, Changjin power plants struck on July 19–21, Sindoku copper and zinc mines hit on July 27, and the Tongyang light metals plant struck on July 30. Night attacks were conducted by B-29s, including sixty-three aircraft in the raid on July 30.[57] An Associated Press article published in Japanese newspapers reported a large air raid on an industrial plant near the border between Korea and Manchuria and included unusual details: sixty-six B-29s from bases in Japan and Okinawa dropped 660 tons of bombs, and it was both the largest attack of the war and the closest to the border.[58] But not one reader in one hundred would have imagined that the base in Japan that was utilized was Yokota within Tokyo itself. The Communist response to this ferocious air assault was inept. The attack on Suiho Dam on June 22 caught the Soviet air force commander by surprise and he kept his planes on the ground; not a single US aircraft was lost.[59] Soviet reports noted that the United States had converted F-80s to fighter-bombers and introduced the F-86 Sabre, which was equal in performance to the Soviets' MiG-15. Another major factor in the outcome of the air assault was the switch from daylight bombing in 1951 to nighttime attacks in 1952. Further, the Soviet reduction from three air divisions to two in North Korea in 1952 put them at a numerical disadvantage. While from September 1951 to January 1952 Soviet defenders shot down an average of seventy-four US aircraft per month (including thirty-seven air-to-ground attack planes), from February to July 1952 an average of twenty-eight US aircraft were downed per month (and only seven were air-to-ground attack planes). The ratio of Soviet kills to losses dropped drastically from 9.2 to 1 to 2.2 or 2 to 1.[60] The Soviet air force could not interdict US bombers, and its losses of fighter planes rose 400 percent.

However, a US National Intelligence Estimate stated that "by US criteria the Communist air force in the Korean-Manchurian-China area is believed to be reaching a fairly high standard. . . . There are indications that Soviet participation in enemy operations is so extensive that a *de facto* air war exists over North Korea between the UN and the USSR."[61] In reality, its early advantage lost, the Soviet air force was now being overwhelmed by US air power.

By this point China had also entered the air war. Mao told Stalin on April 23 that seventeen of China's nineteen fighter regiments were based at Andung and engaged in combat operations, and that China had already lost 154 MiG-15s.[62]

The US bombing offensive dealt a heavy blow to North Korea. Yet, on July 4, after the raids on the Suiho Dam, an unperturbed Mao matter-of-factly assessed American military activities and objectives in a message to Stalin: "Despite some indications that the other side is attempting to cause a change in the Korean truce negotiations, the enemy may prolong the negotiations. . . . In June the enemy increased military activity in part of the frontline area. On June 23 the enemy . . . intensively bombed the Suiho electric power plants and destroyed plants. These facts all show the enemy is attempting to put military pressure on us." Mao asked Stalin for emergency supplies of weapons and ammunition to repel the attacks.[63]

Kim Il Sung did not share Mao's equanimity. The damage to North Korea was too devastating for business as usual, such as requesting more arms from Moscow. On July 6, early in the US blitz, Kim informed the China-Korea Joint Headquarters that the KWP Central Committee's Politburo had decided to reassign Kim Ung to Pyongyang as vice-minister of national defense; that a new KPA Frontline Headquarters led by Kim Kwang-hyop (of the Manchurian faction) would be established; and that Choe Yong-gon would become vice-commander of the Joint Headquarters.[64] It seems that Kim was uneasy now with China's way of conducting the war. The Joint Headquarters accepted the KWP's decisions, except Ch'oe Yong-gon's appointment.

Deeply shaken by the bombing of Pyongyang, Kim Il Sung apparently proposed to Mao that they should accept the US offer on prisoners so as to complete truce negotiations; thus, there would be no forced repatriation of Communist prisoners. The text of Kim's communication to Mao is not available, and Kim probably did not consult with Pak Hon-yong, who would have opposed the move. But Mao's reply to Kim on July 15 read: "After examining this problem for two days, our comrades unanimously concluded that when the enemy is furiously bombing us to agree to a deceitful enemy proposal would be extremely disadvantageous."[65]

Mao summed up the pros and cons of Kim's proposal. Rejection of the US position on prisoners would cause "only one harm," that is, "more losses by the Korean People's Army and the Chinese People's Volunteers." But acceptance of the US position at Panmunjom would cause "great harm," Mao said. The Americans would take advantage of Communist weakness, leading to one defeat after another. But if China and North Korea were steadfast, the enemy would make concessions. "If the enemy breaks off the negotiations without making concessions, we should continue military action," Mao wrote Kim. "The enemy cannot win the war. We should look for a way to change the current situation." Mao also pointed out: "Once the war began, China aided Korea and the Korean people are now sincerely fighting on the frontlines in defense of the peace camp of the entire world. Through the sacrifices of the Korean people positions at the 38th parallel have been strengthened and North Korea and Northeast China are being defended." China would assist Korea to its full capacity, Mao told Kim: "Therefore we make a request of you. In order to resolve urgently the situation in Korea we want you unreservedly to bring all problems to us." If China and North Korea could not find a solution, they would jointly appeal to Stalin. Mao told Kim that he would contact Stalin and heed his view.

Stung by Mao's rebuke, Kim backed down. In a cable to Mao on July 16, he withdrew his suggestion of accepting a truce on US terms and agreed to work in concert with the Chinese leader. "After careful consideration and discussion, we reached a unanimous conclusion. We acknowledge that your analysis of the present situation is correct. At the same time you kindly considered our situation and suggested that we unreservedly present the problem of essential assistance. We thank you from the bottom of our hearts." Kim Il Sung pressed Mao for additional antiaircraft guns, aircraft, and aid that would enable the KPA to engage in limited offensives.[66] If they were to continue the war, Kim reasoned, China and the Soviet Union would have to provide the wherewithal. His report of a "unanimous conclusion" in Pyongyang may, of course, have papered over differences within the North Korean leadership. Or perhaps Pak Hon-yong was consulted and then accepted Kim's view.

Kim wrote to Stalin the same day that he was determined to carry on the war. But he also lamented: "During the year of negotiations we have in effect ceased combat operations and shifted to a passive defense. In this situation the enemy has suffered virtually no losses and continuously inflicted enormous human and material losses on us. For example, recently the enemy disabled all of Korea's electric power plants and it is impossible to restore them because of the U.S. aggressive aerial action. . . . The enemy takes advantage of this situation in the [truce] negotiations to thrust unacceptable demands at us. Naturally, our Chinese friends reject these conditions. We agree with Comrade Mao's views."

Kim realized that if there was no truce, the Communist side would have to resume offensive operations. He thus asked Stalin for equipment for ten antiaircraft regiments, forty TU-2 aircraft, and weapons for the KPA.[67]

Stalin cabled Mao that day: "We consider your position in the truce negotiations to be completely correct. Today we received a message from Comrade Kim Il Sung in Pyongyang that he also approves of your position."[68] Mao forwarded to Stalin his July 15 cable to Kim and Kim's response the following day.

On July 24, Stalin told Kim that it would be very difficult to meet his request, but promised, in view of Korea's severe situation, to provide equipment for five antiaircraft regiments, thirty TU-2 aircraft, one thousand trucks, and twenty-six thousand tons of weapons and medical supplies.[69] At the same time, Stalin informed Mao that the Soviet Union could provide only 20 percent of China's own request for weapons and ammunition.[70] His warm reply to Kim contrasts with his somewhat brusque message to Mao. Stalin was more sympathetic to Kim Il Sung than to Mao. Inferior Soviet air power could not prevent the enormous damage inflicted on North Korea by US bombing, which might explain Stalin's sympathy to Kim.

Kim's attempt to halt the fighting by proposing Communist acceptance of US truce terms on prisoners had been quashed. A deepening rift had emerged between Mao and Kim over the conduct of the war.

POLITICAL CRISIS IN PUSAN

While North Korea was reeling under US bombing, South Korea's temporary capital of Pusan was the scene of a seminal political struggle far from the front lines.

When the ROK National Assembly in January 1952 rejected President Syngman Rhee's proposed constitutional amendment for direct election of the president, Rhee's Liberal Party ordered its mass organizations to organize protests and a signatory campaign against his opponents. A mass rally on February 8 demanded revision of the constitution. In a speech on February 16, President Rhee appealed for the recall of assembly members who had rejected the people's wishes on direct elections. Unbowed, 122 members of the Democratic Party and the internal Liberal Party that was working inside the assembly signed a bill to abolish the presidental system and establish a system in which the premier was responsible to Parliament.[71]

The Truman administration was deeply concerned about the impending confrontation in South Korea. On February 15, US Ambassador to the ROK John Muccio sent a comprehensive report to Washington that included an assessment of Rhee and the potential presidential candidates that might be elected by the National Assembly to succeed him that August: "Rhee is becoming increasingly recalcitrant and senile. While he is president no one else seems to have the guts to stand up to him. Two of the possible candidates, Yi Pom-sok and Shin Ik-hui, are pretty crummy from our point of view. The best two, Chang Myon and Ho Chong, lack popular followings and are somewhat weak. . . . Chang Myon's chances in an election by the National Assembly are probably our best hope." But if American influence on the elections became an issue, "the Assembly's sensitive feelings [about] ROK dignity would flare up," Muccio said, and "Chang's close ties with the United States would be a liability rather than an asset." The United States had to avoid the impression of interference.[72]

Fully aware that Washington preferred Chang Myon, Rhee launched a preemptive attack and fired him as prime minister on April 20. Rhee again submitted a bill before the National Assembly on May 14 for direct election of the president and got the assembly to approve Chang Taek-sang as prime minister. Ten days later, the president named Yi Pom-sok interior minister, and that night martial law was declared in the Pusan area. A roundup of anti-Rhee assembly members began, starting with So Min-ho. Chong Hon-ju and three other assembly members were arrested on charges of using secret funds from the International Communist Party for a plot to establish a "National Leaders Committee to Reform the Government." More than ten assembly members were jailed in a week. Yet the opposition remained defiant.[73] On May 29, Vice-President Kim Song-su resigned in protest and took refuge on a US Navy hospital ship. The American embassy gave Chang Myon protection.[74]

According to Lee Jong-won, opposition political leaders sought US intervention. The day after martial law was imposed, Prime Minister Chang Taek-sang, Rhee's own appointee, tearfully appealed to UNCURK (UN Commission for the Unification and Rehabilitation of Korea) representatives to "save Korea."[75]

Muccio had by then returned to Washington for consultations, leaving Counselor E. Allan Lightner as the senior officer in the US embassy. On May 27, he and US 8th Army commander Gen. James Van Fleet visited Rhee. Lightner carried with him a message from Muccio to Rhee requesting an explanation of the situation in South Korea for President Truman.[76] Van Fleet told Rhee that he feared the measures that had been taken might "reflect unfavorably" on the Korean government and "cause the outside world to lose confidence in ROK." He did not understand why martial law has been declared, Van Fleet said, adding that the transfer of "additional ROK troops to the Pusan area" would "weaken the front." Rhee explained his actions and said that ROKA Chief of Staff Yi Chong-chan was reportedly involved in a plot against him and would be dismissed. When Van Fleet defended General Yi, Rhee countered that a "group of gangsters" controlled a majority of the National Assembly, had connections with the nation's enemies, and planned to seize the government. He had acted to "save Korea and the democratic cause," Rhee said. With Rhee determined "at all costs to rid himself of enemies" and indifferent to overseas criticism, Lightner concluded that "stronger action now seems required." On May 28, UNCURK representatives handed Rhee a request that he lift martial law and release the jailed National Assembly members.[77]

The same day, Van Fleet brought Yi Chong-chan to a meeting with Rhee and brokered a compromise: Rhee revoked Yi's dismissal as ROKA chief of staff in return for the temporary continuation of martial law under the command of Maj. Gen. Won Yong-duk.[78]

Two days later, Lightner delivered a letter to Rhee from the US government that called for an immediate end to martial law and approved the UNCURK statement. Rhee told Lightner that two "Commie underground agents" had been arrested and "'it will all be revealed' . . . in public trials of enemies of democracy," Lightner wrote. When Lightner challenged whether the arrested assemblymen were all involved in a Communist plot, "Rhee waxed wroth" and charged that the United States and UNCURK were interfering in Korea's internal affairs.[79] Lightner thought the United States had been too lenient with Rhee. In the second of two telegrams to the State Department that day, he said: "This is now [a] struggle to death: Either Rhee has his way or Rhee falls." Lightner requested that the "necessary steps" be taken to stop Rhee.[80] Lightner was then in touch with ROKA officers who were planning a coup d'etat against Rhee.

Researchers are divided on the identity of the plotters. In 1984 journalist Cho Kap-che, based on interviews with the conspirators, singled out Yi Yong-mun, chief of the Department of Operations and Education at ROKA headquarters, and his deputy Park Chung-hee.[81] In 1994 Lee Jong-won theorized that General Van Fleet himself suggested a coup to Yi.[82]

But the idea that Van Fleet urged General Yi to overthrow the ROK government strains belief. It was, of course, Van Fleet who had brokered a compromise between President Rhee and General Yi.

Lightner recommended the use of US military force to prevent Rhee from nullifying the upcoming election by the National Assembly of South Korea's next president, and wanted UN Commander Gen. Mark Wayne Clark to pressure Rhee. An uncooperative Rhee should be taken into protective custody, Lightner suggested.[83] Clark demurred. In a message to US Army Chief of Staff Joseph Collins on May 31, Clark said he preferred to avoid a showdown unless Rhee's actions "adversely affect either the combat operations of 8th Army or the social and economic situation in Korea which, in turn, will adversely affect the combat operations of the Army. At such time the military will be forced to act." For the time being, Clark would "continue to urge Rhee to moderate his illegal and unconstitutional action."[84]

On June 2, Clark and Van Fleet met with Rhee. Afterwards, Clark outlined the conversation to Lightner. Rhee had assured the two generals that additional troops would not be withdrawn from the front lines to Pusan, that the ROK's political problems would soon be settled, and that the US commanders need not be concerned, Clark reported.[85] To the extent that Rhee was exhilarated by Clark's conciliatory manner, Lightner must have been disheartened.

The next day Lightner delivered a letter from Truman to Rhee. The US president expressed "shock at the turn of events during the past week. . . . It would be a tragic mockery of the great sacrifices in blood and treasure which the people of many free nations and of Korea have made in the past two years if any changes considered necessary in the political structure of the ROK cannot be carried out in accordance with due process of law." Truman urged Rhee "most strongly to seek acceptable and workable ways to bring this crisis to an end and hope you will take no irrevocable acts."[86] Lightner forcibly supplemented the letter, terming American opposition to Rhee's intention to dissolve the National Assembly "a question of principle, since we could not ignore such developments behind the front lines in a country which was being defended by the collective action of many democratic countries in a cause that was fighting for the very principles of constitutional government, human rights and freedom." Lightner also told Rhee that "no evidence had been presented to prove there was a major Commie conspiracy" behind the assembly's actions in opposition to Rhee's agenda. Rhee responded that Lightner was "grossly misinformed and all would be revealed soon to prove he was right," as Lightner wrote afterward. The meeting with Lightner concluded with Rhee expressing hope that Ambassador Muccio would "understand his position and that US Govt wld let things alone here."[87]

Later in the day, Lightner began to back away from his earlier position advocating the removal of Rhee. Prime Minister Chang Taek-sang had told him that the ROK cabinet had balked at Rhee's dissolution of the National Assembly and that he had drafted a compromise constitutional amendment to end the crisis. Chang's compromise called for: 1) direct election of the president; 2) nomination of the prime minister by the president, confirmation by the National Assembly, and removal by a two-thirds no confidence vote of the National Assembly. In addition, the president could only nominate cabinet ministers proposed by the prime minister and they had to be confirmed by the National Assembly.[88] Though surely ambivalent, Lightner reported the facts to Washington without comment.

In Washington, senior State Department officials and members of the Joint Chiefs of Staff conferred on June 4 about what to do with Syngman Rhee.[89] They agreed to support Chang's compromise and approved messages to Clark and Muccio. Clark was told that Washington strongly hoped "agencies of the United Nations and of the United States Government will join their efforts and use their great powers of persuasion in taking measure short of the grave and distasteful steps of open military intervention."[90] Muccio received similar unequivocal instructions: "(1) Every means must be exhausted to obtain a resolution of this internal crisis by methods short of active military intervention. . . . (2) There has to be some leadership in the ROK Govt. It appears that this leadership can best be provided by Rhee under some controls and in a more chastened mood. It appears here that US and UN interests wld best be served if the end result is that Rhee remains as Pres."[91]

Washington had chosen to stick with Syngman Rhee, and Lightner understood the implications. To withdraw support from Rhee's opponents meant to persuade them to support Chang's compromise. Lightner wrote to Kenneth Young, director of Northeast Asia Affairs in the State Department: "It is not only Rhee himself who is dangerous; it is the little group that surrounds him, eggs him on and carries out his dictates—above all Lee Bum-suk [Yi Pom-sok]."[92] Lightner's point was acceptable to Washington.

Muccio returned to Seoul on June 6 and soon echoed Lightner. After meeting with Rhee, Muccio reported to Washington that the South Korean president "was both physically and mentally exhausted and did not know to whom to turn. . . . I feel strongly that the 'Lee Bum-suk group' has practically taken Rhee over completely. Our main immediate problem is to thwart the Lee Bum-suk group from taking over."[93]

In Washington, Young submitted a memorandum dated June 13 to John Allison, assistant secretary of state for Far Eastern Affairs. His conclusions were shaped by Lightner's letter to him: "Our policy should be to circumscribe Rhee's position and eliminate the Lee-Yim-Yun trio"—Lee Bum-suk (Yi Pom-sok), Louise Yim (Im Yong-shin), and Yun Kyong (Yun Chi-yong). " . . . Let us recognize that there is now no national 'brand' name to substitute for Rhee in the Republic of Korea."[94] Young also recommended: "The United States, in its own interest, should encourage Korean efforts to (1) remove Lee Bum Suk and General Won, (2) install a competent Defense Minister, (3) reestablish an unbroken chain of command from CINCUNC through ROK, Chief of Staff to all military and police units, (4) develop a united cabinet and a national patriotic coalition for the duration of the war, and (5) formulate sound constitutional reforms to take effect after August 15 [sic—August 5], 1952." "The United States should support Rhee *only* if the above items are put into effect with his full cooperation," Young advised.[95] If the program he recommended failed, Rhee continued to defy US advice, and "disturbed conditions threaten the Pusan base area, the United States will have to resort to the ultimate measure of military government," Young wrote. Almost as an afterthought, he added that "the Departments of State and Defense should continue to consult informally on tentative plans for UNC martial rule."[96]

Muccio tried to work out a compromise between Rhee and the National Assembly. Emboldened by America's support, the Rhee camp intensified pressure on the opposition. Still hopeful of American intervention, however, recalcitrant elements in the National Assembly held out. On June 20, Democratic Party assembly members, including Yi Si-yong, Kim Song-su, Chang Myon, and Cho Pyong-ok, organized a mass meeting to preserve the ROK's constitution. A pro-Rhee mob attacked the meeting and many people were injured. The next day, Prime Minister Chang's Silla Association introduced a bill to amend the constitution to permit direct election of the president.[97] On June 23, Muccio reported to Washington that he had spoken with the prime minister, the chairman, and vice-chairman of the National Assembly, and opposition leaders, including the head of the Democratic Party, and urged them to find a way to end the stalemate: "All of these leaders indicated that they were prepared to work towards such a solution. In view of Rhee's and the leaders' reaction, I felt that it should be possible to arrive at a compromise. But jockeying is still going on."[98]

Meanwhile, in Washington, Kenneth Young hastily drafted a proposal to remove Rhee by force. According to Lee Jong-won, Young's proposal "was the first official policy for the United Nations to intervene directly with military force."[99] Alexis Johnson, deputy assistant secretary of state for Far Eastern Affairs, endorsed it, and it was sent to Joseph Collins at the JCS. At Collins' suggestion, the memorandum was forwarded to UN Commander

General Clark in a joint cable from the State and Defense Departments on June 25. The cable noted that the political situation in South Korea might deteriorate to the point that direct intervention could not be avoided, and instructed Clark to confer with Muccio "earliest in order to develop and submit to Wash for approval detailed polit and mil plan." If intervention were authorized, the UN commander would order the ROKA chief of staff to declare martial law in the Pusan area. Use of UN forces would be avoided or kept to a minimum; South Korean forces would do the main work. [100] This was a contingency plan, though, not a policy decision to be implemented at that time.

Clark informed the JCS on June 27 that he still believed diplomatic pressure was the best course of action. But his staff was preparing a detailed operational plan for intervention. He and General Van Fleet of the 8th Army believed the South Korean army and chief of staff were loyal to the UN Command. To avoid suspicion that there was such a plan, Clark suggested that "he and Muccio not meet for the moment, but coordination take place at the staff level." [101] Thus, despite his reluctance to intervene militarily, Clark was now directly involved.

In an assessment of the situation to the State Department on June 28, Ambassador Muccio said that he thought Rhee might "win out without having to resort to or being faced with measures or situations which wld invite UN intervention. . . . Since Rhee probably will maintain martial law and proceed with trials of arrested Assemblymen up to the moment of victory, we will have hard time regarding his victory as having taken place in manner acceptable to free world." [102] The ambassador had probably already informed the South Korean opposition that the United States would not intervene and that they had to cooperate with Rhee.

The National Assembly reconvened for a special session on July 1. Whether from bribes or fear of violence, two-thirds of the assembly voted to amend the constitution to allow for direct election of the president and a bicameral assembly. Sixty-three external Liberal Party assemblymen (those working with civil organizations) voted for the amendment, along with twenty Silla Association assemblymen, nineteen internal Liberal Party assemblymen, eleven Minyu Association assemblymen, six Minguk Party assemblymen, and four independents.

The next day, Prime Minister Chang announced that in order to have a quorum, assemblymen absent from the special session would be "guided and escorted" by police to the Assembly Hall. That night, security forces searched Pusan and brought in members who had been in hiding; seven assemblymen under arrest for the alleged Communist conspiracy against Rhee were also taken to the hall. The legislators were held there from July 2 to July 3. The constitution stipulated a thirty-day interval between filing and adoption of an amendment, but Rhee's followers ruled that the revision could be immediately passed. The opposition's last stand was over. Assembly chairman Shin Ik-hui tearfully told a press conference that Ambassador Muccio had said "he hoped the situation would not get worse." At 7:50 p.m. on July 4, the amendment for direct presidential elections and a bicameral assembly was adopted by a vote of 160 to 0, with three abstentions.[103]

The UN's General Clark sent his contingency plan for military intervention to Washington the next day. The gist of his scenario was that the UN Command would stage a coup d'etat because using the ROKA might bring civil war. Rhee would be enticed from Pusan to Seoul, and the UN Command would move into Pusan "and seize between 5 and 10 key ROK officials who have been ldrs in Rhee's dictatorial actions. . . . [Rhee] wld be urged to sign a proclamation lifting martial law, permitting Natl Assembly freedom of action and estab freedom of the press and radio without interference fr his various strong armed agencies." If the president refused to issue the proclamation, the prime minister would be asked to do so. If both refused, the UN Command would establish an interim government, Clark wrote. Clark thought passage of the constitutional amendment would soon stabilize the situation, but the plan "will be completed and filed here for future use if neces," he reported.[104]

On July 23, Rhee replaced ROKA Chief of Staff Yi Chong-chan, who was sent to the United States for "training," with Paek Sun-yob, commander of the 2nd Army. Rhee also took other conciliatory steps.[105] Martial law was lifted four days later. The court-martial of seven assemblymen arrested for involvement in the alleged Communist plot was dropped, and the death sentence that had been given to Assemblyman So Min-ho was reduced to eight years' imprisonment.

In the elections for president and vice-president on August 5, Rhee won the presidency again, with 5,230,000 of the 7,030,000 votes cast, aided by election irregularities. The Liberal Party had designated Yi Pom-sok as its vice-presidential candidate, but Rhee did not endorse him, and the vote was rigged to elect independent Ham Tae-yong. The Liberal Party later expelled Yi. He was now out of the picture. Rhee, his power base strengthened, was poised to take over the party, and he flaunted his popular support.[106]

The Rhee administration emerged from South Korea's crisis stronger than ever, though President Rhee now went along with Washington's wishes.

ZHOU ENLAI VISITS MOSCOW

At the time of the South Korean elections, there were signs that the Americans would intensify the bombing of North Korea to deliver a knockout punch. The UN Command announced on August 5 the names of seventy-eight centers in North Korea targeted for destruction.[107] The announcement was timed to influence an upcoming top-level Sino-Soviet conference in Moscow to plan Communist strategy for reaching an armistice.

Mao Zedong sent a large Chinese delegation to Moscow led by Premier Zhou Enlai and armed with a full agenda. They would consider not only the war in Korea and an armistice, but China's "internal situation over the past three years and the five-year plan for economic development." They would also discuss extension of the Port Arthur Agreement on the use of Port Arthur in China by the Soviet navy. The delegation arrived on August 17, and Zhou and Stalin met three days later. [108]

After a discussion of Soviet military assistance to China, Zhou spoke of changed circumstances in Korea. Chinese and Korean forces were now confident that they could drive the enemy back, he said. In 1952, they had shown that they could keep their positions and strengthen them. They were now much stronger than before and could continue an operation for longer than seven days. But when Stalin asked whether offensive operations were possible, Zhou responded that to execute a general offensive would be difficult.

Stalin said that the American forces clearly wanted to gain control of more Chinese prisoners of war and that they were refusing to return prisoners to the PRC. The Americans might send them to Chiang Kai-Shek in Taiwan, Stalin said. That would be a violation of international law, he pointed out. Under international law, all belligerents were required to return prisoners to their countries, except those convicted of crimes.

After Stalin asked what Mao thought about the prisoner issue and whether the Chinese would concede to the United States or stick to their present position, Zhou discussed China's disagreement with North Korea on this issue. The American side had offered to return 83,000 prisoners and the North Koreans wanted to accept this, he said. However, they did not understand that the Americans were playing a deceptive game. Of these 83,000 prisoners, 6,400 were Chinese and the remainder were Korean. The Americans were trying to drive a wedge between Chinese and Koreans, Zhou argued.

That was right, Stalin said. Zhou then expanded on the Chinese disagreement with the North Koreans: "Mao Zedong has analyzed the situation and insists on the return of all prisoners. The Korean side thinks continuation of the war [is] disadvantageous because daily losses exceed the number of prisoners at issue." According to the declassified records of this meeting, Zhou said next that "suspension of the war is disadvantageous for America." But from the context it is clear the wording should be "is advantageous." The conference transcript is apparently wrong.

Zhou then stated: "Mao regards continuation of the war as advantageous to us because it prevents America from preparing for a new world war." Stalin responded, "Mao Zedong is right. Americans are turning against the war. North Korea will suffer losses in the war, but they will not be defeated. . . . It is necessary to persist and endure. Of course, we must understand the Korean position. They are suffering huge losses, yet we must persuade them that this is a momentous undertaking. They must have fortitude. They must persevere. . . . We must aid and support the Koreans. What is the grain situation for Koreans? We can help more."

Stalin and Zhou clashed briefly at this point. Zhou emphasized once more that they could not make concessions to the Americans in the negotiations. Stalin insisted softly that if the Americans conceded on some points, it was all right to accept them, with the understanding that negotiations would continue on the unresolved issues. Zhou agreed with Stalin, but asserted that if the Americans did not want peace, Chinese and Koreans must resolve to continue the war, even for another year. Stalin was obliged to admit that Zhou was right.[109]

In this exchange, Stalin did nothing more than approve of Zhou's position; Stalin did not urge China to continue the war, as some scholars contend. He just said that the USSR would help with the war effort until China could get a reasonable ceasefire at Panmunjom.[110]

After Zhou commented that America had no stomach for a third world war, Stalin said that America could not conquer tiny Korea, and then launched into a derisive harangue about American weakness. One doubts that Stalin really believed what he said about American weakness, however; he and Zhou fully understood how powerful the United States was. Then Zhou abruptly began to talk about showing a conciliatory attitude in the negotiations on the prisoner issue. He said that if America offered to return a small number of prisoners and proposed that the return of the remaining prisoners could be resolved with the mediation of neutral countries—for example, India—such a proposal could be accepted. Stalin immediately supported Zhou's idea. He suggested that if America proposed to retain a certain percentage of Korean and Chinese prisoners, North Korea and China could retain the same percentage of South Korean and American prisoners until a final prisoner exchange. This would put pressure on the American side. "The main thing is to propose the cannons stop firing," Stalin said.

At last Stalin had suggested a concrete compromise on the prisoner issue. Zhou then developed Stalin's idea: "First, announce we will hold back the same percentage of South Korean and American prisoners as the percentage of North Korean and Chinese prisoners retained by the Americans and then stick to this position. Second, seek mediation by a neutral country. Third, sign an armistice by separating the prisoner problem and continuing to discuss it."[111]

Toward the end of the meeting, Zhou said that it was Mao's wish that Kim Il Sung and Peng Dehuai be invited to Moscow. Mao wanted Stalin to rebuke Kim for his willingness to accept US truce terms on the prisoner issue. Stalin replied that it would be strange for the Soviet Union to issue such an invitation, but that if Kim and Peng came to Moscow, he would meet with them. Zhou said that Peng wanted to visit Moscow, and that while he did not know about Kim, the North Korean leader probably should talk with Stalin too. Stalin concurred.

Zhou then stated that the Chinese government considered it appropriate to prolong the negotiations at Panmunjom. China was preparing for the possibility that the war might go on for another two or three years, Zhou said, but it could not sustain the fighting by itself. Zhou again raised the issue of Soviet military assistance to China, asking for airplanes, artillery, and artillery ammunition. The Soviet Union would provide as much as it could, Stalin said. He then returned to the hardships of the North Koreans:

Stalin: What is the general mood among Koreans? Are they in a state of shock?

Zhou: There is much destruction in Korea, especially since the bombing of the hydroelectric power plants on the Yalu River. This has affected the spirit of our Korean comrades and made them want to attain peace faster.

Stalin: American tactics are terrorizing. But Chinese are not terrified. Can you say the Koreans will not be terrified?

Zhou: Basically I can say that.

Stalin: If that is correct [the situation] is not so bad.

Zhou: The Koreans are a little unsettled. They have lost some confidence and resolve. A part of the leadership is even panicky.

Stalin: I, too, understood this sentiment from Kim Il Sung's cables to Mao Zedong.

Zhou: Yes, that is right.[112]

Indeed, Kim Il Sung, in a panicky mood, had expressed his wish to Mao Zedong to conclude a truce agreement immediately. Yet Stalin remained sympathetic to the North Koreans.

STALIN SIZES UP KIM IL SUNG AND PAK HON-YONG

Mao Zedong informed Kim Il Sung on August 23 that Stalin would meet with him and other North Korean leaders. Kim replied the next day that he, Pak Hon-yong, and Soviet Ambassador to the DPRK Vladimir Razuvaev would go to Moscow together. CPV commander Peng Dehuai would accompany them. Mao told Zhou Enlai to ask Stalin to send a special aircraft to Pyongyang for the visitors, adding that Pak's presence would be useful.[113] Mao must have known that Pak's views on the war were closer to his own than Kim's.

On August 29, massive air attacks on Pyongyang resumed with deadly force. US Navy and 5th Air Force planes struck in three waves at four-hour intervals—9:30 a.m., 1:30 p.m., and 5:30 p.m. That night, eleven B-29s from Kadena in Okinawa followed up with more bombings. The 1,403 sorties flown exceeded even the July 11 attack. Pyongyang was completely destroyed.[114] In fact, no capital city had ever been bombed so intensively. Soviet aircraft and antiaircraft units were utterly ineffective. Pyongyang was as defenseless as Tokyo had been in the last months of the Pacific War.

With smoldering Pyongyang fresh in their minds, Peng Dehuai, Kim Il Sung, and Pak Hon-yong arrived in Moscow on September 1. They met with Stalin three days later.[115] Also present from the Soviet Union were Politburo members Vyacheslav Molotov, Georgii Malenkov, Anastas Mikoyan, Lavrentii Beria, Nikolai Bulganin, and Lazar Kaganovich. On the Chinese side, Zhou Enlai, Chen Yun, Li Fu-chun, Zhang Wentian, and Su Yu attended along with Peng.

The meeting of September 4 began with this exchange:

Stalin: What is the mood of the Korean people?

Kim Il Sung: The mood is good.

Stalin: Does Pak Hon-yong agree?

Pak Hon-yong: Yes, the mood is good.

Stalin: What about in the armies?

Kim Il Sung: In the armies the mood is also good.

Stalin: And what does Peng Dehuai think?

Peng Dehuai: Good.

Kim Il Sung: The overall situation is favorable, if you do not include the bombing raids.

Stalin: Do you have any fighter aviation?

Kim Il Sung: We have one division.[116]

Kim Il Sung's directness in bringing up the destruction caused by American air raids must have favorably impressed Stalin, who promised to provide from one to three air divisions. When Kim added that "as a result of the constant intensification of the enemy's bombing we need to build up our anti-aircraft artillery," Stalin said, "We will give you the material base for 10 divisions of anti-aircraft artillery."

To test the reactions of Kim Il Sung and Pak Hon-yong in front of the Chinese, Stalin asked a blunt question:

Stalin: They say that you, Chinese and Koreans, have some sort of disagreement about how to conduct negotiations with the Americans. Is that right?

Kim Il Sung: In my opinion, there are no serious conflicts of opinion. We have agreed to the versions suggested by our Chinese comrades. But taking into consideration the grave situation in which the Korean people find themselves, we are interested in signing the armistice as soon as possible. Our Chinese comrades are also interested in that. [117]

This was, politically, a brilliant answer. While stressing unity of purpose with the Chinese, Kim Il Sung had expressed Korea's desire for a quick ceasefire. Then Stalin sounded out the North Koreans on the idea he had run by Zhou Enlai on the prisoner issue: that China and North Korea should detain the same percentage of prisoners that America kept (10 to 20 percent, he said). As for new proposals at the truce talks:

Stalin: Our Chinese comrades believe that at the present time we should not introduce any new proposals and that we should bide our time, until new proposals are introduced by the Americans, in order for us to make revisions. Do you know about this?

Kim Il Sung: We have heard this from Mao Zedong.

Stalin: And what did Mao Zedong say on this issue?

Kim Il Sung: During his conversation with us, Mao Zedong suggested a few alternatives: the first was to continue to insist on the release of all POWs; second—negotiate the question of POWs after the armistice; the third—due to the detention of our POWs by the opponent, we also have to detain a corresponding quantity of their POWs.

In this manner, Mao Zedong's point of view coincides with your point of view, comrade Stalin. We believe that these three options are the most appropriate ones. But I would like to ask for your advice on what steps we should take to secure a resolution of the question.[118]

That was another adroit answer by Kim Il Sung. The conversation then shifted back to Stalin's idea on POWs and, next, to military tactics. Stalin asked about guerilla units behind enemy lines. Kim Il Sung answered that they were in action, although their conditions were very hard. This was Pak Hon-yong's area of expertise, but he said nothing.

During the meeting, Stalin had shown the Chinese his sympathy for North Korea while telling the Koreans his approach for ending the impasse. For his part, Kim Il Sung had stressed his agreement with China while still expressing hope that a settlement could soon be reached at Panmunjom. Stalin appreciated Kim's political savvy. But Stalin became suspicious of Pak Hon-yong, who, aside from his one comment about the mood of the North Korean people, remained silent throughout the meeting.

On September 12, in a night attack in North Korea, six B-26s and twenty-nine B-29s hit the Suiho power plant.[119] That evening in Moscow, Stalin hosted a dinner party, and the next day Kim Il Sung, Pak Hon-yong, and Peng Dehuai returned to North Korea. By order of the China-Korea Joint Headquarters, on September 14 Chinese and North Korean forces launched a tactical counterattack.

Meanwhile, Mexico had unveiled a new proposal on the POW issue: prisoners who wanted to return to their home country would be exchanged immediately, and nonrepatriables would be transferred to a UN member state until an agreement was reached at a future date. They would then be returned to either North Korea, South Korea, China, or Taiwan when normal conditions were restored.

Calling the Mexican initiative an American proposal, Mao cabled Zhou that he thought China and North Korea should reject it and that Zhou should confer with Stalin.[120] On September 17, Stalin agreed with Mao. If the Mexican plan was submitted to the General Assembly, Stalin said, the Soviet UN representative would oppose it in principle and call for an immediate halt to the fighting, the return of all prisoners to their native land according to international norms, and the withdrawal of all foreign troops from Korea. The Soviet delegate would not allude to the proposal discussed earlier to temporarily hold 20 percent of the POWs and repatriate the remainder, Stalin wrote; that idea would be left to Mao to act on.[121] While strongly endorsing Mao's position on the Mexican initiative, Stalin had thus slipped his own compromise proposal back into the game.

At the start of a third meeting with Zhou on September 19, Stalin reiterated his message to Mao that the Mexican resolution was unacceptable and that the Soviet delegation was prepared to respond accordingly at the UN. Zhou asked Stalin to hold off on his compromise proposal for two to three weeks.

Stalin replied: "This is Mao Zedong's business. If Mao Zedong wants us to act, we can submit the second position on proportional retention of POWs to the Assembly." Zhou asked if Stalin could support a third position—the transfer of POWs to a neutral nation until their fate was decided. Stalin was cautious. The Soviet Union wanted all prisoners returned to their home countries, Stalin told Zhou, just as China did. If an agreement could not be reached on this basis, the prisoners could not be transferred to the United Nations because it was a belligerent. Stalin asked about "the view of the Chinese comrades" on which neutral country the prisoners should be sent to. Zhou Enlai answered that he was authorized to say that they were thinking of India. Stalin then stated that this proposal could be acceptable. [122]

Zhou, of course, reported Stalin's ideas to Mao. In effect, the Soviet Union had two proposals ready, but neither was made to the United Nations at that time.

At the end of this latest meeting on September 19, which also included Molotov, Malenkov, Beria, Mikoyan, Bulganin, and Vyshinskii, Zhou and Stalin had a very important and interesting exchange. To bring the meeting to a conclusion, Zhou said that all of the problems he wanted instructions on had been covered:

Stalin: [Were they] instructions or advice?

Zhou Enlai: From Comrade Stalin's perspective it may be advice, but from our point of view they are instructions.

Stalin: We only offer advice, give our opinion. Our Chinese comrades are free to adopt it or not. Instructions would be obligatory.

Zhou: From a Chinese point of view, they were instructions, moreover very valuable ones. The Chinese did not follow them blindly, but realized they needed them.

Stalin: We do not know very much about China so we refrain from giving directions.

Zhou: Comrade Stalin was knowledgeable about the problems we raised. I ask you again if you have instructions.

Stalin: Our advice is this. We should remember that the English and Americans are trying to place many of their people—agents—in the Chinese state organization. This applies to the Americans or the French. They are all the same. The [agents] carry out destructive operations and try to undermine from within. They may even commit such crimes as murder by poisoning. Thus you must be vigilant. Keep this in mind. This is my only advice.

Zhou: That is very valuable instruction. Not only the Americans, British, and French engage in such despicable behavior. They get Chinese to do it too.

Stalin: There are also agents from the national bourgeoisie. [123]

Thus, espionage and subversion by a foreign intelligence service could be a pretext for suppression of domestic opposition, as unfolded a few months later in the Soviet Union with the Doctors' Plot. And if enemy agents had infiltrated China, as Stalin said, they could have penetrated North Korea as well. One can imagine Stalin giving similar instructions to his North Korean comrades.

The Soviet Union had its own spies in other countries at this time. The famous British spies Donald Maclean and Guy Burgess had eluded the Federal Bureau of Investigation and MI5 and fled to the Soviet Union in May 1951. Graduates of Cambridge University, both were Communist agents who had worked in the British government on behalf of the Soviet Union and socialism. Maclean was secretary at the British embassy in Washington, DC, from 1944 to 1948. He was deeply involved in wartime cooperation between the United States and Britain, and in postwar development of nuclear energy and formation of the North Atlantic Treaty Organization. At the time of his defection to the Soviet Union, Maclean was in charge of American affairs at the British Foreign Office. Burgess had moved from the British Broadcasting Corporation to the Foreign Office, where he served for a time as secretary to the deputy foreign minister; he was first secretary in the British embassy in Washington in 1951. [124]

Also, in the 1930s Soviet intelligence had utilized Richard Sorge, an agent who penetrated the German embassy in Tokyo and obtained crucial intelligence on the planned German attack on the Soviet Union. After the Sorge ring was broken up, the Soviet Union still had devoted, talented spies in enemy governments. Several were still active in Britain in 1952. Soviet intelligence successes abroad doubtless reinforced Stalin's conviction that the West had agents in Moscow too.

JAPAN AND KOREA

While the Korean armistice negotiations had stalemated, in Japan—a main rear base of US armed forces for the Korean War—the Japanese Communist Party's project of armed struggle had proven a total failure.

In October 1951, the JCP's Fifth National Party Conference had adopted a new party program, formulated in Moscow under Stalin's guidance. The party's Mountain Village Operations Unit was organized mainly with student party members in the Ogochi Dam district near Tokyo, and Core Defense Units were set up around the country.

On October 21, the organization of Korean JCP members, the National Committee for Fatherland Defense (NCFD), had ordered its Fatherland Defense Units to be militant like the party's Core Defense Units. NCFD had endorsed the JCP's program of armed revolution in November and decided to form numerous "resistance and defense organizations." The JCP quickly produced and distributed textbooks and selected writings on military matters disguised with such titles as "Analytical Nutrition Tables" and "Cultivation of Bulbous Plants."[125] The CPSU's Politburo, in response to a cable from JCP leaders Tokuda Kyuichi and Nosaka Sanzo, agreed on February 10, 1952, to send US$300,000 to the JCP from the so-called International Labor Unions' Fund for Assistance to Left-wing Labor Organizations.[126]

The militant members of the JCP were in fact mainly Koreans. At an NCFD meeting in Nagoya, Japan, on January 17–20, 1952, JCP representative Pak Un-chol reportedly presented the results of an investigation of US military bases, factories producing goods for US forces, and transportation routes. The JCP's new party program had directed its Core Defense Units to target factories making bombs for use in Korea, the rail lines on which the bombs were carried, and the air bases of the bombers. But Pak Un-chol told the NCFD: "Attacks must not harm the general public. For example, the public would be upset by the destruction of power plants and railroad lines."[127] This was no doubt the policy line of the JCP's leadership in Japan, which would not elevate the level of armed struggle beyond use of Molotov cocktails. But Koreans living in Japan were also hesitant to commit deadly acts. In their memoirs that contain accounts of participation in NCFD activities,[128] there is not one mention of committing major violence, such as the destruction of public property.[129] Their activism was essentially limited to propaganda and demonstrations.

Akahata, the JCP's newspaper, resumed publication in late April 1952 after being shut down by the Supreme Commander of the Allied Powers. "Free Japan" radio broadcasts began from Beijing on May 1. Also, the pro-DPRK Unified Democratic Front of Koreans in Japan organized a one-month campaign to confront the occupation authorities. On May 1, at a mass rally at Meiji Shrine Park in Tokyo, the police fired on demonstrators approaching the Imperial Palace Plaza. Two people were killed, 2,300 injured, and 1,232 arrested, including 130 Koreans, in what became famous as "Bloody May Day." Molotov cocktails were thrown for the first time in Japan in Tokyo on May 30, a symbolic date that commemorated the killing by British police of Chinese demonstrators in Shanghai on May 30, 1925. Crowds fought the police, and two police outposts (*koban*) were burned down. Three militants were killed and thirty-six arrested. Clashes broke out that day in Nagoya and Osaka as well.

On June 25, the anniversary of the start of the Korean War, protests were held in 167 places around Japan. Koreans enraged at the US bombing of Suiho and other power stations in North Korea that had begun two days earlier were the most militant elements in the protests. A rally of five thousand protesters in Shinjuku in Tokyo turned into a battle with the police. Of the twenty-nine demonstrators arrested, eight were Koreans. At a more violent rally in Osaka, one thousand antiwar protestors broke into the Suita switchyard and fought with the police. More than 92 of the 250 people arrested there were Koreans. On July 7, about five thousand people rallied in Osu, Aichi Prefecture, to hear a speech by Diet member Hoashi Kei, who had visited the Soviet Union and China. In an unauthorized demonstration after the rally, the crowd fought with police, who arrested 269 people, including 150 Koreans. Prosecutors indicted 150 people.[130] This protest was a response to the second wave of US bombings of North Korea. Koreans were in the forefront, and many Molotov cocktails were thrown.

The violent confrontations in Japan then ended; there were virtually no more street battles with the police. The JCP continued to organize Flying Squads in mountainous areas, but these scattered cells could not kindle a revolution.

Meanwhile, an article by Paek Su-bon entitled "To purify and strengthen the patriotic camp" published in NCFD's *New Korea* on April 28, 1952, had sparked debate over Korean political identity and loyalties. Paek Su-bon, whose true name was Han Tok-su, argued that Koreans in Japan were overseas citizens of the DPRK. The article cast doubt on the notion of unconditionally following the leadership of the JCP.[131] Han seemed to suggest that, rather than being the vanguard of armed revolution in Japan, Koreans there should pursue activities that aided the security and survival of North Korea. The JCP attacked his essay for sowing distrust of its leadership.

In June the party directed Fatherland Defense Units to intensify their militant activities. A month later, the JCP designated the Korean movement in Japan a "parachute unit in the enemy's rear area bases."[132] Although the JCP's line of armed revolution went unchanged, the link with North Korea was emphasized. Han Tok-su's ideas had spread among the leftist Korean community in Japan. Three years later, in 1955, Koreans would collectively withdraw from the JCP and form the pro–North Korean General Association of Korean Residents in Japan, known as Soren, or Chongryun.

Top JCP leader Tokuda Kyuichi went to Moscow in May 1952 for medical treatment and conferred with Stalin. Soviet sources show that they discussed Ito Ritsu, earlier the number three man at JCP headquarters in Beijing, who had been imprisoned twice in the 1930s–1940s in Japan and was suspected of betraying Soviet agent Richard Sorge while in prison. Stalin was probably frustrated at the lack of progress toward revolution in Japan and had suspicions about Ito. But Tokuda defended Ito and managed to assuage Stalin's doubts. [133]

Tokuda's essay "On the thirtieth anniversary of the Japanese Communist Party" appeared in a Cominform publication on July 4. Tokuda's intentions are unknown, but some of his statements, including his criticism of the tendency to disparage participation in elections, were interpreted in Japan to mean that violent struggle should be suspended. [134]

STALIN'S DILEMMA

Amid the JCP's debates, the stalemate in the Korean armistice negotiations continued. On September 28, the UN Command made its final offer on prisoners. All POWs would be moved to the demilitarized zone and their preferences for relocation confirmed. Prisoners who wanted to return to their home countries would be exchanged; those who declined repatriation would be immediately released. [135] Chinese and North Korean negotiators rejected the plan on October 8, insisting that all prisoners be returned to their home countries in accordance with the Geneva Convention. [136] The same day, US Secretary of State Dean Acheson announced that negotiations would not resume until the Communists accepted one of the UN Command's numerous proposals for resolving POW issues. The talks were broken off. [137]

On October 6–14, the Communist Party of the Soviet Union's Nineteenth Congress was held in Moscow. Liu Shaoqi led the Chinese delegation; the North Korean delegation consisted of Pak Chong-ae, Pak Yong-bin, Pae Chol, Kim Il, and Pak Kum-chol. [138] The congress paid international homage to Stalin, who had recently published *Economic Problems of Socialism in the U.S.S.R.* Georgii Malenkov delivered the party Central Committee's report, praising Stalin as "the genius leader and teacher of all progressive mankind." But Stalin was not at ease.

In *Economic Problems of Socialism* he had called the confrontation between capitalism and socialism an "absolute contradiction" [139] and war among capitalist countries a probability. The contest with capitalist countries, especially with the United States, was then a heavy burden on the Soviet Union. The arms race since 1949—spurred on by the Korean War—had enormously expanded US military budgets. Although Soviet scientists had successfully tested a nuclear bomb on August 29, 1949, ending the US nuclear monopoly, Stalin knew the breakthrough had not suddenly made the Soviet Union militarily secure. The first prototype was essentially a copy of the American bomb and was not adaptable as a military weapon. Second and third bombs had then been built and successfully dropped from airplanes on

September 24 and October 18 in 1951. But these types of atomic bombs would not be manufactured on a production line until 1954.[140] A scientific team led by Andrei Sakharov was nearing the experimental detonation stage for a hydrogen bomb, but actual weapons were still years away.[141] While the United States had already deployed atomic weapons in the field, the USSR still had not one usable atomic bomb. And Stalin knew that the Americans were very well aware of this.

In 1947 the Soviet Union had developed the TU-4 bomber, modeled after the B-29, which could deliver a nuclear payload. But the United States was 6,500 kilometers away and the TU-4 could not make a roundtrip flight of that distance.[142] The MiG-15 fighter had performed brilliantly in the early stage of the Korean War until the F-86 Sabre had appeared. From that point, the air war in Korea displayed the growing disparity between Soviet and American air power in favor of the Americans.

On top of these problems that Stalin was then facing, not only had the Japanese revolution that was supposed to destabilize the US rear in Japan fizzled out, but American agents, including Jews, were apparently reaching deep inside the Soviet Union. He worried that the enemy might be searching for an opportunity to get even closer to the center of power in the Soviet Union. Stalin, the man who was effectively leading the war against America on the battlefield in Northeast Asia, was seized by a deep sense of crisis.

Apprehensive and uncertain, Stalin turned on his most loyal subordinates. On October 16, at the first Central Committee meeting after the Communist Party Congress, Stalin accused Vyacheslav Molotov and Anastas Mikoyan of being afraid of American economic power and secretly using their positions in the Politburo to instruct the Soviet ambassador in Washington to make concessions to the United States. S. A. Lozovskii, the vice-minister of foreign affairs, a Jew who had already been exposed as an "enemy of the people," was allegedly involved in the conspiracy.[143] Stalin replaced the Politburo of the Central Committee (eleven members) with a Presidium (twenty-five members) and named Molotov and Mikoyan to it, but he excluded them from the new Bureau of the Presidium (nine members), an equivalent to the Politburo.[144] To avoid allegations of personal responsibility for the Soviet Union's misadventure in Korea, Stalin was apparently setting up his closest associates as scapegoats.

On October 24, Dean Acheson, hoping for a breakthrough in the Korean truce talks, revealed that secret contacts were under way with the Soviet Union. His intentions are not clear. The same day, a US initiative known as the 21-power resolution was submitted to the UN General Assembly. It laid out principles for the nonforcible return of prisoners, principles that the United States knew China and the Soviet Union would not accept.[145] The new Presidium of the CPSU decided on November 3 to deny that secret talks were being held with Washington. Soviet newspapers the next day carried a TASS report of the denial.[146] Secret talks probably were being held, and Stalin must have approved them, although their substance is unknown.

The attention of the Korean War negotiators then shifted to a resolution at the UN General Assembly by Krishna Menon of the Indian delegation. Under this plan, prisoners would be moved to a demilitarized area and placed under the control of a prisoner repatriation commission of four neutral nations that would oversee their return to their desired locations.[147] On November 24, Soviet representative to the UN Andrei Vyshinsky stridently attacked the Indian resolution.[148] The following month, Zhou Enlai and Pak Hon-yong both dismissed it as nothing more than a "revision" of the American 21-power resolution.[149]

The same month, Stalin found some traitors right on his doorstep. On November 9, V. M. Vinogradov, head of the Kremlin hospital, was arrested, and two days later the hospital's doctor M. S. Vovsi was also arrested. They were both part of the infamous Doctors' Plot that resulted in fabricated charges that Jewish doctors were conspiring to poison the Soviet leadership. The Prague Trials of "anti-state elements" in Czechoslovakia then started on November 22. Rudolph Slansky, the Jewish general secretary of the Czechoslovakian Communist Party, and thirteen subordinates, including eleven Jews, were sentenced to death as foreign spies five days later.[150] At a Soviet Presidium Bureau meeting on December 1, during an exchange on the sabotage allegedly committed by treasonous doctors in various medical fields, Stalin said: "The more we succeed, the harder the enemy works to destroy us. Because of our great success, our side forgets this. There are signs we are becoming easygoing, stupid, and overconfident. Every Jewish nationalist is an agent of American intelligence. Jewish nationalists think America has saved their nation. . . . They think they will inevitably become Americans."[151]

The purges, show trials, and anti-Semitic propaganda then unfolding in the Soviet Union were of a piece with Stalin's sham accountability for his failures in Northeast Asia, the hot spot of his growing confrontation with the United States. In each case, scapegoats, spies, or fifth columnists were blamed.

PURGES IN THE JCP AND NORTH KOREA

Stalin had, of course, personally communicated with Mao Zedong and Kim Il Sung on the Communist side's strategy in Korea, including via cables to the Soviet ambassadors in the PRC and the DPRK. Copies of Mao's and Kim's messages to Stalin were circulated to other Politburo members; Stalin's answers under various pseudonyms—Filippov, Fyn Si, and Semenov—apparently were not. Hidden behind these noms de guerre, Stalin had thrown himself into war and revolution in Northeast Asia. For more than two years, together with Mao Zedong and Kim Il Sung, Stalin had lived and breathed Korea. But his risky gamble there was now in deep trouble. He had made the crucial decisions, and thus the losses and defeats were primarily his. He must have been eager to change course and finish the war. But first his misjudgments had to be explained. Other than admitting error, the only explanation was betrayal.

A harsh measure was taken toward a betrayer in the JCP. On December 24, 1952, according to Ito Ritsu's memoirs, Nosaka Sanzo assembled the JCP's Beijing headquarters and announced in the presence of Chinese Communist Party representative Li Chuli that, on instructions from the Communist Party of the Soviet Union, Ito was under investigation and had been imprisoned.[152] When Tokuda Kyuichi had collapsed and been hospitalized two months earlier, Ito had lost his high-level party protector. Nosaka's version is that both the Chinese and Soviet Communist parties had expressed suspicion of Ito.[153] A US occupation study of the Richard Sorge spy ring released in 1949 said that Ito had recanted Communism while under arrest in 1941, and that he had revealed the name of a woman member of the American Communist Party to the police who proved to be a member of the Sorge ring. His confession had led to the discovery of Sorge, the author of the study wrote.[154] Because of his checkered past, accusations that Ito was working for the Supreme Commander for the Allied Powers and the Japanese government after World War II found fertile ground.[155]

Ito's suppression was carried out secretly. But suppression of betrayers in North Korea was more open. At the Fifth Plenum of the Korean Workers' Party Central Committee that began on December 15, 1952, Kim Il Sung's report, "The Organizational and Ideological Consolidation of the Korean Workers' Party is the Foundation of Our Victory," provided the attendees with an overview of the party's accomplishments in the ten months since the Fourth Plenum.[156] Kim quoted extensively from Georgii Malenkov's report to the Nineteenth Congress of the CPSU and was extravagantly loyal to the Soviet line. Since the Fourth Plenum, 363,847 new members had joined the KWP and total membership had risen from 657,386 to 1,021,233, Kim reported. In less than a year after Kim's open-door membership policy had replaced Ho Ka-i's restrictive approach, party membership had increased 50 percent. The new members, one-third of the party, were loyal to Kim, who called for a qualitative improvement in party members. Kim said that Pak Yong, chief of the party committee in South Hamgyong Province, was an example of a person who had appropriated the party line to falsely present himself as a hero of the revolution.

Kim called for "strengthening the Party character and struggle against the remnants of petty bourgeois liberalism and factionalism." He criticized as "petty bourgeois" people who bragged of revolutionary exploits in the past but were incapable of carrying out major assignments, and those who gave positions to relatives, former classmates, friends, and men from their own hometown. These "petty bourgeois" people also included those who were obsessed with local differences between party members from the South and the North. Kim condemned the "remnants of factionalism" who supported members of their own group "even if they betrayed the revolutionary movement." Such people "covered up their dark . . . past and praised and promoted each other in order to join [the party] and obtain high positions in the party and government." While pretending to support party policy and the Central Committee, he said, they actually disregarded them and harmed the KWP. Kim warned that "the experiences of other countries with peoples' democracy and fraternal parties have shown if we leave remnants of factionalism undisturbed, the factionalists in the end become spies for the enemy." The speech was a preemptive attack by Kim Il Sung and his allies on DPRK Foreign Minister Pak Hon-yong and the South Korean Workers' Party faction of the KWP.

At the Plenum, Pak Chong-ae, party secretary, repeatedly lauded Kim's leadership. During "the great war to liberate the fatherland and the period of peaceful reconstruction . . . all the successes and victories of the Korean people are linked to the glory of our party and the name of Comrade Leader Kim Il Sung," Pak Chong-ae gushed. After liberation from Japan, Comrade Kim Il Sung had made North Korea a revolutionary base. "Despite the opposition of many comrades," Pak said, thanks to his leadership the Korean Workers' Party was unified. If Kim Il Sung had not tightened party discipline at the Third Plenum and "corrected leftist tendencies" at the Fourth Plenum, Pak argued, the party would have been weakened and the people might not have been victorious in the battle against American and British imperialism. Kim Il Sung had convened the Fifth Plenum to move further ahead in the revolutionary struggle, Pak said, but the party still had to combat the "remnants of factionalism and bourgeois liberalism": "Many of the leading party organs and party cadres do not understand that our party has only one line and that is the line of the Central Committee and Kim Il Sung."

Pak Chong-ae criticized factionalists who praised the leadership of provincial party committees instead of the central leadership. She also criticized use of the expression "under the correct leadership of the head of the Political Department [of the Korean People's Army] and Front Commander." This was an indirect attack on Pak Hon-yong, who had led the KPA's Political Department until early 1951. "In our party there is no leadership other than that of the Central Committee and Comrade Kim Il Sung, and there cannot be," Pak emphasized.[157]

At the Fifth Plenum, the KWP's Central Committee decided to identify factionalists and launch a campaign of public criticism. But lower echelons of the party were unexpectedly slow to react. Meanwhile factionalism in the

DPRK was linked with espionage. The discovery of the Doctors' Plot in the Soviet Union was reported in North Korea on January 18, 1953, and DPRK Minister of Internal Security Pang Hak-se wrote on February 5, "Let's make the anti-spies struggle [an] all people's movement."[158]

In mid-February the KWP identified specific factionalists and demanded their censure. On February 17, *Nodong Shinmun*, the KWP's newspaper, reported that a Pyongyang municipal party plenum had accused several prominent figures of factionalism. They included Chu Nyong-ha, former DPRK ambassador to the Soviet Union and the vice-minister of foreign affairs; Cho Il-myong (Cho Tu–won), vice-minister of culture and propaganda; Yim Hwa, a poet and staff member of the North Korean General Federation of Literature and Fine Arts; and Yi Che-u, a former member of the Central Committee of the South Korean Workers' Party. Chu Nyong-ha worked for Pak Hon-yong, and Cho Il-myong had been a trusted associate of both Pak Hon-yong and KWP Secretary Yi Sung-yop since the days of the South Korean Workers' Party. Yim Hwa was a close associate of Cho Il-myong. Although the real targets—Pak Hon-yong and Yi Sung-yop—were already obvious, they were not immediately purged. Both were conspicuously present at ceremonies to commemorate the fifth anniversary of the founding of the Korean People's Army on February 7 and the thirty-fifth anniversary of the founding of the Soviet Red Army on February 22.

Four days later, *Nodong Shinmun* reported that at a plenary session of the South Pyongan Province party committee, Secretary Pak Chang-ok had denounced as "factional elements" a group that included Chu Nyong-ha, Yim Hwa, novelist Kim Nam-chon, vice-chief of the party Agitation and Propaganda Department Yi Won-jo, former chief of the Foreign Affairs Department of the North Korean People's Committee Yi Kang-guk, and Chang Si-u, a prewar minister of commerce and wartime head of the Rear Area Department of the KPA Staff. A few days later, Chu Nyong-ha, Chang Si-u, and others were attacked by name at a plenary session of the Pyongyang West District committee of the KWP.[159]

As the denunciations intensified, Chu Nyong-ha, Cho Il-myong, Yim Hwa, and others were probably arrested and interrogated by the DPRK's Ministry of Public Security. Their confessions were fashioned into a narrative of a meeting at Pak Hon-yong's house in September 1952. The meeting was allegedly attended by Yi Sung-yop; Pae Chol, chief of the party Liaison Department; Pak Sung-won, vice-chief of the party Liaison Department; Yun Sun-dal; Cho Il-myong; Yim Hwa; and others. At their subsequent trials, prosecutors described this meeting as the occasion when the accused plotted a coup d'etat against the Kim Il Sung regime and drew up a list of senior members for a Pak Hon-yong government.[160] Pak Hon-yong's group, which advocated continuing the war in Korea, may have imagined a scenario in which China and the Soviet Union would rebuke Kim Il Sung for giving up the struggle and support a Pak administration.

A few days after February 22, no later than March 1, Yi Sung-yop, a member of the KWP Politburo as well as party secretary, and the man in charge of operations against the South, was apparently arrested. So were Pae Chol; Pak Sung-won; Maeng Chong-ho, the chief of the 10th Detachment of the Flying Squadron to Liberate South Korea; and others. On March 4, KWP members in the DPRK's Ministry of Culture and Propaganda criticized Cho Il-myong, Yim Hwa, and writer Yi Tae-jun. Party members at the Ministry of Foreign Affairs denounced Chu Nyong-ha and Ambassador to China Kwon O-jik. While Pak Hon-yong was still listed as a member of the Presidium at the mourning ceremony for Stalin's death on March 9, Yi Sung-yop disappeared from public view.[161]

Many of the targeted individuals—Yi Sung-yop, Cho Il-myong, Yim Hwa, Pak Song-won, Yi Kang-guk, Yi Won-jo, and Maeng Chong-ho—had earlier been arrested by the Japanese police during the colonial period and had renounced Communism under mental and physical torture. Their tainted records now made them suspect of spying for the US military. Chu Kwang-mu (a Soviet Korean), the head of the Preliminary Examination Department of the Ministry of Public Security, personally directed the interrogations and tortured the prisoners to get confessions to the alleged plot against the Kim Il Sung regime.[162]

As North Korea was basically dependent on Soviet guidance and material aid, a person of Yi Sung-yop's stature, a direct subordinate of Pak Hon-yong—the second-highest figure in the KWP and the state—would not have been arrested without an order or approval from Stalin. The Soviet leader must have given the green light to move against Pak Hon-yong himself by his last working day, February 28, before collapsing as a result of a stroke on March 1.[163]

The arrests of the leading cadre from the South who oversaw ongoing clandestine operations against South Korea were tantamount to North Korea declaring a ceasefire. It is unlikely they would have happened without Stalin's permission. The purges would seem to confirm that Stalin wanted to end the Korean War.

FINAL NEGOTIATIONS BETWEEN STALIN AND MAO ZEDONG

Chinese leaders were concerned that when President-Elect Dwight D. Eisenhower took office in January 1953 he would launch an offensive in Korea to break the stalemate in the war. They thought the most likely scenario was an amphibious US landing north of the battle lines. Mao cabled his analysis to Chinese People's Volunteers First Deputy Commander Deng Hua on December 9, 1952, and within a week there was a consensus in the Chinese government and military.[164] Mao issued orders to the Chinese People's Volunteers on December 16 to prepare for the expected US landing. A joint conference of the CPV party committee and military staff concluded that although the enemy's main objective was probably the west coast of North Korea, defensive preparations should also include the east coast. Choe Yong-gon, Pak Il-u, Kim Kwang-hyop, and Soviet military advisers attended the meeting.[165]

Afterwards, Deng Hua and fellow CPV Deputy Commander Yang Dezhi decided to beef up the staffs of the east and west coast commands of the CPV and the KPA. They explained Mao's analysis to Kim Il Sung and requested that senior leaders be assigned to the posts; Kim promised to act. The KWP Politburo put Kim Ung and Pang Ho-san, the most experienced men available, in charge of the east and west coast commands, respectively.[166]

In a long message to Stalin on December 17, Mao said the incoming Eisenhower administration might launch an amphibious operation in northern Korea and asked for additional military aid: "With the truce talks suspended and American casualties not yet on a scale that would compel them to stop military activities, in the spring of 1953 for a certain length of time (for example one year) [the new administration] will probably resume the offensive. Eisenhower is preparing for military operations [in Korea] to be taken immediately after his inauguration."

Mao considered attacks on both coasts possible and sought delivery from the Soviet Union of 624 artillery weapons of various types in the first quarter of 1953. He also sought 805,000 rounds of ammunition in January, and 1,550,000 rounds between February and April.[167]

Stalin replied on December 27 that amphibious operations in Korea had been developed under the Truman administration and "the current U.S. command in Korea. It is very possible that the Eisenhower administration will move toward easing tension on the battlefield in Korea. . . . Yet it is best to assume a worst-case scenario and the probability of a U.S. offensive." The Soviet Union had already promised to provide equipment for twenty Chinese divisions, Stalin said, and could only increase the total amount of equipment by 25 percent.[168] As always with Mao Zedong, Stalin was circumspect, and he did not directly insist that Mao end the fighting in Korea, though he wanted the war to end.

In an interview with the *New York Times*, Stalin spoke of "peaceful coexistence" and sought Eisenhower's cooperation to end the war. The interview appeared on Christmas Day 1952 and was reported in the Soviet Union and China the next day.[169] Stalin had sent Eisenhower a clear message that he wanted to terminate the Korean War, and the people of the Soviet Union and China were now aware of it.

Yet a year-end letter from Kim Il Sung to Stalin is striking for Kim's effusive gratitude for Soviet support. The letter begins: "Respected Iosif

Vissarionovich, we offer our boundless thanks to you and to the Soviet government for the constant aid and attention you have given to the Korean People's Army." The conclusion dripped with appreciation: "Beloved Iosif Vissarionovich please accept the heart-felt wishes of all the Korean people for your good health and long life for the sake of all mankind. With deepest respect and affection, Kim Il Sung."[170]

Why such effusive gratitude? Stalin had both conveyed his approval of a quick end to the fighting and supported the suppression of Pak Hon-yong and the South Korean Workers' Party group that wanted to continue the war. Kim Il Sung had reason to be thankful to Stalin.

Mao Zedong continued to press Stalin for Soviet assistance against the expected American offensive. On January 4, 1953, he asked that a promised 332 artillery cannons and 600,000 rounds of ammunition be delivered by May 1.[171] Four days later, Mao told Stalin that in preparation for a US landing, he wanted to send naval units to Korea as Chinese People's Volunteers, and he asked for warships, land-based artillery, naval aircraft, and Soviet advisers.[172] A week later, Stalin answered that it would be difficult to deliver the artillery weapons and ammunition within the time frame, but that he would try to expedite the transfer.[173] On January 27, Stalin agreed with Mao's decision to dispatch naval units to Korea and promised to provide warships, airplanes, and three advisers.[174] Stalin was still largely accommodating Chinese requests.

Liu Shaoqi and Wang Jiaxing had two interviews with Stalin on January 5–6, 1953.[175] Both Chinese leaders had remained in Moscow after the Nineteenth CPSU Congress to convalesce from illnesses and met with Stalin prior to their return to China. Although the topics of these meetings have not been made public by the Chinese authorities, it would not be surprising if Stalin had secretly tried to persuade Liu and Wang to favor a ceasefire in Korea.

Two and a half years earlier, in June 1950, President Truman had directed the US 7th Fleet to both protect Formosa and ensure that the island would not be used to attack the Chinese mainland. President Eisenhower, in his State of the Union speech on February 2, 1953, ended the latter mission and the neutralization of the Taiwan Straits, ordering that the 7th Fleet would no longer "shield" or be a "defensive arm of Communist China." The *New York Times* headlined the change of policy "Eisenhower frees Chiang to raid mainland."[176]

Eisenhower's speech intensified concern in Beijing about his intentions. Two threats might now be combined: an attack on Chinese territory by Chiang Kai-shek and a landing by US forces on the northern coast of Korea. In a speech to the Chinese People's Political Consultative Conference on February 7, Mao said: "No matter how many years American imperialism intends to wage war we are determined to fight as long as it takes until American imperialism gives up."[177] Mao and Stalin were headed in opposite directions.

The first indication of an open break between North Korea and China on the Korean War occurred on February 5, when Kim Il Sung called back Pak Il-u from the Chinese-Korean Joint Headquarters and appointed Choe Yong-gon deputy commander of the headquarters. Pak Il-u, the Korean leader most trusted by the Chinese Communist Party, had been deputy political commissar at the headquarters.[178] Kim Il Sung was unhappy with a command structure that China completely controlled.

While Pak Il-u's removal may not have fully conveyed to China Kim Il Sung's disenchantment with China and the war, the next steps left no doubt: the campaign to discredit Pak Hon-yong and Yi Sung-yop in late February and the recall of Ambassador Kwon O-jik from Beijing.

In Washington, unbeknownst to Kim and Mao, the Eisenhower administration was actually planning something even more threatening in Korea than an amphibious landing in the North. The new president had in mind using atomic weapons to force the Communists into a settlement. Eisenhower first raised the nuclear option in a meeting of the US National Security Council on February 11. Gen. Mark Wayne Clark of the UN Command had requested permission to attack the so-called "Kaesong sanctuary" for enemy forces. The sanctuary had been created through the armistice negotiations, and the Chinese were thought to be building up men in the area for an attack on UN forces. President Eisenhower said that "the use of tactical atomic weapons on the Kaesong area" should be considered. New Secretary of State John Foster Dulles "discussed the moral problem and the inhibitions on the use of the A-bomb, and Soviet success to date in setting atomic weapons apart from all other weapons as being in a special category," a memorandum of the discussion stated. "It was his opinion that we should try to break down this false distinction."[179] Some in the new administration were dissatisfied with a truce at the current military demarcation line and favored pushing the battle lines north to the narrow part of the peninsula.[180]

Unaware of US strategic machinations, and with no hard evidence that a US landing operation was being planned, China's leaders were not inclined to change course despite the shift in Pyongyang unless the United States showed a willingness to compromise on the prisoner issue. At the request of Premier Zhou Enlai, on February 19 the Chinese delegation at the Panmunjom truce talks led by Qiao Guanhua assessed the situation. If the Communist side offered to resume the truce talks unconditionally, they wrote in a memorandum, the UN Command would most likely refuse. And if the Communist proposal was in the form of a letter from Kim Il Sung and Peng Dehuai, "the other side would see it as a sign of confusion and weakness," they thought. The Chinese delegation's memorandum concluded that China ought to "maintain the present situation and continue [military] action to compel America to compromise."[181] Mao and Zhou reportedly endorsed this recommendation. China would wait until US actions offered a chance to gain a compromise.

General Clark provided that opportunity on February 22 with a proposal for the immediate exchange of sick and wounded prisoners. The idea had originated in a resolution by The League of Red Cross Societies on December 16, 1952. It could be discussed at the UN General Assembly when it reconvened on February 24. The Joint Chiefs of Staff, loath to appear to be acting under pressure, directed Clark to make the proposal before the General Assembly took it up.[182] Ding Guoyu, a member of the Chinese delegation at Panmunjom, asked Beijing on February 25 for instructions.[183] There was no immediate answer; Mao and Zhou could not decide, and they contacted neither Moscow nor Pyongyang. Stalin's opinion apparently was not sought.

Stalin's last action related to Korea before he died, as far as we know, concerned loan repayments. Under the Soviet-Korean Agreement of November 14, 1951, loans for the DPRK to purchase materials provided by the Soviet Union were to be repaid in Korean raw materials and commodities. Kim Il Sung told Soviet Ambassador to the DPRK Vladimir Razuvaev that North Korea wanted to defer payments until the fighting ended. Razuvaev recommended approval, the ministries of foreign trade and foreign affairs concurred, and the matter reached Stalin on February 10. Stalin had approved postponement of a 1949 loan of 212 million rubles and a cabinet order dated July 13, 1952, was drafted in his name.[184] This time Stalin approved postponement of payments for the agreement of 1951. On February 18, 1953, the Presidium Bureau of the Central Committee of the CPSU approved postponement of repayment of all Korean war loans until the war was over.[185] Stalin was responsive to Kim Il Sung to the end.

Chapter Seven

The Armistice

Joseph Stalin's stroke was announced first in the Soviet Union on March 4, 1953, at 6:20. It was 0:20 Korean time. In North Korea the news also became known in the morning of March 4. His death two days later must have shocked Kim Il Sung. At a memorial in Pyongyang, eulogies to Stalin were given by the Chairman of the Presidium of the Supreme People's Assembly Kim Tu-bong, Chief of the Propaganda section of the KWP Pak Chang-ok, Deputy Prime Minister Hong Myong-hui, and Defense Minister Choe Yong-gon.[1] Foreign Minister Pak Hon-yong joined the ceremony, but did not speak. Apparently he was arrested shortly afterwards. His arrest was part of Kim Il Sung's agenda to end the fighting in Korea, which Pak sought to continue.

Zhou Enlai was sent to Moscow to attend Stalin's funeral and was in the Soviet Union from March 8 to 17. During the funeral ceremony in Red Square, Zhou heard Stalin's successor as Soviet premier, Georgii Malenkov, call for the relaxation of international tensions and peaceful coexistence. Two days later, Zhou met with the new Soviet leadership: Malenkov, Vice-Premier Lavrentii Beria, Foreign Minister Vyacheslav Molotov, Party Secretary Nikita Khrushchev, Commerce Minister Anastas Mikoyan, and Vice-Foreign Minister Vasilii Kuznetsov.[2] The war in Korea was probably the main topic, and the collective Kremlin leadership must have urged Zhou to end it quickly. But the conventional view that Stalin's death precipitated an armistice is mistaken. Stalin had already been moving toward a ceasefire, though he did not force that course of action on China or North Korea.

In his meeting with the new Soviet leadership, Zhou Enlai presumably conferred mainly with his counterpart Molotov, who had replaced Andrei Vyshinsky as Soviet minister of foreign affairs. They agreed to respond to the proposal from UN Commander Gen. Mark Clark the previous month for

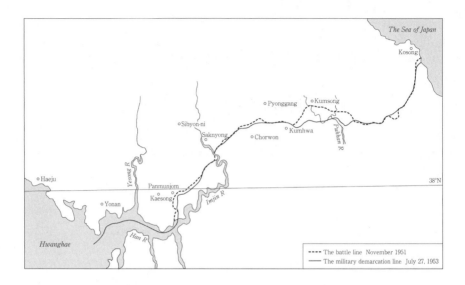

The Military Demarcation Line, July 27, 1953

the immediate exchange of sick and wounded prisoners. But if Molotov asked China to change its position on prisoners of war, Zhou would have balked, though he would have been inclined to agree to Clark's proposal.

Zhou's dialogue with the Kremlin was interrupted on March 17 when he flew to Prague to attend the funeral of Klement Gottwald, president of Czechoslovakia, who had died suddenly on March 14.[3] While Zhou was away, in response to Clark's offer, Molotov circulated within the Soviet government drafts of letters to Mao Zedong and Kim Il Sung and instructions to the Soviet UN representative.[4]

The letter to Kim Il Sung said, "the Soviet government . . . has concluded that continuation of the past policy on this problem would be incorrect." The Communist side must "attempt to use the enemy's initiative to seize the initiative and extricate China and Korea from the war, which would accord with the basic interests of the Chinese and Korean peoples and the interests of all the peace loving peoples of the world." China and Korea should respond positively to Clark's proposal as a start to solving the prisoner problem, leading to a compromise in the ceasefire negotiations, the letter said. Korea and China should insist on the immediate return of all prisoners who wanted to go home and propose the transfer of the remaining prisoners to a neutral country that would fairly arrange their disposition. The letter also stated that a statement should be issued in Beijing and Pyongyang that both countries agreed on their response to Clark and that the Soviet government would add its support.

These steps advised by Molotov were all subsequently implemented by the Communists and must have been based on the points Zhou and Molotov discussed. Molotov's draft of letters to Mao Zedong and Kim Il Sung was signed by Malenkov and approved by the Soviet cabinet on March 19. Zhou Enlai and Soviet Vice-Foreign Minister Kuznetsov would take the letter to Mao Zedong, and Vice-Foreign Minister Jacob Malik would deliver it to Kim Il Sung in Pyongyang.[5]

Zhou received Molotov's draft upon his return to Moscow from Prague on March 21 and met that night with the Soviet leadership, including Malenkov, Beria, Molotov, Khrushchev, Bulganin, Malik, and Kuznetsov. Zhou finally agreed to the Soviets' plan, but till then sent to Mao two telegrams from Moscow.[6] In fact, China found it very difficult to swallow the principle that prisoners who refused repatriation would be transferred to a neutral country. *History of the War to Resist America*, China's recent official history, skirts the dilemma: "The Soviet Union had to resolve internal problems and did not consider prolonging the Korean War. There was a similar desire [to end the war] in Korea. A concession was made on the formula for prisoner repatriation and a Korean armistice was achieved as quickly as possible."[7]

Soviet officials also talked about their response to General Clark's proposal with Korean Workers' Party Secretary Pak Chong-ae, a DPRK representative at Stalin's funeral, who was still in Moscow.[8] Zhou Enlai left Moscow on March 24 and arrived in Beijing two days later.[9] Vice-foreign minister Kuznetsov and Soviet interpreter N. T. Fedorenko apparently accompanied him.

THE TRUCE NEGOTIATIONS RESUME

Mao Zedong on March 23 instructed Ding Guoyu, the senior Chinese Communist Party representative in the Communist delegation at the Panmunjom truce talks, to inform Kim Il Sung and Chinese People's Volunteers commander Peng Dehuai that a response to Clark's proposal was under way: "We are preparing to agree to discuss this matter. A reply will probably take several days to draft. For the time being this must be kept secret."[10]

Zhou reported to Mao the discussion that he had in Moscow on March 26. Kuznetsov also probably met with Mao. According to the *Zhou Enlai Chronology*, "At this time the policy and actions the Chinese government should take were settled." Mao finally decided to concede on prisoner repatriation.[11] That evening, he informed Kim Il Sung that Soviet special envoy Kuznetsov and his party would leave Beijing the next day and enter Korea from Andung. A cable drafted by Zhou and sent in Mao's name the next day informed Kim Il Sung of China's decision. The instructions specified that Kim Il Sung and Peng Dehuai would send similar replies to Clark on the exchange of sick and wounded prisoners. After statements were issued in Beijing, Pyongyang, and Moscow, Peng and Kim were "to make concessions on the return of prisoners and obtain an armistice in Korea. However, in the event an armistice is unattainable, we will prepare to continue fighting."[12] Kim Il Sung must have been ecstatic.

The response to Clark formulated by China and signed by Kim Il Sung and Peng Dehuai was given to the UN Command on March 28. The main provisions were agreement to exchange sick and wounded prisoners, an expectation that a "reasonable" solution to the details of this exchange would lead to an overall solution to the prisoner problem, which in turn should lead to an armistice in Korea, and the immediate resumption of negotiations at Panmunjom.[13]

Kuznetsov and Fedorenko reached Pyongyang on March 29 and, together with Soviet Ambassador to the DPRK Vladimir Razuvaev, gave the Soviets' letter to Kim Il Sung. According to Kuznetsov and Fedorenko's account of the meeting to Moscow, "Kim Il Sung listened to our presentation and was very excited. He said he knew it was good news and he was very happy. He wanted to read the documents carefully and asked to meet us again."[14] Kim was clearly excited at the prospect of an immediate ceasefire, and when the four men met again later that day he approved the Soviet proposal.

At the second meeting on March 29, Kim Il Sung again expressed complete agreement with the Soviet government's proposal on Korea and said he hoped to implement it as soon as possible. Kim Il Sung emphasized that the time had come for their side to take the initiative to end the war and achieve peace. The choice was between renewed military operations or stopping the war, he said. To prolong the present situation was not in the interests of the Democratic People's Republic of Korea or the People's Republic of China. Kim pointed out that North Korean losses on the battlefield and in rear areas were extremely high (about three hundred to four hundred persons a day), and thus that it was inappropriate to continue to dispute with the Americans the number of prisoners to be returned. He concluded, "Under current conditions the Soviet government's proposal was the most appropriate."[15] Now calm and composed (unlike his earlier panicky state that Zhou Enlai and Stalin had noticed), Kim Il Sung had insinuated that Chinese tenacity was no longer "appropriate" and was thankful to the Soviets for cutting the Gordian knot.

Radio Beijing reported Zhou Enlai's answer to Clark on March 30: "The governments of the People's Republic of China and the Democratic People's Republic of Korea propose that after a ceasefire both sides immediately return all prisoners committed to repatriation and guarantee that the remainder will be transferred to a neutral nation and their repatriation fairly resolved." The immediate repatriation provision of the Geneva Convention had not been abandoned. In an attached reservation, China and North Korea rejected the contention by the UN Command that some prisoners had refused repatriation.[16] Nevertheless, as a practical matter, the Chinese had clearly conceded the issue to the Americans, who still demanded that there be no forced repatriation of any prisoners. Although Zhou's proposal was ostensibly a joint Chinese–North Korean proposal, Kim Il Sung's opinion was probably not sought.

The Soviet emissaries persuaded the North Koreans to defer Nam Il's promotion to foreign minister until the truce negotiations were finished. Molotov himself had instructed Ambassador Razuvaev on March 24 that DPRK representative at Panmunjom Nam Il was not to be appointed foreign minister, replacing Pak Hon-yong, before Kuznetsov and Fedorenko arrived in Pyongyang, and that the DPRK vice-foreign minister should be temporarily named to the post. It meant that the DPRK government had already communicated to the Soviets their wish about Nam Il's succession as Foreign Minister to Pak Hon-yong. Kuznetsov and Fedorenko's advice was respected. Nam Il's appointment by the Supreme People's Assembly was thus kept secret, and Vice-Foreign Minister Yi Tong-gon (also a Soviet Korean) temporarily filled the position.[17] The Kremlin had the final say in high-level personnel moves in Pyongyang.

Kim Il Sung ardently endorsed Zhou Enlai's proposal on prisoners, which of course, in genesis, was actually Moscow's plan, on March 31. The next day, Soviet Foreign Minister Molotov issued a statement backing Zhou and Kim's position.[18] Soviet leader Georgii Malenkov had toned down the wording of Molotov's original draft, leaving intact the phrase "move forward from a rational adjustment on the issue of sick and wounded prisoners to a solution of all issue of war prisoners, guided by sincere effort to achieve an armistice in Korea," but eliminating the wording "in the spirit of mutual compromise." Malenkov worried that the latter wording sounded too revealing.[19] China, North Korea, and the Soviet Union had now all responded to the UN's overture by General Clark.

While the Communists were preparing for potentially conclusive negotiations, US officials continued to discuss the use of the atomic bomb. At a National Security Council meeting on March 31, President Eisenhower "raised the question of the use of atomic weapons in the Korean war," *The Foreign Relations of the United States* records. "Admittedly, he said, there were not many good tactical targets, but he felt it would be worth the cost if, through use of atomic weapons, we could (1) achieve a substantial victory over the Communist forces and (2) get to a line at the waist of Korea [push back the military demarcation line]. . . . The President and Secretary Dulles were in complete agreement that somehow or other the taboo which surrounds the use of atomic weapons would have to be destroyed."[20] Such sinister arguments about the use of atomic weapons at this stage of armistice negotiations were truly striking. A CIA memorandum dated April 3 forecast prolonged delay in obtaining a truce: "We believe that so long as the military stalemate in Korea continues, the Communists are unlikely to make concessions on the POW issue to secure an armistice."[21]

But the Communist proposal on prisoners came at an opportune moment. Eisenhower made the exchange of sick and wounded prisoners a test of enemy intentions: if it was implemented, the United States would reopen truce negotiations.[22] Liaison officers on both sides began to meet on April 6, and five days later the senior liaison officers, Gen. Yi Sang-jo and Rear Adm. John C. Daniel, signed an agreement on the exchange of sick and wounded prisoners.

Documents exchanged on December 18, 1951, had given the number of prisoners held by the two sides as shown in table 7.1.

Of these prisoners, the sick and wounded prisoners that were exchanged broke down as shown in table 7.2.

ROK OPPOSES PRISONER EXCHANGE

After the basic obstacle to resuming truce talks was removed, ROK President Syngman Rhee, his political base secure from the 1952 election, intensified his opposition to a truce. In Washington on April 8, ROK Ambassador to the United States Yang Yu-chan presented Rhee's five conditions for a truce: (1) reunification of Korea; (2) withdrawal of all Chinese Communist forces from Korea; (3) disarming of North Korean forces; (4) prevention of any third country from providing arms to the Communists in North Korea; and (5) clarification of ROK sovereignty over all Korea and her voice in the solution of the Korean problem.[23]

In a letter to Eisenhower the next day, Rhee said that if a peace agreement permitted Chinese forces to stay in Korea, South Korea would still "have to ask all the friendly nations whose armed forces are now fighting in Korea and who do not desire to join with us in our determination to defeat aggres-

Table 7.1.

US soldiers	3,198
ROK soldiers	7,142
Other UN countries' soldiers	1,219
Total held by North Korea/China	**11,559**
CPV soldiers	20,700
KPA soldiers	111,773
Total held by South Korea/United States	**132,473**

Table 7.2.

US and other UN countries' soldiers	213
ROK soldiers	471
Total	**684**
KPA soldiers	5,194
CPV soldiers	1,030
Total	**6,224**

sive communism and drive up to the Yalu River, to withdraw from Korea." South Korea would fight on alone.[24] In effect, Rhee demanded that if the Sino-American War ended, the hostilities should revert to a contest for unification exclusively waged between the South and North. Without the United States, however, South Korea on its own had never been able to effectively wage war against the North, and it still couldn't. Thus, if the Eisenhower administration refused to continue the conflict, Rhee wanted a treaty between the United States and the ROK that guaranteed the South's postwar security.

Rhee had ample reason for concern. Washington rejected out of hand his opposition to a truce and desire to continue fighting, and had no intention of concluding a bilateral defense security agreement with the ROK. The US Defense Department, still wedded to the strategy of maintaining a defense perimeter around Japan, the Ryukyus, and the Philippines, "strongly opposed" inclusion of South Korea in the perimeter.[25]

On April 17, the UN Command requested a meeting of liaison officers to prepare for resumption of the truce talks, and two days later the liaison officers agreed to reopen negotiations on April 25. Syngman Rhee and his supporters wasted no time showing their opposition. On April 23–24, throughout South Korea, public rallies and demonstrations demanded "opposition to the death against a truce without national unification" in what the *Tong'a Ilbo* newspaper headlined a "National Movement." In Pusan, still the temporary capital of the ROK, tens of thousands of demonstrators led by more than a hundred National Assembly members closed down the commercial center of the city and some protestors tried to break into the US embassy.[26] In Washington, "as if timed to events in Pusan," ROK diplomats presented a final aide-mémoire to the State Department that was more ominous than Rhee's letter to Eisenhower: "President Syngman Rhee is preparing to withdraw the ROK (Republic of Korea) military forces from the UNC (United Nations Command) when, and if, the UN (United Nations) makes with the Communist aggressors any agreement which, after a cease-fire agreement, would either permit or allow Chinese Communists to remain south of the Yalu River."[27] Rhee had thrown down the gauntlet.

On April 26, the day the truce talks resumed, Gen. Mark Clark advised US Army Chief of Staff Joseph Collins that the UN Command had two options if Rhee withdrew ROK forces from UN control immediately after an armistice was signed: include a provision for withdrawal of all foreign troops from Korea in the truce agreement, or "be prepared to meet the contingency . . . by drastic action."[28] The latter course entailed the arrest and detention of Rhee, taking him into "protective custody"—in plain language, a coup d'état. Clark assured Collins that "plans to carry out such a course of action are all prepd and have been recently brought up to date."[29] The UNC had dusted off the plan prepared in 1952 during the Pusan political crisis. This time Clark expected ROKA Chief of Staff Paek Sun-yop to head a provisional government and suggested that Paek's upcoming visit to the United States be postponed. However, Clark thought Rhee was bluffing and wanted to try again to dissuade him.

On the first day truce negotiations resumed, senior Communist delegate Nam Il submitted a six-point proposal; (1) repatriation within two months of all prisoners who chose to return home; (2) transfer of the remaining POWs to an agreed neutral state within one month; (3) allowance of six months for each side to explain the situation to POWs to eliminate their apprehensions and inform them of all matters related to their return; (4) repatriation of new prisoners who chose it; (5) if after six months any nonrepatriates remain, their disposition would be referred to a political conference specified in the armistice agreement; and (6) the expense of maintaining POWs in a neutral state to be borne by the country of origin. Senior UN Command delegate Gen. William K. Harrison Jr. suggested that Switzerland be the neutral country. Citing the cost of transporting POWs from Korea to Europe, the Communists rejected Switzerland. But Harrison reiterated that Switzerland was the ideal country as a neutral nation and said that the Communist proposals were neither "reasonable nor constructive."[30]

In a private meeting with Rhee in Pusan on April 27 that lasted more than an hour, UN Commander Clark said that he came "as a friend to discuss the problem which might arise in the event he [Rhee] took drastic unilateral action [and] had asked to see him alone and informally." Clark also said he "hoped we could discuss these matters on a frank, personal and friendly basis." Rhee was responsive—"calm, dispassionate and unemotional." Clark expressed his concerns as UN commander, and Rhee repeated his views on the need for Chinese troops to leave Korea and his doubts that a political conference would achieve unification. "Then came the most significant statement from Rhee, to the effect that he was not now even thinking in terms of eventually withdrawing ROK forces from UN control, that if such action were taken, it would only be as a last resort, and then only after thorough and frank discussion with me," Clark recounted on the next day. Relieved to hear that Rhee would not act unilaterally, Clark advised General Collins that Paek Sun-yop proceed with his trip to the United States as planned.[31]

Rhee followed up in a letter to Clark on April 30, suggesting that both US and Chinese troops simultaneously withdraw from Korea. The plan Rhee proposed included: (1) conclusion of a US-ROK mutual defense treaty; (2) UN supervision of a buffer zone on the north bank of the Yalu River; (3) a nonaggression arrangement between China and the ROK; (4) immediate return of US forces to Korea if the Soviet Union attempted to invade Korea; (5) prohibition against Japanese forces participating in combat in Korea; and (6) strengthening of ROK forces by the United States.[32]

But Rhee's statements at the April 29 press conference, which were made public on May 1, upset Clark. If the truce negotiators did not completely accept the ROK government's five conditions for a truce that ROK Ambassador Yang had presented in Washington on April 8, President Rhee reportedly said, "the Republic of Korea will move north on its own."[33] Probably urged by the worried Clark, US 8th Army commander Gen. Maxwell Taylor had his staff draft Operation Plan Everready. According to the plan, when an armistice agreement was signed or immediately prior to the signing, if the ROKA did not follow UNC orders or the ROK government and military acted unilaterally and threatened UN forces, the 8th Army would stage a coup d'état.[34]

On May 7, Nam Il of North Korea countered the UN forces' plan with an eight-point proposal: (1) repatriation of POWs to their country of choice within two months; (2) establishment of a Neutral Nations Repatriation Commission made up of Poland, Czechoslovakia, Switzerland, Sweden, and India; (3) transference of the other POWs to the neutral nations repatriation committee; (4) the sending of personnel of both sides to interview and counsel prisoners within a four-month period; (5) repatriation of POWs who chose a destination in this period; (6) organization of the political conference to decide the disposition of remaining POWs; (7) bearing of the expenses of the Neutral Nations Repatriation Commission for POWs by "the nations to which they belong"; and (8) informing the POWs of these conditions. The new points from Nam Il's earlier proposal were the transfer of POWs to a five-country repatriation commission and reduction of the period for interviewing and counseling POWs from six months to four months.[35]

Clark acknowledged that the proposal was the "first concession of any importance" by the Communists in the current talks, but cautioned Washington that "it contains provisions that can work to the detriment of the UNC and involve US in extreme difficulty with ROK Government."[36] Clark thought this was in fact a new measure that assured the repatriation of all POWs.

At a meeting with Clark on May 12, Syngman Rhee insisted that no Communist custodial forces be allowed into South Korea to monitor prisoners and that "no Korean non-repatriates be transferred to a neutral state." Clark sympathized with Rhee "because his position reflects a realism in the situation which we cannot ignore without jeopardizing the vital interests of our government and the UNC in connection with the armistice negotiations." Clark felt that "the only realistic and workable solution is to release the Korean non-repatriates on the effective date of the armistice."[37] Clark summarized Rhee's views as follows: If a treaty was unattainable, he wanted a guarantee of immediate US assistance if the Communists violated a truce. Clark recommended that the United States make such a guarantee.[38]

The Joint Chiefs of Staff concurred with Clark, and on May 13 the US delegation at Panmunjom submitted a counterproposal to the Communist proposal that accepted many of Nam Il's eight articles "as a basis for negotiations." The US counterproposal included a provision that nonrepatriates be released on the date a truce came into effect.[39] This last provision could not be accepted by the Communist side.

The Communist joint command in Korea started the first summer offensive that same day,[40] and the following day Communist truce negotiators rejected the UNC's counterproposal as "absolutely unacceptable."[41] The Communist offensive continued until May 26. In anticipation of an indefinite recess at Panmunjom, General Clark intended to apply military pressure to the Communists by bombing North Korean dams and attacking Kaesong and Kumsong. If the truce talks were not resumed, Clark also wanted to release the thirty-five thousand North Korean nonrepatriate POWs.[42] But he reconsidered on May 16, suggesting that a compromise offer be made at Panmunjom. If it was rejected, the UN Command should take decisive action. The JCS approved the plan.

UN Command delegate at Panmunjom William Harrison made a new offer on May 25. The proposal stipulated that nonrepatriate prisoners be transferred to a Five Neutral Nations' Repatriation Commission chaired by India, and that only Indian troops be used for custodial duties with the prisoners. Both sides would have ninety days to verify the POWs' intentions and prisoners would be released after 120 days.[43]

This US compromise basically accepted the May 7 Communist proposal presented by Nam Il. To the Rhee administration, it was the worst-case scenario.

COMPROMISE

When UN Commander Clark informed President Rhee of the final UNC position on May 25, just prior to the resumption of truce talks, the president responded, "I am deeply disappointed" and spelled out his objections. Indian troops would not be permitted to enter South Korea, nor would the Communists be allowed to contact nonrepatriates. Rhee also told Clark that Korea "could not wait 6 months and then years for a political conference [to talk about the future of the country] to be effected." US Ambassador to South Korea Ellis O. Briggs, who had replaced John Muccio in April 1952, read a message from President Eisenhower to Rhee, which depressed Rhee even more. Among other things, Eisenhower in his message questioned how Rhee could object to North Korean prisoners of war receiving the same treatment as other prisoners of war opposing repatriation. Rhee replied: "One thing we want is the withdrawal of the Chinese Communists. . . . We want to live, we want to survive. Leaving the Chinese Communists in our country is impossible. You can withdraw all UN Forces, all economic aid. We will decide our own fate. We do not ask anyone to fight for us. We made our mistake perhaps in the beginning in relying upon democracy to assist us. Sorry, but I cannot assure President Eisenhower of my cooperation under the present circumstances."[44]

A second Communist offensive began on May 27. With an eye to the new proposal from US negotiators at Panmunjom, the Communist command changed their operational plan on June 1 and struck mainly ROK positions, with measured attacks on US forces and none on British units. Concentrated on the eastern front, the offensive by June 16 had destroyed the ROKA 5th and 7th Divisions.[45]

On May 29, Ambassador Briggs reported to Washington that Rhee's options included the release of all North Korean prisoners or rejection of a truce and removal of ROK forces from the UN Command. South Korea might also impede a ceasefire by organizing a strike of Korean laborers attached to US units, Briggs noted.[46]

At a joint State Department–JCS meeting on May 29, US Army Chief of Staff Joseph Collins said that he had asked Clark if ROKA Chief of Staff Paek Sun-yop, who was then visiting Washington, should be rushed back to Seoul to detain Syngman Rhee. Clark was negative because a changed itinerary and early return might arouse suspicion, and Collins asked again what Clark thought of arranging a meeting between Paek Sun-yop and Eisenhower. After a review of Operation Plan Everready for a possible coup d'état by the US 8th Army, Assistant Secretary of State Walter Robertson said it might be better to just "get our forces out of there." Deputy Assistant Secretary of State Alexis Johnson said if a coup was mounted, Koreans should be used to carry it out and "any military law or military government should be set up under the cover of South Koreans." Collins was wavering on the idea, but in response to a suggestion of a US-ROK security treaty, he said, "Personally I think we should be prepared to take Rhee into protective custody rather than sweeten him up with a security pact." Collins was impressed by Johnson's comment that "a promise to negotiate a pact rather than the actual conclusion of a pact" might be enough to induce Rhee's cooperation.[47]

Collins then informed Clark that Plan Everready was "under consideration at the highest levels of government," and authorized him to take preliminary measures to ensure the safety of the UN Command in case of an emergency. When Secretary of State John Foster Dulles returned to Washington,
he and President Eisenhower would consider a US-ROK security treaty,
Collins said. If Clark considered it effective in heading off an emergency, he
could then inform Rhee that Dulles would recommend negotiation of a bilateral security treaty. [48] Clark was optimistic that Rhee, one of whose goals was
of course to obtain a security treaty, could be persuaded to temper his opposition to a truce. [49]

Although US security officials had no objection in principle to pushing
Rhee aside, at the end of the day they decided against it. Another joint State
Department–JCS conference on May 30 was followed by a meeting of senior
officials with Eisenhower. General Clark was informed that the administration could not "concur with any action on your part which would establish a
UNC military government in ROK." However, Clark was told to "take whatever other steps you deem appropriate to safeguard the integrity and security
of your forces." The officials had concluded that a mutual security treaty was
the only way to satisfy Rhee, and Eisenhower approved it. Clark was informed that a treaty would be offered. [50]

In a letter to Eisenhower that day, Rhee attacked the May 25 UNC proposal offered by William Harrison as "of such an appeasing nature that it
cannot avoid the appearance of surrender and that, in turn, will lead to a great
disaster to all." After the conclusion of a US-ROK mutual security treaty,
Rhee wanted the "simultaneous withdrawal of both the Communist and United Nations forces from Korea." If that was unacceptable, "Koreans should be
allowed to continue the fighting." [51] Rhee conveyed the impression that if
Chinese and US forces left, he intended to renew combat operations against
the North. On the pretext that truce talks had heated up, Paek Sun-yop returned to Seoul from the United States ahead of schedule in late May. [52] Rhee
may have recalled him because of the May 25 proposal.

The South Korean press reported on May 30 that an emergency cabinet
meeting was scheduled for the next day at Chinhae, and on June 2 it reported
that a statement about the results of this "historic meeting" would soon be
released. [53] The next day, the Soviet Union's foreign minister, Vyacheslav
Molotov, told US Ambassador to the USSR Charles Bohlen that he "was
satisfied that the path was open to a compromise at Panmunjom." [54] Bohlen
was delighted. On June 4 Communist negotiators agreed in principle to the
May 25 UNC proposal. [55] Gradually, a settlement was taking shape. The next
day, Clark and Briggs asked Rhee not to order unilateral action by the ROKA
or issue a statement opposing a truce. But their appeal fell on deaf ears. Rhee
wanted to "speak his piece" against a truce. [56] On June 7 the ROK government summoned Choe Tok-shin, the chief ROK delegate at Panmunjom, to

Seoul. He was officially recalled on June 15 and thereafter took no part in the truce talks.[57] On June 8, Harrison and Nam Il signed an agreement on prisoners. Unless the upcoming political conference decided the fate of POWs who refused repatriation, they would be transferred to the Neutral Nations Repatriation Commission and released after 120 days. Prisoners who chose to go to a neutral nation would be assisted in doing so.[58]

In case Rhee tried to abort the armistice and a new ROK government had to be installed, Clark ordered all subordinate commands to be prepared to implement Operation Plan Everready.[59] Eisenhower wrote Rhee on June 6 that the time had come to pursue Korean unification by political means, not warfare, and promised, in the interest of the ROK's security, that the United States would provide economic and military aid and negotiate a mutual defense treaty.[60] Rhee was preparing a reply on June 9 when Gen. Maxwell Taylor called on him to discuss ROK officer assignments. The conversation turned to the truce, and Taylor asked the president his requirements. Rhee listed four: (1) a sixty-day limit on the political conference; (2) a mutual security treaty with the United States; (3) expansion of the ROKA to twenty divisions; and (4) barring of representatives from India and Communist nations from entry to the ROK.[61] On June 12, in a personal message to Rhee, Secretary of State Dulles cited the urgent need "for a highly confidential exchange of views between our two governments" and invited him to visit the United States.[62] Rhee replied that he could not leave South Korea and asked Dulles to come to Seoul.[63]

Senior US officials were then trying to formulate a posttruce Korea policy. The NSC Planning Board drafted a set of objectives entitled "United States Tactics Immediately Following an Armistice in Korea." Dated June 15, the study assumed that even after a truce Communist China would try to achieve its objectives by force. The danger of aggression remained, particularly in Southeast Asia, the study argued, while differences between the United States and its major allies on policy toward China were likely to widen. "It is important to our national security, as well as to the objective of obtaining an acceptable settlement, that political and economic pressures against Communist China be developed and maintained." The strategy enunciated for Korea was to maintain US military power after a truce; increase ROK military strength; conclude a security treaty with the ROK; strengthen the "democratic institutions" and "economic recovery" of the ROK; and in the upcoming political conference, seek to establish a united, independent, democratic Korea. Specific measures to achieve these objectives were attached to the study.[64] An annex entitled "Agreed 'Greater Sanctions' Statement" said that "if there is a renewal of the armed attack" by the Communists, "we should again be united and prompt to resist." It concluded with a warning that "in all probability, it would not be possible to confine hostilities within the frontiers of Korea."[65]

Also on June 15, Deputy Assistant Secretary of State Walter K. Scott submitted a draft position paper to the NSC Planning Board entitled "To Determine the Basic U.S. Objective with Respect to Korea." It laid out two options: (1) continued division of the peninsula and the ROK as a military ally of the United States, or (2) a "unified, neutralized Korea under a substantially unchanged ROK." The latter alternative entailed "Communist agreement to a unified Korea with a U.S. political orientation in exchange" for the removal of US forces and bases, exclusion of the ROK from "the U.S. military sphere," a guarantee of the ROK's territorial integrity, UN membership, and "limitations on the level and character of the ROK defense forces." China and the Soviet Union might prefer this latter choice, which, although sacrificing North Korea, would be a plus for the security of Manchuria and North China and avoid the burden of providing postwar support for North Korea, Scott's draft paper asserted. US allies, including Japan, would also welcome this second alternative. The security of Japan would be enhanced by the removal of Communist power from Korea to Manchuria. And a unified, neutral Korea under the ROK flag "could be expected to appeal to" South Koreans themselves, Scott argued. Plus, the United States would not have to station forces in Korea. The paper concluded: "It is in the interests of the U.S., and should be the U.S. objective, to secure a unified and neutralized Korea."[66] But to imagine that the Communists would accept a neutralized Korean Peninsula under the South, and "with a U.S. political orientation" no less, was completely unrealistic and showed Washington's imprudent perception of Korea.[67]

Although the NSC Planning Board's study and Scott's draft position paper to the board reached diametrically opposite conclusions about post-truce Korea, Dulles authorized submission of Scott's paper to the board, and it was taken up the same day in a joint State Department–JCS meeting. Deputy Undersecretary of State H. Freeman Matthews led the discussion of the neutralization option; many participants expressed doubts about a neutral post-truce Korea, including whether Eisenhower had even mentioned neutralization to Rhee. Walter Robertson, the assistant secretary of state, who had been designated a special emissary to negotiate with Rhee, replied to the doubters: "No, but he did say we would work for a unified Korea and how we can get a unified Korea without neutralization is very real question. If anybody has the answer, I wish they would let me know since I have to start off for Korea in a couple of days."[68]

In a letter to Eisenhower on June 17, Rhee coupled appreciation for the US promise of a mutual security treaty with a warning that "if it is tied up with the armistice its efficacy would be diminished almost to a vanishing point." He condemned moves toward an armistice and wanted to know what had happened to the UN's objective to establish a unified, independent, democratic Korea and punish the Communist aggressors. "We cannot avoid seeing the cold fact that the counsels of appeasers have prevailed in altering the armistice positions of the United States," Rhee said. "The terms of the armistice being what they are, the Communist build-up will go on unhampered until it is capable of overwhelming South Korea with one swoop at a moment of the Communists' own choosing."[69]

The letter foreshadowed Rhee's bold move a few hours later. Overnight, twenty-five thousand North Korean prisoners were released from four POW camps in South Korea, including those at Pusan and Masan. Rhee's unilateral act was intended to throw a monkey wrench into the truce process. Worried about the Communist reaction, the UN Command protested the release and accused senior ROK officials of staging the "escape."

Eisenhower quipped at the start of an NSC meeting on June 18 that "we seemed to have acquired another enemy instead of a friend." Eisenhower also reported that "he and his advisers had been composing a message which, by implication, informed Rhee that if he continued in this course it was 'goodbye' to Korea." Others present strongly advised against the withdrawal of US forces. Dulles saw a silver lining. The Communist reaction to Rhee's move would show how much they wanted a truce, he said. Yet the United States had to take a very tough line so Rhee would understand who was running the show.[70]

Participants in a joint State Department–JCS damage-control meeting the next day were at a loss for countermeasures. The coup d'état option had already been ruled out. Now they faced the possibility of fighting erupting between ROKA military police and US troops around the POW camps over Rhee's release of the prisoners. ROKA Provost Marshal Won Yong-duk had ordered his men to fire on anyone who blocked the prisoners' escape. Alexis Johnson noted that "Won Yong Duk is Rhee's man. Would it be possible for us to take action against Won Yong Duk without first having made the decision that we were prepared to take action against Rhee?" Adm. Donald Duncan of the US Navy said a move against Won Yong-duk could be justified on the grounds of self-defense. But the group could not come up with options.[71]

THE UNITED STATES PERSUADES RHEE

The measured Communist response to Rhee's prisoner release on June 19, in the names of Kim Il Sung and Peng Dehuai, criticized the UN Command for not preventing the flagrant attempt by the "Syngman Rhee clique" to disrupt the truce process. Kim and Peng's letter asked three questions: "Is the United Nations Command able to control the South Korea Government and Army? If not, does the armistice in Korea include the Syngman Rhee clique? If it is not included, what assurance is there for the implementation of the armistice agreement on the part of South Korea?"[72] It is difficult to tell whether the Communist negotiators were feeling contemptuous compassion toward the UNC given its difficulties with Rhee, or whether they were pressing once more for the Americans to clamp down on the ROK government.

Peng Dehuai arrived in Pyongyang on June 20 on a previously scheduled visit and met with Li Kenong, a senior Chinese member of the Communist delegation at Panmunjom; CPV commander Deng Hua; and others. In a telegram to Mao that night, Peng recommended that they delay the signing of a truce and deal a heavy blow to Syngman Rhee by killing fifteen thousand ROK troops. Mao concurred the next day: "more than 10,000 puppet soldiers must be annihilated."[73]

The Communist command prepared for a third offensive in the area south of the North Korean town of Kumsong from Kumhwa to the Pukhan River. The area was protected by four ROKA divisions. The mission was assigned to five armies of the CPV's 20th Army group and the 9th Army group.[74]

UN Commander Gen. Mark Clark met Syngman Rhee alone on June 22 for more than an hour. The president was "extremely nervous," Clark reported, and "said he had not slept most of the night and he seemed under considerable strain and tension." Yet Rhee was very friendly and said he still wanted to work with President Eisenhower. Clark made no mention of Rhee's prisoner release and instead talked about the future. Rhee had to accept two core American principles, Clark said: the need to achieve an honorable armistice and that the UN Command would not drive the Chinese out of Korea. In a bid to win Rhee over, Clark made a personal suggestion, unauthorized by Washington, on the handling of nonrepatriate North Korean prisoners. He told Rhee that the Korean nonrepatriate POWs must remain under UN custody and that ROK representatives would have full opportunity to approach the POWs.[75]

Clark was leaving for Tokyo the next day, and Rhee gave him a draft aide-mémoire to be forwarded to Washington with his conditions for acceptance of an armistice. South Korea would not sign an armistice, Rhee said, but would comply with UNC orders to implement it if Rhee's terms were met: (1) a political conference to decide all remaining questions on Korea, including the withdrawal of foreign forces and the unification of Korea that would last ninety days. If an agreement for the withdrawal of Chinese forces and the unification of Korea was not reached, the armistice would end and ROK forces, with US air and naval assistance, would attack the North; (2) conclusion of a US-ROK mutual defense treaty before an armistice was signed; (3) US military and economic assistance to the ROK; (4) barring of foreign troops from entering the ROK to guard prisoners of war and Communist representatives from counseling POWs.[76] The first point concerning resuming attack on the North after a failure of political conferences was absolutely unacceptable to Washington.

Walter Robertson left Washington on June 22 as the personal emissary of President Eisenhower and Secretary of State John Foster Dulles carrying a letter from Dulles to Rhee. He was accompanied by Kenneth Young, director of the State Department's Office of Northeast Asian Affairs, and US Army Chief of Staff Joseph Collins. The United States had sent more than a million of its young men to Korea, Dulles wrote Rhee, of whom 24,000 had died, and spent many billions of dollars as "part of the price we paid for loyalty to the principle of unity when you invoked it. . . . It is at this moment that you are apparently considering the rejection of the principle of unity. Because the fighting has not given you all that you had hoped, you seem to be on the verge of wrecking allied unity. . . . Do you have the right to take this action? . . . For your Republic now to attempt to go its separate way would mean a horrible disaster. It would give the Communists their greatest victory. . . . The principle of interdependence involves sacrifice. It will involve sacrifices on your part as it has involved sacrifices on our part."[77] Dulles had mustered powerful arguments to try to sway Rhee to get on board with an armistice.

Robertson conferred with Clark, Collins, and others in Tokyo on June 24–25. A memorandum of the meeting recounts that some participants felt that if ROK obstructionism blocked an armistice, the United Nations would have no choice but to somehow "work out an alternate arrangement with the Communists" and withdraw from Korea. "All the conferees agreed that the time had come to tell Rhee the blunt truth that the United States will have no other alternative but to get out if he pursues his present policy."[78]

At this point the conferees received NSC report 157, "U.S. Objective With Respect to Korea Following an Armistice," which had been submitted to the NSC on June 25.[79] This was the same document as Walter Scott's paper submitted with Dulles' approval to the Planning Board of the NSC on June 15. The "Alternative Feasible Objectives" were the same. A Korea divided with the ROK tied into the US security system or a unified neutralized Korea under a substantially unchanged ROK were presented. Conclusion and recommendation were the same. The latter alternative was recommended. It showed Washington's total helplessness concerning setting the terms on the Korean issue at this moment.

Robertson had hoped to seal a bargain with Rhee on June 26. Although the letter from Dulles had made a strong impression on Rhee, he had ridiculed an armistice the day before to a crowd of 500,000 at a rally to commemorate the start of the war. An about-face would make him look ridiculous, Robertson worried. Robertson was convinced that the United States should try to find a face-saving solution: "We should help him do so with such modification of details which will not compromise our position."[80]

Robertson and Clark drafted a memorandum the next day based on Robertson's conversation with Rhee that included assurances that: (1) if the political conference continued beyond ninety days and was being manipulated by the Communists, the United States and ROK would jointly withdraw; (2) after an armistice was signed the United States would confer with President Rhee on the goals of the political conference; and (3) negotiations would be held on a mutual defense treaty. In return, the ROK would have to accept an armistice and comply with the UNC. [81]

But Rhee rejected Robertson and Clark's aide-mémoire as inconsistent with his meeting the day before with Robertson, and on June 28 he presented his own. The salient points were conclusion of a mutual defense treaty prior to an armistice and the immediate resumption of military operations if the United States and the ROK jointly left the political conference following an armistice. [82]

Dulles realized the South Korean president had not budged an inch and directed Clark to pressure him into compliance. On June 29 Robertson returned Rhee's draft as wholly unacceptable and tried to reason with him. Clark told Rhee that the UNC would resume talks at Panmunjom. Rhee then promised to provide a "more satisfactory version" of his memorandum. [83]

In a letter to the Communist commanders on June 29, Clark carefully addressed the three questions Kim Il Sung and Peng Dehuai had earlier posed "in an earnest endeavor to achieve an early armistice." He proposed resumption of the talks. [84] Chinese Vice-Foreign Minister Wu Xiuquan on July 3 took a draft response to Clark's letter by Peng Dehuai and Kim Il Sung to the Soviet embassy in Beijing, which reported it to Moscow. [85] The next day the Presidium of the Central Committee of the CPSU delegated Georgii Malenkov and Vyacheslav Molotov to draft an affirmative reply. [86] Molotov sent the document to the Soviet embassy in Beijing that day. [87] Fearful of another rash act by South Korea, the Soviet government was against Kim Il Sung attending a truce signing ceremony at Panmunjom.

A major change in US thinking occurred in Washington on June 30. In a report to Secretary of Defense Charles Wilson, the JCS opposed the neutralization of Korea and the removal of US forces. To attain the primary US goal of a "unified, independent, and non-Communist Korea," they recommended "overt and covert programs" to "establish the Republic of Korea as an example, economically and politically, of the advantages of association with the free world" and to "create dissatisfaction and unrest in North Korea" that would lead to unification. [88] This view was characterized by Lee Jon-won as "a big turnabout from the U.S. military's traditional position that had ignored the strategic significance of the Korean Peninsula." [89] The turnabout was a direct result of President Rhee's perseverance.

Robertson gradually came to feel overwhelmed by Rhee while trying to persuade the South Korean president to support an armistice. Robertson sent Dulles a personal assessment on July 1: "Rhee in addition to being a shrewd, resourceful trader is also a highly emotional, irrational, illogical fanatic fully capable of attempting to lead his country into national suicide." At the same time, though, the South Korean president was a potential asset: "Rhee has aroused his country to a determination and will to fight Communism, probably unmatched by any other country in the world including ourselves. Such spirit and fortitude should be preserved, not destroyed. In addition, his army equipped by us is the largest and most effective anti-Communist army in Asia and we badly need it on our side."[90]

Whether Rhee fully understood the mood of senior US officials is unclear. He concluded a long message to Robertson on July 1 with: "We are very near to an agreement not to obstruct the armistice, provided the US definitely pledges to resume fighting with us, in case of failure of the political conference, until the unification of Korea is accomplished. If this cannot be done, I do not see how I can comply with your request in the armistice, for I have no means to convince the Korean people who are definitely opposed to the truce terms as they are now."[91] Rhee had gone too far, and Robertson intended to reiterate that the United States would not pledge to resume the fighting, and that if Rhee did not change his attitude, Robertson would acknowledge that his mission had failed and return to Washington.[92]

The NSC discussed NSC report 154 on July 2. Speaking to the restrictions on trade with Communist China considered in the report, Eisenhower said that "as long as the Chinese remained in any part of Korea they were plain and simple aggressors." He thought the United States could pressure its allies not to trade with China and "hoped we would be quite heavy-handed in exerting such pressure." Paragraph 14-b of NSC 154, in an amended form after some debate at the meeting, stated that the United States would "undertake with respect to the security of Korea, commitments . . . similar to those undertaken by the U.S. under the treaties with the Philippines, Australia and New Zealand." By this amendment the status of the ROK which was tied into the US security system was accepted. The Council then discussed NSC report 157 on US objectives after an armistice. Gen. Omar Bradley, chairman of the Joint Chiefs of Staff acknowledged at the outset that proposing a neutralized Korea might prove to be the only way to achieve a settlement at the upcoming political conference, but he equated the proposed unified and neutralized Korea with a disarmed Korea and argued that it would be a tactical error to lead off with this proposal. Undersecretary of State Walter B. Smith countered JCS objections to the neutralization of Korea point by point. Eisenhower noted that neutral countries like Switzerland and Sweden were armed and thought that the Communists might accept a unified Korea "without offensive capabilities." After further debate, the NSC retained the original wording of paragraph 9, which called for "a unified and neutralized Korea under a substantially unchanged ROK" with "military forces sufficient for internal security and capable of defending Korean territory short of an attack by a major power." The amended document was approved as NSC report 157/1.[93] Thus confusion continued in Washington.

On July 2 Robertson revised his aide-mémoire with Clark of June 27 in preparation for another meeting with Rhee. On the sticking point of US action if the political conference to settle the remaining questions on Korea failed, he inserted "the United States Government would consult immediately" with the ROK under "what courses of action should be taken in the light of circumstances then existing to seek the unification of Korea." In a separate letter to Rhee, Robertson explained that US forces were in Korea under UN resolutions, and that independent military action would require a declaration of war by the US Congress.[94]

Gen. Joseph Collins reported on a trip he had taken to Korea at a State Department–JCS conference on July 3. He quoted Maj. Gen. Thomas W. Herren, former deputy commanding general for civilian affairs of the 8th Army, as saying that Rhee now had "complete control over the Korean people." Generals Taylor and Clark both described ROKA Chief of Staff Gen. Paek Sun-yop as "strongly pro-U.S.," but said "that he is now completely circumscribed in his actions and that there is little he could or would do to help us."[95]

Undersecretary of State Walter Smith was inclined to think Robertson should leave Seoul if his continued presence as special emissary to negotiate with Rhee was pointless.[96] In what they thought of as a final attempt to get Rhee to come around, Robertson and Kenneth Young met Rhee and ROK Foreign Minister Byun on July 4. Rhee apparently accepted the fact that the United States could not reopen the fighting if the political conference failed. Robertson's statements to him that the US Senate had to ratify a mutual defense treaty and that it would be difficult to get Senate approval if Rhee opposed an armistice also had an effect. Rhee wanted assurance from Eisenhower and Dulles that the Senate would quickly ratify a treaty. Robertson asked if Rhee would agree to the revised aide-mémoire he had given him, and Rhee seemed about to consent when Byun interjected that the armistice should be delayed until a mutual defense treaty was ratified; otherwise, the ROK would be unprotected. Young pointed out that a Greater Sanctions statement that was to be issued at the time of the armistice was a warning to the Communists that assured the ROK's security. Rhee and Byun were "somewhat relieved," but Rhee rejected Robertson's entreaty to conclude the negotiations that day.[97]

Four days later the ROK presented a revised aide-mémoire to the United States that sought a guarantee of Senate approval of a mutual defense treaty. If the Senate balked at a pact, language similar to the US-Japan security treaty might be acceptable to the ROK. Since the United States would not agree to resume fighting if the political conference failed, Rhee argued, it should "at least give us moral and material support in our fight for unification." Rhee refused to promise that ROK forces would cooperate with the UN: "So long as the United Nations Command and the Republic of Korea pursue same common objective [unification of Korea] they will remain in same relationship as hitherto. But suppose they do not, the existing relationship will automatically undergo a definite change."[98]

In Washington on July 7, the National Security Council approved NSC 154/1 and 157/1.[99] In Seoul, Robertson, US Ambassador Ellis Briggs, and Young met with Rhee and Byun the next day. Robertson reviewed his and Rhee's aide-mémoires and read part of a telegram from Undersecretary of State Smith which conveyed a message from Senate leaders to Eisenhower and Dulles on ratification of a mutual defense treaty if the Republic of Korea cooperated in an armistice and the upcoming political conference. Robertson said he would be leaving for Washington on July 10 and hoped for an agreement by then.[100] Secretary of State Dulles sent Robertson a personal message from Eisenhower to Rhee to be used at his discretion. Eisenhower wrote: "Throughout these days I have been profoundly sympathetic with you. . . . Your illustrious place in history as a great patriot is due to patient and sober striving. We want to be allied with you in such endeavors."[101]

Rhee's letter to Robertson on July 9 finally made the critical promise the United States sought: "Although we cannot sign truce, we shall not obstruct it, so long as no measure or actions taken under armistice are detrimental to our national survival." Rhee also agreed not to release more nonrepatriate North Korean prisoners and to permit "three months of indoctrination prior to their release" later. Chinese prisoners who refused repatriation would be transferred to Taiwan.[102] Rhee wrote:

> We shall endeavor to cooperate fully and earnestly in political and peaceful achievement of reunification of our nation, which is our most fundamental national objective and necessity. . . .
> When our talks began, we asked that forces of UN or of US should join with ROK forces to achieve joint objectives of reunifying Korea. However, if this proposal is not agreeable to US, we should like to have specific assurances of moral and material support for an effort with our own armed forces to repel aggressors from Korea.[103]

Rhee had dropped his insistence on a US pledge "to resume fighting until the unification of Korea is accomplished," but still wanted US support for South Korean fighting. And the attached draft security treaty made the standard South Korean claim that the ROK's jurisdiction extended "northward to Yalu and Tumen Rivers."[104] Robertson sent Rhee's letter to the State Department, noting that this last point was unresolved and calling attention to the absence of a specific commitment to leave "ROK forces under United Nations Command." But Dulles deemed the "letter satisfactory basis for entering into armistice, leaving the detailed problems which it raises for future discussion and negotiation."[105]

At the reopened truce talks on July 10, though impatient, Nam Il said with tempered wording that the UN Command bore responsibility for recovering the prisoners released unilaterally by Rhee, and asked if ROK forces were included in the armistice. In response, the UN's William Harrison said that ROK forces were under the UN Command and "would abide by the provisions of the agreement."[106] Their mission accomplished, Robertson and Young then met cordially with Rhee and left for Washington on July 12.[107]

Chinese forces launched their third offensive in a violent rainstorm the night of July 13 at Kumsong. The ROK Capital Division initially abandoned its positions and fell back. Later, with US support, ROK units retook some of the high ground. With an armistice imminent, US commanders did not want to sacrifice lives to recapture nonessential terrain, and they established a new main line of resistance. The Communist attack stopped on July 20. Chinese commanders put their casualties at 33,253 men and enemy casualties at 78,000, and reported that 178 square kilometers of ground were recovered. The UN Command estimated Chinese casualties at 72,000, including 25,000 killed, and put friendly casualties at 29,629 killed and wounded.[108] Both sides said about 30,000 troops were killed in the battle.

PURGES AND COUNTERPURGES

At this stage of the conflict, the political currents were swirling in opposite directions in North Korea and the Soviet Union. In Pyongyang, the roundup continued of Pak Hon-yong followers and former South Korean Workers' Party members. So Chol (of the Manchurian faction) replaced the disgraced Kwon O-jik as acting ambassador to China, and Kim Il (also of the Manchurian faction) was named secretary of the Korean Workers' Party Central Committee.[109]

The interrogations of former SKWP members were used to fabricate charges that those detained had committed espionage for the United States and plotted a coup against Kim Il Sung. Ho Ka-i was vilified even after committing suicide. KWP Secretary Pak Chong-ae later told the KWP Central Committee's Sixth Plenum that he had been "assigned to rebuild a residential area destroyed by U.S. bombing, but had not drawn up a specific or organized plan and for a month had wasted the labor of an enormous number of mobilized workers and valuable state equipment and materials, and caused great loss to the nation by delaying an urgent project." The KWP Political Committee had ordered Ho Ka-i to finish the assignment. But "he did not engage in self-criticism, made excuses that more time was needed, avoided the just criticism of the Political Committee, and chose the path of suicide,"

Pak reported to the Plenum.[110] Ho Ka-i's major crime was that "he showed no concern about exposing the infiltration into our Party of an anti-Party and anti-State group that has conspired to commit destructive actions and behaved like a bystander. To commit suicide at this difficult time is a betrayal of the Fatherland and the people."[111]

The interrogations and confessions of the Pak Hon-yong group had probably been shown to Ho Ka-i, who had not been implicated in the plot against Kim Il Sung, but who had to have wondered when his turn would come. Criticized mainly by his comrades, who were Soviet Koreans, Ho Ka-i must have despaired that he had lost favor in the Communist Party of the Soviet Union and could not return there.

In Moscow, a new political wind was blowing. Lavrentii Beria, vice-premier and minister of internal affairs, who had risen after Stalin's death to become the most important person in the Soviet government after Georgii Malenkov, announced on April 4 that the Doctors' Plot was a fabrication and stopped the investigation. Beria hinted that innocent people had been tortured into confessing. Secret accusers who had been awarded the Order of Lenin were stripped of the honor. Two days later, an editorial in *Pravda* criticized Minister of State Security S. D. Ignat'ev and announced the arrest of Vice-Minister M. D. Riumin, the lead investigator in the Doctors' Plot case. Ignat'ev, who had just become secretary of the Central Committee of the CPSU, was dismissed.[112]

Among the charges against Ignat'ev was that he had ignored testimony by witnesses who knew the allegations of US germ warfare in North Korea in 1952 were trumped up. Documents recently published by the *Sankei Shimbun* newspaper in Japan included a letter dated April 21, 1953, from Beria to the Presidium of the CPSU's Central Committee urging prosecution of Ignat'ev. Beria attached the statements of Glukhov, adviser to the DPRK Ministry of Public Security, Igor' Selivanov, adviser to the KPA medical department, and Vladimir Razuvaev, ambassador to the DPRK. Glukhov and Razuvaev reported that when the World Peace Council had visited North Korea in June and July 1952, the North Koreans, with the help of Soviet advisers, had created two bogus contaminated zones and showed them to the WPC as examples of US bacteriological attacks. Selivanov testified that a Soviet investigation had found no evidence of germ warfare. Worried that they could not create a credible contaminated area, the North Koreans had asked the Soviets for advice.[113]

Beria levied the accusation against Ignat'ev that he had ignored evidence that the allegations of US germ warfare were bogus because Ignat'ev was a member of the rival Malenkov faction in the post-Stalin power struggle. On April 24, the Presidium acted against Razuvaev and Ignat'ev. The former was recalled from Pyongyang and stripped of his general's rank. The latter was dismissed from the Central Committee, and his case was referred to the party's Control Committee for disciplinary action. The censure of both was reported to Beijing and Pyongyang. Although annoyed, Mao Zedong promised an investigation.[114] S. P. Suzdalev was named ambassador to Pyongyang.[115]

Threatened by Beria's "reformist" actions, Malenkov and Nikita Khrushchev struck back on June 26. Beria's arrest was announced on July 10. Beria was declared a spy for Britain and the United States, a classic tactic worthy of Joseph Stalin's style. One has to wonder how such Stalinist actions could be reconciled with the so-called thaw of April 1953.[116] The denunciation of Beria as a spy for foreign intelligence agencies provided the perfect opportunity for opponents of Pak Hon-yong and Ito Ritsu to label them traitors, too.

SIGNING THE ARMISTICE

China suggested to the Soviet Union that Kim Il Sung and Peng Dehuai not attend the armistice signing ceremony in late July 1953. Vyacheslav Molotov disagreed and told the Central Committee of the CPSU on July 23 that if Kim and Peng were not present, the US representatives would say they did not know who the plenipotentiary was and that the United States might thus delay the signing. Security should be tightened and Kim and Peng should be present, Molotov argued, and the Central Committee concurred.[117] However, the next day the Presidium approved a letter to the DPRK government which stated that the North Korean vice-premier rather than Kim Il Sung should attend.[118] The Soviets were clearly very anxious about the details.

On July 24 the negotiators at Panmunjom agreed that the armistice would be set at the military demarcation line. With a settlement hours away, Rhee pressed for assurance from Dulles that the United States would provide support if the armistice went awry: "Before deciding the position of my government," Rhee said, he wanted to know if the United States would "resume military efforts to drive the Chinese Red invaders" out of Korea or promise "moral and material support" for ROK military actions if the political conference to decide remaining questions of Korea failed. He also wanted the proposed mutual security pact between the ROK and the United States to include "immediate and automatic military support" if the ROK were attacked.[119] After conferring with Eisenhower, Dulles told Rhee that he and the president were surprised that he was reviving settled issues at the last minute.[120] Yet Rhee's stubborn temerity was rewarded with a firm US commitment to ROK security.

William Harrison and Nam Il signed the armistice agreement at Panmunjom at 10:20 a.m. on July 27, 1953, without a word to each other. Nam Il looked at his watch and left without shaking hands with Harrison. The armistice came into effect twelve hours later.[121] The armistice order was issued by

Gen. Mark Clark for the UN Command and by Kim Il Sung and Peng Dehuai for the Communist side. That afternoon at Munsan, Clark signed the document. Peng Dehuai and Choe Yong-gon went to Kaesong that afternoon in their capacities as commander and vice-commander, respectively, of the Chinese–North Korean Joint Headquarters for a huge celebration with frontline troops. When the armistice began at 10 p.m., Kim Il Sung signed the agreement in Pyongyang as supreme commander of the KPA. The next day at 9:30 a.m., Peng Dehuai signed it as CPV commander.[122]

REACTIONS

On July 28, 110,000 people gathered in Pyongyang's central square for a speech by Kim Il Sung. Standing amid a wasteland of burned-out buildings, North Koreans were relieved at the end of US bombing. Soviet Ambassador to North Korea S. P. Suzdalev had reported Kim's draft speech to Moscow on July 19.[123] The Korean people had crushed the plan of the American imperialists to turn all of Korea into a colony and a military base against the Soviet Union and China, Kim declared; the armistice was the result of their heroic three-year struggle to defend the freedom and independence of the fatherland. The nation and people had won a historic victory. Kim Il Sung was flanked on the podium by Kim Tu-bong, chairman of the Presidium of the Supreme People's Assembly; three KWP secretaries—Pak Chong-ae, Pak Chang-ok, and Kim Il; and four vice-premiers—Choe Yong-gon, Chong Il-yong, Pak Ui-wan, and Choe Chang-ik. Missing were Pak Hon-yong, Yi Sung-yop, Ho Ka-i, and Pak Il-u.

Kim Il Sung's authority was complete, the armistice his personal triumph. The military, political, and moral defeat of the American aggressors was not only a victory for the Korean people but also a great victory for the world's freedom-loving democratic camp, Kim Il Sung went on to say. "The fact that America, the largest power in the imperialist camp, had waged war against our small Korea for three years and been forced to sign an armistice at Panmunjom on the 38th parallel where it began the invasion was best proof that imperialists could no longer attack other countries with impunity," he said.

After noting the spiritual support and economic aid from fraternal countries in the socialist camp led by the great Soviet Union, Kim Il Sung paid special tribute to China for sending the Chinese People's Volunteers to the front line in Korea at the most difficult time in the DPRK's war to liberate the fatherland.

The guns were silent, but a complete victory had not been won, Kim Il Sung also cautioned. The American imperialists had not been driven from the fatherland and were planning to use Japan in their aggressive wars in Asia.

Planes from US bases in Japan had turned peaceful Pyongyang and farming villages across the North into charred ashes, Kim said. The United States had fought the war from depots and rear area bases in Japan.

While shrilly threatening to attack the North, the Rhee administration had begun negotiations with Japan to normalize diplomatic relations, Kim continued. He warned that a US-ROK mutual security treaty would increase the danger of another war. North Korea must strengthen the KPA's war-fighting power, improve "revolutionary vigilance," and rebuild the economy, he said. Not a single spy or saboteur could be allowed to operate in the republic. The "completion of national territory" was now linked to "peaceful unification of the fatherland." Kim did not mention unification by military force. The people's patriotic duty during the armistice was to develop the national economy and make the DPRK a stronger democratic base, he exhorted the crowd.[124] Kim's speech was broadcast nationwide and followed by an artillery salute and a parade of 110,000 citizens that lasted several hours. North Koreans were openly joyful at peace.[125]

In contrast to Kim Il Sung's rhetoric of vindication and hope, the predominant mood in South Korea was bitter disappointment. There were no government-sponsored festivities, not even in Seoul or the temporary capital of Pusan, and citizens did not celebrate the armistice. The civilian population had not been under attack from the skies as North Koreans had, and the ceasefire had no direct impact on them. A *Tong'a Ilbo* newspaper headline summed up the national state of mind: "Desolation of Failed Unification."[126] Of course, ROKA officers and men at the front, who had been under fierce attack and suffered casualties until a few hours before the armistice, must have been relieved.

The day before the armistice was signed, UN Commander Clark asked Rhee to reassure the nonrepatriate North Korean prisoners of war that they would not be forced to return to the North. At first Rhee said that he intended to make a public announcement that his administration would "cooperate with the armistice."[127] However, South Korean press reports on July 29 headlined the president's strident determination to "Accomplish Unification" and his appeal to North Koreans not to despair. Rhee said he had opposed the armistice from a conviction that it would bring greater suffering and destruction and be the prelude to another Communist attack. Now that an armistice had been signed, Rhee said he hoped his assessment was wrong. To achieve the liberation of northern Korea and national unification peacefully the South would not obstruct a political conference, he said. The United States and the Republic of Korea were in accord on effective cooperation and assistance. Rhee urged North Koreans not to abandon hope and promised not to forget their plight. The Republic of Korea remained determined to rescue the North and the United Nations had promised to help, he stated.[128]

The *New York Times* wrote: "If the political conference with the Communists failed to reach a unification agreement acceptable to him, Dr. Rhee's statement said, 'we and the whole world will come to fully realize the futility of peaceful means in solving our problems and then we will be able to pursue our own method of achieving unification with the complete sympathy of world opinion.'"[129] James Reston of the *Times* interviewed Rhee on July 29: "President Syngman Rhee of the Republic of Korea said today it was 'inconceivable' that the United States would fail to reopen the Korean war if the Communists refused to agree to the reunification of this country. . . . The President was fierce in his condemnation of those who were 'foolish enough to believe' there was any way to settle the Korean question by 'peaceful means.'" Rhee "made it clear that in his mind the truce was a 'temporary' expedient designed to achieve one end only, one objective—agreement by the Communists that all Korea should be governed by his regime." Rhee's former personal secretary Robert Oliver was present at the interview with Reston.[130]

On July 28 the new Soviet ambassador to China, Vasilii Kuznetsov, conveyed to Mao Zedong congratulations on the armistice from Malenkov and Molotov. Mao told Kuznetsov that America had been forced into an armistice by a combination of military, political, and economic factors. US forces had not mounted an offensive for the last year and had been unable to hold their defensive positions on the battlefield, Mao said. From a purely military viewpoint, Mao argued, the Communists probably should hammer the UN Command for about another year and gain a military demarcation line along the Han River.[131] Mao was repentant somehow.

Writer Guo Moruo, president of the Chinese Association of the Campaign to Resist America and Assist Korea, led a celebration of the signing of the armistice in Korea at Zhongshan Park Odeum in Beijing. The celebration was attended by 4,500 people.[132] At a meeting of the Central Government People's Committee on September 12, Peng Dehuai made a report, and then Mao spoke. The war was a great victory of enormous significance, Mao said, and listed China's accomplishments: (1) by pushing the Americans back to the 38th parallel and holding positions there, the battlefield had been kept far from the Yalu and Tumen Rivers and a threat was removed from Northeast China; (2) the Chinese military had gained experience, fought US forces for thirty-three months and learned how they operate, and did not fear them; (3) the political consciousness of all Chinese had been raised; and (4) an imperialistic war of aggression against China and a third world war had been delayed.[133] To the leadership in Beijing, the armistice was a great success; the battlefield confrontation with the United States had ended in a draw, the revolution had survived, and China had gained the right to participate in international affairs.

On July 28, the *Izvestiia* newspaper of the Soviet government carried a message from Foreign Minister Molotov to Kim Il Sung and a message from DPRK Vice-Foreign Minister Kim Tong-gon to Molotov on the first page. An editorial on "The Great Victory of the Camp of Peace and Democracy" reflected recent political changes in Moscow.[134] The masses had long awaited an armistice in Korea and believed that a truce there would reduce international tensions and open the way to the resolution of other international problems, the editorial said. The armistice was a major contribution to peace, and success in the difficult negotiations showed that all problems could be settled peacefully. The Soviet government firmly held that all international issues could be settled by negotiations between the countries involved, the editorial stated; the armistice inspired trust in the supporters of the peaceful resolution of international problems. Stalin's successors thus sang the praises of their successful diplomacy.

On July 26, shortly after the armistice was signed, President Eisenhower gave a five-minute speech on national television and radio networks: "For this nation the cost of repelling aggression has been high. . . . It has been paid in terms of tragedy. . . . We have won an armistice on a single battleground— not peace in the world. We may not now relax our guard nor cease our quest." Eisenhower quoted remarks by Abraham Lincoln on the end of the American Civil War. In a separate statement, Secretary of State John Foster Dulles repeated the president's warning and said preserving the right of Communist prisoners to choose where they went after being released was "a victory for the principle of political asylum"; also, unification of Korea had to be achieved by peaceful means.[135] But the US government could not claim the outcome was a victory, given that the declared war aim was not attained.

US troops on the front lines were of course happy to return home. Yet relief at surviving the war was mixed with frustration. Capt. Clyde Fore of the 27th Regimental Combat Team was on a hospital ship returning to the United States when the armistice was signed. "There was no rejoicing—we were just sad and quiet," he said. "This was the first time Americans had ever accepted a no-win war. Everybody else was acclimatized to no-win wars, but we were not. To me, Korea had been an abomination. So many people had died, for what?"[136]

The ROK embassy in Washington held no ceremony to mark the armistice.[137] Americans thought they had been fighting for South Korea's freedom, but the Rhee regime was a far cry from democratic, and it was unappreciative of American sacrifices. The United States tried to forget a war that ended without victory or glory.

The Japan-ROK talks had reopened several months earlier, on April 15, and Kubota Kanichiro spoke for a Yoshida administration that showed no good will toward South Korea. The Korean armistice went unremarked on by the Japanese government. No political party even issued a statement. The only official reaction was by Foreign Minister Okazaki Katsuo in response to a question in the Lower House Foreign Affairs Committee the afternoon of July 27: "As a neighboring country the signing of an armistice is a good development, however, it does not settle all the issues. From this point on I think the political conference will be very important. . . . I do not know if Japan can participate or not. However, as a neighbor Japan will cooperate with [South] Korea and various ties will develop, I think. From the government's point of view we want Japan's intentions as far as possible to be reflected through the participating countries. . . . The United States will probably request Japan to provide materials and so forth for Korea's reconstruction, and I think Japan should cooperate much more than other countries in the Republic of Korea's economic development and postwar recovery."

The *Asahi Shimbun* newspaper reported Okazaki's statement on the front page. An analytical article, "The Korean Armistice and Japan," began innocuously: "The Japanese government response in the Diet and elsewhere showed no sign of concern about the post-armistice situation. The low-key reaction reflects the government's judgment that the armistice will have no sudden impact on Japan." Then the tone turned ominous: "Looking beyond the bland official statements there are dark clouds on the horizon. Self-sustaining economic growth to replace the godsend of special procurements will be difficult."

What optimism there was that the armistice would not hamstring Japan's economic recovery was based on a US guarantee in April 1953 that these special procurements would continue for two years, and on aid expected under the Mutual Security Assistance program. Special procurements for South Korea's recovery were also anticipated. Still, the *Asahi* article concluded that the future of Japan's economy was far from bright.[138] There were obviously economic problems ahead. Bank of Japan Governor Ichimanda Naoto, who had credited special procurements for Japan's earlier recovery, was philosophical at a press conference on July 27: "Although some people talk about economic difficulties to come, it is unfortunate that our economy needed a war in Korea to recover." The story that covered his press conference was headlined "Hard Times Forecast."[139]

The strongest reaction to the armistice in Japan was a jubilant rally by four thousand pro-Pyongyang Koreans at the Hibiya Public Hall on July 27. Across Tokyo at the pro-Seoul Mindan (ROK Association for Korean Residents in Japan) headquarters, the attitude was somber. An armistice without unification was nothing to celebrate.[140] The armistice was unwelcome on Taiwan, too. The Kuomintang had no official reaction until Chiang Kai-shek's message of encouragement to anti-Communist Chinese prisoners on August 3.[141]

The purge trials in North Korea of former SKWP members that began on August 3 were the most important immediate postarmistice developments in this country. In verdicts announced five days later, ten defendants were declared guilty of espionage for the United States and treason, including plotting to overthrow the DPRK. All were sentenced to death: Yi Sung-yop, Cho Il-myong, Yim Hwa, Pak Sung-won, Yi Kan-guk, Pae Chol, Paek Hyong-bok, Cho Yong-bok, Maeng Chong-ho, and Sol Chong-sik. Yun Sun-dal and Yi Won-cho were sentenced to fifteen and twelve years of hard labor, respectively. Pak Chong-ae denounced the southern Communists at the Sixth Plenum of the KWP Central Committee on August 5–9 (the same meeting at which she vilified Ho Ka-i). The Plenum unanimously demanded the expulsion of Pak Hon-yong (who was also behind bars) from the party and prosecution of him for protecting and controlling the Yi Sung-yop spy ring and betrayal of the KWP and the nation. Eight persons were expelled from the party as traitorous subversives: Chu Nyong-ha, Chang Si-u, Pak Hon-yong, Kim O-song (former vice-minister of culture and propaganda), An Ki-song, Kim Kwang-su (vice-minister of light industry), Kim Ung-bin (former head of the Kum Gang Political Institute), and Kwon O-jik. Four former members of the SKWP were dropped from the KWP's Central Committee: Ku Chae-su, Yi Chon-jin, Cho Pok-re, and Yi Chu-sang.[142] Of course, Ho Ka-i, who committed suicide on July 2, was also harshly condemned.[143] The Plenum elected a fifteen-member Standing Committee of the Central Committee. Five members became the Political Committee: Kim Il Sung, Kim Tu-bong, Pak Chong-ae, Pak Chang-ok, and Kim Il. Kim Il Sung was chairman of the KWP, and Pak Chong-ae, Pak Yong-bin, and Kim Il were vice-chairmen. Kim Il Sung completely controlled the government, military, and party.

On August 3, the Communist Party of the Soviet Union's Central Committee approved an aid grant of one billion rubles to the DPRK.[144] Kim Il Sung told Soviet Ambassador Suzdalev on August 12 that he wanted to visit the Soviet Union, and three days later the Presidium of the Central Committee CPSU approved a visit by a North Korean delegation in early September.[145]

The United States and the Republic of Korea signed a provisional mutual defense treaty on August 8 that provided for consultation on appropriate measures if South Korea's independence and security were threatened by an "external armed attack." South Korea granted the United States the right to station "land, air and sea forces" on its territory.[146] The treaty was officially signed in Washington on October 1, 1953.

HUMAN SUFFERING AND PRISONERS OF WAR

The Korean War took an enormous toll on the 30 million Koreans in North and South Korea and the 700,000 Koreans in Manchuria. China and the United States also suffered heavy losses. Accurate figures are still not available, and North Korea never published casualty figures. But David Rees in 1964 cited UN estimates of North Korean dead at 520,000 KPA personnel and one million civilians.[147] Bruce Cumings and Jon Halliday in 1988 put North Korean fatalities at about 500,000 military and more than two million civilians.[148] In my earlier book *Korean War*, I suggested, on the basis of estimates of population change, that North Korea had lost about 2,720,000 people through war-related deaths and refugees who moved to the South. This was 28.4 percent of the DPRK's population in 1949.[149] A large share of the decline was accounted for by people who fled to the South. In 2001 a collection of Soviet Ambassador Razuvaev's reports was published by the Institute of Defense Ministry in the ROK, and a 1954 report about the damages the DPRK suffered during the war contained the following data: deaths from air raids—282,000; abducted to the South or disappeared—796,000; evacuated to China or other "people's democratic" countries—80,000; remained in territories given to the South after the armistice—40,000; mobilized in the army—600,000. The total affected was 1,798,000 people.[150]

Cumings and Halliday estimated South Korean battle-related fatalities at 47,000, with deaths from sickness greater than that, and about a million civilian deaths.[151] The UN Command put ROK military deaths at 237,686.[152] In *Korean War* I calculated a population loss in South Korea of 2,330,000 (including deaths and missing).[153]

The official Chinese figure for Chinese People's Volunteers' combat deaths is 116,000—obviously too low—with another 29,000 Chinese taken prisoner or missing in action.[154] Cumings and Halliday put the figure at one million for Chinese deaths and missing in action.[155] The official US statistic for US war dead is 33,629.[156] Cumings and Halliday, who include deaths from sickness, place the total at 54,246.[157] Reports differed on the number of Soviet pilots killed; one says 110 and another 120. The newest analysis by experts of the General Staff, Russian Federation, that includes antiaircraft gun crews puts total Soviet air force deaths at 315.[158]

Both sides treated prisoners harshly and captivity was a grueling ordeal. Repatriates and anti-Communist prisoners often fought and killed each other in the UN camps. From August 5 to September 6, 1953, the UN Command transferred 75,801 prisoners to Chinese and Korean authorities, while the Communists turned over 12,773 South Korean and US prisoners to the UN side.

On September 23, the UNC transferred to the neutral Indian Custodial Force 22,604 prisoners who rejected repatriation. China and North Korea handed over 359 nonrepatriates.[159] The subsequent disposition of these prisoners was as shown in table 7.3.

On January 21, 1954, 14,209 Chinese POWs left South Korea for Taiwan (the number eventually reached 14,619). As the total number of Chinese POWs, as recorded in December 1951, was 20,700, a full two-thirds went to

Table 7.3.

Chinese and North Korean troops	22,604
Repatriated to PRC or DPRK	629
Returned to UN Command	21,820
Escaped and missing	13
Died in Indian custody	38
Remaining in Indian custody	18
Shipped to India	86
UN Command troops	**359**
Returned to UN Command	9
Returned to DPRK or PRC	347
Escaped	1
Shipped to India	2

Taiwan, and only 6,081 returned to the PRC. This was a great propaganda triumph for the Republic of China.

Hailed as heroes and "anticommunist warriors," January 23, the date they arrived in Taiwan, became "123 Freedom Day." All over the island, welcome bells rang out at noon, and the prisoners issued a "Declaration of Freedom." The next day Chiang Kai-shek thanked Syngman Rhee for sending the prisoners and said that their voluntary choice of the Republic of China proved that the democratic nations had taken the initiative. Given the opportunity, compatriots on the Chinese mainland would fight for freedom, Chiang said.[160] Many ex-prisoners had themselves tattooed with slogans such as "oppose Communism, resist Russia" (*fangong kange*), "exterminate communism" (*miegong*), and "resolutely oppose Communism" (*jianjue fangong*). The tattoos attested to the prisoners' intense emotions and desire to demonstrate loyalty to the Chiang regime. A movie, *Fourteen Thousand Witnesses,* was made about the prisoners, and to this day, every January 23 is commemorated on Taiwan as "123 Freedom Day."[161]

Although the People's Republic initially acclaimed the six thousand POWs who returned to the mainland, the atmosphere quickly changed. The prisoners who had surrendered to the enemy were deemed to have cooperated with it; revealing your name and unit was branded as disclosing military secrets. The POWs were investigated for collaboration and many were removed from military and party rolls.[162] Wei Lin, for example, who at age eleven had headed a PLA children's unit and served in Korea as a regimental vice-chief of staff, was captured. He was expelled from the army and party upon repatriation. His military status was later restored, but his application to rejoin the party in 1960 was rejected. Wei Lin was finally readmitted in 1980.[163]

Many other former Chinese POWs suffered a similar fate. In March 1979, when the reform era of Deng Xiaoping was under way, the PLA General Political Department began to reexamine the POW investigations. In September 1980, after recommendations from major party organs, including the Central Commission for Discipline Inspection and the Central Organization Bureau, the Chinese Communist Party's Central Committee authorized a review. Hearings were held that cleared former POWs of disloyalty charges. After living under a cloud for thirty years, many were allowed to rejoin the party.[164]

The approximately 69,000 Korean People's Army prisoners were repatriated to the DPRK, because of 75,801 prisoners of war transferred into Chinese and North Korean hands, only 6,081 were Chinese. As the total number of KPA POWs, as recorded in December 1951, was 111,773, almost 42,000 refused repatriation to the DPRK. They included the 25,000 North Korean POWs who Syngman Rhee released unilaterally. North Korea had a tradition, from the earlier guerilla operations against the Japanese Imperial Army in Manchuria, of strict discipline. There Japanese army and armed police took prisoners only to make them Japanese agents. As in China, a cruel fate thus probably awaited Korean War returnees to the North. With former members of the SKWP being tried for treason or purged, one can easily imagine that North Korean POWs faced a fate similar to that of their Chinese comrades. The grim Soviet precedent was also an ominous portent. Soviet prisoners held by the Germans who returned to Russia after the Third Reich surrendered in World War II were sent directly to Soviet prison camps.

According to South Korean researcher Heo Man-ho, the ROK government received 8,341 prisoners of war from the DPRK. But Heo challenged the North Korean statistics. He cited the records at the Republic of Korea National Cemetery which show that 102,384 men were missing in action from the three branches of the ROK armed forces. Heo Man-ho put the number of South Korean MIAs in 1951 at 88,000 and estimated that 80 percent were taken prisoner.[165] North Korea probably regarded these South Korean soldiers as loyal supporters who voluntarily joined the KPA, not as prisoners. Whether these men willingly changed sides or were forced to fight for the North, tens of thousands of former ROK soldiers were thus separated from their families.

Twenty-three US prisoners of war were attracted to revolutionary China and refused repatriation.[166] Pvt. James Veneris, for example, was from a Greek immigrant worker's family. In China he was a laborer, married twice to Chinese women, and had children. In September 2001, a Japanese newspaper reported that at age seventy-nine he was teaching English at Shandong University.[167] British prisoner George Blake, an intelligence officer at the

British Legation in Seoul, was captured when the KPA seized the capital in 1950. In captivity he read Lenin's *The State and Revolution* and Marx's *Das Kapital* and was influenced by Communist ideology. Blake was critical of the Rhee regime and thought war inhumane, but he was not sympathetic to North Korea. He returned to the United Kingdom, was hired by M16, and became a double agent for Soviet intelligence.[168]

THE ARMISTICE SYSTEM

The armistice agreement signed in late July 1953 established a demilitarized zone two kilometers north and south of the military demarcation line, under the authority of a Military Armistice Commission made up of five senior officers from the UN Command and five jointly appointed by the CPV and KPA.[169] A Neutral Nations Supervisory Commission was also created. The UN Command nominated Sweden and Switzerland to the commission, and China and North Korea named Poland and Czechoslovakia. Article IV of the armistice agreement stipulated: "In order to insure the peaceful settlement of the Korean question, the military Commanders of both sides hereby recommend to the governments of the countries concerned on both sides that, within three (3) months after the Armistice Agreement is signed and becomes effective, a political conference of a higher level of both sides be held by representatives appointed respectively to settle through negotiation the questions of the withdrawal of all foreign forces from Korea, the peaceful settlement of the Korean question, etc." Article V, Clause 62, stated: "this Armistice Agreement shall remain in effect until expressly superseded either by mutually acceptable amendments and additions or by provision in an appropriate agreement for a peaceful settlement at a political level between both sides."[170] Thus, until the political conference reached an "appropriate agreement for a peaceful settlement," the armistice system would remain in effect.

The preliminary meeting of the political conference opened at Panmunjom on October 26. Huang Hua, the senior Chinese delegate, led the Communist side and dominated DPRK representative Ki Sok-pok (a Soviet Korean). Huang Hua proposed that the Soviet Union and India participate as neutral nations and that the political conference be held in New Delhi. The United States insisted that the Soviet Union was a cobelligerent with China and North Korea and thus was not a neutral nation.[171] As a result, the preliminary meetings were stalemated and indefinitely suspended in January 1954.

The foreign ministers of the United States, Great Britain, France, and the Soviet Union met in Berlin in January 1954 to discuss issues pertaining to Germany and Austria. On February 8, they announced an agreement to hold a conference in Geneva to resolve Asian issues too, and they invited China, the two Koreas, and other belligerents in Korea to participate.[172] The Geneva Conference was to be first the Korean political conference and second the peace conference for the Indochina War.

The Geneva Conference began on April 26, 1954. The next day, the two Korean governments announced their terms for unification. The ROK representative insisted that free elections be held only in the North, because UN-supervised elections had already been held in the South in May 1948, and that the DPRK be incorporated into the Republic of Korea.[173] The United States had rejected this stance when the UN Command crossed the 38th parallel in October 1950, but now immediately endorsed it.[174] Washington had promised to back this position to get the ROK to join the Geneva Conference. North Korean delegate Nam Il made a five-point proposal: (1) establishment of an all-Korea commission and a unified government through a peninsula-wide election; (2) enactment of an election law by representatives of the all-Korean commission and representatives of large social organizations; (3) promotion of economic exchange between the South and North; (4) withdrawal of all foreign forces within six months; and (5) no interference in the election by the United Nations, which had been a belligerent in the war and was not neutral.[175] China and the Soviet Union championed the proposal.[176]

Representatives of the belligerent countries which joined the UN forces except the United States disagreed with the ROK-US proposal that elections be held only in the North and favored a Korea-wide election. On May 23 the ROK presented a revised fourteen-point proposal that called for Korea-wide elections under UN supervision.[177] Per the proposal, the ROK constitution would remain in effect until revised by a unified National Assembly. Another provision of the ROK's proposal said that Chinese forces should be withdrawn a month before the nationwide election, whereas the withdrawal of UN forces would begin before the election but not be completed until the United Nations controlled all of Korea. North Korea, China, and the Soviet Union rejected this plan. On June 15 the Representatives of belligerent countries on the UN side issued a final "Declaration by the Sixteen" stating that there was no purpose to further negotiations.[178]

Peace talks on the Korean question were now over and the armistice system became permanent. The war had started because unification could not be achieved peacefully, but use of military force had failed, and diplomacy had achieved nothing at the conference table. As a result, huge armies faced each other uneasily across the military demarcation line just as they had when the ceasefire started in 1953. Divided into two hostile states, the Korean Peninsula was neither at peace nor at war.

Chapter Eight

Postwar Northeast Asia

THE KOREAS

The war to unify the Korean Peninsula ended in an armistice near the 38th parallel at almost the same place Korea was divided in 1945. In the west, the military demarcation line dipped below the parallel. Pyongyang gained the Kaesong area and the Ongjin Peninsula. In the east, the line was above the parallel and Seoul acquired the southern half of Chorwon County and Yang-gu, Inje, and Kosong Counties. The territorial losses and gains were almost even.

The legacy of war was massive destruction and death. Gutted buildings and shattered towns dotted the peninsula. Savagely bombed by the United States, the North was particularly devastated; the destruction there was widespread and severe. Brig. Gen. Don Z. Zimmerman, deputy for intelligence of the Far East Air Force, observed, "The degree of destruction suffered by North Korea, in relation to its resources, was greater than that which the Japanese islands suffered in World War."[1] Pyongyang was completely destroyed; not a trace of the prewar capital was left intact. A new city which was to be reborn from the ashes was destined to be completely severed from its past.

The total number of fatalities will never be known. Deaths from combat in the two Koreas are estimated at three to four million, higher than the three million Japanese killed in the Pacific War (1931–1945). The combined population of the South and North on June 1, 1949, was 28,650,000.[2] More than 10 percent of the combined population was killed. Many more were wounded and displaced. In addition to the deaths from land combat and aerial bombing, a large number of people were simply massacred on both sides. When cities changed hands, the new occupiers found piles of executed prisoners in the prisons. Many entire villages were slaughtered in ideological cleansings.

The armistice in 1953 locked the division of the peninsula into place, separating two societies that then grew further apart. In the North, Christian churches were now empty. Christianity had been vital in the North on the eve of the war. A survey of church schools in Sonchon County, North Pyongan Province, in January 1950 found forty-four churches in the county; the largest, North Church in Sonchon city, had 23 teachers and 263 pupils and students, and offered classes from kindergarten to high school.[3] By 1953, those Christians had disappeared from the North. They were either dead, had fled to the South, or had abandoned their faith, at least in public.

Similarly, the Communist movement was gone from South Korea. The longtime Communists from the colonial period, members of the Southern Workers' Party, college students in Seoul who had collaborated with the DPRK during the occupation in 1950, and the leaders of People's Committees in farm villages who had risen up against landlords had disappeared. They were either dead or had fled North. Communist sympathizers trapped in the South who formed partisan bands on Mt. Chiri and in the Taebaek mountain range were hunted down, murdered, or imprisoned. Marxism became taboo in the South.

The division of the peninsula ripped families apart. Parents, children, and siblings ended up in different halves, some by choice and others by circumstance. About ten million family members and other relatives—nearly a third of the population in 1949—were cut off from each other.

In the South and North, political systems ideologically driven by the nationalisms of Syngman Rhee and Kim Il Sung, respectively, were strengthened through the war. The competition between them for legitimacy now intensified. Hopes for unification receded into a distant future.

The United States became the guarantor of South Korea's security under the US-ROK mutual defense treaty. US troops were stationed in the South, and the US commander, as head of the UN Command, continues to have operational control of ROK military forces today. One purpose of that arrangement was to restrain South Korea, with its eighteen divisions and 650,000 troops, from attacking the North.[4]

North Korea, its population decimated and many of its cities and towns in ruins, struggled to recover from the war. Shattered social and cultural traditions were replaced by norms and practices based on State socialism of the Soviet type. By the beginning of 1956, 950,000 Chinese People's Volunteers left North Korea and the 250,000 of them that remained in the North in 1958 were finally withdrawn by the end of that year. In 1961, the Soviet Union and China concluded mutual security treaties with North Korea. Neither power would countenance another northern invasion of the South. Pyongyang lacked the military power to try to attack the South again in any event; for many years, the KPA was much smaller than the ROKA.[5]

The two states on the Korean Peninsula settled into a hostile standoff. They were incapable of military action against each other on their own. The peninsula was neither at peace nor in a conventional Cold War, where countries at least maintain diplomatic relations. The armistice had stopped the shooting, but a warlike enmity persisted, and without the safety valve of Cold War détente.

THE UNITED STATES

Paul Pierpaoli has made the most insightful observations on the impact of the war on American policy. He writes:

> The conflict greatly affected American foreign policy, national security policy, and domestic policy. In terms of American foreign policy, the impact of the Korean War is hard to overemphasize. . . . The shock of the North Korean invasion and the American decision to intervene in Korea led to the militarization of containment and resulted in a sustained, if sometimes episodic, militarization of American policy.[6]

The change in US foreign policy extended beyond Northeast Asia. The Truman administration began its involvement in Indochina that led to US intervention in Vietnam. Military intervention began in Europe, too. The North Atlantic Treaty Organization was formed in April 1949. As John Lewis Gaddis wrote, it was "as explicit an invitation as has ever been extended from smaller nations to a great power to construct an empire."[7] In December 1950 the Truman administration greatly increased the deployment of US troops to NATO and named Gen. Dwight Eisenhower the supreme NATO commander. NATO members, European countries, were now politically dominated by, and economically dependent on, the United States. The Truman administration's advocacy of rearming West Germany and membership in NATO gained momentum about this time. As Pierpaoli points out, "the fears unleashed by the war in Korea" led to what had been previously unthinkable—the rearmament of West Germany and Bonn's full participation in NATO.[8]

During the Korean War, US military expenditures rose from 6 percent of Gross National Product in 1950 to 18 percent by 1953. In 1950 US military forces consisted of ten army divisions and twelve regiments of special troops, two hundred navy warships and seven carrier air groups, two marine divisions, and forty-eight air force wings. But by January 1953 there were twenty-one full-strength army divisions, four hundred navy warships and sixteen carrier air groups, three marine divisions, and one hundred air force wings.

Total troop strength reached 3.5 million, double the figure in June 1950. Industrial production also rapidly increased. Aircraft production reached one thousand airplanes a month, four times the output in mid-1950.[9]

The United States was now equipped to fight two wars simultaneously on the scale of Korea, one in Asia and another in Europe. And presidential authority had vastly expanded. The United States had become a military empire. In Korea, for the first time in American history, a president had sent forces overseas and waged war for years without congressional approval. The United States created a network of military bases all over the world and stationed its military forces in these bases.

War and militarization meanwhile distorted domestic American politics as McCarthyism flourished in an atmosphere of fear and suspicion. In fact, the era of McCarthyism in America was impossible without the Korean War. In 1945, in the Republican-dominated Congress after World War II, the House Committee on Un-American Activities (HUAC) became a permanent committee, and the Congress went on a hunt for Reds, including in the entertainment industry. In the most famous case, a group of writers and directors who refused to cooperate with the committee, the Hollywood Ten, was convicted in a federal court in 1949 of contempt of Congress. In February 1950, Republican Senator Joseph McCarthy claimed that a Communist espionage ring was operating in the State Department. McCarthy and HUAC captured public attention and gained influence during the Korean War. Herbert Norman, a Canadian diplomat in Tokyo and a respected historian of modern Japan, was questioned in October 1950 about accusations in the US Senate that he was a member of the Communist Party and a spy. Director Elia Kazan, who was among those who protected colleagues in 1947, later testified against associates in a closed HUAC session in 1952.[10]

Korea was the first war the United States did not win. Though waged against Communist expansion, it was difficult to justify it as a crusade for freedom and democracy, given the dictatorial regime in Seoul. Despite transformation of the American political economy and society, the conflict became "the forgotten war." The Korean War Veterans Memorial on the Mall in Washington, DC, was not dedicated until 1995, after the Vietnam Veterans Memorial was erected and the Republic of Korea had become a democracy.

THE SOVIET UNION

If the United States was obviously affected by the Korean War, change went largely unnoticed in the Soviet Union. Yet the transformation that started there in 1949 was equally profound.

The proximate causes were the Chinese revolution and the armed clashes at the 38th parallel in Korea. On October 26, 1948, the Ministry of State

Security and the Prosecutor's Office jointly ordered the arrests of members of former opposition factions, the White Army, nationalists, and others who had previously been arrested for spying or subversive activities. In 1949 these "repeaters" (*vtorniki*) were sent to gulags.[11] In the Politburo, accusations against P. S. Popkov, first secretary of the Leningrad Party Organization, for "anti-state" actions led to a large-scale purge that included the arrests of A. A. Kuznetsov and N. A. Voznesenskii, former leaders of the Leningrad Party Organization. A crackdown on the Jewish Anti-Fascist Committee began in late 1948, and in January 1949 former Vice-Minister of Foreign Affairs S. A. Lozovskii was arrested for alleged contacts with American spies. A wave of arrests followed. A campaign to discredit Jewish intellectuals in the form of attacks on "cosmopolitanism" began later that year.

By withdrawing his support for Chiang Kai-shek and openly endorsing Mao Zedong in 1949, Stalin moved with trepidation toward a showdown with the United States in the Far East. When North Korea sought approval that year to attack the South, Stalin refused. He worried that the Republic of Korea might then attack the North. In August 1949, Soviet scientists successfully tested a fission weapon, breaking the US monopoly on nuclear weapons. Still fearful of the United States' superior capacity to employ nuclear weapons on the battlefield, the Soviet Union pressed ahead to develop more powerful weapons.

After deciding to cooperate with the Chinese Communists, Stalin in early 1950 ordered the Japan Communist Party to lead a revolution to cripple the US occupation of Japan. Stalin also began to support Pyongyang's plan to unify Korea.

Meanwhile, Soviet troop strength had declined from 11,360,000 at the end of World War II to 2,870,000 by 1948. Soviet military expenditures, which had reached 128.7 billion rubles in 1944, had fallen by almost half to 73.7 billion rubles by 1946.[12] With the start of the Korean War, they rose rapidly again.

Korea was Stalin's war. He was the chief executive officer whose orders from deep within the Kremlin made the Soviet Union the rear base and workshop that supplied weapons and ammunition on deferred payments to North Korean and Chinese forces. The Soviet air force clashed directly with the US air force in the skies over Korea. Those aerial battles were the first and probably the last US-Soviet war.

In response to the US buildup of NATO, the Soviet Union increased military aid to Eastern Europe and stationed more troops there. Soviet military budgets and troop levels rapidly increased during the Korean War. The 2.87 million men under arms in 1948 had reached 5.76 million by 1955.[13] Arms budgets and production also rapidly increased. The total expenditures of the six Soviet ministries involved with armaments production went from

19 billion rubles in 1950 to 35.6 billion rubles in 1953 to 48.3 billion rubles in 1955.[14]

Officially, the Soviet Union was just a sympathetic bystander in the Korean War. The Soviet press carried a daily roundup of articles under the title "War in Korea" that never mentioned direct Soviet involvement. Moscow's role was completely hidden from the Soviet public. In that sense, the war was more personal to Stalin than the Russo-Japanese war was to Tsar Nicholas II, yet more remote to the Soviet man and woman in the street than the battles of the Tsushima Straits and Port Arthur were in 1904–1905. Historian Elena Zubkova writes that in the summer of 1950, rumors that US forces had landed on Sakhalin and the Kurile Islands triggered panic buying of matches, salt, and soap in the Soviet Far East. Elsewhere in the Soviet Union, there was no sense of imminent danger. But anxiety that the United States and the Soviet Union might go to war against each other existed everywhere. When fighting broke out in Korea, many Soviet citizens signed the Stockholm Peace Appeal for a ban on nuclear weapons. Rumors of imminent hostilities with the United States now circulated among the Soviet public.[15]

The crackdown in the Soviet Union on alleged spies and enemy agents that began in the late 1940s continued during the war. Six defendants, former leaders of the Leningrad regional party committee, were tried on September 29–30, 1950, found guilty of antiparty activities and treason, and executed. Arrests of party members in Leningrad continued in 1951 and 1952. Members of the Jewish Anti-Fascist Committee went on trial from May 8 to July 18, 1952, and ten persons were sentenced to death. A total of 110 Jews were punished, including Molotov's Jewish wife, Polina Zhemchuzhina, who was convicted of treason. The infamous arrests of Jewish doctors in the Kremlin hospital began in late 1952 and the Doctors' Plot was made public in January 1953. In preparation for a collision between the Soviet Union and the United States, Jews—potential spies for the CIA—were hunted down and arrested.

As in the United States, the Korean War engendered a sense in the Soviet Union of an impending struggle for survival against an implacable enemy, and the country was transfigured into a militarized state. Yet Stalin's senior colleagues, the bureaucracy, and the general public in the Soviet Union were distanced from the conflict. To them, the Korean War was too adventurous. Stalin was at odds with many in the inner circle and isolated from the people. When he died on the eve of the armistice, his successors adopted a policy of peaceful coexistence and began to dismantle parts of the Soviet system.

US and Soviet conventional arms were a match for each other in Korea, and both sides learned the strengths and weaknesses of the other's arsenal. As the Cold War continued, the two garrison states rushed into an arms race to acquire supremacy in nuclear weapons and missiles.

CHINA

The Korean War was virtually a Sino-US war in Korea. An official Chinese history of this war calls it a "comprehensive test of [American and Chinese] military, political, economic, and diplomatic strength."[16] By that standard, the outcome can be considered a draw. The young, revolutionary People's Republic of China suffered enormous casualties, but secured its place as a force to be reckoned with in the international community. Fighting under the name of the Chinese People's Volunteers, the PLA was "hardened in modern warfare"[17] against US forces and matured into a conventional army capable of holding its own on the contemporary battlefield. In that sense, the PRC gained much from the war and may be considered the victor, despite taking much higher casualties than US forces. Internally, the experience of a total war and national mobilization for war accelerated China's implementation of Soviet-style state socialist changes such as the first Five-Year Plan (1953–1957), the collectivization of agriculture, and nationalization of industry, establishing a social foundation for the party state and state socialism.

US intervention in the Taiwan Straits in June 1950 to protect the Chiang Kai-shek regime, of course, forced the PRC to abort plans for the liberation of Taiwan. Yet with the outbreak of war in Korea, in October 1950 Beijing sent PLA units to Tibet and extended Chinese sovereignty to that area in September 1951. Tibet was incorporated as an autonomous region of China.

The confrontation with the United States persisted after the Korean War armistice of 1953 as China sided with Communist nationalists in East Asia, while the United States supported non-Communist nationalists and anti-Communists. The competition escalated from providing arms and political support to war, with Vietnam as the prime example. China responded to the expansive US role in South Vietnam by intervening in the Vietnamese civil war in 1963 and providing extensive assistance for Hanoi.[18] Outside the Soviet bloc, with the United Kingdom and some Asian countries as exceptions, Communist China came to be regarded as an outlaw state until it was finally admitted to the United Nations in 1971.

TAIWAN

The Republic of China (ROC) benefited from US military intervention at the start of the Korean War. The appearance of the US 7th Fleet in the Taiwan Straits saved threatened Taiwan. Chiang Kai-shek's repeated offers of troops to fight in Korea were then rejected by the United States, with the result that the ROC gained enormously from the war at no cost to itself. With backing from the United States, the ROC concluded a peace treaty with Japan that aided Taiwan's international legitimacy. The price, however, was abandonment of claims for reparations for Japan's earlier invasion and occupation of China, a concession to Tokyo with great repercussions, including freeing Japan from heavy pressure to provide large reparations to mainland China.

Direct ROC involvement in Korea was twofold: personnel from Taiwan interviewed Chinese POWs in South Korea, and two-thirds of these prisoners chose to resettle in Taiwan, no small victory in the ideological struggle of the time. The armistice was nevertheless a bitter pill for Chiang Kai-shek. He had hoped the Korean War would escalate into World War III, enabling the Kuomintang to invade the mainland and defeat the Communists. But a return to the mainland was always an illusion, and the "lost" opportunity was a blessing in disguise for Taiwan, as evidenced by the island's rapid economic development and social transformation. As a result of the Korean War, however, the rivalry between the PRC and Taiwan became entangled with the enmity between the two Korean states.

JAPAN

Speaking of beneficiaries of the Korean War, Japan can be called the greatest one of all. A lasting political system and economic base were built during the conflict. After the defeat of Imperial Japan in World War II, strong pacifist and antimilitary sentiment took root in people's minds, and the public supported Article 9, the no-war clause in the 1947 Japanese constitution. According to the preamble of the constitution, the "security and existence" of a disarmed Japan was to be guaranteed by "the justice and faith of the peace-loving peoples," basically the Allied Powers: the United States, United Kingdom, Republic of China, and Soviet Union. But Mao Zedong's revolution had banished the Nationalists to Taiwan, and war between the United States and the People's Republic of China in Korea undermined the no-war precondition of Article 9. With war raging in a neighboring country, the Japanese people might naturally have considered revising Article 9, rearming to defend Japan, and aiding the Republic of Korea militarily.

But Prime Minister Yoshida understood both the constitutional constraints on militarism and the public's aversion to it, and held back from directly involving Japan on the battlefield in Korea. He drew the line at compliance with Occupation orders and providing bases for US forces throughout the Japanese archipelago. And in the negotiations for a post–World War II peace treaty, Yoshida only agreed to create lightly armed forces, and he concluded a bilateral security treaty with the United States that enabled US forces to remain in Japan in return for a security guarantee.

Under Yoshida's leadership, Japan profited tremendously from its neighbors' war without direct military participation. Progressive political parties, which represented popular sentiment, defended Article 9, opposed an active role in the war and rearmament, fought for a Japanese peace treaty that included the Soviet Union and China, and took issue with the Japan-US security treaty. Through a particular balance between the conservative Yoshida administration and the progressive opposition, Japan rejected major rearmament and established the holy trinity of Article 9, lightly armed self-defense forces, and the Japan-US security treaty. Embraced by the United States, though dependent on it, Japan enjoyed a long peace in East Asia even as a series of New Asian Wars raged. The holy trinity served as a basis for Japan's economic recovery and later high-speed growth. The Korean War itself, which was widely perceived as a "fire across the river" because no Japanese forces were engaged, fueled Japan's rapid economic growth in the 1950s and 1960s.

Shielded by its bilateral alliance with the United States and urged on by Washington, Japan concluded a peace treaty with the Republic of China and held normalization talks with the ROK. Taking advantage of Chiang Kai-shek's weakness to compel the Republic of China to abandon claims for reparations can also be seen as a Japanese diplomatic triumph, despite the damage to future relations with China.

However, the lack of sympathy in Japan for the Republic of Korea and the Korean people as a whole during the Korean War left the Japanese people unaware of their role in support of the US war in Korea even as Japan avoided direct engagement. Granted, solidarity with Taiwan and South Korea would have brought Japan into an anti-Communist military alliance that the Japanese government was reluctant to seal and which the Japanese people adamantly opposed. But there was indifference to the fate of the neighbors and the region. Even inhabitants of Tokyo were virtually unaware that B-29s continued to bomb North Korea from Yokota Air Base in Tokyo right up to the armistice.

THE LEGACY OF THE KOREAN WAR

The Northeast Asian geopolitical system and the new version of the global Cold War which were born out of the Korean War remained virtually intact in the 1960s and contributed to the Vietnam War, the third in a series of the New Asian Wars following the Chinese civil war and the Korean War. Though Sino-Soviet disagreements were growing, China and the Soviet Union both assisted North Vietnam. But in a crucial moment of the Vietnam War, the United States government, desperate for a diplomatic way out of the Vietnamese impasse, took a bold step to seek reconciliation with China, its main foe in Asia. President Nixon visited Beijing and shook hands with Mao Zedong in February 1972. Japanese Prime Minister Tanaka Kakuei then flew to Beijing in September of that year and established diplomatic relations with the PRC, annulling Japan's 1951 peace treaty with the ROC. The North Vietnamese, of course, grew closer to the Soviet Union after Nixon's rapprochement with China. Nevertheless, the United States was defeated ignominiously in Vietnam and Saigon fell in April 1975. South Korean military leaders who fought with American forces in Vietnam were disgraced and lost face with their own people. A small yet brave democratic movement of students and Christians grew in South Korea and finally in 1987 gave birth to a national democratic revolution.

In the Soviet Union, the reform process known as "Perestroika" began impressively in 1987. The Cold War was declared over, and the demise of the State socialist system called the Soviet Union followed. After the end of Soviet Communism and the dissolution of the Soviet empire, China developed a market economy while strengthening its one-party-state under Communist rule. By the end of the first decade of the new millennium, China had become the second greatest economic power in the world after the United States.

The United Nations Command during the war included sixteen nations: the United States, ROK, the United Kingdom, Canada, Australia, New Zealand, the Philippines, Thailand, France, Greece, the Netherlands, Belgium, Luxemburg, Turkey, Ethiopia, and Colombia. The PRC now has diplomatic relations with all sixteen of these countries. To China, the Korean War and the Sino-American War had ended. The DPRK managed to establish diplomatic relations with thirteen of the sixteen countries, all except the United States, the ROK, and France. The last hidden belligerent country which fought on the Communist side, the Soviet Union, succeeded in establishing diplomatic relations with the ROK on the eve of her demise. But an invisible participant of the war on the US side, Japan, has not yet normalized its relations with the DPRK, which was also a victim of Japan's thirty-five-year colonial rule.

Thus, Northeast Asia had changed substantially. In the year 2013, the sixtieth anniversary of the Korean War armistice, a totally different regional landscape exists. Relations between the ROK and the DPRK changed substantially after the Pyongyang Summit in June 2000. Both of them now recognize each other, though mutual relations are strained.

But the United States' wars in Afghanistan and Iraq and President George W. Bush's labeling of the DPRK as a member of the Axis of Evil posed critical problems for the DPRK. The relationship between the DPRK and the United States remains volatile and problematic. And the DPRK's relationship with Japan, which deteriorated in the last decade, is another source of tension. North Korea has not had a chance of normalizing her relations with the United States and Japan. Today, the DPRK, pretending to be a nuclear power, looks totally helpless, perpetually intimidating the United States with aggressive words and military performances and at the same time longing impatiently for dialogue with this giant state. The DPRK's abnormal relationships with the United States and Japan are critical legacies of the Korean War. They hinder a truly new Northeast Asia from emerging. Reconciliation must be brought in this region to put the Korean War to rest as the final legacy of the deadly Cold War era in the Asia-Pacific.

Notes

PREFACE: THE KOREAN WAR:
ITS ORIGINS AND LEGACY

1. I. F. Stone, *The Hidden History of the Korean War* (New York: Monthly Review Press, 1952).
2. Allen S. Whiting, *China Crosses the Yalu: The Decision to Enter the Korean War* (New York: Macmillan, 1960).
3. Roy E. Appleman, *South to the Naktong, North to the Yalu (June–November 1950)* (Washington, DC: Center of Military History, US Army, 1961; 1992).
4. Robert F. Futrell, *The United States Air Force in Korea, 1950–1953* (New York: Duell, Sloan and Pearce,1961).
5. Shinobu Seizaburo, "Gendaishi no kakki toshite no Chosen senso" [The Korean War: a turning point in modern history], *Sekai*, August 1965; and Shinobu Seizaburo, *Chosen senso no boppatsu* [The start of the Korean War] (Tokyo: Fukumura Shuppan, 1969).
6. Kamiya Fuji, *Chosen senso* [The Korean War] (Tokyo: Chuo Koronsha, 1966); and Okonogi Masao, "Minzoku kaiho senso toshite no Chosen senso" [The Korean War as a war of national liberation], *Kokusai Mondai* 182, 1975.
7. *Foreign Relations of the United States, 1950*, vol. 7 (Washington, 1976). (Hereafter *FRUS.*)
8. William W. Stueck Jr., *The Road to Confrontation: American Policy toward China and Korea, 1947–1950* (University of North Carolina Press, 1981); and James I. Matray, *The Reluctant Crusade: American Foreign Policy in Korea, 1941–1950* (University of Hawaii Press, 1985).
9. Okonogi Masao, *Chosen senso: Beikoku no kainyu katei* [The Korean War: The process of the United States intervention] (Tokyo: Chuo Koronsha, 1986).
10. Bruce Cumings, *The Origins of the Korean War: Liberation and the Emergence of Separate Regimes, 1945–1947* (Princeton University Press, 1981), and Cumings, *The Origins of the Korean War, Vol. 2, The Roaring of the Cataract, 1947–1950* (Princeton University Press, 1990).
11. Ibid., vol. 2, 619, 621.
12. Pang Sun-joo, "Nohoek pukhan pipchamunso haeje" [Captured North Korean materials with commentary] (1), *Asea Munhwa*. First issue, Institute of Asian Culture, Hallym University, 1986.

13. Jon Halliday and Bruce Cumings, *Korea: The Unknown War* (New York: Penguin Books, 1988).

14. Gavan McCormack, *Cold War, Hot War* (Sydney: Hale and Iremonger, 1983).

15. Callum A. MacDonald, *Korea: The War before Vietnam* (London: Macmillan, 1986).

16. *FRUS, 1951*, vol. 7, part 1–2 (Washington, 1983); and *FRUS, 1952–1954*, vol. 15, part 1–2 (Washington, 1984).

17. Rosemary Foot, *A Substitute for Victory: The Politics of Peacemaking at the Korean Armistice Talks* (Cornell University Press, 1990).

18. Billy C. Mossman, *Ebb and Flow, November 1950–July 1951* (Washington, DC: Center of Military History, US Army, 1990).

19. Sasaki Harutaka, *Chosen senso: Kankoku-hen* [The Korean War; Republic of Korea], 3 vols. (Tokyo: Hara Shobo, 1976).

20. Kim Hak-joon, *Chosen senso; tsukon no minzoku shototsu* [The Korean War: a tragic clash], trans. Kaneda Mitsuto, (Tokyo: Saimaru Shuppankai, 1991).

21. Wada Haruki, "Chosen senso o kangaeru" [Rethinking the Korean War], *Shiso* (May 1990).

22. Xu Yan, *Diyici jiaoliang: kangmei yuanchao zhanzheng de lishi huigu yu fansi* [The first test of strength: a historical review and evaluation of the war to resist America and assist Korea] (Beijing: Chinese Broadcasting and Television Press, 1990); Qi Dexue, *Chaoxian zhanzheng juece neimu* [Inside story of decision making during the Korean War] (Shenyang: Liaoning University Press, 1991); Heng Xueming, *Shengsi sanba xian: Zhongguo zhiyuanjun zai Chaoxian zhanzheng shimo* [Life and death on the 38th parallel: the Chinese volunteers in the Korean War] (Anhui: Anhui Literature Publisher, 1992).

23. Shu Ken Ei (Zhu Jianrong), *Mo Taku To no Chosen senso* [Mao Zedong's Korean War] (Tokyo: Iwanami Shoten, 1991).

24. Wada Haruki, "Chosen senso o kangaeru" [Rethinking the Korean War], *Shiso* (May, June, July, 1993).

25. Chen Jian, *China's Road to the Korean War: The Making of the Sino-American Confrontation* (NY: Columbia University Press, 1994); and Shu Guang Zhang, *Mao's Military Romanticism: China and the Korean War, 1950–1953* (University of Kansas Press, 1995).

26. Wada Haruki, *Chosen senso* [The Korean War] (Tokyo: Iwanami Shoten, 1995).

27. Hagiwara Ryo, *Chosen senso: Kin Nichi-sei to Makassa no inbo* [The Korean War: a conspiracy by Kim Il Sung and Gen. Douglas MacArthur] (Tokyo: Bungei Shunju, 1993).

28. Park Myung-lim, *Hanguk chonjaengui palbal kwa kiwon* [The outbreak of the Korean War and its origins], vol. 1–2 (Seoul: Nanamu Chulpan, 1996).

29. Suh Dong-man, "Kita Chosen ni okeru shakaishugi no seiritsu" [The establishment of socialism in North Korea] (PhD diss., University of Tokyo, 1995).

30. Kathryn Weathersby, "New Russian Documents on the Korean War," *Cold War International History Project Bulletin* no. 6–7 (Winter 1995/1996): 30–84, hereinafter *CWIHP Bulletin*; Alexandre Y. Mansourov, "Stalin, Mao, Kim, and China's Decision to Enter the Korean War, Sept. 16–Oct. 15, 1950: New Evidence from the Russian Archives," Ibid., 94–119; Kathryn Weathersby, "Stalin and a Negotiated Settlement in Korea, 1950–1953" (paper presented at the International Conference on the New Evidence on the Cold War in Asia, Hong Kong, Jan. 9–12, 1996); and Alexandre Y. Mansourov, "Soviet-North Korean Relations and the Origins of the Korean War," Ibid.

31. Haruki Wada, "Stalin and the Japanese Communist Party, 1945–1953: In the Light of New Russian Archival Documents" (paper presented at the International Conference on the New Evidence on the Cold War in Asia, Hong Kong, Jan. 9–12, 1996). See also my essays, "Rekishi toshiteno Nosaka Sanzo" [Nosaka Sanzo as history], *Shiso* (March, April, and May, 1994). Later Wada Haruki, *Rekishi toshiteno Nosaka Sanzo* (Tokyo: Heibonsha, 1996).

32. This document was obtained by the British Broadcasting Corporation in 1994 and is included in Weathersby's article in *CWIHP Bulletin* no. 6–7 (Winter 1995/1996): 39–40. It was also obtained by the Sankei Shimbun and made public with other materials in *Seiron*, November 1995, 110–116, and December 1995, 228–241.

33. *CWIHP Bulletin* no. 11 (Winter 1998): 176–185. See also Milton Leitenberg, "New Russian Evidence on the Korean War Biological Warfare Allegations: Background and Analysis," Ibid., 185–199.

34. Evgenii Bajanov and Natalia Bajanova, *Soryonui charyoro pon Hanguk chonjaengui chonmal* [The Korean War as seen in Soviet documents] (Seoul: Toso chulpan Yollim, 1998).

35. A. V. Torkunov, *Zagadochnaia voina: Koreiskii konflikt 1950–1953 godov* [An enigmatic war: the Korean conflict, 1950–1953] (Moscow, 2000).

36. Trans. Shimotomai Nobuo and others, *Chosen senso no nazo to shinjitsu; Kin Nichi-sei, Sutarin, Mo Taku To no kimitsu denbun ni yoru* [Enigmas and reality of the Korean War in the secret cables of Kim Il Sung, Stalin, and Mao Zedong] (Tokyo: Soshisha, 2001).

37. Kathryn Weathersby, "Stalin, Mao, and the End of the Korean War," in *Brothers in Arms: The Rise and Fall of the Sino-Soviet Alliance, 1945–1963*, ed. Odd Arne Westad (Stanford University Press, 1998), 96–116.

38. Cumings' letter to Weathersby, July 11, 1995 and Weathersby's reply to Cumings, in *CWIHP Bulletin* no. 6–7 (Winter 1995/1996): 120–122.

39. Bruce Cumings, *The Korean War: A History* (New York: The Modern Library, 2010), 9.

40. Alexandre Y. Mansourov, "Communist War Coalition Formation and the Origins of the Korean War" (PhD diss., Columbia University, 1997).

41. Vojtech Mastny, *The Cold War and Soviet Insecurity: The Stalin Years* (Oxford University Press, 1996).

42. Shen Zhihua, *Zhongsu tongmeng yu Chaoxian zhanzheng yanjiu* [Studies on the Sino-Soviet alliance and the Korean War] (Guilin: Guangxi Pedagogical University Press, 1999).

43. Wada, *Hanguk chonjaeng* [The Korean War], trans. Suh Dong-man (Seoul: Changjak kwa Pipyongsa, 1999).

44. Academy of Military Sciences, Military Historical Studies Section, *Kangmei yuanchao zhangzhengshi* [A history of the war to resist America and aid Korea], vols. 1–3 (Beijing: Military Sciences Press, 2000).

45. Pang Xianzhi and Li Jie, *Mao Zedong yu kangmei yuanchao* [Mao Zedong and the cause of resistance to America and aid to Korea] (Beijing: The Central Press of Historical Documents, 2000).

46. Chen Jian, *Mao's China and the Cold War* (Chapel Hill: University of North Carolina Press, 2001).

47. Wada Haruki, "The Korean War, Stalin's Policy, and Japan," *Social Science Japan Journal* 1, no. 1 (1998).

48. Yamazaki Shizuo, *Shijitsu de kataru Chosen senso; kyoryoku no zenbo* [Japan's cooperation in the Korean War] (Tokyo: Hon no Izumi-sha, 1998).

49. Nam Ki-jong, "Chosen senso to Nihon; 'kichi kokka' ni okeru senso to heiwa" [The Korean War and Japan; war and peace in a "military base state"] (PhD diss., University of Tokyo, 2000).

50. Paul G. Pierpaoli, Jr., "Alpha and Omega: Understanding the Meaning of the Korean War" (paper presented at the international symposium, "The Korean War and Searching for Peace on the Korean Peninsula in the 21st Century," Seoul, June 24, 2000).

51. Paul G. Pierpaoli, Jr., *Truman and Korea: The Political Culture of the Early Cold War* (University of Missouri Press, 1999).

52. Heo Man-ho, "Human Rights and Legacies of the Korean War: Civilian Genocide and South Korean POWs Detained in North Korea" (paper presented at international symposium "The Korean War and Searching for Peace on the Korean Peninsula in the 21st Century," Seoul, June 24, 2000).

53. Kim Tong-chun, *Chonjaeng kwa sahoe: uriege Hanguk chonjaengun muosi onna?* [War and society: what was the Korean War to us?] (Seoul: Tolbegae, 2000).

54. Shen Zhihua, *Mao Zedong, Sudalin yu Chaoxian zhanzheng* [Mao Zedong, Stalin and the Korean War] (Guangdong People's Press, 2003), 458–461. English translation: Zihua Shen, *Mao, Stalin and the Korean War: Trilateral Communist Relations in the 1950s* (Milton Park, Abingdon: Routledge, 2012). See also, Shen Zihua, "Sino-North Korean Conflict and its Resolution during the Korean War," *CWIHP Bulletin* no. 14–15 (Winter 2003–Spring 2004): 19–21.

55. Chong Pyong-jun, *Hanguk chonjaeng: 38 son chongdol kwa chonjaengui hyongsong* [The Korean War: clashes at the 38th parallel and formation of the war] (Seoul: Tolbegae, 2006).

56. *Soryon kunsakomundanjang Rajubayep ui 6. 25 chonjaeng pogoso* [Reports from the June 25 War by V. N. Razuvaev, Soviet chief military advisor], vol. 1–3 (Seoul: Institute for Compiling Military History, Defense Ministry, ROK, 2001).

57. Yom In-ho, *To hanaui Hanguk chonjaeng: Manju Chosoninui 'choguk' kwa chonjaeng* [Another Korean War: the fatherland for Manchurian Koreans and the war] (Seoul: Yoksa Pipyongsa, 2010).

58. Park Myung-lim, *Hanguk 1950: chonjaeng kwa pyonghwa* [Korea 1950: war and peace] (Seoul: Nanamu Chulpan, 2002).

59. "Russian Documents on the Korean War: 1950–53," introduction by James Hershberg and translation by Vladislav Zubok, *CWIHP Bulletin* no. 14–15 (Winter 2003–Spring 2004): 369–383.

60. Shen Zihua (ed.), *Chaoxian zhanzheng: Eguo dang'anguande jiemiwenjian* [The Korean War: declassified materials of Russian Archives], vol. 1–3 (Taipei: Institute of Modern History, Central Academy, 2003).

61. William W. Stueck Jr., *The Korean War: An International History* (Princeton University Press, 1995), 3.

62. Wada Haruki. "Tohoku Azia senso toshiteno Chosen senso" [The Korean War as a Northeast Asian war], *Shien* (Rikkyo University) 56, no. 2 (1996).

63. Wada Haruki, *Tohoku Azia Kyodo no Ie: Shinchiikishugi Sengen* [The Northeast Asian Common House: a manifesto of new regionalism] (Tokyo: Heibonsha, 2003); *Tongbuk Asia kongdongui jip* (Seoul: Ilchogak, 2004).

1. TWO STATES AND UNIFICATION BY FORCE

1. So Chung-sok, "Yi Sung-man kwa pukchintongil" [Syngman Rhee and advancing northward], *Yoksa Pipyong* (Summer 1995): 111.

2. *Inmin*, September 1948, 2. The expression *kukto anjong* ("stabilize national territory") is used in place of *kukto wanjong* ("complete national territory") to conceal the meaning. In the October 1948 issue of *Inmin* (page 15) "*kukto wanjong*" is used.

3. Wada Haruki, "The Korean War, Stalin's Policy, and Japan," *Social Science Japan Review* 1, no. 1 (1998): 6. For relations with the Japanese Communist Party and Nosaka Sanzo, see Wada Haruki, *Rekishi toshiteno Nosaka Sanzo* [Nosaka Sanzo as history] (Tokyo: Heibonsha, 1996), 138–139. In his report on Nosaka (October 29, 1949), K. Ses'kin wrote: "Nosaka is in contact with one of our agents in Tokyo and provides information on domestic politics, economic conditions, Allied Occupation policy, and the activities of several political parties, including the Japanese Communist Party. On occasion he offers advice, in the name of the Politburo Central Communist Party, or in his own name from his perspective and that of Tokuda and others . . ." TsKhSD, 1/d I-I, 127–128.

4. Vojtech Mastny, *The Cold War and Soviet Insecurity: The Stalin Years* (Oxford University Press, 1996), 11–29. David Holloway, *Stalin and the Bomb: The Soviet Union and Atomic Energy, 1939–1956* (Yale University Press, 1994), 224–272.

5. Wada, "Korean War, Stalin's Policy," 11.

6. A. Ledovskii, "Sekretnaia missiia A. I. Mikoiana v Kitai (ianvar'-fevral' 1949 g.)" [The secret mission of A. I. Mikoyan to China (January–February 1949)], *Problemy Dal'nego Vostoka* no. 2 (1995): 97–100.

7. For the full text of six telegrams see S. L. Tikhvinskii, "Perepiska I. V. Stalina s Mao Tsedunom v ianvare 1949 g" [Stalin's correspondence with Mao Zedong in January 1949], *Novaia i noveishaia istoriia* no. 4–5 (1994), 133–139.

8. Mikoyan's memoir on this trip was presented to the Presidium, CC, CPSU, on Sept. 22, 1960. See A. Ledovskii, "Secret mission," 100–110; no. 3 (1995), 94–105.

9. Mastny, *Cold War and Soviet Insecurity,* 47–58.

10. *Izvestiia TsK KPSS*, no. 12 (1989), 35–40. *Evreiskii antifashistskii komitet v SSSR 1941–1948; dokumentirovannaia istoriia* [The Jewish anti-fascist committee in the USSR, 1941–1948: a documentary history] (Moscow, 1996), 388–389; and Wada Haruki, "Sengo Sorenni okeru rekishika to rekishigaku sono ichi" [Historians and historiography in the postwar Soviet Union, part 1], *Roshiashi kenkyu* no. 25 (June 1976): 24–32.

11. Wada Haruki, *Chosen Senso* [The Korean War] (Tokyo: Iwanami Shoten, 1995), 52–53. Regarding Ho Ka-i, see note 87.

12. *Hanguk inmyong taesajon* [Korean biographical encyclopedia] (Seoul: Shinku Munhwa-sa, 1995), 403. Everett Drumright, Counselor, US Embassy, Seoul, wrote of Shin on March 29, 1949: "New Minister Defense Shin [Sung Mo] impresses us as a man of ability and integrity. In our view his new appointment will give Rhee more effective and loyal control of security forces than has been case Lee Bum Suk. By virtue new appointment Shin in position control both army and police. This together with fact he enjoys fullest confidence President Rhee, makes him second most powerful official in Korean Government." *FRUS, 1949*, vol. 7, part 2, 979.

13. *Korean biographical encyclopedia*, 927; *Chong Il-gwon hoegorok* [Chong Il-gwon's memoirs] (Seoul: Koryo Sojok, 1999), 71–75; Chong Il-gwon, *Genbaku ka, kyusen ka* [Atomic bomb or truce?] (Tokyo: Nihon Kogyo Shimbun-sha, 1989); Paek Sun-yop, *Kaisoroku, Kanko-ku senso, issennichi* [Memoirs of Paek Sun-yop: the Korean War's thousand days] (Tokyo: Miritari rebyu, 1988), 28–34, 211.

14. *Korean biographical encyclopedia*, 199; Cumings, *Origins*, vol. 2, 492–495; and Park, *Outbreak*, vol. 2, 577–578.

15. Shtykov to Foreign Ministry, January 14, 1949, APRF (Presidential Archive, Russian Federation), f. 3, op. 65, d. 3, 1–2.

16. Wada Haruki, "Soren no Chosen seisaku, senkyuhyaku yonjugonen hachigatsu–jugatsu" [The Soviet Union's Korean policy, August–September, 1945], *Shakai Kagaku Kenkyu* 33, no. 4 (1982): 116–117.

17. Shtykov to Molotov, January 27, 1949, APRF, f. 3, op. 65, d. 3, 3–5. See Chong Pyong-jun, *Korean War*, 266.

18. Shtykov to Molotov, February 3, 1949, Ibid., 6–7.

19. Ibid., February 3, 1949, Ibid., 8–9.

20. S. S. Biriuzov to Shtykov, February 4, 1949, Ibid., 10.

21. Shtykov to Molotov, February 4, 1949, Ibid., 11–12.

22. *Kin Nichi-sei chosakushu* [Writings of Kim Il Sung], vol. 5 (Pyongyang, 1981), 39. According to Mansourov, Shtykov's report was based on an appeal from Kim Il Sung who "believed that the South was building up military pressure along the border as a preparatory step for a preventive strike against the North." Alexandre Mansourov, "Communist War Coalition Formation and the Origins of the Korean War" (PhD diss., Columbia University, 1997), 91–92. Shtykov does not mention Kim Il Sung in his reports at this time.

23. *Haebanghu 4 nyonganui kungnaewoe chungyo ilchi, chungbopan* [Chronology of important foreign and internal events in four years after liberation (expanded edition)] (Pyongyang: Minju Choson-sa, 1949), 231.

24. Shtykov had already reported this announcement to Molotov, February 3, 1949, Ibid., 13–16.

25. Shtykov to Foreign Ministry, February 4, 1949, Ibid., 13–16.

26. *FRUS, 1949*, vol. 7, part 2, 956–958. On February 17, 1949, President Syngman Rhee angrily complained to Robert Oliver that the United States had provided only a small amount of weapons and had refused to give tanks on the grounds that Korean terrain was not suitable. Robert Oliver, *Syngman Rhee and American Involvement in Korea, 1942–1960* (Seoul: Panmun, 1979), 223. See also Park, *Outbreak*, vol. 2, 596.

27. Shtykov to Molotov, February 9, 1949, APRF, f. 3, op. 65, d. 3, 18–19.

28. I disagree with Mansourov's interpretation that this proposal "was intended to convey a strong message to any potential aggressor that the Soviet Union would get reinvolved if its North Korean client was endangered." See Mansourov, "Communist War Coalition," 110.

29. Shtykov to Molotov, February 14, 1949, APRF, f. 3, op. 65, d. 3, 22.

30. Foreign Ministry to Shtykov, February 23, 1949, Ibid., 23.

31. Purkaev to Shtykov, February 24, 1949, Ibid., 24.

32. *Izvestiia TsK KPSS*, no. 2 (1989), 126–134.

33. Record of meeting between Stalin and North Korean delegation, March 5, 1949, APRF, f. 45, op. 1, d. 346, 13–14.

34. Mansourov, "Soviet-North Korea Relations and the Origins of the Korean War" (paper presented at the International Conference on the New Evidence on the Cold War in Asia, 5); and Mansourov, "Communist War Coalition," 99–100.

35. *Istoricheskii arkhiv* no. 5–6 (1996): 50.

36. Evguени Bajanov, "Assessing the Politics of the Korean War, 1949–51," *CWIHP Bulletin* no. 6–7, 54, 87. This is not mentioned in the Korean language version of his book. According to the chronology apparently prepared by a foreign ministry official, during the March visit to the Soviet Union Kim Il Sung expressed hope for unification through military action, but Stalin disapproved and said the North could only strike in response to a Southern attack. "*Khronologiia osnovnykh sobytii kanuna i nachal'nogo perioda Koreiskogo voiny*" [Chronology of basic events on the eve and in the early period of the Korean War], 5.

37. *Seoul Shinmun*, May 15, 1995, 5.

38. *Otnosheniia Sovetskogo Soiuza s narodnoi Koreei 1945–1980. Dokumenty i materialy* [The Soviet Union's relations with the People's Korea, 1945–1980, documents and materials] (Moscow, 1981), 404.

39. *FRUS, 1949*, vol. 7, 969–978.

40. Foreign Ministry to Shtykov, April 17, 1949, APRF, f. 3, op. 65, d. 3, 25.

41. *FRUS, 1949*, vol.7, part 2, 987–988.

42. *Memorandum*, Vasilevsky and Shtemenko to Stalin, April 20, 1949, APRF, f. 3, op. 65, d. 839, 13–14.

43. Sasaki Harutaka, *Chosen senso: Kankoku-hen* [The Korean War: Republic of Korea], vol. 1 (Tokyo: Hara Shobo, 1976), 356, 422–423.

44. Shtykov to Foreign Ministry, April 20, 1949, APRF, f. 3, op. 65, d. 3, 28–29.

45. Vasilevskii to Shtykov, April 21, 1949, Ibid., 30.

46. *FRUS, 1949*, vol. 7, 989–991.

47. Ibid., 993.

48. Shtykov to Stalin, May 1, 1949, APRF, f. 3, op. 65, d. 3, 31–40.

49. Mansourov, "Communist War Coalition," 115–117.

50. Kovalev to Stalin, May 18, 1949, APRF, f. 45, op. 1, d. 331, 59–61.

51. Shtykov to Vyshinsky, May 15, 1949, Ibid., f. 3, op. 6, d. 3, 47.

52. *Yonbyon Munhwa* [Yonbyon Culture] no. 1 (Oct. 1948): 16–17.

53. Ibid., 18–19.

54. Yi Han, "Choson minjujuui inmin Konghwaguk songnip kyongsuk taehoe" [Celebration rally for the founding of the DPRK], *Yonbyon Munhwa* no. 2 (November 1948): 9.

55. Yi Chong-sok has disputed my assertion that at the time Koreans in China held Chinese citizenship, quoting the memoirs of Liu Jun-xiu, "Haesok kwa silchungui chonggyohan mannam" [Elaborate combination of interpretation and fact finding], *Yoksa Hakbo* no. 164 (1999): 414–415. For Liu's memoirs, see Liu Jun-xiu, "Chosonjok inmindul soge" [Among the Korean people], *Sungni* [Victory] (Chungguk Choson minjok palchachui chongsa, 5) (Beijing, Nationalities Press, 1992), 711.

56. The 164th Division records contain this statement: "We received orders and, under the command of Comrade Yi Tok-san, departed Changchun on July 17, 1949, and headed for a new front." *Choson uiyonggun samchidae* [The Korean Volunteer Army. The third unit.] (Harbin: Korean Nationalities Press, 1987), 325. But according to a noncommissioned officer's testimony of the former 166th Division, on July 23, in the morning of departure, the division's destination was announced in a meeting of commanders down to the company level. But the rank and file came to know it only on a train, many hours after the departure. Kim Jung-saeng, *Choson uiyonggunui milippuk kwa 6.25 chonjaeng* [The secret arrival in North Korea of the Korean volunteer unit and the Korean War] (Seoul: Myongji Chulpansa, 2000), 144–145.

In 2010 Korean scholar Yom In-ho criticized my assertions, saying that Korean officers and soldiers in the PLA shared the ardent desire to go back to Korea and join the struggle for revolutionary unification of the fatherland. Therefore they were not sent to Korea by PLA headquarters, but returned home to their fatherland, Yom wrote; his assertions were based first of all on the case of the Korean division which left China last in April 1950. Yom called this division the 156th division of the PLA, which became the 12th division of the KPA on arrival in Korea. Yom In-ho, *To hanaui Hanguk chonjaeng: Manju Chosoninui 'choguk' kwa chon-jaeng* [Another Korean War: the fatherland for Manchurian Koreans and the war] (Seoul: Yoksa pipyongsa, 2010), 266–278. Our disagreement should be verified by closer study of the documents of the general staff of the PLA and the CCP.

57. Shtykov to Vyshinsky, May 15, 1949, APRF, f. 45, op. 1, d. 346, 46–47.

58. Shin Yom, "Ilbone taehan miguk paengchangjuuichadul ui chongchaek" [American expansionists' policy toward Japan], *Kulloja* (March 1948): 53–88.

59. Shtykov to Foreign Ministry, May 2, 1949, APRF, f. 45, op. 1, d. 346, 41–44.

60. *FRUS, 1949*, vol. 7, 1003–1005.

61. Park, *Outbreak*, vol. 2, 620–621. Park cited *United States Armed Forces in Korea, G-2, Periodical Report*, May 6, 1949.

62. Sasaki, *Korean War*, vol. 1, 354–356. Chong Pyong-jun, *Korean War*, 333–334, 350–355.

63. Mansourov, "Communist War Coalition," 124.

64. Shtykov to Gromyko and Shtemenko, May 21, 1949, APRF, f. 45, op. 1, d. 346, 49–50.

65. *FRUS, 1949*, vol. 7, 1012.

66. Ibid., 1013.

67. Ibid., 1017.

68. *Soguk tongil minjujuui chonson kyolsongtaehoe munhonjip* [Documents related to the formation of the Fatherland Unification Democratic Front] (Pyongyang: Choson Minpo-sa, 1949), 183–184. For the proposals from Southern parties and responses from Northern parties, see 148–1157. For the Fatherland Front's program, see 114.

69. Shtykov to Foreign Ministry, June 5, 1949, APRF, f. 45, op. 1, d. 346, 59–63.

70. Mansourov, "Communist War Coalition," 129–132. Mansourov has apparently confused Shtykov's June 5 telegram with the telegram on June 28.

71. Mensh'kov and Shtemenko to Shtykov, June 4, 1949, APRF, f. 45, op. 1, d. 346, 53–58.

72. *FRUS, 1949*, vol. 7, 1030–1031.

73. Ibid., 1033–34.

74. Ibid., 1034–1035.

75. Ibid., 1035–1036.

76. Sasaki, *Korean War*, 372.

77. Shtykov to Vyshinsky, June 18, 1949, APRF, f. 3, op. 65, d. 3, 64–67.

78. *FRUS, 1949*, vol. 7, 1041–1043.

79. Shtykov to Vyshinsky, June 22, 1949, APRF, f. 3, op. 65, d. 3, 68–75.

80. NRC, USFEC, RG 242, SA 2010, item 2/76.

81. Vyshinsky to Shtykov, June 24, 1949. APRF, f. 3, op. 65, d. 3, 76.

82. *Fatherland Front Documents*, 184, 19, 62.

83. Vyshinsky to Shtykov, June 28, 1949, APRF, f. 3, op. 65, d. 3, 78–79.

84. For Chang Sun-myong's speech, see *Fatherland Front Documents*, 73–78. For the conference process, see Ibid., 187–188. Mori Yoshinori contends that Pak Hon-yong's Southern Workers' Party was the main force behind the Fatherland Front and advocated peaceful unification to block Kim Il Sung's use of force. Mori incorrectly links Chang Sun-myong's speech to this attempt. Mori Yoshinori, "Sokoku toitsu minshushugi sensen no kessei" [Formation of the Fatherland Unification Democratic Front], *Toyama Kokusai Daigaku Kiyo* 7 (March 1997).

85. *Fatherland Front Documents*, 17; Federation of Korean Residents in Japan mentioned in the lists of organizations which sent delegates, Ibid., 144; and Song Sung-chol as a member of the preparatory committee, Ibid., 160.

86. Tsuboi Toyokichi, *Zainichi Chosenjin undo no gaikyo* [The Movement of Koreans in Japan: an overview], Reprint (Tokyo: Jiyu Seikatsu-sha, 1959), 93–95. Hagiwara argues that Han Dok-su alone was selected over Kim Chon-hae, Pak Un-chol, and other Koreans from Japan for the Central Committee of the Fatherland Front because Kim Il Sung wanted to use Han to control the Korean movement in Japan, a so-called conspiracy by Kim Il Sung and Han Tok-su. Hagiwara, *Kita Chosenni kieta tomo to watashi no monogatari* [My friends who

disappeared in North Korea] (Tokyo: Bungei Shunju, 1998), 314–318. This interpretation is unconvincing. Pak Un-chol was a leader of the Japanese Communist Party, not of the League of Koreans in Japan. Kim Chon-hae became head of the Social Division, CC KWP, and the chairman of the Fatherland Front when he moved to Pyongyang in the next year. Han Tok-su was probably named to the Fatherland Front Central Committee because he was in Pyongyang.

87. *Choson chonsa: nyonpyo* [History of Korea, chronology], vol. 2 (Pyongyang: Kwahak paekka sajon, 1991), 162. There are no direct records of high officials. For the positions of Kim Il Sung and Pak Hon-yong, see Sbornik reshenii Politsoveta i Orgkomiteta TsK Trudovoi partii Korei za 1951 god [Decisions of the Central Committee Politburo and Organization Committee, Korean Workers Party, 1951], RGASPI, f. 17, op. 137, d. 730, 2–269; and *Kulloja* no. 11 (1951): 37 (as noted by Mori Yoshinori). For Ho Ka-i's position as vice-chairman, see *Minju Choson*, Sept. 12, 1950. For his position as party secretary, see "Materialy 4-go plenuma TsK Trudovoi partii Korei" [Materials of fourth plenum, Central Committee, Korean Workers Party], RGASPI, f. 17, op. 137, d. 731,110. For Yi Sung-yob's position as party secretary, see the *Nodong Shinmun*, February 28, 1952. Ho Ka-i was party secretary but lost his party position when he became vice-premier. See Materials of fourth plenum, d. 731, 110. Kim Sam-yong, an underground operative for the Southern Workers' Party, has been listed as the third party secretary, however, Pak Chong-ae was also party secretary before November 1951. See Materials of fourth plenum. According to the verdict in the trial of Yi Sung-yob and others, Kim Sam-yong was just a member of the Political Committee, Korean Workers' Party. See *Namnodang yongu charyojip* [Collected materials on the South Korean Workers' Party], vol. 2 (Seoul: Korea University Press, 1974), 621.

88. *FRUS, 1949*, vol. 7, 1046–1057. For the comparison of troop strength, 1048; conclusion, 1052; Option C, 1054; and the strategic evaluation of South Korea by the Joint Chiefs of Staff, 1056–1057.

89. Shtykov to Vyshinsky, July 13, 1949, APRF, f. 3, op. 65, d. 5, 25–27.

90. So Chung-sok, *Syngman Rhee*, 112.

91. "Posetiteli kremlevskogo kabineta I. V. Stalina. Zhurnaly zapisi lits, priniatykh pervym gensekom. 1924–1953 gg" [Visitors of Stalin's cabinet in the Kremlin: the lists of men received by the first general secretary, 1924–1953], *Istoricheskii arkhiv* no. 5–6 (1996): 56–58. The record of the meeting on June 27 is also open to researchers. A. M. Ledovskii, *SSSR i Stalin v sud'bakh Kitaia: Dokumenty i svidetel'stva uchastnika sobytii 1937–1952* [The USSR and Stalin in the destiny of China. Documents and testimonies of a participant in the events, 1937–1952] (Moscow, 1999), 83–84, 85–88.

92. Ishii Akira, *Chu-So kankeishi no kenkyu, 1937–1952* [Studies in the history of Sino-Soviet relations, 1937–1952] (Tokyo: University of Tokyo Press, 1990), 233–234. Shi Zhe, *Zai lishi juren shenbian* [Living around the historical giant] (Beijing: The Central Press of Historical Documents, 1991), 414–415.

93. Vyshinsky to Shtykov, August 3, 1949, APRF, f. 3, op. 65, d. 3, 88–89.

94. Sasaki, *Korean War*, 379–380. See Chong Pyong-jun, *The Korean War*, 404–410.

95. Cumings, *Origins*, vol. 2, 393–394.

96. Shao Yulin, "Shihan huiyilu" [Memoirs of the ambassador to Korea], 13, *Zhuanji wen shue* (Taipei) vol. 32, no. 3 (March 1977): 111–114.

97. Cumings, *Origins*, vol. 2, 393–394.

98. Wada, *The Korean War*, 24.

99. For Pang Ho-san's career before he went to the Soviet Union, see the records of CCP members compiled in 1937 by Piao Yuanbin, secretary of the Xiajiang special committee, CCP, RGASPI, f. 514, op. 1, d. 1078, 28–29. For Pang's career after returning to China, see *Zhu Dehai yisheng* [The life of Zhu Dehai] (Beijing: Nationalities Press, 1987), 687. For his military record in the Chinese civil war, see *Hyogmyong hoesanggi Li Hong-gwan chidae* [A memoir of the revolution: Li Hong-gwan's unit] (Shenyang: Liaoning National Press, 1986), 5, 23, and 41.

100. A. V. Torkunov, *Zagadochnaia voina: Koreskii konflikt 1950–1953 godov* [An enigmatic war: the Korean conflict, 1950–1953] (Moscow, 2000), 30–31; *Khronologiia*, 12–14; and Bajanov and Bajanova, *Korean War*, 23–25.

101. This section is not in Torkunov. See *Khronologiia*, 12–14; and Bajanov and Bajanova, *Korean War*, 25.

102. Torkunov, *Enigmatic war*, 31–32.

103. Ibid., 32; *Khronologiia*, 14; and Bajanov and Bajanova, *Korean War*, 26.

104. *FRUS, 1949*, vol. 7, 1075–1076. The list of weapons has not been made public.

105. *Zhongguo renmin jiefangjun disi yezhanjun zhanshi* [A history of the 4th Field Army, Chinese People's Liberation Army] (Beijing: People's Liberation Army Press, 1998), 502–503.

106. *Izvestiia TsK KPSS* no. 2 (1989): 130. Anastas Mikoyan, *Tak bylo* [This was the past] (Moscow: Vagrius, 1999), 566.

107. *Sovetskii atomnyi proekt: Konets atomnoi monopolii. Kak eto bylo . . .* [The Soviet atomic project: the end of monopoly of atomic bombs] (Nizhnii Novgorod, 1995), 175–178.

108. Wada, *The Korean War*, 113–116. For argument about the September Revolution, see Yamada Munemitsu, *Sengo shisoshi* [History of postwar thought] (Tokyo: Sanichi Shobo, 1959), 123.

109. Tunkin to Vyshinsky, Sept. 3, 1949, APRF, f. 3, op. 65, d. 775, 116–119.

110. Foreign Ministry to Tunkin, Sept. 11, 1949, Ibid., 122.

111. Tunkin to Foreign Ministry, Sept. 14, 1949, Ibid., d. 837, 94–101.

112. F. Fejt, *Minzoku shakaishugi kakumei: Hangaria junen no higeki* [A national socialist revolution: the tragic decade in Hungary] (Tokyo: Kindai Seikatsu-sha, 1957), 30.

113. Shtykov, *Memorandum*, Sept. 15, 1949, APRF, f. 3, op. 65, d. 776, 121.

114. Drafts of instructions to Shtykov, Ibid., f. 3, op. 65, d. 839, 5–16. Draft no. 1, 11–13: no. 2, 14–16; no. 3, 8–10; and no. 4, 5–7. The written comments on draft no. 3 are by Stalin. Torkunov, *Enigmatic war*, 51.

115. *Memorandum*, Molotov to Politburo members, Sept. 23, 1949, APRF, f. 3, op. 65, d. 776, 2, 33–38. Draft no. 4 is 2, 34–36. According to Mansourov, Politburo members reviewed all the drafts. He attributes my no. 1 to Bulganin, no. 2 to Kaganovich, no. 3 to Mikoyan, and no. 4 to Beriia. "Communist War Coalition," 162–164. I disagree.

116. Decision by Politburo, Communist Party Soviet Union, Sept. 24, 1949, APRF, f. 3, op. 65, d. 776, II, 30–32.

117. *Pravda*, Sept. 26, 1949. Holloway, *Stalin and the Bomb*, 265.

118. Shtykov to Foreign Ministry, Oct. 4, 1949, APRF, f. 43, op. 1, d. 346, 59.

119. For the partisan movement in South Korea, see Yi Tae, *Nambugun* [Guerrilla units in the South] (Seoul: Ture-sa, 1988).

120. TsKhSD, 1/d I-I, 122–128. Full translation in Wada, *Nosaka Sanzo*, 296–302.

121. A. N. Mamin, "K polozheniiu v Kompartii Iaponii" [On the situation in the Japanese Communist Party], June 26, 1950, RGASPI, f. 17, op. 137, d. 413, 130. For details, see Wada, *Nosaka Sanzo*, 221.

122. TsKhSD, f. 89, op. 50, d. 2, 1–2.

123. Sasaki, *Korean War*, 382–384. Chong Pyong-jun, *Korean War*, 441–442.

124. Gromyko to Shtykov, Oct. 26, 1949. *APRF,* f. 3, op. 65, d. 6, 103.

125. Shtykov to Foreign Ministry, Oct. 31, 1949, Ibid., 104–106.

126. Gromyko to Shtykov, Nov. 20, 1949, Ibid., 107.

127. *FRUS, 1949*, vol. 7, 1079–1080.

128. Ibid., 1080–1084.

129. Park, *Outbreak*, vol. 2, 609.

130. This letter was captured by the North Koreans when they occupied Seoul and published *Jijitsuwa kataru: Chosen senso chohatsu no uchimaku* [The facts speak: inside story of the outbreak of the Korean War] (Pyongyang: Gaikokubunshuppansha, 1960, photo edition), 31. Regarding the letter's veracity, see Wada, *The Korean War*, 146–147. In an interview with United Press correspondent Joseph Jones on October 7, 1949, Rhee bragged: "I am confident we can occupy Pyongyang in three days." Park, *Outbreak*, vol. 2, 609.

131. Pang, "Captured North Korean materials," 154.

132. Ibid., 155–156.

133. *FRUS, 1949*, vol. 7, 1093.

134. Park, *Outbreak*, vol. 2, 617. Park notes that Syngman Rhee's rhetoric about "advance northward" had four functions: (1) maintain internal tension as domestic policy; (2) obtain

more support from the United States; (3) exaggerate South Korea's strength to thwart an invasion by North Korea and the Soviet Union; (4) encourage a desire to invade the North if South Korea became strong enough. Park supports Professor Yi Ho-jae's terminology of an "intimidation policy" (611–615). Rhee's statement on December 30 shows his resolve to go to war, according to Park.

135. Cumings, *Origins*, vol. 2, 163–167. Kan Hideteru, *Bei-So reisen to Amerika no Ajia seisaku* [The Cold War and US Asian policy] (Osaka: Minerva Shobo, 1992), 246–247.

2. NORTH KOREA GOES TO WAR

1. Stalin-Mao conference, December 16, 1949. APRF, f. 45, op. 1, d. 329, 9–17.
2. *Wang Dongxing riji* [Wang Dongxing's diary] (Beijing: Chinese Social Sciences Press, 1993), 164–166.
3. N. Fedorenko, "Nochnye besedy" [Conversations at night], *Pravda*, October 23, 1988, 4.
4. "Zapis' besedy P. F. Iudina s Mao Tsedunom" [Conversation of P. F. Iudin and Mao Zedong, March 31, 1956], *Problemy Dal'nego Vostoka* [Problems of the Far East] no. 5 (1994): 103–109.
5. Dieter Heinzig, "Stalin, Mao, Kim and Korean War Origins, 1950: A Russian Documentary Discrepancy," *CWIHP Bulletin* no. 8–9, 240.
6. Fedorenko, op. cit.
7. M. V. Gorbanevskii, *V. nachale bylo slovo . . . Maloizvestnye stranitsy istorii sovetskoi lingvistiki* [In the beginning there was a word—unknown pages of the history of Soviet linguistics] (Moscow, 1991), 50.
8. Wang, *Diary*, 171–173.
9. Shi, *Historical giant*, 440.
10. Stalin to Shtykov, January 8, 1950. APRF, CWIHP file, per. 3, 110.
11. Shtykov to Foreign Ministry, January 11, 1950, Ibid., 111–112.
12. *Nie Rongzhen huiyilu* [Nie Rongzhen's memoirs] (Beijing: People's Liberation Army Press, 1984), 744; and Wada, *The Korean War*, 25.
13. Wada, *The Korean War*, 80–81.
14. *Pravda*, January 4, 1950.
15. *Nihon kyosanto gojunen mondai shiryoshu* [Documents on the 1950 controversy in the Japanese Communist Party] vol. 1 (Tokyo: Shin Nihon Shuppansha, 1957), 9–11.
16. *Jianguo yilai Mao Zedong wengao* [Mao Zedong's manuscripts since the founding of the PRC], vol. 1 (Beijing: The Central Press of Historical Documents, 1987), 237.
17. Cumings, *Origins*, vol. 2, 433–435.
18. Park, *Outbreak*, vol. 2, 556–569.
19. Wada, *The Korean War*, 135–136.
20. Song Sung-chol, "Yosida passyo chongchaekul pantaehanun Ilbon inmindul ui tujaeng" [The Japanese people's struggle against the fascist policies of Yoshida], *Kulloja* no. 19 (1949): 124–125.
21. Record of conference, Molotov, Vyshinsky, and Mao Zedong in Shen Zhihua, *Zhongsu tongmeng yu Chaoxian zhanzheng yanjiu* [Studies on the Sino-Soviet alliance and the Korean War] (Guilin: Guangxi Pedagogical University Press, 1999), 335–340. This work is based on documents in the Russian Foreign Ministry Archives. Also see Shi, *Historical giant*, 454–457. The Soviet statement is in *Pravda*, January 21, 1950.
22. Record of Conference, Stalin-Mao, January 22, 1950, APRF, f. 45, op. 1, d. 329, 32. Gaddis, also relying on these conversations, contends the Acheson speech changed Stalin's thinking on the risk of war. John Lewis Gaddis, *We Now Know: Rethinking Cold War History* (Oxford: Clarendon Press, 1997), 73.
23. APRF, f. 45, op. 1, d. 329, 30.
24. Shen, *Sino-Soviet alliance*, 265; and Shen, "Chu-So joyaku kosho ni okeru rieki no shototsu to sono kaiketsu" [Conflicts of interests in negotiations of Soviet-Chinese Treaty and

their solution], *Shiso*, August 2001, 83. The author speculates that having lost rights in Port Arthur and Dalian, Stalin supported Kim Il Sung's plans to attack South Korea in order to gain access to an ice-free port on the Korean peninsula. I cannot agree with this conclusion.

25. Shtykov to Vyshinsky, January 6, 1950, APRF, CWIHP file, per. 3, 108–109.
26. Shtykov to Vyshinsky, January 19, 1950, Ibid., 113–117.
27. Shtykov to Vyshinsky, January 28, 1950, Ibid., 118–121.
28. Stalin to Shtykov, January 30, 1950, Ibid., 122.
29. Shtykov to Stalin, January 31, 1950, Ibid., 123–124. See *CWIHP Bulletin* no. 6–7, 36.
30. APRF, f. 45, op. 1, d. 347, 12, in Torkunov, *Enigmatic War*, 56.
31. Shtykov to Vyshinsky, February 9, 1950, APRF, f. 45, op. 1, d. 346, 74–75.
32. Vyshinsky to Shtykov, February 9, 1950, Ibid., 76.
33. Shtykov to Vyshinsky, February 10, 1950, Ibid., 77.
34. Shtykov to Vyshinsky, February 23, 1950, APRF, CWIHP file, per. 3, 130.
35. A. M. Samsonov, *Moskva, 1941 god; Ot tragedii porazhenii—k velikoi pobede* [Moscow 1941: from the tragedy of defeat to the great victory] (Moscow, 1991), 227. Samsonov, *Stalingradskaia bitva* [The Battle for Stalingrad], 2nd ed. (Moscow, 1985), 540. *Osvobozhdenie gorodov. Spravochnik po osvobozhdeniiu gorodov v period Velikoi Otechestvennoi voiny 1941–1945* [Emancipation of cities in the Great Fatherland War: a guidebook] (Moscow, 1985), 85–86, 131–132, 154, 258–259.
36. Shtykov to Vyshinsky, March 9, 1950, and March 16, 1950. APRF, CWIHP file, per 3, 131–132. The total amount was 134,050,500 rubles, according to the original document. For Kim Il Sung's list, see Shtykov to Vyshinsky, March 16, 1950, Ibid., 133–140.
37. *Khronologiia*, 26.
38. KLO 498-C, May 15, 1950. *KLO-TLO munsojip* [Documents of the KLO and TLO], vol. 1 (Chunchon: Institute of Asian Cultural Studies, Hallym University, 2000), 77. See also Pang, "Captured North Korean materials," 145. According to Hagiwara, "The accuracy of this report was demonstrated by subsequent events. Kim Il Sung did just what he said and moved against the South." Hagiwara, *Conspiracy*, 268. This is incorrect.
39. KLO 384-A, March 10, 1950; KLO 395-A, March 15, 1950; KLO 396-B, March 16, 1950. *KLO-TLO documents*, vol. 1, 32, 35–36.
40. Pang, "Captured North Korean materials," 125–126.
41. I. F. Stone, *The Hidden History of the Korean War* (Boston: Little, Brown, 1988), 60. See also Okonogi, *Korean War*, 74.
42. Shtykov to Foreign Ministry, March 21, 1950, APRF, CWIHP file, per. 3, 130.
43. A copy of this document is in the *Seoul Shinmun*, May 24, 1995, and it is cited in Bajanov and Bajanova, *Korean War*, 51. See also Torkunov, *Enigmatic war*, 57.
44. I read "namerennye." It means "intend." Bajanov translated it as "the mood to carry out armed unification." He reads "nastroennye." Tokunov reads it as "namerenie" (intention).
45. Matsui Noriaki, "Maboroshii no Saharin tonneru" [The mysterious Sakhalin tunnel], *Suzutani* (Hokkaido Toyohara-kai), no. 12 (September 1994): 98–103. Matsui, *Shiryo Sutarin-Meriniku kaidan, 1950 sangatsu* [Stalin-Melnik meeting, March 1950], Ibid. no. 13 (September 1995): 76–84. This is a translation of Melnik's report to the staff conference of the Sakhalin Province committee, CPSU, April 17, 1950.
46. *Istoricheskii arkhiv* no. 1 (1997): 11.
47. *Seoul Shinmun*, May 24, 1995; Bajanov and Bajanova, *Korean War*, 52–55; and Torkunov, *Enigmatic war*, 58–59. Torkunov wrote that he did not discover the conference record.
48. Nikita Khrushchev, *Khrushchev Remembers* (Boston: Little, Brown, 1970), 367–368.
49. Report by A. M. Ignat'ev of the meeting between Ambassador Yi Chu-yon and Mao Zedong. Ignat'ev to Vyshinsky, April 10, 1950. APRF, f. 3, op. 65, d. 3, 148–149.
50. Ignat'ev to Vyshinsky, April 25, 1950, Ibid., 150.
51. Shtykov to Vyshinsky, May 12, 1950, Ibid., 151–152.
52. Ibid., 152.
53. Roshchin to Foreign Ministry for Filippov, May 13, 1950, Ibid., 155–156.
54. Vyshinsky to Embassy, Beijing (Filippov to Mao Zedong), May 14, 1950, APRF, f. 45, op. 1, d. 331, 55.

316   *Notes*

55. Bajanov and Bajanova, *Korean War*, 66–68; *Khronologiia*, 29–31; and Torkunov, *Enigmatic war*, 69.

56. Yo Chong [pseud.], "Pihwa: Kim Il-sung kwa Pukhan" [The secret story: Kim Il Sung and North Korea], *Tong'a Ilbo*, April 29, 1990. Japanese translation, *Kin Nichi-sei: sono shogekino jitsuzo* [Kim Il Sung: the shocking reality] (Tokyo: Kodansha, 1992), 190–191. This division was believed to have been first designated the 7th Division and later changed to the 12th Division. However, in an earlier book I followed the account of Yo Chong, the senior party committee member in the 32nd Regiment of this division from Zhengzhou days, who says the unit was always the 12th Division. Hagiwara contends this is wrong and the 7th Division is listed in an order issued by Artillery Commander Mu Chong dated May 31, 1950 (*Shokun*, April, 1995, 149–150). The source he cites only lists the 825th Unit as the seventh of the twelve addressees. *Miguk kungnip kongmunsogwan sojang Pukhan haebanchikhu kukpicharyo* [Secret materials related to North Korea immediately after liberation, in US National Archives, August 1945–June 1951], vol. 3 (Seoul: Koma solim, 1998), 206 and 224. This is an unauthorized reprint edition of Hagiwara Ryo's publications, *Kitachosen no Gokuhibunsho*, 3 vols. (Tokyo: Natsu no shobo, 1995). From this source one can only say that the KPA had seven divisions and the 825th Unit was the seventh. North Korea numbered the unit the 12th Division to create the illusion that the KPA had a dozen divisions and frighten the enemy. How odd that Hagiwara, who has made such an effort to decipher camouflaged unit designations, did not understand such an elementary ploy. He says the division was changed from the 7th Division to the 12th Division when the commander was relieved because the unit was late in attacking Chunchon. That is not sufficient grounds to redesignate a unit in the middle of combat. Hagiwara found the wording "7th Division (12th Division)" in a US military history, but this expression meant that its author could not confirm the number assigned to the seventh KPA division in order. A KLO agent report (May 25, 1950) notes a "Rumor of the formation of a new PA 7th Division." In a KLO report dated April 1950 on the "inspection of all units of the armed forces in North Korea" the 7th Division was rated "7th class." This may be the 7th Division. However, US intelligence could not locate the division (*KLO-TLO documents*, vol. 1, 98). According to Hagiwara, the 12th Division first appears in a document dated June 30; he concludes the name was changed the day before. However, the Russian language documents captured by the US Army include a draft reconnaissance order dated June 18 from the chief of staff of the commander in chief in the field addressed to the chief of staff, 12th Division (ATIS Enemy Documents, no. 6, Item 2, Document number 200564). Hagiwara quotes Choe Yonghwan, a political officer with the KPA 6th Division. Yo Chong, an officer actually in the 12th Division, should be a more reliable source. A recently published study, based on sources familiar with the events, flatly states, "it is incorrect that the volunteer unit [from Manchuria] became the 7th Division upon entry in North Korea and was re-designated during the war." Kim Jung-saeng, *Choson uiyonggunui milippuk kwa 6.25 chonjaeng* [The secret arrival in North Korea of the Korean volunteer unit and the Korean War] (Seoul: Myongji Chulpansa, 2000), 188. Also in his more fundamental study on Manchurian Koreans' participation in the Korean War, Yom In-ho clearly pointed out that on April 25, 1950 a ceremony on the foundation of the 12th Division was held in Wonsan with participation of Defense Minister Choe Yongon, Yom In-ho, *Another Korean War*, 276.

57. Mansourov, "Communist War Coalition," 329–333.

58. Ibid., 333.

59. Torkunov, *Enigmatic war*, 74, 76. In the text the date for this report is given as May 27; the correct date of May 29 is in the note.

60. Mansourov, "Communist War Coalition," 334–335.

61. Park, *Outbreak*, vol. 1, 287–304.

62. Mansourov, "Communist War Coalition," 337–338.

63. Ibid., 347–348. The cited document is Shtykov to Stalin, June 12, 1950, Tsentral'nyi arkhiv Ministerstva oborony (TsAMO) [Central archives of Ministry of Defense], d. 120, 10–30. See also Wada, *The Korean War*, 54–55.

64. Mansourov, "Communist War Coalition," 348–350.

65. *Khronologiia*, 33; Bajanov and Bajanova, *Korean War*, 74.

66. Cumings, *Origins*, vol. 2, 595–596.

67. Hagiwara, *Conspiracy*, 184–188; and Park, *Outbreak*, vol. 1, 363.

68. Choson Inmingun che 655 gunbutae munhwabu, *Chonsi chongchi munhwa saop* [Politi-co-cultural work in wartime], June 13, 1950 (NA, RG 242, SA 2009, Item 10/58,2). I was able to examine this document thanks to the kindness of Pang Sun-joo.

69. Ibid., 12.

70. Torkunov, *Enigmatic war*, 75; *Khronologiia*, 33; and Bajanov and Bajanova, *Korean War*, 74.

71. NA. RG 242, ATIS, *Enemy Documents*, no. 6, Item 3, Doc. No. 200686. I am indebted to Pang Sun-joo for the use of these Russian language materials. The document is classified "Sov. Sekretno" or "Top Secret," which is given in English as "Soviet Secret." Cumings disputes its credibility, *Origins*, vol. 2, 585–591. Park Myung-lim found the document consistent with other material and credible. *Outbreak*, vol. 1, 409–415.

72. NA. RG 242, ATIS, *Enemy Documents*, no. 6 Item 2, Doc. No. 200564.

73. Wada, "Rethinking the Korean War," *Shiso* (May, 1993), 38; and Wada, *The Korean War*, 52.

74. Pang, "Captured North Korean materials," 69–70. The photographs are on 107–111. See also Wada, "Rethinking the Korean War," *Shiso* (September 1990): 11; and Wada, *The Korean War*, 11–12. These materials are also quoted in Hagiwara, *Conspiracy*, 211–215. According to Hagiwara, "This document is the most vivid account of the condition of KPA soldiers, including their state of mind, immediately before they attacked the South." Hagiwara's identification of Unit 353 as the self-propelled artillery battalion of the 3rd Division is very helpful. Hagiwara explains the military situation in detail, including that all KPA divisions had begun to move toward the 38th parallel from about June 10. *Conspiracy*, 172.

75. *Khronologiia*, 33–34; and Bajanov and Bajanova, *Korean War*, 75; and Mansourov, "Communist War Coalition," 367–368.

76. *Khronologiia*, 33–34; and Mansourov, "Communist War Coalition," 371–372.

77. Torkunov, *Enigmatic war*, 75; *Khronologiia*, 34; Bajanov and Bajanova, *Korean War*, 75–76; and Mansourov, "Communist War Coalition," 372–374.

78. Only the use of naval personnel was rejected, according to *Khronologiia*, 34. Bajanov cites two points in "Assessing the Politics," 76. Mansourov speculates on the two points in "Communist War Coalition," 375–377. Torkunov was unable to find Stalin's response to Kim Il Sung. *Enigmatic war*, 75.

79. Paul G. Pierpaoli, Jr., *Truman and Korea: The Political Culture of the Early Cold War* (University of Missouri Press, 1999), 25–26. For the drafting process, see Cumings, *Origins*, vol. 2, 177–181.

80. KLO 423, April 4, 1950. *KLO-TLO documents*, vol. 1, 47.

81. KLO 424, April 4, 1950. Ibid., 48.

82. KLO 435 E, April 10, 1950. Ibid., 51.

83. KLO 437, April 10, 1950. Ibid., 52–53.

84. KLO 457 B, April 21, 1950. Ibid., 64.

85. KLO 518, May 25, 1950. Ibid., 97–99.

86. Pang, "Captured North Korean materials," 124–125. This evaluation is similar to that in a document in the Willoughby Paper, "Intelligence in War: A Brief History of MacArthur's Intelligence Services, 1941–1951," appendix 4, "The North Korean Pre-Invasion Build-up." For the complete document, see *KLO-TLO documents*, vol. 3, 289–300.

87. Cumings, *Origins*, vol. 2, 615.

88. Pang, "Captured North Korean materials," 84.

89. Okonogi, *Korean War*, 74. For the differences between my interpretation and those of Cumings and Pang, see Wada, *The Korean War*, 139–144. Although Hagiwara has examined few of the KLO materials, he concludes that: "The capacity of the US military and the United States. . . is so great that it scares one truly . . . nevertheless the US military, particularly MacArthur and Willoughby, pretended to be unaware [of the DPRK's military preparations] and allowed Kim Il Sung to move South." Hagiwara, *Conspiracy*, 269.

90. Cumings, *Origins*, vol. 2, 612.

91. Ibid., 500–507.

92. Ibid., 552, 876; Sasaki, *Korean War*, vol. 2, 112; Harold Joyce Noble, *Embassy at War* (Seattle: University of Washington, 1975), 10–11.

93. *FRUS, 1950*, vol. 7, 110,120. Curiously, Cumings says this document has not been made public. *Origins*, vol. 2, 613.

94. Chong Il-gwon, *Atomic bomb*, 19–20.

95. Kankoku Kokubo gunshikenkyusho [Republic of Korea, National Defense History Research Institute], ed. *Kankoku Senso* [Korean War], vol. 1 (Tokyo: Kaya shobo, 2000), 121.

96. Chong Il-gwon, *Atomic bomb*, 38; and *Chong Il-gwon's memoirs*, 133.

97. Park, *Outbreak*, vol. 2, 586–588.

98. *FRUS, 1950*, vol. 7, 43–44.

99. *Paeksa Yi Yun-yong hoegorok* [Yi Yun-yong's memoir] (Seoul: Sacho, 1984), 157–158.

100. *FRUS, 1950*, vol. 7, 60; and Cumings, *Origins*, vol. 2, 492–493.

101. *Chong Il-gwon's memoirs*, 134.

102. *FRUS 1950*, vol. 7, 65–66.

103. Ibid., 83–84.

104. Ibid., 85.

105. Ibid., 84–85.

106. Yun Kyong-chol, *Bundangono Kankoku seiji, 1945–1986* [Politics in the Republic of Korea, 1945–1986] (Tokyo: Bokutakusha, 1986), 103; and Cumings, *Origins*, vol. 2, 486.

107. Park, *Outbreak*, vol. 2, 589–591. Cumings is skeptical of Clay Blair's account of SL-17. *Origins*, vol. 2, 614–615.

108. Park, *Outbreak*, vol. 2, 569–582.

109. Sasaki, *Korean War*, vol. 2, 74.

110. Ibid., 96–100.

111. Ibid., 146–148.

3. ATTACK

1. Pang, "Captured North Korean materials," 65. For unit designations, see Hagiwara, *Conspiracy*, 192.

2. Pang, "Captured North Korean materials," 88–90. Unit designations are in Hagiwara, *Conspiracy*, 227.

3. Related materials are in Wada, *The Korean War*, 49–52.

4. Shtykov to Zakharov, June 26, 1950, in *Seiron*, November 1995, 110–112. The British Broadcasting Corporation also obtained these materials. An English translation is in *CWIHP Bulletin* no. 6–7, 37–40.

5. *Kin Nichi-sei senshu* [Selected works of Kim Il Sung], vol. 2 (Tokyo: San'ichi Shobo, 1952), 13–20.

6. *Haebang Ilbo* (Seoul), July 2, 1950, 1.

7. Roy Appleman, *South to the Naktong, North to the Yalu, June–November 1950* (Washington, DC: Center of Military History, US Army, 1992), 16; G. K. Plotnikov, "Otechestvennaia osvoboditel'naia voina koreiskogo naroda (obzor voennykh deistvii)" [The fatherland liberation war of the Korean people], in *Za mir na zemle Korei: Vospominaiia i stat'i* [For peace on the land of Korea: reminiscences and articles] (Moscow, 1985), 41.

8. Sasaki, *Korean War*, vol. 2, 172, 174–177, and 202.

9. *FRUS, 1950*, vol. 7, 131; and Cumings, *Origins*, vol. 2, 585.

10. *FRUS, 1950*, vol. 7, 142–143; Noble, *Embassy*, 72; and Sasaki, *Korean War*, vol. 2, 342, 369, and 373–376.

11. Noble, *Embassy*, 72–73.

12. Wada, *The Korean War*, 60.

13. Kim Song-chil, *Yoksa appeso: han sahakcha ui 6:25 ilgi* [Witness to history: a historian's diary of the Korean War] (Seoul: Changjak kwa pipyongsa, 1993), 68–69.

14. *Haebang Ilbo*, July 18, 1950.

15. Ibid., July 3, 1950.

16. Kim Song-chil, *Witness*, 90, 185–186.
17. *Haebang Ilbo*, July 2, 1950.
18. Ibid., July 3, 1950.
19. *FRUS, 1950*, vol. 7, 140.
20. Appleman, *South to the Naktong*, 39.
21. *FRUS, 1950*, vol. 7, 237–238.
22. Ibid., 140.
23. Ibid., 125–126.
24. Cumings, *Origins*, vol. 2, 625.
25. *FRUS, 1950*, vol. 7, 144–147. For the complete text of the resolution, see 155–156.
26. Ibid., 157–160.
27. Cumings, *Origins*, vol. 2, 627.
28. *FRUS, 1950*, vol. 7, 178–183.
29. Ibid., 202–203.
30. Okonogi, *Korean War*, 97.
31. Cumings, *Origins*, vol. 2, 628.
32. *Zhou Enlai nianpu 1949–1979* [A chronology of Zhou Enlai, 1949–1976], vol. 1 (Beijing: The Central Press of Historical Documents, 1997), 51.
33. *FRUS, 1950*, vol. 7, 211.
34. I first made this point in "Rethinking the Korean War," *Shiso* (May 1990). O Chunggun later reached virtually the same conclusion in "Chosen senso to Soren—Kokuren Anpo Rijikai kesseki o chushinni" [The Soviet Union and the Korean War—boycott of the security council], *Hogaku Kenkyu* 65, no. 2 (February 1992).
35. A. A. Gromyko, *Pamiatnoe* [The unforgettable], vol. 1 (Moscow, 1988), 206–207.
36. *FRUS, 1950*, vol. 7, 148.
37. Ibid., 209.
38. Ibid., 229.
39. Ibid., 220.
40. Ibid., 229–230.
41. For the meeting, see Okonogi, *Korean War*, 101–102. For the directive, see *FRUS, 1950*, vol. 7, 240–241.
42. Ibid., 249–250.
43. Okonogi, *Korean War*, 108–113.
44. Chong Il-gwong, *Atomic bomb*, 25–27 and 37–39.
45. Ibid., 42–44; and Noble, *Embassy*, 105–108.
46. Appleman, *South to the Naktong*, 59–60.
47. McCormack, *Cold War*, 100.
48. *FRUS, 1950*, vol. 7, 291.
49. Ibid., 307.
50. Ibid., 312–313.
51. For the messages from Clement Attlee and Ernest Bevin, see Ibid., 314–315 and 329–331, respectively.
52. Ibid., 327–328.
53. Ibid., 329.
54. Chong Il-gwong, *Atomic bomb*, 58.
55. Appleman, *South to the Naktong*, 195–196.
56. *Asahi Shimbun*, June 26, 1950.
57. Yoshida Kasei, "Gaku no dokuritsu miyako no seihoku ni hibiku [A refrain "The independence of university" reverberated in northwest Tokyo], in *Waseda 1950 nen shiryo to shogen* [Waseda University in 1950: materials and testimonies] vol. 1 (Tokyo, 1997), 125.
58. Ando Jinbei, *Sengo Nihon Kyosanto shiki* [A private story of the postwar Japanese Communist Party] (Tokyo: Bunshun Bunko, 1995), 108.
59. *Akahata*, June 26, 1950.
60. *Asahi Shimbun*, June 27, 1950; and Sodei Rinjiro, ed., *Correspondence between General MacArthur, Prime Minister Yoshida and Other High Japanese Officials [1945–1951]* (Tokyo: Hosei University Press, 2000), 201–202.

61. Sodei, *MacArthur-Yoshida correspondence*, 205–206; and Miyake Akimasa, *Reddo paji to wa nanika? Nihon senryo no kage* [What was the Red Purge?: behind the Occupation] (Tokyo: Otsuki Shoten, 1994), 5–12, 55–57.

62. *Asahi Shimbun*, June 27, 1950.

63. *Asahi Shimbun*, June 25–28, 1950.

64. *Asahi Shimbun*, June 27, 1950.

65. Yamazaki Shizuo. *Shijitsu de kataru Chosen senso; kyoryoku no zenbo* [Japan's cooperation in the Korean War]. Tokyo: Hon no Izumisha, 1998, 66.

66. Ibid., 112–113; and Nam Ki-jong. "Chosen senso to Nihon; 'kichi kokka' ni okeru senso to heiwa" [The Korean War and Japan; war and peace in a "military base state"]. PhD diss., University of Tokyo, 2000, 36.

67. Yamazaki, *Japan's cooperation*, 86–87; and Nam, *Korean War and Japan*, 104–105.

68. Robert F. Futrell, *The United States Air Force in Korea, 1950–1953* (New York: Duell, Sloan and Pearce, 1961), 5–6; and Appleman, *South to the Naktong*, 50–51.

69. *Asahi Shimbun*, June 29, 1950.

70. Futrell, *Air Force*, 87–88.

71. Ibid., 131, 182.

72. *Asahi Shimbun*, July 4–5, 1950.

73. Shinobu Seizaburo, *Sengo Nihon seijishi* [A political history of postwar Japan], vol. 4 (Tokyo: Keiso Shobo, 1967), 1153–1154.

74. *Nihon Shakaito no sanjunenshi* [The Japan Socialist Party: a thirty year history] (Tokyo: Newspaper Division, Central Headquarters, Japan Socialist Party, 1976), 134–135.

75. *Asahi Shimbun*, July 9, 1950; and Sodei, *MacArthur-Yoshida correspondence*, 203–204.

76. *Kokkai Dai 8 kai Shugiin kaigiroku* [Japanese Diet proceedings, the 8th Diet, house of representatives], vol. 3 (July 14, 1950), 19–20.

77. *Asahi Shimbun*, July 15, 1950.

78. *Diet proceedings*, the 8th Diet, vol. 4 (July 15, 1950), 35, 37.

79. Ibid., 31.

80. *Kokkai Dai 8 kai Shugiin gaimuiinkai kaigiroku* [Japanese Diet proceedings, the 8th Diet, house of representatives, diplomatic committee], vol. 2 (July 21, 1950), 7.

81. Ibid, 11.

82. Ibid., vol. 4 (July 26, 1950), 13.

83. Ibid., vol. 5 (July 29, 1950), 11.

84. Cumings, *Origins*, vol. 2, 508, 525–526.

85. Ibid., 512–525.

86. Ibid., 531–543.

87. Shao Yulin, *Memoirs*, 16, *Zhuanji wen shue*, vol. 32, no. 6 (June 1977): 103.

88. *Zhonghua minguo dashiji* [A chronology of the Republic of China] (Taipei, 1957), 606–607.

89. *Gu Weijun huigulu* [Memoirs of Wellington Koo], vol. 8 (Beijing: Zhongua Shuju Chuban, 1989), 11–14.

90. *History of the war to resist America*, vol. 1, 46–47.

91. Ibid., 61–62.

92. Fyn Si to Shtykov, July 1, 1950, APRF, f. 45, op. 1, d. 346, 104.

93. Torkunov, *Enigmatic war*, 104–105.

94. Bajanov, "Assessing the Politics," 104–105.

95. Shtykov to Fyn Si, July 4, 1950, APRF, f. 45, op.1, d. 346, 136–139. See also *CWIHP Bulletin* no. 6–7, 42–43.

96. The announcement of Kim Il Sung's appointment as Supreme Commander appeared in *Minju Choson*, July 6, 1950.

97. So Pyong-gon, "Mu Chong changgun irdaegi" [General Mu Chong: a biography], *Shinchonchi* vol. 1, no. 2 (March 1946): 238–241; and *Oruta* [Organ of the Korean Communist Party committee] (South Hamgyong Province) no. 18 (January 1, 1946).

98. Kim Ung used the name Wang Xinhu in China. Ye Quanhong, "Huangpu junxiao hanji xuesheng kaoshi" [A study of Korean students in the Huangpu military school], *Hanguk nianpo* (Taipei), no. 14 (1996):162; Chong Kil-un, "Chosun uiyongun Hwajung chidae kwa Jiluyu

chidae" [Korean Volunteers Army—Hwachung unit and Jiluyu unit], in *Kyolchon* [Decisive battle] (Beijing: Minjok Chulpansa, 1991), 376–378; Kim Jung-saeng, *Korean Volunteer Army*, 128. For Kang Kon, see Li Changyi, *Jiang Xintai junlu shengya* [Kang Shintae's life in wars and journeys], *Zhongguo chaoxianzushi yanjiu*, vol. 2 (Yanbian University Press), 291–304.

99. Fyn Si to Shtykov, July 6, 1950, *APRF,* f. 45, op. d. 346, 140.See also *CWIHP Bulletin* no. 6–7, 43.

100. Filippov to Zhou Enlai, July 5, 1950, *APRF,* f. 45. op. d. 346, 79.

101. Du Ping, *Zai zhiyuanjun zongbu* [My days at the headquarters of the Chinese People's Volunteers] (Beijing: Liberation Army Press, 1989), 13–14.

102. Letter, Kim Il Sung to Stalin, *APRF,* f. 3, op. 65, d. 826, 88. Shtykov telegram transmitting letter, July 8, 1950. *APRF,* f. 45, op. 1, d. 346, 143–144. See also *CWIHP Bulletin* no. 6–7, 43–44.

103. Filippov to Soviet Ambassador, Beijing, for Zhou Enlai or Mao Zedong, July 13, 1950. APRF, f. 45, op. 1, d. 329, 85. See also *CWIHP Bulletin* no. 6–7, 44.

104. Filippov to Soviet Ambassador, Pyongyang, July 13, 1950, APRF, f. 45. op. 1, d. 346, 149–150. Letter, Kim Il Sung to Shtykov, July 14, 1950, APRF, f. 3, op. 65, d. 826, 108–109. See also *CWIHP Bulletin* no. 6–7, 44.

105. Appleman, *South to the Naktong*, 164–177.

106. *Hangyore 21* (Seoul), no. 292 (January 20, 2000); and *Newsweek*, Japanese edition (February 2, 2000): 54–55.

107. Appleman, *South to the Naktong*, 195–197.

108. Ibid., 199.

109. U Ryong-ho, *Chosen no gyakusatsu* [Massacre in Korea] trans. Ohata Kenji et al., (Tokyo: Ota Shuppan, 2001), 14–62. Compare this account with Pang Sun-joo, "Hanguk chonjaeng tangsi pukhan charyoro pon Nogulli sakon" [The Nogulli incident in the light of North Korean materials], *Chongsin Munhwa Yongu* vol. 23, no. 2 (Summer 2000).

110. Appleman, *South to the Naktong*, 215–221.

111. Kang Kon's death was officially announced on Sept. 7, 1950. Judging from the memoir of Yu Song-chol, who was present at Kang's death, it may have occurred immediately after the occupation of Taejon. Yu Song-chol, "Naui chungon" [My testimony], *Hanguk Ilbo*, Nov. 1–30, 1990. See also Hanguk Ilbo, eds., *Chungon: Kim Il Sungul marhanda* [Testimony: Kim Il Sung] (Seoul: Hanguk Ilbosa, 1991). These recollections are collected in the Japanese translation *Kin Nichisei sono shogekino jitsuzo* [Kim Il Sung: the shocking reality] (Tokyo: Kodansha, 1992). Quotes are from the Japanese translation as Yu, *Testimonies*. Yu, *Testimonies*, 118. Based on Yu's memoirs, I previously wrote that Choe Chun-guk had reportedly died in mid-July. Wada, *The Korean War*, 64. Choe's name appears on orders issued by the commander of the 12th Division from July 10 to July 31. *Miguk kungnip kongmunsogwan sojang Pukhan haebanchikhu kukpicharyo* [Secret materials related to the occupation of North Korea immediately after Liberation in US National Archives], vol. 5 (Seoul: Koryo sorim, 1998), 104–136. The official date of July 30 seems correct.

112. Yu, *Testimony*, 52–81.

113. Futrell, *Air Force*, 92–96.

114. Appleman, *South to the Naktong*, 262.

115. Appleman, *South to the Naktong*, 382; and McCormack, *Cold War*, 100–102.

116. *Life of Zhu Dehai*, 68; and Kim Jung-saeng, *Korean Volunteer Army*, 128.

117. Appleman, *South to the Naktong*, 580. *Hanguk chonjaeng-sa puto*, [History maps of the Korean War] (Seoul: Ilshin-sa, 1991), 53, 67, and 69.

118. *Kim Sa-ryang chakpumjip* [Selected works of Kim Sa-ryang] (Pyongyang: Munye chulpansa, 1987), 289. Regarding Kim Sa-ryang's presence with the 6th Division at this time, see Hagiwara Ryo, *Chosen senso shuzai no–to* [A journalist's notes on the Korean War] (Kyoto: Kamogawa Shuppan, 1995), 75.

119. Futrell, *Air Force*, 118–122; and Appleman, *South to the Naktong*, 376–372.

120. Futrell, *Air Force*, 127–128.

121. Regarding Mao Zedong's statement at this meeting, Qi Dexje has pointed out that Mao, speaking as the "center," said, "If America uses nuclear weapons, so be it . . . We are not afraid. We will use hand grenades." Qi Dexue, *Chaoxian zhanzheng juece neimu* [Inside story of

decision making during the Korean War] (Shenyang: Liaoning University Press, 1991), 30. Based on materials in Beijing, Zhu Jianrong has written that Mao Zedong said that if America was going to use nuclear weapons, China had no choice but to fight to the end. Zhu Jianrong, *Mao's Korean War*, 120. For more detailed accounts of this meeting see Yasuda Jun, "Chugoku kenkoku shoki no anzen hosho to Chosen senso e no kainyu" [Security issues in the initial phase of the PRC and China's intervention in the Korean War], *Hogaku kenkyu* 67, no. 8 (August 1994): 45–47.

122. Nie, *Memoirs*, 734.

123. Du Ping, *My days at the headquarters*, 19–20. Zhu Jianrong attributes this spirit to the dissemination of Mao's strong views by participants in this meeting. Zhu Jianrong, *Mao's Korean War*, 125.

124. Nie, *Memoirs*, 734.

125. *Khronologiia*, 45; and Torkunov, *Enigmatic war*, 105–106.

126. Kim Tong-chun, *Chonjaeng kwa sahoe: uriege Hanguk chonjaengun muosi onna?* [War and society: what was the Korean War to us?] (Seoul: Tolbegae, 2000), 174; and *Minju Choson*, July 10, 1950.

127. Kim, *War and society*, 174; and Joseph C. Goulden, *Korea: The Untold Story of the War* (New York: Times Books, 1982), 130.

128. Kim Song-chil, *Witness*, 96–100.

129. *Konghwaguk nanbanbu chiyok e tojikaehyok ul silsi han gose kwanhan chonryong mit sihaeng sechik* [Directives and detailed rules concerning the implementation of land reform in the southern half of the Republic] NRC, USFEC, RG242, SA 2009, Box 7, Item 4.

130. *Haebang Ilbo*, July 18, July 28, August 19, August 29, 1950.

131. *Choson inminui chonguiui chogukhaebang chonjaengsa* [A history of the righteous war of the Korean people to liberate the fatherland], vol. 1 (Pyongyang: Sahoekwahak Chulpansa, 1983), 344.

132. *Haebang Ilbo*, August 5, August 8, September 5, 1950.

133. *Choson minjujuui inmin konghwaguk naegak kongbo* [Cabinet announcements, Democratic People's Republic of Korea], no. 146 (August 1, 1950), 549–550; no. 148 (August 18, 1950), 550–552.

134. Kim Song-chil, *Witness*, 137–138.

135. *Haebang Ilbo*, July 18, 1950.

136. Cumings, *Origins*, vol. 2, 671.

137. *Minju Choson*, August 17, 1950.

138. *Haebang Ilbo*, August 23, 1950.

139. Noble, *Embassy*, 170–173.

140. Appleman, *South to the Naktong*, 382, 384.

141. Futrell, *Air Force*, 130–131.

142. *Asahi Shimbun*, August 17, 1950.

143. Appleman, *South to the Naktong*, 382.

144. Cumings, *Origins*, vol. 2, 661.

145. *Khronologiia*, 47; and Torkunov, *Enigmatic war*, 106.

146. Shu Yinwen, "Deng Hua," *Zhonggong dangshi renwuzhuan* [Biographies of figures of the Chinese Communist Party], vol. 32 (Xian: Shanxi People's Press, 1987), 148–149.

147. Shtykov to Vishinsky, August 28, 1950, in *Seiron*, November 1995, 110–116.

148. Fyn Si to Shtykov, August 28, 1950, APRF, f. 45, op. 1, d. 347, 5–6 and 10–11. See also *CWIHP Bulletin* no. 6–7, 45.

149. Shtykov to Fyn Si, August 31, 1950, APRF, f. 45, op. 1, d. 347, 12–13. See also *CWIHP Bulletin* no. 6–7, 45–46.

150. Shtykov to Fyn Si, August 31, 1950, APRF, f. 45, op. 1, d. 347, 14–15. See also *CWIHP Bulletin* no. 6–7, 46.

151. Bajanov and Bajanova, *Korean War*, 109.

152. *Asahi Shimbun*, August 20, 1950.

153. Sodei, *MacArthur-Yoshida correspondence*, 206.

154. *Asahi Shimbun*, August 20, 21, 1950.

Notes 323

155. *Sekai*, December 1950, 25–40. *Sekai Rinji Zokan Sengo heiwaron no genryu* [Sekai special issue: the origins of postwar pacifism] (July 1985): 3–16.
156. *Sekai*, "Postwar pacifism," 28.
157. *Sekai*, December, 1950, 25–40.
158. Ibid., 41–48.
159. Igarashi Takeshi, *Tainichi kowa to reisen: sengo Nichi-Bei kankei no keisei* [The peace treaty with Japan and the Cold War; the formulation of postwar Japan-US relations] (University of Tokyo Press, 1986), 243.
160. Futrell, *Air Force*, 133–136.
161. Futrell, *Air Force*, 137–138; and Appleman, *South to the Naktong*, 454–487.
162. Appleman, *South to the Naktong*, 488.
163. Ibid., 489–491.
164. Ibid., 501–502.
165. Max Hastings, *The Korean War* (New York: Simon & Schuster, 1987), 123.
166. Yamazaki, *Japan's cooperation*, 88.
167. Sodei, *MacArthur–Yoshida correspondence*, 207.
168. These instructions are in Filippov to Mao Zedong or Chou Enlai, October 1, 1950, APRF, f. 45. op. 1, d. 347, 97–98.
169. *Khronologiia*, 52–54.
170. Academy of Military Science, *War to resist America*, vol. 1, 123. For Zhou Enlai's telegram, see *Zhou Enlai junshi wenxuan* [Selected military papers of Zhou Enlai]. vol. 4 (Beijing: People's Press, 1997), 56–57.
171. *Khronologiia*, 54–55; and Bajanov and Bajanova, *Korean War*, 112–113.
172. *Khronologiia*, 55–56; and Bajanov and Bajanova, *Korean War*, 114.
173. Vasilevskii, memorandum, Sept. 21 and 23, 1950, APRF, f. 3, op. 65, d. 827, 79–80 and 81–82.
174. *Khronologiia*, 58–60.
175. Matveev to Fyn Si, Sept. 21, 1950, APRF. f. 3, op. 65, d. 827, 103–106. "Matveev" was a pseudonym for Army Gen. Matvei Vasil'evich Zakharov, the deputy chief of the general staff of the Soviet Armed Forces. Mansourov, "Stalin, Mao, Kim, And China's Decision to Enter the Korean War, Sept. 16–Oct. 15, 1950: New Evidence from the Russian Archives," *CWIHP Bulletin* no. 6–7 (Winter 1995/1996): 106. For Zakharov's career, see M. V. Zakharov, *General'nyi shtab v predvoennye gody* [The general staff in the prewar years] (Moscow, 1988), 293–309.
176. Politburo decision, Sept. 27, 1950, APRF, f. 3, op. 65, d. 827, 90–93. "Rekomendatsii Fyn Si" [Fyn Si's recommendations], *Rodina* no. 4 (1993): 79–80.
177. For the massacre of the people arrested, see Kim Tong-chun, *War and society*, 162–163. For members of the National Assembly, see *Pukhan chongnam, 1945–1968* [North Korea big reference book, 1945–1968] (Seoul: Kongsangwon Munje yonguso, 1983), 1012–1018. The treatment of "abducted heroes" is described in Yi Tae-ho, *Oryokko no fuyu* [Winter on the Yalu], trans. Aoyagi Junichi (Tokyo: Shakai Hyoronsha, 1993). The original was published in Korean in 1991 by Tassosure, Seoul. The story was based on the testimony of Shin Kyong-wan, former vice-division chief of the Fatherland Front, who later fled from North Korea.
178. Kim Song-chil, *Witness*, 226–227.
179. Chong Il-gwon, *Atomic bomb*, 169–172.
180. Shtykov to Gromyko, Sept. 30, 1950, APRF, f. 45, op. 1, d. 347, 46–49.
181. Shtykov to Gromyko, Sept. 30, 1950, APRF, f. 45, op. 1, d. 347, 41–45. The original text in Korean is attached. This translation is by Alexandre Mansourov, *CWIHP Bulletin* no. 6–7, 112.
182. The complete text of major documents is in Academy of Military Science, *War to resist America*, vol. 1, 148–149. Hong Xuezhi, *Kangmei yuanchao zhanzheng huiyi* [Recollections of the war to resist America and assist Korea] (Beijing: Liberation Army Press, 1990), 14–15. Although Hong says Pak Hon-yong was the messenger, the official history named Pak Il-u, which seems more likely. *War to resist America*, vol. 1, 148.
183. Politburo decision, Sept. 30, 1950, APRF, f. 3, op.65, d. 827, 100–101.
184. Yu Song-chol, *Testimony*, 119, 122–124.

185. I infer this from the order dated Dec. 7 and jointly signed by Kim Il Sung, Supreme Commander, KPA, and Kim Ung, Chief of the General Staff, KPA, *Secret materials related to North Korea*, vol. 5, 69.

186. Fyn Si to Shtykov, Oct. 1, 1950, *Rodina* no. 4 (1993): 80–81.

187. Filippov to Mao Zedong or Zhou Enlai, Oct. 1, 1950, *APRF*, f. 45, op. 1, d. 347, 97–98.

188. Film, "Densetsu no maihime Choe Sung-hui" [Legendary dancer Ch'oe Sung-hui], directed by Fujiwara Tomoko, 2000.

189. Yi Tae, *Guerrilla units in the South*, chapter 1.

190. *A History of the Righteous war of the Korean people*, vol. 2, 88–90. *Kim Il Sung's Selected Works*, vol. 6, 133–139.

191. In an earlier work I said "Pak Hon-yong and Ho Ka-i had repeated Kim Il Sung's criticism of the party organization within the military and the personnel of the KPA Political Division." Wada, *The Korean War*, 195. Yi Chong-sok has commented that "from the general retreat until the final mobilization Kim Il Sung requested Pak Hon-yong to share tasks in military matters and made him equally accountable." "Haesok kwa silchungui chonggyohan mannam" [Elaborate combination of interpretation and fact finding], *Yoksa Hakpo* no. 164 (1999): 416–417. Yi is correct, and I have revised my treatment here. Kim Il Sung and Pak Hon-yong were still in joint control at this stage.

192. *Choson inmingun choegosaryonggwan myongryong* [Order, Supreme Commander, KPA, October 14, 1950], NRC, USFEC, RG 242, SA 2010, item 8/117. *Secret materials related to North Korea* vol. 5, 63–66. For details on this order, see Hagiwara, *Conspiracy*, 323–325. When I wrote *Korean War*, I was only aware of the description in Appleman, *South to the Naktong*, 630. Regarding this order, Hagiwara writes, "Kim Il Sung issued a half-crazed order on October 14" and "a desperate Kim Il Sung not only turned guns on South Koreans but ruthlessly killed North Koreans too." In the epilogue of *Korean War* (352–354) I criticized Hagiwara's appraisal, incorrectly stating that only English-language materials were available. However, I stand by my assessment that such extreme measures are not rare.

193. The order is recorded in the diary of an KPA soldier. Pang, "Captured North Korean materials," 110.

194. *Russkii arkhiv: Velikaia Otechestvennaia: Prikazy narodnogo komissara oborony SSSR, 22 iiunia 1941 g.–1942 g.* [Russian archives: Orders of the People's commissar of defense, USSR, June 22, 1941–1942], vol. 13 (2–2), (Moscow, 1997), 59–60.

195. Ibid., 277.

196. See Suh Dong-man, *Pukchoson sahoejuui cheje songnipsa 1945–1961* [A history of formation of the socialist system in North Korea]. (Seoul: Son'in, 2005), 398–421.

4. US-ROK FORCES REACH THE YALU AND CHINA ENTERS THE WAR

1. *FRUS, 1950*, vol. 7, 569–570.

2. George F. Kennan, *Memoirs, 1925–1950* (Boston: Little, Brown, 1967), 488–489.

3. Okonogi, *Korean War*, 136.

4. Cumings, *Origins*, vol. 2, 710.

5. Ibid., 711.

6. Okonogi, *Korean War*, 127.

7. Cumings, *Origins*, vol. 2, 711, 905.

8. Ibid., 712.

9. *FRUS, 1950*, vol. 7, 543–544.

10. *FRUS, 1950*, vol. 6, 256.

11. Cumings, *Origins*, vol. 2, 711; and Okonogi, *Korean War*, 129.

12. *FRUS, 1950*, vol. 7, 685–693.

13. Ibid., 707–708.

14. Ibid., 705–707.

15. Ibid., 712–721.
16. Ibid., 781–782.
17. Ibid., 735.
18. Ibid., 736–741.
19. Ibid., 751–752.
20. Ibid., 796.
21. Chong Il-gwon, *Atomic bomb*, 172–176.
22. Appleman, *South to the Naktong*, 608.
23. Ibid., 631–633.
24. *FRUS, 1950*, vol. 7, 904–906.
25. Ibid., 913–914.
26. Appleman, *South to the Naktong*, 623.
27. Chong Il-gwon, *Atomic bomb*, 185.
28. Paek Sun-yop, *Memoirs*, 28–29, 119–122.
29. *Kin Nichi-sei senshu* [Selected works of Kim Il Sung], vol. 2, 92–100.
30. Okonogi, *Korean War*, 166–170.
31. *Selected military papers of Mao Zedong*, 345–347. Also see *Mao Zedong's manuscripts*, vol. 1, 539.
32. Zhu Jianrong, *Mao Zedong's Korean War*, 186–188; and Wada, *The Korean War*, 185.
33. Pang Xianzhi and Li Jie, *Mao Zedong yu kangmei yuanchao* [Mao Zedong and the cause of resistance to America and aid to Korea] (Beijing: The Central Press of Historical Documents, 2000), 18–19. Photo copies are among frontispieces.
34. Chen Jian, *Mao's China and the Cold War* (The University of North Carolina Press, 2001), 90. Chen Jian explained his discovery to me at an international conference to commemorate the fiftieth anniversary of the Korean War, Seoul, August 2000.
35. Roshchin to Filippov, Oct. 3, 1950. APRF, f. 45, op. 1, d. 334, 105–106. See also *CWIHP Bulletin* no. 6–7, 114–116. Mao Zedong's telegram is an attachment to the cable.
36. Roshchin to Filippov, Oct. 4, 1950, Ibid., d. 329, 107–109. Mao's telegram is an attachment to the cable.
37. This cable was quoted by Stalin in his cable to Kim Il Sung. See Fyn Si to Kim Il Sung, Oct. 8, 1950, Ibid., d. 347, 65–67. See also *CWIHP Bulletin* no. 6–7, 116.
38. Mansourov says the cable was sent Oct. 5, 1950, but I disagree. See Mansourov, "Stalin, Mao and Kim," *CWIHP Bulletin* no. 6–7, 101.
39. Zhu, *Mao's Korean War*, 191–199, 217.
40. Fyn Si to Kim Il Sung, October 8, 1950. APRF, f. 45, op. 1, d. 347, 67.
41. *Mao Zedong's manuscripts*, vol. 1, 543, 545.
42. Accounts of Zhou's mission abound. I have relied heavily on the memoirs of interpreter Shi Zhe. The new Russian materials accord with Shi Zhe; records of the Stalin-Zhou meetings have not been found. For my interpretation as of 1995, see Wada, *The Korean War*, 185–186.
43. The date was unclear. For the latest interpretation, see *Zhou Enlai nianpu 1949–1976* [A chronology of Zhou Enlai, 1949–1976], vol. 1 (Beijing: The Central Press of Historical Documents, 1997), 85.
44. Shi, *Historical giant*, 495–496.
45. Ibid., 498.
46. *Chronology of Zhou Enlai*, vol. 1, 85.
47. Torkunov, *Enigmatic war*, 97.
48. Shtykov to Fyn Si, Oct. 14, 1950. APRF, f. 45, op. 1, d. 335, 3. See also *CWIHP Bulletin* no. 6–7, 118.
49. *Mao Zedong wenji* [Mao Zedong's writings], vol. 6 (Beijing: People's Press, 1999) 103–104. Clauses 3, 4, and 5 were not previously made public.
50. Fyn Si to Kim Il Sung, October 13, 1950. APRF, f. 45, op. 1, d. 347, 74–75.
51. Shi, *Historical giant*, 499–501.
52. *Chronology of Zhou Enlai*, vol. 1, 86–87.
53. Roshchin to Filippov, October 14, 1950, APRF, f. 45, op. 1, d. 335, 1–2. See also *CWIHP Bulletin* no. 6–7, 118–119.

54. Fyn Si to Shtykov for Kim Il Sung, October 14, 1950. Ibid., d. 347, 77. See also *CWIHP Bulletin* no. 6–7, 119.

55. *Asahi Shimbun*, November 8, 15, 1950.

56. Toyoshita Narahiko, *Anpo joyaku no seiritsu—Yoshida gaiko to tenno gaiko* [The peace treaty: Yoshida Shigeru's diplomacy and the emperor] (Tokyo: Iwanami Shoten, 1996), 25–28.

57. Appleman, *South to the Naktong*, 633.

58. Okubo Takeo, *Uminari no hibi—kakusareta sengoshi no danso* [Roaring waves: the hidden pages of the postwar history] (Tokyo: Kaiyo Mondai Kenkyukai, 1978), 209.

59. Ibid., 209–211.

60. Ibid., 212.

61. Ibid., 213.

62. Appleman, *South to the Naktong*, 633–634.

63. Okubo, *Roaring waves*, 216–226.

64. Appleman, *South to the Naktong*, 634.

65. Okubo, *Roaring waves*, 227–228.

66. Okubo Takeo, *Mutekinariyamazu* [The foghorn kept blowing] (Tokyo: Kaiyo Mondai Kenkyukai, 1984), 317.

67. Okubo, *Roaring waves*, 217, 260.

68. *Tong'a Ilbo*, October 19, 1950.

69. *New York Times*, October 19, 1950.

70. Paek Sun-yop, *Memoirs*, 129–134.

71. *Tong'a Ilbo*, October 12, 1950.

72. *FRUS, 1950*, vol. 7, 938–939.

73. Ibid., 963.

74. Ibid., 984–985.

75. *Tong'a Ilbo*, November 4, 1950.

76. *Tong'a Ilbo*, October 26, November 5, 1950.

77. Joseph C. Goulden, *Korea: The Untold Story of the War* (New York: Times Books, 1982), 251.

78. *New York Times*, October 23, 1950; and Cumings, *Origins*, vol. 2, 718.

79. An Yong-hyon, *Secret history*, vol. 3, 111.

80. *Korean biographical encyclopedia*, 118.

81. *Tong'a Ilbo*, October 30, 1950; and Chong Il-gwon, *Atomic bomb*, photograph, 210.

82. An Yong-hyon, *Secret history*, vol. 5, 253–260.

83. *Hanguk chonjaengsa pudo* [History maps of the Korean War], 110; and Appleman, *South to the Naktong*, 663–666.

84. Conrad Crane, *American Airpower Strategy in Korea, 1950–1953* (University of Kansas Press, 2000), 44.

85. *New York Times*, October 31, 1950.

86. *Tong'a Ilbo*, November 15, 1950. Kim Sam-gyu fled to Japan in September 1951, founded the monthly journal *Koria Hyoron*, and never returned to South Korea. For a memoir, see Kim Sam-gyu, "Kojinshi no naka no Chosen to Nihon" [Korea and Japan in my life], in *Chosen to Nihon no aida* [Between Korea and Japan] (Tokyo: Asahi Sensho, 1980).

87. *Tong'a Ilbo*, November 16, 1950.

88. *New York Times*, November 2, 1950.

89. An Yong-hyon, *Secret history*, vol. 3, 112.

90. *Tong'a Ilbo*, October 15, 1950.

91. *Tong'a Ilbo*, October 19, 1950.

92. Decision, Politburo, Central Committee, CPSU, October 25, 1950, APRF, f.3, op. 65, d. 827, 141–143.

93. Nam Ki-jong, "Korean War and Japan," 141.

94. Appleman, *South to the Naktong*, 385–387; and Nam Ki-jong, "Korean War and Japan," 36–37.

95. Deng Lifeng, ed., *Xin Zhongguo Junshi Huodong Jishi, 1945–1959* [A chronology of the military activities of new China, 1945–1959] (Beijing: CCP History Literature Press, 1989), 136–137, 141.

96. Hong Xuezhi, *Kangmei yuanchao zhanzheng huiyi* [Recollections of the war to resist America and assist Korea] (Beijing: Liberation Army Press, 1990), 48.

97. *Mao Zedong's manuscripts*, vol. 1, 600.

98. *Zhongguo renmin zhiyuanjun kangmei yuanchao zhanshi* [A History of the Chinese People's Volunteers' war to resist America and assist Korea], 2nd ed. (Beijing: Military Science Press, 1990), 13–30; and Yasuda Jun, "Chugoku no Chosen senso daiichiji, dainiji seneki" [China's first and second offensives in the Korean War], *Hogaku Kenkyu* 68, no. 2 (February 1995): 385–391.

99. *History of the CPV's War*, 34, and appendix 3.

100. Appleman, *South to the Naktong*, 715–716.

101. "Uchastie SSSR v koreiskoi voine (Novye dokumenty)" [The participation of the USSR in the Korean War (new documents)], *Voprosy istorii* no. 11 (1995): 3.

102. Okonogi, *Korean War*, 183–190; and Appleman, *South to the Naktong*, 763.

103. *History of the CPV's War*, 30–47; and Yasuda, *China's first and second offensives*, 391–396.

104. Wada, *The Korean War*, 193.

105. *Choson Inmingun*, November 22, 1950.

106. Ibid., November 27, 1950. Regarding Yi Pang-nam, see Kim Jung-saeng, *Secret arrival*, 200.

107. *Peng Dehuai junshi wenxuan* [Selected military papers of Peng Dehuai] (Beijing: The Central Press of Historical Documents, 1988), 354; "Choe Hyon tongjiui yangnyok" [A biographical sketch of comrade Choe Hyon], *Nodong Sinmun*, April 10, 1982; Yo Chong's memoires in *Kim Il Sung: the shocking reality* (Kodansha, 1992), 300; and Academy of Military Science, Military Historical Studies Section, *Kangmei yuanchao zhanzhengshi* [A history of the war to resist America and aid Korea], vol. 2 (Beijing: Military Sciences Press, 2000), 369.

108. Du Ping, *Zai zhiyuanjun zongbu* [My days at the headquarters of the Chinese People's Volunteers] (Beijing: Liberation Army Press, 1989), 141.

109. Shtykov to Zakharov, October 31, 1950, APRF, f. 45, op. 1, d. 347, 81–83. For place names, see Shen, *Sino-Soviet alliance*, 394.

110. Fyn Si to Shtykov, November 1, 1950, Ibid., 84. See also *CWIHP Bulletin* no. 6–7, and Shtykov to Fyn Si, letter from Kim Il Sung attached, November 2, 1950, Ibid., 87.

111. Mao Zedong to Filippov, November 8, 1950, Ibid., d. 335, 80–81. Zhou Enlai to Filippov, November 16, 1950, Ibid., 117–118, and November 17, 1950, Ibid., 122–123. See also *CWIHP Bulletin* no. 6–7, 48–50.

112. Filippov to Zhou Enlai, November 17, 1950, Ibid., 124. See also *CWIHP Bulletin* no. 6–7, 80.

113. Kim Il Sung to Stalin, November 18, 1950, Ibid., d. 347, 88–89.

114. Filippov to Kim Il Sung, November 20, 1950, Ibid., 90–91. See also *CWIHP Bulletin* no. 6–7, 50–51.

115. Stalin to Zhou Enlai, November 10, 1950, Ibid., d. 335, 85–86.

116. *History of the CPV's War*, appendix 5, 10.

117. Billy C. Mossman, *Ebb and Flow: November 1950–July 1951* (Washington, 1990), 150–155.

118. Ibid., 167–173.

119. Yi Ho-chol, "Sirhyangmin" [The uprooted], *Wolgan Taehwa*, January 1977, 307. This is the preface to the serialized novel *Pohyang yahwa* [Nostalgic talks]. Hwang Sok-yong's novel is included in *Kakuchi* [Foreign land], trans. Takasaki Soji (Tokyo: Iwanami Shoten, 1986).

120. *Choson Inmingun*, December 9, 1950.

121. Filippov to Mao Zedong, December 1, 1950, APRF, f. 45, op. 1, d. 336, 5. See also *CWIHP Bulletin* no. 6–7, 51.

122. *A Chronology of Zhou Enlai*, vol. 1, 102.

123. *History of the war to resist America*, vol. 2, 162.

124. Ibid., 168–169.

125. Du Ping, *My days at the headquarters*, 141–142.

126. Yu Song-chol, "Pipadaui pihwa" [Secret stories: the sea of blood] *Koryo Ilbo* (Alma Ata), May 31, 1991. Nam Il was dismissed as vice-minister of education on September 29,

1950. See *Choson minjujuui inmin konghwaguk naegak kongbo* [Cabinet announcements, Democratic People's Republic of Korea (DPRK)], no. 15, 1950 (September 30), 588.
127. *FRUS, 1950*, vol. 7, 1237–1238.
128. Ibid., 1242–1249; and Okonogi, *Korean War*, 211–214.
129. *FRUS, 1950*, vol. 7, 1253.
130. Ibid., 1253–1254.
131. Okonogi, *Korean War*, 216.
132. Ibid., 234.
133. *FRUS, 1950*, vol. 7, 1279–1280.
134. Ibid., 1262.
135. Cumings, *Origins*, vol. 2, 748–749.
136. Futrell, *Air Force*, 356.
137. Mossman, *Ebb and Flow*, 35.
138. Cumings, *Origins*, vol. 2, 750.
139. *Chong Il-gwon's memoirs*, 304–306.
140. Ibid., 323.
141. *Asahi Shimbun*, October 21, November 5, 7, 1950.
142. Gromyko's Diary, December 4, 1950, APRF, f. 3, op. 65, d. 515, 35–37.
143. Wada, *The Korean War*, 198, 209.
144. Shtykov to Fyn Si, November 22, 1950, APRF, f. 45, op. 1, d. 347, 94. A letter from Vyshinsky, January 3, 1951, V. N. Razuvaev's letter attached. Ibid., f. 3, op. 65, d. 828, 88–100.
145. *Istochnik* no. 1 (1996): 136. According to Embassy First Secretary V. I. Petukhov, Shtykov was in Korea "until the end of 1950." *Za mir na zemle Korei. Vospominaniia i stat'i* [For peace on the Korean land: reminiscences and articles] (Moscow, 1985), 119.
146. *Bol'shaia Sovetskaia entsiklopedia* [Soviet encyclopedia], 3-e izd., vol. 29 (Moscow, 1978), 507.
147. *Kto byl kto v Velikoi Otechestvennoi voine 1941–1945. Kratkii spravochnik* [Who's who in the Great Fatherland War, 1941–1945: a short biographical dictionary] (Moscow, 1995), 207. See also Vladimir Nikolaevich Razuvaev (biograficheskii ocherk) [V. N. Razuvaev—biography], *Soryon kunsakomundanjang Rajubayep ui 6. 25 chonjaeng pogoso* [Reports from the June 25 War by V. N. Razuvaev, Soviet Chief Military Advisor], vol. 1 (Seoul: Institute for Compiling Military History, Defence Ministry, ROK, 2001), 26–45. Here it is stated that Razuvaev arrived at Korea in November 1950.
148. Shu Guang Zhang, *Mao's Military Romanticism*, 123.
149. Heng Xueming, *Shengsi sanba xian: Zhongguo zhiyuanjun zai Chaoxian zhanchang shimo* [Life and death on the 38th parallel: the Chinese volunteers in the Korean War] (Anhui: Anhui Literature Publisher, 1982), 185.
150. *Mao Zedong's manuscripts*, vol. 1, 719–720.
151. Mossman, *Ebb and Flow*, 158–159.
152. *Mao Zedong's manuscripts*, vol. 1, 722.
153. *Selected military papers of Peng Dehuai*, 355.
154. Yang Fengan and Wang Tiancheng, *Jiayu chaoxian zhanzhengde ren* [A man who commanded the Korean War] (Beijing: CCP Central Party School Press, 1993), 203–204.
155. Ibid., 204; and Heng Xueming, *Life and death*, 185–186.
156. *Mao Zedong's manuscripts*, vol. 1, 741–742.
157. In *Korean War* I incorrectly said that Ambassador Shtykov was transferred after January 25, 1951. *Korean War*, 203–204.
158. Roshchin to Stalin, December 7, 1950, APRF, f. 45, op. 1, d. 336, 17–19.
159. Filippov to Zhou Enlai, December 7, 1950, Ibid., 20–21.
160. Decision of the Politburo, Central Committee, CPSU, December 7, 1950, Ibid., 23–24.
161. Yasuda, *China's first and second offensives*, 407–408.
162. This report was published in Kim Il Sung, *Chayu kwa tongnipul uihan uidaehan hae-bang tujaeng* [Great liberation struggle for freedom and independence] (Pyongyang, March 1951). See *Selected works of Kim Il Sung*, vol. 2 (August 1952). However, part of the original text has been deleted. A complete Russian language translation is in the former Communist

Party Archive in Moscow (Doklad Kim Ir Sena na plenume TsK Trudovoi partii Korei 21 dekabria 1950 goda, RGASPI, f. 17, op. 137, d. 731, 2–62). I basically used the text in *Selected Works*; for the omitted portion I followed the Russian language translation.

163. Doklad Kim Ir Sena, 13–14.

164. In *Korean War* (p. 196) I said "Kim Il Sung tacitly raised the issue of Pak Hon-yong's responsibility." I was wrong. The confrontation had not yet started.

165. In Manchuria Mu Chong executed the director of a hospital for professional negligence. Kim Il Sung telephoned Yi Sang-jo, assistant chief of staff, who organized three army corps, and ordered him to send Mu Chong back to North Korea, where he was relieved of all his positions. Interview with Yi Sang-jo, Minsk, April 27, 1990; and "Kim Il tongjiui yangnyok" [Biographical sketch of comrade Kim Il], *Nodong Shinmun*, March 10, 1984.

166. *Selected military papers of Peng Dehuai*, 357–358.

167. Futrell, *Air Force*, 256, 258.

168. *Selected military papers of Peng Dehuai*, 359–360.

169. Mossman, *Ebb and Flow*, 192–208; and *History of the CPV's War*, 61–63.

170. Mao Zedong to Filippov, January 8, 1951, APRF, f. 45, op. 1, d. 336, 88–90.

171. For details, see my *Korean War*, 200–201; Ye Yumeng, *Chubing Chaoxian: Kangmei yuanchao lishi jishi* [Historical records of Chinese military intervention in Korea] (Beijing: October Literature Press, 1990), 302–303; and Heng Xueming, *Life and death*, 193–196.

172. *New York Times*, December 16, 1950; and Pierpaoli, *Truman and Korea*, 26, 44–46.

173. Okonogi, *Korean War*, 258–259.

174. *FRUS, 1950*, vol. 7, 1625–1626.

175. *Ashida Hitoshi nikki* [Diary of Ashida Hitoshi], vol. 3 (Tokyo: Iwanami Shoten, 1986), 406–409.

176. Ibid., 413–414.

177. *Asahi Shimbun*, December 17, 1950.

178. Ibid., December 28, 1950.

179. Ibid., December 29, 1950.

180. Ibid.; and *Thirty years of the Japan Socialist Party*, 140–141.

181. *FRUS, 1950*, vol. 7, 1630–1633.

182. *FRUS, 1951*, vol. 7, 41–43.

183. Ibid., 55–57.

184. Ibid., 64.

185. Ibid., 71–72.

186. Zakharov to Filippov, January 13, 1951, APRF, f. 45, op. 1, d. 336, 121.

187. Roshchin to Moscow, January 13, 1951, Ibid., 122.

188. Mao Zedong to Filippov, January 16, 1951, Ibid., f. 45, op. 1, d. 337, 1–3.

189. Heng, *Life and death*, 208.

190. *Mao Zedong's manuscripts*, vol. 2, 28.

191. Heng Xueming, *Life and death*, 209.

192. *FRUS, 1951*, vol. 7, 76.

193. Ibid., 91–93.

194. Mossman, *Ebb and Flow*, 234–236.

195. Mao Zedong to Filippov, January 27, 1951, APRF, f. 45, op. 1, d. 337, 37–40.

196. Du Ping, *My days at the headquarters*, 188.

197. *Selected military papers of Peng Dehuai*, 364–367.

198. Du Ping, *My days at the headquarters*, 191.

199. Ibid., 191–192; and Hong Xuezhi, *Kangmei yuanchao zhanzheng huiyi* [Recollections of the war to resist America and assist Korea] (Beijing: Liberation Army Press, 1990), 115.

200. Mossman, *Ebb and Flow*, 240–247.

201. Heng Xueming, *Life and death*, 206–207.

202. *Kim Il Sung Chosakushu* [Writings of Kim Il Sung], vol. 6, (Pyongyang: Gaikokubun-shuppansha, 1981), 267.

203. Gao Gang's report, Russian language translation, RGASPI, f. 17, op. 137, d. 947, 20.

204. Ibid., 18.

205. Mao Zedong to Filippov, January 29, 1951, APRF, f. 45, op. 1, d. 337, 41–43. For a translation from Chinese sources, see Wada, *The Korean War*, 207.
206. Filippov to Mao Zedong, January 30, 1951, Ibid., 44.
207. Shu Guang Zhang, *Mao's Military Romanticism*, 137.
208. Du Ping, *My days at the headquarters*, 192.
209. *Choson Inmingun*, February 3, 1951.
210. *Selected military papers of Peng Dehuai*, 371–372.
211. Fyn Si to Razuvaev, January 30, 1951, APRF, f. 45, op. 1, d. 337, 12–13.
212. Ibid., Filippov to Mao Zedong, January 30, 1951, Ibid., 47–48.
213. Razuvaev to Filippov, January 31, 1951, Ibid., d. 338, 15–19.
214. *Selected military papers of Peng Dehuai*, 371–382; and *History of the war to resist America*, vol. 2, 227, 373.
215. Mao Zedong to Filippov, February 9, 1951, APRF, f. 45, op. 1, d. 337, 54–55.
216. *History of the CPV's War*, 78–81.
217. Mao Zedong to Filippov, March 2, 1951, APRF, f. 45, op. 1, d. 337, 78–82.
218. Filippov to Mao Zedong, March 4, 1951, Ibid., 89.
219. Citing a report on the condition and combat successes of the 64th Fighter Airforce Corps from November 1950 to September 15, 1951, General Belov said the zone from Antung to Sonchon was almost completely defensible but not the zone from Anju to Pyongyang. *Voprosy istorii* no. 11 (1994), 11.
220. *History of the CPV's War*, 81–86.

5. FIGHTING WHILE NEGOTIATING

1. *FRUS, 1951*, vol. 7, 263–264.
2. Ibid., 265–266.
3. Ibid., 298–299.
4. Ibid., 337.
5. Cumings, *Origins*, vol. 2, 750–751, 916.
6. Futrell, *Air Force*, 336–338.
7. *History of CPV's War*, 94–100; and Mossman, *Ebb and Flow*, 398–437.
8. *History of CPV's War*, 100–105; and Futrell, *Air Force*, 339–340.
9. Futrell, *Air Force*, 341.
10. *History of CPV's War*, 106–110; and Mossman, *Ebb and Flow*, 465–487.
11. *FRUS, 1951*, vol. 7, 401–410, 421–422.
12. The secretaries of Defense and State expressed a similar opinion in a draft memorandum to President Truman dated September 7, 1950. Igarashi Takeshi, *Sengo Nichi-Bei kankei no keisei—kowa anpo to reisengo no shiten ni tatte* [The formation of postwar US-Japan relations: the peace settlement and the security pact] (Tokyo: Kodansha Gakujutsu Bunko, 1995), 256–257. Toyoshita has written that to Dulles the most important issue in the peace negotiations was "whether the US military would retain the same rights to use military bases throughout Japan as during the Occupation." See Toyoshita, *Peace treaty*, 48.
13. *FRUS, 1951*, vol. 7, 833–834.
14. Diplomatic Archives of Ministry of Foreign Affairs, Japan, B. 4, 0.0.0, Sori-Allison kaidanroku [Transcript, meeting of Prime Minister (Yoshida)—(John) Allison], 0074–0075.
15. Igarashi, *Formation*, 199–200; and *FRUS, 1951*, vol. 7, 849.
16. *FRUS, 1951*, vol. 7, 944–950.
17. See Wada, *The Korean War*, chapter 3.
18. *Nihon Kyosanto tosei koyo bunken* [Japanese Communist Party documents related to strengthening party spirits] (Tokyo: Sundaisha, 1952), 68, 74.
19. Ibid, 145–154.
20. N. B. Adyrkhaev, *Sutarin to Nihon no Kyosanshugisha to no kaigo* [Stalin's meeting with Japanese Communists], *Kyokuto no shomondai* [Problems of the Far East] vol. 19, no. 4

(August 1990): 155–160; and Hakamada Satomi, *Watashi no sengoshi* [My postwar history] (Tokyo: Asahi Shimbunsha, 1978), 89–102.

21. *FRUS, 1951*, vol. 7, 1024–1036.

22. Filippov to Mao Zedong or Zhou Enlai, May 6, 1951, APRF, f. 45, op. 1, d.338, 67–69.

23. Mao Zedong to Filippov, May 6, 1951, Ibid., 77.

24. B. Slavinskii, "San-Frantsisskaia konferentsiia 1951 g. po mirnomu uregulirovaniiu s Iaponiei i sovetskaia diplomatsiia" [San Francisco peace conference and Soviet diplomacy], *Problemy Dal'nego Vostoka* no. 1 (1994): 87.

25. *FRUS, 1951*, vol. 7, 1119–1121.

26. Hong Sa-jung, "Kungmin pangwigun sakon" [The National Defense Corps incident], in *Chonhwanki ui naemak* [Inside story of the turning point] (Seoul: Chosun Ilbosa, 1982), 550.

27. *Tong'a Ilbo*, January 10, 1951.

28. Hong, "National Defense Corps incident," 551–565.

29. Yi Yong-hui, "Senjo to ningen" [The battlefield and human beings], in *Bundan minzoku no Kuno* [The anguish of a divided people], trans. Takasaki Soji (Tokyo: Ochanomizu Shobo, 1985), 125–126.

30. *Tong'a Ilbo*, January 21 and 27, 1951; and Hong, "National Defense Corps incident," 566–568.

31. *Tong'a Ilbo*, February 3, 1951.

32. *Tong'a Ilbo*, March 30, 1951; and Yi, "Battlefield," 148–152.

33. Yi, "Battlefield," 152–153.

34. *Tong'a Ilbo*, April 26 and 28, May 1 and 3, 1951.

35. *Tong'a Ilbo*, May 8, 1951; and *FRUS, 1951*, vol. 7, 464.

36. *Tong'a Ilbo*, May 10 and 17, 1951.

37. *FRUS, 1951*, vol. 7, 389–390.

38. Ibid., 419.

39. Ibid., 416–419. Muccio was angry at the resignation of Cho Pyong-ok. Syngman Rhee wrote to Robert Oliver that "Cho Pyong-ok is Muccio's man." Lee Jong Won, "Bei-Kan kankei ni okeru kainyu no genkei: 'Evuaredei keikaku' saiko" [Operation Everready reexamined: the prototype of interference in US-Korean relations], *Hogaku* 58, no. 1 (April 1994): 6.

40. *FRUS, 1951*, vol. 7, 493.

41. Ibid., 497.

42. Ibid., 503.

43. Ibid., 527.

44. Ibid., 526–527.

45. *Tong'a Ilbo*, June 16 and 25, 1951.

46. Hong, "National Defense Corps Incident," 570–573. In South Korea, coverage of the Kochang massacre was taboo until 1982, when many newspapers carried articles about the incident. According to the June issue of the magazine *Madan*, the number of residents killed was 719, not the official figure of 187. Yi, "Battlefield," 153–157.

47. *Pravda*, May 19, 1950.

48. *FRUS, 1951*, vol. 7, 483–486.

49. Filippov to Mao Zedong, May 22, 1951, APRF, f. 45, op. 1, d. 338, 87, and Mao Zedong to Filippov, May 26, 1951, Ibid., 89.

50. Mao Zedong to Filippov, May 26, 1951, Ibid., 91.

51. Mao Zedong to Filippov, May 27, 1951, Ibid., 95–97. In the Russian language text the letter to Peng Dehuai is dated May 16. However, in the Chinese text the date is May 26. See *Mao Zedong's manuscripts*, vol. 2 (Beijing: The Central Press of Historical Documents, 1988), 331–332.

52. Chen Jian considers Nie Rongzhen's account highly credible (*Nie Rongzhen's memoirs*, 741–742), and contends that after the fifth offensive, Mao Zedong and other Chinese leaders were ready to end the war. Chen quotes only from the first half of Mao Zedong's letter to Peng Dehuai. Chen Jian, "China's Strategies to End the Korean War" (paper presented at the Cold War International History Project conference, Hong Kong, January 1996, 11–12). Nie Rongzhen says a reassessment meeting was held at the general staff and "many comrades favored a halt near the 38th parallel and continue the fighting while negotiating and resolve all the issues

by negotiations . . . With Comrade Mao Zedong presiding, the meeting decided the policy of negotiating while fighting." The date of this meeting is unclear. Shu Guang Zhang and Kathryn Weathersby also rely on Nie Rongzhen to explain this change of policy. See Shu Guang Zhang, *Mao's Military Romanticism*, 217–218; and Kathryn Weathersby, "Stalin, Mao, and the End of the Korean War," in *Brothers in Arms: The Rise and Fall of the Sino-Soviet Alliance, 1945–1963*, ed. Odd A. Westad (Stanford University Press, 1998), 99. In my earlier work, without citing evidence I also wrote that Mao Zedong in late May "apparently decided to respond to the truce proposal." *Korean War*, 213.

53. Filippov to Mao Zedong, May 29, 1951, APRF, f. 45, op. 1, d. 338, 98–99.

54. Filippov to Razuvaev, May 29, 1951, Ibid., d. 348, 29. See also *CWIHP Bulletin* no. 6–7, 59.

55. Razuvaev to Filippov, May 30, 1951, Ibid., 30.

56. *Peng Dehuai nianpu* [A chronology of Peng Dehuai] (Beijing: People's Press, 1998), 500–501.

57. S. A. Krasovskii to Filippov, June 4, 1951, APRF, f. 45, op. 1, d. 339, 10–16.

58. Ibid., June 4, 1951, Ibid., 4–6.

59. Filippov to Mao Zedong, June 5, 1951, Ibid., 17–18. See also *CWIHP Bulletin* no. 6–7, 59–60.

60. *FRUS, 1951*, vol. 7, 507–511.

61. Chen Jian, "China's Strategies," 12; and Shu Guan Zhang, *Mao's Military Romanticism*, 218. Both works are based on Chai Chengwen and Zhao Yong-chon, *Banmendian tanpan* [Negotiations at Panmunjom] (Beijing: Liberation Army Press, 1988), 125. Weathersby cites Chen ("Stalin, Mao," 95). I also thought the Chinese had been unable to persuade Kim Il Sung and asked Stalin to change Kim's mind. *Korean War*, 213.

62. *Mao Zedong's manuscripts*, vol. 2, 350 and 355.

63. Mao Zedong to Filippov, June 5, 1951, APRF, f. 45, op. 1, d. 339, 23. See also *CWIHP Bulletin* no. 6–7, 60.

64. Filippov to Mao Zedong, June 7, 1951, Ibid., 26. See also *CWIHP Bulletin* no. 6–7, 60.

65. Shi, *Historical Giants*, 505–508.

66. Filippov to Mao Zedong, June 13, 1951, APRF, f. 45, op. 1, d. 339, 31–32. See also *CWIHP Bulletin* no. 6–7, 60–61. The heading "Three problems were presented" in Russian is "Byli postavleny tri voprosa." However, Torkunov read this as "Vami postavleny tri voprosa." Torkunov, *Enigmatic war*, 165. This mistake occurred because Torkunov thought Gao Gang and Kim Il Sung had persuaded Stalin of the need for a truce.

67. Roshchin to Filippov, June 13, 1951, APRF, f. 45, op. 1, d. 339, 55–56. See also *CWIHP Bulletin* no. 6–7, 61.

68. Memorandum, Gao Gang and Kim Il Sung to Stalin, June 14, 1951, Ibid., 57–60. See also *CWIHP Bulletin* no. 6–7, 61–62.

69. Mao Zedong to Filippov, June 21, 1951, Ibid., 64–65. See also *CWIHP Bulletin* no. 6–7, 62.

70. William Stueck, *The Korean War: An International History* (Princeton University Press, 1995), 208–209.

71. Filippov to Mao Zedong, June 24, 1951, APRF, f. 45, op. 1, d. 339, 78. See also *CWIHP Bulletin* no. 6–7, 62.

72. *FRUS, 1951*, vol. 7, 548.

73. Ibid., 574–576.

74. Ibid., 588–589.

75. Ibid., 601–604.

76. Ibid., 604–605.

77. *Tong'a Ilbo*, July 1, 1951.

78. *FRUS, 1951*, vol. 7, 607.

79. Ibid., 611.

80. *Tong'a Ilbo*, July 10, 1951.

81. Mao Zedong to Filippov, June 30, 1951, APRF, f. 45, op. 1, d. 339, 92. See also *CWIHP Bulletin* no. 6–7, 63.

82. Mao Zedong to Filippov, June 30, 1951, Ibid., 90–91. See also *CWIHP Bulletin* no. 6–7, 64.

83. Mao Zedong to Filippov, June 30, 1951, Ibid., 93–94. See also *CWIHP Bulletin* no. 6–7, 64.

84. Filippov to Mao Zedong, June 30, Ibid., 95–96. See also *CWIHP Bulletin* no. 6–7, 64–65.

85. Razuvaev to Filippov, July 1, 1951, Ibid., d. 340, 3–4. See also *CWIHP Bulletin* no. 6–7, 65.

86. Filippov to Razuvaev, July 2, 1951, Ibid., 5.

87. Mao Zedong to Filippov, July 3, 1951, Ibid., d. 339, 6–7. See also *CWIHP Bulletin* no. 6–7, 65.

88. Mao Zedong to Filippov, July 3, 1951, Ibid., 8–10. See also *CWIHP Bulletin* no. 6–7, 66.

89. Filippov to Mao Zedong, July 3, 1951, Ibid., 11. See also *CWIHP Bulletin* no. 6–7, 66–67.

90. Wada, *The Korean War*, 215.

91. Mao Zedong to Filippov, July 3, 1951, APRF, f. 45, op. 1, d. 339, 14–15. See also *CWIHP Bulletin* no. 6–7, 67.

92. Wada, *The Korean War*, 215–216.

93. *Mao Zedong's manuscripts*, vol. 2, 390.

94. *FRUS, 1951*, vol. 7, 1119–1120.

95. Hong Xuezhi, *Recollections*, 191; and *Mao Zedong's manuscripts*, vol. 2, 386.

96. Paek Sun-yob, *Memoirs*, 176–178.

97. Mao Zedong to Filippov, July 10, 11, 13, 16, and 17, 1951, APRF, f. 45, op. 1, d. 340, 22–24, 25–28, 29–30, 35–42, 54–55, 56–61, and 64–67.

98. Mao Zedong to Filippov, July 13, 1951, Ibid., 43–45.

99. Filippov to Mao Zedong, July 14, 1951, Ibid., 48.

100. Mao Zedong to Filippov, July 18, 1951, Ibid., 68–70.

101. Mao Zedong to Filippov, July 19 and 21, 1951, Ibid., 71–75, 85–87, and 95–96.

102. Mao Zedong to Filippov, July 21, 1951, Ibid., 83–84.

103. Mao Zedong to Filippov, July 21, 1951, Ibid., 88–91.

104. Filippov to Mao Zedong, July 21, 1951, Ibid., 92.

105. Mao Zedong to Filippov, July 26, 27, 29, 30, and 31, 1951, Ibid., 98–99, 100–102, 111–113, 116–122, 123–124, 125–129, 130–131, and 132–138.

106. Mao Zedong to Filippov, August 1, 2, 3, 4, 5, 11, 12,13, 17, and 20, 1951, Ibid., d. 341, 1–2, 3–4, 19–20, 22–23, 27–28, 37–39, 40–44, 59–60, 61–62, 73–74, 75–76, 77–78, 79–80, and 84–85.

107. Rosemary Foot, *A Substitute for Victory: The Politics of Peacemaking at the Korean Armistice Talks* (Cornell University Press, 1990), 46–47.

108. Mao Zedong to Filippov, August 2, 1951, APRF, f. 45, op. 1, d. 341, 7.

109. Mao Zedong to Filippov, August 4, 1951, Ibid., 30.

110. Mao Zedong to Filippov, August 11, 1951, Ibid., 45–46.

111. Torkunov, *Enigmatic War*, 174.

112. Mao Zedong to Filippov, August 13, APRF, f. 45, op. 1, d. 341, 56–58. See also *CWIHP Bulletin* no. 6–7, 67–68.

113. Mao Zedong to Filippov, August 13, 1951, Ibid., 53–55.

114. Central Committee, CPSU to Mao Zedong, August 17, 1951, Ibid., d. 340, 82.

115. Mao Zedong to Filippov, August 27, 1951. Ibid., 86–88. See also *CWIHP Bulletin* no. 6–7, 68–69.

116. Filippov to Mao Zedong, August 29, 1951, Ibid., 89. Decision of the Politburo, CPSU, APRF, f. 3, op. 65, d. 829, 4–5. See also *CWIHP Bulletin* no. 6–7, 69.

117. Mao Zedong to Filippov, August 30, 1951, APRF, f. 45, op. 1, d. 341, 97. See also *CWIHP Bulletin* no. 6–7, 70.

118. *FRUS, 1951*, vol. 7, 694–695.

119. Ibid., 707–709.

120. Ibid., 745.

121. On July 27, 1951, Kim Chae-uk presented a report to the Political Committee, Central Committee, KWP, on "Regarding the plan to establish a Korean Workers' Party organization in the Korean People's Army." Kim is believed to have been head of the Political Department, KPA. See his report, RGASPI, f. 17, op. 137, d. 730, 96–101.

122. Ibid., 100–113. This decision is discussed in Kim Nam-sik, *Namnodang yongu* [A study of The Southern Workers' Party] (Seoul: Tolbegae, 1984), 463–464.

123. For materials from the trial of Pae Chol and Pak Sung-won, see "Michegukchuui koyong kanchop Pak Hon-yong,Yi Sung-yop todangui Choson minjujuui inmin konghwaguk chonggwon chonbok ummo wa kanchop sakon kongban munhon" [Materials from the trial of the conspiracy of the agents of US imperialism Pak Hon-yong, and Yi Sung-yop clique to overthrow the Democratic People's Republic of Korea]. *"Nam-Nodang" yongu charyojip* [Materials on the 'Southern Workers' Party'], vol. 2 (Seoul: Korea University Press, 1974), 492–493 and 544–545. Kim Nam-sik, *Southern Workers' Party*, 468–470.

124. Kim Nam-sik, *Southern Workers' Party*, 470–471; and Yi Tae, *Guerrilla units in the South*, 290–294.

125. Kim Hak-Joon, *The Unification Policy of South and North Korea* (Seoul National University Press, 1977), 139. Kim Hak-Joon, *Chosen Senso: tsukon no minzoku shototsu* [The Korean War: a tragic clash] (Tokyo: Saimaru Shuppankai, 1991), 252–253. This study is based on North Korean radio broadcasts.

126. *FRUS, 1951*, vol. 7, 813.

127. *Writings of Kim Il Sung*, vol. 6, 393–394.

128. Kim Hak-Joon expresses this view in *Unification Policy*, 138, and *Korean War*, 252. I did too in *Korean War*, 217.

129. Ambassador Razuvaev sent a telegram to Moscow on September 10, 1951 in which he pointed out that "Korean leaders cherish some wariness toward armistice negotiations, only they cannot express it openly and directly." "Korean leaders' thinking is under a certain pressure. This war, which will destroy the state, cannot make Koreans achieve unification. Therefore, at present in the worst conditions, they cannot but agree to the restoration of the situation before the war." Shtykov also mentioned some differences in attitude between Chinese and Koreans, "Kim Il Sung and other Korean leaders already recognized the military and political necessity of the armistice agreement, but they thought that the negotiations should be done lest the prestige of the DPRK should be injured . . . Chinese tend to make concession to Americans only to come to armistice agreement" Shen Zihua, ed., *Korean War*, vol. 3, 1022, 1024.

130. RGASPI, f. 17, op. 137, d. 731, 66–91.

131. Ibid., 95–104.

132. Pak Il-u, *Choson inmingun kwa Chungguk inmin chiwongun ui kongdong chakchon* [Joint operations by the Korean People's Army and the Chinese People's Volunteers] (Pyongyang: Choson rodongdang chulpansa, 1951), 24 and 30.

133. Ibid., 76.

134. Adyrkhaev, *Stalin's meetings*, 155–160; and Hakamada, *My postwar history*, 89–102.

135. *Nihon Kyosanto gojunen mondai shiryoshu* [Documents on the 1950 controversy in the Japanese Communist Party], vol. 3, Tokyo: Shin Nihon Shuppansha, 1987, 172–173.

136. Kameyama Kozo, *Sengo Nihon Kyosanto no nijuchobo* [The postwar Japanese Communist Party's double accounting] (Tokyo: Gendai Hyoronsha, 1978), 153–160.

137. For the Soviet proposal, see AVPRF, Fond Vyshinskogo, 1951 op. 24, p. 32, d. 396, part 2, 93–94; and Slavinskii, "San Francisco peace conference," 96–97.

138. Ministry of Foreign Affairs, Treaty Bureau, ed., *Kaisetsu heiwa joyaku* [Commentary on San Francisco peace treaty] (Tokyo, 1951).

139. Watanabe Yozo, Yoshioka Yoshinori, eds., *Nichibei Anpojoyaku Zensho* [Documents on the Japan-US security pact] (Tokyo: Rodojunposha, 1968), 65–67.

140. *Japanese Communist Party documents*, 7–20.

141. Shinobu, *Political history of postwar Japan*, vol. 4, 1158.

142. For the situation in the vicinity of US bases in Japan, see Inomata Kozo, Kimura Kihachiro, and Shimizu Ikutaro, eds., *Kichi Nihon—Ushinawareteiku Sokoku no sugata* [Japan as US bases: our disappearing homeland] (Tokyo: Wakosha, 1953).

143. Yamamoto Takeshi, "Chosen tokuju" [Korean War special procurements], in *Showa no senso* [The War of Showa], vol. 10, ed. Yamamuro Hideo (Tokyo: Kodansha, 1985), 96.

144. *Teijin no ayumi* [History of the Teijin company], 7 (Tokyo: Teijin Kabushiki Kaisha, 1972), 79.

145. Ibid., 80.

146. *Toyota Jidosha Nijunenshi* [Twenty-year history of the Toyota automobile company] (Toyota: Toyota Jidosha Kabushikigaisha, 1958), 300–314.

147. Ibid., 315–317.

148. Ibid., 318–319.

149. *Tokuju ni kansuru tokei* [Special procurement statistics] (Tokyo: Keizai Shingicho Chosabu Tokeika, 1954), 12–13.

150. *Nihon Gaikoshi* [Diplomatic history of Japan], vol. 28 (Tokyo: Kashima Kenkyujo Shuppankai, 1971), 33–34.

151. Lee Jong Won, "Kannichi Kaidan to Amerika—'Fukainyu seisaku'no seiritsu o chushin ni" [The Japan-ROK conference and the United States: formation of the "nonintervention policy"], *Kokusai Seiji* 105 (January 1994): 165.

152. Sodei Rinjiro, ed., *Correspondence between General MacArthur, Prime Minister Yoshida and Other High Japanese Officials [1945–1951]* (Tokyo: Hosei University Press, 2000), 147. This letter was first published by Sodei in *Hogaku Shirin* 79, no. 2. Subsequently Tanaka Hiroshi quoted it in "Sengo Nihon to posuto shokuminchi mondai" [Postwar Japan and postcolonial problems], *Shiso*, August 1985, 44–45.

153. Mihashi Osamu, Robert Riketto, Yi Yong-nang, and Ebina Yoshinori, "Senryoka ni okeru taizainichi Chosenjin kanri seisaku keisei katei no kenkyu (1)" [Formulation of Japanese policy to control Koreans in Japan during the Occupation (1)], *Seikyu gakujutsu ronshu* no. 6 (1995): 268.

154. *FRUS, 1951*, vol. 7, 1007–1008; and Tanaka, "Postwar Japan," 44.

155. Yi Won-dok, "Nihon no sengo shori gaiko no ichi kenkyu—Nikkan kokko seijoka kosho (1951–65) o chushin ni shite" [An aspect of Japan's diplomacy to settle postwar issues—negotiations to normalize relations between Japan and the ROK] (PhD diss., University of Tokyo, 1994), 30. Takasaki Soji, *Kensho Nikkan kaidan* [The Japan-ROK conferences revisited] (Iwanami Shoten, 1996), 22–23.

156. Yu Chin-o, "*Han-Il Hoedam*" [ROK-Japan conferences], 23, *Chung'ang ilbo*, September 26, 1983.

157. *Diplomatic history of Japan*, vol. 28, 39–40.

158. Yu Chin-o, "ROK-Japan conferences," 21, *Chung'ang ilbo*, Sept. 23, 1983.

159. Lee Chong-Sik, *Japan and Korea: The Political Dimension* (Stanford University Press, 1985), 37.

160. *History of CPV's War*, 124–126; *History of the war to resist America*, vol. 3, 183–187; and Matthew B. Ridgway, *The Korean War* (New York: Doubleday, 1967), 185–190.

161. Mao Zedong to Filippov, August 27, 1951, APRF, f. 45, op. 1, d. 340, 87. See also *CWIHP Bulletin* no. 6–7, 68–69.

162. Mao Zedong to Filippov, September 8, 1951, Ibid., d. 341, 98–99. See also *CWIHP Bulletin* no. 6–7, 70.

163. Filippov to Mao Zedong, September 10, 1951, Ibid., 109. See also *CWIHP Bulletin* no. 6–7, 70.

164. Filippov to Mao Zedong, September 12, 1951, Ibid., 120.

165. Mao Zedong to Filippov, September 20, 1951, Ibid., 125–127.

166. Filippov to Mao Zedong, September 26, 1951, and Mao Zedong to Filippov, October 5, 1951, Ibid., 128–129 and 134–135.

167. Filippov to Mao Zedong, October 7, 1951, Ibid., 136–137.

168. Jon Halliday, "Air Operations in Korea: The Soviet Side of the Story," in *A Revolutionary War: Korea and the Transformation of the Postwar World*, ed.William J. Williams (Chicago: Imprint Publications, 1993), 152.

169. *Voprosy istorii*, no. 12 (1994): 32.

170. Mao Zedong to Filippov, October 24, 1951, APRF, f. 45, op. 1, d. 341, 141.

171. *Voprosy istorii*, no.12 (1994): 30–31.

172. *History of the war to resist America*, vol. 3 (2000), 108–111. For Pak Chong-dok, see Kim Jung-saeng, *Secret arrival*, 186.

173. Kim Jung-saeng, *Secret arrival*, 114–127.

174. Foot, *Substitute for Victory*, 50.

175. Mao Zedong to Filippov, October 19, 1951, APRF, f. 45, op. 1, d. 341, 139–140.

176. Mao Zedong to Filippov, October 25, 1951, Ibid., 144–146.

177. Mao Zedong to Filippov, October 25, 1951, Ibid., 147–149.

178. Mao Zedong to Filippov, October 31, 1951, Ibid., 160.

179. Mao Zedong to Filippov, November 14, 1951, Ibid., f. 45, op. 1, d. 342, 16–19. See also *CWIHP Bulletin* no. 6–7, 70–71.

180. Razuvaev to Vasilevskii, October 17, 1951, Ibid., d. 358, 38. Matveiev (Zakharov) to Razuvaev, November 13, 1951, Ibid., 39.

181. Razuvaev to Zakharov, November14, 1951, Ibid., 43.

182. Filippov to Mao Zedong, November 19, 1951, Ibid., d. 342, 23. For the Politburo decision, see Ibid., f. 3, op. 65, d. 828, 42–43. See also *CWIHP Bulletin* no. 6–7, 72.

183. Politburo decision, Central Committee, CPSU, November 19, 1951, Ibid., f. 3, op. 65, d. 828, 44–45. See also *CWIHP Bulletin* no. 6–7, 72.

184. Draft telegram to Razuvaev, and Gromyko to Malenkov, November 20, 1951, Ibid., 46–48. See also *CWIHP Bulletin* no. 6–7, 72–73.

185. Telegram from Pyongyang to Gromyko, November 21, 1961, Ibid., 49–53.

186. A. I. Lan'kov, *Severnaia Koreia: vchera i segodnia* [North Korea: yesterday and today] (Moscow, 1995), 50–56. *VKP (b), Komintern i Iaponiia, 1917–1941* [The All-Union Communist Party (b.), Comintern and Japan, 1917–1941] (Moscow, 2001), 712.

187. RGASPI, f. 17, op. 137, d. 731, 111–145. See Kim Il Sung, *Writings of Kim Il Sung*, vol. 6, 429–452. Although this section of the text has been considerably modified, the gist of the speech has not been revised.

188. RGASPI, f. 17, op. 137, d. 731, 146–149.

189. Ibid., 149–151.

190. Ibid., 151–152.

191. Ibid., 152–159.

192. Ibid., 160–179 and 180–196. Kim Il Sung, *Writings of Kim Il Sung*, vol. 6, 453–467.

193. RGASPI, f. 17, op. 137, d. 731, 110. The text says only that Ho Ka-i was dismissed as secretary.

194. "Kim Il tongjiui yangnyok" [Biographical sketch of comrade Kim Il], *Nodong Shinmun*, March 10, 1984. Kim Il is known to have been chairman of the Party committee in South Pyongan Province in March 1952. Wu Ruilin wrote in his memoirs that his unit was visited in March 1952 by Kim Il, secretary of the Party committee in North Pyongan Province. Wu Ruilin, *Kangmei yuanchao zhongde Disishi'er jun* [The 42nd Army in the war to resist America and assist Korea] (Beijing: Jincheng Press, 1995), 188. But it was not the case. That Kim Il was top party leader in South Pyongan Province was verified by Suh Dong-man. See Suh, *Formation of Socialist System*, 938.

195. Lee Jong Won, "Operation Everready," 7. Yun Kyong-chol, *Politics in the Republic of Korea*, 133.

196. Kim Mun-nyong, "Palsu kaehon" [Abridged constitutional revision], in *Turning point*, 586–587. Yun Kyong-chol, *Politics in the Republic of Korea*, 134.

197. Kim Mun-nyong, "Abridged constitutional revision," 593–594.

198. Foot, *Substitute for Victory*, 109, 111–112.

199. Shao Yulin, "Shihan huiyilu" [Memoirs of the ambassador to Korea], 24, "Han zhan-chang wo moulue xinzhanxhi peihe yunyong" [Our psychological warfare operations on the Korean battlefield], *Zhuanji wenshue* 34, no. 2 (1979): 122.

200. Foot, *Substitute for Victory*, 114–116.

201. Ibid., 96–97; and *FRUS, 1952–1954*, vol. 15, 6.

202. Mao Zedong to Filippov, January 31, 1952, APRF, f. 45, op. 1, d. 342, 73–77. See also *CWIHP Bulletin* no. 6–7, 74–75.

203. Filippov to Mao Zedong, February 2, 1952, Ibid., 78. See also *CWIHP Bulletin* no. 6–7, 75.

204. Mao Zedong to Filippov, February 4, 1952, Ibid., 81–82.
205. Ibid., 81.
206. Ibid., 81–82.
207. Ibid., 82–83.
208. Politburo decision, Central Committee, CPSU, April 14, 1952, Ibid., f. 3, op. 65, d. 778, 22–23. Babkin to Shtemenko, attachment, letter from Kim Il Sung to Stalin, April 16, 1952, Ibid., f. 45, op. 1, d. 348, 60–61. See also *CWIHP Bulletin* no. 6–7, 76–77.
209. *FRUS, 1952–1954*, vol. 15, 36–38.
210. Ibid., 40–43.
211. Ibid., 44–45.
212. Foot, *Substitute for Victory*, 87, 116.

6. THE THIRD YEAR

1. *History of the war to resist America*, vol. 3, 186, 190.
2. Hastings, *The Korean War*, 272.
3. Soviet materials about the antibacteriological campaign were published in the *Sankei Shimbun* on January 8, 1998. The Japanese newspaper got handwritten copies of documents in the Russian Presidential Archive that were subsequently retyped. Kathryn Weathersby of the CWIHP concluded that they are credible and published English-language translations in Kathryn Weathersby, "Deceiving the Deceivers: Moscow, Beijing, Pyongyang, and the Allegations of Bacteriological Weapons Use in Korea," *CWIHP Bulletin* no. 11 (Winter 1998): 176–185. Milton Leitenberg concurred with Weathersby's conclusions. See Leitenberg, "New Russian Evidence on the Korean War Biological Warfare Allegations: Background and Analysis," Ibid., 185–199. The first document in Weathersby's publication is an excerpt from Mao Zedong's telegram to Stalin on February 21, 1952. It accords in content with the plan by Zhou Enlai dated February 19, 1952. We also can confirm the fact that this topic was discussed at the Politburo, Central Committee, CPSU, on February 23, 1952. I consider the excerpt authentic.
4. Yang Dezhi, *Weile heping* [For the peace] (Beijing: Long March Publisher, 1987), 101–102.
5. *A Chronology of Peng Dehuai*, 524–525; and *History of the war to resist America*, vol. 3, 213.
6. *A Chronology of Zhou Enlai*, vol. 1, 217. Bacteriological warfare is not mentioned prior to February 21, 1952.
7. Ibid., 218.
8. *Choson inminui chonguiui chogukhaebang chonjaengsa* [A history of the righteous war of the Korean people to liberate the fatherland], vol. 3 (Pyongyang: Sahoekwahak Chulpansa, 1983), 150.
9. *Nodong Shinmun*, February 23, 1952.
10. *CWIHP Bulletin* no. 11, 180. According to the Explanatory Note from former Ambassador Razuvaev to Beriia (April 18, 1953), when the Chinese government informed Kim Il Sung and Pak Hon-yong of US germ warfare, the Korean leaders consulted him. Razuvaev doubted the allegations and advised them to ask the Chinese for an explanation. Instead the North Koreans quickly issued a statement and "two days later the statement of Zhou Enlai followed."
11. *Politbiuro TsK RKP (b)-VKP (b). Povestki dnia zasedanii 1919–1952. Katalog* [Politburo, CPSU 1919–1952: Meeting agendas, list], vol. 3 (Moscow, 2001), 872.
12. *Pravda*, February 24, 1952, 4.
13. *A Chronology of Zhou Enlai*, vol. 1, 220.
14. *Nodong Shinmun*, February 27, 1952.
15. *Nie Rongzhen nianpu* [A chronology of Nie Rongzhen] (Beijing: People's Liberation Army Press, 1999), 546.
16. *History of the war to resist America*, vol. 3, 213–214, 222–223; and *Mao Zedong's manuscripts*, vol. 3, 303.
17. *Politbiuro TsK RKP (b)-VKP (b)*, vol. 3, 874.

18. *Pravda*, March 8, 1952, 4.

19. *A Chronology of Zhou Enlai*, vol. 1, 223–224.

20. *Nodong Shinmun*, March 2, 1952.

21. Gromyko' s memorandum, March 5, 1952, APRF, f. 3, op. 65, d. 830, 3. See also *CWIHP Bulletin* no. 6–7, 76.

22. Politburo decision, March 7, 1952, APRF, f. 3, op. 65, d. 830, 1–2.

23. *A Chronology of Zhou Enlai*, vol. 1, 224–227; and *A Chronology of Nie Rongzhen*, vol. 1, 547.

24. Leitenberg, "New Russian Evidence," 186–187.

25. Weathersby, "Deceiving the Deceivers," 180–181.

26. Chen, *Mao's China and the Cold War*, 110; and Leitenberg, "New Russian Evidence," 188.

27. Gromyko to the Soviet Ambassador, Beijing, March 9, 1952, APRF, f. 45, op. 1, d. 342, 100.

28. Mao Zedong to Filippov, March 10, 1952, Ibid., 102–103.

29. *History of the war to resist America*, vol. 3, 194.

30. Mao Zedong to Filippov, March 29, 1952, APRF, f. 45, op. 1, d. 342, 126–130.

31. Filippov to Mao Zedong, April 2, 1952, Ibid., d. 343, 2–3.

32. Hosoya Chihiro, *Sanfuranshisuko kowa e no michi* [The road to the San Francisco peace treaty] (Tokyo: Chuo Koronsha, 1984), 279–301.

33. For outstanding research on this topic based on Nationalist Chinese and Japanese documents, see Ishii Akira, "Nikka heiwa joyaku teiketsu kosho o meguru jakkan no mondai" [Some issues of the negotiations on a Japan-Republic of China peace treaty], *Tokyo Daigaku Kyoyo Gakubu, Kyoyo Gakka kiyo* no. 21 (March 1988). See also "Nikka heiwa joyaku no koshokatei; Nihon gawa daiichiji soan o megutte" [Negotiation of the Japan-Republic of China peace treaty: Japan's first proposal], *Chugoku—shakai to bunka* [China: society and culture] no. 3 (June 1988). For my article, which draws heavily on Ishii's work, see Wada Haruki, "Economic Co-operation in Place of Historical Remorse: Japanese Post-war Settlements with China, Russia and Korea in the Context of the Cold War," in *The Political Economy of Japanese Society*, vol. 2 (Oxford University Press, 1998).

34. Diplomatic Archives of Ministry of Foreign Affairs, Japan, "Nikka heiwajoyaku kankei ikken" [Documents related to the Japan-ROC peace treaty], vol. 3, 28–29.

35. Ibid., vol. 1, 433.

36. Ibid., 435–436.

37. Ibid., 436.

38. Ishii, "Some Issues," 86–88.

39. Diplomatic Archives of MOFA, Japan, File cited, vol. 1, 611–612.

40. Ibid., vol. 3, 232, 259.

41. Ibid., vol. 2, 294–295.

42. *A Chronology of Zhou Enlai*, vol. 1, 237.

43. Lee Jong Won, "Japan-ROK conference and the United States," 167–169; and Yi Won-dok, "Aspect of Japan's diplomacy," 34–35.

44. *Diplomatic history of Japan*, vol. 28, 46–47; and *Han-Il kwangye charyojip* [Materials on ROK-Japan relations], vol. 1 (Seoul: Asiatic Research Center, Korea University, 1976), 92–94; Yi Won-dok, "Aspect of Japan's diplomacy," 35–42; and Takasaki, *Japan-ROK conferences*, 35–37.

45. Kim Nam-sik, *Southern Workers' Party*, 470.

46. Yi Tae, *Guerrilla units in the South*, 295–296.

47. *Nodong Shinmun*, April 10, 1952.

48. Ibid., April 15, 1952.

49. Futrell, *Air Force*, 448–449, 480.

50. Ibid., 449–452. See also the description of the damage from the Soviet side, Razintsev's report, July 11, 1952, attached to Razuvaev to Sokolovskii, July 28, 1952, Razuvaev, *June 25 war reports*, vol. 3, 106–130.

51. The *Asahi Shimbun* headlined these air raids: "Suiho among Five Power Plants Bombed on the Korean-Manchuria Border" (June 24, 1952); "Four Power Plants Attacked Again" (June

25, 1952); "North Korean Power Plants Knocked Out, US Far East Navy Announces," (June 25, evening edition); "US Bombing of Suiho Criticized, Prime Minister Atlee in House of Commons," (June 26, 1952); "Power Plants Bombed Three Times" (June 27, 1952); and "Soviet Newspaper Condemns Bombing of Suiho" (June 27, 1952, evening edition).

52. *Asahi Shimbun*, June 25, 1952, evening edition.

53. Futrell, *Air Force*, 480–481.

54. *Asahi Shimbun*, July 4, 1952, evening edition.

55. Futrell, *Air Force*, 482.

56. *Asahi Shimbun*, July 12, 1952, morning and evening editions; July 13, 1952.

57. Futrell, *Air Force*, 483.

58. *Asahi Shimbun*, July 31, 1952, evening edition.

59. *FRUS, 1952–1954*, vol. 15, 357.

60. *Voprosy istorii* no. 12 (1994), 31–32. The MiG 15 and F-86 had a maximum air speed of 1,100 KPH. The MiG 15's weight and wingspan were less than those of the F-86. The Soviet fighter was armed with one 37 mm canon and two 23 mm cannons; the US plane had four 20 mm cannons. The aircraft were about equal in overall operational capability. Combat results varied depending on pilot experience. V. K. Babich, *Vozdushnyi boi (Zarozhdenie i razvitie)* [The air fighting: how it began and developed] (Moscow, 1991), 159.

61. National Intelligence Estimate, "Communist Capabilities and Probable Courses of Action in Korea," *FRUS, 1952–1954*, vol. 15, 439–440.

62. Mao Zedong to Filippov, April 22, 1952, APRF, f. 45, op. 1, d. 343, 22–23.

63. Mao Zedong to Filippov, July 4, Ibid., 55–57.

64. *History of the war to resist America*, vol. 2, 269.

65. Mao Zedong to Filippov, July 18, 1952, APRF, f. 45, op. 1, d. 343, 72–75. This cable includes Mao's telegram to Kim Il Sung dated July 15, 1952. See also *CWIHP Bulletin* no. 6–7, 78–79.

66. Kim Il Sung's reply dated July 16 is also included in Mao's July 18 cable.

67. Razuvaev to Vasilevskii and Vyshinskii. Kim Il Sung's letter to Stalin is attached. July 17, 1952, APRF f. 45, op. 1, d. 348, 65–68. See also *CWIHP Bulletin* no. 6–7, 77. This episode of Kim Il Sung's failed attempt to dissent from Mao's position was long overlooked by scholars. I first pointed out this fact in my article "East Asia and the Cold War: Reinterpreting Its Meaning in the New Millenium," in *Ending the Cold War in Korea*, ed. Chung In Moon (Yonsei University Press, 2001), 79–80. Shen Zihua also paid attention to this episode in his article "Sino-North Korean Conflict and its Resolution during the Korean War," *CWIHP Bulletin* no. 14–15 (Winter 2003–Spring 2004): 19–20.

68. Filippov to Mao Zedong, July 16, 1952, Ibid., d. 343, 69.

69. Filippov to Kim Il Sung, July 24, 1952, Ibid., d. 348, 70.

70. Filipov to Mao Zedong, July 24, 1952, Ibid., d. 343, 76.

71. Yun Kyong-chol, *Politics in the Republic of Korea*, 134–135.

72. *FRUS, 1952–1954*, vol. 15, 50–51.

73. Ibid., 16.

74. Lee Jong Won, "Operation Everready," no. 1, 15.

75. Ibid., 16.

76. *FRUS, 1952–1954*, vol. 15, 251–252.

77. Ibid., 252–256, 266.

78. Lee Jong Won, "Operation Everready," no. 1, 17. The authority for this assertion is not provided.

79. *FRUS, 1952–1954*, vol. 15, 266–267.

80. Ibid., 268–269.

81. Cho Kap-che, "Yi Sung-man taetongnyong chego kyehoek" [The plan to remove President Syngman Rhee], *Wolgan Choson*, June 1984; and Lee Jong Won, "Operation Everready," no. 1, 18–19.

82. Lee Jong Won, "Operation Everready," no. 1, 20–22. See also Jong Yil Ra, "Political Crisis in Korea, 1952: Administration, Legislature, Military and Foreign Powers," *Journal of Contemporary History* 27 (1992): 313–314. Edward C. Keefer, "The Truman Administration

and the South Korean Political Crisis of 1952: Democracy's Failure?" *Pacific Historical Review* 60, no. 2 (May 1991): 158.

83. *FRUS, 1952–1954*, vol. 15, 280.

84. Ibid., 274–276.

85. Ibid., 289.

86. Ibid., 285–286.

87. Ibid., 290–293.

88. Ibid., 293–295.

89. Ibid., 299–301.

90. Ibid., 301–302.

91. Ibid., 302–305.

92. Ibid., 308.

93. Ibid., 325.

94. Ibid., 334.

95. Ibid., 336–337.

96. Ibid., 337. Young strongly opposed Syngman Rhee and wanted the State and Defense departments to develop a plan for the ROKA to declare martial law and establish a transitional government by Koreans. Lee Jong Won, "Operation Everready," no. 1, 34.

97. Yun Kyong-chol, *Politics in the Republic of Korea*, 137.

98. *FRUS, 1952–1954*, vol. 15, 349–350.

99. Lee Jong Won, "Operation Everready," no. 1, 35–36. In *Korean War*, I did not examine the crisis and dated Operation Everready from the spring of 1953. Lee shows that the prototype was conceived in June 1952, a very instructive insight.

100. *FRUS, 1952–1954*, vol. 15, 358–360.

101. Ibid., 377. This letter, which has not been made public, is cited in the note.

102. Ibid., 362–363.

103. Ibid., 376–377; Kim Mun-nyong, "Abridged constitutional revision," 605–607; and Yun Kyong-chol, *Politics in the Republic of Korea*, 137–138.

104. *FRUS, 1952–1954*, vol. 15, 377–379. Lee Jong Won says the Clark proposal was reactive, put a heavy burden on the United States, and would have been difficult to execute, compared to the Defense Department proposal to use the ROKA. On the contrary, under wartime conditions it may have been more feasible despite the chief of staff's negative stand.

105. Sasaki, *Korean War*, vol. 1, 459, 469.

106. Kim Mun-nyong, "Abridged constitutional revision," 607–611; and Yun Kyong-chol, *Politics in the Republic of Korea*, 140–141.

107. Futrell, *Air Force*, 484.

108. I utilized the transcripts of the Moscow meetings for my account of them. Russian transcript of meeting between Stalin and Zhou Enlai, August 20, 1952, APRF, f. 45, op. 1, d. 329, 64–65. See also *CWIHP Bulletin* no. 6–7, 12.

109. APRF, f. 45, op. 1, d. 329, 66–67. See also *CWIHP Bulletin* no. 6–7, 12–13.

110. Weathersby writes that Chinese leaders wanted a settlement while Stalin "continued to press for continuation of the war." For this interpretation, see Weathersby, "Stalin, Mao," 104–105; Bajanov and Bajanova, *The Korean War*, 213; and Torkunov, *Enigmatic War*, 257.

111. Stalin and Zhou Enlai, August 20, 1952, APRF, f. 45, op.1, d. 329, 68–70. See also *CWIHP Bulletin* no. 6–7, 13. Weathersby finds Stalin's remarks and proposal on prisoners of war inconsistent. She concludes that Stalin pressured Zhou to continue the war (Weathersby, "Mao, Stalin," 106), she could not understand why Stalin would speak that way. Chen Jian, too, even in his later book, repeats this standard interpretation. Chen makes China the driving force in truce negotiations, finds no disagreement between Beijing and Moscow on ending the war, and mistakenly asserts that Stalin's proposal was an amalgam of Zhou's three proposals. (Chen, *Mao's China and the Cold War*, 112–114).

112. APRF, f. 45, op. 1, d. 329, 71–72. See also *CWIHP Bulletin* no. 6–7, 14.

113. Zhou Enlai to Stalin, including Mao Zedong's letter, August 25, 1952, APRF, f. 45, op.1, d. 343, 89–90.

114. Futrell, *Air Force*, 489.

115. The record of this unique meeting only became available in 2003. "Russian Documents on the Korean War: 1950–53," introduction by James Hershberg and translation by Vladislav Zubok, *CWIHP Bulletin* no. 14–15 (Winter 2003–Spring 2004): 378–381. This document was published in Chinese at the same time. Shen Zhihua, ed., *The Korean War*, vol. 3, 1214–1221.

116. *CWIHP Bulletin* no. 14–15, 378.

117. Ibid., 379.

118. Ibid., 379–380.

119. Futrell, *Air Force*, 491.

120. Zhou Enlai to Stalin, including letter from Mao Zedong, September 16, 1952, APRF, f. 45, op. 1, d. 343, 94–96. See also *CWIHP Bulletin* no. 6–7, 79.

121. Semenov (Stalin) to Mao Zedong, September 17, 1952, Ibid., 97–103. See also *CWIHP Bulletin* no. 6–7, 79.

122. Stalin and Zhou Enlai meeting, September 19, 1952, Ibid., d. 329, 91–93. See also *CWIHP Bulletin* no. 6–7, 17–18.

123. Ibid., 99–100. See also *CWIHP Bulletin* no. 6–7, 19.

124. Phillip Knightley, *Philby: The Life and Views of the K.G.B. Master Spy* (London, 1992); Genrich Borovik, *The Philby Files: The Secret Life of Master Spy Kim Philby* (Boston: Little, Brown, 1994); and Richard Deacon, *The Cambridge Apostles: A History of Cambridge University's Elite Intellectual Secret Society* (London: Farrar, Straus & Giroux, 1986).

125. Wada, *The Korean War*, 242–243.

126. TsKhSD, f. 89, op. 50, d. 5, 1.

127. Nam Ki-jong, "Korean War and Japan," 263–264.

128. Chon Jin-sik, *Waga Chosen, watashi no Nihon* [Our Korea, my Japan] (Tokyo: Heibonsha, 1993), 205–206; Kang Che-on, "Minsen jidai no watashi" [My role in the Unified Democratic Front], in *Taiken de kataru kaihogo zai-Nichi Chosenjin undo* [The postwar Korean movement in Japan: personal accounts] (Kobe: Kobe Gakusei Seinen Center Shuppanbu, 1989), 146–150.

129. Kobayashi Tomoko, a specialist on the Korean minority in Japan, has written: "I am certain that Koreans in Japan did not commit acts of violence such as blowing up freight trains during the Korean War." "Sengo ni okeru zai-Nichi Chosenjin to 'sokoku'—1945–1952" [The postwar Korean minority in Japan and the 'fatherland'—1945–1952] (PhD diss., Ewha Women's University, 1996), 60. Nam Ki-jong, "Korean War and Japan," also found no major acts of violence committed by Koreans.

130. *Asahi Shimbun*, June 25, 1952, evening edition; and Wada Haruki, *Rekishi toshiteno Nosaka Sanzo* [Nosaka Sanzo as history] (Tokyo: Heibonsha, 1996), 247–248.

131. Hokkyokusei [The North Star], no. 7, June 10, 1952; in Pak Kyong-shik, ed., *Chosen mondai shiryo sosho* [Materials on Korean problems, series], vol. 15 (Tokyo: Ajia Mondai Kenkyujo, 1991), 152–159.

132. Nam Ki-jong, "Korean War and Japan," 266–273; and Kobayashi, "Postwar Korean minority," 95–96.

133. Watanabe Tomiya, *Itsuwari no rakuin: Ito Ritsu supaisetsu no hokai* [Stigma: Ito Ritsu was not a spy] (Tokyo: Gogatsu Shobo, 1993), 323.

134. Tsuboi Toyokichi, *Zai-Nichi Chosenjin undo no gaikyo* [Political activity by the Korean minority in Japan: an overview], reprint, (Tokyo: Jiyu Seikatsu-sha, 1959), 381–382.

135. *FRUS, 1952–1954*, vol. 15, 545–547.

136. Ibid., 554–557.

137. Ibid., 557.

138. *Sovieto domei kyosanto daijukyukai taikai gijiroku* [Nineteenth Congress, Communist Party of the Soviet Union, record] (Tokyo: Gogatsu Shobo, 1953), 34.

139. Stalin, *Sodomei ni okeru shakai shugi no keizaiteki shomondai* [Some economic problems of socialism in the USSR] (Tokyo: Kokumin Bunko, 1953), 42–46.

140. *Sovetskii atomnyi proekt: Konets atomnoi monopolii. Kak eto bylo . . .* [The Soviet atomic project: the end of monopoly of atomic bombs], Nizhnii Novgorod, 1995, 189, 191–192.

141. Ibid., 196–198.

142. L. L. Kerber, *Tupolev* [Andrei Tupolev] (Saint Petersburg, 1999), 227, 242.

342   *Notes*

143. Anastas Mikoyan, *Tak bylo: Razmyshleniia o minuvshem* [This was the past. Thoughts about the past] (Moscow: Vagrius, 1999), 574. Novelist Konstantin Simonov wrote of these events in *Glazami cheloveka moego pokoleniia* [By the eye of a member of my generation] (Moscow, 1990), 236–239.

144. Mikoyan, *This was the past*, 572–573.

145. Foot, *Substitute for Victory*, 154.

146. Memorandum, Pushkin, October 30, 1952, APRF, f. 3, op. 65, d. 830, 33–34. Decision, Presidium Bureau, Central Committee, CPSU, November 3, 1952, Ibid., 31–32. There is also a Tass announcement.

147. Foot, *Substitute for Victory*, 154.

148. William Stueck, *The Korean War*, 301.

149. *History of the war to resist America*, vol. 3, 333.

150. *Renmin Ribao*, November 30, 1952.

151. The diary note of V. A. Malyshev (1937–1951) was found in his office after his death and preserved in the Party Archives. *Istochnik* no. 5 (1997): 140–141.

152. *Ito Ritsu kaisoroku: Beijing sanjunananen* [Ito Ritsu's memoirs: thirty-seven years in Beijing] (Tokyo: Bungei Shunshu, 1993), 14–16.

153. Nosaka Sanzo, "'Beijing kikan' ni kansuru Ito Ritsu no "shogen" ni tuite" [Ito Ritsu's 'testimony' regarding the 'Beijing center'], *Akahata*, January 26, 1981. Nosaka Sanzo, "Ito Ritsu shogen e no hansho: watashi no iibun" [A refutation of Ito Ritsu's account], *Asahi Shimbun*, February 16, 1981.

154. This G-2 report is known as Willoughby's report, which was released by GHQ SCAP to the public on February 11, 1949. Later it was published in 1952 in the United States. Charles A. Willoughby, *Shanghai Conspiracy, The Sorge Spy Ring* (New York: Dutton, 1952). The report aimed partly to damage the reputation of the JCP by disclosing the dark past of its central figure. This version of Ito's responsibility for the exposure of Sorge's ring was carefully studied by Chalmers Johnson in the appendix "Was Ito a Judas?" attached to his book *An Instance of Treason: Ozaki Hotsumi and the Sorge Spy Ring* (Stanford University Press, 1990). It is now challenged by Ito Ritsu himself and researcher Watanabe Tomiya with persuasion. Watanabe Tomiya, *Itsuwari no Rakuin: Ito Ritsu Supaisetsu no hokai* [Stigma: Ito Ritsu was not a spy] (Tokyo: Gogatsu Shobo, 1993). See Ito's confession, Ibid., 382–404.

155. *Ito Ritsu's memoirs*, 47–48. Ito returned to Japan in September 1980 after twenty-seven years in a Chinese prison.

156. RGASPI, f. 17, op. 137, d. 947, 146–210.

157. Ibid., 211–228.

158. *Nodong Shinmun*, January 5, 18, and 26, 1953, and February 5, 1953.

159. Ibid., February 5, 17, 18, 23, 26, and 31, 1953.

160. "Materials from the trial of the agents of US imperialism", 467–469.

161. *Nodong Shinmun*, March 4, 5, and 10, 1953. One interpretation mistakenly puts Pak Hon-yong's arrest on March 5 (Miyamoto Satoru, "Chosen Jinmingun no 'seikika'" ["Normalization" of the Korean People's Army], *Rokkodai ronshu (Hogakuseijihen)* 47, no. 1 (July 2000): 134.

162. Kang Sang-ho's memoirs, *Chung'ang Ilbo*, April 6, 1993 and June 28, 1993. According to court records Yun Sun-dal and Yi Won-jo were arrested on March 13, 1953, and April 12, 1953, respectively.

163. Dimitrii Volkogonov, *Triumf i tragediia. Politicheskii portret I. V. Stalina* [Triumph and tragedy: Stalin's political portrait], vol. 2, part 2 (Moscow: Agentstvo Novosti, 1989), 191–196.

164. *Mao Zedong's manuscripts*, vol. 3, 632; and Shu Guang Zhang, *Mao's Military Romanticism*, 234–235.

165. *History of the war to resist America*, vol. 3, 353.

166. Ibid., 355.

167. Mao Zedong to Semenov, December 17, 1952, APRF, f. 45, op. 1, d. 343, 105–114.

168. Semenov to Mao Zedong, December 27, 1952, Ibid., 115–116. See also *CWIHP Bulletin* no. 6–7, 79–80. Weathersby says of Stalin, "advising the Chinese to prepare for a new

American attack served to maintain the status quo in Korea," but I cannot agree. Weathersby, "Mao, Stalin," 108.

169. *Izvestiia*, December 26, 1952; and *Renmin Ribao*, December 26, 1952.
170. Razuvaev to Sokolovskii, Kim Il Sung's letter to Stalin is attached, January 3, 1953, APRF, f. 45, op. 1, d. 348, 83–87.
171. Memorandum, Vasilevskii and Sokolovskii to Stalin, January 3, 1953, Ibid., d. 343, 133–135.
172. Mao Zedong to Semenov, January 8, 1953, Ibid., 125–128.
173. Semenov to Mao Zedong, January 15, 1953, Ibid., 137.
174. Ibid., January 27, 1953, Ibid., 139.
175. *Istoricheskii arkhiv* no. 1 (1996): 34–35. Such a description is not in *Liu Shaoqi Nianpu* [a chronology of Liu Shaoqi], vol. 2 (Beijing: Central Press of Historical Documents, 1996).
176. *New York Times*, February 3, 1953.
177. Shu Guang Zhang, *Mao's Military Romanticism*, 329.
178. Qi Dexue, *Inside story of decision making*, 330; Du Ping, *My days at the headquarters*, 142; and *History of the war to resist America*, vol. 3, 394.
179. *FRUS, 1952–1954*, vol. 15, 770.
180. Nakatsuji Keiji, "Aizenhawa- seiken to Chosen teisen—'tairyo hofuku' senryaku o jiku ni" [The Eisenhower administration and the Korean armistice: the strategy of "massive retaliation"] *Hiroshima Daigaku Sogo Kagakubu kiyo*, 2, *Shakai bunka kenkyu* 14 (1988): 40.
181. Chai and Zhao, *Negotiations at Panmunjom*, 255–256, and *History of the war to resist America*, vol. 3, 380.
182. *FRUS, 1952–1954*, vol. 15, 785–786, 788–790.
183. *History of the war to resist America*, vol. 3, 380.
184. Memorandum, Borisov and Vyshinskii, February 10, 1953, APRF, f. 3, op. 65, d. 778, 100.
185. Decision, Presidium Bureau, Central Committee, CPSU, February 18, 1953, Ibid., 101–102.

7. THE ARMISTICE

1. *Haebanghu simnyon ilchi* [Chronology of ten years after liberation, 1945–1955] (Korean Central News Agency, n.d.), 133; and *Nodong Shinmun*, March 10, 1953.
2. *A Chronology of Zhou Enlai*, vol. 1, 289–290.
3. Ibid.
4. Memorandum and proposal, Molotov to Malenkov and Beria, March 18, 1953, APRF, f. 3 op. 65, d. 830, 72, 74–82.
5. Decision of the Cabinet, USSR, March 19, 1953, Ibid., 60–71. See also *CWIHP Bulletin* no. 6–7, 80–82.
6. *A Chronology of Zhou Enlai*, vol. 1, 290.
7. *History of the war to resist America*, vol. 3, 381.
8. *Izvestiia*, March 9, 1953.
9. *A Chronology of Zhou Enlai*, vol. 1, 290.
10. *Mao Zedong's Manuscripts*, vol. 4, 148–149.
11. *A Chronology of Zhou Enlai*, vol. 1, 291. Yang Kuisong has written that Stalin supported Beijing's position on Chinese prisoners, but his successors pressured China and Mao Zedong had to change his position. See Yang Kuisong, *Mao Zhedong he Mosike de enen yuanyuan* [Mao Zhedong and Moscow's love and hate] (Nanchang: Jiangxi People's Publisher, 1999), 363–365. Zhang Min and Zhang Xiujuan believe Zhou Enlai favored the Soviet proposal to concede on prisoners and persuaded Mao to agree. See Zhang Min and Zhang Xiujuan, *Zhou Enlaihe kangmeiyuanchao zhanzheng* [Zhou Enlai and the war to resist America and assist Korea] (Shanghai: Shanghai People's Publisher, 2000), 500. Chen Jian emphasizes Chinese factors: "In this context, China's shifting attitude toward the POW issue in late March 1953 appears much more logical and less dramatic than it would seem otherwise. Stalin's death

might have contributed to this reversal, but it was more an outgrowth of Beijing's existing policies based on Chinese leaders' assessment of the changing situation than a reflection of altering Soviet directives." Chen, *Mao's China and the Cold War*, 115.

12. *A Chronology of Zhou Enlai*, vol. 1, 291.

13. *FRUS, 1952–1954*, vol. 15, 818–819.

14. Torkunov, *Enigmatic war*, 279; and Kuznetsov and Fedorenko to Moscow, March 29, 1953, APRF, f. 3, op. 65, d. 830, 98.

15. Kuznetsov and Fedorenko to Moscow, March 29, 1953, 97–98. See also *CWIHP Bulletin* no. 6–7, 83.

16. *Renmin Ribao*, March 30, 1953.

17. Kuznetsov and Fedorenko to Moscow, March 29, 1953. For Yi Tong-gon's status as a Soviet Korean, see *Pirok: Choson Minjujuui Inmin Konghwaguk* [Secret records: the Democratic People's Republic of Korea], vol. 1 (Seoul: Chung'ang Ilbosa, 1992), 182.

18. *Izvestiia*, April 2, 1953.

19. Memorandum, Molotov to Malenkov, March 31, 1953, APRF, f. 3, op. 65, d. 830, 110.

20. *FRUS, 1952–1954*, vol. 15, 826–827.

21. Ibid., 874–876.

22. Ibid., 857.

23. *FRUS, 1952–1954*, vol. 15, 897–898.

24. Ibid., 902–903.

25. Ibid., 896. Nakatsuji Keiji, "Chosen teisen to Bei-Kan kankei" [The truce in Korea and United States-Republic of Korea relations], *Shiso* no. 5 (1990): 50; and Lee Jong Won, "Aizenhawa-seiken no tai-Kan seisaku to 'Nihon'" (1) [The Eisenhower administration's policy toward Korea and "Japan"], *Kokka Gakkai Zasshi* 10, nos. 1–2 (February 1994): 45–46.

26. *Tong'a Ilbo*, April 24, 1953.

27. *FRUS, 1952–1954*, vol. 15, 935.

28. Ibid., 941.

29. In *Korean War*, I did not appreciate the significance of Clark's message. See Lee Jong Won, "Operation Everready," (2). 5 ff.

30. *FRUS, 1952–1954*, vol. 15, 950–951; and Chai and Zhao, *Negotiations at Panmunjom*, 259–260.

31. *FRUS, 1952–1954*, vol. 15, 947–950.

32. Ibid., 955–956.

33. *Tong'a Ilbo*, May 1, 1953.

34. *FRUS, 1952–1954*, vol. 15, 967.

35. Ibid., 980–981.

36. Ibid., 987.

37. Ibid., 1008–1010.

38. Ibid., 1011.

39. *Department of State Bulletin*, May 25, 1953, 755–757.

40. *History of the CPV's War*, 198–200.

41. *FRUS, 1952–1954*, vol. 15, 1020.

42. Ibid., 1022–1023.

43. Ibid., 1090–1093.

44. Ibid., 1106–1108.

45. *History of the CPV's War*, 200–204.

46. *FRUS, 1952–1954*, vol. 15, 1102–1104.

47. Ibid., 1115–1119.

48. Ibid., 1119–1120.

49. Ibid., 1121.

50. Ibid., 1128.

51. Ibid., 1124–1126.

52. Paek Sun-yop, *Memoirs*, 199.

53. *Tong'a Ilbo*, May 30 and June 2, 1953.

54. Molotov Diary, meeting with US Ambassador Charles Bohlen, June 3, 1953, ARPF, f. 3, op. 65, d. 812, 6–13.

55. *FRUS, 1952–1954*, vol. 15, 1137.
56. Ibid., 1144–1146.
57. Ibid., 1148.
58. *Department of State Bulletin*, June 22, 1953, 866–867.
59. *FRUS, 1952–1954*, vol. 15, 1152–1154.
60. *Department of State Bulletin*, June 15, 1953, 835–836.
61. *FRUS, 1952–1954*, vol. 15, 1159–1160.
62. Ibid., 1166.
63. Ibid., 1168.
64. Ibid., 1172–1173.
65. Ibid., 1173–1174.
66. Ibid., 1180–1183.
67. According to Lee Jong Won, the State Department was focused on the possibility of agreement by the Soviet Union and underestimated the reactions of China and North Korea. Lee Jong Won, "Eisenhower administration's policy," 51. There was no chance of an agreement with the Soviet Union either.
68. *FRUS, 1952–1954*, vol. 15, 1187.
69. *Department of State Bulletin*, July 6, 1953, 13–14.
70. *FRUS, 1952–1954*, vol. 15, 1200–1205.
71. Ibid., 1217.
72. *Department of State Bulletin*, June 29, 1953, 907.
73. Yang Dezhi, *For the peace*, 218–219.
74. Ibid., 219–220.
75. *FRUS, 1952–1954*, vol. 15, 1231–1232.
76. Ibid., 1241–1242.
77. Ibid., 1238–1240.
78. Ibid., 1265–1269.
79. Ibid., 1272–1274.
80. Ibid., 1278–1279.
81. Ibid., 1279–1280.
82. Ibid., 1283.
83. Ibid., 1286.
84. *Department of State Bulletin*, July 13, 1953, 46–47.
85. Nas'kov to Moscow, July 3, 1953, APRF, f. 3, op. 65, d. 812, 136–147.
86. Decision of the Presidium Bureau, Central Committee, CPSU, July 4, 1953, Ibid., 135.
87. Molotov to Soviet ambassador in China, July 4, 1953, Ibid., d. 830, 148–150.
88. *FRUS, 1952–1954*, vol. 15, 1290–1291.
89. Lee Jong Won, "Eisenhower administration's policy," 50.
90. *FRUS, 1952–1954*, vol. 15, 1291.
91. Ibid., 1294–1295.
92. Ibid., 1295.
93. Ibid., 1300–1308.
94. Ibid., 1314.
95. Ibid., 1318.
96. Ibid., 1324.
97. Ibid., 1326–1329.
98. Ibid., 1351.
99. Ibid., 1341–1346.
100. Ibid., 1353–1354.
101. Ibid., 1354.
102. Ibid., 1358.
103. Ibid., 1358–1359.
104. Ibid., 1360.
105. Ibid., 1362.
106. Ibid., 1364–1365.
107. Ibid., 1374.

108. *History of the CPV's War*, 212. John Miller, Jr., Owen J. Carroll, and Margaret E. Tackley, *Korea 1951–1953* (Office of the Chief of Military History, 1982), 283; and Kojima Noboru, *Chosen senso* [Korean War], vol. 3 (Tokyo: Bungeishunju, 1984), 485.

109. Kang Sang-ho memoirs, *Chung'ang Ilbo*, May 10 and 17, 1993; *Renmin Ribao*, August 16, 1953; and "Kim Il tongjiui yangnyok" [Biographical sketch of comrade Kim Il], *Nodong Shinmun*, March 10, 1984.

110. [Pak Chong-ae], *Choekun tangnaeesso barrodoen Yi Sung-yob, Pae Chol, Pak Sung-won, Yun Sun-dal, Cho Il-myong, Yi Kang-gukdung pantang pankukkajok kanchop totangdului sakone kwanhayo* [On the case of the antiparty and antistate spies clique Yi Sung-yop, Pae Chol, Pak Sung-won, Yun Sun-dal, Cho Il-myong, Yi Kan-guk, and others,which was discovered recently in our party] (Pyongyang, 1953), 40. On the first page of the document no author's name is written, only stamps of "Top Secret" and "10,000 copies printed." Pang Sun-joo found this document among captured North Korean materials and kindly allowed me to use it. The document is believed to be the report by Pak Chong-ae to the Sixth Plenum of CC, KWP, August 1953.

111. Ibid., 41.

112. *Pravda*, April 6, 1953.

113. *CWIHP Bulletin* no. 11, 180–182. Igor' Selivanov read a paper, "Soviet medical aid during the Korean War," at a symposium at Kyonghui University, June 20, 1992, in which he disclosed that Soviet experts conducted an extensive epidemiological survey in North Korea and confirmed that germ warfare projectiles were not used. See *Toitsu Nippo* (Tokyo), June 23, 1992.

114. *CWIHP Bulletin* no. 11, 182–184. Ignat'ev was dismissed by the Plenum of Central Committee on April 28. See *Lavrentii Beriia, 1953. Stenogramma iiul'skogo Plenuma TsK KPSS i drugie dokumenty* [Lavrentii Beriia, 1953. Stenographic record of the July 1953 plenary meeting of CC CPSU and other documents] (Moscow, 1999), 347 and 398. The *Sankei Shimbun* materials show the Central Committee expelled Ignat'ev from the party on June 2. See *CWIHP Bulletin* no. 11, 184. The most recent materials related to Beriia made public in Russia, however, do not show that Ignat'ev's expulsion was implemented. On July 7, after Beriia was arrested, Ignat'ev was restored to favor and returned to the Central Committee. See *Lavrentii Beriia, 1953*, 348. In short, Ignat'ev was not actually ousted. Either he was not expelled on June 2 or, improbably, the decision was kept secret until Beriia was arrested on June 26.

115. V. I. Petukhov, *U istokov bor'by za edinstvo i nezavisimost' Korei* [At the beginning of the struggle for Korean unification and independence] (Moscow, 1987), 191. Suzdalev's name first appears on a telegram to Moscow dated July 19, 1953. APRF, f. 3, op. 65, d. 830, 154–164.

116. Wada Haruki, "Sutarin hihan: 1953–1956" [Criticism of Stalin: 1953–1956], in *Gendai shakaishugi—sono tagenteki shoso* [Contemporary socialism: its multiple dimensions] (University of Tokyo Press, 1977), 15–16.

117. Memorandum, Molotov to Malenkov and Khrushchev, July 23, 1953, APRF, f. 3, op. 65, d. 830, 167–168.

118. Decision of the Presidium Bureau, Central Committee, CPSU, July 24, 1953, Ibid., 167–168.

119. *FRUS, 1952–1954*, vol. 15, 1428.

120. Ibid., 1430–1432.

121. Ibid., 1443–1444.

122. Chai and Zhao, *Negotiations at Panmunjom*, 280–282.

123. Suzdalev to Moscow, July 19, 1953, APRF, f. 3, op. 65, d. 830, 154–164.

124. *Nodong Shinmun*, special edition, July 28, 1953. See also Kim Il Sung, *Writings of Kim Il Sung*, vol. 7 (Pyongyang: Gaikokubunshuppansha, 1981), 480–499. In the 1981 edition the term "completion of national territory" was changed to "preservation of national territory."

125. *Nodong Shinmun*, July 29, 1953.

126. *Tong'a Ilbo*, July 28, 1953.

127. *FRUS, 1952–1954*, vol. 15, 1442–1443.

128. *Tong'a Ilbo*, July 29, 1953.

129. *New York Times*, July 29, 1953.

130. Ibid., July 30, 1953; Stueck, *The Korean War*, 342–343.

131. Kuznetsov to Moscow, July 29, 1953, APRF, f. 3, op. 65, d. 830, 187–189. See also *CWIHP Bulletin* nos. 6–7, 83.

132. *History of the war to resist America*, vol. 3, 465.

133. Ibid., 466–467.

134. *Izvestiia*, July 28, 1953.

135. *New York Times*, July 27, 1953.

136. Hastings, *The Korean War*, 326.

137. Ibid., 325–326.

138. *Asahi Shimbun*, July 28, 1953.

139. Ibid. A Japanese Foreign Ministry report on the prospects for a truce anticipated economic difficulties. *Chukyo shinteian o meguru Chosen kyusen kosho no seihi narabini sono eikyo* [The new Chinese Communist proposal: the outlook for truce negotiations in Korea]. Nam Ki-jong, "Korean War and Japan," 100.

140. *Asahi Shimbun*, July 27, 1953, evening edition.

141. *Zhonghua minguo dashiji* [Chronology of the Republic of China] (Taipei, 1957), 641.

142. *Renmin Ribao*, August 13, 1953.

143. [Pak Chong-ae], *Report to the Sixth Plenum*, 40–41.

144. Decision of the Presidium Bureau, Central Committee, CPSU, August 3, 1953, APRF, f. 3, op. 65, d. 779, 1.

145. Ibid., August 19, 1953, Ibid., 25.

146. For the treaty text, see Yang Tae-hyon, *Testimony of history*, 490–492.

147. David Rees, *The Limited War* (London: Macmillan, 1964), 460–461.

148. Halliday and Cumings, *Unknown war*, 200.

149. Wada, *The Korean War*, 326.

150. Razuvaev, *June 25 war reports*, vol. 3, 36.

151. Halliday and Cumings, *Unknown war*, 200.

152. An Yong-hyon, *Secret history*, vol. 5, 508.

153. Wada, *The Korean War*, 323.

154. Qi Dexue, *Inside story of decision making*, 358.

155. Halliday and Cumings, *Unknown war*, 200–201.

156. An Yong-hyon, *Secret history*, vol. 5, 508.

157. Halliday and Cumings, *Unknown war*, 200.

158. *Voprosy istorii* no. 12 (1994): 45; and *Rossiia i SSSR v voinakh XX veka. Kniga poter.* [Russia and USSR in wars of the 20th century: a book of losses] (Moscow: Veche, 2010), 554.

159. Foot, *Substitute for Victory*, 190.

160. 14,619 Chinese POWs went to Taiwan finally. *Chronology of the Republic of China*, 650.

161. Huang Kewu, "Yiersanziyouri—congyigejieride yanbiankan dangdai Taiwan fangong-shenhua de xingshuai" [The rise and fall of a contemporary Taiwanese anti-Communist myth as seen through the change of a national holiday], in *1949 nian—zhongguo de guanjian niandai xueshu taolunhui lunwenji* [Year 1949—a collection of articles from a symposium on key years of Chinese history] (Taipei, 2000), 643–669.

162. Da Ying, *Zhiyuanjun zhanfu jishi* [Prisoners of war of the Chinese People's Volunteers] (Beijing: Kunlun, 1987), 274–276.

163. Ibid., 282–284.

164. Ibid., 291–292.

165. Heo Man-ho, "Human Rights Legacies of the Korean War: Civilian Genocide and South Korean POWs Detained in North Korea" (a paper presented at the International Symposium in Commemoration of the 50th Anniversary of the Korean War, Seoul, June 24, 2000).

166. Foot, *Substitute for Victory*, 190.

167. *Asahi Shimbun*, September 11, 2001.

168. Dzhorzh Bleik [George Blake], *Inogo vybora net* [No other choice] (Moscow, 1991), 151–156. Blake fled to the Soviet Union in the 1960s.

169. The armistice agreement text is in *Department of State Bulletin*, August 3, 1953, 132–139.

170. Ibid., 139.
171. Foot, *Substitute for Victory*, 201; and Heng, *Life and death*, 372–373.
172. *Asahi Shimbun*, February 19, 1954. Japan tried unsuccessfully to participate in the political conference on the Korean War. Nam Ki-jong, "Korean War and Japan," 156–158.
173. *Asahi Shimbun*, April 28, 1954.
174. Ibid., April 29, 1954.
175. Ibid., April 28, 1954.
176. Ibid., April 29, 1954.
177. Ibid., May 23, 1954, evening edition.
178. Ibid., June 16, 1954.

8. POSTWAR NORTHEAST ASIA

1. Callum A. MacDonald, *Korea: The War before Vietnam* (MacMillan Press, 1986), 258.
2. An Yong-hyon, *Secret history*, vol. 5, 515; and *Chosen Minshushugi Jinmin Kyowakoku kokumin keizai hatten tokeishu, 1946–1963* [Economic development statistics for the Democratic People's Republic of Korea, 1946–1963] (Tokyo: Nihon Chosen Kenkyujo, 1965), 6.
3. Sawa Masahiko, *Nam-Boku Chosen kurisutokyo shiron* [The history of Christianity in South and North Korea] (Nihon Kirisutokyo-dan Shuppankai, 1982), 320–321; and NRC, USFEC, RG 242, SA 2005, item 4/41.
4. Murata Koji, *Daitoryo no zasetsu— Ka-ta-seiken no zaikanbeigun tettai seisaku* [The president fails: the Carter administration's policy of US troop withdrawal from the Republic of Korea] (Yuhikaku, 1998), 39.
5. Wada Haruki, *Kitachosen: Yugekitai Kokka no Genzai* [North Korea: the guerrilla unit state today] (Tokyo: Iwanami Shoten, 1998), 209. Wada Haruki, *Kitachosen Gendaishi* [A contemporary history of North Korea] (Tokyo: Iwanami Shoten, 2012), 73, 97.
6. Paul G. Pierpaoli, Jr., "Alpha and Omega: Understanding the Meaning of the Korean War" (paper presented at the international symposium, "The Korean War and Searching for Peace on the Korean Peninsula in the 21st Century," Seoul, June 24, 2000, 5–6).
7. John Lewis Gaddis, *We Now Know: Rethinking Cold War History* (Oxford: Clarendon Press, 1997), 49.
8. Paul G. Pierpaoli, Jr., "Alpha and Omega," 8.
9. Paul G. Pierpaoli, Jr., *Truman and Korea: The Political Culture of the Early Cold War* (University of Missouri Press, 1999), 149, 187, 227–228.
10. See Kamijima Haruhiko, *Red Purge Hollywood: Akagari ni idonda Blacklist eigajin retsuden* [Red Purge Hollywood: Lives of blacklisted moviemen who challenged the Purge] (Tokyo: Sakuhinsha, 2006). Roger Bowen, *Innocence Is Not Enough: The Life and Death of Herbert Norman* (Vancouver: Douglas and McIntyre, 1986).
11. Elena Zubkova, *Poslevoennoe sovetskoe obshchestvo: politika i povsednevnost' 1945–1953* [Postwar Soviet society: politics and everyday life, 1945–1953] (Moscow, 2000), 201.
12. I. V. Bystrova, *Voenno-ekonomicheskaia politika SSSR: ot "demilitarizatsii" k gonke vooruzhenii. Stalinskoe desiatiletie kholodnoi voiny; fakty i gipotezy* [The Soviet military-economic policy; from demilitarization to the arms race, Stalin's ten years of the Cold War, facts and hypothesis] (Moscow, 1999), 176–177.
13. Ibid., 176.
14. Ibid., 184.
15. Zubkova, *Postwar Soviet society*, 130.
16. *History of the war to resist America*, vol. 3, 547.
17. Ibid., 555.
18. Shu Kenei (Zhu Jianrong), *Motakuto no Betonamu senso—chugoku gaiko no daitenkan to bunka daikakumei no kigen* [Mao Zedong and the Vietnam War: the turnabout of China's foreign policy and the origin of the cultural revolution] (Tokyo: Daigaku Shuppankai, 2001), 23–24.

Bibliography

I. OFFICIAL SOURCES

Unpublished Sources

Arkhiv Prezidenta Rossiiskoi Federatsii (APRF) [Russian presidential archives], fond 3, opis' 65, delo 3, 371, 511, 515, 775, 776, 777, 778,779, 812, 826, 827, 828, 829, 830, 839; fond 45, opis' 1, delo 329, 331, 334, 335, 336, 337, 338, 339, 340, 341, 342, 343, 346, 347, 348. Cold War International History Project (CWIHP) file.

Arkhiv vneshnei politiki Rossiiskoi Federatsii (AVPRF) [Russian archives of foreign policy] fond Vyshinskogo, 1951, opis' 24, papka 32, delo 396, part 2.

Diplomatic Archives of Ministry of Foreign Affairs, Japan. Nikka heiwajoyaku kankei ikken [Documents related to the Japan-ROC peace treaty]. Vol. 1, 2, 3.

Diplomatic Archives of Ministry of Foreign Affairs, Japan. Sori-Allison kaidanroku [Transcript, meeting of Prime Minister (Yoshida)—(John) Allison], B4, 0, 0, 0, 6.

Elityn file of ROK Foreign Ministry from the Institute for Diplomatical and Security Studies, ROK.

Khronologiia osnovnykh sobytii kanuna i nachal'nogo perioda Koreiskogo voiny (ianvar' 1949–oktiabr' 1950 gg.) po materialam Arkhiva vneshnei politiki Rossii Ministerstva inostrannykh del Rossiiskoi Federatsii [Chronology of basic events on the eve and in the early period of the Korean War according to the materials of the Russian Foreign Ministry].

Pak Chong-ae. *Choegun tangnaeesso ballodoen Yi Sung-yob, Pae Chol, Pak Sung-won, Yun Sun-dal, Cho Il-myong, Yi Kang-gukdung pandang pankukkajok kanchop todangdului sakone kwanhayo* [On the case of the antiparty and antistate spies clique Yi Sung-yop, Pae Chol, Pak Sung-won, Yun Sun-dal, Cho Il-myong, Yi Kan-guk, and others which was discovered recently in our party]. (A report in the Plenary Meeting of CC KWP, August 1953.)

Rossiiskii gosudarstvennyi arkhiv sotsial'no-politicheskoi istorii (RGASPI) [Russian state archives on social-political history], fond 17, opis' 128, delo 415, 618; opis' 137, delo 414, 730, 731, 947, 4134; fond 514, opis' 1, delo 1078.

Tsentr khraneniia sovremennoi dokumentatsii (TsKhSD) [Center for storage of contemporary documents] (Now Rossiiskii gosudarstvennyi arkhiv noveishei istorii=RGANI), 1/d I-I, ll. 127–128; fond 89, opis' 50, delo 2.

US National Records Center (NRC), United States, Far East Command (USFEC). Record Group (RG) 242 "Captured Enemy Documents." ATIS Enemy Documents, no. 6, Item 2, 200564; Item 3, 200686.

US National Records Center (NRC), United States Military Government in Korea. Record Group (RG) 319.
US National Records Center (NRC), G-2, Intelligence Summaries—North Korea.
United States, Far East Command (USFEC). Record Group (RG) 331. General Headquarters/ Supreme Command of Allied Forces (GHQ SCAP). (National Library of Parliament, Japan Microfiche.)

Published Sources

Korean Language

Choson minjujuui inmin konghwaguk naegak kongbo [Cabinet announcements, Democratic People's Republic of Korea (DPRK)]. No. 146, 148, 1950; no. 2, 1951.
Hangukchonjaengki pilla [Leaflets in the period of the Korean War]. N.p.: Institute of Asian Culture Studies, Hallym University, 2000.
Han-Il kwangye charyojip [Materials on ROK-Japan relations]. Vol. 1. Seoul: Asiatic Research Center, Korea University, 1976.
Kim Il Sung. *Chayu kwa tongnibul uihan uidaehan haebang tujaeng* [Great liberation struggle for freedom and independence]. Pyongyang, March 1951.
Kim Sa-ryang chakpumjip [Selected works of Kim Sa-ryang]. Pyongyang: Munye chulpansa, 1987.
Kim Song-chil. *Yoksa appeso: han sahakcha ui 6:25 ilgi* [Witness to history: a historian's diary of the Korean War]. Seoul: Changjak kwa pipyongsa, 1993.
KLO-TLO munsojip [Documents of the KLO and TLO]. Vol. 1. Chunchon: Institute of Asian Culture Studies, Hallym University, 2000.
"Michegukchuui koyong kanchop Pak Hon-yong,Yi Sung-yop todangui Choson minjujuui inmin konghwaguk chonggwon chonbok ummo wa kanchop sakon kongban munhon" [Materials from the trial of the conspiracy of the agents of US imperialism Pak Hon-yong, Yi Sung-yop clique to overthrow the Democratic People's Republic of Korea]. *"Nam-Nodang" yongu charyojip* [Materials on the "Southern Workers' Party"]. Vol. 2. Seoul: Korea University Press, 1974.
Miguk kungnip kongmunsogwan sojang Pukhan haebanchikhu kukpicharyo [Secret materials related to North Korea immediately after liberation, in US National Archives, August 1945–June 1951]. Vol. 3–6. Seoul: Koryo sorim, 1998. (This is an unauthorized reprint edition of Hagiwara Ryo's publications, *Kitachosen no Gokuhibunsho*. 3 vols. Tokyo: Natsu no shobo, 1995.)
Pak Il-u. *Choson inmingun kwa Chungguk inmin chiwongun ui kongdong chakchon* [Joint operations by the Korean People's Army and the Chinese People's Volunteers]. Pyongyang: Choson Rodongdang chulpansa, 1951.
Propaganda and Agitation Bureau. *Kim Il Sung changgunui ryakchon* [General Kim Il Sung's short biography]. N.p.: Central Committee, KWP, April 15, 1952.
Pukchoson rodongdang cheicha chondang taehoe hoeuirok [Records of the Second Congress of NKWP]. Pyongyang: Central Committee, NKWP, 1948.
Shin Yom. "Ilbone taehan Miguk paengchangjuuichadul ui chongchaek" [American expansionists' policy toward Japan]. *Kulloja* (March 1948).
Soguk tongil minjujuui chonson kyolsongtaehoe munhonjip [Documents related to the formation of the Fatherland Unification Democratic Front]. Pyongyang: Choson Minpo-sa, 1949.
Song Sung-chol. "Yosida passyo chongchaekul pantaehanun Ilbon inmindul ui tujaeng" [The Japanese people's struggle against the fascist policies of Yoshida]. *Kulloja* no. 19 (1949).
Soryon kunsakomundanjang Rajubayep ui 6. 25 chonjaeng pogoso [Reports from the June 25 War by V. N. Razuvaev, Soviet chief military advisor]. Vol. 1–3. Seoul: Institute for Compiling Military History, Defense Ministry, ROK, 2001.
Yi Han, "Choson minjujuui inmin konghwaguk songnip kyongsuk taehoe" [Celebration rally for the founding of the DPRK], *Yonbyon Munhwa* no. 2 (November 1948).

Chinese Language

Jianguo yilai Liu Shaoqi wengao [Liu Shaoqi's manuscripts since the founding of the PRC].Vol. 1–2. Beijing: The Central Press of Historical Documents,1996.
Jianguo yilai Mao Zedong wengao [Mao Zedong's manuscripts since the founding of the PRC]. Vol. 1–4. Beijing: The Central Press of Historical Documents, 1987–1988.
Mao Zedong junshi wenxuan [Selected military papers of Mao Zedong]. Beijing: PLA Soldiers Press, 1981(Reprint in Japan, 1985).
Mao Zedong wenji [Mao Zedong's writings] Vol. 6. Beijing: People's Press, 1999.
Peng Dehuai junshi wenxuan [Selected military papers of Peng Dehuai]. Beijing: The Central Press of Historical Documents, 1988.
Shen Zihua, ed. *Chaoxian zhanzheng: Eguo dang'anguande jiemiwenjian* [The Korean War: declassified materials of Russian archives]. Vol. 1–3. Taipei: Institute of Modern History, Central Academy, 2003.
Wang Dongxing riji [Wang Dongxing's diary]. Beijing: Chinese Social Sciences Press, 1993.
Zhou Enlai junshi wenxuan [Selected military papers of Zhou Enlai]. Vol. 4. Beijing: People's Press, 1997.

English Language

Department of State Bulletin. May 25, 1953; June 15, 1953; June 22, 1953; June 29, 1953; July 6, 1953; July 13, 1953; August 3, 1953.
Foreign Relations of the United States 1949. Vol. 7, part 2. Washington, DC: 1976.
Foreign Relations of the United States, 1950. Vol. 7. Washington, DC: 1976.
Foreign Relations of the United States, 1951. Vol. 7. Washington, DC: 1983.
Foreign Relations of the United States, 1952–1954. Vol. 15. Washington, DC: 1984.
Mansourov, Alexandre. "Stalin, Mao, Kim, and China's Decision to Enter the Korean War, Sept. 16–Oct. 15, 1950: New Evidence from the Russian Archives," *Cold War International History Project Bulletin* no. 6–7 (Winter 1995/1996).
"Russian Documents on the Korean War: 1950–53," introduction by James Hershberg and translation by Vladislav Zubok, *CWIHP Bulletin* no. 14–15 (Winter 2003/Spring 2004).
Sodei Rinjiro, ed. *Correspondence between General MacArthur, Prime Minister Yoshida and Other High Japanese Officials [1945–1951].* Tokyo: Hosei University Press, 2000.
"Talks with Mao Zedong and Zhou Enlai, 1949–1953," commentary by Chen Jian, *CWIHP Bulletin* no. 6–7 (Winter 1995/1996).
Weathersby, Kathryn. "Deceiving the Deceivers: Moscow, Beijing, Pyongyang, and the Allegations of Bacteriological Weapons Use in Korea," *CWIHP Bulletin* no. 11 (Winter 1998).
——— "New Findings on the Korean War," Ibid. no. 3 (Fall 1993).
——— "Korea, 1949–50: To Attack or Not to Attack? Stalin, Kim Il Sung, and the Prelude to War," Ibid. no. 5 (Spring 1995).
——— "New Russian Documents on the Korean War," Ibid. no. 6–7 (Winter 1995/1996): 30–84.

Russian Language

Evreiskii antifashistskii komitet v SSSR 1941–1948: dokumentirovannaia istoriia [The Jewish antifascist committee in the USSR, 1941–1948: A documentary history]. Moscow, 1996.
"Kommunisticheskii antikoreiskii sgovor" [A Communist anti-Korean intrigue]. *Kuranty*, August 6, 1993.
Lavrentii Beriia, 1953. Stenogramma iiul'skogo Plenuma TsK KPSS i drugie dokumenty [Lavrentii Beriia, 1953. Stenographic record of the July 1953 plenary meeting of CC CPSU and other documents]. Moscow, 1999.
"Okazat' voennuiu pomoshch' koreiskim tovarishcham: perepiska vozhdei" [Military aids to Korean comrades; correspondence of leaders]. *Istoricheskii arkhiv* no. 1 (1996): 123–136.

352 Bibliography

Otnosheniia Sovetskogo Soiuza s narodnoi Koreei 1945–1980. Dokumenty i materialy [The Soviet Union's relations with the People's Korea, 1945–1980, documents and materials]. Moscow, 1981.
Politbiuro TsK RKP(b)-VKP(b). Povestki dnia zasedanii 1919–1952. Katalog [Politburo, CC, CPSU Meeting agendas,1919–1952, List]. Vol. 3. Moscow, 2001.
"Posetiteli kremlevskogo kabineta I. V. Stalina. Zhurnaly zapisi lits, priniatykh pervym gensekom. 1924–1953 gg." [Visitors of Stalin's cabinet in the Kremlin: the lists of men received by the first general secretary, 1924–1953]. Istoricheskii arkhiv nos. 5–6 (1996); no. 1 (1997).
"Proidet desiatok let, i eti vstrechi ne vosstanovish' uzhe v pamiati" [Ten years passed (from the diary of people's komissar V. A. Malyshev)]. Istochnik no. 5 (1997).
"Rekomendatsii Fyn Si" [Fyn Si's recommendations]. Rodina no. 4 (1993).
Russkii arkhiv: Velikaia Otechestvennaia: Prikazy narodnogo komissara oborony SSSR, 22 iiunia 1941 g.–1942 g. [Russian archives: Great Fatherland War: Orders of the People's commissar of defense, USSR, June 22, 1941–1942]. Vol. 13 (2–2). Moscow, 1997.
"Uchastie SSSR v koreiskoi voine (Novye dokumenty)" [The participation of the USSR in the Korean War (new documents)]. Voprosy istorii nos. 11–12 (1995).
VKP(b), Komintern i Iaponiia,1917–1941 [The All-Union Communist Party (b.), Comintern and Japan, 1917–1941]. Moscow, 2001.
"Zapis' besedy P. F. Iudina s Mao Tsedunom" [Conversation of P. F. Iudin and Mao Zedong, March 31, 1956]. Problemy Dal'nego Vostoka [Problems of the Far East] no. 5 (1994).

Japanese Language

Ashida Hitoshi nikki [Diary of Ashida Hitoshi]. Vol. 3. Tokyo: Iwanami Shoten, 1986.
Chosen Minshushugi Jinmin Kyowakoku kokumin keizai hatten tokeishu, 1946–1963 [Economic development statistics for the Democratic People's Republic of Korea, 1946–1963]. Tokyo: Nihon Chosen Kenkyujo, 1965.
Jijitsuwa kataru: Chosen senso chohatsu no uchimaku [The facts speak: Behind the outbreak of the Korean War]. Pyongyang: Gaikokubun- shuppansha, 1960.
Kin Nichi-sei chosakushu [Writings of Kim Il Sung]. Vol. 5–7. Pyongyang: Gaikokubunshuppansha, 1981.
Kin Nichi-sei senshu [Selected works of Kim Il Sung]. Vol. 2., Vol. extra. Tokyo: San'ichi Shobo, 1952.
Kokkai Dai 8 kai Shugiin gaimuiinkai kaigiroku [Japanese Diet proceedings, the Eighth Diet, house of representatives, diplomatic committee]. No. 2, 4, 5. August 21, 26, 29, 1950.
Kokkai Shugiin kaigiroku [Japanese Diet proceedings, house of representatives] No. 3, 4. July 15, 16, 1950.
Kominforumu Juyo Bunkenshu [Important documents of Cominform]. Tokyo: Nikkan Rodotsushinsha, 1953.
Ministry of Foreign Affairs, Treaty Bureau. Kaisetsu heiwa joyaku [Commentary on San Francisco peace treaty]. Tokyo, 1951.
Nihon kyosanto gojunen mondai shiryoshu [Documents on the 1950 controversy in the Japanese Communist Party]. Vols. 1, 2, 3. Tokyo: Shin Nihon Shuppansha, 1957.
Nihon Kyosanto tosei koyo bunken [Japanese Communist Party documents related to strengthening party spirits]. Vols. 1, 2. Tokyo: Sundaisha, 1952.
Pak Kyong-shik, ed. Chosen mondai shiryo sosho [Materials on Korean problems, series]. Vols. 10, 15. Tokyo: Ajia Mondai Kenkyujo, 1991.
Sekai. Special issue, Sengo heiwaron no genryu [The origins of postwar pacifism] (July 1985).
Shiryo zainichi chosenjin kyousanshugiundo [Korean Japanese Communist movements: documents]. Tokyo: Revolt-sha, 1970.
Sovieto domei kyosanto daijukyukai taikai gijiroku [Nineteenth Congress, Communist Party of the Soviet Union, record].Tokyo: Gogatsu Shobo, 1953.
Stalin, I. V. Sodomei ni okeru shakai shugi no keizaiteki shomondai [Some economic problems of socialism in the USSR]. Tokyo: Kokumin Bunko, 1953.

Tokuju ni kansuru tokei [Special procurement statistics]. Tokyo: Keizai Shingicho Chosabu Tokeika, 1954.
Watanabe Yozo, and Yoshioka Yoshinori eds. *Nichibei anpojoyaku zensho* [Documents on the Japan-US security pact]. Tokyo: Rodojunposha, 1968.

II. PERIODICALS

Akahata [Organ of the Japanese Communist Party], 1949, 1950.
Asahi Shimbun, 1950, 1952, 1953, 1954, 2001.
Choson Ilbo, 1990–1993.
Choson Inmingun, July, August, September, November, December, 1950; January, February, 1951.
Chung'ang Ilbo, 1990–1993.
Haebang Ilbo (Seoul), July 2, 3, 4, 10, 18, 19, 28, 29, 1950; August 1, 3, 4, 5, 8, 11, 23, 1950; September 5, 6, 1950.
Hangyore 21 (Seoul), no. 292 (January 20, 2000).
Inmin, September–October 1948; nos. 1–7 (1950).
Istochnik no. 1 (1996)
Izvestiia, 1952–1953.
Izvestiia TsK KPSS, no. 2, 12 (1989).
Koryo Ilbo (Alma Ata), November 1990–December 1993.
Kulloja nos. 1–12, 14 (1950); no. 2, 7, 11 (1951); no. 1 (1953).
Minju Choson, July, August, September, 1950.
New York Times, October–December, 1950; February, July 1953.
Newsweek, Japanese edition, (February 2, 2000).
Nodong Shinmun, January, February, March, July, August, September, 1950; January, February, March, 1951; January–December, 1952; January–August, 1953; 1982; 1984.
Oruta [Organ of the Korean Communist Party committee] (South Hamgyong Province) no. 18 (January 1, 1946).
Pravda, 1949, 1950, 1952.
Renmin Ribao, 1951–1953.
Sankei Shinbun, April 6, 1977; January 8, 1998.
Seiron. November and December 1995.
Sekai, December 1950.
Seoul Shinmun, May–August, 1995
Toitsu Nippo (Tokyo), 1990–1993.
Tong'a Ilbo, 1950–1953.
Yonbyon Munhwa [Yonbyon Culture], Inaugural issue, October 1948; no. 2 (November 1948).

III. INTERVIEWS

Chong Sang-jin, Alma-Ata, April 21, 1990.
Chu Hong-sun, Yenji, August 17, 1991.
Kang Sang-ho, Leningrad, May 29, 1990.
Suzuki Ichizo, Tokyo, April 19, 1992.
Yi Sang-jo, Minsk, April 27, 1990.

IV. REMINISCENCES

Korean Language

Choe Tae-hwan. "6. 25 chonjaeng palbalui silsangul parkhinda" [The truth of the beginning of the Korean War]. *Yoksapipyong* no. 2 (Summer 1988).

Chong Il-gwon hoegorok [Chong Il-gwon's memoirs]. Seoul: Koryo Sojok, 1999.

Choson uiyonggun samchidae [The Korean Volunteer Army. The third unit.]. Harbin: Korean Nationalities Press, 1987.

Hyogmyong hoesanggi Li Hong-gwan chidae [A memoir of the revolution: Li Hong-gwan's unit]. Shenyang: Liaonin National Press, 1986.

Kang Sang-ho, interview, *Choson Ilbo*, June 20, 1990.

——— "Naega chirun pukhan sukchong" [Repression in North Korea, which I experienced]. *Chung'ang Ilbo* nos. 1–35 (January 11–October 12, 1993).

Liu Jun-xiu. Chosonjok inmindul soge [Among the Korean people], *Sungni* [Victory] (Chungguk Choson minjok palchachui chongso, 5). Beijing: Minjok Chulpansa, 1992.

Paeksa Yi Yun-yong hoegorok [Yi Yun-yong's memoir]. Seoul: Sacho, 1984.

Yi Tae. *Nambugun* [Guerrilla units in the South]. Seoul: Ture-sa, 1988.

Yo Chong [pseud.]. "Pihwa: Kim Il-sung kwa Pukhan" [The secret story: Kim Il Sung and North Korea]. *Tong'a Ilbo* (April 22–July 15, 1990).

Yu Chin-o. "Han-Il Hoedam" [ROK-Japan conferences]. (21) *Chung'ang Ilbo* (September 26, 1983).

Yu Song-chol. "Naui chungon" [My testimony]. *Hanguk Ilbo* (Nov. 1–30, 1990).

——— *Chungon: Kim Il Sungul marhanda* [Testimony: Kim Il Sung]. Seoul: Hanguk Ilbosa, 1991.

——— "Pipadaui pihwa" [Secret stories: the sea of blood]. *Koryo Ilbo* (Alma Ata), May 24, 28–31, June 4–5, 1991.

Chinese Language

Chai Chengwen, and Zhao Yong-chon. *Banmendian tanpan* [Negotiations at Panmunjom]. Beijing: Liberation Army Press, 1988.

Du Ping. *Zai zhiyuanjun zongbu* [My days at the headquarters of the Chinese People's Volunteers]. Beijing: Liberation Army Press, 1989.

Gu Weijun huigulu [Memoirs of Wellington Koo]. Vol. 8. Beijing: Zhongua Shuju Chuban, 1989.

Hong Xuezhi. *Kangmei yuanchao zhanzheng huiyi* [Recollections of the war to resist America and assist Korea]. Beijing: Liberation Army Press, 1990.

Nie Rongzhen huiyilu [Nie Rongzhen's memoirs]. Beijing: People's Liberation Army Press, 1984.

Pen Dehuai zishu [The autobiography of Pen Dehuai]. Beijing: People's Press, 1981.

Shao Yulin. "Shihan huiyilu" [Memoirs of the ambassador to Korea]. 13, 16, 24, *Zhuanji wen shue* (Taipei) 32, no. 3, 6 (March, June 1977); 34 (February 1979).

Shi Zhe. *Zai lishi juren shenbian* [Living around the historical giant]. Beijing: The Central Press of Historical Documents, 1991.

Wu Ruilin. *Kangmei yuanchao zhongde Disishi'er jun* [The 42nd Army in the war to resist America and assist Korea]. Beijing: Jincheng Press, 1995.

Yang Dezhi. *Weile heping* [For the peace]. Beijing: Long March Publisher, 1987.

English Language

Kennan, George F. *Memoirs, 1925–1950*. Boston: Little, Brown, 1967.

Khrushchev, N. *Khrushchev Remembers*. Boston: Little, Brown, 1970.

Knox, Donald. *The Korean War: Pusan to Chosin: An Oral History.* San Diego, CA: Harcourt Brace Jovanovich, 1985.
Noble, Harold Joyce. *Embassy at War.* Seattle: University of Washington Press, 1975.
Oliver, Robert. *Syngman Rhee and American Involvement in Korea, 1942–1960.* Seoul: Panmun book Company, 1979.
Ridgway, Matthew B. *The Korean War.* New York: Doubleday, 1967.

Russian Language

Bleik, Dzhorzh [George Blake]. *Inogo vybora net* [No other choice]. Moscow, 1991.
Borzenko, S. *Koreia v ogne. Ocherki* [Korea in fire: sketches]. Moscow, 1951.
Fedorenko, N. "Nochnye besedy" [Conversations at night]. *Pravda*, October 23, 1988.
Gromyko, A. A. *Pamiatnoe* [The unforgettable]. Vol. 1. Moscow, 1988.
Lobov, G. "V nebe severnoi Korei" [In the sky over North Korea]. *Aviatsiia i kosmonavtika* nos. 10–12 (1991); nos. 1–5 (1990).
Meretskov, K. A. *Na sluzhbe narodu* [Serving the people]. Moscow, 1983.
Mikoyan, Anastas. *Tak bylo* [This was the past]. Moscow: Vagrius, 1999.
Petukhov, V. I. *U istokov bor'by za edinstvo i nezavisimost' Korei* [At the beginning of the struggle for Korean unification and independence]. Moscow, 1987.
Simonov, Konstantin. *Glazami cheloveka moego pokoleniia* [By the eye of a member of my generation]. Moscow, 1990.
Smorchkov, A. P. "Prikaz: 'V boiu govorit' po-koreiski'" [The order "Speak Korean in battle"]. *Komsomol'skaia Pravda*, June 9, 1990.
Volk, I., Kornilov, V. and Vasil'ev, A. "Koreia v bor'be" [Korea in battle]. *Novyi mir* no. 4 (1951).
Zakharov, M. V. *General'nyi shtab v predvoennye gody* [The general staff in the prewar years]. Moscow, 1988.
Za mir na zemle Korei. Vospominaniia i stat'i [For peace on the Korean land: reminiscences and articles]. Moscow, 1985.
Zhukov, G. K. *Vospominaniia i razmyshleniia* [Reminiscences and thoughts]. Moscow, 1969.

Japanese Language

Adyrkhaev, N. B. *Sutarin to Nihon no Kyosanshugisha to no kaigo* [Stalin's meeting with Japanese Communists], *Kyokuto no shomondai* [Problems of the Far East], vol. 19, no. 4, August 1990.
Ando Jinbei. *Sengo Nihon Kyosanto shiki* [A private story of the postwar Japan Communist Party]. Tokyo: Bunshun Bunko, 1995.
Chon Jin-sik. *Waga Chosen, watashi no Nihon* [Our Korea, my Japan]. Tokyo: Heibonsha, 1993.
Chong Il-gwon. *Genbaku ka, kyusen ka* [Atomic bomb or truce?]. Tokyo: Nihon Kogyo Shimbun-sha, 1989.
Hakamada Satomi. *Watashi no sengoshi* [My postwar history]. Tokyo: Asahi Shimbunsha, 1978.
Ito Ritsu. *Ito Ritsu kaisoroku: Beijing sanjunananen* [Ito Ritsu's memoirs: thirty-seven years in Beijing]. Tokyo: Bungei Shunju, 1993.
Kameyama Kozo. *Sengo Nihon Kyosanto no nijuchobo* [The postwar Japanese Communist Party's double accounting]. Tokyo: Gendai Hyoronsha, 1978.
Kang Che-on. "Minsen jidai no watashi" [My role in the Unified Democratic Front]. In *Taiken de kataru kaihogo zai-Nichi Chosenjin undo* [The postwar Korean movement in Japan: personal accounts]. Kobe: Kobe Gakusei Seinen Shuppanbu, 1989.
Kim Sam-gyu. "Kojinshi no naka no Chosen to Nihon" [Korea and Japan in my life]. In *Chosen to Nihon no aida* [Between Korea and Japan]. Tokyo: Asahi Sensho, 1980.

Kin Nichi-sei: sono shogeki no jitsuzo [Kim Il Sung: the shocking reality]. Tokyo: Kodansha, 1992.

Nosaka Sanzo. "'Beijing kikan' ni kansuru Ito Ritsu's no 'shogen' ni tsuite" [Ito Ritsu's 'testimony' regarding the 'Beijing organization']. *Akahata*, January 26, 1981.

——— "Ito Ritsu shogen e no hansho: watashi no iibun" [A refutation of Ito Ritsu's account]. *Asahi Shimbun*, February 16, 1981.

Okubo Takeo. *Mutekinariyamazu* [The foghorn kept blowing]. Tokyo: Kaiyo Mondai Kenkyu-kai, 1984.

——— *Uminari no hibi—kakusareta sengoshi no danso* [Roaring waves: the hidden pages of the postwar history]. Tokyo: Kaiyo Mondai Kenkyukai, 1978.

Paek Sun-yop. *Kaisoroku, Kankoku senso issennichi* [Memoirs of Paek Sun-yop: the Korean War's thousand days]. Tokyo: Miritari rebyu, 1988.

Yi Tae. *Nambu gun: shirarezaru Chosen senso* [Guerrilla units in the South]. Translated by An U-sik. Tokyo: Heibonsha, 1991.

Yi Yong-hui. "Senjo to ningen" [The battlefield and human beings]. In *Bundan minzoku no Kuno* [The anguish of a divided people]. Translated by Takasaki Soji. Tokyo: Ochanomizu Shobo, 1985.

Yo Chong [pseud.]. "Shuki: Abakareta rekishi" [Secret story]. In *Kin Nichi-sei: sono shogekino jitsuzo* [Kim Il Sung: the shocking reality]. Tokyo: Kodansha, 1992.

Yoshida Kasei. "Gaku no dokuritsu miyako no seihoku ni hibiku" [A refrain "The independence of university" reverberated in northwest Tokyo]. In *Waseda 1950 nen shiryo to shogen* [Waseda University in 1950: materials and testimonies] vol. 1, 1997.

Yu Song-chol. "Shogen: kakusareta shinjitsu" [Testimonies]. In *Kin Nichi-sei: sono shogekino jitsuzo* [Kim Il Sung: the shocking reality]. Tokyo: Kodansha, 1992.

V. STUDIES AND DESCRIPTIONS

Korean Language

An Yong-hyon. *Hanguk chonjaeng pisa* [Secret history of the Korean War]. Vol. 1–5. N.p.: Kyongin Munhwasa, 1992.

Bajanov, Evgenii, and Bajanova, Natalia. *Soryonui charyoro pon Hanguk chonjaengui chon-mal* [The Korean War as seen in Soviet documents]. Seoul: Toso chulpan Yollim, March 1998.

"Choe Hyon tongjiui yangnyok" [A biographical sketch of comrade Choe Hyon]. *Nodong Sinmun*, April 10, 1982.

Cho Kap-che. "Yi Sung-man taetongnyong chego kyehoek" [The plan to remove President Syngman Rhee]. *Wolgan Choson*, June 1984.

Chong Kil-un. "Choson uiyongun Hwajung chidae kwa Jiluyu chidae" [Korean Volunteers Army—Hwachung unit and Jiluyu unit]. In *Kyolchon* [Decisive battle]. Beijing: Minjok Chulpansa, 1991.

Chong Pyong-jun. *Hanguk chonjaeng: 38 son chongdol kwa chonjaengui hyongsong* [The Korean War: clashes at the 38th parallel and configuring the war]. Seoul: Tolbegae, 2006.

Choson chonsa: nyonpyo [History of Korea, chronology]. Vol. 2. Pyongyang: Kwahak paekka sajon, 1991.

Choson inminui chonguiui chogukhaebang chonjaengsa [A history of the righteous war of the Korean people to liberate the fatherland]. Vol. 1–3. Pyongyang: Sahoekwahak Chulpansa, 1983.

Documentary Hanguk chonjaeng [Korean War]. Vol. 1–2. Seoul: KBS Munhwa saoptan, 1990.

Haebanghu 4 nyonganui kungnaewoe chungyo ilchi, chungbopan [Chronology of important foreign and internal events in four years (expanded edition)]. Pyongyang: Minju Choson-sa, 1949.

Haebanghu simnyon ilchi [Chronology of ten years after liberation, 1945–1955]. Pyongyang: Korean Central News Agency, n.d.

Hanguk chonjaengsa pudo [History maps of the Korean War]. Seoul: Ilshinsa, 1991.

Hanguk inmyong taesajon [Korean biographical encyclopedia]. Seoul: Shinku Munhwa-sa, 1995.

Hong Sa-jung. "Kungmin pangwigun sakon" [The National Defense Corps incident]. In *Chonhwanki ui naemak* [Inside story of the turning point]. Seoul: Chosun Ilbosa, 1982.

"Kim Il tongjiui yangnyok" [Biographical sketch of comrade Kim Il]. *Nodong Shinmun*, March 10, 1984.

Kim Jung-saeng. *Choson uiyonggunui milippuk kwa 6.25 chonjaeng* [The secret arrival in North Korea of the Korean volunteer unit and the Korean War]. Seoul: Myongji Chulpansa, 2000.

Kim Mun-nyong. "Palsu kaehon" [Abridged constitutional revision]. In *Chonhwanki ui naemak* [Inside story of the turning point]. Seoul: Chosun Ilbosa, 1982.

Kim Nam-sik. *Namnodang yongu* [A study of the Southern Workers' Party]. Seoul: Tolbegae, 1984.

Kim Tong-chun. *Chonjaeng kwa sahoe: uriege Hanguk chonjaengun muosi onna?* [War and society: what was the Korean War to us?]. Seoul: Tolbegae, 2000.

Pang Sun-joo. "Nohoek pukhan pipchamunso haeje" [Captured North Korean materials with commentary] (1) *Asea Munhwa*, first issue (Institute of Asian Culture, Hallym University), 1986.

——— "Hanguk chonjaeng tangsi pukhan charyoro pon Nogulli sakon" [The Nogulli incident in the light of North Korean materials]. *Chongsin Munhwa Yongu* 23, no. 2 (Summer 2000).

Park Myung-lim, *Hanguk chonjaengui palbal kwa kiwon* [The outbreak of the Korean War and its origins]. Vol. 1–2. Seoul: Nanamu Chulpan, 1996.

——— *Hanguk 1950: chonjaeng kwa pyonghwa* [Korea 1950: war and peace]. Seoul: Nanamu Ch'ulpan, 2002.

Pirok: Choson Minjujuui Inmin Konghwaguk [Secret records: the Democratic People's Republic of Korea]. Vol. 1–2. Seoul: Chung'ang Ilbosa, 1992.

Pukhan chongnam, 1945–1968 [North Korea big reference book, 1945–1968]. Seoul: Kongsangwon Munje yonguso, 1983.

Pukhan inmyong sajon [North Korean biographical dictionary]. Seoul: Chun'ang Ilbosa, 1990.

So Pyong-gon. "Mu Chong changgun ildaegi" [General Mu Chong: a biography]. *Shinchonchi* 1, no. 2 (March 1946).

So Chung-sok. "Yi Sung-man kwa pukchintongil" [Syngman Rhee and advancing northward]. *Yoksa Pipyong*, Summer 1995.

Suh Dong-man. *Pukchoson sahoejuui cheje songnipsa 1945–1961* [A history of formation of the socialist system in North Korea]. Seoul: Son'in, 2005.

Uidaehan suryong Kim Il Sung tonjigeso yondohasin chosoninminui chonguiui chogukhaebang chonjaengsa [A history of the righteous fatherland liberation war of the Korean people led by the great leader Kim Il Sung]. Vol. 1–3. Pyongyang: Kwahak paekwa sajon chonghap chulpansa, 1993.

Volkogonov, D. *Sutarin* [Stalin]. Seoul: Segyon-sa, 1993.

Wada Haruki. *Hanguk chonjaeng* [The Korean War]. Translated by Suh Dong-man. Seoul: Changjak kwa pipyongsa, 1999.

——— *Kim Il Sung kwa Manju hangil chonjaeng* [Kim Il Sung and the anti-Japanese war in Manchuria]. Translated by Yi Chong-sok. Seoul: Changjak kwa pipyongsa, 1992.

——— *Tongbuk Asia kongdongui jip* [The Northeast Asian Common House]. Translated by Yi Won-dok. Seoul: Ilchogak, 2004.

Yang Tae-hyon. *Yoksaui chungon: hyujonhoedam pisa* [Testimony of history: the secret history of the armistice negotiations]. Seoul: Keisol chulpansa, 1993.

Yi Chong-sok. "Haesok kwa silchungui chonggyohan mannam" [Elaborate combination of interpretation and fact finding]. *Yoksa Hakpo* no. 164 (1999).

Yi Ho-chol. "Sirhyangmin" [The uprooted]. *Wolgan Taehwa*, January 1977.

Yom In-ho. *To hanaui Hanguk chonjaeng: Manju Chosoninui 'choguk' kwa chonjaeng* [Another Korean War: the fatherland for Manchurian Koreans and the war]. Seoul: Yoksa pipyongsa, 2010.

Chinese Language

Academy of Military Science, Military Historical Studies Section. *Kangmei yuanchao zhanzhengshi* [A history of the war to resist America and aid Korea]. Vols. 1–3. Beijing: Military Sciences Press, 2000.

Da Ying. *Zhiyuanjun zhanfu jishi* [Prisoners of war of the Chinese People's Volunteers]. Beijing: Kunlun Publisher, 1987.

Deng Lifeng, ed. *Xin Zhongguo Junshi Huodong Jishi, 1945–1959* [A chronology of the military activities of new China, 1945–1959]. Beijing: CCP History Literature Press, 1989.

Heng Xueming. *Shengsi sanba xian: Zhongguo zhiyuanjun zai Chaoxian zhanchang shimo* [Life and death on the 38th parallel: the Chinese volunteers in the Korean War]. Anhui: Anhui Literature Publisher, 1992.

Huang Kewu. "Yiersanziyouri—congyigejieride yanbiankan dangdai Taiwan fangongshenhua de xingshuai" [The rise and fall of a contemporary Taiwanese anti-Communist myth as seen through the change of a national holiday]. In *1949 nian—zhongguo de guanjian niandai xueshu taolunhui lunwenji* [Year 1949—a collection of articles from a symposium on key years of Chinese history]. Taipei, 2000.

Kanmei yuanchao zhanzheng [War to resist America and assist Korea]. Beijing: Chinese Social Science Press, 1990.

Li Changyi. *Jiang Xintai junlu shengya* [Kang Shintae's life in wars and journeys]. *Zhongguo chaoxianzushi yanjiu*. Vol. 2. Yanbian University Press.

Liu Shaoqi Nianpu [A chronology of Liu Shaoqi]. Vol. 2. Beijing: Central Press of Historical Documents, 1996.

Nie Rongzhen Nianpu [A chronology of Nie Rongzhen]. Vol. 1. Beijing: People's Liberation Army Press, 1999.

Pang Xianzhi, and Li Jie. *Mao Zedong yu kangmei yuanchao* [Mao Zedong and the cause of resistance to America and aid to Korea]. Beijing: The Central Press of Historical Documents, 2000.

Peng Dehuai Nianpu [A chronology of Peng Dehuai]. Beijing: People's Press, 1998.

Qi Dexue. *Chaoxian zhanzheng juece neimu* [Inside story of decision making during the Korean War]. Shenyang: Liaoning University Press, 1991.

Shen Zhihua. *Mao Zedong, Sudalin yu Chaoxian zhanzheng* [Mao Zedong, Stalin and the Korean War] (Guangdong People's Press, 2003).

———— *Zhongsu tongmeng yu Chaoxian zhanzheng yanjiu* [Studies on the Sino-Soviet alliance and the Korean War]. Guilin: Guangxi Pedagogical University Press, 1999.

Shu Yinwen, "Deng Hua." *Zhonggong dangshi renwuzhuan* [Biographies of figures of the Chinese Communist Party]. Vol. 32. Xian: Shanxi People's Press, 1987.

Xu Yan. *Diyici jiaoliang: kangmei yuanchao zhanzheng de lishi huigu yu fansi* [The first test of strength: a historical review and evaluation of the war to resist America and assist Korea]. Beijing: Chinese Broadcasting and Television Press, 1990.

Yang Fengan, and Wang Tiancheng. *Jiayu Chaoxian zhanzhengde ren* [A man who commanded the Korean War]. Beijing: CCP Central Party School Press, 1993.

Yang Kuisong. *Mao Zhedong he Mosike de enen yuanyuan* [Mao Zhedong and Moscow's love and hate]. Nanchang: Jiangxi People's Publisher, 1999.

Yao Xu. "Kanmei yuanchao de yingming juece" [A clever policy of resistance to America and aid to Korea]. *Dangshi yanjiu* [Study of party history] no. 5 (1980).

Ye Quanhong. "Huangpu junxiao hanji xuesheng kaoshi" [A study of Korean students in the Huangpu military school]. *Hanguk nianpo* (Taipei), no. 14 (1996).

Ye Yumeng. *Chubing Chaoxian: Kangmei yuanchao lishi jishi* [Historical records of Chinese military intervention in Korea]. Beijing: October Literature Press, 1990 (the first part *Heixue* and the second *Hanjiang Xue* were each published in 1989–1990).

Zhang Min, and Zhang Xiujuan. *Zhou Enlaihe kangmeiyuanchao zhanzheng* [Zhou Enlai and the war to resist America and assist Korea]. Shanghai: Shanghai People's Publisher, 2000.

Zhonghua minguo dashiji [A chronology of the Republic of China]. Taipei, 1957.

Zhongguo renmin jiefangjun disi yezhanjun zhanshi [A history of the 4th Field Army, Chinese People's Liberation Army]. Beijing: People's Liberation Army Press, 1998.

Zhongguo renmin zhiyuanjun kangmei yuanchao zhanshi [A history of the Chinese People's Volunteers' war to resist America and assist Korea]. 2nd ed. Beijing: Military Science Press, 1990.
Zhou Enlai nianpu 1949–1976 [A chronology of Zhou Enlai, 1949–1976]. Vol. 1. Beijing: The Central Press of Historical Documents, 1997.
Zhu Dehai yisheng [The life of Zhu Dehai]. Beijing: Nationalities Press, 1987.

English Language

Appleman, Roy E. *South to the Naktong, North to the Yalu (June–November 1950)*. Washington, DC: Center of Military History, US Army, 1961; 1992.
Bajanov, Evgueni. "Assessing the Politics of the Korean War, 1949–51," *CWIHP Bulletin* no. 6–7 (Winter 1995/1996).
Borovik, Genrikh. *The Philby Files; The Secret Life of Masterspy Kim Philby*. Boston: Little, Brown, 1994.
Bowen, Roger. *Innocence Is Not Enough: The Life and Death of Herbert Norman*. Vancouver: Douglas and McIntyre, 1986.
Chen Jian. *China's Road to the Korean War: The Making of the Sino-American Confrontation*. NY: Columbia University Press, 1994.
—— "China's Strategies to End the Korean War." Paper presented at the Cold War International History Project Conference, Hong Kong, January 1996.
—— *Mao's China and the Cold War*. NC: University of North Carolina Press, 2001.
Cotton, James, and Ian Neary, eds. *The Korean War in History*. Manchester University Press, 1989.
Crane, Conrad. *American Airpower Strategy in Korea 1950–1953*. University Press of Kansas, 2000.
Cumings, Bruce. "The Course of Korean-American Relations, 1943–1953." In *Child of Conflict*. University of Washington Press, 1983.
—— *The Origins of the Korean War: Liberation and the Emergence of Separate Regimes, 1945–1947*. Princeton University Press, 1981.
—— *The Origins of the Korean War: Vol. 2. The Roaring of the Cataract, 1947–1950*. Princeton University Press, 1990.
—— *The Korean War: A History*. New York: The Modern Library, 2010.
Deacon, Richard. *The Cambridge Apostles: A History of Cambridge University's Elite Intellectual Secret Society*. London: Farrar, Straus & Giroux, 1986.
Dvorchak, Robert J. *Battle for Korea: A History of the Korean Conflict*. 50th anniversary ed., Pennsylvania: Combined Publishing, 2000.
Foot, Rosemary. *A Substitute for Victory: The Politics of Peacemaking at the Korean Armistice Talks*. Cornell University Press, 1990.
Futrell, Robert F. *The United States Air Force in Korea, 1950–1953*. New York: Duell, Sloan and Pearce, 1961.
Gaddis, John Lewis. *We Now Know: Rethinking Cold War History*. Oxford: Clarendon Press, 1997.
Goncharov, Sergei N., John W. Lewis, and Xue Litai. *Uncertain Partners: Stalin, Mao and the Korean War*. Stanford University Press, 1993.
Goulden, Joseph C. *Korea: The Untold Story of the War*. New York: Times Books, 1982.
Halliday, Jon. "Air Operations in Korea: The Soviet Side of the Story." In *A Revolutionary War: Korea and the Transformation of the Postwar World*, edited by William J. Williams. Chicago: Imprint Publications, 1993.
Halliday, Jon, and Bruce Cumings. *Korea: The Unknown War*. New York: Penguin Books, 1988.
Hao Yufan, and Zhai Zhihai. "China's Decision to Enter the Korean War: History Revisited," *China Quarterly* no. 121 (March 1990).
Hastings, Max. *The Korean War*. New York: Simon & Schuster, 1987.
Heinzig, Dieter, "Stalin, Mao, Kim and Korean War Origins, 1950: A Russian Documentary Discrepancy," *CWIHP Bulletin*, no. 8–9 (Winter 1996/1997).

Heo Man-ho. "Human Rights Legacies of the Korean War: Civilian Genocide and South Korean POWs Detained in North Korea." Paper presented at the International Symposium "The Korean War and Searching for Peace on the Korean Peninsula in the 21st Century," Seoul, June 24, 2000.

Holloway, David. *Stalin and the Bomb: The Soviet Energy and Atomic Energy 1939–1956.* Yale University Press, 1994.

Johnson, Chalmers. *An Instance of Treason: Ozaki Hotsumi and the Sorge Spy Ring.* Stanford University Press, 1990.

Jun Sang-In. "The Sociology of the Korean War: Societal Transformation and Social Legacies." Paper presented at the International Symposium "The Korean War and Searching for Peace on the Korean Peninsula in the 21st Century," Seoul, June 24, 2000.

Keefer, Edward C. "The Truman Administration and the South Korean Political Crisis of 1952: Democracy's Failure?" *Pacific Historical Review* 60, no. 2 (May 1991).

Kim Hak-Joon. *The Unification Policy of South and North Korea.* Seoul National University Press, 1977.

Knightley, Phillip. *Philby: The Life and Views of the K.G.B. Master Spy,* London, 1992.

Lee Chong-Sik. *Japan and Korea: The Political Dimension.* Stanford University Press, 1985.

Leitenberg, Milton. "New Russian Evidence on the Korean War Biological Warfare Allegations: Background and Analysis," *CWIHP Bulletin* no. 11 (Winter 1998).

——— "The Korean War Biological Weapon Allegations: Additional Information and Disclosures," *Asian Perspective* 24, no. 3 (2000).

Lowe, Peter. *The Korean War.* London: Macmillan, 2000.

MacDonald, Callum A. *Korea: The War before Vietnam.* London: Macmillan, 1986.

——— "'So Terrible a Liberation'—The UN Occupation of North Korea," *Bulletin of Concerned Asian Scholars* 23, no. 2 (1991):

Mansourov, Alexandre. "Soviet-North Korean Relations and the Origins of the Korean War." Paper presented at the International Conference on the New Evidence on the Cold War in Asia, Hong Kong, January 9–12, 1996.

——— "Stalin, Mao, Kim, and China's Decision to Enter the Korean War, Sept. 16–Oct. 15, 1950: New Evidence from the Russian Archives," *CWIHP Bulletin* no. 6–7 (Winter 1995/1996).

Mastny, Vojtech. *The Cold War and Soviet Insecurity: The Stalin Years.* Oxford University Press, 1996.

Matray, James I. *The Reluctant Crusade: American Foreign Policy in Korea, 1941–1950.* University of Hawaii Press, 1985.

McCormack, Gavan. *Cold War, Hot War.* Sydney: Hale and Iremonger, 1983.

Merril, John. "Khrushchev Remembers," *The Journal of Korean Studies* 3 (1981).

Miller, John, Owen J. Carroll, and Margaret E. Tackley. *Korea 1951–1953.* Office of the Chief of Military History, 1982.

Mossman, Billy C. *Ebb and Flow, November 1950–July 1951.* Washington, DC: Center of Military History, US Army, 1990.

Pierpaoli, Paul G., Jr. "Alpha and Omega: Understanding the Meaning of the Korean War," Paper presented at the International Symposium "The Korean War and Searching for Peace on the Korean Peninsula in the 21st Century," Seoul, June 24, 2000.

——— *Truman and Korea: The Political Culture of the Early Cold War.* University of Missouri Press, 1999.

Ra, Jong Yil. "Political Crisis in Korea, 1952: Administration, Legislature, Military and Foreign Powers," *Journal of Contemporary History* 27 (1992).

Rees, David. *The Limited War.* London: Macmillan, 1964.

Shen, Zihua. *Mao, Stalin and the Korean War: Trilateral Communist Relations in the 1950s.* Milton Park, Abingdon: Routledge, 2012.

———"Sino-North Korean Conflict and its Resolution during the Korean War," *CWIHP Bulletin* no. 14–15 (Winter 2003–Spring 2004).

Stone, I. F. *The Hidden History of the Korean War.* New York: Monthly Review Press, 1952; Boston: Little, Brown, 1988.

Stueck, William W., Jr. *The Road to Confrontation: American Policy toward China and Korea, 1947–1950*. University of North Carolina Press, 1981.
——— *The Korean War: An International History*. Princeton University Press, 1995.
Wada Haruki. "East Asia and the Cold War: Reinterpreting Its Meaning in the New Millennium," In *Ending the Cold War in Korea*, edited by Chung In Moon. Seoul: Yonsei University Press, 2001.
——— "Economic Co-operation in Place of Historical Remorse: Japanese Post-war Settlements with China, Russia and Korea in the Context of the Cold War." In *The Political Economy of Japanese Society*. Vol. 2. Oxford University Press, 1998.
——— "The Korean War, Stalin's Policy, and Japan," *Social Science Japan Journal*, vol. 1, no. 1 (April 1998).
——— "Stalin and the Japanese Communist Party, 1945–1953: In the Light of New Russian Archival Documents." Paper presented at the International Conference on the New Evidence on the Cold War in Asia, Hong Kong, January 9–12, 1996.
Weathersby, Kathryn. "Deceiving the Deceivers: Moscow, Beijing, Pyongyang, and the Allegations of Bacteriological Weapons Use in Korea," *CWIHP Bulletin* no. 11 (Winter 1998).
——— "New Russian Documents on the Korean War," *CWIHP Bulletin* no. 6–7 (Winter 1995/1996).
——— "Soviet Aims in Korea and the Origins of the Korean War, 1945–1950: New Evidence from Russian Archives," *CWIHP Working Paper* no. 8 (November 1993).
——— "Stalin and a Negotiated Settlement in Korea, 1950–53." Paper presented at the International Conference on the New Evidence on the Cold War in Asia, Hong Kong, January 9–12, 1996.
——— "Stalin, Mao, and the End of the Korean War." In *Brothers in Arms: The Rise and Fall of the Sino-Soviet Alliance 1945–1963*, edited by Odd Arne Westad. Stanford University Press, 1998.
Whiting, Allen S. *China Crosses the Yalu: The Decision to Enter the Korean War*. New York: Macmillan, 1960.
Willoughby, Charles A. *Shanghai Conspiracy, The Sorge Spy Ring*. New York: Dutton, 1952.
Zhang, Shu Guang. *Mao's Military Romanticism: China and the Korean War, 1950–1953*. University of Kansas Press, 1995.
Zubok, Vladislav M. "Stalin's Goals in the Far East: From Yalta to Sino-Soviet Treaty of 1950 (New Archival Evidence from Moscow)." Paper presented at the International Conference on the New Evidence on the Cold War in Asia, Hong Kong, January 9–12, 1996.
Zubok, Vladislav, and Constantine Pleshakov. *Inside the Kremlin's Cold War: From Stalin to Khrushchev*. Harvard University Press, 1996.

Russian Language

Babich, V. K. *Vozdushnyi boi (zarozhdenie i razvitie)* [The air fighting: how it began and developed]. Moscow, 1991.
Bol'shaia Sovetskaia entsiklopedia [Soviet encyclopedia], 3-e izd., vol. 29, Moscow, 1978.
Bystrova, I. V. *Voenno-ekonomicheskaia politika SSSR: ot "demilitatlizatsii" k gonke voorvzhenii, Stalinskoe desiatiletie kholodnoi voiny; fakty i gipotezy* [The Soviet military-economic policy; from demilitarization to the arms race, Stalin's ten years of the Cold War, facts and hypothesis]. Moscow, 1999.
Gorbanevskii, M. V. *V nachale bylo slovo . . . Maloizvestnye stranitsy istorii sovetskoi lingvistiki* [In the beginning there was a word—unknown pages of the history of Soviet linguistics]. Moscow, 1991.
Kerber, L. L. *Tupolev* [Andrei Tupolev]. Saint Petersburg, 1999.
Kto byl kto v Velikoi Otechestvennoi voine 1941–1945. Kratkii spravochnik [Who's who in the Great Fatherland War, 1941–1945: a short biographical dictionary]. Moscow, 1995.
Lan'kov, A. "Bor'ba fraktsii i stanovlenie rezhima edinolichnoi vlasti v KNDR" [Struggles among factions and formation of one man's power regime in DPRK]. *Dal'nii vostok* no. 10 (1992).

——— Severnaia Korea: vchera i segodnia [North Korea: yesterday and today]. Moscow, 1995.

Ledovskii, A. "Sekretnaia missiia A. I. Mikoiana v Kitai (ianvar'–fevral' 1949 g.)" [The secret mission of A. I. Mikoyan to China (January–February 1949)]. Problemy Dal'nego Vostoka no. 2–3 (1995).

——— SSSR i Stalin v sud'bakh Kitaia: Dokumenty i svidetel'stva uchastnika sobytii 1937–1952 [The USSR and Stalin in the destiny of China. Documents and testimonies of two participants in the events, 1937–1952]. Moscow, 1999.

Naitli, Fillip. Kim Filbi—supershpion KGB [Kim Philby: a master spy]. Moscow, 1992.

Osvobozhdenie gorodov. Spravochnik po osvobozhdeniiu gorodov v period Velikoi Otechestvennoi voiny 1941–1945 [Emancipation of cities in the Great Fatherland War: a guidebook]. Moscow, 1985.

Plotnikov, G. K. "Otechestvennaia osvoboditel'naia voina koreiskogo naroda (obzor voennykh deistvii)" [The fatherland liberation war of the Korean people]. In Za mir na zemle Korei: Vospominaiia i stat'i [For peace on the land of Korea: reminiscences and articles]. Moscow, 1985.

Rossiia i SSSR v voinakh XX veka. Kniga poter. [Russia and the USSR in wars of the 20th century: a book of losses]. Moscow: Veche, 2010.

Samsonov, A. M. Moskva, 1941 god: Ot tragedii porazhenii—k velikoi pobede [Moscow 1941: from the tragedy of defeat to the great victory]. Moscow, 1991.

——— Stalingradskaia bitva [The battle for Stalingrad]. 2nd ed. Moscow, 1985.

Slavinskii, Boris. "Sovetskii Soius eshche v 1951 godu podgotovil proekt mirnogo dogovora s Iaponiei" [The Soviet Union had already prepared its version of a peace treaty with Japan in 1951]. Nezavisimaia gazeta, October 12, 1993.

——— "San-Frantsisskaia konferentsiia 1951 g. po mirnomu uregulirovaniiu s Iaponiei i sovetskaia diplomatsiia" [San Francisco peace conference and the Soviet diplomacy]. Problemy Dal'nego Vostoka no. 1 (1994).

Sovetskaia voennaia entsiklopediia [Soviet military encyclopedia]. Moscow, 1977.

Sovetskii atomnyi proekt: Konets atomnoi monopolii. Kak eto bylo . . . [The Soviet atomic project: the end of monopoly of atomic bombs]. Nizhnii Novgorod, 1995.

Semiriaga, M. I. Tainy stalinskoi diplomatii 1939–1941[Secrets of Stalin's diplomacy]. Moscow, 1992.

Tikhvinskii, S. L. "Perepiska I.V. Stalina s Mao Tsedunom v ianvare 1949 g." [Stalin's correspondence with Mao Zedong in January 1949]. Novaia i noveishaia istoriia no. 4–5 (1994).

Titenskii, Aleksandr. "'Za chto srazalis'?: 40 let nazad zavershilas' Koreiskaia voina" [For what did they fight? 40 years ago the Korean War ended]. Nezavisimaia gazeta, July 23, 1993.

Torkunov, A. V. Zagadochnaia voina: Koreiskii konflikt 1950–1953 godov [An enigmatic war: the Korean conflict, 1950–1953]. Moscow, 2000.

Tumanov, Grigorii. "Shtykovaia ataka Kim Ir Sena" [Kim Il Sung's attack with bayonets]. Novoe vremia no. 26 (1993).

Vada, Kharuki. "Koreiskaia voina i Iaponiia: politika Stalina" [The Korean War and Japan: Stalin's policy]. In Rossiia kak problema vsemirnoi istorii [Russia as a problem of world history]. Moscow: AIRO-XX, 1999.

Vanin, Iurii V. Koreiskaia voina (1950–1953) i OON [The Korean War and the United Nations]. Moscow, 2006.

Volkogonov, Dimitrii. Triumf i tragediia. Politicheskii portret I. V. Stalina [Triumph and tragedy: Stalin's political portrait]. Vol. 2, part 2. Moscow: Agentstvo Novosti, 1989.

Zubkova, Elena. Poslevoennoe sovetskoe obshchestvo: politika i povsednevnost' 1945–1953 [Postwar Soviet society: politics and everyday life, 1945–1953]. Moscow, 2000.

Japanese Language

Akagi Kanji, ed. Chosen seno (The Korean War: collection of articles). Tokyo: Keiogijuku University Press, 2003.

Fejt, F. *Minzoku shakaishugi kakumei: Hangaria junen no higeki* [A national socialist revolution: the tragic decade in Hungary]. Tokyo: Kindai Seikatsu-sha, 1957.

Hagiwara Ryo. *Kita Chosenni kieta tomo to watashi no monogatari* [My friends who disappeared in North Korea]. Tokyo: Bungei Shunju, 1998.

—— *Chosen senso: Kin Nichi-sei to Makassa no inbo* [The Korean War: a conspiracy by Kim Il Sung and Gen. Douglas MacArthur]. Tokyo: Bungei Shunju, 1993.

—— *Chosen senso shuzai no–to* [A journalist's notes on the Korean War]. Kyoto: Kamogawa Shuppan, 1995.

Hosoya Chihiro. *Sanfuranshisuko kowa e no michi* [The road to the San Francisco peace treaty]. Tokyo: Chuo Koronsha, 1984.

Hwang Sok-yong, *Kakuchi* [Foreign land] Translated by Takasaki Soji. Tokyo: Iwanami Shoten, 1986.

Igarashi Takeshi. *Sengo Nichi-Bei kankei no keisei—kowa anpo to reisengo no shiten ni tatte* [The formation of postwar US-Japan relations: the peace settlement and the security pact]. Tokyo: Kodansha Gakujutsu Bunko, 1995.

—— *Tainichi kowa to reisen: sengo Nichi-Bei kankei no keisei* [The peace treaty with Japan and the Cold War; the formulation of postwar Japan-US relations]. University of Tokyo Press, 1986.

Inomata Kozo, Kimura Kihachiro, and Shimizu Ikutaro, eds. *Kichi Nihon—Ushinawareteiku Sokoku no sugata* [Japan as US bases: our disappearing homeland]. Tokyo: Wakosha, 1953.

Ishii Akira. *Chu-So kankeishi no kenkyu, 1937–1952* [Studies in the history of Sino-Soviet relations, 1937–1952]. University of Tokyo Press, 1990.

—— "Nikka heiwa joyaku no koshokatei; Nihon gawa daiichiji soan o megutte" [Negotiation of the Japan-Republic of China peace treaty: Japan's first proposal]. *Chugoku—shakai to bunka* [China: society and culture] no. 3 (June 1988).

—— "Nikka heiwa joyaku teiketsu kosho o meguru jakkan no mondai" [Some issues in the negotiations on a Japan-Republic of China peace treaty]. *Tokyo Daigaku Kyoyo Gakubu, Kyoyo Gakka kiyo* no. 21 (March 1988).

Kamijima Haruhiko. *Red Purge Hollywood: Akagari ni idonda Blacklist eigajin retsuden* [Red Purge Hollywood: Lives of blacklisted movie men who challenged the Purge]. Tokyo: Sakuhinsha, 2006.

Kamiya Fuji. *Chosen senso* [The Korean War]. Tokyo: Chuo Koronsha, 1966.

Kan Hideteru. *Bei-So reisen to Amerika no Ajia seisaku* [The Cold War and US Asian policy]. Osaka: Minerva Shobo, 1992.

Kankoku Kokubo gunshikenkyusho [Republic of Korea, National Defense History Research Institute] ed. *Kankoku Senso* [Korean War], vol. 1, Tokyo: Kaya Shobo, 2000.

Kim Hak-joon. *Chosen senso; tsukon no minzoku shototsu* [The Korean War: a tragic clash]. Translated by Kaneda Mitsuto. Tokyo: Saimaru Shuppankai, 1991.

Kojima Noboru. *Chosen senso* [Korean War]. Vol. 1– 3. Tokyo: Bungei Shunju, 1984 (first edition, 1977).

Lee Jong Won. "Aizenhawa-seiken no tai-Kan seisaku to 'Nihon'" [The Eisenhower administration's policy toward Korea and "Japan"]. *Kokka Gakkai Zasshi* 10, nos. 1–2 (February 1994).

—— "Bei-Kan kankei ni okeru kainyu no genkei 'Evua-redei keikaku' saiko" [Operation Everready reexamined: the prototype of interference in US-Korean relations]. *Hogaku* 58, no. 1 (April 1994); 59, no. 4 (April 1995).

—— "Kannichi Kaidan to Amerika—'Fukainyu seisaku'no seiritsu o chushin ni" [The Japan-ROK conference and the United States: formation of the "nonintervention policy"]. *Kokusai Seiji* no. 105 (January 1994).

Matsui Noriaki. "Maboroshii no Saharin tonneru" [The mysterious Sakhalin tunnel]. *Suzutani* (Hokkaido Toyohara-kai) no. 12 (September 1994): 89–103.

—— *Shiryo Sutarin-Meriniku kaidan, 1950 sangatsu* [Stalin-Melnik meeting, March 1950]. Ibid. no. 13 (September 1995).

Mihashi Osamu, Robert Riketto, Yi Yong-nang, and Ebina Yoshinori. "Senryoka ni okeru taizainichi Chosenjin kanri seisaku keisei katei no kenkyu (1)" [Formulation of Japanese policy to control Koreans in Japan during the Occupation (1)]. *Seikyu gakujutsu ronshu* no. 6 (1995).

Miyake Akimasa. *Reddo paji to wa nanika? Nihon senryo no kage* [What was the Red Purge?: behind the Occupation]. Tokyo: Otsuki Shoten, 1994.

Miyamoto Satoru. "Chosen Jinmingun no 'seikika'" ["Normalization" of the Korean People's Army]. *Rokkodai ronshu* [Rokkodai Papers] (Hogakuseijihen) 47, no. 1 (July 2000).

Mori Yoshinori."Sokoku toitsu minshushugi sensen no kessei" [Formation of the Fatherland Unification Democratic Front]. *Toyama Kokusai Daigaku Kiyo* 7 (March 1997).

—— *6 gatsu no raigeki: Chosen senso to Kim Il Sung taisei no keisei* (Thunderbolt in June: the Korean War and the formation of the Kim Il Sung system). Tokyo: Shakaihyoronsha, 2007.

Murata Koji. *Daitoryo no zasetsu—Ka-ta-seiken no zaikanbeigun tettai seisaku* [The president fails: the Carter administration's policy of US troop withdrawal from the Republic of Korea]. Tokyo: Yuhikaku, 1998.

Nakatsuji Keiji. "Aizenhawa-seiken to Chosen teisen—'tairyo hofuku' senryaku o jiku ni" [The Eisenhower administration and the Korean armistice: the strategy of "massive retaliation"]. *Hiroshima Daigaku Sogo Kagakubu kiyo*, 2 *Shakai bunka kenkyu* 14 (1988).

—— "Chosen teisen to Bei-Kan kankei" [The truce in Korea and United States-ROK relations]. *Shiso* no. 5 (1990).

Nihon Gaikoshi [Diplomatic history of Japan]. Vol. 28. Tokyo: Kashima Kenkyujo Shuppankai, 1971.

Nihon Shakaito no sanjunenshi [The Japan Socialist Party: a thirty year history]. Tokyo: Newspaper Division, Central Headquarters, Japan Socialist Party, 1976.

O Chunggun. "Chosen senso to Soren—Kokuren Anpo Rijikai kesseki o chushinni" [The Soviet Union and the Korean War—boycott of the security council]. *Hogaku Kenkyu* 65, no. 2 (February 1992).

Okonogi Masao. *Chosen senso: Beikoku no kainyu katei* [The Korean War: The process of the United States intervention]. Tokyo: Chuo Koron-sha, 1986.

—— "Minzoku kaiho senso toshite no Chosen senso" [The Korean War as a war of national liberation]. *Kokusai Mondai* 182 (1975).

Onuma Hisao, ed. *Chosen senso to Nihon* (The Korean War and Japan: collection of articles). Tokyo: Shinkansha, 2006.

Pak Kyon-shik. *Kaihougo zainichichosenjin undoshi* [A history of movements of Japanese Koreans after 1945]. Tokyo: Sanichi shobo, 1989.

Republic of Korea, National Defense History Research Institute. *Kankoku senso* [Korean War]. Vol. 1–2. Tokyo: Kaya shobo, 2000–2001.

Sasaki Harutaka. *Chosen senso: Kankoku-hen* [The Korean War: Republic of Korea]. 3 vols. Tokyo: Hara Shobo, 1976.

Sawa Masahiko. *Nam-Boku Chosen kurisutokyo shiron* [The history of Christianity in South and North Korea]. Tokyo: Nihon Kirisutokyo-dan Shuppankai, 1982.

Shen Zhihua. "Chu-So joyaku kosho ni okeru rieki no shototsu to sono kaiketsu" [Conflicts of interest in negotiations of the Soviet-Chinese treaty and their solution]. *Shiso*, August 2001.

Shinobu Seizaburo. "Gendaishi no kakki toshite no Chosen senso" [The Korean War: a turning point in modern history]. *Sekai*, August 1965.

—— *Chosen senso no boppatsu* [The start of the Korean War]. Tokyo: Fukumura Shuppan, 1964.

—— *Sengo Nihon seijishi* [A political history of postwar Japan]. Vol. 3–4. Tokyo: Keiso Shobo, 1967.

Shu Ken Ei (Zhu Jianrong). *Mo Taku To no Chosen senso* [Mao Zedong's Korean War]. Tokyo: Iwanami Shoten, 1991.

——*Motakuto no Betonamu senso—chugoku gaiko no daitenkan to bunka daikakumei no kigen* [Mao Zedong and the Vietnam War: the turnabout of China's foreign policy and the origin of the cultural revolution] (Tokyo: Daigaku Shuppankai, 2001),

Takasaki Soji. *Kensho Nikkan kaidan* [The Japan-ROK conferences revisited]. Tokyo: Iwanami Shoten, 1996.

Bibliography 365

Tanaka Hiroshi. "Sengo Nihon to posuto shokuminchi mondai" [Postwar Japan and postcolonial problems]. *Shiso*, August 1985.

Teijin no ayumi [History of the Teijin company]. 7. Tokyo: Teijin Kabushiki Kaisha, 1972.

Torkunov A. V. *Chosen senso no nazo to shinjitsu; Kin Nichi-sei, Sutarin, Mo Taku To no kimitsu denbun ni yoru* [Enigmas and reality of the Korean War in the secret cables of Kim Il Sung, Stalin, and Mao Zedong]. Tokyo: Soshisha, 2001.

Toyoshita Narahiko. *Anpo joyaku no seiritsu—Yoshida gaiko to tenno gaiko* [The peace treaty: Yoshida Shigeru's diplomacy and the emperor]. Tokyo: Iwanami Shoten, 1996.

Toyota Jidosha Nijunenshi [Twenty-year history of the Toyota automobile company]. Tokyo: Toyota Jidosha Kabushikigaisha, 1958.

Tsuboi Toyokichi. *Zainichi Chosenjin undo no gaikyo* [The Movement of Koreans in Japan: an overview]. Reprint, Tokyo: Jiyu Seikatsu-sha, 1959.

Yamada Munemitsu. *Sengo shisoshi* [History of postwar thought]. Tokyo: Sanichi Shobo, 1959.

Yamamoto Takeshi. "Chosen tokuju" [Korean War special procurements]. In *Showa no senso* [The War of Showa], edited by Yamamuro Hideo. Vol. 10. Tokyo: Kodansha, 1985.

Yamazaki Shizuo. *Shijitsu de kataru Chosen senso; kyoryoku no zenbo* [Japan's cooperation in the Korean War]. Tokyo: Hon no Izumi-sha, November 1998.

Yasuda Jun. "Chugoku kenkoku shoki no anzen hosho to Chosen senso e no kainyu" [Security issues in the initial phase of the PRC and China's intervention in the Korean War]. *Hogaku kenkyu* 67, no. 8 (August 1994).

—— "Chugoku no Chosen senso daiichiji, dainiji seneki" [China's first and second offensives in the Korean War]. *Hogaku Kenkyu* 68, no. 2 (February 1995).

Yi Tae-ho. *Oryokko no fuyu* [Winter on the Yalu]. Translated by Aoyagi Junichi. Tokyo: Shakai Hyoronsha, 1993.

Yun Kyong-chol. *Bundangono Kankoku seiji, 1945–1986* [Politics in the Republic of Korea, 1945–1986]. Tokyo: Bokutakusha, 1986.

U Ryong-ho. *Chosen no gyakusatsu* [Massacre in Korea]. Translated by Ohata Kenji et al. Tokyo: Ota Shuppan, 2001.

Wada Haruki. *Chosen senso* [The Korean War]. Tokyo: Iwanami Shoten, 1995.

—— "Chosen senso o kangaeru" [Rethinking the Korean War] 1-4, *Shiso* May 1990; May, June, July 1993.

—— *Chosen senso zenshi* [The Korean War: a history]. Tokyo: Iwanami Shoten, 2002.

—— *Kim Il Sung to manshu konichi senso* [Kim Il Sung and anti-Japanese war in Manchuria]. Tokyo: Heibonsha, 1992.

—— *Kitachosen Gendaishi* [A contemporary history of North Korea]. Tokyo: Iwanami Shoten, 2012.

—— *Kitachosen: Yugekitai Kokka no Genzai* [North Korea: the guerrilla unit state today]. Tokyo: Iwanami Shoten, 1998.

—— *Rekishi toshiteno Nosaka Sanzo* [Nosaka Sanzo as history]. Tokyo: Heibonsha, 1996.

—— "Sengo Sorenni okeru rekishika to rekishigaku sono ichi" [Historians and historiography in the postwar Soviet Union, part 1]. *Roshiashi Kenkyu* no. 25 (June 1976).

—— "Soren no Chosen seisaku, senkyuhyaku yonjugonen hachigatsu-jugatsu" [The Soviet Union's Korean policy, August–September, 1945]. *Shakai Kagaku Kenkyu* 33, no. 4 (1982).

—— "Sutarin hihan: 1953–1956" [Criticism of Stalin: 1953–1956]. In *Gendai shakaishugi— sono tagenteki shoso* [Contemporary socialism: its multiple dimensions]. University of Tokyo Press, 1977.

—— *Tohoku Azia Kyodo no Ie: Shinchiikishugi sengen* [The Northeast Asian Common House: a manifesto of new regionalism]. Tokyo: Heibonsha, 2003.

—— "Tohoku Azia senso toshiteno Chosen senso" [The Korean War as a Northeast Asian war]. *Shien* (Rikkyo University) 56, no. 2 (1996).

Watanabe Tomiya. *Itsuwari no rakuin: Ito Ritsu supaisetsu no hokai* [Stigma: Ito Ritsu was not a spy]. Tokyo: Gogatsu Shobo, 1993.

VI. UNPUBLISHED DISSERTATIONS

Kobayashi Tomoko. "Sengo ni okeru zai-Nichi Chosenjin to 'sokoku'—1945 –1952" [The postwar Korean minority in Japan and the 'fatherland'—1945–1952]. PhD diss., Ewha Women's University, 1996.
Mansourov, Alexandre Y. "Communist War Coalition Formation and the Origins of the Korean War." PhD diss., Columbia University, 1997.
Nam Ki-jong. "Chosen senso to Nihon; 'kichi kokka' ni okeru senso to heiwa" [The Korean War and Japan; war and peace in a "military base state"]. PhD diss., University of Tokyo, 2000.
Suh Dong-man. "Kita Chosen ni okeru shakaishugi no seiritsu" [The establishment of socialism in North Korea]. PhD diss., University of Tokyo, 1995.
Yi Won-dok. "Nihon no sengo shori gaiko no ichi kenkyu—Nikkan kokko seijoka kosho (1951–65) o chushin ni shite" [An aspect of Japan's diplomacy to settle postwar issues— negotiations to normalize relations between Japan and the ROK]. PhD diss., University of Tokyo, 1994.

VII. FILM

"Densetsu no maihime Choe Sung-hui" [Legendary dancer Choe Sung-hui]. Directed by Fuji-wara Satoko, 2000.

Index

About the Author

Wada Haruki is professor emeritus, University of Tokyo, and fellow, Center for Northeast Asian Studies, Tohoku University. He studies Modern Russian history and Contemporary Korea. He is the author of *Kim Il Sung and the Anti-Japanese Guerrilla War* (Tokyo and Seoul), *The Russo-Japanese War: Its Origins and the Beginning*, 2 vols. (Tokyo), and *A Contemporary History of North Korea* (Tokyo).

44.00   1/17/14